CASES AND MATERIALS ON

HOUSING LAW

CASES AND MATERIALS ON

HOUSING LAW

Professor David Hughes
Professor of Housing and Planning Law, De Montfort
University, Leicester

Martin Davis
Principal Lecturer in Law, De Montfort University,
Leicester

Veronica Matthew
Principal Lecturer in Law, De Montfort University,
Leicester

Nicholas Smith
Lecturer in Law, University of Leicester

BLACKSTONE
PRESS LIMITED

First published in Great Britain 1999 by Blackstone Press Limited,
Aldine Place, London W12 8AA. Telephone (020) 8740 2277
www.blackstonepress.com

© David Hughes, Martin Davis, Veronica Matthew, Nicholas Smith, 2000

ISBN: 1 85431 936 1

British Library Cataloguing in Publication Data
A CIP catalogue record for this book is available from the British Library

Typeset by Style Photosetting Ltd, Mayfield, East Sussex
Printed by Ashford Colour Press, Gosport, Hampshire

Contents

Preface

The authors of this book have been teaching housing law at undergraduate and postgraduate level for many years, and have been providing continuing professional development in the housing field for lawyers, housing managers and advice centre workers.

Those who study and practise housing law need to be conversant with both case law and legislation in order to determine what exactly the law is on a given point. The statutory language is often opaque, and so are many of the judgments. Students of housing law therefore need to use the original sources and it is often not easy for them to have access to a properly stocked law library. This book gives extensive quotations from case and statute law; there are also comments and questions, to enable students to consider whether the law is logical or just.

We are grateful to our publishers for their patience while we produced this book. We would especially like to thank Alison Mather for dealing with the complex manuscript both cheerfully and efficiently.

Acknowledgements

The authors of this work gratefully acknowledge the co-operation of the following publishers in allowing publication of portions of their copyright material.

HMSO (Copyright Unit) for extracts from DoE Circular 6/90, DoE Circular 3/97 and the Code of Guidance on Parts VI and VII of the Housing Act 1996.

Crown Copyright is reproduced with the permission of the Controller of Her Majesty's Stationery Office. The Incorporated Council of Law Reporting for England and Wales for extracts from the Law Reports and Weekly Law Reports. The Butterworths Division of Reed Elsevier (UK) Ltd for extracts from the All England Law Reports. International Thomson Publishing Services Limited for extracts from the Housing Law Reports and Property and Compensation Law Reports.

Table of Cases

Cases reported in full are shown in heavy type. The page at which the report is printed is shown in heavy type.

Table of Statutes

Introduction

The title of this book presupposes that there is such a subject as 'The Law of Housing'. Certainly from a teaching point of view, in many universities and colleges there is a subject labelled 'Housing Law' which is taught, perhaps at undergraduate and/or postgraduate level, perhaps as a 'stand alone' module or double module, as part of a 'Welfare Law' course or for courses for the Chartered Institute of Housing's qualifications. That in itself is a sufficient reason for the authors of the present volume to produce a collection of those cases and materials which, in their experience, are most germane to the needs of teachers and students on such courses. The aims of such a collection must be to inform and stimulate study by the provision of a comprehensive selection of material from both Parliament and the courts, coupled with textual matter that elucidates, analyses, informs and challenges the reader. Within the confines of these covers we hope that we have achieved those aims.

Nevertheless, we return to the presupposition with which we began. Though it is clear that there is in educational terms a subject known as 'Housing Law', there is amongst academics much less certainty and agreement than the curricula of universities and colleges would tend to suggest. While not pretending to be able to settle the various debates about whether there is in reality any such subject – and if there is, what its content should be – it would be contrary to our stated aims of elucidation and stimulation if we did not address some of the issues involved.

Housing Law as the product of history

Housing Law is primarily a subspecies of the law of Landlord and Tenant, and many of the concepts which will be encountered in this book are shared in common with that general body of law, for example notions such as covenants, weekly and monthly tenancies, and bedrock issues such as whether an individual is a tenant with a legal interest in land, or a mere licensee with only a personal permission to be present on land. What differentiates Housing Law from Landlord and Tenant Law in general, however, is that, first, it deals only with residential accommodation and, secondly, by longstanding conventional understanding it also deals with housing conditions, houses in multiple occupation and standards not just in rented property but in virtually all residential accommodation, and with the promotion of the interests of those who have no residential property at all, i.e. the homeless – thus drawing in elements of what we may call 'public law'. The reasons for this are historical.

With the industrial revolution of the mid- to late 18th century came a considerable change in the pattern of population distribution. The United Kingdom gradually ceased to be a rural nation: indeed, the year 1850 marked the point at which the urban and rural populations were even, ever since which we have been an increasingly urban nation. As the people moved from the countryside into the towns they increased in number, and the nature of their legal interests in land and accommodation changed.

It should never be thought that in pre-industrial Britain there was a kind of rural paradise in which everyone was well housed. William Blake's 'Jerusalem' does us all something of a disservice by talking about 'dark, satanic mills', for many may be led to suppose that before their creation people worked and lived in healthy and happy surroundings: they did not. The average rural labourer lived in appalling conditions – cave dwelling, for example, did not fully disappear until the early years of the 20th century, and most of the attractive country cottages we see today are either the product of 19th-century building, or of even more recent combinations of smaller, older dwellings into acceptable units. It was not uncommon for rural dwellers to live in tiny, cramped 'one up–one down' houses, with access to the upper floor by ladder, and the cattle and domestic animals living in adjacent rooms. The poor – and most people were poor – lived badly, and their legal entitlements to the land they occupied were frequently determined by local manorial custom, often dating from medieval times.

Those moving from the countryside to the towns thus did not expect high standards of accommodation; nor did they find them. Though in London, from the 18th century onwards, there were some attempts to impose certain standards on the building of properties, such legislation did not exist elsewhere. Moreover, the great majority of dwellings were available, irrespective of the social class of the tenant, on a leasehold basis only, and their condition thus deteriorated where lessors were concerned only to receive rent and not to take effective steps to ensure that repairs were carried out and property maintained. The influx of people from the countryside led to more overcrowding of existing properties and, where new accommodation was built, to the provision of filthy, insanitary slums. As many houses as possible per acre were squeezed in; these were often built on a 'back-to-back' basis, so that the only entrance was via the front of the house, and no natural light or ventilation reached the rear rooms of dwellings. An alternative was the court system, with dwellings built around a common courtyard – often back-to-back and court housing were combined. Such dwellings were available on weekly lettings, which thus became the standard tenure for the poorer classes of society.

In the early years of the 19th century, to propose any alleviation of these poor conditions was seen as running against two basic legal principles which had almost the status of constitutional fundamentals – freedom of contract and freedom of property. Freedom of contract depended on the notion that all persons are of equal bargaining power, and thus if a tenant wished to secure better conditions on his home he should negotiate these freely with his landlord. The vast disparity of economic power between landlords and tenants was utterly ignored by the law. That is not to say that tenants had absolutely no remedy – they could, in some cases, simply get out and find other accommodation; something which could often be done in larger towns with an abundance of landlords in competition with one another. Very often tenants would depart without paying rent owed – the famous 'moonlight flit' celebrated in the old music hall song 'My Old Man':

> We had to move away, for the rent we couldn't
> pay. The moving van came round right after
> dark.
> There was me and my old man piling things
> inside the van, which we've often done before, let me
> remark.

Indeed, from time to time so prevalent was this habit that landlords complained they could not make an economic return on their property. However, for most of the 19th century the 'whip hand' lay with landlords, and they were largely able to dictate the rent and conditions of letting of property on a 'take it or leave it' basis. Freedom of property drew much of its intellectual justification from what was seen as a most important issue in the Constitutional struggle between 1642 and 1688 – namely, the right of freeborn Englishmen to enjoy their property without interference by the state. Furthermore, if a man had property it was seen as a mark of divine favour – the just reward for thrift, hard work, self-denial and assiduous attention to business.

What led to a gradual, and bitterly contested, erosion of these principles was the clear evidence of ill health and suffering caused by the insanitary living conditions of the urban poor. These were first systematically investigated by Edwin Chadwick in 1845, and were then unmistakably manifested to the whole nation in the great cholera epidemics of the 1850s. Infant mortality ran at an appallingly high level, and for those children who survived infancy life expectancy was low. In the mid-19th century in Leicester, it has been calculated that the average life expectancy of a working class woman was about 20 years, of a middle class woman about 30 years and of an upper class woman 40 years. A combination then of genuine social concern for suffering, and fear on the part of those anxious lest disease should yet further spread, led to legislation to deal with nuisances, though the effect of this in practice took a long time to produce positive results.

What may be called the first substratum of the modern law of housing was thus concerned with the eradication of public health hazards and the removal of 'nuisances' such as foul water courses and piles of rotting human and animal waste. Local Boards of Health and Sanitary Authorities – the ancestors of our modern local authorities – were given a series of powers to deal with conditions that were prejudicial to health, from the 1840s onwards. However, it was not until 1875 that they were given power under the Public Health Act to prescribe minimum building standards for new houses. What they were not given was power to build new homes, and early slum clearances, coupled with the building of railways into town centres and their voracious demands for land, often led to the poor being forced from one area into another which was just as bad, often with increased overcrowding.

The other substratum of Housing Law, namely the provision of housing on a non-speculative, non profit-making basis, did not begin to emerge until the end of the 19th century, and is in reality a 20th-century phenomenon.

There has been since the Middle Ages a tradition of philanthropic housing provision in England and Wales, as the survival of almshouses shows. In the 19th century this was continued by a number of charitable trusts such as the Guinness, Peabody and Sutton foundations. At the same time a number of employers, both rural and urban, built 'model' dwellings for their employees, as witness, for example, Saltaire, Swindon, Eastleigh, Crewe, Wolverton, and a little later Bourneville and Port Sunlight. However, such provision did little to help the vast mass of the unskilled, urban labouring poor. To meet their housing needs accommodation had to be provided that was available for rent on a non profit-making basis, and the capital cost of construction of which was subsidised.

Though a hesitant start was made on the creation of publicly-provided housing towards the end of the 19th century, the legal strands of which were consolidated in the first recognisable modern 'housing act' – the Housing of the Working Classes Act 1890 – it was not until after the end of the First World War, when social pressures made it clear that there was a need to build 'a land fit for heroes' (as the then Prime Minister David Lloyd-George put it in an electoral address in Wolverhampton), that on a nationwide basis major programmes of subsidised housing got under way, with central funding from the Exchequer under the Housing Act of 1923.

It was not the voluntary and philanthropic sectors which undertook the building of subsidised housing, however, for they were not willing to take on the task, but local authorities. Thus there came together local oversight of housing conditions and local housing provision.

Housing Law as the product of policy

What the local authorities faced in the early 1920s was a housing market in which the vast majority of homes were still owned by private landlords – they accounted for 90 per cent of housing provision at the turn of the century. Much of that housing was of very poor quality and little new housing for rent was being built. Moreover, in an effort to defuse public unrest over rising rent levels during the war, in 1915 the Government had introduced rent controls, and these were to remain a generally important feature of the private rented sector until 1988. There was at the same time a small, but growing, owner-occupied sector which was fostered by generally rising levels of income, making it possible for an increasing number of people to own their own homes with assistance from the burgeoning building society movement, and the encouragement of builders more than ready to build for sale as opposed to renting.

It is at this point that the confused nature of what we call the 'Law of Housing' emerges. All housing, irrespective of who owns it or how it is occupied, is a matter of social concern, for everyone needs shelter and the health and the cohesion of society is affected when that need is not met for a number of its members. Therefore a truly 'social' system of housing law would be concerned with both those who rent and those who own, and would deal with their rights, the financing and the upkeep and maintenance of their homes in a comprehensive and coherent fashion. While it is possible to trace themes and issues of this sort on a cross-sectoral basis, it has to be admitted that for the vast majority of those who teach and study the Law of Housing it is not how they proceed.

The law relating to owner-occupation is treated by most housing lawyers as part of the law relating to conveyancing and town and country planning – the former to deal with acquisition and transfer, the latter to govern location and siting. 'Housing Law' thus has come to be the law of rented housing in both the public and private sectors, but with the addition of the law relating to housing conditions on a cross-sectoral basis – though the worst housing conditions are still to be found in rentals. A further addition which most housing practitioners need to know is that portion of Family Law relating to the occupation and transfer of rented dwellings.

When pressed then to give a description of 'Housing Law', most teachers and practitioners would identify the 'core' as the various housing and homelessness functions of local housing authorities. In England these are the London Borough Councils (e.g., Camden), the Metropolitan District Councils (e.g., Birmingham), the Shire District Councils (e.g., Cambridge) and, where they exist, Unitary Authorities (e.g., Leicester); and in Wales the single-tier County Councils (predominantly in rural areas) and County Boroughs (predominantly in urban areas). Around this core most people would place the law of the private rented sector and the law of other 'registered social landlords', of which more below, together with some Family Law as described above.

That is a description, not a definition, of Housing Law because a satisfactory definition remains elusive. What is studied, and what is dealt with in this book, is, frankly, a somewhat eclectic set of rules and principles. There is, however, one generally unifying feature bringing together these various elements, and that is the social welfare issue, or (to be blunt) the issue of poverty.

Looking back from the end of the 20th century, one could be forgiven for thinking that local authorities would inevitably take on a 'welfare' role in relation to housing given their combination of powers to demolish unfit properties and provide new dwellings. However, in the 1920s this was far from clear. The first great council building programmes were designed to provide accommodation, which, while subsidised, was still intended for the class of skilled workers. Thus in the 1920s local authorities built housing that was spacious and architecturally attractive – but at a price. It was only in the 1930s that Government policy changed and authorities were encouraged to build larger numbers of cheaper homes primarily to rehouse those displaced from demolished slum dwellings.

The Second World War interrupted that process, and public house building did not truly recommence until after the passing of the Housing Act 1949 which enabled authorities to build for all social groups, not just the working classes – an indication that in post-1945 Britain the public sector was to supersede the private landlord as a provider of rented accommodation. However, under the Conservative Government from 1951 to 1964 there was a return to building properties largely to rehouse slum dwellers, while a totally independent body – the Commission for the New Towns – oversaw the creation of 'New Town Corporations' in places as far apart as Harlow, Crawley, Washington and Skelmersdale, to house people identified as 'overspill' from overcrowded industrial centres.

'New Towns' continued to be established throughout the 1960s, with the final phase being the massive expansion of existing towns such as Peterborough and Northampton, though by then much of the new housing was built for sale, not rent. At the same time local authorities were encouraged, particularly via central subsidy arrangements, to continue building replacements for slum housing, increasingly on a 'high-rise–system built' basis, largely because it was thought that that was the only way to provide sufficient 'units of accommodation' to meet the needs of an increasing population, and to replace all the unfit properties still standing. The council slum clearance and new building programmes continued into the mid-1970s. What was built, however, was often inner urban housing of a most unlovely and unloved variety – tower blocks and medium rise 'deck-access' housing. Shortly thereafter, in 1977, local housing authorities were also placed under legal duties to house homeless persons whose increasing numbers throughout the 1960s became a cause of social concern and led to the creation of the charity 'Shelter'.

By this time it was becoming clear that Britain was polarising socially according to housing tenure. Owner-occupation developed rapidly as the major housing tenure as real incomes continued to rise. Those who could afford to bought their own homes. Indeed, it is arguable that many who could barely afford to buy were encouraged to do so by various means, including tax relief on mortgage payments and the extremely generous discounts for tenants under the 'right to buy' policy introduced under the Housing Act 1980, which will be dealt with below. Council housing became increasingly the place for the less well-off, those with insecure or no employment and, of course, the homeless. At the same time the private rented sector continued a seemingly inexorable decline. There arose calls for a 'third arm' in housing, something midway between local authority and owner-occupied housing. In an attempt to answer that call, the Labour Government in 1974 sought to foster the philanthropic and voluntary non profit-making sector by boosting housing associations with public funding provided by a central body, the Housing Corporation, set up by the Housing Act 1964. A housing association is a group of people who band together to provide housing on a non profit-making, grant-aided basis. Though some such bodies had been created in the early years of the century, it was only after the 1974 Act, when these associations were prepared to register with – and thus be subject to control by – the Housing Corporation, that this sector in housing began to grow.

Alongside the emergence of housing associations there was also a growing questioning of the role of local authorities as landlords and of the way in which they discharged their functions – particularly with regard to the rights of the tenants which, as a matter of law, hardly existed at all. The idea that tenants of both authorities and associations should enjoy a new legal status and a package of associated rights – the 'secure tenancy' – was initially enshrined in the Labour Government's Housing Bill of 1979. However, with the election to power of the Conservatives in 1979 this Bill was radically transformed into the Housing Act 1980, where the principal right given to secure tenants was the 'right to buy', i.e. a right to cease to be a tenant and to become an owner-occupier at a heavily discounted price. Under this popular policy over 1 million local authority dwellings have been sold to their occupiers, very often leaving authorities with the least attractive stock. Before 1980 local authorities had had a discretionary power to sell their homes, but whether or not this was used depended very often on the political control of individual councils. Labour-controlled authorities were less inclined to sell than Conservative ones. The radical change made by the 1980 Act was that authorities lost the ability to decline to sell.

The right to buy, however, was only the first in a number of policy initiatives which sought to take away from local authorities their role as housing providers, and to give that function, in a way limited by the amount of public money available for grants in aid of new construction, to housing associations. In 1988, under the Housing Act of that year, the Conservative Government introduced the policies of 'tenants' choice' and 'the Housing Action Trust'. The former was designed to enable the transfer of council estates to new landlords, ostensibly at the wish of tenants but in reality at the initiative of those new landlords; the latter was an initiative designed to regenerate whole sections of run-down council housing in inner urban areas by transferring their ownership to new appointed bodies who would improve them, and at the same time seek to enhance employment prospects for their occupiers, with a view to their transfer to the private sector. Neither policy succeeded: 'tenants' choice' floundered when there was a dearth of bodies willing to become new landlords; while the Housing Action Trusts (HATs) were resisted by tenants who regarded them as an imposition. Only a limited number of HATs were created following assurances by ministers, and appropriate modifications of the law, enabling tenants to return to local authority ownership after a HAT had done its work. Much more successful as a means of reducing the local authority stock was the Large Scale Voluntary Transfer (LSVT) developed by authorities themselves where they were ideologically opposed to being landlords, or saw the scheme as a way of raising money for much needed repairs of stock. Using their general powers to dispose of housing and land, a number of authorities began to dispose of their housing either to existing housing associations or to purposely created new ones. Beginning in the mid-1980s, by the late 1990s there had been 64 LSVTs involving the transfer of 260,000 homes. On the whole, however, it was the stock of rural and suburban authorities which was transferred, leaving the large urban authorities with less attractive, often 'hard-to-let' stock, and thus further reinforcing the negative perception of council housing as welfare property available for the poor and the socially deprived.

The current position

The start of the 1990s saw the stock of local authority dwellings continuing to erode as a result of right to buy sales and large-scale voluntary transfers, the stock of housing associations slowly increasing (albeit from a small base compared with that of local authorities), the beginnings of a slight revival in the fortunes of private landlords consequent on the removal of rent controls over new lettings under the Housing Act 1988, and the continued consolidation of the owner-occupied sector as the dominant tenure in housing. The increase in the number of properties rented from private landlords was also partly attributable to difficulties experienced by some owner-occupiers in the early years of the decade as economic recession led to job losses and a consequent inability of some owner-occupiers to meet mortgage commitments. Of the stock held by local authorities, much was in the form of urban estates suffering from multiple deprivation in the form of a lack of educational, health, welfare, social and employment opportunities, and often so afflicted by crime and vandalism that people grew unwilling to live in them, thus rendering such stock 'hard-to-let'. Some of these estates were to be found in inner-urban areas, others were in peripheral locations away from easy access to central facilities such as hospitals and shopping areas. Furthermore, there was evidence on a nationwide basis that entry into council housing was increasingly less available to general applicants as authorities used their available stock to accommodate the homeless – in the Greater London area over 60 per cent of allocations being generally made each year to homeless applicants. These figures should be treated with a degree of reserve, in that many so called 'homeless' applicants might well have qualified for being housed anyway under general allocation rules. However, the seeming bias in the figures led to apparently radical changes in the law in the Housing Act 1996. These, though, did nothing to reverse the generally held view amongst concerned professionals that housing had become a welfare service, that social housing was welfare housing and that the Law of Housing, far from relating to the residentially occupied built environment generally, had become an aspect of Welfare Law concerned with the problems, rights and aspirations of one part of the community only.

What the 1996 Act did achieve was to bring a legislative end to what had become, in many places, an effective right to a council house for homeless people. It also created a new concept in social housing, that of the 'registered social landlord'. Most members of this new class of bodies were already in existence as housing associations. However, the idea behind the legislation was yet further to vary the ownership of public rented housing by creating 'local housing companies' to whom transfers of houses could be made. These would operate at a distance from local authorities, though their management structures would include local authority representatives, tenant representatives and other people prominent in the local business and social community. Such bodies would be able to seek funding for new construction outside the very strict public finance borrowing limits otherwise imposed on local authorities.

Back to the future?
The ink was hardly dry on the 1996 Act when the Labour Party returned to power in May 1997. One of the first tasks of the Blair Government was to initiate a Comprehensive Public Spending Review, the implications of which for public sector housing remained somewhat unclear at the end of 1999. There are indications, however, that:

(a)   there will be no major public sector building programme because there is no willingness to devote public resources to a major new wave of public sector housebuilding, and the official argument is that only about 17,000 new units per annum are needed, while those unable to work need 24,000 new tenancies per annum, and many of those will be available in the existing stock of public dwellings;

(b)   most public investment in housing will be devoted to renovating local authority stock, with authorities thus being favoured in preference to housing associations;

(c)   in return for increased funding authorities will be expected to produce the 'best practice' value for money results obtained by the most efficient and effective councils, and these will be enforced by an external inspectorate, with the Secretary of State for the Environment being given new powers to take housing functions away from those authorities who fail to come up to standard;

(d)   it may take up to 20 years to remedy the most run-down, inner-urban areas, though as a start, in September 1998 the Government announced new public investment of £800m – the 'New Deal' – with £12m being initially

available for 17 'pathfinder' areas in which local partnerships of local
authorities, voluntary groups and community organisations will identify ways
of regenerating areas not just by undertaking work on houses but also by
improving shopping, recreational, health and education facilities;

(e)   there will, however, be a competitive element in the regeneration
process, for the regeneration 'packages' will be submitted in the form of 'bids'
for funding and only those considered successful will be financed.

What is clear, however, is that, as the Government's Social Exclusion Unit
has shown in its reports, there is a sector of our society which does not
participate in the generally comfortable style of life enjoyed by most people.
The majority who live in their own homes are, overall, comfortably off. That
is not to say that there are no problems in the owner-occupied sector. There
are problems in relation to those owner-occupiers who, having been encouraged to buy, now find that their employment is insecure and that they cannot
meet their mortgage commitments. There are problems for those who, being
encouraged to believe that house prices would inexorably always climb, now
find that prices have fallen and that their homes are worth less than the sums
for which they are mortgaged – the so-called 'negative equity' effect. There
are problems for those owner-occupiers who have purchased older houses –
and a very large proportion of our housing stock dates from before 1919 –
and who have made no long-term provision to fund the expensive capital
repairs, such as new roofs and damp proof courses, such properties are
already needing. Even so, the overall picture of the owner-occupied sector is
one of reasonable comfort.

It is also true that in the public sector all is not gloom. Not all council
tenants live in poverty and social deprivation – far from it in fact. But what
is true is that for much of this century, and increasingly since the 1970s,
council accommodation has been a refuge for those who are the most
vulnerable in our society. That may not have been the intention of the
framers of housing policy and law in the 1920s, but it is a fate that has
increasingly overtaken council housing since the 1930s, though down to the
1950s and 1960s a substantial number of council tenants would have been in
secure, well-paid employment. Of course it has been the better-off tenants
who have largely exercised the right to buy. Council accommodation has now
become the place where those in insecure accommodation, elderly non
owner-occupiers, single parents, the jobless, and the disabled look to find a
home. That of itself does not, of course, produce urban decay: to follow that
line of argument would indeed be to blame victims for their own misfortune.
What does appear to be the case, however, is that where vulnerable persons
are congregated together in housing from which they have little chance to
move, because more desirable properties have been disposed of and no new
property is being built, and they then suffer the 'double (or more) whammy'
of poor educational and employment opportunities, their areas begin to
decline still further. Those who can move out do so, and what is left is
decaying houses, many of which are empty, in areas prone to crime and social

disorder. Furthermore, in earnings terms the gap between the poorest 10 per cent of the population and those on average earnings is now wider than at any time since the 19th century.

It is a sad reflection on a society which has seen such a general improvement in the living conditions of most of its citizens throughout the 20th century that pockets of relative deprivation continue to exist. No one should suppose that even in the most run-down estates living conditions are as vile as those that existed in pre-industrial rural England, or those that developed as the pace of urbanisation grew throughout the 19th century. But that is little comfort to those who currently live in the stigmatised hard-to-let estates, or who have nowhere to live at all. For it should be remembered that while the official estimate is that only 17,000 new units are needed per annum, other estimates, for example those of Shelter, are that there is a hidden, unmet need for decent, healthy accommodation which requires the building of 100,000–130,000 units per annum.

The role of law
Housing Law, it was argued earlier, is the product of housing policy, and housing policy has come increasingly to be an aspect of social welfare policy, or, to be more frank, policy about those who are the less well-off and most insecure in our society. The reality is that Housing Law has little to say about owner-occupation – that is the preserve of the conveyancers and, insofar as a public law element is concerned, the Law of Town and Country Planning. For better or worse, Housing Law is largely concerned with the poor and the vulnerable – and they are largely found in rented accommodation, much of it rented from social landlords such as local authorities and housing associations. That being so, what is the role of the law?

No one should suppose that bad housing conditions can be eradicated by law. The role of the law from the mid-19th century onwards was to declare unacceptable certain types and conditions of housing, and then to provide frameworks and procedures within which by the deployment of public resources that unacceptable housing could be demolished, and, in time, replaced. However, the key element in that was not the law but the willingness to devote public finances to the eradication of bad housing and the creation of better conditions. In more recent years the law has been developed so as to recognise the rights and entitlements of those who live in the units of accommodation provided. This was a rather belated development which came about in response to a slow recognition that the vast majority of tenants suffered in terms of status when compared to owner-occupiers who enjoyed numerous rights consequent on their status as freeholders.

The law is still concerned with eradicating poor housing conditions, even though the desire to fund major new public housing programmes no longer seems to exist. It is also concerned to protect the interests of individual tenants. What may now be emerging, however, is a new emphasis in the law which has a crisis-driven feel about it. Given the poor conditions found on many estates, there is a new realisation that it is not enough to protect the individual rights of tenants, such as security of tenure and succession. What is now needed are provisions to ensure the collective safety of tenants – 'security' in the non-legal sense. Urban squalor and decay do not just mean poor housing conditions, they also bring with them crime, prostitution, vandalism, noise, drug dealing and general anti-social behaviour. Much attention in Housing Law is now directed to how these problems may be most appropriately tackled.

What follows in this book is primarily concerned with the issues that have been identified in the previous two paragraphs. That is, Housing Law as it has come to be. The majority of teachers and practitioners of the subject, being pragmatic types, accept that situation – albeit with varying degrees of grace. It is not the whole of the law relating to housing; it largely ignores owner-occupation, and it concentrates instead on the problems of one sector in society. It is, perhaps also the most interesting part of the law relating to housing, and it demands a degree of intellectual commitment and rigour on the part of students. Most conveyancing does appear to be a rather bloodless exercise compared to the cut and thrust of possession actions taken in respect of unruly tenants. However, in the din of battle it should always be remembered that the conveyancers deal with the majority of houses. That limited role for Housing Law is not, however, of itself a problem, for it retains an intellectual excitement all of its own. What is a problem is when students of Housing Law forget that all the statutes ever passed and all the judgments ever made have not by themselves ensured that a single house has ever been built or improved – that process demands in addition finance and political will. Without those elements the law remains a somewhat sterile intellectual exercise – a forum within which arguments take place over the allocation of increasingly scarce resources.

So this introduction ends not with a 'let the buyer beware', but with a 'let the student beware'. Enjoy the rest of this book and its contents, but never by seduced into believing that law alone can solve overall housing problems. They can be solved only by efforts of political will, and that is something about which we must think not as lawyers but as fellow members of a human civil society.

1 THE CATEGORIES OF OCCUPATION AND THE STATUS OF OCCUPANTS

(A) Introduction

As explained in the introductory chapter, 'Housing Law', although potentially a subject of enormous width, is normally (and for the purposes of this book) confined to the rights and duties, statutory and common law, of landlords of residential premises and their tenants. The crucial question to ask, therefore, is whether a landlord and tenant relationship has been created or not.

It is first necessary to determine the *status* of the parties. Even if owner-occupation is excluded, it is not self-evident that the occupier of residential premises is a tenant. First, the occupation may be unlawful and the occupier consequently a trespasser (or in popular speech a 'squatter'). The legal position of 'squatters' has been steadily weakened over the past 25 years; through a combination of simplified possession procedures to evict them (see now, for example, County Court Rules Ord. 24, r. 1) and increasing 'criminalisation' of their entry into and continued occupation of residential premises (see most recently ss. 72–76, Criminal Justice and Public Order Act 1994). Secondly, the occupier may be viewed as a *licensee* rather than as a *tenant*. A *licensee* is someone who has a right or permission to be on the premises (so that no issue of trespass arises) but whose right is a *personal* rather than a *proprietary* one so that no legal interest in the land is acquired. A licensee's rights are primarily contractual, stemming from the licence agreement. The classic definition of a licence was given as long ago as 1673 in the case of *Thomas v Sorrell* (1673) Vaugh 330, at 351:

A dispensation or licence properly passeth no interest, nor alters or transfers property in anything, but only makes an action lawful, which without it had been unlawful.

Licences arise naturally in many situations where it would be inappropriate to impose the formality of landlord and tenant relationships on the parties, for example occupiers of hotel rooms and holiday accommodation, or where the extent of the services provided or degree of 'care' provided indicates that the essence of the arrangement is the provision of the service/care rather than the creation of residential property rights. Good examples would include being a lodger in another's house, or being looked after as a long-term resident in a nursing or retirement home (and see, most recently, *Gray* v *Taylor* [1998] 4 All ER 17, for a similar approach in relation to an almsperson occupying a flat, under a trust, in an almshouse). However, in other cases the lease/licence issue is a highly contentious one.

(B) Licensees, tenants and private sector rights

In a number of respects a licensee is at a disadvantage in terms of residential status and rights; most importantly, in relation to a lack of statutory rent controls and effective statutory security of tenure (these issues are discussed further in chapter 2). Correspondingly, the legal position of a licensor 'landlord' is significantly stronger. If the matter was to be seen by the courts as merely one of drafting, of contract 'construction', then few well-advised 'landlords' would fail to avail themselves of the licence 'loophole'. Prior to the key decision of *Street* v *Mountford* (below), the law was in danger of accommodating landlords in just this way. However, Lord Templeman, in giving the unanimous judgment of the House of Lords in *Street*, was at pains to emphasise that merely calling something a licence did not necessarily make it one. Instead, the 'reality' of what had been agreed had to be discerned. Above all, what distinguished a tenancy from a licence was that in reality a *tenant* enjoyed *exclusive possession* of the property occupied (the right to exclude others from the property for the duration of the term granted), whereas a licensee did not.

Street v *Mountford*
[1985] AC 809; [1985] 2 All ER 289

LORD TEMPLEMAN: My Lords, by an agreement dated 7 March 1983, the respondent Mr Street granted the appellant Mrs Mountford the right to occupy the furnished rooms numbers 5 and 6 at 5, St Clements Gardens, Boscombe, from 7 March 1983 for £37 a week, subject to termination by 14 days' written notice and subject to the conditions set forth in the agreement. The question raised by this appeal is whether the agreement created a tenancy or a licence.

A tenancy is a term of years absolute. This expression, by section 205(1)(xxvii) of the Law of Property Act 1925, reproducing the common law, includes a term from week to week in possession at a rent and liable to determination by notice or re-entry. Originally a term of years was not an estate in land, the lessee having merely a personal action against his lessor. But a legal estate in leaseholds was created by the Statute of Gloucester 1278 and the Act of 1529 21 Hen. VIII, c. 15. Now by section 1 of the Law of Property Act 1925 a term of years absolute is an estate in land capable of subsisting as a legal estate. In the present case if the agreement dated 7 March 1983 created a tenancy, Mrs Mountford having entered into possession and made weekly payments acquired a legal estate in land. If the agreement is a tenancy, the occupation of Mrs Mountford is protected by the Rent Acts.

A licence in connection with land while entitling the licensee to use the land for the purposes authorised by the licence does not create an estate in the land. If the agreement dated 7 March 1983 created a licence for Mrs Mountford to occupy the premises, she did not acquire any estate in the land. If the agreement is a licence then Mrs Mountford's right of occupation is not protected by the Rent Acts, hence the practical importance of distinguishing between a tenancy and a licence.

In the course of argument, nearly every clause of the agreement dated 7 March 1983 was relied upon by the appellant as indicating a lease and by the respondent as indicating a licence. The agreement, in full, was in these terms:

I Mrs Wendy Mountford agree to take from the owner Roger Street the single furnished room number 5 and 6 at 5 St Clements Gardens, Boscombe, Bournemouth, commencing 7 March 1983 at a licence fee of £37 per week.

I understand that the right to occupy the above room is conditional on the strict observance of the following rules:

1. No paraffin stoves, or other than the supplied form of heating, is allowed in the room.

2. No one but the above-named person may occupy or sleep in the room without prior permission, and this personal licence is not assignable.

3. The owner (or his agent) has the right at all times to enter the room to inspect its condition, read and collect money from meters, carry out maintenance works, install or replace furniture or for any other reasonable purpose.

4. All rooms must be kept in a clean and tidy condition.

5. All damage and breakages must be paid for or replaced at once. An initial deposit equivalent to 2 weeks' licence fee will be refunded on termination of the licence subject to deduction for all damage or other breakages or arrears of licence fee, or retention towards the cost of any necessary possession proceedings.

6. No nuisance or annoyance to be caused to the other occupiers. In particular, all music played after midnight to be kept low so as not to disturb occupiers of other rooms.

7. No children or pets allowed under any circumstances whatsoever.

8. Prompt payment of the licence fee must be made every Monday in advance without fail.

9. If the licence fee or any part of it shall be seven days in arrear or if the occupier shall be in breach of any of the other terms of this agreement or if (except by arrangement) the room is left vacant or unoccupied, the owner may re-enter the room and this licence shall immediately be terminated (without prejudice to all other rights and remedies of the owner).

10. This licence may be terminated by 14 days' written notice given to the occupier at any time by the owner or his agent, or by the same notice by the occupier to the owner or his agent.

Occupier's signature
Owner/agent's signature
Date 7 March 1983

I understand and accept that a licence in the above form does not and is not intended to give me a tenancy protected under the Rent Acts.

Occupier's signature.

On 12 August 1983 on Mrs Mountford's application a fair rent was registered. Mr Street then made application under section 51(a) of the County Courts Act 1959 for a declaration that Mrs Mountford's occupancy was a licence and not a tenancy. The recorder in the county court held that Mrs Mountford was a tenant entitled to the protection of the Rent Acts and made a declaration accordingly. The Court of Appeal held that Mrs Mountford was a licensee not entitled to the protection of the Rent Acts. Mrs Mountford appeals.

. . .

In the present case, it is submitted, the provisions of the agreement dated 7 March 1983 and in particular clauses 2, 4, 7 and 9 and the express declaration at the foot of the agreement manifest the clear intention of both parties that the rights granted are to be those of a personal nature and not those of a tenant.

My Lords, there is no doubt that the traditional distinction between a tenancy and a licence of land lay in the grant of land for a term at a rent with exclusive possession. In some cases it was not clear at first sight whether exclusive possession was in fact granted. For example, an owner of land could grant a licence to cut and remove standing timber. Alternatively the owner could grant a tenancy of the land with the right to cut and remove standing timber during the term of the tenancy. The grant of rights relating to standing timber therefore required careful consideration in order to decide whether the grant conferred exclusive possession of the land for a term at a rent and was therefore a tenancy or whether it merely conferred a bare licence to remove the timber.

. . .

In the case of residential accommodation there is no difficulty in deciding whether the grant confers exclusive possession. An occupier of residential accommodation at a rent for a term is either a lodger or a tenant. The occupier is a lodger if the landlord provides attendance or services which require the landlord or his servants to exercise unrestricted access to and use of the premises. A lodger is entitled to live in the premises but cannot call the place his own. In *Allan* v *Liverpool Overseers* (1874) LR 9 QB 180, 191–192 Blackburn J said:

> A lodger in a house, although he had the exclusive use of rooms in the house, in the sense that nobody else is to be there, and though his goods are stowed there, yet he is not in exclusive occupation in that sense, because the landlord is there for the purpose of being able, as landlords commonly do in the case of lodgings, to have his own servants to look after the house and the furniture, and has retained to himself the occupation, though he has agreed to give the exclusive enjoyment of the occupation to the lodger.

If on the other hand residential accommodation is granted for a term at a rent with exclusive possession, the landlord providing neither attendance nor services, the grant is a tenancy; any express reservation to the landlord of limited rights to enter and view the state of the premises and to repair and maintain the premises only serves to emphasise the fact that the grantee is entitled to exclusive possession and is a tenant. In the present case it is conceded that Mrs Mountford is entitled to exclusive possession and is not a lodger. Mr Street provided neither attendance nor services and only reserved the limited rights of inspection and maintenance and the like set forth in clause 3 of the agreement. On the traditional view of the matter, Mrs Mountford not being a lodger must be a tenant.

There can be no tenancy unless the occupier enjoys exclusive possession; but an occupier who enjoys exclusive possession is not necessarily a tenant. He may be owner in fee simple, a trespasser, a mortgagee in possession, an object of charity or a service occupier. To constitute a tenancy the occupier must be granted exclusive possession for a fixed or periodic term certain in consideration of a premium or periodical payments. The grant may be express, or may be inferred where the owner accepts weekly or other periodical payments from the occupier.

Occupation by service occupier may be eliminated. A service occupier is a servant who occupies his master's premises in order to perform his duties as a servant. In those circumstances the possession and occupation of the servant is treated as the possession and occupation of the master and the relationship of landlord and tenant is not created; see *Mayhew* v *Suttle* (1854) 4 El & Bl 347. The test is whether the servant requires the premises he occupies in order the better to perform his duties as a servant:

'Where the occupation is necessary for the performance of services, and the occupier is required to reside in the house in order to perform those services, the occupation being strictly ancillary to the performance of the duties which the occupier has to perform, the occupation is that of a servant'; *per* Mellor J in *Smith* v *Seghill Overseers* (1875) LR 10 QB 422, 428.

The cases on which Mr Goodhart relies begin with *Booker* v *Palmer* [1942] 2 All ER 674. The owner of a cottage agreed to allow a friend to install an evacuee in the cottage rent free for the duration of the war. The Court of Appeal held that there was no intention on the part of the owner to enter into legal relationships with the evacuee. Lord Greene MR, said, at p. 677:

To suggest there is an intention there to create a relationship of landlord and tenant appears to me to be quite impossible. There is one golden rule which is of very general application, namely, that the law does not impute intention to enter into legal relationships where the circumstances and the conduct of the parties negative any intention of the kind. It seems to me that this is a clear example of the application of that rule.

The observations of Lord Greene MR were not directed to the distinction between a contractual tenancy and a contractual licence. The conduct of the parties (not their professed intentions) indicated that they did not intend to contract at all.

In the present case, the agreement dated 7 March 1983 professed an intention by both parties to create a licence and their belief that they had in fact created a licence. It was submitted on behalf of Mr Street that the court cannot in these circumstances decide that the agreement created a tenancy without interfering with the freedom of contract enjoyed by both parties. My Lords, Mr Street enjoyed freedom to offer Mrs Mountford the right to occupy the rooms comprised in the agreement on such lawful terms as Mr Street pleased. Mrs Mountford enjoyed freedom to negotiate with Mr Street to obtain different terms. Both parties enjoyed freedom to contract or not to contract and both parties exercised that freedom by contracting on the terms set forth in the written agreement and on no other terms. But the consequences in law of the agreement, once concluded, can only be determined by consideration of the effect of the agreement. If the agreement satisfied all the requirements of a tenancy, then the agreement produced a tenancy and the parties cannot alter the effect of the agreement by insisting that they only created a licence. The manufacture of a five pronged implement for manual digging results in a fork even if the manufacturer, unfamiliar with the English language, insists that he intended to make and has made a spade.

It was also submitted that in deciding whether the agreement created a tenancy or a licence, the court should ignore the Rent Acts. If Mr Street has succeeded, where

owners have failed these past 70 years, in driving a coach and horses through the Rent
Acts, he must be left to enjoy the benefit of his ingenuity unless and until Parliament
intervenes. I accept that the Rent Acts are irrelevant to the problem of determining
the legal effect of the rights granted by the agreement. Like the professed intention of
the parties, the Rent Acts cannot alter the effect of the agreement.

In *Marcroft Wagons Ltd* v *Smith* [1951] 2 KB 496 the daughter of a deceased tenant
who lived with her mother claimed to be a statutory tenant by succession and the
landlords asserted that the daughter had no rights under the Rent Acts and was a
trespasser. The landlords expressly refused to accept the daughter's claims but
accepted rent from her while they were considering the position. If the landlords had
decided not to apply to the court for possession but to accept the daughter as a tenant,
the moneys paid by the daughter would have been treated as rent. If the landlords
decided, as they did decide, to apply for possession and to prove, as they did prove,
that the daughter was not a statutory tenant, the moneys paid by the daughter were
treated as mesne profits. The Court of Appeal held with some hesitation that the
landlords never accepted the daughter as tenant and never intended to contract with
her although the landlords delayed for some six months before applying to the court
for possession. Roxburgh J said, at p. 507:

> Generally speaking, when a person, having a sufficient estate in land, lets another
> into exclusive possession, a tenancy results, and there is no question of a licence.
> But the inference of a tenancy is not necessarily to be drawn where a person
> succeeds on a death to occupation of rent-controlled premises and a landlord
> accepts some rent while he or the occupant, or both of them, is or are considering
> his or their position. If this is all that happened in this case, then no tenancy would
> result.

In that case, as in *Booker* v *Palmer* the court deduced from the conduct of the parties
that they did not intend to contract at all.

Errington v *Errington and Woods* [1952] 1 KB 290 concerned a contract by a father
to allow his son to buy the father's house on payment of the instalments of the father's
building society loan. Denning LJ referred, at p. 297, to the judgment of Lord Greene
MR in *Booker* v *Palmer* [1942] 2 All ER 674, 677 where, however, the circumstances
and the conduct of the parties negatived any intention to enter into legal relationships.
Denning LJ continued, at pp. 297–298:

> We have had many instances lately of occupiers in exclusive possession who have
> been held to be not tenants, but only licensees. When a requisitioning authority
> allowed people into possession at a weekly rent: . . . when a landlord told a tenant
> on his retirement that he could live in a cottage rent free for the rest of his days:
> . . . when a landlord, on the death of the widow of a statutory tenant, allowed her
> daughter to remain in possession, paying rent for six months: *Marcroft Wagons Ltd*
> v *Smith* [1951] 2 KB 496; when the owner of a shop allowed the manager to live
> in a flat above the shop, but did not require him to do so, and the value of the flat
> was taken into account at £1 a week in fixing his wages: . . . in each of those cases
> the occupier was held to be a licensee and not a tenant . . . The result of all these
> cases is that, although a person who is let into exclusive possession is prima facie to
> be considered a tenant, nevertheless he will not be held to be so if the circumstances
> negative any intention to create a tenancy. Words alone may not suffice. Parties
> cannot turn a tenancy into a licence merely by calling it one. But if the circumstan-
> ces and the conduct of the parties show that all that was intended was that the

occupier should be granted a personal privilege, with no interest in the land, he will be held to be a licensee only.

In *Errington* v *Errington and Woods* [1952] 1 KB 290 and in the cases cited by Denning LJ at p. 297 there were exceptional circumstances which negatived the prima facie intention to create a tenancy, notwithstanding that the occupier enjoyed exclusive occupation. The intention to create a tenancy was negatived if the parties did not intend to enter into legal relationships at all, or where the relationship between the parties was that of vendor and purchaser, master and service occupier, or where the owner, a requisitioning authority, had no power to grant a tenancy. These exceptional circumstances are not to be found in the present case where there has been the lawful, independent and voluntary grant of exclusive possession for a term at a rent.

If the observations of Denning LJ are applied to the facts of the present case it may fairly be said that the circumstances negative any intention to create a mere licence. Words alone do not suffice. Parties cannot turn a tenancy into a licence merely by calling it one. The circumstances and the conduct of the parties show that what was intended was that the occupier should be granted exclusive possession at a rent for a term with a corresponding interest in the land which created a tenancy.

In *Cobb* v *Lane* [1952] 1 TLR 1037, an owner allowed her brother to occupy a house rent free. The county court judge, who was upheld by the Court of Appeal, held that there was no intention to create any legal relationship and that a tenancy at will was not to be implied. This is another example of conduct which negatives any intention of entering into a contract, and does not assist in distinguishing a contractual tenancy from a contractual licence.

In *Facchini* v *Bryson* [1952] 1 TLR 1386, an employer and his assistant entered into an agreement which, inter alia, allowed the assistant to occupy a house for a weekly payment on terms which conferred exclusive possession. The assistant did not occupy the house for the better performance of his duty and was not therefore a service occupier. The agreement stipulated that 'nothing in this agreement shall be construed to create a tenancy between the employer and the assistant.' Somervell LJ said, at p. 1389:

If, looking at the operative clauses in the agreement, one comes to the conclusion that the rights of the occupier, to use a neutral word, are those of a lessee, the parties cannot turn it into a licence by saying at the end 'this is deemed to be a licence;' nor can they, if the operative paragraphs show that it is merely a licence, say that it should be deemed to be a lease.

Denning LJ referred to several cases including *Errington* v *Errington and Woods* and *Cobb* v *Lane* and said, at pp. 1389–1390:

In all the cases where an occupier has been held to be a licensee there has been something in the circumstances, such as a family arrangement, an act of friendship or generosity, or such like, to negative any intention to create a tenancy . . . In the present case, however, there are no special circumstances. It is a simple case where the employer let a man into occupation of a house in consequence of his employment at a weekly sum payable by him. The occupation has all the features of a service tenancy, and the parties cannot by the mere words of their contract turn it into something else. Their relationship is determined by the law and not by the label which they choose to put on it: . . .

The decision, which was thereafter binding on the Court of Appeal and on all lower courts, referred to the special circumstances which are capable of negativing an intention to create a tenancy and reaffirmed the principle that the professed intentions of the parties are irrelevant. The decision also indicated that in a simple case a grant of exclusive possession of residential accommodation for a weekly sum creates a tenancy.

In *Murray Bull & Co. Ltd* v *Murray* [1953] 1 QB 211 a contractual tenant held over, paying rent quarterly. McNair J found, at p. 217:

> both parties intended that the relationship should be that of licensee and no more
> . . . The primary consideration on both sides was that the defendant, as occupant
> of the flat, should not be a controlled tenant.

In my opinion this case was wrongly decided. McNair J citing the observations of Denning LJ in *Errington* v *Errington and Woods* [1952] 1 KB 290, 297 and *Marcroft Wagons Ltd* v *Smith* [1961] 2 KB 496 failed to distinguish between first, conduct which negatives an intention to create legal relationships, secondly, special circumstances which prevent exclusive occupation from creating a tenancy and thirdly, the professed intention of the parties. In *Murray Bull & Co. Ltd* v *Murray* the conduct of the parties showed an intention to contract and there were no relevant special circumstances. The tenant holding over continued by agreement to enjoy exclusive possession and to pay a rent for a term certain. In those circumstances he continued to be a tenant notwithstanding the professed intention of the parties to create a licence and their desire to avoid a controlled tenancy.

In *Addiscombe Garden Estates Ltd* v *Crabbe* [1958] 1 QB 513 the Court of Appeal considered an agreement relating to a tennis club carried on in the grounds of a hotel. The agreement was:

> 'described by the parties as a licence . . . . the draftsman has studiously and
> successfully avoided the use either of the word "landlord" or the word "tenant"
> throughout the document' *per* Jenkins LJ at p. 522.

On analysis of the whole of the agreement the Court of Appeal came to the conclusion that the agreement conferred exclusive possession and thus created a tenancy. Jenkins LJ said, at p. 522:

> The whole of the document must be looked at; and if, after it has been examined,
> the right conclusion appears to be that, whatever label may have been attached to
> it, it in fact conferred and imposed on the grantee in substance the rights and
> obligations of a tenant, and on the grantor in substance the rights and obligations
> of a landlord, then it must be given the appropriate effect, that is to say, it must be
> treated as a tenancy agreement as distinct from a mere licence.

In the agreement in the *Addiscombe* case it was by no means clear until the whole of the document had been narrowly examined that exclusive possession was granted by the agreement. In the present case it is clear that exclusive possession was granted and so much is conceded. In these circumstances it is unnecessary to analyse minutely the detailed rights and obligations contained in the agreement.

In the *Addiscombe* case Jenkins LJ referred, at p. 528, to the observations of Denning LJ in *Errington and Errington and Woods* to the effect that 'The test of exclusive possession is by no means decisive'. Jenkins LJ continued:

> I think that wide statement must be treated as qualified by his observations in
> *Facchini* v *Bryson* [1952] 1 TLR 1386, 1389; and it seems to me that, save in

exceptional cases of the kind mentioned by Denning LJ in that case, the law remains that the fact of exclusive possession, if not decisive against the view that there is a mere licence, as distinct from a tenancy, is at all events a consideration of the first importance.

Exclusive possession is of first importance in considering whether an occupier is a tenant; exclusive possession is not decisive because an occupier who enjoys exclusive possession is not necessarily a tenant. The occupier may be a lodger or service occupier or fall within the other exceptional categories mentioned by Denning LJ in *Errington v Errington and Woods* [1952] 1 KB 290.

In *Isaac v Hotel de Paris Ltd* [1960] 1 WLR 239 an employee who managed a night bar in a hotel for his employer company which held a lease of the hotel negotiated 'subject to contract' to complete the purchase of shares in the company and to be allowed to run the nightclub for his own benefit if he paid the head rent payable by the company for the hotel. In the expectation that the negotiations 'subject to contract' would ripen into a binding agreement, the employee was allowed to run the nightclub and he paid the company's rent. When negotiations broke down the employee claimed unsuccessfully to be a tenant of the hotel company. The circumstances in which the employee was allowed to occupy the premises showed that the hotel company never intended to accept him as a tenant and that he was fully aware of that fact. This was a case, consistent with the authorities cited by Lord Denning in giving the advice of the Judicial Committee of the Privy Council, in which the parties did not intend to enter into contractual relationships unless and until the negotiations 'subject to contract' were replaced by a binding contract.

In *Abbeyfield (Harpenden) Society Ltd v Woods* [1968] 1 WLR 374 the occupier of a room in an old people's home was held to be a licensee and not a tenant. Lord Denning MR said, at p. 376:

> The modern cases show that a man may be a licensee even though he has exclusive possession, even though the word 'rent' is used, and even though the word 'tenancy' is used. The court must look at the agreement as a whole and see whether a tenancy really was intended. In this case there is, besides the one room, the provision of services, meals, a resident housekeeper, and such like. The whole arrangement was so personal in nature that the proper inference is that he was a licensee.

As I understand the decision in the *Abbeyfield* case the court came to the conclusion that the occupier was a lodger and was therefore a licensee, not a tenant.

In *Shell-Mex and B.P. Ltd v Manchester Garages Ltd* [1971] 1 WLR 612 the Court of Appeal after carefully examining an agreement whereby the defendant was allowed to use a petrol company's filling station for the purposes of selling petrol, came to the conclusion that the agreement did not grant exclusive possession to the defendant who was therefore a licensee. At p. 615 Lord Denning MR in considering whether the transaction was a licence or a tenancy said:

> Broadly speaking, we have to see whether it is a personal privilege given to a person (in which case it is a licence), or whether it grants an interest in land (in which case it is a tenancy). At one time it used to be thought that exclusive possession was a decisive factor. But that is not so. It depends on broader considerations altogether. Primarily on whether it is personal in its nature or not: see *Errington v Errington and Woods* [1952] 1 KB 290.

In my opinion the agreement was only 'personal in its nature' and created 'a personal privilege' if the agreement did not confer the right to exclusive possession of the filling station. No other test for distinguishing between a contractual tenancy and a contractual licence appears to be understandable or workable.

Heslop v *Burns* [1974] 1 WLR 1241 was another case in which the owner of a cottage allowed a family to live in the cottage rent free and it was held that no tenancy at will had been created on the ground that the parties did not intend any legal relationship. Scarman LJ cited with approval, at p. 1252, the statement by Denning LJ in *Facchini* v *Bryson* [1952] 1 TLR 1386, 1389:

> In all the cases where an occupier has been held to be a licensee there has been something in the circumstances, such as a family arrangement, an act of friendship or generosity, or such like, to negative any intention to create a tenancy.

In *Marchant* v *Charters* [1977] 1 WLR 1181 a bedsitting room was occupied on terms that the landlord cleaned the rooms daily and provided clean linen each week. It was held by the Court of Appeal that the occupier was a licensee and not a tenant. The decision in the case is sustainable on the grounds that the occupier was a lodger and did not enjoy exclusive possession. But Lord Denning MR said, at p. 1185:

> What is the test to see whether the occupier of one room in a house is a tenant or a licensee? It does not depend on whether he or she has exclusive possession or not. It does not depend on whether the room is furnished or not. It does not depend on whether the occupation is permanent or temporary. It does not depend on the label which the parties put upon it. All these are factors which may influence the decision but none of them is conclusive. All the circumstances have to be worked out. Eventually the answer depends on the nature and quality of the occupancy. Was it intended that the occupier should have a stake in the room or did he have only permission for himself personally to occupy the room, whether under a contract or not? In which case he is a licensee.

> But in my opinion in order to ascertain the nature and quality of the occupancy and to see whether the occupier has or has not a stake in the room or only permission for himself personally to occupy, the court must decide whether upon its true construction the agreement confers on the occupier exclusive possession. If exclusive possession at a rent for a term does not constitute a tenancy then the distinction between a contractual tenancy and a contractual licence of land becomes wholly unidentifiable.

> In *Somma* v *Hazelhurst* [1978] 1 WLR 1014, a young unmarried couple H and S occupied a double bedsitting room for which they paid a weekly rent. The landlord did not provide services or attendance and the couple were not lodgers but tenants enjoying exclusive possession. But the Court of Appeal did not ask themselves whether H and S were lodgers or tenants and did not draw the correct conclusion from the fact that H and S enjoyed exclusive possession. The Court of Appeal were diverted from the correct inquiries by the fact that the landlord obliged H and S to enter into separate agreements and reserved power to determine each agreement separately. The landlord also insisted that the room should not in form be let to either H or S or to both H and S but that each should sign an agreement to share the room in common with such other persons as the landlord might from time to time nominate. The sham nature of this obligation would have been only slightly more obvious if H and S had been married or if the room had been furnished with a double bed instead of two single beds. If the landlord had served notice on H to leave and had required S to share the room with a strange man, the notice would only have been a disguised notice to quit on both H and S. The room was let and taken as residential accommodation with exclusive possession in order that H and S might live together in undisturbed

quasi-connubial bliss making weekly payments. The agreements signed by H and S constituted the grant to H and S jointly of exclusive possession at a rent for a term for the purposes for which the room was taken and the agreement therefore created a tenancy. Although the Rent Acts must not be allowed to alter or influence the construction of an agreement, the court should, in my opinion, be astute to detect and frustrate sham devices and artificial transactions whose only object is to disguise the grant of a tenancy and to evade the Rent Acts. I would disapprove of the decision in this case that H and S were only licensees and for the same reason would disapprove of the decision in *Aldrington Garages Ltd* v *Fielder* (1978) 37 P & CR 461 and *Sturolson & Co.* v *Weniz* (1984) 272 EG 326.

In the present case the Court of Appeal, 49 P & CR 461 held that the agreement dated 7 March 1983 only created a licence. Slade LJ, at p. 329 accepted that the agreement and in particular clause 3 of the agreement 'shows that the right to occupy the premises conferred on the defendant was intended as an exclusive right of occupation, in that it was thought necessary to give a special and express power to the plaintiff to enter . . .' Before your Lordships it was conceded that the agreement conferred the right of exclusive possession on Mrs Mountford. Even without clause 3 the result would have been the same. By the agreement Mrs Mountford was granted the right to occupy residential accommodation. The landlord did not provide any services or attendance. It was plain that Mrs Mountford was not a lodger. Slade LJ proceeded to analyse all the provisions of the agreement, not for the purpose of deciding whether his finding of exclusive possession was correct, but for the purpose of assigning some of the provisions of the agreement to the category of terms which he thought are usually to be found in a tenancy agreement and of assigning other provisions to the category of terms which he thought are usually to be found in a licence. Slade LJ may or may not have been right that in a letting of a furnished room it was 'most unusual to find a provision in a tenancy agreement obliging the tenant to keep his rooms in a "tidy condition"' (p. 329). If Slade LJ was right about this and other provisions there is still no logical method of evaluating the results of his survey. Slade LJ reached the conclusion that 'the agreement bears all the hallmarks of a licence rather than a tenancy save for the one important feature of exclusive occupation': p. 329. But in addition to the hallmark of exclusive occupation of residential accommodation there were the hallmarks of weekly payments for a periodical term. Unless these three hallmarks are decisive, it really becomes impossible to distinguish a contractual tenancy from a contractual licence save by reference to the professed intention of the parties or by the judge awarding marks for drafting. Slade LJ was finally impressed by the statement at the foot of the agreement by Mrs Mountford 'I understand and accept that a licence in the above form does not and is not intended to give me a tenancy protected under the Rent Acts.' Slade LJ said, at p. 330:

> it seems to me that, if the defendant is to displace the express statement of intention embodied in the declaration, she must show that the declaration was either a deliberate sham or at least an inaccurate statement of what was the true substance of the real transaction agreed between the parties; . . .

My Lords, the only intention which is relevant is the intention demonstrated by the agreement to grant exclusive possession for a term at a rent. Sometimes it may be difficult to discover whether, on the true construction of an agreement, exclusive possession is conferred. Sometimes it may appear from the surrounding circumstances that there was no intention to create legal relationships. Sometimes it may appear from the surrounding circumstances that the right to exclusive possession is referable to a legal relationship other than a tenancy. Legal relationships to which the grant of exclusive possession might be referable and which would or might negative the grant of an estate or interest in the land include occupancy under a contract for the sale of the land, occupancy pursuant to a contract of employment or occupancy referable to the holding of an office. But where as in the present case the only circumstances are that residential accommodation is offered and accepted with exclusive possession for a term at a rent, the result is a tenancy.

The position was well summarised by Windeyer J sitting in the High Court of Australia in *Radaich* v *Smith* (1959) 101 CLR 209, 222, where he said:

> What then is the fundamental right which a tenant has that distinguishes his position from that of a licensee? It is an interest in land as distinct from a personal permission to enter the land and use it for some stipulated purpose or purposes. And how is it to be ascertained whether such an interest in land has been given? By seeing whether the grantee was given a legal right of exclusive possession of the land for a term or from year to year or for a life or lives. If he was, he is a tenant. And he cannot be other than a tenant, because a legal right of exclusive possession is a tenancy and the creation of such a right is a demise. To say that a man who has, by agreement with a landlord, a right of exclusive possession of land for a term is not a tenant is simply to contradict the first proposition by the second. A right of exclusive possession is secured by the right of a lessee to maintain ejectment and, after his entry, trespass. A reservation to the landlord, either by contract or statute, of a limited right of entry, as for example to view or repair, is, of course, not inconsistent with the grant of exclusive possession. Subject to such reservations, a tenant for a term or from year to year or for a life or lives can exclude his landlord as well as strangers from the demised premises. All this is long established law: see *Cole on Ejectment* (1857) pp. 72, 73, 287, 458.

My Lords, I gratefully adopt the logic and the language of Windeyer J. Henceforth the courts which deal with these problems will, save in exceptional circumstances, only be concerned to inquire whether as a result of an agreement relating to residential accommodation the occupier is a lodger or a tenant. In the present case I am satisfied that Mrs Mountford is a tenant, that the appeal should be allowed, that the order of the Court of Appeal should be set aside and that the respondent should be ordered to pay the costs of the appellant here and below.

Questions
1.   Was *Street* definitive? Could it be assumed that any residential occupation lacking 'lodger' (or other distinct) characteristics would henceforward be treated as a tenancy?
2.   To what extent was previous case law on the issue approved or disapproved? (Note in particular Lord Templeman's discussion of *Addiscombe* v *Crabbe* [1958] 1 QB 513; *Abbeyfield* v *Woods* [1968] 1 WLR 374; *Marchant* v *Charters* [1977] 1 WLR 1181 and *Somma* v *Hazelhurst* [1978] 1 WLR 1014.)
3.   Was Lord Templeman correct to state that 'An occupier of residential accommodation at a rent for a term is either a lodger or a tenant'?
4.   What types of situations do you think Lord Templeman had in mind when (at the end of his judgment) he states that in 'exceptional circumstances' the usual test(s) for determining tenant status might not apply?

5.   Above all, how were the courts to, in the future, approach the determination of the licensee/tenant question if the form of the agreement was not to be
seen as conclusive? Was it, in effect, a policy issue – that any attempt to treat a
'normal' residential arrangement as 'non-exclusive' would be treated as a
'sham' unless the *property owner* could prove that this was a true indication of
how the agreement was likely to operate *in practice*? (Note, in *Street* the
solicitor/landlord admitted that there had been in reality exclusive possession.)

Following *Street* the Court of Appeal attempted to resolve some of the above
issues. However, no consistent 'line' emerged. In some cases a wide 'policy
orientated' view of *Street* was taken. In other cases the landlord's continuing
right to 'contract out' of protective legislation was underlined (see in
particular the widely divergent approaches of the Court of Appeal in *A. G.
Securities* v *Vaughan* and *Antoniades* v *Villiers*, below). Finally, the House of
Lords returned to the issue again in the linked cases of *A. G. Securities* v
Vaughan and *Antoniades* v *Villiers*. The decision of the House was unanimous,
although all of their Lordships delivered judgments. Lord Templeman's
judgment and part of Lord Oliver's are reproduced here.

A. G. Securities v *Vaughan and Others*; *Antoniades* v *Villiers*
[1990] 1 AC 417; [1988] 3 All ER 1058

LORD TEMPLEMAN: My Lords, in each of the two appeals now under consideration, the question is whether the owner of residential accommodation granted a
tenancy or granted licences.
   In the first appeal, the appellant company, A.G. Securities, owned a block of flats,
Linden Mansions, Hornsey Lane, London. Flat No. 25 consists of six living rooms in
addition to a kitchen and bathroom. The company furnished four living-rooms as
bedrooms, a fifth as a lounge and a sixth as a sitting-room. In 1974 furnished lettings
became subject to the Rent Acts. If the company granted exclusive possession of the
flat to one single occupier or to two or more occupiers jointly in consideration of
periodical payments, the grant would create a tenancy of the flat. If the company
granted exclusive possession of one bedroom to four different occupiers with joint use
of the lounge, sitting-room, kitchen and bathroom, each of the four grants would
create a tenancy of one bedroom. Exclusive possession means either exclusive
occupation or receipt of rent and profits.
   The company entered into separate agreements with four different applicants. Each
agreement was in the same form, and was expressed to be made between the company
as 'the owner' and the applicant as 'licensee.' The agreement contained, inter alia, the
following relevant clauses:

   1.   The owner grants to the licensee the right to use in common with others who
   have or may from time to time be granted the like right the flat known as 25, Linden
   Mansions, Hornsey Lane, N6 but without the right to exclusive possession of any
   part of the said flat together with fixtures furniture furnishings and effects now in
   the said flat for six months from the ———— day of —————— 19—— and
   agreements signed by them respectively, they became tenants of the flat.
. . .

The company contends that each respondent is a licensee.

In the second appeal, the appellant, Mr Antoniades, is the owner of the house, 6, Whiteley Road, Upper Norwood. The attic was converted into furnished residential accommodation comprising a bedroom, a bed sitting-room, kitchen and bathroom. The furniture in the sitting-room consisted of a bed-settee, a table-bed, a sideboard and a chair.

The appellants, Mr Villiers and Miss Bridger, spent three months looking for a flat where they could live together. In February 1985 they were shown the attic flat. The bedroom lacked a bed; the appellants expressed a preference for a double bed which Mr Antoniades agreed to provide. Mr Antoniades and Mr Villiers entered into an agreement dated 9 February 1985. The agreement was described as a licence, Mr Antoniades was described as 'the licensor' and Mr Villiers was described as 'the licensee'. The agreement recited that

'the licensor is not willing to grant the licensee exclusive possession of any part of the rooms hereinafter referred to' and that 'the licensee is anxious to secure the use of the rooms notwithstanding that such use be in common with the licensor and such other licensees or invitees as the licensor may permit from time to time to use the said rooms.'

The material provisions of the agreement were as follows:

By this licence the licensor licences the licensee to use (but not exclusively) all those rooms (hereinafter referred to as 'the rooms') on the top flat (1 bedroom, 1 bed-sitting-room, the kitchen and bathroom) of the building . . . 6, Whiteley Road SE19 . . . together with the use of the furniture fixtures and effects now in the rooms (more particularly set out in the schedule of contents annexed hereto) from 14 February 1985 for the sum of £87 per calendar month on the following terms and conditions: (1) The licensee agrees to pay the said sum of £87 (on the 14th of each month) monthly in advance . . . (3) The licensee shall use his best endeavours amicably and peaceably to share the use of the rooms with the licensor and with such other licensees or invitees whom the licensor shall from time to time permit to use the rooms and shall not interfere with or otherwise obstruct such shared occupation in any way whatsoever . . . (10) The licensee shall not do or suffer to be done in the rooms any act or thing which may be a nuisance cause of damage or annoyance to the licensor and the other occupiers or uses of the rooms . . . (12) The licensee . . . will not use the rooms in any illegal or immoral way . . . (16) The licensor shall be entitled at any time to use the rooms together with the licensee and permit other persons to use all of the rooms together with the licensee . . . (17) This license is personal to the licensee and shall not permit the use of the rooms by any person whatsoever and only the licensor will have the right to use or permit the use of the rooms as described in clause 16. The licensee under no circumstances will have the right to allow any other people of his choice to use the rooms in any way . . . (22) The licensee (occupier) declares that he is over 18 years old and understands this licence . . . (23) The real intention of the parties in all surrounding circumstances is to create this licence which is not coming under the Rent Acts and is binding as written . . . (24) This licence represents the entire agreement of the parties and no oral or other agreements were made and no different explanations or representations were made and only agreements in writing will be legally binding . . . . (25) The licensee read and understood this licence and received copy and the licensee understands that all rooms and all parts of the dwelling will be shared and no exclusive possession of any part of the whole will be allowed to the licensees by the licensor under any circumstances.

There then followed the schedule of furniture and then a new clause as follows:

26. Subject to clause 21 this licence may be terminated by one month's notice in writing given by either party at any time and the licensor reserves the right of eviction without court order.

That agreement was signed by Mr Villiers in five places and each of his signatures was witnessed.

Either then or thereafter, Mr Villiers signed an addendum to the agreement whereby Mr Villiers:

Agrees that the licence signed on 9 February 1985 does not come under the Rent Acts and the flat is for single people sharing and if Mr Villiers marries any occupier of the flat then Mr Villiers will give notice and vacate the flat at 6, Whiteley Road London SE19. The owner Mr Antoniades did not promise any other accommodation in any way. No persons will have exclusive possession of the above flat as agreed.

Mr Antoniades entered into a separate agreement and a separate addendum with Miss Bridger. The agreement and the addendum were in the same form, bore the same date, were executed on the same day and were signed and witnessed in the same way as the agreement and addendum entered into by Mr Villiers.

Thereupon Mr Villiers and Miss Bridger entered into occupation of the rooms comprised in the agreement. Mr Antoniades has never attempted to use any of the rooms or authorised any other person to use the rooms.

The appellants, Mr Villiers and Miss Bridger, claim that they became tenants of the whole of the attic flat. Mr Antoniades contends that each appellant is a licensee.

My Lords, ever since 1915 the Rent Acts have protected some tenants of residential accommodation with security of tenure and maximum rents. The scope and effect of the Rent Acts have been altered from time to time and the current legislative protection is contained in the Rent Act 1977. Section 1 of the Act of 1977, reproducing earlier enactments, provides:

Subject to this Part of this Act, a tenancy under which a dwelling-house (which may be a house or part of a house) is let as a separate dwelling is a protected tenancy for the purposes of this Act.

Parties to an agreement cannot contract out of the Rent Acts; if they were able to do so the Acts would be a dead letter because in a state of housing shortage a person seeking residential accommodation may agree to anything to obtain shelter. The Rent Acts protect a tenant but they do not protect a licensee. Since parties to an agreement cannot contract out of the Rent Acts, a document which expressed the intention, genuine or bogus, of both parties or of one party to create a licence will nevertheless create a tenancy if the rights and obligations enjoyed and imposed satisfy the legal requirements of a tenancy. A person seeking residential accommodation may concur in any expression of intention in order to obtain shelter. Since parties to an agreement cannot contract out of the Rent Acts, a document expressed in the language of a licence must nevertheless be examined and construed by the court in order to decide whether the rights and obligations enjoyed and imposed create a licence or a tenancy. A person seeking residential accommodation may sign a document couched in any language in order to obtain shelter. Since parties to an agreement cannot contract out of the Rent Acts, the grant of a tenancy to two persons jointly cannot be concealed, accidentally or by design, by the creation of two documents in the form of licences. Two persons seeking residential accommodation may sign any number of documents in order to obtain joint shelter. In considering one or more documents for the purpose of deciding whether a tenancy has been created, the court must consider the surrounding circumstances including any relationship between the prospective occupiers, the course of negotiations and the nature and extent of the accommodation and the intended and actual mode of occupation of the accommodation. If the owner of a one-bedroomed flat granted a licence to a husband to occupy that flat provided he share the flat with his wife and nobody else and granted a similar licence to the wife provided she shared the flat with the husband and nobody else, the court would be bound to consider the effect of both documents together. If the licence to the husband required him to pay a licence fee of £50 per month and the licence to the wife required her to pay a further licence fee of £50 per month, the two documents read together in the light of the property to be occupied and the obvious intended mode of occupation would confer exclusive occupation on the husband and wife jointly and a tenancy at the rent of £100.

Landlords dislike the Rent Acts and wish to enjoy the benefits of letting property without the burden of the restrictions imposed by the Acts. Landlords believe that the Rent Acts unfairly interfere with freedom of contract and exacerbate the housing shortage. Tenants on the other hand believe that the Acts are a necessary protection against the exploitation of people who do not own the freehold or long leases of their homes. The court lacks the knowledge and the power to form any judgment on these arguments which fall to be considered and determined by Parliament. The duty of the court is to enforce the Acts and in so doing to observe one principle which is inherent in the Acts and has been long recognised, the principle that parties cannot contract out of the Acts.

The enjoyment of exclusive occupation for a term in consideration of periodical payments creates a tenancy, save in exceptional circumstances not relevant to these appeals: see Street v Mountford [1985] AC 809, 826–827. The grant of one room with exclusive occupation in consideration of a periodic payment creates a tenancy, although if the room is not a dwelling, the tenant is not protected by the Rent Acts: see Curl v Angelo [1948] 2 All ER 189. The grant of one room with exclusive occupation as a dwelling creates a tenancy but if a tenant shares some other essential living premises such as a kitchen with his landlord or other persons, the room is not let as a separate dwelling within the meaning of section 1 of the Rent Act 1977: see Neale v Del Soto [1945] KB 144 and Cole v Harris [1945] KB 474. Section 21 of the Act of 1977 confers some rights on a tenant who shares essential living premises with his landlord, and section 22 confers protection on a tenant who shares some essential living premises with person other than the landlord.

If, under an agreement, the owner of residential accommodation provides services or attendance and retains possession for that purpose the occupier is a lodger and the agreement creates a licence. Under an agreement for the exclusive occupation of a room or rooms consisting of a dwelling for periodic payments then, save in the exceptional circumstances mentioned in Street v Mountford [1985] AC 809, 826–827, a single occupier, if he is not a lodger, must be a tenant. The agreement may provide, expressly or by implication, power for the owner to enter the dwelling to inspect or repair but if the occupier is entitled to the use and enjoyment of the dwelling and is not a lodger he is in exclusive occupation and the agreement creates a tenancy.

Where residential accommodation is occupied by two or more persons the occupiers may be licensees or tenants of the whole or each occupier may be a separate tenant of part. In the present appeals the only question raised is whether the occupiers are licensees or tenants of the whole.

In the first appeal under consideration the company entered into four separate agreements with four separate persons between 1982 and 1985. The agreements were in the same form save that the periodical sum payable under one agreement did not correspond to the sum payable pursuant to any other agreement. The company was not bound to make agreements in the same form or to require any payment. The agreement signed by Mr Vaughan in 1982 did not and could not entitle or compel Mr Vaughan to become a joint tenant of the whole of the flat with Mr Cook in 1985 on the terms of Mr Vaughan's agreement or on the terms of Mr Cook's agreement or on the terms of any other agreement either alone with Mr Cook or together with any other persons. In 1985 Mr Vaughan did not agree to become a joint tenant of the flat with Mr Cook or anybody else. In 1985, in the events which had happened, the company possessed the right reserved to the company by clause 2(3) of Mr Vaughan's agreement to authorise Mr Cook to share the use of the flat in common with Mr Vaughan. In 1985 Mr Vaughan orally agreed with Mr Cook that if the company authorised Mr Cook to use the flat in common with Mr Vaughan, then Mr Vaughan would allow Mr Cook to occupy a specified bedroom in the flat and share the occupation of the other parts of the flat excluding the other three bedrooms. Mr Vaughan's agreement with the company did not prevent him from entering into this oral agreement with Mr Cook. Under the standard form agreement the company did not retain power to allocate the four bedrooms but delegated this power to the occupiers for the time being. If the occupiers had failed to allocate the bedrooms the company would have been obliged to terminate one or more of the agreements. The respondents claim that they are joint tenants of the flat. No single respondent claims to be a tenant of a bedroom.

The Court of Appeal [1988] 2 WLR 689 (Fox and Mustill LJJ, Sir George Waller dissenting), concluded that the four respondents were jointly entitled to exclusive occupation of the flat. I am unable to agree. If a landlord who owns a three-bedroom flat enters into three separate independent tenancies with three independent tenants each of whom is entitled to one bedroom and to share the common parts, then the three tenants, if they agree, can exclude anyone else from the flat. But they do not enjoy exclusive occupation of the flat jointly under the terms of their tenancies. In the present case, if the four respondents had been jointly entitled to exclusive occupation of the flat then, on the death of one of the respondents, the remaining three would be entitled to joint and exclusive occupation. But, in fact, on the death of one respondent the remaining three would not be entitled to joint and exclusive occupation of the flat. They could not exclude a fourth person nominated by the company. I would allow the appeal.

In the first appeal the four agreements were independent of one another. In the second appeal the two agreements were interdependent. Both would have been signed or neither. The two agreements must therefore be read together. Mr Villiers and Miss Bridger applied to rent the flat jointly and sought and enjoyed joint and exclusive occupation of the whole of the flat. They shared the rights and the obligations imposed by the terms of their occupation. They acquired joint and exclusive occupation of the flat in consideration of periodical payments and they therefore acquired a tenancy jointly. Mr Antoniades required each of them, Mr Villiers and Miss Bridger, to agree to pay one half of each aggregate periodical payment, but this circumstance cannot convert a tenancy into a licence. A tenancy remains a tenancy even though the landlord may choose to require each of two joint tenants to agree expressly to pay one half of the rent. The tenancy conferred on Mr Villiers and Miss Bridger the right to occupy the whole flat as their dwelling. Clause 16 reserved to Mr Antoniades the power at any time to go into occupation of the flat jointly with Mr Villiers and Miss Bridger. The exercise of that power would at common law put an end to the exclusive occupation of the flat by Mr Villiers and Miss Bridger, terminate the tenancy of Mr Villiers and Miss Bridger, and convert Mr Villiers and Miss Bridger into licensees. But the powers reserved to Mr Antoniades by clause 16 cannot be lawfully exercised because they are inconsistent with the provisions of the Rent Acts.

When Mr Antoniades entered into the agreements dated 9 February 1985 with Mr Villiers and Miss Bridger and when Mr Antoniades allowed Mr Villiers and Miss Bridger to occupy the flat, it is clear from the negotiations which had taken place, from the surrounding circumstances, and from subsequent events, that Mr Antoniades did not intend in February 1985, immediately or contemporaneously, to share occupation or to authorise any other person to deprive Mr Villiers and Miss Bridger of exclusive occupation of the flat. Clause 16, if genuine, was a reservation by a landlord of a power at some time during the currency of the tenancy to share occupation with the tenant. The exclusive occupation of the tenant coupled with the payment of rent created a tenancy which at common law could be terminated and converted into a licence as soon as the landlord exercised his power to share occupation. But under the Rent Acts, if a contractual tenancy is terminated, the Acts protect the occupiers from eviction.

If a landlord creates a tenancy under which a flat is let as a separate dwelling the tenancy is a protected tenancy under section 1 of the Rent Act 1977. After the termination of a protected tenancy the protected tenant becomes a statutory tenant under section 2 of the Act. By section 3(1):

> So long as he retains possession, a statutory tenant shall observe and be entitled to the benefit of all the terms and conditions of the original contract of tenancy, so far as they are consistent with the provisions of this Act.

By section 98 a court shall not make an order for possession of a dwelling house which is subject to a protected tenancy or a statutory tenancy unless the court considers that it is reasonable to make such an order and is satisfied either that alternative accommodation is available or that certain other conditions are satisfied. The landlord cannot dispense with an order of the court and enter into possession in exercise of his common law powers.

Where a landlord creates a tenancy of a flat and reserves the right to go into exclusive occupation at any time of the whole or part of the flat with or without notice, that reservation is inconsistent with the provisions of the Rent Acts and cannot be enforced without an order of the court under section 98. Where a landlord creates a tenancy of a flat and reserves the right to go into occupation of the whole or part of the flat with or without notice, jointly with the existing tenants, that reservation also is inconsistent with provisions of the Acts. Were it otherwise every tenancy agreement would be labelled a licence and would contract out of the Rent Acts by reserving power to the landlord to share possession with the tenant at any time after the commencement of the term.

Clause 16 is a reservation to Mr Antoniades of the right to go into occupation or to nominate others to enjoy occupation of the whole of the flat jointly with Mr Villiers and Miss Bridger. Until that power is exercised Mr Villiers and Miss Bridger are jointly in exclusive occupation of the whole of the flat making periodical payments and they are therefore tenants. The Rent Acts prevent the exercise of a power which would destroy the tenancy of Mr Villiers and Miss Bridger and would deprive them of the exclusive occupation of the flat which they are now enjoying. Clause 16 is inconsistent with the provisions of the Rent Acts.

There is a separate and alternative reason why clause 16 must be ignored. Clause 16 was not a genuine reservation to Mr Antoniades of a power to share the flat and a power to authorise other persons to share the flat. Mr Antoniades did not genuinely intend to exercise the powers save possibly to bring pressure to bear to obtain possession. Clause 16 was only intended to deprive Mr Villiers and Miss Bridger of the protection of the Rent Acts. Mr Villiers and Miss Bridger had no choice in the matter.

In the notes of Judge Macnair, Mr Villiers is reported as saying that: 'He [Mr Antoniades] kept going on about it being a licence and not in the Rent Act. I didn't know either but was pleased to have a place after three or four months of chasing.' The notes of Miss Bridger's evidence include this passage: 'I didn't understand what was meant by exclusive possession or licence. Signed because so glad to move in. Had been looking for three months.'

In *Street* v *Mountford* [1985] AC 809, 825, I said:

Although the Rent Acts must not be allowed to alter or influence the construction of an agreement, the court should, in my opinion, be astute to detect and frustrate sham devices and artificial transactions whose only object is to disguise the grant of a tenancy and to evade the Rent Acts.

It would have been more accurate and less liable to give rise to misunderstandings if I had substituted the word 'pretence' for the references to 'sham devices' and 'artificial transactions'. *Street* v *Mountford* was not a case which involved a pretence concerning exclusive possession. The agreement did not mention exclusive possession and the owner conceded that the occupier enjoyed exclusive possession. In *Somma* v *Hazelhurst* [1978] 1 WLR 1014 and other cases considered in *Street* v *Mountford*, the owner wished to let residential accommodation but to avoid the Rent Acts. The occupiers wished to take a letting of residential accommodation. The owner stipulated for the execution of agreements which pretended that exclusive possession was not to be enjoyed by the occupiers. The occupiers were obliged to acquiesce with this pretence in order to obtain the accommodation. In my opinion the occupiers either did not understand the language of the agreements or assumed, justifiably, that in practice the owner would not violate their privacy. The owner's real intention was to rely on the language of the agreement to escape the Rent Acts. The owner allowed the occupiers to enjoy jointly exclusive occupation and accepted rent. A tenancy was created. *Street* v *Mountford* reasserted three principles. First, parties to an agreement cannot contract out of the Rent Acts. Secondly, in the absence of special circumstances, not here relevant, the enjoyment of exclusive occupation for a term in consideration of periodic payments creates a tenancy. Thirdly, where the language of licence contradicts the reality of lease, the facts must prevail. The facts must prevail over the language in order that the parties may not contract out of the Rent Acts. In the present case clause 16 was a pretence.

The fact that clause 16 was a pretence appears from its terms and from the negotiations. Clause 16 in terms conferred on Mr Antoniades and other persons the right to share the bedroom occupied by Mr Villiers and Miss Bridger. Clause 16 conferred power on Mr Antoniades to convert the sitting-room occupied by Mr Villiers and Miss Bridger into a bedroom which could be jointly occupied by Mr

Villiers, Miss Bridger, Mr Antoniades and any person or person nominated by Mr Antoniades. The facilities in the flat were not suitable for sharing between strangers. If clause 16 had been genuine there would have been some discussion between Mr Antoniades, Mr Villiers and Miss Bridger as to how clause 16 might be operated in practice and in whose favour it was likely to be operated. The addendum imposed on Mr Villiers and Miss Bridger sought to add plausibility to the pretence of sharing by forfeiting the right of Mr Villiers and Miss Bridger to continue to occupy the flat if their double-bedded romance blossomed into wedding bells. Finally and significantly, Mr Antoniades never made any attempt to obtain increased income from the flat by exercising the powers which clause 16 purported to reserve to him. Clause 16 was only designed to disguise the grant of a tenancy and to contract out of the Rent Acts. In this case in the Court of Appeal [1988] 3 WLR 139, 148, Bingham LJ said:

> The written agreements cannot possibly be construed as giving the occupants, jointly or severally, exclusive possession of the flat or any part of it. They stipulate with reiterated emphasis that the occupants shall not have exclusive possession.

My Lords, in Street v Mountford [1985] AC 809, this House stipulated with reiterated emphasis that an express statement of intention is not decisive and that the court must pay attention to the facts and surrounding circumstances and to what people do as well as to what people say.

In Somma v Hazelhurst [1978] 1 WLR 1014, a young unmarried couple applied to take a double bedsitting-room in order that they might live together. Each signed an agreement to pay £38.80 per month to share the use of the room with the owner and with not more than one other person at any one time. The couple moved into the bedsitting-room and enjoyed exclusive occupation. In terms the owner reserved the right to share living and sleeping quarters with the two applicants. If the couple parted and the youth moved out, the owner could require the damsel to share her living and sleeping quarters with the owner and with a stranger or with one of them or move out herself. The couple enjoyed exclusive occupation until the owner decided to live with them or until one of their agreements was terminated. The right reserved to the owner to require the applicants or one of the applicants to share with the owner or some other third party was contrary to the provisions of the Rent Acts and, in addition was, in the circumstances, a pretence intended only to get round the Rent Acts.

In Aldrington Garages Ltd v Fielder (1978) 37 P & CR 461, Mr Fielder and Miss Maxwell applied to take a self-contained flat in order that they might live together. Each signed an agreement to pay £54.17 per month to share the use of the flat with one other person. The couple moved into the flat and enjoyed exclusive occupation. In terms if the couple parted and Mr Fielder moved out, the owner could require Miss Maxwell to share her living and sleeping quarters with a stranger or move out herself. Mr Fielder and Miss Maxwell enjoyed exclusive occupation unless and until one of their agreements was terminated. The right reserved to the owner to require Miss Maxwell to share with a third party if Mr Fielder's agreement was terminated and to require Mr Fielder to share with a third party if Miss Maxwell's agreement was terminated was contrary to the provisions of the Rent Acts and in addition was, in the circumstances, a pretence intended only to get round the Rent Acts.

In Sturolson & Co. v Weniz (1984) 17 HLR 140, the defendant and a friend applied to take a self-contained flat for the occupation of the defendant, his wife and the friend. The defendant and his friend signed agreements to pay £100 per month to share the flat with such other persons as might be nominated or approved by the owner from time to time. The defendant, his wife and the friend, moved into the flat and enjoyed exclusive occupation. In terms the defendant and the friend paid between them £200 per month for a flat which could be invaded by one or more strangers at any time. The owner's agent gave the game away by saying that the owner was happy so long as he received £200 per month from the flat. The defendant and the friend enjoyed exclusive occupation. The right reserved to the owner to require them to share with others was contrary to the provisions of the Rent Acts and was in any event a pretence intended only to get round the Rent Acts.

In *Street* v *Mountford* [1985] AC 809, 825, this House disapproved of the decisions of the Court of Appeal in *Somma* v *Hazelhurst* [1978] 1 WLR 1014, *Aldrington Garages Ltd* v *Fielder*, 37 P & CR 461 and *Sturolson and Co.* v *Weniz*, 17 HLR 140, which held that the occupiers were only licensees and not tenants.

In *Crancourt Ltd* v *Da Silvaesa* (1986) 18 HLR 265, 276 in which leave was given to defend proceedings under RSC, Ord. 113, Ralph Gibson LJ referring to the disapproval by this House in *Street* v *Mountford* [1985] AC 809, 825, of the decision of the Court of Appeal in *Somma* v *Hazelhurst*, said:

As I understand the reference to the 'sham nature of the obligation,' namely that of sharing the room in common with other persons nominated by the landlord, the House of Lords is there saying, first, that the agreement in that case constituted the grant of exclusive possession; secondly, that the written obligation to share the room was not effective to alter the true nature of the grant; and, thirdly, that, on the facts of the case, it should have been clear to the Court of Appeal that the landlord cannot have intended the term as to sharing occupation to be a true statement of the nature of the possession intended to be enjoyed by the 'licensees'.

I agree with this analysis.

In *Hadjiloucas* v *Crean* [1988] 1 WLR 1006, two single ladies applied to take a two-roomed flat with kitchen and bathroom. Each signed an agreement to pay £260 per month to share the use of the flat with one other person. The two ladies moved into the flat and enjoyed exclusive occupation. In terms, if the agreement of one lady was terminated, the owner could require the other to share the flat with a stranger. The judge in the county court decided that the agreements only created licences. The Court of Appeal ordered a retrial in order that all the facts might be investigated. Since, however, the two ladies applied for and enjoyed exclusive occupation unless and until one of their agreements was terminated, the ladies acquired a tenancy protected by the Rent Acts. The reservation to the owner of the right at common law to require one of the ladies to share the flat with a stranger was a pretence.

My Lords, in each of the cases which were disapproved by this House in *Street* v *Mountford* [1985] AC 809, and in the second appeal now under consideration, there was, in my opinion, the grant of a joint tenancy for the following reasons. (1) The applicants for the flat applied to rent the flat jointly and to enjoy exclusive occupation. (2) The landlord allowed the applicants jointly to enjoy exclusive occupation and accepted rent. A tenancy was created. (3) The power reserved to the landlord to deprive the applicants of exclusive occupation was inconsistent with the provisions of the Rent Acts. (4) Moreover in all the circumstances the power which the landlord insisted upon to deprive the applicants of exclusive occupation was a pretence only intended to deprive the applicants of the protection of the Rent Acts.

The Court of Appeal [1988] 3 WLR 139 (Bingham and Mann LJJ) decided in the second appeal under consideration that Mr Villiers and Miss Bridger were licensees. I would restore the order of Judge MacNair who declared that Mr Villiers and Miss Bridger were tenants protected by the Rent Acts.

LORD OLIVER OF AYLMERTON: My Lords, since lettings of residential property of an appropriate rateable value attract the consequences of controlled rent and security of tenure provided by the Rent Acts, it is not, perhaps, altogether surprising that those who derive their income from residential property are constantly seeking to attain the not always reconcilable objectives on the one hand of keeping their property gainfully occupied and, on the other, of framing their contractual arrangements with the occupants in such a way as to avoid, if they can, the application of the Acts. Since it is only a letting which attracts the operation of the Acts, such endeavours normally take the form of entering into contractual arrangements designed, on their face, to ensure that no estate is created in the occupant for the time being and that his occupation of the land drives merely from a personal and revocable permission granted by way of licence. The critical question, however, in every case is not simply how the arrangement is presented to the outside world in the relevant documentation, but what is the true nature of the arrangement. The decision of this House in *Street v Mountford* [1985] AC 809 established quite clearly that if the true legal effect of the arrangement entered into is that the occupier of residential property has exclusive possession of the property for an ascertainable period in return for periodical money payments, a tenancy is created, whatever the label the parties may have chosen to attach to it. Where, as in that case, the circumstances show that the occupant is the only occupier realistically contemplated and the premises are inherently suitable only for single occupation, there is, generally, very little difficulty. Such an occupier normally has exclusive possession, as indeed she did in *Street v Mountford*, where such possession was conceded, unless the owner retains control and unrestricted access for the purpose of providing attendance and services. As my noble and learned friend, Lord Templeman, observed in that case, the occupier in those circumstances is either a lodger or a tenant. Where, however, the premises are such as, by their nature, to lend themselves to multiple occupation and they are in fact occupied in common by a number of persons under different individual agreements with the owner, more difficult problems arise. These two appeals, at different ends of the scale, are illustrations of such problems.

Antoniades v Villiers and Another

. . .

If the documents fall to be taken seriously at their face value and to be construed according to their terms, I see, for my part, no escape from the conclusion at which the Court of Appeal arrived. If it is once accepted that the respondent enjoyed the right – whether he exercised it or not – to share the accommodation with the appellants, either himself or by introducing one or more other persons to use the flat with them, it is, as it seems to me, incontestable that the appellants cannot claim to have had exclusive possession. The appellants' case therefore rests, as Mr Colyer frankly admits, upon upholding the judge's approach that the true transaction contemplated was the appellants should jointly enjoy exclusive possession and the licences were mere sham or window-dressing to indicate legal incidents which were never seriously intended in fact, but which would be inconsistent with the application to that transaction of the Rent Acts. Now to begin with, I do not, for my part, read the notes of the judge's judgment as showing that he construed the agreement in the light of what the parties subsequently did. I agree entirely with the Court of Appeal that if he did that he was in error. But though subsequent conduct is irrelevant as an aid to construction, it is certainly admissible as evidence on the question of whether the documents were or were not genuine documents giving effect to the parties' true intentions. Broadly what is said by Mr Colyer is that nobody acquainted with the circumstances in which the parties had come together and with the physical lay-out and size of the premises could seriously have imagined that the clauses in the licence which, on the face of them, contemplate the respondent and an apparently limitless number of other persons moving in to share the whole of the available accommodation, including the bedroom, with what, to all intents and purposes, was a married couple committed to paying £174 a month in advance, were anything other than a smoke-screen; and the fact the respondent, who might be assumed to want to make the maximum profit out of the premises, never sought to introduce anyone else is at least some indication that that is exactly what it was. Adopting the definition of a sham formulated by Purchas LJ in *Hadjiloucas v Crean* [1988] 1 WLR 1006, 1013, Mr Colyer submits that the licences clearly incorporate clauses by which neither party intended to be bound and which were obviously a smoke-screen to cover the real intentions of both contracting parties. In the Court of Appeal [1988] 3 WLR 139, 149, Bingham LJ tested the matter by asking the two questions, viz.: (1) on what grounds, if one party had left the premises, could the remaining party have been made liable for anything more than the £87 which he or she had agreed to pay, and (2) on what ground could they have resisted a demand by the respondent to introduce a further person into the premises? For my part, however, I do not see how this helps. The assumed negative answers prove nothing, for they rest upon the assumption that the licences are not sham documents, which is the very question in issue.

If the real transaction was, as the judge found, one under which the appellants became joint tenants with exclusive possession, on the footing that the two agreements are to be construed together, then it would follow that they were together jointly and severally responsible for the whole rent. It would equally follow that they could effectively exclude the respondent and his nominees.

Although the facts are not precisely on all fours with *Somma v Hazelhurst* [1978] 1 WLR 1014, they are strikingly similar and the judge was, in my judgment, entitled to conclude that the appellants had exclusive possession of the premises. I read his finding that, 'the licences are artificial transactions designed to evade the Rent Acts' as a finding that they were sham documents designed to conceal the true nature of the transaction. There was, in my judgment, material on which he could properly reach this conclusion and I, too, would allow the appeal.

A.G. Securities v Vaughan and Others

The facts in this appeal are startlingly different from those in the case of *Antoniades*. To begin with the appeal concerns a substantial flat in a mansion block consisting of four bedrooms, a lounge, a sitting-room and usual offices. The trial judge found, as a fact, that the premises could without difficulty provide residential accommodation for four persons. There is no question but that the agreements with which the appeal is concerned reflect the true bargain between the parties. It is the purpose and intention of both parties to each agreement that it should confer an individual right on the licensee named, that he should be liable only for the payment which he had undertaken, and that his agreement should be capable of termination without reference to the agreements with other persons occupying the flat. The judge found that the agreements were not shams and that each of the four occupants had arrived independently of one another and not as a group. His finding was that there was never a group of persons coming to the flat all together. That has been challenged because, it is said, the evidence established that initially in 1977 and 1978 there was one occupant who was joined by three others who, although they came independently and not as a trio, moved in at about the same time. Central heating was then installed, so that the weekly payments fell to be increased and new agreements were signed by the four occupants contemporaneously. Speaking for myself, I cannot see how this can make any difference to the terms upon which the individuals were in occupation. If they were in as licensees in the first instance, the mere replacement of their agreements by new agreements in similar form cannot convert them into tenants, and the case has, in my judgment, to be approached on the footing that agreements with the occupiers were entered into separately and individually. The only questions are those of the effect of each agreement vis-à-vis the individual licensee and whether the agreements collectively had the effect of creating a joint tenancy among the occupants of the premises for the time being by virtue of their having between them exclusive possession of the premises.

. . .

The respondents are compelled to support their claims by a strange and unnatural theory that, as each occupant terminates his agreement, there is an implied surrender by the other three and an implied grant of a new joint tenancy to them together with the new incumbent when he enters under his individual agreement. With great respect to the majority in the Court of Appeal, this appears to me to be entirely unreal. For my part, I agree with the dissenting judgment of Sir George Waller in finding no unity of interest, no unity of title, certainly no unity of time and, as I think, no unity of possession. I find it impossible to say that the agreements entered into with the respondents created either individually or collectively a single tenancy either of the entire flat or of any part of it. I agree that the appeal should be allowed.

Notes
1. The above decision(s) go some way to resolving the questions left unanswered by *Street* v *Mountford*. Above all, covert 'contracting out' of the Rent Act and other 'protective' legislation via the use of purported licences is not to be allowed. Lord Templeman's judgment is probably the clearest on this point (at p. 458):

> Parties to an agreement cannot contract out of the Rent Acts; if they were able to do so the Acts would be a dead letter because in a state of housing shortage a person seeking residential accommodation may agree to anything to obtain shelter. . . . Since parties . . . cannot contract out of the Rent Acts, a document which expresses the intention, genuine or bogus, of both parties or of one party to create a licence will nevertheless create a tenancy if the rights and obligations enjoyed and imposed satisfy the legal requirements of a tenancy.

However, Lord Oliver is almost as clear, and Lords Ackner and Bridge agreed with Lords Oliver and Templeman. Secondly, it is clear that although the form of the agreement cannot be ignored, it must give way to the 'substance and reality' of the agreement. In coming to a decision as to the 'substance' of the agreement, evidence as to how it was likely to work and indeed did work in practice is of particular importance. Lord Oliver is particularly clear on this (in relation to *Antoniades* v *Villiers*) (at p. 467):

> There is equally no question but that the premises are not suitable for occupation by more than one couple save on a very temporary basis . . . the size of the accommodation and the facilities available clearly do not make the flat suitable for

multiple occupation . . . There is an air of total unreality about the documents read as separate and individual licences in the light of the circumstance that the appellants were together seeking a flat as a quasi matrimonial home.

2. The decisions also give further indication as to situations where the normal approach might not apply, or as to where an agreement is likely to be seen as a licence, even if the normal approach is followed. For example, in overturning the majority ruling in *A.G. Securities* v *Vaughan* that a joint tenancy had been created, the House of Lords was at pains to point out that it was not solely a policy issue with which they were concerned, there had to be a realistic claim that (sole or joint) exclusive possession had been created/granted. As Lord Oliver stated (at p. 470):

> The facts in this appeal are startlingly different from those in the case of *Antoniades*. To begin with, the appeal concerns a substantial flat in a mansion block consisting of four bedrooms, a lounge, a sitting-room and usual offices . . . . There is no question but that the agreements with which the appeal is concerned reflect the true bargain between the parties. It is the purpose and intention of both parties to each agreement that it should confer an individual right on the licensee named, that he should be liable only for the payment which he had undertaken, and that his agreement should be capable of termination without reference to the agreements with other persons occupying the flat . . . . I agree with the dissenting judgment of Sir George Waller in finding no unity of interest, no unity of title, certainly no unity of time and, as I think, no unity of possession. I find it impossible to say that the agreements entered into with the respondents created either individually or collectively a single tenancy either of the entire flat or of any part of it.

It is clear from this that there must be some credibility in the claim that either sole or joint exclusive possession was granted; and that where there is a 'shifting population' owing little affinity to one another, such a claim will be harder to sustain. For further exemplification of this point, see *Stribling* v *Wickham* (1989) 21 HLR 381 and *Nicolaou* v *Pitt* (1989) 21 HLR 487. In *Stribling*, a county court finding of a joint tenancy was overturned where a flat, originally occupied by three friends, was at the time of legal proceedings occupied by only one of the original three plus two others. In the words of Parker LJ (at p. 389):

> The flat was suitable for use by a multiple but shifting population, and was so used. . . . Each licensee had a specific obligation to pay the amount reserved by his agreement only. In my judgment there is no process of 'legal alchemy' by which the agreement can be placed into the mould of a tenancy.

In *Nicolaou*, a county court finding of a tenancy was upheld where a small flat (two rooms, bathroom and kitchen) was at the time of the legal proceedings occupied by the ex-husband of one of the original three occupants (none of whom was any longer in occupation). The Court of Appeal felt that there was ample justification for the judges finding that *de facto* exclusive possession had been granted to the husband and wife, of which the husband was the 'successor'.

3.   As to exceptional cases, a clear instance would be a loose arrangement between members of the same family where the formality of a landlord and tenant relationship was not intended (although *Ward* v *Warnke* (1990) 22 HLR 496 indicates that caution is needed before drawing this conclusion). Another example is the 'service' licence, under which an employee occupies a property to facilitate discharge of his/her employment responsibilities (in traditional language, to facilitate 'the better performance of [his] duties'). In such cases, *Norris* v *Checksfield* confirmed that even if the employee had *de facto* exclusive possession and paid rent, a tenancy was not necessarily created.

Norris v *Checksfield*
[1991] 1 WLR 1241

WOOLF LJ: . . . For the purposes of both issues I can summarise the facts quite briefly, basing myself on the note of the judgment of Judge Hammerton. In 1988 the employee worked for the employer as a semi-skilled mechanic. In 1989 he was invited to resume that employment and started in July 1989. At that time he was living in lodgings approximately one mile away. In August 1989 the employee was seen by the employer and asked if he would like to reside at the bungalow, which was the subject of the proceedings, which had previously been occupied by another employee. The employee wanted to occupy the premises and he was allowed into possession on two specific terms which the employer made clear. The first was not of any relevance. The second was that the employee would be able to drive coaches for the employer's business and would apply for a PSV licence for this purpose. In the employer's opinion, for this work, it was clearly desirable that the employee should be in the bungalow since this would make him readily available in an emergency or if there was urgent work. The judge found that it was on 'that condition' that occupancy of the bungalow was granted to the employee.

Before the employee moved into the premises he was asked to, and did, sign a document confirming the terms of his occupation. That document referred to the employee having a licence and so far as relevant provided:

It is a condition of your employment that you shall occupy (the premises) or such other alternative property the employer may provide and that on termination of your employment your licence to occupy such property shall cease forthwith.

It was arranged that the employee would have the sum of £5 per week deducted from his salary in relation to his occupation.

At a later date, 13 October 1989, the employee was given a statement of the main particulars of his employment. These showed that he was to be employed as a semi-skilled mechanic, his normal hours of work were eight to five, Monday to Friday, Saturday if agreed. He was to give and receive one week's notice to terminate the employment but could be dismissed instantly for misconduct.

Possibly because he was unaware of this until October 1989, as he contended, the employee did not tell the employer that he was disqualified from driving. About the same time the employer learned that this was the situation from the police and this, together with his no longer being a satisfactory employee, caused the employer to dismiss the employee summarily. About ten days later, by letter delivered on 11 December 1989, the employer informed the employee that he was required to vacate the bungalow. The proceedings for possession were instituted on 18 December 1989.

In relation to the thorny issue as to when an employee is a licensee and not a tenant of premises belonging to his employer which he is allowed to occupy, Mr Seaward, who appeared on behalf of the employee, was prepared to accept Mr Zeidman's submission on behalf of the employer. Mr Zeidman submitted that an employee can be a licensee, although his occupation of the premises is not *necessary* for the purposes of the employment, if he is genuinely *required* to occupy the premises for the *better performance* of his duties. In my judgment this submission accurately reflects the law. We have been referred to a number of authorities which set out different tests. The most helpful decision is that of the House of Lords in *Glasgow Corporation* v *Johnstone* [1965] AC 609. In that case Lord Reid, with whose speech Lord Wilberforce agreed, said, at p. 618:

> So, if necessity were the criterion, the appeal would succeed. But if it is sufficient for the respondents to show that their servant is bound to reside there, and that his residing there is of material assistance to them in the carrying out of their activities, then the appellants must fail on this point.

Lord Reid then went on to examine a number of English authorities and concluded this part of his speech by saying, at p. 619:

> In requiring that the occupation should be necessary I think that Mellor J's judgment (in *Smith* v *Seghill Overseers* (1875) LR 10 QB 422] is out of line with the other authorities, and the authorities on this topic appear to me to support the respondent's contention in the present case.

Lord Reid was therefore of the opinion that it would be sufficient if the employee's occupation was of 'material assistance' to his employment. It need not be *'necessary'* for his employment. The same view was taken by Lord Evershed and Lord Hodson. Lord Guest stated the position which must exist for there to be a licence in the following terms, at p. 629:

> The residence must be ancillary to the duties which the servant has to perform (*Smith* v *Seghill Overseers*) or, put in another way, the requirement must be with a view to the more efficient performance of the servant's duties (*Fox* v *Dalby* (1874) LR 10 CP 285).

As Mr Seaward correctly submitted, it would not suffice if the occupation was a 'fringe benefit' or merely an inducement to encourage the employee to work better. Unless the occupation fulfilled this test, the fact that the employee had exclusive possession and paid rent would almost inevitably establish a service tenancy: see generally *Street* v *Mountford* [1985] AC 809 and *A. G. Securities* v *Vaughan* [1990] 1 AC 417, 459, *per* Lord Templeman.

If in this case, as was contemplated, when the employee went into occupation he had obtained a PSV licence and had changed the nature of his job so that he became a coach driver, the judge would undoubtedly have been entitled to regard the employee as a licensee. He would then have entered into occupation under a document which described the relationship in terms of a licence and the occupation would be beneficial to the employee's employment on the judge's findings. His occupation would enable him to assist his employer in cases of emergency or on short notice.

However Mr Seaward submitted that the employment situation which has to be considered is that which existed in fact at the time the licence was entered into. Not the situation which might exist in the future. The situation which existed at the time the licence was entered into was that the employee's occupation of the premises was irrelevant to his employment as a semi-skilled mechanic. In that employment he was not required to assist with emergencies and he could perform the work equally as well from the lodgings at which he was previously living or indeed from any other address which was within travelling distance to his place of work. Occupation was beneficial to the employee but not beneficial to his employment.

There is no previous decision of the courts which directly conflicts with Mr Seaward's approach. However, I have no hesitation in coming to the conclusion that notwithstanding this argument the judge was entitled to come to the conclusion that the employee was a licensee. Although the employee was unable to obtain the necessary PSV licence to drive coaches, he was on the judge's finding only allowed into occupation on the basis that he would obtain the necessary qualifications and work as a coach driver. In my judgment it would not be sensible, unless compelled to do so, to restrict an employer's ability to grant a licence to situations where the employment which would be benefited by the employee taking up occupation commenced simultaneously with or prior to the occupation of the premises. There may be many circumstances where it would be desirable for the employee to take up occupation before the relevant work commenced. What is required is that there should be a sufficient factual nexus between the commencement of the occupation of the premises and the employment which would benefit from that occupation. If for some reason it becomes apparent that the employee is not going to be able to fulfil the requirements of that employment within a reasonable time, then the position may be different. However, if the situation is one where it is contemplated, as was the position here, that the employee would, within a reasonable time, be able to take up the relevant employment, that will suffice. The fact that the employee during the interval may be performing some other duties which are not affected by the occupation of the premises does not prevent a licence coming into existence.

On the facts found by the judge in this case, this was therefore a case where it was proper to regard the employee as going into occupation as a licensee in order to better perform his duties when he became a coach driver.

4.   It might be thought that the easiest way to bolster a 'licence' argument would be to demonstrate that services were provided or rights over the property were retained, so as to undermine any wholly *'exclusive'* possession in the occupants. However, while the provision of substantial services is likely to convert an occupant into a lodger (and so a licensee), the court will be vigilant to detect pretences and shams aimed solely at undermining tenancy status. This is demonstrated by the following case:

Aslan v *Murphy*
[1990] 1 WLR 766

LORD DONALDSON MR: *Aslan v Murphy (No. 1)*
The defendant was the occupier of Room 2A at 54 Redcliffe Gardens, London SW10. It is a basement room measuring 4'3" by 12'6". He occupied this room under an agreement which recited that 'the licensor is not willing to grant the licensee exclusive

possession of any part of the room hereinafter referred to [and] the licensee is anxious to secure the use of the room notwithstanding that such use be in common with the licensor and such other licensees or invitees as the licensor may permit from time to time to use said room' [adding that] 'this licence is entered into by the licensor and the licensee solely upon the above basis'.

The introduction to the operative part of the agreement provided:

By this licence the licensor licences the licensee to use (but not exclusively) all the furnished room known as room no. 2A (hereinafter referred to as 'the room') on the basement floor of the building situated and known as 54 Redcliffe Gardens (hereinafter referred to as 'the building') on each day between the hours of midnight and 10.30 a.m. and between noon and midnight, but at no other times, for the purpose of temporary accommodation for the licensee's personal use only and for no other purposes whatsoever, and the licensee shall also be entitled to use, in common with all other persons having the like right, the common parts of the building. The licensee shall pay the licensor a licence fee of £25 per week for the use of the room commencing on 15 May 1988.

Other clauses reflected the shared nature of the occupancy. Thus:

1. The licensor shall at all times have the right to decide the use and occupancy of the room and each part of the room together with the positioning of the furniture of the room.

. . .

3.(a) The licensee shall be personally liable for and shall pay for all services such as electricity, gas, telephone or whatever use[d] by the licensee in the room and will indemnify the licensor against all such expenses.

(b) The licensee agrees to share the expense of such services (apart from those services provided by the licensor under Clause 4 of this licence) as are used jointly with any other person occupying or using the room or using the common parts of the building.

(c) The licensee shall use his best endeavour amicably and peaceably to share the use of the room with the licensor and/or with such other licensees or invitees whom the licensor shall from time to time permit to use the room and shall not interfere with or otherwise obstruct such shared accommodation in any way whatsoever.

In holding that [Mr Murphy] was a licensee, Judge McDonnell said:

The submission that the written agreement in the present case was a sham designed to conceal the grant of exclusive possession and therefore the creation of a tenancy rested upon (i) the size of the room which made it impracticable for the landlord or anyone else to share occupation with the defendant, and (ii) the fact that the plaintiff said that he [sic] did not intend to put anyone else into the room or to object to the defendant using it between 10.30 am and noon. In my judgment the first submission fails because the plaintiff made it quite plain that he never intended to grant the defendant exclusive possession of the room for the very good reason that he had been advised that to do so might lead to the creation of a tenancy protected by the Rent Act and the defendant never suggested that there was any other agreement expressed or implied than that to which he had put his signature.

As to the second submission 'the Rent Acts must not be allowed to alter or influence the construction of an agreement' – *Street* v *Mountford* AC 809, 825.

'It is not a crime, nor is it contrary to public policy for a property owner to license occupiers to occupy property on terms which do not give rise to a tenancy . . . Where a written agreement is not held to be a sham the task of the court, as with any other agreement, is to construe it and give fair effect to its terms in the context of all the relevant surrounding circumstances.' *Antoniades* v *Villiers* [1988] 3 WLR 139 at 147 *per* Bingham LJ. In this case the written agreement made it quite plain that the exclusive possession was not to be granted, and there are no surrounding circumstances to suggest that effect should not be given to it according to its terms. I am fortified in the conclusion because it is clear that the plaintiff was not prepared to grant any legal or enforceable right to exclusive possession or any right at all to occupy the room between 10.30 am and noon and the defendant realised this.

In fairness to the judge, it should be said that he gave judgment before the House of Lords reversed the decision of this court in *Antoniades* v *Villiers* [1990] AC 417 and therefore without the benefit of the guidance contained in the speeches. In the light of that guidance, the judge's decision is unsupportable on this ground and no attempt was made to support it.

The judge was, of course, quite right to approach the matter on the basis that it is not a crime, nor is it contrary to public policy, for a property owner to license occupiers to occupy a property on terms which do not give rise to a tenancy. Where he went wrong was in considering whether the whole agreement was a sham and, having concluded that it was not, giving effect to its terms, *i.e.* taking it throughout at face value. What he should have done, and I am sure would have done if he had known of the House of Lords approach to the problem, was to consider whether the whole agreement was a sham and, if it was not, whether in the light of the factual situation the provisions for sharing the room and those depriving Mr Murphy of the right to occupy if for 90 minutes out of each 24 hours were part of the true bargain between the parties or were pretences. Both provisions were wholly unrealistic and were clearly pretences.

In this court an attempt to uphold the judge's decision was made upon a different basis, namely, the landlord's right to retain the keys. The provisions relevant to this aspect of the agreement are as follows:

1.   . . . The licensor will retain the keys to the room and has absolute right of entry at all times for the purpose of exercising such control and (without prejudice to the generality of the foregoing) for the purpose of effecting any repairs or cleaning to the room or building or for the purpose of providing the attendance mentioned in Clause 4 hereof or for the purpose of removing or substituting such articles of furniture from the room as the licensor might see fit. The said right of entry is exerciseable by the licensor or his servants or agents with or without any other persons (including prospective future licensees of the room).
. . .

4.   The licensor will provide the following attendance for the licensee:
   (1)   housekeeping
   (2)   lighting of common parts
   (3)   cleaning of common parts
   (4)   window cleaning
   (5)   intercom
   (6)   telephone coin box
   (7)   cleaning of room
   (8)   collection of rubbish

(9)   provision and laundering of bed linen
(10) hot water
(11) provision of household supplies.

Provisions as to keys are often relied upon in support of the contention that an occupier is a lodger rather than a tenant. Thus in *Duke* v *Wynne*, to which we turn next, the agreement required the occupier 'not to interfere with or change the locks on any part of the premises, [or] give the key to any other than an authorised occupier of the premises.' Provisions as to keys, if not a pretence which they often are, do not have any magic in themselves. It is not a requirement of a tenancy that the occupier shall have exclusive possession of the keys to the property. What matters is what underlies the provisions as to keys. Why does the owner want a key, want to prevent keys being issued to the friends of the occupier or want to prevent the lock being changed?

A landlord may well need a key, in order that he may be able to enter quickly in the event of emergency: fire, burst pipes or whatever. He may need a key to enable him or those authorised by him to read meters or to do repairs which are his responsibility. None of these underlying reasons would of themselves indicate that the true bargain between the parties was such that the occupier was in law a lodger. On the other hand, if the true bargain is that the owner will provide genuine services which can only be provided by having keys, such as frequent cleaning, daily bed-making, the provision of clean linen at regular intervals and the like, there are materials from which it is possible to infer that the occupier is a lodger rather than a tenant. But the inference arises not from the provisions as to keys, but from the reason why those provisions formed part of the bargain.

On the facts of this case, the argument based upon the provisions as to keys must and does fail for the judge found that 'during the currency of the present agreement virtually "no services" had been provided.' These provisions may or may not have been pretences, but they are without significance in the context of the question which we had to decide.

(C)   Public sector licensees

As will be explained in chapter 5, since 1980, most occupiers of council accommodation are tenants who enjoy 'secure' status (now under the Housing Act 1985, Pt IV). Such tenants have the benefit of security of tenure in their homes and a catalogue of rights (commonly known as the 'tenants charter'), ranging from the right to buy to rights of succession. Many local authorities expressed concern that this development would lead to them having diminished control over occupiers they wished to house only temporarily (for example, some homeless persons, the temporary occupiers of accommodation pending works and the occupiers of short life properties). Moreover, most local authorities were (initially at least) concerned, where possible, to protect their housing stock from erosion by the right to buy.

Quite apart from statutory exceptions to secure status which cover some of the above categories (Housing Act 1985 Sch. 1,) councils have often been attracted to the device of granting licences rather than tenancies. However, two difficulties appeared to bar the way to the successful use of licences in most situations by public sector landlords. First, *Street* v *Mountford* applied in principle as much to public sector landlords as to private sector ones, so that (particularly after *Antoniades* v *Villiers*) most occupants paying rent with *de facto* exclusive possession will be tenants whatever the form of the agreement they have signed. This appeared to be confirmed by the Court of Appeal in *FHA* v *Jones* [1990] 1 WLR 779. Secondly, in any event, s. 79(3) of the Housing Act 1985 states that 'The provisions of this Part apply in relation to a licence to occupy a dwelling house . . . as they apply in relation to a tenancy' — the 'part' referred to being the key Pt IV of the Act. This suggests that even if the occupier is a licensee, he or she still enjoys the benefits of the 'tenants charter' and security of tenure.

However, both the above assumptions were significantly undermined by the House of Lords decision in the following case:

Westminster City Council v Clarke
[1992] 2 AC 288; [1992] 1 All ER 695

Lord Templeman delivered the unanimous judgment of the House.

LORD TEMPLEMAN: My Lords, the appellants, Westminster City Council, have provided accommodation for the respondent, Mr Clarke, and the question is whether Mr Clarke is a licensee or a secure tenant.

Part III of the Housing Act 1985 which begins at section 58 and ends with section 78 requires a local housing authority to provide accommodation to certain persons who are homeless and in need.

By section 58:

(1) A person is homeless if he has no accommodation in England, Wales, Scotland. (2) A person shall be treated as having no accommodation if there is no accommodation which he, together with any other person who normally resides with him as a member of his family . . . (a) is entitled to occupy by virtue of an interest in it or by virtue of an order of a court, or (b) has an express or implied licence to occupy . . . or (c) occupies as a residence by virtue of an enactment or rule of law giving him the right to remain in occupation or restricting the right of another person to recover possession.

By section 59(1) certain homeless persons are classified as having:

a priority need for accommodation—(a) a pregnant woman . . . (b) a person with whom dependent children reside . . . (c) a person who is vulnerable as a result of old age, mental illness or handicap or physical disability or other special reason . . . (d) a person who is homeless or threatened with homelessness as a result of an emergency such as flood, fire or other disaster.

By section 62:

(1) If a person (an 'applicant') applies to a local housing authority for accommodation . . . and the authority have reason to believe that he may be homeless or threatened with homelessness, they shall make such inquiries as are necessary to satisfy themselves as to whether he is homeless or threatened with homelessness. (2) If they are so satisfied, they shall make any further inquiries necessary to satisfy themselves as to—(a) whether he has a priority need, and (b) whether he became

homeless or threatened with homelessness intentionally; and if they think fit they may also make inquiries as to whether he has a local connection with the district of another local housing authority.

Section 63 makes provision for the temporary accommodation of some applicants where the local authority is making the necessary inquiries:

> (1) If the local housing authority have reason to believe that an applicant may be homeless and have a priority need, they shall secure that accommodation is made available for his occupation pending a decision as a result of their inquiries under section 62.

On completing their inquiries under section 62 the local housing authority must decide whether the applicant is homeless, if so, whether he has a priority need, and if so, whether he became homeless intentionally and whether they propose to refer him to another local authority on grounds of local connection. By section 64 these decisions must be notified to the applicant supported by reasons. By section 65 where a local authority are satisfied that the applicant is homeless and:

> (2) . . . they are satisfied that he has a priority need and are not satisfied that he became homeless intentionally, they shall, unless they notify another local housing authority in accordance with section 67 (referral of application on grounds of local connection), secure that accommodation becomes available for his occupation

Section 65(3) imposes on a local housing authority a duty to house temporarily an applicant found to have a priority need but to have become homeless intentionally and also a duty to house an applicant pending a determination as to whether the conditions for the referral of the application to another local housing authority are satisfied.

The appellant council are a local housing authority. The respondent, Mr Clarke, satisfied that council that he was homeless, and that he had a priority need as a vulnerable person under section 59(1)(c) of the Act. The council were not satisfied that Mr Clarke had become homeless intentionally and they did not refer Mr Clark's application for accommodation to another local housing authority. The council accepted towards Mr Clarke the duty imposed on them by section 65(2) to 'secure that accommodation becomes available for his occupation'.

The council own a terrace of houses 131–137, Cambridge Street. The premises are used by the council as a hostel. There are 31 single rooms each with a bed and limited cooking facilities. There was originally a common room which has since been vandalised. The occupiers of the hostel are homeless single men, including men with personality disorders or physical disabilities, sometimes eccentric, sometimes frail, sometimes evicted from domestic accommodation or discharged from hospital or from prison. Experience has shown the possibility that the hostel may have to cope with an occupier who is suicidal or alcoholic or addicted to drugs. There is a warden supported by a resettlement team of social workers. The hope is that after a period of rehabilitation and supervision in the hostel, each occupier will be able to move on to permanent accommodation where he will be independent and look after himself. In the case of Mr Clarke, the hostel was designed to be a halfway house for rehabilitation and treatment en route to an independent home. In these circumstances Mr Clarke was provided with accommodation at the hostel pursuant to an agreement entitled 'Licence to occupy' dated 5 February 1987, addressed to Mr Clarke and, so far as material, in the following terms:

Westminster City Council by this licence which is personal to you will allow you to occupy in common with the council and any other persons to whom the same right is granted accommodation at the single persons hostel at 131–137 Cambridge Street, SW1 in the City of Westminster. The terms of the licence under which you agree to occupy the accommodation are set out below and the current conditions of occupation are set out hereafter. . . . 1. This licence does not give you and is not intended to give you any of the rights or to impose upon you any of the obligations of a tenant nor does it give you the right of exclusive occupation of any particular accommodation or room which may be allotted to you or which you may be allowed to use nor does it create the relationship of landlord and tenant. The accommodation allotted to you may be changed from time to time without notice as the council directs and you may be required to share such accommodation with any other person as required by the council. Any furniture provided or services of whatever nature may be changed or withdrawn at any time. 2. The licence permits you only and not any person invited by you to occupy accommodation in common with the council whose representative may enter the accommodation at any time. You may use the accommodation as living accommodation only and not for any other purpose. 3. The council may terminate the licence at any time by giving you not less than seven days notice in writing and you must leave at the end of that time except that if you fail to pay the charges hereinafter provided or if you break the terms of the licence or the conditions of occupation in any other way the licence may be terminated forthwith . . .

Undertaking by licensee(s)
I have read and I agree to observe the above licence and the conditions of occupation set out overleaf. I agree to pay regularly in advance on Monday of each week the charge of £16.79 for the accommodation and for the services provided. I understand that this charge is assessed on my present financial circumstances and that the charge will be amended if the council's scale of charges is amended or if my circumstances alter. I understand that failure to pay the weekly charge or to observe the terms of the licence or the conditions of occupation may result in the council requiring me to leave the accommodation.

Conditions of occupation
In the interest of the council and of other residents certain conditions have to be made and these conditions may be changed from time to time as the council considers necessary. You are asked to co-operate with the council's staff and in particular you are required: (1) Not to invite any person to share the accommodation with you nor allow any person to stay overnight. (2) To keep the accommodation allocated to you in a clean condition and to take care of all furniture, bed linen or other articles provided. (3) To clean and leave tidy on each occasion after use by you the bathroom and toilet accommodation. (4) To pay for any damage caused . . . (5) To be in your accommodation by not later than 11 pm and to ensure that visitors leave by not later than this time . . . (6) To do nothing which may cause nuisance, annoyance or discomfort to other residents and to be responsible for the behaviour of your visitors . . . (10) To comply with the directions of the council's warden or other staff in charge of the hostel.

Mr Clarke was allocated room E on the first floor of 131, Cambridge Street. On 13 April 1988 the council gave Mr Clarke notice terminating his licence. The notice was issued because of complaints by residents and others that Mr Clarke had caused nuisance and annoyance and noise. On 13 November 1988 the council issued the summons in these proceedings for possession. Mr Clarke, by this defence, claimed to be a 'secure tenant' entitled to the protection of Part IV of the Act of 1985. Subsequently Mr Clarke smashed up room E and threw the council's furniture and his clothes into the street. He was taken away by the police and subsequently returned. The incident is an illustration of the need for the council to be able to evict an occupier at short notice. The trial judge, Mr Recorder Langan QC made an order for possession in favour of the council but his decision was reversed by the Court of Appeal (Dillon, Balcombe and Ralph Gibson LJJ) (1991) 89 LGR 917 who held that Mr Clarke was a secure tenant of room E and dismissed the council's claim for possession. The council now appeal.

Part IV of the Act of 1985 entitled 'Secure tenancies and rights of secure tenants' begins with section 79 and ends with section 117. By section 79:

> (1) A tenancy under which a dwelling-house is let as a separate dwelling is a secure tenancy at any time when the conditions described in sections 80 and 81 as the landlord condition and the tenant condition are satisfied. (2) Subsection (1) has effect subject to—(a) the exceptions in Schedule 1 (tenancies which are not secure tenancies) . . . (3) The provisions of this Part apply in relation to a licence to occupy a dwelling-house (whether or not granted for a consideration) as they apply in relation to a tenancy.

The landlord condition prescribed by section 80 is that the interest of the landlord belongs to certain authorities or bodies including a local authority. In the present case, therefore, the landlord condition is satisfied. The tenant condition prescribed by section 81 is: 'that the tenant is an individual and occupies the dwelling-house as his only or principal home; . . .'.

Mr Clarke occupies room E as his only home. If room E is a separate dwelling house occupied under a tenancy or licence by Mr Clarke as his only home, then Mr Clarke is a secure tenant. The exceptions set forth in Schedule 1 do not apply.

If Mr Clarke is a secure tenant the council cannot obtain possession unless they first serve a notice prescribed by regulations made under section 83 of the Act of 1985 and institute proceedings within the time-limit prescribed by that section. By section 84, as applied to the present case, the court will then only be able to make an order for possession if Mr Clarke has been guilty of conduct which is a nuisance or annoyance to neighbours and if the court considers that it is reasonable to make the order. If therefore Mr Clarke is a secure tenant, the council may not be able to obtain possession of room E and cannot speedily obtain possession of any of the hostel rooms. If Mr Clarke is not a secure tenant then he has no defence to the council's present action for possession.

Section 112 of the Act of 1985 provides that for the purposes of Part IV a dwelling house may be a house or part of a house. Under the Rent Acts, in order to create a letting of part of a house as a separate dwelling there must be an agreement by which the occupier has exclusive possession of essential living rooms of a separate dwelling house. Essential living rooms provide the necessary facilities for living, sleeping and cooking. Thus a bed-sitting room with cooking facilities may be a separate dwelling house even though bathroom and lavatory facilities might be elsewhere and shared with other people: see *Neale v Del Soto* [1945] KB 144; *Cole v Harris* [1945] KB 474 and *Goodrich v Paisner* [1957] AC 65, 79. Room E provides facilities for living, sleeping and cooking. Room E is occupied by Mr Clarke as his only home. Section 79(1) of the Act of 1985 employs the language of the Rent Acts. Accordingly Mr

Clarke is a secure tenant of room E if he enjoys exclusive possession of room E. In order to determine whether Mr Clarke enjoys exclusive possession of room E, the rights conferred on Mr Clarke and the rights reserved to the council by the licence to occupy must be considered and evaluated.

Mr Sedley, who appeared on behalf of Mr Clarke, submitted that Mr Clarke was a secure tenant even if he was not granted exclusive possession of room E. Section 79(3), he said, applied to any licence to occupy a dwelling house. This submission would confer security of tenure on a lodger and on a variety of licensees and is contrary to the language of section 79(3) which applies the provisions of Part IV of the Act to a licence 'as they apply in relation to a tenancy'. Part IV only applies to a tenancy of a dwelling house let as a separate dwelling, namely with exclusive possession. Part IV therefore applies to a licence which has the same characteristics. A tenant or licensee can only claim to be a secure tenant if he has been granted exclusive possession of a separate dwelling house.

The predecessor of section 79(3) of the Act of 1985 was section 48 of the Housing Act 1980 which provided that where under a licence

> the circumstances are such that, if the licence were a tenancy, it would be a secure tenancy then . . . this Part of this Act applies to the licence as it applies to a secure tenancy.

The result of section 48 of the Act of 1980 was that, whether the occupier was a tenant or a licensee, he must be granted exclusive possession in order to become a secure tenant. The Court of Appeal so held in *Family Housing Association* v *Miah* (1982) 5 HLR 94 and *Royal Borough of Kensington and Chelsea* v *Hayden* (1984) 17 HLR 114.

The Rent Acts do not apply to a licence and section 48 of the Act of 1980 was enacted at a time when some private landlords were granting exclusive possession of residential accommodation at a rent but in the form of a licence. Section 48 of the Act of 1980 made clear that such a licence created a secure tenancy. Subsequently in *Street* v *Mountford* [1985] AC 809 this House reaffirmed the general principle that a grant of exclusive possession of residential accommodation at a rent created a tenancy protected by the Rent Acts notwithstanding that the parties intended to grant and expressed themselves as having granted a licence and not a tenancy. The decision of this House in *Street* v *Mountford* [1985] AC 809 was published on 2 May 1985. The Act of 1985 received the Royal Assent on 30 October 1985. In *Family Housing Association* v *Jones* [1990] 1 WLR 779, 790 Balcombe LJ held that in these circumstances section 79(3) of the Act of 1985 must have been intended to alter the law and to confer the status of a secure tenant on a licensee who did not enjoy exclusive possession. The Court of Appeal in the instant case, 89 LGR 917, felt bound to follow its decision in *Family Housing Association* v *Jones* though Dillon LJ doubted the soundness of that decision so far as it construed section 79(3) and Balcombe LJ to some extent resiled from his earlier views. In my opinion section 79(3) did not alter the law. The Act of 1985 was an enactment which consolidated various statutes including the Act of 1980 and gave effect to certain recommendations of the Law Commission. Those recommendations did not relate to section 48 of the Act of 1980. Therefore section 79(3) was a consolidating measure and in redrafting section 48 of the Act of 1980 in the form of section 79(3) of the Act of 1985 the draftsman had no power to alter the law. In my opinion, on the true construction of section 48 of the Act of 1980 and on the true construction of section 79(3) of the Act of 1985, whether those sections be considered together or separately a licence can only create a secure tenancy if it confers exclusive possession of a dwelling house.

So the question is whether the 'licence to occupy' followed by the allocation of room E and the payment of rent conferred on Mr Clarke exclusive possession of room E. In *Street* v *Mountford* the landlord agreed to grant a licence of residential accommodation for a weekly fee. The agreement was designated a licence and contained a declaration that the licence did not create and was not intended to create a tenancy protected by the Rent Acts. Nevertheless the licensee enjoyed exclusive possession; a third party could not lawfully interfere with that possession and the landlord only reserved limited power to enter to protect his own interests as a landlord. The licence created a tenancy.

In *A. G. Securities* v *Vaughan* [1990] 1 AC 417 four separate bedrooms in a house were occupied by four separate individuals under four separate and independent agreements, all four occupiers being entitled to share the house in common. But they did not enjoy exclusive possession of the house jointly. Each had exclusive possession of one bedroom but shared possession of the other parts of the house. The bedroom was not a dwelling house and the house was shared. In these circumstances each occupier was a licensee. In *Antoniades* v *Villiers* also reported at [1990] 1 AC 417 a one-bedroomed flat was occupied by a couple on the terms of licences which expressly reserved to the owner the right to share and permit other persons to share the flat. The reservation, which was not and could not reasonably be acted upon, was a pretence designed to disguise the fact that the couple were granted exclusive possession at a rent and were therefore tenants. In the present case no pretence is involved. The question is whether upon the true construction of the licence to occupy and in the circumstances in which Mr Clarke was allowed to occupy room E, there was a grant by the council to Mr Clarke of exclusive possession of room E.

From the point of view of the council the grant of exclusive possession would be inconsistent with the purposes for which the council granted the accommodation at Cambridge Street. It was in the interest of Mr Clarke and each of the occupiers of the hostel that the council should retain possession of each room. If one room became uninhabitable another room could be shared between two occupiers. If one room became unsuitable for an occupier he could be moved elsewhere. If the occupier of one room became a nuisance he could be compelled to move to another room where his actions might be less troublesome to his neighbours. If the occupier of a room had exclusive possession he could prevent the council from entering the room save for the purpose of protecting the council's interests and not for the purpose of supervising and controlling the conduct of the occupier in his interests. If the occupier of a room had exclusive possession he could not be obliged to comply with the terms and the conditions of occupation. Mr Clarke could not, for example, be obliged to comply with the directions of the warden or to exclude visitors or to comply with any of the other conditions of occupation which are designed to help Mr Clarke and the other occupiers of the hostel and to enable the hostel to be conducted in an efficient and harmonious manner. The only remedy of the council for breaches of the conditions of occupation would be the lengthy and uncertain procedure required by the Act of 1985 to be operated for the purpose of obtaining possession from a secure tenant. In the circumstances of the present case I consider that the council legitimately and effectively retained for themselves possession of room E and that Mr Clarke was only a licensee with the rights corresponding to the rights of a lodger. In reaching this conclusion I take into account the object of the council, namely the provision of accommodation for vulnerable homeless persons, the necessity for the council to retain possession of all the rooms in order to make and administer arrangements for the suitable accommodation of all the occupiers and the need for the council to retain possession of every room not only in the interests of the council as the owners of the terrace but also for the purpose of providing for the occupiers supervision and assistance. For many obvious reasons it was highly undesirable for the council to grant to any occupier of a room exclusive possession which obstructed the use by the council of all the rooms of the hostel in the interest of every occupier. By the terms of the licence to occupy Mr Clarke was not entitled to any particular room, he could be required to share with any other person as required by the council and he was only entitled to 'occupy accommodation in common with the council whose representative may enter the accommodation at any time.' It is accepted that these provisions of the licence to occupy were inserted to enable the council to discharge its responsibilities to the vulnerable persons accommodated at the Cambridge Street terrace and were not inserted for the purpose of enabling the council to avoid the creation of a secure tenancy. The conditions of occupancy support the view that Mr Clarke was not in exclusive occupation of room E. He was expressly limited in his enjoyment of any accommodation provided for him. He was forbidden to entertain visitors without the approval of the council staff and was bound to comply with the council's warden or other staff in charge of the hostel. These limitations confirmed that the council retained possession of all the rooms of the hostel in order to supervise and control the activities of the occupiers, including Mr Clarke. Although Mr Clarke physically occupied room E he did not enjoy possession exclusively of the council.

This is a very special case which depends on the peculiar nature of the hostel maintained by the council, the use of the hostel by the council, the totality, immediacy and objectives of the powers exercisable by the council and the restrictions imposed on Mr Clarke. The decision in this case will not allow a landlord, private or public, to free himself from the Rent Acts or from the restrictions of a secure tenancy merely be adopting or adapting the language of the licence to occupy. The provisions of the licence to occupy and the circumstances in which that licence was granted and continued lead to the conclusion that Mr Clarke has never enjoyed that exclusive possession which he claims. I would therefore allow the appeal and restore the order for possession made by the trial judge.

Notes

1.   Lord Templeman stated that this was 'a very special case', which should not encourage landlords (public or private) to think that by calling something a licence, or by purporting to deny exclusive possession they would thereby avoid protective legislation. Indeed, it is hard to see how the House of Lords *could* have countenanced such a development only four years after explicitly rejecting it in *Antoniades/Vaughan*. However, it is not clear that the situation is *Clarke*, though distinct, was necessarily 'very special'. Indeed, it seems typical of a significant number of hostels operated by local authorities. The difficulty lies in knowing where the line should be drawn: at one extreme is the type of hostel where it would be absurd to suggest that any form of 'exclusivity' was granted (for example, a refuge where there is no guarantee of a particular room, or indeed of any room, being available on a particular day); at the other is something which is a 'hostel' in name only, where the occupier does not receive social service care requiring constant access, and is able to live in an independent and self-contained manner. *Clarke*, whatever Lord Templeman's views, appears to be somewhere in the middle, and the court appears to approach the *realities* of exclusive possession in a somewhat

'cavalier' manner (for example, is it ever asked whether the 'mobility clause' was operated in practice?).

2. 'Policy' considerations clearly underpin the judgment, as indicated by the constant references by Lord Templeman to the considerable inconvenience which an opposite finding would cause to the local authority concerned. No doubt the House was aware that none of the exceptions to security that are set out in Sch. 1 of the Housing Act 1985 specifically excludes hostel accommodation from protection. However, did the House overstate the difficulties in such cases for public sector landlords? It is *possible* for a landlord to obtain an expedited hearing for a possession claim, and injunctions may be available where an occupant breaks the terms of an agreement.

3. In seeking to protect the position of the public landlord, it is also possible to argue that the House of Lords made a nonsense of s. 79(3) of the 1985 Act referred to above. This subsection appears to state that a licensee fulfilling the conditions for a secure tenancy would gain equivalent protection to a secure tenant, i.e. it creates the concept of the *secure licence*.

Many hostel dwellers will fail to attain this status because they do not occupy a 'separate dwelling' as required by s. 79(1) of the Act, most typically because they share kitchen facilities with other residents of the hostel (see *Central YMCA Housing Association Ltd* v *Saunders* [1990] 23 HLR 212 in chapter 5). This is a quite separate concept to that of exclusive possession, focusing on whether essential living accommodation is in practice shared with others, rather than on whether there is a legal right to exclude others from the separate accommodation undoubtedly occupied. By accident, or design, Lord Templeman conflates the two notions (at p. 299) 'Part IV only applies to a tenancy of a dwelling house let as a separate dwelling, *namely* with exclusive possession' (emphasis added). This interpretation seems to leave s. 79(3) largely without content, since if there is exclusive possession there will normally be a tenancy in any case. Moreover, it might be thought that licensees who do share kitchens and bathrooms are exactly those whom local authorities most need to 'manage' and control, whereas where there is relatively separate living this need is much reduced.

4. Since *Clarke* the 'licence' issue has come before the Court of Appeal in a number of further cases concerning hostels. For example, in *Brennan* v *Lambeth LBC* (1997) 30 HLR 481, a homeless applicant was provided with accommodation, with his 14-year-old son, at a hostel while his application was considered. The hostel consisted of seven large Victorian houses, converted into shared units (kitchen, bathrooms and toilets were all shared). Hostel officers had an office in one of the houses. Residents of the hostel were responsible for cleaning their own rooms, but common parts were cleaned by council staff. In agreeing with the county court, that no court order was required to secure the applicant's removal from the hostel, the Court of Appeal held that his occupational status in the hostel was that of licensee. *Clarke* was referred to, but not analysed in any detail. Brooks LJ clearly felt that the applicant's status was beyond argument. Potter LJ emphasised, again, how significant a role is played by policy in this area (at p. 485):

'. . . it is necessary to keep an eye on . . . the problems which face a Local Authority in the management of hostels . . . [even where] the residents may require a lower level of care . . . [since] the need to reconcile the interests of short term occupants, plainly call for an effective power and genuine need to remove tenants from room to room during their occupancy . . .'

In *Mohamed* v *Manek and Royal Borough of Kensington and Chelsea* (1995) 27 HLR 439, another homeless applicant was placed in temporary (private sector) bed and breakfast accommodation. This consisted of a room on the fourth floor of a hotel, with its own bathroom/toilet plus shared use of a kitchen (along with 35 other occupiers of the hotel!). In allowing the authority's appeal from the county court's granting of an injunction preventing the applicant's eviction, the Court of Appeal held that not only did the applicant merely have a licence (this point was barely discussed), but that s. 3 of the Protection from Eviction Act 1977 (see further chapter 2) did not apply so as to require a court order. Section 3(2B) applies the normal requirement of a court order to licences as well as to tenancies, so long as they are not 'excluded licences' and so long as the premises involved are 'occupied as a dwelling'. Hostels of the *Brennan* type, operated by authorities themselves, are excluded from s. 3 if licences are involved (see s. 3A(8)). In *Manek* this exclusion could not apply, but the court found that temporary occupation of the hotel room by a homeless applicant did not amount to occupying 'a dwelling'. In the words of Nourse LJ (at p. 452): 'Without some element of more than transient occupation, premises cannot properly be called a dwelling'.

5.   The trend of the post *Clarke* case law has generally been to protect public sector landlords from the full impact of *Street* v *Mountford* and its offspring. In similar vein, cases such as *LB Camden* v *Shortlife Community Housing* (1992) 25 HLR 330 were concerned to avoid conferring the status of tenant on the occupiers of flats and houses under 'short life' housing schemes. Indeed, such decisions, although clearly coloured by policy considerations, seemed to flow reasonably naturally from the reasoning in *Street* v *Mountford*. In a typical arrangement, the local authority licensed the properties to a housing cooperative, or other community housing organisation, which either lacked the legal personality to acquire a secure tenancy, or in any event was not granted exclusive possession. The cooperative then purported to license the properties to the individual occupiers. Even if these occupiers initially appeared to have exclusive possession, quite apart from the policy context, it seemed impossible for them to acquire tenancies. Briefly, because their immediate landlord (the cooperative) had no legal estate themselves, they could not pass one on to the occupiers. The words of Denning L.J. in *Lewisham BC* v *Roberts* [1949] 2 KB 608 (at p. 622) seemed to sum matters up clearly '[The Crown] . . . cannot grant a lease or create any legal interest in the land in favour of any other person, because it has itself no estate in the land out of which to carve any interest.' However, the very recent House of Lords decision in *Bruton (A.P)* v *London and Quadrant Housing Trust* (24 June 1999) has thrown all the above into doubt, and in so doing has raised

fundamental doubts about the very nature of a 'tenancy' itself. (The following note was prepared from the court transcript, although *Bruton* is now reported at [1999] 3 All ER 481.)

In 1975 the London Borough of Lambeth acquired a block of flats, intending to demolish it and build new flats on the site. However, financial and other considerations delayed this scheme, and on 27 March 1986 an agreement was made between the authority and Quadrant Housing Trust that the latter should have a 'licence' to use the property for their charitable housing purposes, including short term housing for the homeless. It was further agreed that no legal estate or proprietary interest passed to the Trust. On 31 January 1989 Bruton agreed with the Trust that he would occupy a flat in the block. His agreement stated that the property was 'short life' that the Trust itself only held a licence, that he was to occupy on a weekly licence, and that he must vacate the flat on being given 'reasonable' notice by the Trust (normally four weeks). Subsequently the authority abandoned its redevelopment scheme and the flat fell into disrepair. Were the Trust in breach of the implied covenant to repair in s. 11, Landlord and Tenant Act 1985 (see further Chapter 7)? Aside from other considerations this section would only apply if a relationship of landlord and tenant existed between Bruton and the Trust. Bruton sought to enforce the repairing covenant and the Trust then served notice to quit on him, and sought a declaration that he was merely a licensee. In the County Court and the Court of Appeal ([1998] QB 834) Bruton was found to be merely a licensee. However, the House of Lords overturned this, unanimously. The leading judgment is that of Lord Hoffmann, with which the majority of the remainder of the House expressly agreed. Lord Hoffmann's judgment is in outline, as follows. Firstly he took from *Street* v *Mountford* the proposition that 'a . . . tenancy is a contractually binding agreement, not referable to any other relationship between the parties, by which one person gives another the right to exclusive possession of land, for a fixed or renewable period . . . usually in return for a periodic payment in money. An agreement having these characteristics creates a relationship of landlord and tenant to which the common law or statute then attach various incidents. The fact that the parties use language more appropriate to a different kind of agreement, such as a licence, is irrelevant if upon its true construction it has the identifying characteristics of a lease'. His lordship felt that (here) 'the agreement, construed against the relevant background, plainly gave Mr Bruton a right to exclusive possession', and, as such, he was, prima facie, to be classified as a tenant. Secondly, there were no 'special circumstances' in the case to negative this prima facie assumption; '[The only] circumstances were that the Trust was a responsible landlord performing socially valuable functions, it had agreed within the council not to grant tenancies, Mr Bruton had agreed that he was not to have a tenancy and the Trust had no estate out of which it could grant one. In my opinion none of the circumstances can make an agreement to grant exclusive possession something other than a tenancy'. Finally, as regards the 'lack of title' issue concerning the Housing Trust. His Lordship stated, somewhat startlingly that 'the term "lease" or "tenancy" describes a relationship between two parties which are designated landlord and tenant. It is not concerned with the question of whether the agreement creates an estate or other proprietary interest which may be binding upon third parties. A lease may, and usually does, create a proprietary interest called a leasehold estate, or, technically, a "term of years absolute". This will depend upon whether the landlord had an interest out of which he could grant it. But it is the fact that the agreement is a lease which creates the proprietary interest. It is putting the cart before the horse to say that whether the agreement is a lease depends upon whether it creates a proprietary interest'. Therefore the fact that the landlord lacked a proprietary interest in the property did not preclude the granting a tenancy sufficient to bind the parties to the immediate agreement, although the landlord might not be able to pass on an estate in land sufficient to bind third parties, lacking such an interest themselves.

The implications of this decision are potentially, enormously wide ranging, although considerable uncertainty will still attach to it until it is considered further by the courts.

- On its immediate facts it demonstrates that 'short life' agreements are now generally at risk of being classified as tenancies, and not licences. Certainly the simple fact that the 'intermediate' landlord lacks an estate in land, is forbidden to grant tenancies and specifically alludes to these facts in the purported licence(s) with the property occupiers unable to alter the position as all these points were present, and were dismissed, in *Bruton* itself. In principle there could be situations where 'short life' occupiers lacked exclusive possession (perhaps because they were occupying something akin to a hostel) and so no tenancy would be created.

  However, in the typical case, a tenancy seems the likely result. This seems to 'sit' very uneasily with *Clarke* and the general trend of post-*Clarke* case law concerned to facilitate local authority flexibility in matters of housing management. The impact of *Bruton* would appear to hamper the freedom of authorities and charitable bodies to use 'short life' agreements to assist the homeless.

- The *extent* to which local authority freedom *is* curbed depends on issues left somewhat uncertain in *Bruton*. As regards the relationship between the trust and Bruton a tenancy clearly existed. However, what kind of tenancy was this? The House of Lords leaves the matter open; Lord Hoffmann states 'I should add that I express no view on whether (Mr Bruton) was a secure tenant, or on the rights of the council to recover possession of the flat', whereas Lord Jauncey cites Slade LJ in *Family Housing Association* v *Jones* [1990] 1 WLR 779 (at p. 793) to the effect that 'whatever their wishes or intentions, it may at least be difficult for bodies charged with responsibilities for the housing of the homeless to enter into any arrangement pursuant to section 65(2) of the Housing Act 1985 under which the person housed is to enjoy exclusive occupation of premises, however temporarily, without conferring on that person security of tenure by virtue of the Act'. *These* views (echoed by Lord Slynn) *suggest* (but no more) that a secure tenancy might have come into being in *Jones*, which was possible, when that case was decided, as Housing Associations before 1989 could grant such tenancies. The approving references to *Family Housing Association* v *Jones* are particularly confusing, since the case appeared to have been substantially overruled in *Clarke*. In the case of Bruton the likeliest conclusion as to his status is that he acquired an assured tenancy under the Housing Act 1988.

- What *is* clear is that by (however inadvertently) creating a tenancy the trust was in breach of its obligations to the authority, and most of their lordships in *Bruton* are at pains to point out that a tenancy *not* constituting an estate in land would not necessarily bind third parties. Does this mean that occupiers such as *Bruton* have only common law tenancies, or that their rights as secure or assured tenants could be determined by the authority terminating their immediate landlords interest for breach of *their* licence terms (in either scenario the occupiers would have no long term security in the property. In the latter case because the sub-agreements would come to an end at the same time as the head licence ends)? These are murky waters which the judgments in *Bruton* do nothing to clear.

However

- Worrying though the above uncertainties are, they are of much less significance than the startling new proposition which lies at the heart of Lord Hoffmann's judgment, in effect that although a typical consequence of a tenancy is the creation of an estate in land, this is not invariable, and that 'it is putting the cart before the horse to say that whether the agreement is a lease depends upon whether it creates a proprietary interest.' As Lords Hope, Slynn and Hobhouse all expressly agreed with Lord Hoffmann's reasoning this proposition must clearly be taken to represent the courts collective view. The view can perhaps, most easily be characterised as exemplifying Maitland's famous dictum of the move from 'status to contract' – above all a tenancy is seen as a species of contractual relationship. Of course there has always been a tension between the proprietary and contractual attributes of a tenancy; a tension which has caused the courts considerable difficulty in recent years, in areas as diverse as the applicability of contractual doctrines such as frustration and repudiatory breach to tenancies (see *National Carriers* v *Panalpina (Northern) Ltd* [1981] AC 675 and *Hussein* v *Mehlman* [1992] 2 EGLR 87), and the capacity of one joint tenant to determine the interests of another by the service of a notice to quit (see Chapter 8). In a key decision on the later issue, *Hammersmith* and *Fulham LBC* v *Monk* [1992] 1 AC at p. 483B, Lord Bridge stated 'As a matter of principle I see no reason why this question should receive any different answer in the context of the contractual relationship of landlord and tenant than that which it would receive in any other contractual context', although Lord Browne-Wilkinson, more cautiously noted that 'instinctive reactions' to the correct analysis could be 'diametrically' opposed dependent on whether a contract or property perspective were adopted ([1992] 1 AC at p. 491F). He continued 'The contract of tenancy confers on the tenant a legal estate in the land: such legal estate gives rise to rights and duties incapable of being founded in contract alone'. It is a very large step from such cautious analysis to the sweeping certainties of Lord Hoffmann. It is one thing to advert to the tension between the contractual and proprietary attributes of a tenancy, but quite another to deny that a tenancy need have any proprietary attributes at all (even Lord Bridge in *Monk* (at p. 484) refers to a tenancy as an 'estate' without there seeming to be any dispute on the point). Lord Hoffmann's heterodoxy, which seems to have 'carried the day' did not balk at a highly partial reading of *Lewisham* ('cannot create a lease' is rendered as 'cannot bind third parties'!) nor at the fact that throughout Lord Templeman's definitive judgment in *Street* v *Mountford* it is, at least, assumed that a tenancy is an interest in land.

The dilemma which subsequent courts will face is very clear; if a tenancy is not (of necessity) an interest in land, what is it? There is no assistance in *Bruton* on this point. To put it even more simply: if a tenancy need not be an interest in land, how is it, at root, conceptually different from a licence? The traditional position is well summarised by Windeyer J in *Radaich Smith* (1959) 101 CUR 209 (at p. 222), cited with approval by Lord Templeman in *Street* v *Mountford* 'what then is the fundamental right which a tenant has that distinguishes his position from that of a licensee? It is an interest in land as distinct from a personal permission to enter the land, and use it for some stipulated purpose, or purposes. And how is it to be ascertained whether such an interest in land has been given? By seeing whether the grantee was given a legal right of exclusive possession of the land for a term. . . . If he was, he is a tenant. And he cannot be other than a tenant, because a legal right of exclusive possession is a tenancy, and the creation of such a right is a demise . . . a tenant for a term . . . can exclude his landlord as well as strangers from the demised premises. All this is long established law'. In other words, it is the reality of exclusive possession which inevitably creates a leasehold estate, with its accompanying right to exclude others. The two are interwoven, indeed inextricable and so there can be no question of 'putting the cart before the horse' (Lord Hoffmann in *Bruton*). It seems likely that the House of Lords has 'boxed itself in' by failing to clearly distinguish between exclusive *possession* and (mere) exclusive *occupation* of premises (a tendency which can be traced back to Lord Templeman in *Street* v *Mountford*). Exclusive *occupation* characterises many licenses. Sole *occupation in fact* is often the preserve of contractual licensees such as residents in a hotel, or persons living in a retirement home. Exclusive *possession* is, of course, not merely about sole occupation, but overall *control* of the premises, entailing crucially the right to *exclude*. By blurring this, the House of Lords in *Bruton* has raised the spectre that 'licensees' with sole occupation rights, but no overall control of the premises they occupy will now be able to argue that they have some form of tenancy. The 'fall out' from this decision is likely to be considerable!

Questions
1.   Section 79(3) (above) is the successor to a similar provision in s. 48 of the Housing Act 1980. What do you think the intention was in drafting such

a provision into the earlier legislation? Could it be argued that the need for the subsection was largely removed by subsequent case law developments?

2.   Would it have been preferable for the House of Lords in *Clarke* to recognise the deficiency in the legislation (in failing to make specific provision for hostels) and perhaps recommend reform, while acknowledging that the occupier in *Clarke* did have a secure licence since he was not sharing living accommodation?

3.   Is it now possible to know with any certainty how any given public sector dispute involving a purported 'hostel' will be decided?

4.   *Manek* holds that the Protection from Eviction Act 1977 does not apply to the 'temporary housing' of homeless people by housing authorities. What is the status of other 'bed and breakfast' occupants? Are they (normally) at least licensees protected by the 1977 Act? Could they even be tenants if they have exclusive possession of relatively self-contained accommodation? If either/both of those questions is answered 'Yes', does this mean that families, perhaps identical in size and with similar housing needs, living in adjoining hotel rooms have very different housing rights?

5.   What would be the legal position of Mr Bruton if, subsequent to the House of Lords decision in *Bruton*, the local authority terminated the Trusts licence and sought to repossess the property?

(D)   Conclusion

Much of the law in this area is now relatively clear. It seems certain, for example, that private sector landlords cannot evade protective legislation by spurious claims to have created a licence. Equally, aside from 'special cases', there remain situations where the transience of the occupants, and the consequent lack of any joint or sole exclusive possession over the dwelling house (or any part of it), indicates a licence. The issue of rent can be a decisive factor; if a property is occupied by sharers who lack exclusive possession vis-à-vis each other, but who equally have separate rent obligations, this may undermine any claim that they have joint exclusive possession and so are joint tenants. Clearly it is not enough merely to draft out separate agreements with separate obligations, where the *reality* is one rent for the whole property (see *Antoniades*). However, where the separate obligations appear to affect the reality of the situation, this may well support a finding of 'licence'. A good example is *Mikeover Ltd v Brady* [1989] 3 All ER 618. The plaintiff company advertised a two-room flat for two people to share. The layout of the flat was such that it was only suitable for occupation by persons who were personally acceptable to each other. The defendant and a Miss Guile saw the flat, and having decided to rent it signed identical agreements which provided in cl. 1 that 'The owner grants to the licensee the right to use in common with others who have been granted the like right [the flat and furniture therein]'; by cl. 2(1) that the licensee agreed with the owner 'To pay the sum of £86.66 per month for the right to share in the use of the said rooms . . .'; and by cl. 2(4) that the licensee agreed with the owner 'Not to impede the use of the said rooms ... by such other persons not exceeding one in number to whom the owner shall grant a licence'. Miss Guile subsequently moved out and the defendant remained in occupation on his own paying, with the agreement of the plaintiffs, his share of the rent. The plaintiffs did not attempt to replace Miss Guile with another occupant. The defendant fell into arrears and an order for possession was made by Judge Honig in the Clerkenwell County Court on the basis that the defendant had a licence which had been properly determined. The defendant appealed.

The Court of Appeal upheld the judgment of the county court. Specifically, on the issue of the separate rent obligations, Slade LJ stated (at p. 625):

It is, however, well settled that four unities must be present for the creation of a joint tenancy, namely the unities of possession, interest, title and time (see Megarry & Wade *The Law of Real Property* (5th edn, 1984) pp. 419 *et seq.*). In the present case . . . the dispute concerns unity of interest. The general principle, as stated in Megarry & Wade (at p. 420) is that 'the interest of each joint tenant is the same in extent, nature and duration, for in theory of law they hold but one estate'. 'Interest' in this context, must, in our judgment, include the bundle of rights and obligations representing that interest. The difficulty, from the defendant's point of view, is that the two agreements instead of imposing a joint liability on him and Miss Guile to pay a deposit of £80 and monthly payments of £173.32, on their face, imposed on each of them individual and separate obligations to pay only a deposit of £40 and monthly payments of only £86.66. On the face of it, the absence of joint obligations of payment were inconsistent with the existence of a joint tenancy . . .

In agreement with the judge, we . . . conclude that as a matter of substance and reality, each of the two parties to the agreements placed himself or herself under merely individual obligations to pay monthly sums of £86.66 and a deposit of £40, but no joint monetary obligations. What then is the effect? . . .

On [the] authorities, it appears to us that unity of interest imports the existence of joint rights and joint obligations. We therefore conclude that the provisions for payment contained in these two agreements (which were genuinely intended to impose and did impose on each party an obligation to pay no more than the sums reserved to the plaintiffs by his or her separate agreement) were incapable in law of creating a joint tenancy, because the monitary obligations of the two parties were not joint obligations and there was accordingly no complete unity of interest. It follows that there was no joint tenancy. Since inter se Miss Guile and the defendant had no power to exclude each other from occupation of any part of the premises, it also follows that their respective several rights can never have been greater than those of licensees during the period of their joint occupation. It has not been submitted (and we think in all the circumstances it could not be submitted) that the defendant's status became that of tenant after Miss Guile's departure, if it was not that before . . .

However, the result of *Clarke* is somewhat to muddy the waters in public sector cases, particularly where anything akin to a hostel is involved.

Lastly, as the next chapter will indicate, recent legislative changes in the private sector, and particularly the introduction of the assured shorthold tenancy, have themselves removed a substantial degree of tenant protection and have removed the need for landlords to deploy the licence device in the majority of situations.

Questions
1. X lets out her holiday bungalow, on a commercial basis, to Y. The property is normally empty in the winter months, but Y agrees to take it from December to February to have a quiet and secluded place to complete his novel. Y has effective exclusive occupation of the bungalow and pays an agreed rent of £500 per month for the three-month term.

Does Y have a tenancy or a licence?

2. A owns a large Victorian house which had been left to her in the will of an uncle. She lives in the house but is concerned about the high maintenance costs and the waste of space (she uses only three of the seven rooms). A has decided to (as she describes it) 'take in lodgers'. However, on closer examination you discover that no food will be provided. A, however, is concerned to keep the house in good condition, and intends to provide cleaning and general maintenance facilities. She also intends to keep spare keys for the locks on the four rooms she intends to make available. The house has only one bathroom and one kitchen.

Will the proposed 'lodgers' occupy as tenants or as licensees?

3. Hopetown District Council owns a property at Anystreet, Hopetown. The property was formerly a hotel. The council have divided the hotel into flats. These consist of a bathroom, a small kitchen and a main bed-sitting room, with a smaller room leading off where there is another bed. In general the flats are made available to single female parents who have only one child. Jane was admitted to the hotel, with Ben her eight-year-old son, following a dispute with her parents, with whom she was living. She was given what was called a 'licence to occupy' a flat.

Has a tenancy or a licence been created in the above situation?

2 PRIVATE SECTOR TENANCIES: CLASSIFICATION AND STATUS

(A) Introduction

At the end of the previous chapter reference was made to the removal of substantial amounts of tenant protection by recent legislation (more specifically, Pt 1 of the Housing Act 1988). The form that these changes take renders the structure of this area of the law particularly complex. In general, Pt 1 of the Housing Act 1988 is not retrospective in effect so that two distinct legislative codes stand side by side: first, the Rent Act 1977 and associated legislation; and, secondly, the Housing Act 1988. In general, a tenancy entered into before 15 January 1989 is governed by the Rent Act, and a tenancy entered into from 15 January 1989 onwards by the Housing Act. Each code has a distinct set of categories into which a tenancy might fall: in the case of the Rent Act, protected tenancies, statutory tenancies and restricted contracts; in the case of the Housing Act, assured tenancies, statutory periodic tenancies and assured shorthold tenancies. Such classification has fundamental implications for the rights attaching to landlords and tenants under the tenancies in question. The Housing Act 1988 has now been, in its turn, amended by the Housing Act 1996, as explained below.

Legislative involvement in the private sector dates back to the Increase of Rent and Mortgage Interest (War Restrictions) Act 1915. As its name suggests, this was intended as a temporary measure, aimed at curbing excessive rent increases during wartime. It was envisaged that 'normal service' would be resumed after the war, and indeed, the Hunter Committee of 1918 broadly recommended this. However, the reality was a continuation of a system of rent control based on rateable values which lasted until the introduction of the more flexible 'fair rent' scheme in the Rent Act 1965.

Over the intervening years there were numerous calls by those supporting landlords' interests for wholesale 'decontrol' of the market, but this never occurred (although the provisions in the Housing Act 1957 to 'decontrol' all properties with rateable values over £30 (£40 in London) came close). The Rent Act 1965 introduced a less rigid system focusing on individual 'fair rent' evaluations by rent officers. However, any 'creeping decontrol' implicit in the Housing Act 1957 was sharply reversed, the new measures applying to most private sector tenancies (even, from 1974 onwards, to furnished ones). The Rent Act 1977, Pts III and IV now contain the relevant 'fair rent' legislation for those tenancies still governed by the Act.

As the titles of most of the relevant legislation suggest, the main purpose of the above measures was rent control. However, it was acknowledged from the outset (see s. 1(3) of the 1915 Act) that unless this was coupled with security of tenure (i.e. security from eviction save on specified grounds) it was likely to be ineffective. All legislation from 1915 to 1977 centred on the two basic issues of rent control and security of tenure.

As in so many other areas, the Conservative Government in power from 1979, broke up the consensus which had emerged in favour of substantial market intervention and regulation in the private rented sector. All legislation introduced from 1979 to 1988 had the effect of reducing the scope of full Rent Act controls (most obviously by the introduction of the protected shorthold tenancy). However, not until 1988 was a direct assault made on the general framework of protection and rent control. Prior to the legislation, a White Paper (*Housing: The Government's Proposals* (1987) Cm. 214) had indicated the depth of the Government's opposition to the existing system:

1.3　Too much preoccupation since the War with controls in the private rented sector . . . has resulted in substantial numbers of rented houses and flats which are badly . . . maintained and which fail to provide decent homes. The return to private sector landlords has been inadequate to persuade them to stay in the market, or to keep their property in repair . . .
1.8　Rent controls have prevented property owners from getting an adequate return on their investment. People who might have been prepared to grant a temporary letting have also been deterred by laws on security of tenure which made it impossible to regain their property when necessary. These factors have contributed to shortages of supply and poor maintenance.

The 1988 Act swept away all rent control in the traditional sense and reintroduced the primacy of the market. Security of tenure was provided for (albeit on a more limited basis) through the concept of the assured tenancy; but the significance of this is substantially undermined by the facility for landlords to create assured shorthold tenancies, to which no true security of tenure attaches. Indeed, s. 96 of the Housing Act 1996 (inserting a new s. 19A into the 1988 Act) seems to introduce a presumption that all 'new' tenancies are to be as assured shorthold tenancies unless the agreement provides to the contrary, or one of the other (limited) exceptions in the (new) Sch. 2A applies.

The likelihood is that most private sector tenancies are now governed by the Housing Act 1988. Therefore, attention is first given to the provisions as to classification and status contained in the 1988 Act. Following this, the distinct provisions in the Rent Act 1977 are considered.

Questions
1.   '. . . the linchpin of the 1988 Act is the abolition of rent control' (Partington and Hill). Do you agree?
2.   If the above statement *is* true, why do you think that the Government was at pains to 'toughen up' the assured shorthold 'regime' in the 1996 Act? (Assured tenancies also lack effective rent control.)

(B)   Housing Act 1988 tenancies

(i)   Assured Tenancies
Despite the predominance in practice of the assured shorthold tenancy, the starting point has to be the concept of the assured tenancy. Indeed, the definition of an assured shorthold tenancy initially requires that the tenancy fulfils the definition of an assured tenancy (Housing Act 1988, s. 20(1)).

The basic definition is contained in s. 1 of the Housing Act 1988, which provides (in part):

(1)   A tenancy under which a dwelling-house is let as a separate dwelling is for the purposes of this Act an assured tenancy if and so long as—
(a)   the tenant or, as the case may be, each of the joint tenants is an individual; and
(b)   the tenant or, as the case may be, at least one of the joint tenants occupies the dwelling-house as his only or principal home; and
(c)   the tenancy is not one which, by virtue of subsection (2) or subsection (6) below, cannot be an assured tenancy.
(2)   Subject to subsection (3) below, if and so long as a tenancy falls within any paragraph in Part I of Schedule 1 to this Act, it cannot be an assured tenancy; and in that Schedule—
(a)   'tenancy' means a tenancy under which a dwelling-house is let as a separate dwelling;
(b)   Part II has effect for determining the rateable value of a dwelling-house for the purposes of Part I; and
(c)   Part III has effect for supplementing paragraph 10 in Part I.

The key concepts in the above all derive from previous legislation, principally the Rent Act 1977 and its predecessors or the (public sector) Housing Act 1985. There is, therefore, a considerable amount of case law to draw on. For example:

(a)   'Dwelling-house'
Section 45(1) states clearly that a 'dwelling-house' may be a 'house or part of a house' (echoing s. 1 of the Rent Act 1977). It is clear that a flat or even

a room can constitute (for this purpose at least) a 'dwelling-house' (although whether a room constitutes a separate dwelling is another matter). This is supported by 'Rent Act' cases such as *Curl* v *Angelo* [1948] 2 All ER 189 at p.192 and *Langford Property Co.* v *Goldrich* [1949] 1 KB 511. Equally two distinct properties, can, for this purpose, constitute one 'dwelling house'.

Whitty v *Scott-Russell*
[1950] 2 KB 32

In 1937 the predecessor in title of Whitty leased to the defendant tenant (at a rent of £75 a year) a house and a cottage, plus all the attached garden and land. The house and cottage were semi-detached, but lacked any internal communication. The tenant agreed to use the premises only as a private dwelling. He occupied the house and (with the consent of the lessor) sub-let the cottage. Subsequently Whitty (who acquired the reversion as executor of the original landlord) served a notice to quit, and commenced possession proceedings claiming that the (then) Rent and Mortgage Interest Restrictions (Amendment) Act 1933 did not protect the tenant, because the house and cottage could not be taken together as one 'dwelling-house'. However, the county court held that they *did* constitute a single dwelling-house, and the Court of Appeal dismissed the appeal. The approach of the Court is clearly indicated by the following extract from the judgment of Asquith LJ (at p. 37)

Was the 'complex' let a 'dwelling-house'? The material definition of a dwelling-house for the present purpose is that contained in s. 16, sub-s. 1of the Rent and Mortgage Interest Restrictions (Amendment) Act 1933. This definition is expressed to mean the same as the corresponding definition in the Act of 1920, though the language of the Act of 1933 is slightly different, and runs as follows: 'A house let as a separate dwelling, or a part of a house, being a part so let'. In the present case, is what is let 'a house' or two houses, and is it let as a 'separate dwelling' or as two separate dwellings? Or is only part of it let as a separate dwelling?

The main authority relied on by the tenant on this issue is *Langford Property Co. Ltd* v *Goldrich* [1949] 1 KB 511. That was a case in which two flats, not contiguous but forming part of the same block of flats under a single roof, were held to be a 'dwelling-house' within the definition. Somervell LJ, in a judgment with which the other two members of the court concurred, says: 'In my opinion, if the facts justify such a finding, two flats, or indeed so far as I can see two houses could be a separate dwelling-house within the meaning of the definition'.

The Lord Justice, if he had wished to adhere precisely to the terms of the definition, would have said 'two houses' could be 'a house let as a separate dwelling', and therefore a 'dwelling-house'. He appears to base this conclusion partly on the terms of the lease, under which the subject-matter let is expressed to be two flats; partly on the Interpretation Act, whereby the singular prima facie includes the plural, hence 'house' in the definition includes houses; but partly also (in relation to the part of the definition which reads 'let as a separate dwelling') on the fact that the tenant in that case wanted the two flats as a home for his family or its overflow, which one flat would not have been able to accommodate.

If the Interpretation Act alone were concerned, this reasoning would be open to the comment that, if the inclusion of the plural in the singular permitted us to read 'house' as including houses, it would equally permit (or perhaps require) us to read 'let as a separate dwelling' as including 'let as two separate dwellings'. An impartial application of the Interpretation Act might lead to odd results.

It is unnecessary, however, to speculate on this, since we are bound by the decision in *Langford Property Co. Ltd* v *Goldrich*, of which this was part of the ratio decidendi. It enables us to read 'house' as covering two houses. But is this (composite) 'house' in the present case 'let as a separate dwelling'? In *Langford Property Co. Ltd* v *Goldrich*, the tenant's purpose in taking two flats was that his family should occupy both, as in fact they did. 'What happened here', says Somervell LJ 'was that the tenant wished to accommodate in his home these relatives to whom I have referred, and he wanted more accommodation than could be found or conveniently found in one flat. He . . . thereupon took the two flats and made those two flats his home'. It would seem that the circumstance that the tenant intended to make the two flats – the totality of the parcels let – his home, was thought material, and indeed necessary, by Somervell LJ, to his decision that the flats were let 'as a separate dwelling'. If the flats had been let to the tenant, one to be dwelt in by him and his family, the other not to be so dwelt in the decision might, it appears, have been different. In the present case the tenant only took the cottage along with the house because the lessor refused to let the one without the other. He never lived in, and never from the start intended to live in, the cottage.

. . .

In other words, where the original contract was for a particular user, but by the time the plaint is issued has been superseded by a subsequent contract providing for a different user, the subsequent contract may be looked to in deciding whether the premises are let as a 'dwelling' or 'separate dwelling'. This qualification (which was obiter in *Wolfe* v *Hogan* [1949] 2 KB 194, 203) does not apply to the facts of the present case, in which there have not been two successive contracts providing for different users; and the principle is asserted without any such qualification in earlier decisions of the Court of Appeal.

In these circumstances, we are of opinion that the complex 'let' in this case was a dwelling-house within the definition, and we are fortified in that opinion by the concession, in argument, that if X took a tenancy of a house consisting of, say, three floors, and sub-let one floor at once and permanently, the fact of the sublease would not deprive the subject-matter of the head lease of its character as a dwelling-house, provided that in other respects it possessed that character. It cannot in our view make a crucial difference that in the case supposed the part sub-let and the part not sub-let possess internal intercommunication through the common stair, whereas in this case the two units, one of which is sub-let, are two houses clamped together and without such internal intercommunication. Indeed, the judgment of Somervell LJ, in *Langford Property Co. Ltd* v *Goldrich* appears to decide that two houses, even if wholly detached can be 'a house' within the definition; and *Barrett* v *Hardy* [1925] 2 KB 220, *Epsom Grand Stand Association* v *Clarke* [1919] WN 170, and, as we read the case, *Wolfe* v *Hogan* decide that 'a house' expressed in the contract of tenancy to be let 'as a private dwelling-house' is none the less a house 'let as a dwelling' and a 'separate dwelling' because one of its components was sub-let from the start . . .

(b)   'Is let'

This of course raises the tenancy or licence question discussed in the previous chapter. True licences are outside the scope of assured tenancy protection.

(c) 'As a separate dwelling'

Although this compound phrase needs, ultimately, to be read as a whole (see elements in the judgment of Asquith LJ in *Whitty* v *Scott-Russell* (above)), each word also carries an individual significance requiring individual comment:

(i) The word 'as' in the above phrase indicates that the key is the purpose for which the property was originally let and not any subsequent use that may have taken place. The leading case, consistently referred to in the subsequent authorities, is *Wolfe* v *Hogan*. (It was recently applied again by the Court of Appeal specifically in relation to s. 1 of the Housing Act 1988 in *Andrews* v *Brewer* (1997) 30 HLR 203.)

Wolfe v *Hogan*
[1949] 2 KB 194

In August 1939, Mr Noller, a tenant of No. 15, Anderson Street, Chelsea, sub-let to Miss Hogan (the 'tenant') a large room on the ground floor, divided by means of two folding doors and, behind that, a small brick-built edifice attached to the larger room. The large room, when let, contained a number of articles of furniture and junk, Mr Noller being a dealer in such articles elsewhere. It was plain that the tenant's intention was to carry on the business of an antique and junk dealer at this shop. No water was laid on to these rooms and there was no sanitary convenience. Mr Noller arranged with his other tenants upstairs that the tenant Miss Hogan could have the use of their lavatory and bathroom, which was on a halfway floor. It was found by the trial judge that there was no express covenant by the tenant that she would not use the premises as a dwelling-house, but that the whole of the negotiations proceeded on the footing that the tenant was taking this composite room to use it as an antique shop.

Later, when London was exposed to air bombing, the tenant asked Mr Noller whether he would have any objection to her sleeping on the premises, and he, feeling that she might well be in a difficulty in going home in air raids, assented to that request. In 1942, the freeholders parted with the freehold, Mr Noller's lease came to an end and the tenant's sub-tenancy died with it, but she remained in occupation as a tenant of the freeholder. Mr Wolfe, the plaintiff, was now the freeholder and the landlord of the tenant Miss Hogan.

Mr Wolfe, the landlord, having given due notice to terminate the tenancy, and the tenant continuing in possession of the premises after the date for which notice was given, brought an action claiming possession. The tenant resisted the claim, contending that her rooms were let to her 'as a separate dwelling', within the meaning of the (then) s. 12(2), of the Rent and Mortgage Interest (Restrictions) Act, 1920. It was proved that for some time, at any rate, Miss Hogan lived in the rooms as well as conducting her business there. Mr Noller and Mr Wolfe denied that they knew that she was living there, but this was contested. There was no evidence of the knowledge of Mr Wolfe's father who, before Mr Wolfe, was her landlord for a period.

Stable J found that there was merely a letting of premises described as a shop and held that there should be implied in the contract a convenant against the use of the premises otherwise that as a shop. He gave judgment for the plaintiff for possession. The defendant appealed.

The Court of Appeal unanimously upheld the first instance decision, ruling that the premises had been originally let as a 'lock-up' shop, and that nothing subsequently had occurred to change this.

EVERSHED LJ: . . . the matter is more accurately stated by Mr Megarry in the fourth edition of his book on the Rent Acts, and I quote and adopt as part of my judgment the brief summary of the position which I find on p. 19 of his book: 'Where the terms of the tenancy provide for or contemplate the use of the premises for some particular purpose, that purpose is the essential factor, not the nature of the premises or the actual use made of them. Thus, if premises are let for business purposes, the tenant cannot claim that they have been converted into a dwelling-house merely because somebody lives on the premises.' . . . a little later on he writes: 'If, however, the tenancy agreement contemplates no specified use, then the actual use at the time when possession is sought by the landlord must be considered,' and then various instances are given. I may add that in such a case, the lease being quite silent, plainly one cannot get any help from the terms of the lease on the question whether the premises were or were not let as a dwelling, and you have to find the answer to the question by reference to the facts as they have occurred. Again I wish to make it quite plain that I am saying nothing that should be taken as indicating that if a tenant does change the user and creates out of what was formerly a shop a dwelling-house, and if that fact is fully known to and accepted by the other party to the contract, whether or not there is a prohibition, the result may not very well be that there will then be inferred a contract to let as a dwelling-house, although it may be a different contract in essentials from the contract that was originally made and expressed.

But as I have already said, these facts do not arise here. What does arise here is plainly, I think, a contemplation, according to the terms and circumstances of the letting, of user as a shop.

DENNING LJ (as he then was): In determining whether a house or part of a house is 'let as a dwelling' within the meaning of the Rent Restriction Acts, it is necessary to look at the purpose of the letting. If the lease contains an express provision as to the purpose of the letting, it is not necessary to look further. But, if there is no express provision, it is open to the court to look at the circumstances of the letting. If the house is constructed for use as a dwelling-house, it is reasonable to infer the purpose was to let it as a dwelling. But if, on the other hand, it is constructed for the purpose of being used as a lock-up shop, the reasonable inference is that it was let for business purposes. If the position were neutral, then it would be proper to look at the actual user. It is not a question of implied terms. It is a question of the purpose for which the premises were let.

These premises were let in 1939 by the head lessee to Miss Hogan. On the facts, there was ample material on which the judge could find that the purpose of the letting was for use as a shop. At the beginning of the tenancy, therefore, the premises were not within the Act. But the point that has arisen in the course of argument is this: What is the effect of the tenant changing the use she made of the premises? She changed its use from one for business purposes to one partly for business and partly for dwelling purposes. During the air-raids in 1940 she started to sleep on the premises and continued to sleep there. She has thereafter continued to use a part for dwelling purposes. Indeed, when the notice to quit was given in 1947, she was for all practical purposes permanently residing in the back part of the room. Moreover, there is ground for supposing that the landlord accepted rent, knowing of the change of user: because, in 1942, after the original letting to the head lessee under the lease had come to an end, the head landlord became the immediate landlord of Miss Hogan and, knowing the position of affairs in the house, accepted rent from her.

What is the effect of that? In my opinion, it does not give the tenant the protection of the Act. A house or a part of a house originally let for business purposes does not become let for dwelling purposes, unless it can be inferred from the acceptance of rent that the landlord has affirmatively consented to the change of user.

(ii)   The Court of Appeal twice ruled in the 1970s that the phrase 'let as *a* dwelling' could only be interpreted in the singular (notwithstanding the Interpretation Act). So, a house let as *several* dwellings fell outside Rent Act protection, and will equally fall outside the Housing Act 1988. The cases were *Horford Investments Ltd* v *Lambert* [1976] 2 Ch 39, and *St Catherine's College* v *Dorling* [1980] 1 WLR 66.

St Catherine's College v *Dorling*
[1980] 1 WLR 66

An Oxford firm of estate agents, with the cooperation of a large number of Oxford colleges, introduced a scheme whereby the owners of properties would let premises to the college, which would then make the accommodation available to students, typically by sub-letting the properties. (Such arrangements are now widespread as a means of increasing the amount of university 'managed' accommodation. They are often termed 'head tenancy' schemes.) On what basis did the college(s) let the property? If they did so as a protected tenant under the (then) Rent Act provisions, they would acquire a number of important rights — most obviously the potential to apply for a fair rent (the advantages of which could, no doubt, then be passed onto the student sub-tenants). This action was then something of a 'test' case; the particular arrangements were that each student had the exclusive use of one room, as a study bedroom, and shared the kitchen and bathroom. The college had covenanted 'not to use the demised premises other than for occupation by a person or persons . . . pursuing or intending to pursue a course of study' provided by the college.

The college applied to the county court for a declaration that it had a protected tenancy. The judge rejected this application, finding that the house has not been let as *a* dwelling-house, but as a building for multiple occupation. The Court of Appeal dismissed the college's appeal, in essence because the terms of the agreement, and the surrounding circumstances, showed that there had been from the *outset* a letting of premises containing a number of units of accommodation, and not 'a' dwelling.

EVELEIGH LJ: The premises consisted of three rooms upstairs and two rooms downstairs. There was a small kitchen, a bathroom, and two WCs, one inside and one outside. One of the two downstairs rooms had a dining table and four chairs. There were no locks on the doors of the rooms. Each room was equipped with sufficient furniture for its use as a bedroom, a study and a sitting-room. The premises were occupied by the five undergraduates. Each took a room. Each gave a cheque for his share of the total rent; and generally speaking one of them would take all the cheques to Runyards. The dining table was taken from the room where it was when they first occupied the premises and set up in the kitchen. The general practice was for these occupants to cook in relays, providing their own individual food, although on occasions, at weekends in particular, they might eat together around that table.

The question in this case is whether the premises were let as a separate dwelling within the meaning of section 1. The important point in answering that question is to determine the contemplated use of the premises. In *Ponder* v *Hillman* [1969] 1 WLR 1261, 1263, Goff J referred to *Wolfe* v *Hogan* [1949] 2 KB 194 and to a particular passage in the judgment of Evershed LJ and then continued:

. . . [Evershed LJ] approved the following passage in *Megarry on the Rent Acts* (1967) 4th ed., p. 19: 'Where the terms of the tenancy provide for or contemplate the use of the premises for some particular purpose, that purpose is the essential factor, not the nature of the premises or the actual use made of them. Thus, if the premises are let for business purposes, the tenant cannot claim that they have been converted into a dwelling-house merely because somebody lives on the premises'.

So it follows that one has to consider the terms of the lease and the surrounding circumstances at the time that the lease was granted. It may be that in some cases assistance can be obtained from the subsequent user of the premises. In my opinion generally speaking such assistance will be found to be a matter of last resort.

I turn to consider the terms of the tenancy agreement in this case. There is the usual habendum and reddendum, and then I turn to clause 2(1), in which the tenant covenants:

(i) Not to use the demised premises otherwise than for occupation by a person or persons who are as specified by section 8 of the Rent Act 1977 pursuing or intending to pursue a course of study provided by the tenant whether the said person or persons occupy the demised premises as sub-tenants or licensees. (ii) Not to assign sub-let with possession or share possession or occupation of all or part of the demised premises furniture fixtures fittings or effects or any part thereof provided that there shall be no breach of this clause if the tenant shall be a specified educational institution as defined by section 8 of the Rent Act 1977 and either the tenant sub-lets only to a person who is pursuing or intending to pursue a course of study provided by the tenant or the tenant grants a licence for the use of the demised premises to such person.

Then clause 2(m), the user clause reads:

Not to carry on or permit to be carried on upon the demised premises any profession trade or business whatsoever or let apartments or receive paying guests in the demised premises but to use or permit the same to be used as private residence only in the occupation of one person per room and not in any way to contravene the Town and Country Planning Acts and not to exhibit any notice or poster on any portion of the demised premises.

Mr Boyle has submitted that here a group of students, or undergraduates, intended to occupy the premises as joint occupants of the whole, and that this was the object and purport of the tenancy granted to the college. He particularly relied upon sub-clause (m) and invited the court to say that the words 'to be used as private residence only' should be read to include the indefinite article: that is to say, 'to be used as a private residence only'.
. . .

On the other hand, Mr Etherton, for the landlord respondent, has contended that clause 2(m) comes to his aid. He has invited the court to construe the phrase 'as private residence' as meaning: for residential purposes. I would myself accept that submission. One cannot read the words 'as private residence' without reading the words that follow, namely, 'in the occupation of one person per room'. In my opinion it is no accidental omission of the indefinite article. There is an intentional omission and the phrase 'as private residence' is used similarly to the expression 'as business premises'. It is descriptive of the user and not of the premises themselves.

When one then sees that what is envisaged is the occupation of one person per room, using that for private purposes, and then turns to the other provision in sub-clause (1) which I have read, one sees that subletting or a licence to use is contemplated, and the words used are 'sub-lets only to a person'. The importance, to my mind, of the words in that sub-clause is that they show that a subletting is envisaged. That envisages, as I see it – for one must read this as a whole – that the college is permitted to sublet to a person who is to occupy a single room as a private residence. If the college is to be allowed to 'sub-let to a person' (to use the words of the sub-clause) any part of the building, it would follow that it should be allowed to let to more than one person, or the building would otherwise have another part unused. Quite clearly it was never contemplated that the college itself should occupy or make any particular use of the premises – other, that is to say, than as accommodation for undergraduates. Furthermore, of course, the plural is used in sub-clause (1)(i), where we see the words 'for occupation by a person or persons'.

I therefore read these two sub-clauses as saying that the college shall be in a position to sublet, and shall be in a position to sublet to 'persons'; but they must be persons 'pursuing or intending to pursue a course of study'. The use of the singular in sub-paragraph (ii) is simply because it is describing the type of person who may be a sub-tenant; and, as the college may sublet to a particular type of sub-tenant and must do so only for occupation of one person per room, it follows, in my opinion, that the purpose of this letting was that the college should be in a position to do just that. In other words, what was being granted to the college here was a tenancy of a building which contained a number of units of habitation, as they have been called. From that interpretation of this lease I would conclude that the premises were not let as separate dwellings.

In *Horford Investments Ltd* v *Lambert* [1976] Ch. 39, a landlord let to a tenant two houses. Those houses had been converted into a number of 'units of accommodation', and at the time of the lease those units were in fact occupied. The question arose in that case as to whether this was a letting of a dwelling-house, and indeed a separate dwelling-house, so as to attract the protection of the Rent Act 1968. Russell LJ said, at p. 48:

Accordingly, in my judgment the tenancy of each of the two houses in this case is not within the definition of a protected tenancy because of the plurality of dwellings, or, as I have labelled them, units of habitation, comprised in the premises when let and obliged by the terms of the letting to be so maintained.

In that case the covenant in regard to one of the two flats – the user clause in the lease – was in these terms:

> The lessee will not use . . . the . . . premises or any part of thereof for the purposes of any trade or business nor for any purpose other than residential in multiple occupation.

In my opinion, clause 2(m) of the lease which this court has to consider is to the same effect: it is not to use for any purpose other than residential in multiple occupation.

Mr Boyle, however, has argued that the rooms in this house were not dwellings and, consequently, *Horford Investments Ltd* v *Lambert* [1976] Ch. 39 has no application. He further submitted that there is a distinction in that the individual units were already let in that case. I cannot accept that those arguments prevent, or in any way militate against, the construction of the lease which I have just stated.

He referred the court to *Wright* v *Howell* (1947) 204 LTJ 299, where the appellant was the tenant of an unfurnished room in a flat of the respondent landlord. He used as toilet and other facilities those that existed in another flat in the same building which was occupied by the parents-in-law. It was held that, in those circumstances:

> . . . as the room, when let to the tenant, was devoid of cooking arrangements and water supply, and as the word 'dwelling' on its true construction included all the major activities of life, particularly sleeping, cooking and feeding, and as one of those activities, sleeping, was at all relevant times no longer being carried on there, the room was not a dwelling and the tenancy was not protected.

I do not myself see a parallel, on the facts of that case. In the present case the undergraduates were sleeping on the premises; there were facilities provided. It is not necessary, as the many cases under the Rent Acts show, for those facilities to exist in the room itself. Mr Boyle argued that these rooms themselves did not attract the protection of the Rent Acts: as some accommodation was shared they would be outside that protection, and from this he inferred – in what I regard as a non sequitur – that, as they were not themselves protected dwellings, the whole of the house was itself let as a separate individual dwelling. As I say, that to my mind is a non sequitur. The fact (and I would not concede this) that the rooms might not be protected by the Rent Act 1977 does not mean that they were not let. There are many cases where accommodation has been let but by virtue of the sharing of other accommodation – essential accommodation – has been held not to come within the terms of the Rent Act because of the words 'let as a separate dwelling.' But that does not in any way deny the finding of the judge in this case – on ample evidence to support it – that the undergraduates in fact had the exclusive use of their own particular rooms. Further-more, on the facts of this case, in my judgment, the judge was justified in concluding that it was the intention of the landlord and the tenant college that that should be so.

Mr Etherton has submitted, and I agree with the submission, that such an arrangement is not consistent, generally speaking anyway, with the conception of a 'dwelling-house . . . let as a separate dwelling'. Generally speaking, 'a dwelling-house . . . let as a separate dwelling' envisages that at least someone – that someone being in most cases the tenant in occupation – will have the right to go to any part of the premises he chooses. It may well be that a tenant who takes a separate dwelling-house will sublet so as to preclude himself, vis-à-vis the sub-lessee, from entering another part of the premises for the period of the subletting; but that is something which occurs after the lease has been entered into and in no way detracts from the right of the tenant vis-à-vis the landlord to go to another room. The existence of someone able to go in his own right to all the rooms of the premises is one of the hallmarks of a dwelling-house. That is completely absent on the findings in this case. That being so, I would agree with Mr Etherton's submission that the arrangement envisaged in this case was inconsistent with the concept of a building which itself could be described as a separate dwelling.

For those reasons I would dismiss this appeal.

(iii) The word 'separate' is a key concept which involves the idea that the accommodation occupied is (relatively) 'self-contained'. Therefore any sharing of essential living accommodation (other than with other joint tenants) will result in the accommodation falling outside protection. The case law suggests that 'living accommodation' involves living rooms, bedrooms and kitchens, but not bathrooms or toilets. For example in *Cole v Harris* [1945] KB 474 (at p. 479) Mackinnon LJ said: '. . . a dwelling-house is that in which a person dwells or lives, and it seems reasonable that a separate dwelling should be one containing essential living rooms. A WC may be essential in modern days, but I do not think it is a living room, whereas a kitchen, I think is.' The issues were fully explored in the following case:

Neale v Del Soto
[1945] 5 KB 144

By an oral agreement the landlord (Del Soto) sub-let to the tenant, Neale, two unfurnished rooms in a house containing seven rooms of which she was the lessee. The agreement provided for the use by the tenant, jointly with the landlord, of the garage, kitchen, bathroom, lavatory, coalhouse and conservatory. On 11 July 1944 the tenant applied under the then s.12(3) of the Increase in Rent and Mortgage Act 1920, to the county court for an apportionment of the standard rent as at 7 August 1943. The county court judge dismissed the application, holding that a letting of two unfurnished rooms in a house, together with use, jointly with the landlord, of the kitchen, bathroom, lavatory, garage and other rooms, was not a letting of part of a house as a separate dwelling within s. 12 of the Act of 1920. The tenant appealed.

The Court of Appeal dismissed the appeal.

MORTON LJ: . . . The county court judge found as follows: 'I find as a fact from the evidence, as also appeared in the rent book before it was altered, that what was let was two unfurnished rooms for the sole use and occupation by the tenant, and the garage, kitchen, bathroom, lavatory, coalhouse and conservatory for use and occupation by him jointly with the landlord.' Again, in another portion of his judgment, he described the case as follows: 'When, as in this case, a person has got in a lease at a rent two rooms and the use in common with the owner of other rooms, such as the kitchen, that is a sole tenancy of two rooms and a joint tenancy, as it were, of the other rooms, since he has a right to use them in every way, not merely as an accessory to something else.' It was contended by counsel for the plaintiff, relying on the latter passage, that the county court judge had taken the view that there were, in fact, here

two lettings. I do not so read his judgment. There was only one letting, and the county court judge recognised that fact. The use of the phrase 'as it were' indicates that he was not speaking of a separate joint tenancy in the full sense of those words.
. . .

Were the two rooms in question in the present case a part of a house let as a separate dwelling? In my view, they were not. What was let was the two rooms together with the use, in common with the landlord, of the garage, kitchen, bathroom, lavatory, coalhouse and conservatory, and it would be a misuse of language, to my mind, to say that the two rooms, and nothing more, were let as a separate dwelling. The real substance of the matter was that there was a sharing of the house. Each party had the exclusive use of some rooms and the two parties together had the use in common of the other rooms.

Strange results might follow if we were to find that a letting such as this was a letting of the two rooms as a separate dwelling. If, for instance, the owner of a house let to a tenant an attic-bedroom with the right to use all the other rooms in the house, jointly with the landlord, it might be said that that was a letting within the Act, that there could be apportionment of rent under s. 12, sub-s. 3, of the Act as between the attic-bedroom on the one hand and the rest of the house on the other hand, and that a statutory tenancy would arise of the attic-bedroom carrying with it the right to use all the other rooms in the house.
. . .

It was suggested in the course of the argument for the tenant that, if the county court judge's decision is upheld, the result might follow that a letting of the two rooms, together with the use, in common with the landlord, of, for instance, a WC, would be outside the Act. I am content to leave the matter to be dealt with if, and when, it arises, but it may be – I express no view on the matter – that this question is one of degree and, as the judge below observed in his judgment, in the present case a very substantial part of the dwelling was shared, including such a very important room as the kitchen.

For these reasons I am satisfied, on the facts of this case, that the county court judge's decision was right and this appeal ought to be dismissed.

(iv)   With regard to the term 'dwelling' even if none of the living accommodation is shared with others, the accommodation may fall outside protection if it is not 'the "home" of anybody' (Lord Greene MR in *Curl* v *Angelo* [1948] 2 All ER 189, at p. 190). So, if one of the essential features of 'normal living' is carried on elsewhere, and never in the accommodation, then the accommodation may not (for this purpose) be a 'dwelling'. Into the category of 'essential features' would come sleeping and eating. As a general approach it would be realistic to say that if a person rarely if ever sleeps or eats in the accommodation it is not a 'dwelling'; but, of course, any case may have features so that this norm will not be applied. (A good example of this is *Palmer* v *McNamara* (1990) 23 HLR 168 where a person was still seen as a resident landlord – still occupying premises *as his home* – even though he never cooked or slept there. This case is dealt with in more detail below.)

(d)   'Individual'

The word 'individual' in s. 1(1)(a) indicates that the letting must be to a natural person and not to a company, or other form of 'artificial' person. If the courts are not astute to detect 'shams' there is considerable scope here for avoidance of the legislation by landlords via the drafting ploy of the letting being to a company, albeit that the only member of that company is the occupant of the premises. This issue was discussed in *Hilton* v *Plustitle Ltd* (the facts appear in the judgment of Croom-Johnson LJ (at p. 150):

Hilton v Plustitle Ltd
[1989] 1 WLR 149

CROOM-JOHNSON LJ: If a dwelling house is let to a limited company, the company cannot become a statutory tenant under the terms of section 2 of the Rent Act 1977, on the termination of the tenancy. This has been so since *Hiller* v *United Dairies (London) Ltd* [1934] 1 KB 57. This rule has remained unchanged during re-enactments of the Rent Acts ever since. If a tenancy is granted to one person, e.g. a company, on the terms that someone else is to reside in the house, there will be no statutory tenancy in favour of that other person: *S. L. Dando Ltd* v *Hitchcock* [1954] 2 QB 317. In *Firstcross Ltd* v *East West (Export/Import) Ltd* (1980) 255 EG 355 the tenants' nominee was their director and was actually named in the agreement: it was held he acquired no statutory tenancy. Accordingly, if a landlord does not want to be saddled with a statutory tenant he lets on what is known as a 'company let'.

The plaintiff in this action, Mr Hilton, is a civil engineer who has in recent years reconstructed a number of premises in London and therein created flats which are high quality flats. They also contain built-in furniture made in his own workshop. They are let at not excessive but market rents for flats of that quality. He is a good landlord who provides value for money. His policy is to let only as company flats, and his flats are advertised as such.

The second defendant, Miss Rose, is an actress. She saw in an evening newspaper on 8 August 1986 an advertisement referring to one of the plaintiff's flats. The advertisement made it clear that the letting was to be a company let. She knew what that meant. She got in touch with the plaintiff and saw several flats. Eventually she saw one at 45, Priory Road, London, NW6. Miss Rose, as an actress, had no need for a company, but the plaintiff made it clear that any letting would have to be a company let and that the rent would have to be guaranteed by a third party. He gave her the name and telephone number of his accountant, who would be able to provide her with a company which could become the tenant and then nominate her as the person who would reside in its flat. As the judge found, the plaintiff told her that the letting to the company would be for a limited period, with a possibility of renewal if everything was satisfactory. Miss Rose did not go to the accountant. She took advice from her solicitors, and went to a firm called Jordans, from whom she bought a company, the first defendant, off the shelf. It was called Plustitle Ltd. It cost her £150. She became a shareholder and a director.

On 1 September 1986 the company entered into a written agreement with the plaintiff to take the flat for an initial term of six months at a rent of £345 per month. Miss Rose signed the agreement as managing director of the company. The agreement gave the company the right to nominate the occupiers of the property, who would pay no rent. The agreement contained all the usual tenant's covenants. The plaintiff consented to maintain the services in good condition. The rent and fees to be paid by the company were guaranteed by John Rose, who is Miss Rose's brother. Before that agreement was made, the plaintiff obtained a banker's reference for Miss Rose for an amount which was the obligation to pay the monthly rent of £345.

In February 1987 the term was by mutual agreement extended for three months till May. It was followed by an offer for a further three months' extension. There was a dispute about a slight increase in the rent and so the offer was withdrawn by the plaintiff. He asked for possession. Miss Rose sought legal advice and refused to leave. The result has been the present proceedings, in which the plaintiff has asked for an order for possession on the basis that this was a company letting. Miss Rose defends the claim on the basis that the letting to the company was a sham. That has been the only issue before the court.

The judge found the defence was not made out, and he made an order for possession. He gave a long and careful judgment. He found that Miss Rose fully understood what she was doing, and acted after obtaining legal advice. After moving in she paid the rent by her personal cheques, the company not having a bank account. After reviewing all the evidence, the judge said:

> . . . I find without the slightest hesitation that it was both parties' clear intention, with all knowledge of what this involved, that the flat should be let to a company and not to Miss Rose personally. I find that as a fact, having heard the evidence, and having noted submissions made on behalf of Miss Rose in that respect.
> . . .

Mr Walter, for Miss Rose, says that the employment of the company was a sham in that it was a device to prevent Miss Rose from being the tenant, and so far from her being the company's nominee, the company was her agent. Accordingly, he submits, the reality of the letting was that it was to her and not the company.

The mere fact that the purpose of the legal arrangement was to prevent the creation of the statutory tenancy is by itself not enough. On *Aldrington Garages Ltd* v *Fielder* (1978) 37 P & CR 461, 468, Geoffrey Lane LJ said:

> There is no reason why, if it is possible and properly done, agreements should not be entered into which do not fall within the Rents Acts, and the mere fact that those agreements may result in enhanced profits for the owners does not necessarily mean that the agreements should be construed as tenancies rather than as licences.

Roskill LJ said, at p. 473:

> persons are entitled to arrange their affairs to their best advantage so long as the law allows it. That has long been the position in tax cases, and equally long been the position in Landlord and Tenant and Rent Acts cases.

This subject was given a detailed summary in *Antoniades* v *Villiers* [1988] 3 WLR 139, 147, by Bingham LJ, who added to the quotations from Geoffrey Lane LJ and Roskill LJ his own observation:

> It is not a crime, nor is it contrary to public policy, for a property owner to license occupiers to occupy property on terms which do not give rise to a tenancy.

Nevertheless, as Bingham LJ stated, at p. 146:

> The court should be astute to detect and frustrate sham devices and artificial transactions whose only object is to disguise the grant of a tenancy and to evade the Rent Acts: *Street* v *Mountford* [1985] AC 809, 825H . . .

He went on to say:

> The court has to be especially wary and especially careful to see that things like premiums are not being used to conceal payments of rent . . .

'Shams' must be considered in many contexts. The accepted definition, to which the judge in the present case was referred, is that given by Diplock LJ in *Snook* v *London and West Riding Investments Ltd* [1967] 2 QB 786, 802:

As regards the contention of the plaintiff that the transactions between himself, Auto Finance and the defendants were a 'sham,' it is, I think, necessary to consider what, if any, legal concept is involved in the use of this popular and pejorative word. I apprehend that, if it has any meaning in law, it means acts done or documents executed by the parties to the 'sham' which are intended by them to give to third parties or to the court the appearance of creating between the parties legal rights and obligations different from the actual rights and obligations (if any) which the parties intend to create. But one thing, I think, is clear in legal principle, morality and authorities (see *Yorkshire Railway Wagon Co.* v *Maclure* (1882) 21 Ch D 309 and *Stoneleigh Finance Ltd* v *Phillips* [1965] 2 QB 537), that for acts or documents to be a 'sham,' with whatever legal consequences follow from this, all the parties thereto must have a common intention that the acts or documents are not to create the legal rights and obligations which they give the appearance of creating.

As Bingham LJ expressed it in *Antoniades* v *Villiers* [1988] 3 WLR 139, 147:

Put more shortly, a sham exists where the parties say one thing intending another: *Donald* v *Baldwyn* [1953] NZLR 313, 321, *per* FB Adams J.

In the present case the judge found as a fact that it was the intention of both parties, with all knowledge of what this involved, that the flat should be let to the company and not to Miss Rose personally. This finding has not been challenged. Directing himself in accordance with the law as stated by Diplock LJ in the *Snook* case, he held that this transaction was not a sham. We do not find it possible to fault this reasoning.
. . .

In the present case, the company was the only tenant to whom he was prepared to let the property, and the covenants in the lease were perfectly capable of being complied with by the company through its nominee, Miss Rose, and enforced against the company by the plaintiff. Unlike *Street* v *Mountford* the transaction did represent the true position. The company obtained a protected tenancy with the benefits attached to that but neither it nor Miss Rose obtained a statutory tenancy when the protected tenancy came to an end.

We conclude that if the facts are consistent with the purported transaction, we see no reason why, by analogy with *Gisborne's* case, public policy should override the transaction which was deliberately intended to avoid, but not evade, the Rent Acts. Otherwise, public policy would be contradicting s. 2 of the Rent Act 1977 and all the decisions which have preceded it. We would dismiss the appeal.

(e)   'Only or principal home'

The requirement in s. 1(1)(b) that the tenant must occupy the dwelling-house as his only or principal home is *not* one with a long legislative pedigree in the private sector. The equivalent Rent Act formula is broader in scope – 'as his residence' (s. 2(1)(a), Rent Act 1977) – but narrower in application (affecting only the 'secondary' definition of a statutory tenancy). There is, however, a directly equivalent provision to be found in s. 81 of the Housing Act 1985 as part of the statutory definition of a (public sector) secure tenant. Relevant case law is, therefore, dealt with in chapter 5.

Notes

1. The advantages of being classified as an assured tenant are fewer than being classified as a Rent Act protected or statutory tenant. Meaningful rent control does not attach to such tenancies, and even security of tenure is less substantial. It is likely, therefore, that although many of the basic criteria involved in the process of classification as an assured tenant are carried over from the Rent Acts, there will be far fewer contested cases on s. 1 of the Housing Act 1988 than was true under s. 1 of the Rent Act 1977 and its predecessors (this is certainly reflected in the small number of relevant reported cases in the period 1989 to 1998). However, to be outside even assured or assured shorthold status eliminates security altogether (leaving only the procedural controls in the Protection from Eviction Act 1977) and leaves rent as a wholly 'market' issue. (On all the above see chapter 3.) Disputes are likely, therefore, particularly in areas such as 'company lets' and where accommodation is claimed only to be a 'subsidiary' residence of the tenant's.

2. When considering cases such as *St Catherine's College* v *Dorling*, it must be remembered that sub-letting by a tenant will not, of itself, take the dwelling outside the Housing Act 1988, Pt I. (Although sub-letting without landlord permission is a breach of an implied term of the tenancy (s. 15(1)(b), Housing Act 1988), and sub-letting the whole premises *de facto* precludes them being the tenant's only or principal home.) Equally, as illustrated by *Whitty* v *Scott-Russell*, several parts of houses can constitute one dwelling-house. The key is how the property was let in the first place – as one property or a number of dwellings under one roof. In *St Catherine's College* v *Dorling*, the letting was seen to be of a number of dwellings from the beginning.

3. The requirement of 'separateness' of the dwelling can throw up difficult cases, particularly where the premises are shared. At one extreme, the premises occupied are shared in all respects with others – living rooms; kitchens; bathroom; even bedrooms. In such a case the lack of any distinct 'separate' accommodation would not only preclude an assured tenancy arising, but would lead to the conclusion that no tenancy exists at all but merely a licence (in effect this was the aim of the 'non-exclusive occupation' agreements discussed in the previous chapter). Of course such 'separateness' is not required if a joint tenancy exists between the various parties, the sole requirement then being that the joint tenancy 'unit' itself occupies separate accommodation. At the other extreme all that is 'shared' is 'facilities' – toilets/bathrooms, etc. – rather than 'living' accommodation. In such a case assured tenancy status should not normally be affected. On the other hand, *prima facie*, the sharing of (say) a living room *would* undermine such status, the requirement of complete 'separateness' (or 'self-containedness') being breached. Such was indeed the position at first under the Rents Acts (see *Curl* v *Angelo* [1948] 2 All ER 189). However, the matter was eventually dealt with by a specific section in the Rent Act (s. 22 in the 1977 Act) and there is an equivalent provision in s. 3 of the Housing Act 1988:

Housing Act 1988

3.—(1) Where a tenant has the exclusive occupation of any accommodation (in this section referred to as 'the separate accommodation') and—
    (a) the terms as between the tenant and his landlord on which he holds the separate accommodation include the use of the other accommodation (in this section referred to as 'the shared accommodation') in common with another person or other persons, not being or including the landlord, and
    (b) by reason only of the circumstances mentioned in paragraph (a) above, the separate accommodation would not, apart from this section, be a dwelling-house let on an assured tenancy,
the separate accommodation shall be deemed to be a dwelling-house let on an assured tenancy. . . .

The key is, therefore, whether the tenant has exclusive use of at least one room (the 'separate' accommodation), even if this is not wholly self-contained.
4.   Implicit in all the above is the fact that the sharing is with persons other than the landlord of the property. Sharing with the landlord complicates matters considerably. First, s. 3 does not apply (see s. 3(1)(a) above) so that any sharing of essential living accommodation with the landlord prevents an assured tenancy arising (this is quite apart from the specific exclusions concerning 'resident landlords' contained in Sch. 1 para. 10 of the 1988 Act – see below). However, the position is even less favourable for a tenant when ss. 31 and 32 of the Housing Act 1988 are considered. As relevant, these read as follows:

Housing Act 1988

31.   After section 3 of the 1977 Act there shall be inserted the following section—

'Excluded tenancies and licences
3A.—(1) Any reference in this Act to an excluded tenancy or an excluded licence is a reference to a tenancy or licence which is excluded by virtue of any of the following provisions of this section.
    (2) A tenancy or licence is excluded if—
    (a) under its terms the occupier shares any accommodation with the landlord or licensor; and
    (b) immediately before the tenancy or licence was granted and also at the time it comes to an end, the landlord or licensor occupied as his only or principal home premises of which the whole or part of the shared accommodation formed part.
    (3) A tenancy or licence is also excluded if—
    (a) under its terms the occupier shares any accommodation with a member of the family of the landlord or licensor;
    (b) immediately before the tenancy or licence was granted and also at the time it comes to an end, the member of the family of the landlord or licensor occupied as his only or principal home premises of which the whole or part of the shared accommodation formed part; and

(c)   immediately before the tenancy or licence was granted and also at the time it comes to an end, the landlord or licensor occupied as his only or principal home premises in the same building as the shared accommodation and that building is not a purpose-built block of flats.

(4)   For the purposes of subsections (2) and (3) above, an occupier shares accommodation with another person if he has the use of it in common with that person (whether or not also in common with others) and any reference in those subsections to shared accommodation shall be construed accordingly, and if, in relation to any tenancy or licence, there is at any time more than one person which is the landlord or licensor, any reference in those subsections to the landlord or licensor shall be construed as a reference to any one of those persons.

(5)   In subsections (2) to (4) above—

(a)   'accommodation' includes neither an area used for storage nor a staircase, passage, corridor or other means of access;

(b)   'occupier' means, in relation to a tenancy, the tenant and, in relation to a licence, the licensee; and

(c)   'purpose-built block of flats' has the same meaning as in Part III of Schedule 1 to the Housing Act 1988;

and section 113 of the Housing Act 1985 shall apply to determine whether a person is for the purposes of subsection (3) above a member of another's family as it applies for the purposes of Part IV of that Act.'

. . .

32.—(1)   In section 5 of the 1977 Act (validity of notices to quit) at the beginning of subsection (1) there shall be inserted the words 'Subject to subsection (1B) below'.

(2)   After subsection (1) of that section there shall be inserted the following subsections—

'(1A)   Subject to subsection (1B) below, no notice by a licensor or a licensee to determine a periodic licence to occupy premises as a dwelling (whether the licence was granted before or after the passing of this Act) shall be valid unless—

(a)   it is in writing and contains such information as may be prescribed, and

(b)   it is given not less that 4 weeks before the date on which it is to take effect.

(1B)   Nothing in subsection (1) or subsection (1A) above applies to—

(a)   premises let on an excluded tenancy which is entered into on or after the date on which the Housing Act 1988 came into force unless it is entered into pursuant to a contract made before that date.'

The '1977 Act' amended (see s. 32(1)) is the Protection from Eviction Act 1977. In effect, these amendments mean that a landlord who has been sharing *any* 'accommodation' (subject to s. 3A(5)(a)) with a tenant is not even hindered by the procedural hurdles of statutory notices to quit and court orders if possession is sought against the tenant. These matters are explored further in chapter 3.

Questions

1.   In *St Catherine's College* v *Dorling* was the college's scheme within the spirit of the Rent Acts? If not, could this go some way to explaining the Court's decision?

2.   'A living room is a room where you cook, eat, sleep, and put your feet on the fender' (counsel in *Goodrich* v *Paisner* [1957] AC 65, at 91). How helpful is this in attempts to define the scope and meaning of 'dwelling'?

3. Is the approach of the Court of Appeal in *Hilton* v *Plustitle Ltd* consistent with that adopted in lease/licence cases such as *Antoniades* v *Villiers* in the House of Lords (see chapter 1)? If not, can you give any explanation for that? In the light of the House of Lords decision in *Antoniades*, do you think that a case like *Hilton* would be decided the same way today?

(ii) Non-assured tenancies
The next section and chapter 3 will serve to indicate how limited in *practice* remaining tenant protection is, given the increasing predominance and ease of creation of the assured shorthold tenancy. Nevertheless, a tenant's rights are still fewer and a landlord's position is still stronger if the tenancy falls outside the scheme of statutory regulation altogether. The most obvious instance of a contract falling outside protection is, of course, where it creates a licence not a tenancy, but the significance of this has been much diminished (at least in the private sector!) since *Antoniades* v *Villiers* (chapter 1). Secondly, if the provisions in s. 1 of the Housing Act. 1988 are not complied with then the tenancy cannot be an assured one. A decision like *Hilton* v *Plustitle Ltd* (above), if followed, effectively allows a landlord to 'contract out' of the legislation. However, in addition, Sch. 1 of the 1988 Act provides for a disparate group of tenancies which 'cannot be assured tenancies' (it is not entirely clear what they should be called instead, but 'non-assured' should suffice). Many of these replicate equivalent provisions in the Rent Act 1977 and bear (at least) a resemblance to the list of 'non-secure' tenancies in the Housing Act 1985.

Housing Act 1988

SCHEDULE 1
TENANCIES WHICH CANNOT BE ASSURED TENANCIES
PART I
THE TENANCIES

Tenancies entered into before commencement

1. A tenancy which is entered into before, or pursuant to a contract made before the commencement of this Act.

Tenancies of dwelling-houses with high rateable values

2.—(1) A tenancy—
    (a) which is entered into on or after 1st April 1990 (otherwise than, where the dwelling-house had a rateable value on 31st March 1990, in pursuance of a contract made before 1st April 1990), and
    (b) under which the rent payable for the time being is payable at a rate exceeding £25,000 a year.
    (2) In sub-paragraph (1) 'rent' does not include any sum payable by the tenant as is expressed (in whatever terms) to be payable in respect of rates, [council tax] services, management, repairs, maintenance or insurance, unless it could not have been regarded by the parties to the tenancy as a sum so payable.

2A.   A tenancy—

(a)   which was entered into before 1st April 1990, or on or after that date in pursuance of a contract made before that date, and

(b)   under which the dwelling-house had a rateable value on 31st March 1990 which, if it is in Greater London, exceeded £1,500 and, if it is elsewhere, exceeded £750.

Tenancies at a low rent

3.   A tenancy under which for the time being no rent is payable.

3A.   A tenancy—

(a)   which is entered into on or after 1st April 1990 (otherwise than, where the dwelling-house had a rateable value on 31st March 1990, in pursuance of a contract made before 1st April 1990), and

(b)   under which the rent payable for the time being is payable at a rate of, if the dwelling-house is in Greater London, £1,000 or less a year and, if it is elsewhere, £250 or less a year.

3B.   A tenancy—

(a)   which was entered into before 1st April 1990 or, where the dwelling-house had a rateable value on the 31st March 1990, on or after 1st April 1990 in pursuance of a contract made before that date, and

(b)   under which the rent for the time being payable is less than two-thirds of the rateable value of the dwelling-house on 31 March 1990.

3C.   Paragraph 2(2) above applies for the purposes of paragraphs 3, 3A and 3B as it applies for the purposes of paragraph 2(1).

Business tenancies

4.   A tenancy to which Part II of the Landlord and Tenant Act 1954 applies (business tenancies).

Licensed premises

5.   A tenancy under which the dwelling-house consists of or comprises premises licensed for the sale of intoxicating liquors for consumption on the premises.

Tenancies of agricultural land

6.—(1)   A tenancy under which agricultural land, exceeding two acres, is let together with the dwelling-house.

(2)   In this paragraph 'agricultural land' has the meaning set out in section 26(3)(a) of the General Rate Act 1967 (exclusion of agricultural land and premises from liability for rating).

Tenancies of agricultural holdings

7.   A tenancy under which the dwelling-house—

(a)   is comprised in an agricultural holding (within the meaning of the Agricultural Holdings Act 1986); and

(b)   is occupied by the person responsible for the control (whether as tenant or as servant or agent of the tenant) of the farming of the holding.

Lettings to students

8.—(1)   A tenancy which is granted to a person who is pursuing, or intends to pursue, a course of study provided by a specified educational institution and is so granted either by that institution or by another specified institution or body of persons.

(2)   In sub-paragraph (1) above 'specified' means specified, or of a class specified, for the purposes of this paragraph by regulations made by the Secretary of State by statutory instrument.

(3)   A statutory instrument made in the exercise of the power conferred by sub-paragraph (2) above shall be subject to annulment in pursuance of a resolution of either House of Parliament.

Holiday lettings

9.   A tenancy the purpose of which is to confer on the tenant the right to occupy the dwelling-house for a holiday.

Resident landlords

10.—(1)   A tenancy in respect of which the following conditions are fulfilled—

(a)   that the dwelling-house forms part only of a building and, except in a case where the dwelling-house also forms part of a flat, the building is not a purpose-built block of flats; and

(b)   that, subject to Part III of this Schedule, the tenancy was granted by an individual who, at the time when the tenancy was granted, occupied as his only or principal home another dwelling-house which—

(i)   in the case mentioned in paragraph (a) above, also forms part of the flat; or

(ii)   in any other case, also forms part of the building; and

(c)   that, subject to Part III of this Schedule, at all times since the tenancy was granted the interest of the landlord under the tenancy has belonged to an individual who, at the time he owned that interest, occupied as his only or principal home another dwelling-house which—

(i)   in the case mentioned in paragraph (a) above, also formed part of the flat; or

(ii)   in any other case, also formed part of the building; and

(d)   that the tenancy is not one which is excluded from this sub-paragraph by sub-paragraph (3) below.

(2)   If a tenancy was granted by two or more persons jointly, the reference in sub-paragraph (1)(b) above to an individual is a reference to any one of those persons and if the interest of the landlord is for the time being held by two or more persons jointly, the reference in sub-paragraph (1)(c) above to an individual is a reference to any one of those persons.

(3)   A tenancy (in this sub-paragraph referred to as 'the new tenancy') is excluded from sub-paragraph (1) above if—

(a)   it is granted to a person (alone, or jointly with others) who, immediately before it was granted, was a tenant under an assured tenancy (in this sub-paragraph referred to as 'the former tenancy') of the same dwelling-house or of another dwelling-house which forms part of the building in question; and

(b)   the landlord under the new tenancy and under the former tenancy is the same person or, if either of those tenancies is or was granted by two or more persons jointly, the same person is the landlord or one of the landlords under each tenancy.

Crown tenancies

11.—(1)   A tenancy under which the interest of the landlord belongs to Her Majesty in right of the Crown or to a government department or is held in trust for Her Majesty for the purpose of a government department.

(2)   The reference in sub-paragraph (1) above to the case where the interest of the landlord belongs to Her Majesty in right of the Crown does not include the case where that interest is under the management of the Crown Estate Commissioners.

Local authority tenancies etc.

12.—(1)   A tenancy under which the interest of the landlord belongs to—
   (a)   a local authority, as defined in sub-paragraph (2) below;
   (b)   the Commission for the New Towns;
   (c)   the Development Board for Rural Wales;
   (d)   an urban development corporation established by an order under section 135 of the Local Government, Planning and Land Act 1980;
   (e)   a development corporation, within the meaning of the New Towns Act 1981;
   (f)   an authority established under section 10 of the Local Government Act 1985 (waste disposal authorities);
   (g)   a residuary body, within the meaning of the Local Government Act 1985;
   [(gg)   the Residuary Body for Wales (Corff Gweddiolliol Cymru);]
   (h)   a fully mutual housing association; or
   (i)   a housing action trust established under Part III of this Act.

Transitional cases

13.—(1)   A protected tenancy, within the meaning of the Rent Act 1977.
   (2)   A housing association tenancy, within the meaning of Part VI of that Act.
   (3)   A secure tenancy.
   (4)   Where a person is a protected occupier of a dwelling-house, within the meaning of the Rent (Agriculture) Act 1976, the relevant tenancy, within the meaning of that Act, by virtue of which he occupies the dwelling-house.

Notes
1.   Many of the above provisions are reasonably self-explanatory and require little further comment. Of those that do require comment, para. 10 is the most complex and interesting.
2.   The current complexity of paras 2 and 3 is largely a consequence of the abolition of domestic rates – with their attached rateable values – in 1990. For tenancies covered by paras 2(1)(b), and 3A, s. 1(2A) of the Act gives the Secretary of State power to vary the sums involved by regulation. As they stand, few tenancies will be excluded because their rents are too high (for this the rent must exceed £25,000 per year – or well over £2,000 per month – *excluding* (para. 2(2)) any sums payable by the tenant for service charges, repairs, maintenance, etc.). The main example of those paying very low rents are tenants with 'owner-occupier' type long leases.
3.   Paragraph 4 seems clear enough at first glance. The main difficulty is that there is no requirement that the premises should have been *originally* let *as a business*. This is because s. 23(1) of the Landlord and Tenant Act 1954 applies 'to any tenancy where the property comprised in the tenancy is or includes premises which are occupied for the purpose of a business carried on by him or for those and other purposes'. Therefore the essence is the purpose for which the premises are *occupied* rather than the purpose for which they were originally *let* (quite contrary to the 'original purpose' requirement

under s. 1 – see *Wolfe* v *Hogan*, above). The provision has a long pedigree, given the transparent need to exclude true 'business lets' from the scope of protective residential legislation. Probably the clearest analysis is to be found in Lord Denning MR's judgment in *Cheryl Investments* v *Saldanha; Royal Life Saving Society* v *Page* [1978] 1 WLR 1329 (at 1331):

Here we have a topsy-turvy situation. Two landlords contend that their tenants are 'business tenants' and entitled to have their tenancies continued under the statute in that behalf: whereas the tenants contend that they are not so entitled at all. The reason for this oddity is because, if the tenants are not 'business tenants', their tenancies are 'regulated tenancies' and they are protected by the Rent Acts. The protection under the Rent Acts is much better for the tenants than the protection under the business statute. So the landlords seek to chase them out of the Rent Acts and put them into the business Acts.

. . .

The application of the statute
There was much discussion before us as to the meaning of the Business Tenancy Act 1954 (I use those words because I think 'Landlord and Tenant Act 1954' is a little confusing), especially the word 'purposes' in section 23(1) and the time or times at which those 'purposes' had to exist: and the effect of a change by the tenant in the use to which he put the property. Could he take himself in or out of the Act at his option? I found all these matters so confusing that I do not propose to attempt a solution today. I am only going to take four simple illustrations to show how the statute works: for they will suffice for our present cases.
   First, take the case where a professional man is the tenant of two premises: one his office where he works, the other his flat, conveniently near, where he has his home. He has then a 'business tenancy' of his office and a 'regulated tenancy' of his home. This remains the situation even though he takes papers home and works on them at evenings or weekends and occasionally sees a client at home. He cannot in such a case be said to be occupying his flat 'for the purpose of' his profession. He is occupying it for the purpose of his home, even though he incidentally does some work there: see *Sweet* v *Parsley* [1970] AC 132, 155 *per* Lord Morris of Borth-y-Gest.
   Second, take the case where a professional man takes a tenancy of one house for the very purpose of carrying on his profession in one room and of residing in the rest of the house with his family, like the doctor who has a consulting room in his house. He has not then a 'regulated tenancy' at all. His tenancy is a 'business tenancy' and nothing else. He is clearly occupying part of the house 'for the purpose of' his profession, as one purpose; and the other part for the purpose of his dwelling as *another* purpose. Each purpose is significant. Neither is merely incidental to the other.
   Third, suppose now that the first man decides to give up his office and do all his work from his home: there being nothing in the tenancy of his home to prevent him doing it. In that case he becomes in the same position as the second man. He ceases to have a 'regulated tenancy' of his home. He has only a 'business tenancy' of it.
   Fourth, suppose now that the second man decides to give up his office at home and to take a tenancy of an office elsewhere so as to carry on his profession elsewhere. He then has a 'business tenancy' of his new premises. But he does not get a 'regulated tenancy' of his original home, even though he occupies it now only as his home, because it was never let to him as a separate dwelling: unless the landlord agrees to the change.
   Those illustrations point to the solution of the present two cases.

Royal Life Saving Society v Page

No. 14, Devonshire Street is a house with four floors. It is owned by the Howard de Walden Marylebone Estate. In 1945 they let it on a long lease to the Royal Life Saving Society for 64½ years. That society occupy most of the house themselves: but in 1960 they let the top two floors as a maisonette to a Mr Gut for 14 years at a rent of £600 a year. There was a covenant prohibiting assignment without the landlord's consent. There was no restriction on the use which the tenant made of the premises. But it would appear that the maisonette was constructed for use as a separate dwelling: and that the letting was 'as a separate dwelling' within the tests laid down in *Wolfe* v *Hogan* [1949] 2 KB 194, 204–205.

In 1963 Mr Gut made arrangements to assign the lease to the present tenant, Dr Page. He was a medical practitioner who had his consulting rooms at no. 52, Harley Street. His major appointment was medical adviser to Selfridges and he held clinics there five days a week. Dr Page took the maisonette in Devonshire Street so that he could live there as his home. But he thought that in the future he might possibly want to use it occasionally to see patients there. So, when he took the assignment, he asked for consent to do so. Such consent was readily given by the Royal Life Saving Society (his immediate landlords) and by the Howard de Walden Estate (the head landlords). It was a consent for Dr Page to carry on his profession in the maisonette. After the assignment he moved in and occupied it as his home. He put both addresses (Harley Street and Devonshire Street) in the medical directory. He had separate notepaper for each address and put both telephone numbers on each. This was, of course, so that anyone who wished to telephone him could get him at one or other place. But he did very little professional work at the maisonette. Over the whole period of the tenancy he had only seen about one patient a year there. The last patient was in distress 18 months ago. He summarised the position in one sentence: 'Harley Street is my professional address, and the other is my home.'

On those facts it is quite clear that no. 14, Devonshire Street was let as a separate dwelling and occupied by Dr Page as a separate dwelling. There was only one significant purpose for which he occupied it. It was for his home. He carried on his profession elsewhere in Harley Street. His purpose is evidenced by his actual use of it. Such user as he made in Devonshire Street for his profession was not a significant user. It was only incidental to his use of it as his home. He comes within my first illustration. He is, therefore, protected by the Rent Acts as a 'regulated tenancy'.

The landlords later alleged that he was a business tenant and gave him notice to terminate under the Business Tenancy Act 1954. He was quite right to ignore it. He is entitled to stay on as a statutory tenant under the Rent Acts. I agree with the judge, and would dismiss the appeal.

Cheryl Investments Ltd v Saldanha

Beaufort Gardens is a fine London square, in which there were in former times large houses occupied by well-to-do families and their servants. These houses have long since been converted into apartment houses. In particular nos. 46/47 Beaufort Gardens have been turned into 25 separate apartments. These are owned by a property company called Cheryl Investments Ltd, which is run by a Mr Welcoop. In December 1975 the company advertised the apartments in the 'Evening Standard' in these words: 'Knightsbridge. Essex House, near Harrods, serviced flat and flatlets. Doubles from 20 guineas, Flats from 27 guineas. Short–long lets.'

Mr Roland Saldanha answered the advertisement. He had been living in Weybridge, but he wanted a permanent residence in the centre of London. He was shown one of the flats which he liked. It had a large double room with twin beds in it, a bathroom and a toilet. It had no separate kitchen, but there was an entrance hall with a cooker in it which could be used as a kitchen. The landlords provided the furniture and service in the shape of a maid to clean it and change the towels etc. It took her half an hour a day. The charge was £36.75 a week, plus five per cent surcharge.

Mr Saldanha's stay there turned out to be very unhappy with quarrels between him and the landlords. Eventually on February 9, 1977, the landlords gave him notice to quit on March 26, 1977. He claimed the protection of the Rent Acts. He said: 'I am a fully fledged tenant entitled to full protection under the Rent Acts.' The landlords took proceedings in the county court claiming that he was not a tenant but a licensee. They relied on *Appah* v *Parncliffe Investments Ltd* [1964] 1 WLR 1064. But the judge held that he was a tenant, and that the amount in respect of attendance did not form a substantial part of the whole rent: see section 7 of the Rent Act 1977 and *Palser* v *Grinling* [1948] AC 291. So the judge decided those points in favour of Mr Saldanha, and there is no appeal on them.

But on the day of the trial, September 27, 1977, after previous notice, the landlords amended their particulars of claim so as to assert that Mr Saldanha occupied the flat for business purposes and was, therefore, not entitled to the protection of the Rent Acts; and they sought a declaration accordingly. The judge rejected this claim. It is from this decision that the landlords appeal to this court.

On this point the evidence was that Mr Saldanha is an accountant by profession and a partner in a firm called Best Marine Enterprises. They carry on the business of importing sea foods from India and processing them in Scotland. The firm has no trade premises. The two partners carry on the business from their own homes. The other partner works at his home in Basildon. Mr Saldanha works at the flat in Beaufort Gardens; and goes from there out to visit clients. When he went into the flat he had a telephone specially installed for his own use, with the number 589 0232. He put a table in the hall. He had a typewriter there, files and lots of paper: 'The usual office equipment,' said the manageress. He had frequent visitors carrying briefcases. He had notepaper printed: 'Best Marine Enterprises. Importers of Quality Sea-foods. Telephone 589 0232' – that is the number I have just mentioned – 'PO Box 211, Knightsbridge, London, SW3'.

He issued business statements on that very notepaper. A copy of one was found by the maid in a wastepaper basket showing that the firm had imported goods at a total cost of £49,903.30 and sold them for £58,152.35. The maid (whose evidence the judge explicitly accepted in preference to Mr Saldanha's) said: 'I presumed Mr Saldanha conducted business there'.

On that evidence I should have thought it plain that Mr Saldanha was occupying the flat, not only as his dwelling, but also for the purposes of a business carried on by him in partnership with another. When he took the flat it was, no doubt, let to him as a separate dwelling. It was obviously a residential flat with just one large room with twin beds in it. No one can doubt that it was constructed for use as a dwelling and let to him as such within the test in *Wolfe* v *Hogan* [1949] 2 KB 194, 204. But as soon as he equipped it for the purposes of his business of importing sea foods – with telephone, table and printed notepaper – and afterwards used it by receiving business calls there, see customers there and issuing business statements from there – it is plain that he was occupying it 'for the purposes of a business carried on by him'. This was a significant purpose for which he was occupying the flat, as well as a dwelling. It was his only home, and he was carrying on his business from it. It comes within my second illustration.

He did it all surreptitiously. He tried to keep all knowledge of it from the landlord: but that does not alter the fact that, once discovered, his was a 'business tenancy' within section 23 of the Landlord and Tenant Act 1954. Some may say: 'This is a very strange result. It means that he can alter the nature of his tenancy surreptitiously without the consent of his landlord, and thus get a statutory continuation of it: with all the consequences that this entails for the landlord.' That is true: but I see no escape from the words of the Acts. Section 40 of the Act of 1954 clearly contemplates that the landlord may sometimes be quite unaware of the purposes for which a tenant is occupying the premises. It enables a landlord to serve a notice on the tenant so as to find out. But, strange as the result may be, it does open a way to the landlord by which he can get possession. He can give notice of termination to the tenant and oppose any grant of a new tenancy on the ground that he has surreptitiously without the consent of the landlord changed the use of the holding: see section 30(1)(c) of the Act of 1954. I should have thought that the landlord might well be successful. It places him in a better position to evict the tenant than if the tenancy was a 'regulated tenancy' protected under the Rent Acts.

The judge took a different view. He said:

I think [Mr Saldanha] is carrying on some business on the premises, but of a nominal kind, and not worth even considering. It is, in my view, *de minimis*. It amounts to having a few files at home and making a few telephone calls at home.

It is to be noticed that the judge is there speaking of the actual 'use' made of the premises: whereas the statute requires us to look at 'the purpose' for which he is occupying it. A professional man may occupy premises for the 'purpose' of seeing clients, but he may make little 'use' of them because no clients come to see him. On the evidence it seems to me that Mr Saldanha is in the same position as the man in my second illustration. He has only one home – the flat in Beaufort Gardens – and he is occupying it, not only for the purpose of his home, but also for the purpose of a business carried on by him; and that was a significant purpose. It cannot be dismissed by invoking the maxim *de minimis non curat lex*. That maxim must not be too easily invoked. A man cannot excuse himself from a breach of contract by saying that it did no damage. Nor is it permissible for a man sued in tort to say: 'It was only a little wrong and did only a little damage'. So here, I do not think the 'purpose' of Mr Saldanha can be excused by saying: 'It was only little used'.

I would ask: what is the alternative? It could only be that Mr Saldanha would be protected by the Rent Acts and be able to stay there, using his flat for business purposes as much as he liked.

In the case of Mr Saldanha, therefore, I take a different view from the judge. I think that at the expiry of the notice to quit Mr Saldanha was occupying this flat for the purposes of a business carried on by him. So the landlords are entitled to a declaration to that effect. I would allow the appeal in this case.

4.   As regards para. 8 (lettings to students), the list of specified institutions is to be found in the Assured and Protected Tenancies (Lettings to Students) Regulations 1988 (SI 1998 No. 1967). A wide variety of universities and colleges are included, thereby taking the (increasingly common) situation of the university or college sub-letting to its own students (often called 'head tenancy' schemes) outside true statutory regulation.

5.   The equivalent provision to para. 9 (holiday lettings) proved contentious under the Rent Acts (see s. 9, Rent Act 1977), for if the courts were not 'astute' to detect shams, the provision would obviously be attractive to landlords anxious to avoid protective legislation (this is particularly likely when it is borne in mind that most true holiday 'lets' will be construed as merely conferring licences in any event – see chapter 1). The extent to which the courts were mindful of this is open to debate (the number of reported decisions is, in any event, small). In *Buchmann* v *May* [1978] 2 All ER 993, a tenancy agreement for a term of three months contained the following clause: 'It is mutually agreed and declared that the letting hereby made is solely for the purpose of the tenant's holiday in the London area'. The Court of Appeal held that the clause was, *prima facie*, conclusive as to the parties' intentions, and added that 'The court would be astute to detect a sham when it appeared in the context of the Rent Acts, but the burden was on the tenant to prove it, not on the landlord to show that the agreement was correct'. (Sir John Pennycuick, at p. 998).

On the other hand, the tenant (a New Zealand national) did lack permanent residence status in this country, giving some credibility to the stated 'holiday' purpose of the agreement, and in the later case of *R* v *Rent Officer for LB Camden, ex parte Plant* (1980) 257 EG 713 a markedly different approach was taken by the court. Again, the tenancy agreement stated that the accommodation was occupied 'for a holiday', despite the landlord knowing that the prospective tenants were students! As Glidewell J (as he then was) stated (at p. 718)

Prima facie this agreement . . . was to occupy and use this flat for a holiday . . . but . . . both parties knew perfectly well that [the tenants] were going to occupy it for the purpose of their work as students. I so find, and that seems to me to be conclusive of the matter . . . I find that there is clear evidence that the purpose expressed in the tenancy agreement was not the true purpose of that agreement.

This approach is far more in line with that adopted in the most recent lease/licence cases discussed in chapter 1. (*Buchmann* of course pre-dates even *Street* v *Mountford* by some seven years.)

In any event, although prior to the Housing Act 1988 the use of (claimed) 'holiday lets' was fairly widespread (particularly in London), the same is not true under the 1988 Act given the availability of the assured shorthold tenancy.

6.   Paragraph 10 *is* of considerable significance still. Unlike many of the other exceptions its pedigree is relatively short, dating originally from the 1974 Rent Act. Paragraph 10 and its ancillary paragraphs have much in common with the Rent Act provisions (now s. 12, Rent Act 1977), but there are significant differences. The principal paragraph is supplemented by paras 17–22, the key elements of which are reproduced below.

Housing Act 1988

SCHEDULE 1

PART III
PROVISIONS FOR DETERMINING APPLICATION OF
PARAGRAPH 10
(RESIDENT LANDLORDS)

17.—(1) In determining whether the condition in paragraph 10(1)(c) above is at any time fulfilled with respect to a tenancy, there shall be disregarded—

(a) any period of not more that twenty-eight days, beginning with the date on which the interest of the landlord under the tenancy becomes vested at law and in equity in an individual who, during that period, does not occupy as his only or principal home another dwelling-house which forms part of the building or, as the case may be, flat concerned;

(b) if, within a period falling within paragraph (a) above, the individual concerned notifies the tenant in writing of his intention to occupy as his only or principal home another dwelling-house in the building or, as the case may be, flat concerned, the period beginning with the date on which the interest of the landlord under the tenancy becomes vested in that individual as mentioned in that paragraph and ending—

(i)   at the expiry of the period of six months beginning on that date, or

(ii)   on the date on which that interest ceases to be so vested, or

(iii) on the date on which that interest becomes again vested in such an individual as is mentioned in paragraph 10(1)(c) or the condition in that paragraph becomes deemed to be fulfilled by virtue of paragraph 18(1) or paragraph 20 below, whichever is the earlier; and

(c) any period of not more than two years beginning with the date on which the interest of the landlord under the tenancy becomes, and during which it remains, vested—

(i)   in trustees as such; or

(ii)   by virtue of section 9 of the Administration of Estates Act 1925, in [the Probate Judge, or the Public Trustee].

(2) Where the interest of the landlord under a tenancy becomes vested at law and in equity in two or more persons jointly, of whom at least one was an individual, sub-paragraph (1) above shall have effect subject to the following modifications—

(a) in paragraph (a) for the words from 'an individual' to 'occupy' there shall be substituted 'the joint landlords if, during that period none of them occupies'; and

(b) in paragraph (b) for the words 'the individual concerned' there shall be substituted 'any of the joint landlords who is an individual' and for the words 'that individual' there shall be substituted 'the joint landlords'.

18.—(1) During any period when—

(a) the interest of the landlord under the tenancy referred to in paragraph 10 above is vested in trustees as such, and

(b) that interest is held on trust . . . who or for two or more persons of whom at least one occupies as his only or principal home a dwelling-house which forms part of the building or, as the case may be, flat referred to in paragraph 10(1)(a),
the condition in paragraph 10(1)(c) shall be deemed to be fulfilled and accordingly, no part of that period shall be disregarded by virtue of paragraph 17 above.

(2) If a period during which the condition in paragraph 10(1)(c) is deemed to be fulfilled by virtue of sub-paragraph (1) above comes to an end on the death of a person who was in occupation of a dwelling-house as mentioned in paragraph (b) of that sub-paragraph, then, in determining whether that condition is at any time thereafter fulfilled, there shall be disregarded any period—
(a)   which begins on the date of the death;
(b)   during which the interest of the landlord remains vested as mentioned in sub-paragraph (1)(a) above; and
(c)   which ends at the expiry of the period of two years beginning on the date of the death, or on any earlier date on which the condition in paragraph 10(1)(c) becomes again deemed to be fulfilled by virtue of sub-paragraph (i) above.
. . .
22. For the purposes of paragraph 10 above, a building is a purpose-built block of flats if as constructed it contained, and it contains, two or more flats; and for this purpose 'flat' means a dwelling-house which—
(a)   forms part only of a building; and
(b)   is separated horizontally from another dwelling-house which forms part of the same building.

Although the degree of 'permanence' attaching to an assured tenancy is significantly less than that attaching to a Rent Act protected tenancy, the observation of J. T. Farrand (commenting on the Rent Act 1977, s. 12) that 'This resident landlord exception rests on the elementary idea of allowing an owner-occupier to let off a spare room or two without creating any awkwardly permanent protected tenancies' still has pertinence. Indeed, it is, at least, arguable that para. 10 is more obviously focused on the *true* owner-occupier than s. 12.

The main features of para. 10 are:

(a)   The dwelling-house in question must be part only of a building.
(b)   The building must not be a purpose-built block of flats (see para. 22, above).
(c)   The tenancy in question was granted by an individual who occupied as his/her *only or principal home* another dwelling-house also part of the building.

The concept of 'only or principal home' is also to be found in the definition of 'assured tenant' and has been discussed earlier. It is clear that landlords can no longer claim to take advantage of this statutory exception, except in respect of dwellings which form (at least) their *main* residence. The key concept not fully defined in paras 10 and 17 is that of 'building'. Obvious questions to ask are: Is a pair of semi-detached houses *one* building? Is a terrace of eight houses *one* building? What of a flat structurally 'tied in' to another building but with its own access? The permutations are endless! *Some* help is provided by the case of *Bardrick* v *Heycock* particularly in the judgment of Scarman LJ (on this point the Rent Act definition is the same as the Housing Act one).

Bardrick v *Heycock*
(1976) 31 P & CR 420

A house, originally built as a family house in one occupation, was converted into six self-contained flats. The freeholder subsequently demolished a garage, which was structurally an extension of the house, and built in its place a two-storey residential extension. The extension was tied structurally into the main house, but there were no internal communications between it and the main house, and it had its own front door. The freeholder let out the self-contained flats in the main house, and lived himself in the extension. The three flats in question in the present action were let furnished to various of the defendants. In actions by the freeholder for possession of the flats it was common ground that each flat formed part only of a building and that the building was not a purpose-built block of flats. The judge held that the question whether the freeholder occupied as his residence a dwelling-house which also formed part of the building was one of fact and he concluded that the extension occupied by the freeholder did not form part of the same building as the defendants' flats. He accordingly held that the freeholder did not bring himself within the exemption in s. 5A(1) of the Rent Act 1968 and that accordingly the defendants were entitled to the protection of the Act, and he refused the orders for possession sought.

The freeholder appealed, contending that the judge had erred in law and that as a matter of statutory interpretation he should have held that the freeholder's extension and the defendants' flats were all part of the same building.

The Court of Appeal dismissed the appeal, holding that 'building' was an ordinary English word and could not be given a defined or precise meaning as a matter of law; and that the question whether the defendants' flats were part of the same building as the freeholder's extension was one of fact for the judge; and that he had been entitled to conclude that the freeholder's extension was not part of the same building.

SCARMAN LJ: . . . The point to which this court has to direct its attention is whether on a proper construction of section 5A of the Act of 1968 the question which we are considering has been left as one of fact for the judge. I think that it has. The judge must, of course, direct himself in law correctly, and he must, therefore, pay attention to the context of section 5A, occurring as it does within the code of the Rent Act 1968.

The English word 'building' covers an immense range of all sorts of structures. It is an ordinary English word, and its meaning must therefore be a question of fact, always assuming that the court directs itself correctly as to the intention and meaning of the statute which uses it. As a matter of law, to give a defined or precise meaning to the word 'building' is an impossibility. It is beyond the capacity of even the most consummate master of the English language to do so. This itself is, in my judgment, an indication that Parliament is leaving the question of fact to the judge. One must, moreover, remember that the county court judge is likely to be in the best possible position to determine within the area of his jurisdiction what are the housing circumstances, what is the local situation, and the way in which he should approach an answer to this question of fact.

(iii) Assured Shorthold Tenancies

The 'jewel in the crown' of the Housing Act 1988 is undoubtedly the assured shorthold tenancy, which gives landlords maximum flexibility over the long-term future of the property, while providing for only limited controls on the rents which can be charged (see further on these matters chapter 3). In short, as originally conceived in the 1988 Act an assured shorthold tenancy is a short (the minimum period is six months) fixed-term tenancy which satisfies the requirements of an assured tenancy but in relation to which a statutory notice has been served indicating that it is merely to be an assured shorthold. In its original form, the key section (s. 20) reads as follows:

Housing Act 1988

20.—(1) Subject to subsection (3) below, an assured shorthold tenancy is an assured tenancy—

(a) which is a fixed term tenancy granted for a term certain of not less than six months; and

(b) in respect of which there is no power for the landlord to determine the tenancy at any time earlier than six months from the beginning of the tenancy; and

(c) in respect of which a notice is served as mentioned in subsection (2) below.

(2) The notice referred to in subsection (1)(c) above is one which—

(a) is in such form as may be prescribed;

(b) is served before the assured tenancy is entered into;

(c) is served by the person who is to be the landlord under the assured tenancy on the person who is to be the tenant under that tenancy; and

(d) states that the assured tenancy to which it relates is to be a shorthold tenancy.

(3) Notwithstanding anything in subsection (1) above, where—

(a) immediately before a tenancy (in this subsection referred to as 'the new tenancy') is granted, the person to whom it is granted or, as the case may be, at least one of the persons to whom it is granted was a tenant under an assured tenancy which was not a shorthold tenancy, and

(b) the new tenancy is granted by the person who, immediately before the beginning of the tenancy, was the landlord under the assured tenancy referred to in paragraph (a) above,

the new tenancy cannot be assured shorthold tenancy.

(4) Subject to subsection (5) below, if, on the coming to an end of an assured shorthold tenancy (including a tenancy which was an assured shorthold but ceased to be assured before it came to an end), a new tenancy of the same or substantially the same premises comes into being under which the landlord and the tenant are the same as at the coming to an end of the earlier tenancy, then, if and so long as the new tenancy is an assured tenancy, it shall be an assured shorthold tenancy, whether or not it fulfils the conditions in paragraphs (a) to (c) of subsection (1) above.

(5) Subsection (4) above does not apply if, before the new tenancy is entered into (or, in the case of a statutory periodic tenancy, takes effect in possession), the landlord serves notice on the tenant that the new tenancy is not to be a shorthold tenancy.

As its name (and s. 20(1)) indicates, an assured shorthold tenancy is a sub-species of assured tenancy, so that for a valid assured shorthold to exist the tenancy must fulfil all the requirements of a valid assured tenancy, and not (for example) be within one of the Sch. 1 exceptions (although if wholly non-assured a tenant's rights are even fewer than under an assured shorthold). The key to an assured shorthold in its original form was that a statutory notice (s. 20(2) and Assured Tenancies (etc) (Forms) Regulations 1988 (SI 1988/ No. 2203)) had to be served on the tenant prior to the tenancy being entered into, indicating that the tenancy was to be an assured shorthold. There was to be no power to dispense with the strict requirements relating to the service of this notice, although the regulations (reg. 2) do state that 'a form substantially to the same effect' as the specified form (Form 7) will suffice. Indeed the procedural safeguard of the notice appeared fundamental to the concept of the assured shorthold in that at least, by this mechanism a prospective tenant would have an inkling of the restricted nature of the agreement. Most of the limited amount of case law on s. 20 (and assured shortholds in general) has been generated by disputes over the validity of such notices. For example, see the following case:

Panayi & Pyrkos v Roberts
(1993) 25 HLR 421

On 6 November 1990, the plaintiffs granted the defendant a tenancy of a flat for a term of 12 months from 7 November. Prior to the grant, she was served with notice of an assured shorthold tenancy which described the term of the tenancy as being 'from November 7, 1990, to May 6, 1991', i.e. for six months.

On 4 November 1991, a further tenancy for six months was granted to the defendant. On 16 March 1992 a notice requiring possession on 25 May 1992 was served on the defendant and the plaintiffs took possession proceedings. At trial, the judge ordered possession in accordance with s. 21 of the Housing Act 1988. The defendant appealed on the grounds that:

(1)   The notice of assured shorthold tenancy served in November 1991 was defective in that it described a different term for the tenancy than the tenancy agreement itself.

(2)   The notice of 16 March 1992 was defective in that it did not comply with s. 8 of the 1988 Act.

The Court of Appeal held that:

(1)   The prescribed form for creation of an assured shorthold tenancy requires for its completion the specification of a date of termination and must therefore predicate the insertion of the correct date for the tenancy 'in respect of which a notice is served';

(2)   A notice with an incorrect date is not substantially to the same effect as a notice with the correct date and in this case the mistake was not

obvious; accordingly the appellant was not granted an assured shorthold tenancy because there was no proper prefatory notice.

(3) Although unnecessary to decide the point, no legislative purpose would be served by subjecting a notice under s. 21 to the requirements of s. 8.

MANN LJ: . . . The issue can be narrowed. There is a statutory precondition that a notice should have been served in the prescribed form. The prescribed form requires for completion a specification of the date on which the tenancy in respect of which a notice is served both commences and ends. The narrow issue is whether a notice which gives a wrong date (here a termination) is 'substantially to the same effect' as one which gives the correct date. Authority and an evident error apart, I would exclude a quality of obtuseness as being extraordinary. The writing of '1793' for '1993' would be an evident error. The writing in this case of 'May' rather than 'November' in my judgment would be a perplexity rather than an evident error to an ordinary recipient proposing and taking a tenancy of 64, Granville Road.

We were referred to *Tegerdine* v *Brooks* (1977) 36 P & C R 261 and *Morrow* v *Nadeem* [1986] 1 WLR 1381, which are both decisions of this court in regard to whether particular notices served under section 25 of the Landlord and Tenant Act 1954 were in sufficient compliance with a statutory requirement to serve a notice in the prescribed form or in one substantially to the like effect. In the earlier decision Roskill LJ (as he then was) said (at page 266):

> If, as Bridge LJ said during the argument, a notice is incomplete or inaccurate in a relevant respect, then it does not matter that the tenant has not been misled by that inaccuracy. If, however, the omission or inaccuracy is wholly irrelevant, as was the omission here of notes 4, 5 and 7, then *a fortiori* there can be no question of the tenant being misled and I see no reason why we should hold here that this was a bad notice.

In this case there is no evidence as to whether or not the appellant was actually misled. In the light of Roskill LJ's endorsement of the observation of Bridge LJ (as he then was) I would have regarded any such evidence as irrelevant had it been tendered.

In *Morrow* v *Nadeem* the document which had been served failed correctly to identify the landlord. Nicholls LJ (as he then was) said of the prescribed form (at page 1386B):

> That form predicates that the blank spaces preceding the phrase 'landlord of the above-mentioned premises' will be duly completed with the name and address of the person who is correctly so described.

Later he said (at page 1387G):

> There might perhaps be an exceptional case in which, notwithstanding the inadvertent mis-statement or omission of the name of the landlord, any reasonable tenant would have known that that was a mistake and known clearly what was intended.

Neill LJ (at page 1391F) spoke of an 'exceptional case' and Slade LJ agreed with both of the preceding judgments.

Those observations confirm the view which I independently formed. Form No. 7 requires for its completion the specification of a date of termination and must therefore predicate the insertion of the correct date for the tenancy 'in respect of which a notice is served'. A notice with an incorrect date is not substantially to the same effect as a notice with the correct date and in this case the mistake was not obvious. The short answer to Mr Shah's submission is that although the legislative purpose of the primary legislation could perhaps be met without a specification of date, the legislative requirement of the secondary legislation is that there should be a date, and a correct one, in respect of the tenancy granted.

I wish to give no encouragement to arguments which are based on what were described to us as 'slips of the pen' and which I have exemplified as '1793' for '1993'. However, an insistence on accuracy seems to me likely to simplify the task of the county court and more importantly to enable tenants to know with certainty of their status. I would thus allow this appeal on the ground that the appellant was not granted an assured shorthold tenancy because there was no proper prefatory notice. The consequences must be that the appellant is an assured tenant enjoying the protection appropriate to that status.

It is unnecessary to determine Mr Bartlett's second head of argument which developed to the effect that a notice to recover possession of an assured shorthold tenancy should be in the form prescribed for the purpose of section 8 of the Act (which relates to the recovery of possession of dwelling-houses let on assured tenancies). The books give conflicting answers but without reasons. In deference to Mr Bartlett's arguments I express my own opinion that no legislative purpose would be served by subjecting a notice under section 21 (for which no form is prescribed) to the requirements of section 8. Those requirements are understandable in the context of a shorthold tenancy where possession can be recovered only on certain grounds but they have no apparent relevance to the termination of an assured shorthold. My opinion accords with that expressed in *Megarry, The Rent Acts* (11th edition, 1989, volume 3, pages 163–64) and (for what it is worth) with the admonition in the form prescribed for section 8 (which is Form No. 3 to the 1988 Regulations) that it is not to be used where possession is sought under section 21. Section 21 (which I need not recite) seems to me to provide a special code in relation to that species of assured tenancies which are assured shortholds. For the reasons I have given I would allow this appeal.

However, the courts have equally been concerned not to allow minor inaccuracies or deficiencies to invalidate a s. 20 notice and (therefore) an assured shorthold.

Bedding v *McCarthy*
(1994) 27 HLR 103

An agreement was expressed to be for a fixed term from 18 December 1990 until 17 June 1991 (i.e. six months) and was stated to be an assured shorthold tenancy. On the morning of 18 December the prospective tenant was handed a 's. 20' notice which he signed and returned to the landlord. Later that morning the tenancy agreement was signed, and the defendant took possession of the house in the afternoon. Subsequently (in 1993) the landlord sought possession of the property. The tenant contended that, since the agreement was not entered into until some hours into 18 December it did not confer a tenancy for at least six months. Alternatively, the tenant argued that if the agreement took effect from the beginning of

18 December, the 's. 20' notice was not served before the tenancy was entered into. In both the county court, and the Court of Appeal these arguments failed, the Court of Appeal finding:

(1) That tenancy agreements dealt with years, months, weeks and even days, but not with hours, minutes or seconds. Therefore a fixed term for a minimum six-month period was wholly consistent with the description in the notice of the tenancy running from 18 December 1990 to 17 June 1991.

(2) It was a question of fact whether the 's. 20' notice was, or was not, served before the tenancy was entered into and the judge at first instance had been entirely satisfied that the documents were not signed/served contemporaneously but that the notice *did* precede the agreement.

NOLAN LJ (as he then was): . . . The respondent landlords in their skeleton argument referred us to *Halsbury's Laws* (4th ed.), Vol. 45, para. 1143. In that paragraph we find quoted what is described as the general rule relating to fractions of a day, and I need only read the first two sentences:

In computing a period of time, at any rate when counted in years or months, no regard is, as a general rule, paid to fractions of a day, in the sense that the period is regarded as complete although it is short to the extent of a fraction of a day. In cases in which the day of the date of an instrument of lease is included in the term it is immaterial that the tenant's enjoyment cannot begin with the beginning of that day.

This proposition which is supported by copious and ancient authority in the notes to the text of *Halsbury*, appears to me to dispose completely of the initial argument put forward by the appellant/defendant. It is, of course, a commonplace that tenancy agreements and leases deal with years, months and weeks and sometimes days, but not with hours, minutes or seconds, so the lease in the present case is described as a tenancy agreement for a period of six months. That is, in my judgment, perfectly consistent with the description of the proposed tenancy in the notice as one running from 18 December 1990 to 17 June 1991. That is precisely how it would be construed and understood in the ordinary law of landlord and tenant, and I can see no reason why one different standard or approach should be adopted for the purposes of the Housing Act 1988. The remarks of Russell LJ were directed solely to the common form of tenancy agreement dealing with, in that case, years and months. They were not directed or supportive of the proposition that the term of the tenancy should be measured by reference for something less than a whole day.

Mr Naish says if that is so, and if it be the case that the tenancy agreement signed during the morning of 18 December dates back to the beginning of that day, then the landlords fail to satisfy the condition specified in section 20(2)(b), namely the condition that the notice must be served before the tenancy is entered into. This seems to me to confuse the time when the tenancy is entered into with the time when, as a matter of law, it is deemed to commence. It would seem to me clear that the tenancy was entered into when the agreement was signed. It is not the less clear that it was entered into at that point in time because it was deemed to commence some hours earlier.

We come to the question which appears to me to be a pure question of fact: was the notice served before the tenancy was entered into? Mr Naish says it is not consistent for that purpose to look at the fractions of a day. If you are going to ignore fractions of a day, you must do so consistently. But again, I think that is wrong. In paragraph 1144 of *Halsbury's Laws* it is stated:

> The general rule that fractions of a day are to be disregarded does not apply where the object of the statute would be defeated unless the precise hour of an occurrence were noted, or where conflicting claims depend upon the question which of two events was first in order of time, for then the particular hour when the events occurred may become material.

It seems to me the question posed by section 20(2)(b) falls within that category. It is a pure question of fact whether the notice was or was not served before the tenancy was entered into, and the agreed statement of facts on its natural reading establishes that it was served before the tenancy was entered into. In terms, the agreed statement of facts states, 'The defendant signed document 5', that is the notice, 'and returned it, and then all parties signed document 4,' that is the tenancy agreement. Mr Naish argued that these should be regarded essentially as contemporaneous events. He submitted that on their most favourable reading there can only have been a short time between the two events, and it is not therefore to be assumed that the purpose of the Act was fulfilled because this, he submitted, must contemplate a reasonable period of time being given to the proposed tenant to study the document and determine what it is that he is entering into. The difficulty here is that the Act says nothing to suggest that there must be any particular minimum time.

Also in *Andrews* v *Brewer* (1997) 30 HLR 203, an error in a 's. 20' notice which provided that a tenancy would begin on 29 May 1993 and end on 28 May 1993 was held, by the Court of Appeal *not* to have invalidated the notice. In the words of Auld LJ (at p. 210) it was 'an obvious clerical error . . . [which] does not in any way detract from the effect of the notice'.

From the above it seems clear that, even as originally drafted, the foundations required for the creation of an assured shorthold tenancy were not unduly burdensome, and that those foundations which did exist could be seen as necessary safeguards to (at least) ensure that tenants were sufficiently forewarned. However, government thinking was clearly that even this did not go far enough; errors in notices and 'slips' (such as letting a tenant into possession prior to the service of a 's. 20' notice) could result in the inadvertent creation of an assured tenancy. The (apparent) undesirability of this has led to the significant amendments contained in ss. 96–99 of the Housing Act 1996. Although s. 20 (as above) will continue to contain the relevant law for tenancies entered into prior to 28 February 1997 (the commencement date of the amendments), all tenancies claimed to be assured shortholds which are entered into on or after that date are to be governed by the new law.

Section 96 and Sch. 7 of the 1996 Act provide (by inserting s. 19A and Sch. 2A into the 1988 Act) that any assured tenancy coming into force on or after the commencement date is to be an assured shorthold unless it falls within certain parameters (the majority of which are contained in Sch. 7).

Housing Act 1996

ASSURED TENANCES

Assured shorthold tenancies

96.—(1)   In Chapter II of Part I of the Housing Act 1988 (assured shorthold tenancies) there shall be inserted at the beginning—

'Assured shorthold tenancies: post-Housing Act 1996 tenancies
19A.   An assured tenancy which—

(a)   is entered into on or after the day on which section 96 of the Housing Act 1996 comes into force (otherwise than pursuant to a contract made before that day), or

(b)   comes into being by virtue of section 5 above on the coming to an end of an assured tenancy within paragraph (a) above,
is an assured shorthold tenancy unless it falls within any paragraph in Schedule 2A to this Act.'

(2)   After Schedule 2 to that Act there shall be inserted the Schedule set out in Schedule 7 to this Act.

SCHEDULE 7

ASSURED TENANCIES: SCHEDULE INSERTED AFTER SCHEDULE 2 TO THE HOUSING ACT 1988

'SCHEDULE 2A

ASSURED TENANCIES: NON-SHORTHOLDS

Tenancies excluded by notice

1.—(1)   An assured tenancy in respect of which a notice is served as mentioned in sub-paragraph (2) below.

(2)   The notice referred to in sub-paragraph (1) above is one which—

(a)   is served before the assured tenancy is entered into,

(b)   is served by the person who is to be the landlord under the assured tenancy on the person who is to be the tenant under that tenancy, and

(c)   states that the assured tenancy to which it relates is not to be an assured shorthold tenancy.

2.—(1)   An assured tenancy in respect of which a notice is served as mentioned in sub-paragraph (2) below.

(2)   The notice referred to in sub-paragraph (1) above is one which—

(a)   is served after the assured tenancy has been entered into,

(b)   is served by the landlord under the assured tenancy on the tenant under that tenancy, and

(c)   states that the assured tenancy to which it relates is no longer an assured shorthold tenancy.

Tenancies containing exclusionary provision

3.   An assured tenancy which contains a provision to the effect that the tenancy is not an assured shorthold tenancy.

Tenancies under section 39

4. An assured tenancy arising by virtue of section 39 above, other than one to which subsection (7) of that section applies.

Former secure tenancies

5. An assured tenancy which became an assured tenancy on ceasing to be a secure tenancy.

Tenancies under Schedule 10 to the Local Government and Housing Act 1989

6. An assured tenancy arising by virtue of Schedule 10 to the Local Government and Housing Act 1989 (security of tenure on ending of long residential tenancies).

Tenancies replacing non-shortholds

7.—(1) An assured tenancy which—
    (a) is granted to a person (alone or jointly with others) who, immediately before the tenancy was granted, was the tenant (or, in the case of joint tenants, one of the tenants) under an assured tenancy other than a shorthold tenancy ('the old tenancy'),
    (b) is granted (alone or jointly with others) by a person who was at that time the landlord (or one of the joint landlords) under the old tenancy, and
    (c) is not one in respect of which a notice is served as mentioned in sub-paragraph (2) below.
    (2) The notice referred to in sub-paragraph (1)(c) above is one which—
    (a) is in such form as may be prescribed,
    (b) is served before the assured tenancy is entered into,
    (c) is served by the person who is to be the tenant under the assured tenancy on the person who is to be the landlord under that tenancy (or, in the case of joint landlords, on at least one of the persons who are to be joint landlords), and
    (d) states that the assured tenancy to which it relates is to be a shorthold tenancy.
    8. An assured tenancy which comes into being by virtue of section 5 above on the coming to an end of an assured tenancy which is not a shorthold tenancy.
    . . .'

The commentary in the original Bill simply observed that these changes made 'it possible to create an assured shorthold tenancy without serving a prior notice'. This is, of course, grossly misleading – the law prior to 28 February 1997 is that a tenancy is *assured* unless a valid 's. 20' notice is served, whereas from 28 February all this is reversed so that all tenancies will be assured shortholds (assuming they fulfil 'assured' requirements) unless declared to be assured or falling within one of the other exceptions. This even applies to periodic tenancies as well as to fixed-term ones. Indeed the only 'assurance' most private sector tenants will continue to have is that a normal assured shorthold possession order cannot take effect until six months have elapsed from the beginning of the tenancy (s. 99, Housing Act 1996, and see chapter 3). It should, however, also be noted that s. 97 adds a new s. 20A to the 1988 Act which does, at least, enable a tenant to receive a written notice of the basic terms of the tenancy (though application must be made by the tenant before the duty to provide such information arises).

Housing Act 1996

97. After section 20 of the Housing Act 1988 there shall be inserted—

'Post-Housing Act 1996 tenancies: duty of landlord to provide statement as to terms of tenancy

20A.—(1) Subject to subsection (3) below, a tenant under an assured shorthold tenancy to which section 19A above applies may, by notice in writing, require the landlord under that tenancy to provide him with a written statement of any term of the tenancy which—

(a) falls within subsection (2) below, and

(b) is not evidenced in writing.

(2) The following terms of a tenancy fall within this subsection, namely—

(a) the date on which the tenancy began or, if it is a statutory periodic tenancy or a tenancy to which section 39(7) below applies, the date on which the tenancy came into being,

(b) the rent payable under the tenancy and the dates on which that rent is payable,

(c) any term providing for a review of the rent payable under the tenancy, and

(d) in the case of a fixed term tenancy, the length of the fixed term.

(3) No notice may be given under subsection (1) above in relation to a term of the tenancy if—

(a) the landlord under the tenancy has provided a statement of that term in response to an earlier notice under that subsection given by the tenant under the tenancy, and

(b) the term has not been varied since the provision of the statement referred to in paragraph (a) above.

(4) A landlord who fails, without reasonable excuse, to comply with a notice under subsection (1) above within the period of 28 days beginning with the date on which he received the notice is liable on summary conviction to a fine not exceeding level 4 on the standard scale.

(5) A statement provided for the purposes of subsection (1) above shall not be regarded as conclusive evidence of what was agreed by the parties to the tenancy in question.
. . .'

Notes

1. The attractiveness of assured shortholds to landlords could well lead less scrupulous ones to 'winkle out' their existing tenants to replace them with those holding under an assured shorthold. In part such deviousness is deterred by the provisions on unlawful eviction and harassment contained in ss. 27 and 28 of the Housing Act 1988. However, other landlords may use persuasion rather than pressure or threats to achieve the desired result; for example, an offer of a new contract on superficially improved terms could be attractive to (say) a Rent Act tenant unaware that the proposed new contract was on an assured shorthold basis. Section 34(1)(b) of the 1988 Act attempts to deal with such 'ploys' by providing that:

(1) A tenancy which is entered into on or after the commencement of this Act cannot be a protected tenancy, unless—
. . .

(b) it is granted to a person (alone or jointly with others) who, immediately before the tenancy was granted, was a protected or statutory tenant and is so granted by the person who at that time was the landlord (or one of the joint landlords) under the protected or statutory tenancy; . . .

The drafting deficiencies in this are obvious enough; above all, the section does not state that such a tenancy *cannot* be an assured shorthold, but merely that it *can* be a protected tenancy. This could leave the way open for the argument that the protected tenant had voluntarily and expressly relinquished his or her existing rights. In practice, however, it is likely that the courts will give the section a fairly broad 'reading' and block most attempts at the conversion of protected tenancies into assured shortholds. On the other hand, if the landlord transfers his or her interest so that the assured shorthold is under the aegis of a new landlord, the section appears not to apply.

Similar provisions apply under the new 'regime' to curb the attempted transfer of assured tenants into assured shorthold tenants (Sch. 7, para. 7, above).

2.   Another limitation on the creation of assured shortholds is that (under s. 20(3) of the 1988 Act) once a tenancy *is* an assured tenancy it cannot subsequently become an assured shorthold, whether a 's. 20' notice is served on it or not. It is likely that certain well-publicised cases of landlords 'inadvertently' letting prospective tenants into possession and accepting rent prior to a service of 's. 20' notice – thereby *arguably* creating an assured tenancy and precluding an assured shorthold – were significant factors in the Housing Act 1996 'reforms'.

3.   From 28 February 1997, a periodic tenancy can as readily be an assured shorthold as a fixed-term tenancy. Under the original provisions, for the initial creation of an assured shorthold, the tenancy had to be fixed-term (see s. 20(1)(a)). However, even under the original provisions (s. 20(4)) 'continuation' tenancies (whether by new grant or simply by allowing the tenant to continue in possession and carry on paying rent) would be assured shortholds even if periodic. In such cases there may be differences in the form of a notice required by the landlord (in advance of possession proceedings) and the length of notice required (although the minimum two-month notice requirement still applies – see chapter 3).

In *Lower Street Properties Ltd* v *Jones* (1996) 28 HLR 877, the plaintiffs granted the defendant's partner an assured shorthold tenancy of a house for a term of six months. The defendant lived there with the tenant. After the initial term expired, the plaintiffs allowed the tenant to stay for another three months. Subsequently, further three-month and six-month 'concessions' were granted. After the expiry of the last of these (January 1991) the tenant and the defendant continued to live in the property. In February 1992 the tenant died, and the defendant continued to occupy the property alone. In June 1994, the plaintiffs served the defendant with a two-month notice (see further chapter 3) requiring possession of the property, and subsequently sued for possession. The defendant counterclaimed for a declaration that she was an assured tenant by succession (see further chapter 3). The county court dismissed the claim for possession because the plaintiffs had commenced proceedings one day before the notice had expired (!), but equally dismissed the counterclaim – s. 20(4) of the 1988 Act could operate not only on the first tenancy consequent upon the initial assured shorthold, but on any number of subsequent agreements. The tenant remained an assured shorthold tenant until his death, and the defendant succeeded to an assured shorthold periodic tenancy. The Court of Appeal upheld the county court on both points. On the s. 20(4) point, see Kennedy LJ (at p. 881):

In the context of the present case the effect of section 20(4) is to make it clear that Mr van Praag was an assured shorthold tenant until 27 December 1989. What happened then? It is the case for the appellant that section 20(4) can only operate once, at the end of an assured shorthold tenancy created pursuant to section 20(1), so that in December 1989 Mr van Praag became, by virtue of section 5 of the Act, a tenant under an assured tenancy which was not a shorthold tenancy. If she is right, or if at any time before he died Mr van Praag became an assured shorthold tenant, no further assured shorthold tenancy could have come into existence because section 20(3) prevents the grant of an assured shorthold tenancy to an assured tenant. But, for the plaintiff/respondents Mr James contends that section 20(4) can operate again and again, and is intended if necessary so to operate until either the tenant vacates or the landlord brings the situation to an end by serving notice pursuant to section 20(5). The whole purpose of Chapter II of the 1988 Act was to prevent stagnation in the property market by, amongst other things, preventing a tenant who entered as an assured shorthold tenant acquiring the rights of an assured tenant without the consent of the landlord.

. . .

In my judgment Mr van Praag became an assured shorthold tenant, pursuant to section 20(4), for the second time in late 1989 and the process was repeated thereafter at intervals until his death. Sometimes he had a periodic tenancy, sometimes the tenancy was for a fixed term, but always it was an assured shorthold tenancy and always, as it seems to me, the tenancy took effect pursuant to section 20(4) because the two attempts to create an assured shorthold tenancy pursuant to section 20(1) in April 1990 and July 1990 were ineffective. The result was that when Mr van Praag died the tenancy which vested in the defendant was an assured shorthold tenancy.

Questions
1.   What is the logic and justification of the tenancies of resident landlords being outside the framework of statutory protection and regulation?
2.   In what ways (if any) can an assured shorthold tenancy be seen as 'assured'?
3.   In what situations are landlords likely to serve notices or include tenancy provisions to the effect that the tenancies affected are *not* to be assured shortholds? (See the Housing Act 1996, Sch. 7, paras 1, 2 and 3.)

(C)   Rent Act 1977 Tenancies

As indicated in the introduction to this chapter, the last two decades have seen a steady erosion of the substantial degree of tenant security and rent control provided for under the Rent Acts (most recently the Rent Act 1977). In particular, the Housing Acts 1988 and 1996 have largely replaced a 'regime' based on long-term tenant security and rent control, with one based on short-term contracts and market rents (see further chapter 3). However, quite apart from the fact that, as already noted, many Rent Act concepts have been carried forward into the new law, the 1977 Act still continues to govern most tenancies entered into prior to 15 January 1989 and a significant number of tenancies acquired by succession after that date.

Acquiring full rights under the Rent Act 1977 involves possessing the status of either a contractual protected tenant, or a statutory tenant – and it is to these two key concepts that attention is first paid.

(i)   Full Rent Act protection: protected and statutory tenancies
The starting point in determining Rent Act status is s. 1 of the Rent Act 1977, which states:

Subject to this Part of this Act, a tenancy under which a dwelling-house (which may be a house or part of a house) is let as a separate dwelling is a protected tenancy for the purposes of this Act.

The requirement of a 'dwelling house . . . let as a separate dwelling' is also at the foundation of the definition of an assured tenancy and has already been discussed. The principal definitional difference between s. 1 of Rent Act 1977 and s. 1 Housing Act 1988 is that there is no requirement in the Rent Act for the 'dwelling-house' to be the 'only or principal home' of the tenant(s) concerned. Indeed, there appears to be no need (as far as s. 1 is concerned) for the tenant to occupy the property at all! As Scarman LJ stated in *Horford Investments Ltd* v *Lambert* [1976] Ch 39 (at p. 54):

A house (or part of a house) must be let as *a* dwelling, that is to say, as a single dwelling, for the tenancy to be protected for the purposes of the Act. If it is let as a single dwelling, the fact that the tenant does not himself live there, or that he carries on a business as well as a living there, or that he sub-lets part or the whole, or that he uses only part of the premises for habitation does not put the letting outside the Act – unless what is done either modifies the terms of the letting, or brings the house within some specific exclusion stated in the Act.

Further, there is no requirement in s. 1 of the Rent Act 1977 that the tenant should be an individual, so that a tenancy granted to a company can still, in principle, be a protected tenancy.

However, the significance of this is minimised by the fact that tenant residence *is* a key element in the linked concept of the *statutory tenancy*. Broadly, any contractual protected tenancy may be brought to an end by the service of a notice to quit (so long as the formalities of s. 5 of the Protection from Eviction Act 1977 are complied with – see further chapter 3). Continued tenant security is maintained by the device of the statutory tenancy, a highly idiosyncratic 'animal' which confers a 'status of irremoveability' (Stephenson LJ in *Jessamine Investment Co.* v *Schwarz* [1977] 2 WLR 145, at p. 147) rather than a property right. As relevant, s. 2 of the 1977 Rent Act provides as follows (emphasis added):

2.—(1) Subject to this Part of this Act—
   (a) after the termination of a protected tenancy of a dwelling-house the person who, immediately before that termination, was the protected tenant of the dwelling-house shall, *if and so long as he occupies the dwelling-house as his residence,* be the statutory tenant of it; . . .

Unlike, however, the requirement for assured tenancies that the dwelling-house must be the tenant's 'only or principal home' (s. 1(1)(b), 1988 Act), s. 2 only requires that the dwelling-house be a residence of the tenant. From this it is clear that a tenant can live elsewhere part or even most of the time and yet still maintain a statutory tenancy of the property in dispute.

As to what in law *is* a residence (as against a mere convenience), it is necessary to turn to case law, the Rent Act being empty of further definition. Similar provisos have existed for many years, and the case law is equivalently extensive. Two cases, *Brown* v *Brash* and *Brickfield* v *Hughes*, perhaps best illustrate the issues involved.

Brown v *Brash*
[1948] 2 KB 247

In 1941, Cooper, the freeholder of a dwelling-house, café, and petrol pump station, let the premises to the plaintiff on a quarterly tenancy at a quarterly rent of £26. On 20 September 1945, Cooper served on the plaintiff a three months' notice to quit. The plaintiff continued in possession after that date, remaining as a statutory tenant under the Rent Restriction Acts. Shortly after the notice had been given the plaintiff had been sentenced to two years' imprisonment, leaving in physical possession of the premises, Mould, his cohabitee for seven years, and two children. On 11 January 1946, Cooper sold the freehold of the premises to Metters and two brothers named Plant. On 9 March 1946 Mould left the premises taking with her a substantial part of the furniture and leaving the two children elsewhere with the plaintiff's mother. There was evidence that only three articles of domestic furniture remained in the house.

In July 1946, Metters and the Plant brothers brought an action in the county court against the plaintiff, claiming possession of the premises on the ground amongst others that he had abandoned possession of them. On 12 September 1946, judgment was given for the defendant, the present plaintiff, the judge basing his decision on findings that the present plaintiff had not abandoned possession of the premises and that, although he had failed in some of his obligations under the tenancy, it was not reasonable to make an order for possession against him. Between September and late in December 1946, a man named Mulholland and his wife, relations of the plaintiff, spent two or three hours two or three times a week cleaning the premises. On 9 December 1946, Metters and the brothers Plant sold the freehold to the present defendants, Brash and Ambrose, under a contract which provided that the purchasers might at their own risk take immediate possession on paying a deposit of £500. Brash, the first defendant, entered into possession of the premises. A few days later on 25 January 1947, the plaintiff was released from prison and sought to repossess the premises but Brash refused to leave and continued in possession of them. On 14 April 1947, the plaintiff brought this action in the county court claiming possession of the premises and damages for trespass. The defendants, although in possession, counterclaimed (*inter alia*) for possession. The county court judge upheld the plaintiff's claim for possession, awarded him £100 damages for trespass and rejected the defendants' counterclaim for possession. The defendants appealed. The Court of Appeal allowed the appeal, finding that the plaintiff had lost his status as a statutory tenant.

ASQUITH LJ delivering the judgment of the court: . . . The facts of the present case disclose a situation clearly not foreseen or provided for by the Rent Restriction Acts. Anomalous consequences result whether we adopt the principle contended for by the defendants or that contended for by the plaintiff. If the defendants' argument is accepted, the plaintiff must be taken, as at 9 March 1946, simultaneously to intend to return, and to be abandoning possession – an abandonment through the act on that date of someone, Miss Mould, who, so far as the evidence goes, was not authorised by the plaintiff to do that act. If the plaintiff's contention is accepted, then it would apply equally if the plaintiff had been sent to gaol (or had gone away) for ten or fifteen years, leaving no licensee or furniture, provided he intended to return at the end of that period, a result contrary to the clear policy of the Acts, which is to keep a roof over the tenant's or someone's head, not over an unoccupied shell, and to economise rather than sterilise housing accommodation.

We are of opinion that a 'non-occupying' tenant prima facie forfeits his status as a statutory tenant. But what is meant by 'non-occupying'? The term clearly cannot cover every tenant who, for however short a time, or however necessary a purpose, or with whatever intention as regards returning, absents himself from the demised premises. To retain possession or occupation for the purpose of retaining protection the tenant cannot be compelled to spend twenty-four hours in all weathers under his own roof for three hundred and sixty-five days in the year. Clearly, for instance, the tenant of a London house who spends his week-ends in the country or his long vacation in Scotland does not necessarily cease to be in occupation. Nevertheless, absence may be sufficiently prolonged or unintermittent to compel the inference, prima facie, of a cesser of possession or occupation. The question is one of fact and of degree. Assume an absence sufficiently prolonged to have this effect: The legal result seems to us to be as follows: (1.) The onus is then on the tenant to repel the presumption that his possession has ceased. (2.) In order to repel it he must at all events establish a de facto intention on his part to return after his absence. (3.) But we are of opinion that neither in principle nor on the authorities can this be enough. To suppose that he can absent himself for five or ten years or more and retain possession and his protected status simply by proving an inward·intention to return after so protracted an absence would be to frustrate the spirit and policy of the Acts, as affirmed in *Keeves v Dean* [1924] 1 KB 685 and *Skinner v Geary* [1931] 2 KB 546. (4.) Notwithstanding an absence so protracted the authorities suggest that its effect may be averted if he couples and clothes his inward intention with some formal, outward, and visible sign of it; that is, instals in the premises some caretaker or representative, be it a relative or not with the status of a licensee and with the function of preserving the premises for his own ultimate home-coming. There will then, at all events, be someone to profit by the housing accommodation involved, which will not stand empty. It may be that the same result can be secured by leaving on the premises, as a deliberate symbol of continued occupation, furniture; though we are not clear that this was necessary to the decision in *Brown v Draper* [1944] KB 309. Apart from authority, in principle, possession in fact (for it is with possession in fact and not with possession in law that we are here concerned) requires not merely an 'animus possidendi' but a 'corpus possessionis', namely, some visible state of affairs in which the animus possidendi finds expression. (5.) If the caretaker (to use that term for short) leaves or the furniture is removed from the premises, otherwise than quite temporarily, we are of opinion that the protection, artificially prolonged by their presence, ceases, whether the tenant wills or desires such removal or not. A man's possession of a wild bird, which he keeps in a cage, ceases if it escapes, notwithstanding that his desire to retain possession of it continues and that its escape is contrary thereto. We do not think in this connection that it is open to the plaintiff to rely on the fact of his imprisonment as preventing him from taking steps to assert possession by visible action. The plaintiff, it is true, had not intended to go to prison; he committed intentionally the felonious act which in the events which have happened, landed him there; and thereby put it out of his power to assert possession by visible acts after March 9, 1946. He cannot, in these circumstances, we feel, be in a better position than if his absence and inaction had been voluntary.

Applying these general propositions to the facts of the present case, we hold that the plaintiff ceased to possess the premises or to enjoy the protection of the Acts when Miss Mould and the children left in March, 1946; and that nothing which happened after this date (for instance, his resistance to the Metters and Plant action brought in July, 1946, or the visits of the Mulhollands starting in September of that year) could restore his possession or statutory status. As regards the three items of domestic furniture which on the evidence Miss Mould left behind (apart from questions of de minimis) there is no evidence that either the plaintiff or Miss Mould, or indeed anyone, intended these to remain on the premises as symbols of continued possession by the plaintiff. Nor was it either pleaded or argued that the judgment of the county court judge in the previous proceedings (amounting to a decision in September 1946 that the plaintiff had not abandoned possession) was res judicata or created an estoppel in the present case. From March, 1946, on, in our view, the plaintiff lost the protection of the Acts and with it his only rights in respect of the premises. The order for possession and the award of damages for trespass in his favour cannot stand. As regards the counterclaim the defendants, in substance, succeed. It is true that their claim for an order for possession of premises of which they were already in physical occupation is anomalous, but the question in substance is which of these parties is entitled in law to possession, and it follows from our decision on the claim that on this issue the defendants have prevailed. Questions of relative hardship and the reasonableness of making an order for possession for the defendants cannot arise where the tenant by abandoning possession has entirely removed himself from the protective orbit of the Acts. The appeal must be allowed.

Brickfield v *Hughes*
(1987) 20 HLR 108

The defendant tenant was aged 74. In 1968 he had become the statutory tenant of a flat in London, on the expiry of a seven-year lease. In 1970 his wife had inherited a cottage in Lancashire. It had been used initially as a holiday home, but from 1978 the tenant and his wife remained there permanently. Between that time and March 1987 the defendant had not returned to the flat in London at all and his wife made only three visits.

Their adult children had remained in the flat after their departure, and at the time of the trial it was occupied by three of them and the defendant's son-in-law. The defendant and his wife also left furniture and books in the property. The landlord sought possession of the flat, on the basis that the defendant no longer occupied it as his residence. At the trial, evidence was given that the defendant intended to return to London if his wife, who was 71 and in poor health, predeceased him, or if they were unable to manage on their own in Lancashire, which he thought might occur in about five years' time. His daughter gave evidence that she thought that they might well not be able to manage very soon and would not last another winter in the cottage.

The judge found that the defendant had sufficient *animus revertendi* and refused to grant possession. The landlord appealed.

The Court of Appeal dismissed the appeal. Although they clearly felt that it was a marginal case, Neil and Ralph Gibson LJJ did not feel that the finding of the county court judge was so clearly wrong that it should be disturbed.

NEIL LJ: . . . What then is the law, because, as the judge put it in his judgment (at page 44 of the bundle), 'in ordinary terms and language' Mr and Mrs Hughes were living in the cottage between 1978 and the date of the trial.

Section 2(1) of the Rent Act 1977 is in these terms:

Subject to this Part of this Act—
    (a)   after the termination of a protected tenancy of a dwelling-house the person who, immediately before that termination, was the protected tenant of the dwelling-house shall, if and so long as he occupies the dwelling-house as his residence, be the statutory tenant of it.

It is also necessary to read section 2(3). That subsection provides:

In subsection (1)(a) above and in Part I of Schedule 1, the phrase 'if and so long as he occupies the dwelling-house as his residence' shall be construed as it was immediately before the commencement of this Act (that is to say, in accordance with section 3(2) of the Rent Act 1968).

This takes one to the 1968 Act. Section 3(2) of the 1968 Act is in these terms:

In paragraph (a) of subsection (1) above and in Schedule 1 to this Act, the phrase 'if and so long as he occupies the dwelling-house as his residence' shall be construed as requiring the fulfilment of the same, and only the same, qualifications (whether as to residence or otherwise) as had to be fulfilled before the commencement of this Act to entitle a tenant, within the meaning of the Increase of Rent and Mortgage Interest (Restrictions) Act 1920, to retain possession, by virtue of that Act and not by virtue of a tenancy, of a dwelling-house to which that Act applied.

The effect of section 3(2) of the Rent Act 1968 was considered by Cairns LJ in *Gofor Investments Limited* v *Roberts and Another* (1975) 29 P & CR 366. At page 369 the learned Lord Justice said:

So the effect of that subsection was that in considering whether a person did retain a dwelling-house as his residence one had to look at the authorities prior to 1968 to see what the position was.

It was laid down in a number of cases from the 1920s onwards that the fact that the person was not physically in residence at any particular time did not mean that the house had ceased to be his residence. I take as a convenient summing-up for the purpose of this case one sentence from the judgment of Ormerod LJ in *Tickner* v *Hearn* [as expressed in the headnote [1961] 1 All ER 65]: 'In such cases' – that is cases of the kind to which I have been referring – 'there must be a real hope of return coupled with the practical possibility of its fulfilment within a reasonable time.'

Cairns LJ then went on to cite a passage from the judgment of the Court of Appeal delivered by Asquith LJ in *Brown* v *Brash and Ambrose* [1948] 2 KB 247. *Brown* v *Brash* can be regarded as the leading authority in this branch of the law.

From these passages (I would extract the following guidelines) . . .

(1)   Where the tenant's absence is more prolonged than is to be explained by holiday or ordinary business reasons and is unintermittent, the onus lies on the tenant of establishing an intention to return if he seeks the protection of the Act.

(2)   An inward intention, however, is not enough. It must be accompanied by some outward and visible sign of the tenant's intention. The continued occupation by a caretaker or relative or the continued presence of furniture may be sufficient, but in each case the question is whether or not the person or furniture can be regarded as a genuine symbol of his intention to return 'home'.

(3)   In addition the tenant must show that there is a 'practical possibility' – to use the phrase used in *Tickner* and by Ormerod LJ in *Gofor* – or a 'real possibility' – to use Lord Upjohn's expression in *Gofor* – of the fulfilment of that intention within a reasonable time. What is a reasonable time depends on the circumstances, but it is to be noted that in *Gofor* the Court of Appeal declined to interfere with the judge's finding that in the circumstances of that case ten years was a reasonable time.

(4)   The protection of the Act can be claimed even though the tenant has another home or residence – the two words appear to be synonymous in this context (see Lord Brandon in *Hampstead Way Ltd* v *Lewis-Weare* [1985] 1 WLR 164, 169) – but the court will look with particular care at two-home cases.

Before turning to the facts of the present case, I propose to remind myself finally of the words used by Lawton LJ in *Gofor* when considering the approach of an appellate court where the judge had correctly directed himself as to the law. Having decided that the judge had asked himself the correct question, Lawton LJ continued (at p. 375):

This court next has to inquire whether the evidence was sufficient to support his findings. Another way of putting this issue is to ask whether his findings on the evidence were so unreasonable as to be perverse. The judge gave most careful attention to the evidence in this case and he came to the conclusion, surprising, perhaps, to some, that there was a real intention to return and a sufficient *corpus possessionis*.

I return to the case presently before the court. I can deal shortly with what is called the *corpus possessionis*. Mr Hughes relied on the fact that the flat was occupied by members of his family and on the fact that, though he had taken his clothes with him, he had left his furniture and books behind. It was argued on behalf of the landlords that, though these facts were not disputed, there was no evidence that either the family or the furniture were there for the purpose of the alleged home-coming, and the only reason why the furniture had not been taken was because the cottage was fully furnished.

The judge, however, disposed of this matter in a few words. According to the note of his judgment with which we have been provided he said (at p. 46):

> I move to the '*corpus possessionis*'; it *is* in dispute. However, I feel I can deal with that matter pretty shortly on a simple finding. Listed in the Further and Better Particulars are the items of furniture, etc., left by the first defendant in the flat. Mr Hughes spoke of them in evidence. That is the first element. Secondly, quite apart from that, it cannot be disputed that he left behind some of his children. There is a dispute as to their status in the flat. I believe, however, that I am entitled to find, and do find from the facts that the bulk of his possessions and his loved ones are left in the flat, that Mr Hughes does quite easily establish *corpus possessionis*'.

It seems to me that there was evidence on which the learned judge could reach that finding, and it is not a finding with which I think this court can or should interfere.

The arguments concerning Mr Hughes' intention, however, are more difficult . . . The question which the judge had to consider was whether, on the facts there was a real possibility that Mr Hughes' intention to return would be fulfilled in a reasonable time. As to this the judge was clearly impressed by the daughter's evidence that she did not think that they could last another winter in the cottage. It seems to me that, though the prospect of Mr Hughes coming back because his wife had predeceased him might well have failed the test of a real possibility, the judge was entitled to infer and did infer that there was a real possibly that with advancing years they will both have to come back to the flat quite soon. As the judge put it 'The time cannot be far away.'

I confess that I have found this a troublesome case, but in the end I have come to the conclusion that it is impossible, in the light of the authorities, to interfere with the decision which the judge reached after what was clearly a very careful review both of the law and on the facts. Accordingly I for my part would dismiss the appeal.

RALPH GIBSON LJ: It is clear that when a tenant claims to be the statutory tenant of a dwelling-house on the ground that, although he is not residing there, nevertheless he 'occupies it as his residence' by reason of his intention to return to it, the question whether any intention he has is sufficient for the purposes of the Rent Act is one of fact and degree to be decided by the judge in all the circumstances of the case: see *Gofor Investments Ltd* v *Roberts*, per Cairns LJ at page 373 and Lawton LJ at p. 374.

It is open to this court to set aside the finding of the county court judge on that issue if it should appear to the court that, on the evidence, the intention which the tenant had was not such as to satisfy the requirements of the Rent Acts because, for example, it was too 'contingent' or remote as to implementation (see *Cove* v *Flack* [1954] 2 QB 326, *per* Somervell LJ at p. 328).

I think that the phrase 'real intention to return' used by Lawton LJ in the *Gofor Investments* case at page 375 includes not only the reality of any purpose of returning which the defendant may assert but also the remoteness in time and contingency of any likely implementation of that purpose.

References have been made to remoteness in terms of the number of years; thus in *Brown* v *Brash*, already cited by my Lord, Asquith LJ said:

> . . . To suppose that [a non-occupying tenant] can absent himself for 5 or 10 years or more and retain possession and his protected status simply by proving an inward intention to return after so protracted an absence would be to frustrate the spirit and policy of the Acts.

But Asquith LJ continued: '. . . Notwithstanding an absence so protracted . . . its effect may be averted if he couples and clothes his inward intention with some formal, outward and visible sign of it.'

. . .

I said that I had found this part to this case to be difficult. My reason is that I find it hard to see by reference to what principles the county court judge is required to make his decisions 'in the context of all the circumstances.' He is concerned with the fact of occupation as a residence and not with general reasonableness or greater hardship. Parliament has not enacted that a statutory tenant may retain a dwelling-house 'as his residence' if he uses it in fact to provide a place to live for his children. The test to be applied is that the tenant will remain a statutory tenant under the Act 'if and so long as he occupies the dwelling-house as his residence,' but that phrase is to be construed and applied in accordance with the case law established immediately before the commencement of the Rent Act 1968; see *Hall* v *King* (1987) 19 HLR 440, decided in this court by Sir John Donaldson, MR, Lloyd and Balcombe LJJ.

In the *Gofor Investments Ltd* case the county court judge thought that for the wife of a man on a pension to go with him to Morocco or Malta to live for 10 years while the children were educated in Malta was more 'reasonable' than if the visit abroad was for 'mere pleasure.' That showed – since his view was approved by this court – that some prolonged absences may be seen as more meritorious than others for the purposes of the Rent Acts.

It seems to me to be clear that there is a relevant distinction between an absence caused by employment or government service or through illness, on the one hand, and an absence which is more truly voluntary, on the other. Examples of less voluntary absences are the sea captain mentioned in the early cases, and in *Tickner* v *Hearn* [1960] 1 WLR 1406, to which my Lord has referred, the tenant, a voluntary patient in a hospital, who wished to return to her home but remained in hospital at all times after a short period of certification because she was advised to stay and was too unwell to leave.

. . .

On first reading the papers I found it surprising that this learned judge reached the conclusion which he did reach in this case. It is not easy to say of Mr Hughes that, by reason of an intention to return to it, he has throughout been occupying the flat (the dwelling-house) as his residence. Mr Hughes has in fact at no time had a present desire or purpose to return to the flat: he has had no more than what the judge called 'the basic intention,' that is to say, as it seems to me, the recognition and acceptance that the time will come when he will have to return to be cared for there by his children, and a purpose to return when that time arrives. The distinction between Mr Hughes and the tenant in *Tickner* v *Hearn* is obvious. The only dwelling-house of her own which that tenant had was the house of which she was tenant, and throughout it was her immediate wish to return to it; but Mr Hughes has throughout lived in the dwelling-house which he and his wife have preferred to occupy as a residence, namely the cottage in Lancashire.

I see force in this submission; and I think that a judge, in trying such cases, might on similar facts find such a submission decisive; but in my judgment it is impossible for this court to apply the point made by Mr Neuberger so as to rule that the judge's conclusion was not open to him as a matter of law. The absence of 10 years intended by Mrs Boyd, the tenant the *Gofor Investments* case, was, so far as I can see, in no relevant sense less voluntary than the absence of Mr Hughes. Mrs Boyd and her husband found it financially convenient, and, no doubt, agreeable to live in Morocco and Malta. Mr and Mrs Hughes had found it agreeable, and it may be also cheaper, to live during their active retirement in a cottage in Lancashire. In the light of the decision of this court in the *Gofor Investments* case it was open to the learned judge to decide the case as he did and I therefore agree that this appeal should be dismissed.

(ii) Excepted tenancies

Even if the conditions in s. 1 or s. 2 of the 1977 Act are fulfilled, a tenancy will not acquire full legal protection if it falls within one of the exceptions contained in ss. 4–26 of the Act. (This is the significance of the phrase 'Subject to this Part of this Act' which begins both s. 1 and s. 2.) The majority of these exceptions are the same as, or very similar to, those contained in Sch. 1 to the Housing Act 1988 and have already been discussed. The most significant exception to have no direct equivalent in the Housing Act 1988 relates to lettings involving payments for board and attendance (s. 7). To come within the exception the board and attendance 'linkage' must be *bona fide* (see *Palser* v *Grinling* [1948] AC 291). 'Board' implies service as well as the provision of food (see *Otter* v *Norman* [1989] AC 129). Under the Rent Acts this provided a convenient (if controversial) loophole for landlords who wished to minimise their long-term obligations and retain letting control and rent flexibility. However, as the vast majority of such lettings were on a short-term basis and/or attached to transient tenants, it is unlikely that much significance still attaches to this exception more than nine years after the demise of (most) new Rent Act lettings.

Perhaps of most remaining interest is the exception contained in s. 12, concerning resident landlords – particularly in the contrast it provides with the resident landlord exception contained in Sch. 1, para. 10 of the Housing Act 1988. Whereas Sch. 1, para. 10 requires that the landlord occupy another dwelling-house in the same building as the tenant as his or her *only or principal home*, s. 12 merely requires that it is 'occupied as his residence'. This parallels s. 2 discussed above, and clearly suggests that a landlord can live relatively irregularly in the dwelling-house and still come within the exception (although there must be more than merely 'token' or 'convenience' occupation, assuming equivalence of interpretation of s. 2 and s. 12). The question arose relatively recently in the following case:

Palmer v McNamara
(1990) 23 HLR 168

In 1987, the defendant was granted a tenancy of the front room of a flat with a kitchen-diner at the rear end of the room. The plaintiff landlord occupied and kept his belongings in a back room of the flat, including a fridge and a kettle. The bathroom was to be shared.

Although the plaintiff spent each day in his room, he had no cooker as he was unable to cook. If he wished to eat there he bought food that did not need to be cooked, or hot take-away meals. Also as a result of a medical condition which prevented him from dressing or undressing himself, the plaintiff did not sleep in his room but went each night to stay with a friend.

The plaintiff sought possession against the defendant on the basis that he was a resident landlord. He succeeded at first instance and the defendant appealed.

The appeal was dismissed.

DILLON LJ: . . . Does he then occupy the dwelling-house as his residence? He used to beyond any question. Indeed in this field of law the terms used, which have now been part of the jurisprudence on the subject for 70 years, are very well understood – residence, dwelling-house, occupied as his residence – and so the cases that come before the courts tend to be cases where the facts are unusual. To that generality the present case is no exception. Apart from his inability to cook, which has had the result that he does not have a cooker in the room, the plaintiff suffers from ailments as a result of which he has not slept in the room since before the tenancy was granted to the defendant. The plaintiff's evidence is that he has diabetes, but more seriously he has a three-inch shortening of his left leg and osteo-arthritis in his left hip which has caused serious deterioration. That is supported by a doctor's certificate which refers to it as 'long-standing hip joint disease.' The effect of that, particularly if the climate is damp, is that he needs help to dress and undress himself. Therefore since 1987 he has spent his night in the spare room of the house of a very old friend, a Miss Ducker, who lives about a mile or mile-and-a-half away from Drakefield Road. The plaintiff has a car and can travel between the two houses. He uses her spare room and keeps a change of clothes there. He probably now has baths there, because of the difficulty in dressing and undressing, and sometimes has his evening meal or Sunday lunch with Miss Ducker at her home. He may keep the odd book there, but he does not keep his other possessions there. The furniture in the spare room is Miss Ducker's furniture.

It is said that because he sleeps at Miss Ducker's home he does not use his room at 84 Drakefield Road as his residence. He does not use Miss Ducker's spare room as a residence either, and he is therefore in the position, which is not impossible but perhaps unusual, of a man with accommodation but no residence. He spends his days at 84 Drakefield Road. He does his writing and reading there. He watches television and video and has meals that he brings in. But it is said that because he does not sleep there he does not occupy it as his residence.

The question whether a dwelling-house is occupied as a residence is commonly paraphrased as 'does he occupy it as his home?' See the observations of Lord Brandon in *Hampstead Way Investments* v *Lewis-Weare* [1985] 1 All ER 564 at 568A. He said:

My Lords, in order to determine this appeal, it is necessary to examine the more important cases decided between 1920 and 1968 on what is meant by the occupation of a dwelling-house by a person as his residence, or, as it is put in many of the cases (without, in my view, any difference of meaning), the occupation of a dwelling-house by a person as his home.

The word 'home' was used by Scrutton LJ in the leading case of *Skinner* v *Geary* [1931] 2 KB 546. It was also used by Lord Evershed MR in *Beck* v *Scholz* [1953] 1 QB 570 at 575 and by May LJ in *Regalian Securities* v *Sheuer* (1982) 5 HLR 48.

Applying that test, which raises a question of fact and degree to be determined by applying ordinary commonsense, I have no doubt that the judge was entitled, and indeed right, to take the view that the plaintiff occupied his back room as his home. That is enough to determine this appeal.

We were referred to authorities which are concerned with the question, whether, if a person has ceased, for whatever reason, to occupy a dwelling-house as his home, he can nonetheless save the position for the purposes of the Rent Act if he has an intention or desire to return to the dwelling-house, and we had argument on whether it was relevant that at one stage the plaintiff had had it in mind to sell 84 Drakefield Road. But this does not to my mind arise as a question for decision if I am right in the view, which the judge also took, that he is currently occupying the room as his residence or home. I would dismiss this appeal.

(iii)   Restricted contracts
Section 19 of the Rent Act 1977 creates a class of 'restricted' tenancy agreements which fall midway between full legal protection and lacking any protection save procedural controls under the Protection from Eviction Act 1977. Initially the main protection attaching to restricted contracts was the right to seek six-month 'stays of execution' once a landlord sought to repossess (see further chapter 3), but this right was effectively removed by the Housing Act 1980. The power in rent tribunals to fix 'reasonable' rents concerning such tenancies remained. The key to the existence of a restricted contract is that the rent includes payment for the use of furniture, or for services (s. 79(2)) (save in relation to resident landlord cases, where no payment for furniture or services is required (ss. 20 and 21)), and the tenancy does not fall within one of the 'exceptions' seen to be wholly unprotected (most obviously holiday lets). Restricted contracts are being swiftly phased out, s. 36(1) of the 1988 Act providing that there can be no new restricted contracts from the commencement of the 1988 Act.

Questions
1.   Can a tenant be a statutory tenant under the Rent Acts if he regularly occupies more than one dwelling-house as a residence? (See *Hampstead Way Investments Ltd* v *Lewis-Weare* [1985] 1 WLR 164)
2.   Do you think that county court judgments such as the one in *Brickfield* v *Hughes* are dictated by sympathy for the position of the tenant(s) in question?
3.   How would you characterise the legal nature of a statutory tenancy?
4.   How should the status of the following private sector tenants be defined?

   (a)   A tenant granted a six-month fixed-term tenancy in February 1994, who is allowed (after the expiry of this tenancy) to remain in possession of the property, paying rent on a monthly basis (no new tenancy being formally entered into).
   (b)   A tenant granted a tenancy as in (a) in April 1988.
   (c)   A tenant granted a tenancy as in (a) in March 1997.

3 PRIVATE SECTOR TENANCIES: RIGHTS AND REMEDIES

(A) Introduction

The previous chapter examined in detail the criteria determining tenancy status in the private sector. The status of the tenancy – protected, statutory, assured, assured shorthold and so on – largely determines the rights of the parties on such key matters as security of tenure, rent control and rights of succession (although the tenancy agreement itself may still provide the legal basis for matters on which the legislation is silent). Correspondingly, this chapter is concerned with the detailed examination of these various rights, dependent on the prior classification of the tenancy.

In general the trend over the past 20 years has been to strip away the curbs on landlord freedom which Rent Act legislation provides, and in so doing to curtail tenants' rights. The culmination of this process is the assured shorthold tenancy, which, despite its name, gives few 'assurances' other than an initially guaranteed six-month right of occupancy.

Assured shortholds now comprise the overwhelming majority of new lets in the private sector, and probably a near majority of private sector tenancies overall (40 per cent in 1994/95, Department of the Environment, *Housing and Construction Statistics*, 1996).

The following material is organised around the three issues mentioned above, i.e. security of tenure, rent control and succession, examined in turn with reference to assured tenancies, assured shorthold tenancies, protected and statutory tenancies and common law tenancies.

(B) Security of tenure

(i) Assured Tenancies
The Department of the Environment White Paper (1987), *Housing: The Government's Proposals* (Cmnd 214) para. 3.9, recognised that the abolition of all tenant security was questionable:

It is reasonable that, when entering a tenancy, the tenant should expect to have to pay the market rent for the property, with suitable adjustments over time. But once a tenant has a market rent tenancy and is occupying a property as his or her home it is right that he or she should have a reasonable degree of security of tenure. This will continue to require some degree of statutory backing.

Assured tenancies *do* provide for such partial security (although equally clearly assured shortholds do not). The starting point is s. 5 of the Housing Act 1988, which provides (in part) as follows:

Housing Act 1988

Security of tenure
5.—(1)   An assured tenancy cannot be brought to an end by the landlord except by obtaining an order of the court in accordance with the following provisions of this Chapter or Chapter II below or, in the case of a fixed term tenancy which contains power for the landlord to determine the tenancy in certain circumstances, by the exercise of that power and, accordingly, the service by the landlord of a notice to quit shall be of no effect in relation to a periodic assured tenancy.

(2)   If an assured tenancy which is a fixed term tenancy comes to an end otherwise than by virtue of—

(a)   an order of the court, or

(b)   a surrender or other action on the part of the tenant,

then, subject to section 7 and Chapter II below, the tenant shall be entitled to remain in possession of the dwelling-house let under that tenancy and, subject to subsection (4) below, his right to possession shall depend upon a periodic tenancy arising by virtue of this section.

(3)   The periodic tenancy referred to in subsection (2) above is one—

(a)   taking effect in possession immediately on the coming to an end of the fixed term tenancy;

(b)   deemed to have been granted by the person who was the landlord under the fixed term tenancy immediately before it came to an end to the person who was then the tenant under that tenancy;

(c)   under which the premises which are let are the same dwelling-house as was let under the fixed term tenancy;

(d)   under which the periods of the tenancy are the same as those for which rent was last payable under the fixed term tenancy; and

(e)   under which, subject to the following provisions of this Part of this Act, the other terms are the same as those of the fixed term tenancy immediately before it came to an end, except that any term which makes provision for determination by the landlord or the tenant shall not have effect while the tenancy remains an assured tenancy.

The principal 'provisions' referred to in s. 5(1) are contained in ss. 7–9 of the 1988 Act. As relevant, these state as follows:

Housing Act 1988

Orders for possession
7.—(1)   The court shall not make an order for possession of a dwelling-house let on an assured tenancy except on one or more of the grounds set out in Schedule 2 to this

Act; but nothing in this Part of this Act relates to proceedings for possession of such a dwelling-house which are brought by a mortgagee, within the meaning of the Law of Property Act 1925, who has lent money on the security of the assured tenancy.

(2) The following provisions of this section have effect, subject to section 8 below, in relation to proceedings for the recovery of possession of a dwelling-house let on an assured tenancy.

(3) If the court is satisfied that any of the grounds in Part I of Schedule 2 to this Act is established then, subject to subsection . . . (6) below, the court shall make an order for possession.

(4) If the court is satisfied that any of the grounds in Part II of Schedule 2 to this Act is established, then, subject to subsection (6) below, the court may make an order for possession if it considers it reasonable to do so.

(5) Part III of Schedule 2 to this Act shall have effect for supplementing Ground 9 in that Schedule and Part IV of that Schedule shall have effect in relation to notices given as mentioned in Grounds 1 to 5 of that Schedule.
. . .

(6) The court shall not make an order for possession of a dwelling-house to take effect at a time when it is let on an assured fixed term tenancy unless—

(a) the ground for possession is Ground 2 or Ground 8 in Part I of Schedule 2 to this Act or any of the grounds in Part II of that Schedule, other than Ground 9 or Ground 16; and

(b) the terms of the tenancy make provision for it to be brought to an end on the ground in question (whether that provision takes the form of a provision for re-entry, for forfeiture, for determination by notice or otherwise).

(7) Subject to the preceding provisions of this section, the court may make an order for possession of a dwelling-house on grounds relating to a fixed term tenancy which has come to an end; and where an order is made in such circumstances, any statutory periodic tenancy which has arisen on the ending of the fixed term tenancy shall end (without any notice and regardless of the period) on the day on which the order takes effect.

Notice of proceedings for possession [as amended by Housing Act 1996]
8.—(1) The court shall not entertain proceedings for possession of a dwelling-house let on an assured tenancy unless—

(a) the landlord or, in the case of joint landlords, at least one of them has served on the tenant a notice in accordance with this section and the proceedings are begun within the time limits stated in the notice in accordance with subsections (3) to (4B) below; or

(b) the court considers it just and equitable to dispense with the requirement of such a notice.

(2) The court shall not make an order for possession on any of the grounds in Schedule 2 to this Act unless that ground and particulars of it are specified in the notice under this section; but the grounds specified in such a notice may be altered or added to with the leave of the court.

(3) A notice under this section is one in the prescribed form informing the tenant that—

(a) the landlord intends to begin proceedings for possession of the dwelling-house on one or more of the grounds specified in the notice; and

(b) those proceedings will not begin earlier than a date specified in the notice in accordance with subsections (4) to (4B) below; and

(c) those proceedings will not begin later than twelve months from the date of service of the notice.

(4)   If a notice under this section specifies in accordance with subsection (3)(a) above Ground 14 in Schedule 2 to this Act (whether with or without other grounds), the date specified in the notice as mentioned in subsection (3)(b) above shall not be earlier than the date of the service of the notice.

(4A)   If a notice under this section specifies in accordance with subsection (3)(a) above, any of Grounds 1, 2, 5 to 7, 9 and 16 in Schedule 2 to this Act (whether without other grounds or with any ground other than Ground 14), the date specified in the notice as mentioned in subsection (3)(b) above shall not be earlier than—

(a)   two months from the date of service of the notice; and

(b)   if the tenancy is a periodic tenancy, the earliest date on which, apart from section 5(1) above, the tenancy could be brought to an end by a notice to quit given by the landlord on the same date as the date of service of the notice under this section.

(4B)   In any case, the date specified in the notice as mentioned in subsection (3)(b) above shall not be earlier than the expiry of the period of two weeks from the date of the service of the notice.

(5)   The court may not exercise the power conferred by subsection (1)(b) above if the landlord seeks to recover possession on Ground 8 in Schedule 2 to this Act.

(6)   Where a notice under this section—

(a)   is served at a time when the dwelling-house is let on a fixed term tenancy, or

(b)   is served after a fixed term tenancy has come to an end but relates (in whole or in part) to events occurring during that tenancy,

the notice shall have effect notwithstanding that the tenant becomes or has become tenant under a statutory periodic tenancy arising on the coming to an end of the fixed term tenancy.

Additional notice requirements: ground of domestic violence

8A.—(1)   Where the ground specified in a notice under section 8 (whether with or without other grounds) is Ground 14A in Schedule 2 to this Act and the partner who has left the dwelling-house as mentioned in that ground is not a tenant of the dwelling-house, the court shall not entertain proceedings for possession of the dwelling-house unless—

(a)   the landlord or, in the case of joint landlords, at least one of them has served on the partner who has left a copy of the notice or has taken all reasonable steps to serve a copy of the notice on that partner, or

(b)   the court considers it just and equitable to dispense with such requirements as to service.

(2)   Where Ground 14A in Schedule 2 to this Act is added to a notice under section 8 with the leave of the court after proceedings for possession are begun and the partner who has left the dwelling-house as mentioned in that ground is not a party to the proceedings, the court shall not continue to entertain the proceedings unless—

(a)   the landlord or, in the case of joint landlords, at least one of them has served a notice under subsection (3) below on the partner who has left or has taken all reasonable steps to serve such a notice on that partner, or

(b)   the court considers it just and equitable to dispense with the requirement of such a notice.

(3)   A notice under this subsection shall—

(a)   state that proceedings for the possession of the dwelling-house have begun,

(b)   specify the ground or grounds on which possession is being sought, and

(c)   give particulars of the ground or grounds.

Extended discretion of court in possession claims

9.—(1) Subject to subsection (6) below, the court may adjourn for such period or periods as it thinks fit proceedings for possession of a dwelling-house let on an assured tenancy.

(2) On the making of an order for possession of a dwelling-house let on an assured tenancy or at any time before the execution of such an order, the court, subject to subsection (6) below, may—

(a) stay or suspend execution of the order, or

(b) postpone the date of possession,

for such period or periods as the court thinks just.

(3) On any such adjournment as is referred to in subsection (1) above or on any such stay, suspension or postponement as is referred to in subsection (2) above, the court, unless it considers that to do so would cause exceptional hardship to the tenant or would otherwise be unreasonable, shall impose conditions with regard to payment by the tenant of arrears of rent (if any) and rent or payments in respect of occupation after the termination of the tenancy (mesne profits) and may impose such other conditions as it thinks fit.

(4) If any such conditions as are referred to in subsection (3) above are complied with, the court may, if it thinks fit, discharge or rescind any such order as is referred to in subsection (2) above.

In effect, these provisions require that an appropriate notice (normally referred to as a Notice of Possession Proceedings (NOPP) or 's. 8' notice) is served on an assured tenant, or (in the case of fixed-term assured tenancies) an appropriate contractual 'break' clause is triggered. In the latter case, s. 5(2) and s. 5(3) clearly indicate that a periodic assured tenancy will normally then arise. The principal exception is where the fixed-term in question is an assured shorthold tenancy or (following amendments contained in s. 96 of the Housing Act 1996, adding a new s. 19A to the Housing Act 1988) where it stems from a contract entered into on or after 28 February 1997 (the commencement date of the relevant parts of Housing Act 1996). A 's. 8' notice should:

(a) be in the prescribed statutory form (see Assured Tenancy and Agricultural Occupancies (Forms) Regulations 1988 (SI 1988 No. 2203));

(b) contain the ground on which possession is sought and particulars of that ground; and

(c) give prescribed minimum periods of notice (s. 8(3)–(4B) above).

The Housing Act 1996 has amended s. 8 so as to, in particular, allow possession proceedings to be commenced virtually simultaneously with the service of the statutory notice in cases of nuisance/illegal conduct by tenants; and in the case of the new 'domestic violence' ground for possession, so as to require reasonable steps to be taken to serve notice on partners.

A 's. 8' notice remains in force for 12 months from the date of service (s. 8(3)(c)).

The importance of compliance by landlords with these formalities has led to s. 8 coming under close judicial scrutiny.

Mountain v *Hastings*
(1993) 25 HLR 427

In June 1990, the plaintiff granted the defendant an assured tenancy of a flat, at a monthly rent of £160. On 30 July 1992 the defendant was served with a notice of proceedings for possession which was allegedly in accordance with s. 8 of the Housing Act 1988. The notice specified that the plaintiff intended to seek possession on grounds 8, 10, 11, 12, 13 and 14 of Sch. 2 to the Act. In response to the note on Form 3 that he should give the full text of each ground being relied upon, the plaintiff gave summaries of the statutory text. In respect of ground 8 he wrote 'At least three months rent is unpaid.' Later in the form, under the heading 'particulars,' the plaintiff stated: 'The monthly rent is £160. No payment has been received since November 2, 1991. The total arrears due and payable amount to £1,280.' In reliance on the notice, the plaintiff took possession proceedings.

On the first date for hearing, the defendant sought an adjournment to allow her to serve a defence and counterclaim. She admitted that no rent had been paid since November 1991, but alleged that this was because of difficulties with housing benefit. The plaintiff contended that since Ground 8 gave a mandatory right to possession he was entitled to an immediate order for possession. The judge accepted the plaintiff's submission and made an order for possession in 28 days. The defendant appealed on the basis that the s. 8 notice was invalid.

Held (allowing the appeal):

(1)   The ground in Sch. 2 to the Housing Act 1988 may validly be specified in the notice in words different from those in which the ground is set out in the Schedule, provided that the words used set out fully the substance of the ground so that the notice is adequate to achieve the legislative purpose of the provision; that purpose is to give to the tenant the information which the provision requires to be given in the notice to enable the tenant to consider what she should do and, with or without advice, to do that which is in her power and which will best protect her against the loss of her home; but that

(2)   The notice was defective because the words 'At least three months rent is unpaid' did not specify Ground 8; the omitted information was that the ground which must be proved included the requirement that 'both at the date of the service of the notice . . . and at the date of the hearing . . . at least . . . three months' rent is unpaid and . . . "rent" means rent lawfully due from the tenant'; without the omitted words, the description of Ground 8 was not substantially to the like effect; the provision of full information as to the terms in which Ground 8 is expressed in the Schedule is part of that which must be stated if the ground is to be specified and if the notice is to be substantially to the like effect as the notice in the prescribed form.

RALPH GIBSON LJ: . . . For the following reasons, which are substantially in acceptance of Mr Luba's admirable argument, I would allow this appeal on the ground that the notice was bad. I will consider first the arguments directed to the validity of the notice. I will give my reasons later for holding that the defendant must be permitted to raise that point in this court.

As to the submission that the notice was defective because ground 8 was not specified by the full text of that ground as set out in Schedule 2, I do not decide this issue upon that basis. I prefer the view that the ground in Schedule 2 may validly be 'specified in the notice' as required by Parliament, in words different from those in which the ground is set out in the schedule, provided that the words used set out fully the substance of the ground so that the notice is adequate to achieved the legislative purpose of the provision. That purpose, in my judgment, is to give to the tenant the information which the provision requires to be given in the notice to enable the tenant to consider what she should do and, with or without advice, to do that which is in her power and which will best protect her against the loss of her home.

Thus, in *Torridge District Council* v *Jones* (1985) 18 HLR 107, with reference to section 33 of the Housing Act 1980 (later section 83 of the Housing Act 1985 which contains a similar provision), the issue related not to the words in which the ground was specified but to the sufficiency of the particulars of the ground given in the notice. Oliver LJ said at p. 113:

. . . as it seems to me, in the case of the instant statute, we are really concerned with quite a different type of notice. This is a warning shot across the bows of the tenant and the object of it is to warn him that unless he repairs what is stated as the ground on which possession is going to be sought, he is going to be liable to court proceedings. It seems to me as plain as a pikestaff that the object of the notice is to bring to the tenant's notice the defect of which complaint is made to enable him to make a proper restitution before proceedings are commenced and to deal with them.

Later, at p. 114, he said:

It seems to me that it is plain that this subsection does require a specification sufficient to tell the tenant what it is he has to do to put matters right before the proceedings are commenced. In my judgment, therefore, the notice which was served upon the appellant in this case was not a proper notice that complied with section 33(3). Accordingly . . . the notice not complying with the subsection, the court was then prohibited from entertaining the proceedings at all.

If, with reference to the specification of the ground upon which the landlord intends to begin proceedings for possession, the ground is specified in words which give to the tenant every piece of information which Parliament has said that he shall have and in words which are clear, then, as it seems to me, the legislative purpose of the provision would be satisfied and there would be no effective requirement of the ground to be specified in the very words set out in Schedule 2 unless Parliament has made that requirement.

The word 'specified' takes its particular meaning from the context in which it is used and from the matter to which it is applied. The Shorter Oxford Dictionary gives the first meaning of the word as: 'to speak or make relation of some matter fully or in detail.'

The requirement in section 8(2) is to specify the ground: it is not that the ground be set out as in Schedule 2. I would add that it is also not merely to identify the ground. If the ground is specified in the notice in terms which set out all the necessary information, i.e. the substance of the ground, it seems to me that the requirement that the ground be specified would be met. I would add that it is difficult to think of any good reason why a person, given the task of settling a form of notice, should choose to use words different from those in which the ground is stated in the schedule.

The notice must also be in the prescribed form. The regulation by which the form is prescribed requires the form used to be in the form there set out or 'substantially to the same effect.' If the form served is to be completed fully in accordance with the form, it will set out the text of the ground as it appears in Schedule 2 because the form in paragraph 3 says: 'the landlord intends to seek possession on ground(s) . . . in Schedule 2 *which reads*' and Note (3) in the margin says: 'give the full text of each ground which is being relied on.'

The regulation, however, expressly permits the notice to be effective in the prescribed form if it is 'substantially to the same effect.' which I take to mean to be showing no difference in substance having regard to the legislative purpose of the provisions as a whole. I, therefore, am not persuaded that there is a statutory requirement that the ground be set out verbatim from the schedule. I am troubled by the risk that, if the tenant is faced with a set of words which effectively set out the substance of a ground but in markedly different words, the tenant may, if he has access to the words of Schedule 2, be puzzled and troubled by the difference. There is something to be said in favour of the use of the words in which the ground was enacted by Parliament. I do not decide this point, however, because the case can be, and I think should be, decided on the ground that the plaintiff's notice was not 'substantially to the same effect' as that required by the Act and regulations.

Further, on the question of any requirement to state the words of the ground in full as in Schedule 2, it is to be noted that this case does not raise any question as to parts of the text of a particular ground which could properly be considered surplusage to the ground upon which the landlord will rely. Examples are one of the alternatives in ground 1 and one or more of the alternatives in ground 6. The point has not been argued. It seems that, if the omitted material can be regarded as irrelevant in the circumstances of the particular case, the omission may not invalidate the notice: see *Tegerdine* v *Brooks* (1977) 36 P & CR 261. If the omission or inaccuracy was inadvertent, and if it was obvious such a mistake had been made, and what was intended, again the error may not invalidate the notice: see *Morrow* v *Nadeem* [1986] 1 WLR 1381, *per* Nicholls LJ.

I would hold this notice to be defective because, in my judgment, it did not specify ground 8 by the words: 'at least three months rent is unpaid.' The omitted information is that the ground which must be proved includes the requirement that 'both at the date of the service of the notice . . . and the date of the hearing . . . at least . . . three months rent is unpaid and . . . "rent" means rent lawfully due from the tenant.'

Mr Nance submitted that the description of ground 8 was substantially to the like effect as that required by the prescribed form because the omitted words with reference to rent unpaid at the hearing related to the future and the tenant in fact had all that she needed to know in order to decide what to do. That submission is, I think, unacceptable because the tenant who is three months in arrears might suppose from the plaintiff's notice that the mandatory ground of possession, upon which the court must make an order, was thereby established although he or she might be able, if aware of the significance of it, to pay all or part of the arrears before the date of the hearing and therefore prevent proof of such a mandatory ground. It was not submitted, rightly as I think that for this purpose it matters whether or not the particular tenant could or would have paid before the hearing so as to be able to prove any specific detriment caused by the deficiency in the notice: see *per* Roskill LJ in *Tegerdine* v *Brooks* (*supra*) at p. 266. The provision of full information as to the terms in which ground 8 is expressed in the schedule, and in which it must be proved, is, therefore, in my judgment part of that which must be stated if the ground is to be specified and if the notice is to be substantially to the like effect as the notice in the prescribed form.

A possession order will be granted against an assured tenant (once the matter is validly before the courts) only if (at least) one of the grounds listed in the Housing Act 1988, Sch. 2 is made out (s. 7(1)). These grounds are of two general types: Part I grounds, where the court must make an order if the provisions of the ground are satisfied (often termed *mandatory grounds*); and Part II grounds, where, in addition to being satisfied that a ground has been made out, a court should order possession if it considers it *reasonable* to do so (often termed *discretionary grounds*). On this, see s. 7(3) and (4).

(a)   Mandatory grounds for possession

The following grounds are as amended by the Housing Act 1996.

Housing Act 1988

SCHEDULE 2
GROUNDS FOR POSSESSION OF DWELLING-HOUSES LET ON ASSURED TENANCIES
PART I
GROUNDS ON WHICH COURT MUST ORDER POSSESSION

Ground 1

Not later than the beginning of the tenancy the landlord gave notice in writing to the tenant that possession might be recovered on this ground or the court is of the opinion that it is just and equitable to dispense with the requirement of notice and (in either case)—

(a)   at some time before the beginning of the tenancy, the landlord who is seeking possession or, in the case of joint landlords seeking possession, at least one of them occupied the dwelling-house as his only or principal home; or

(b)   the landlord who is seeking possession or, in the case of joint landlords seeking possession, at least one of them requires the dwelling-house as his or his spouse's only or principal home and neither the landlord (or in the case of joint landlords, any one of them) nor any other person who, as landlord, derived title under the landlord who gave the notice mentioned above acquired the reversion on the tenancy for money or money's worth.

Ground 2

The dwelling house is subject to a mortgage granted before the beginning of the tenancy and—

(a)   the mortgagee is entitled to exercise a power of sale conferred on him by the mortgage or by section 101 of the Law of Property Act 1925; and

(b)   the mortgagee requires possession of the dwelling-house for the purpose of disposing of it with vacant possession in exercise of that power; and

(c)   either notice was given as mentioned in Ground 1 above or the court is satisfied that it is just and equitable to dispense with the requirement of notice; and for the purposes of this ground ('mortgage' includes a charge and 'mortgagee' shall be construed accordingly.

Ground 3

The tenancy is a fixed term tenancy for a term not exceeding eight months and—

(a)   not later than the beginning of the tenancy the landlord gave notice in writing to the tenant that possession might be recovered on this ground; and

(b)   at some time within the period of twelve months ending with the beginning of the tenancy, the dwelling-house was occupied under a right to occupy it for a holiday.

Ground 4

The tenancy is a fixed term tenancy for a term not exceeding twelve months and—

(a)   not later than the beginning of the tenancy the landlord gave notice in writing to the tenant that possession might be recovered on this ground; and

(b)   at some time within the period of twelve months ending with the beginning of the tenancy, the dwelling-house was let on a tenancy falling within paragraph 8 of Schedule 1 to this Act.

Ground 5

The dwelling-house is held for the purpose of being available for occupation by a minister of religion as a residence from which to perform the duties of his office and—

(a)   not later than the beginning of the tenancy the landlord gave notice in writing to the tenant that possession might be recovered on this ground; and

(b)   the court is satisfied that the dwelling-house is required for occupation by a minister of religion as such a residence.

Ground 6

The landlord who is seeking possession or, if that landlord is a registered housing association or charitable housing trust, a superior landlord intends to demolish or reconstruct the whole or a substantial part of the dwelling-house or to carry out substantial works on the dwelling-house or any part thereof or any building of which it forms part and the following conditions are fulfilled—

(a)   the intended work cannot reasonably be carried out without the tenant giving up possession of the dwelling-house because—

(i)   the tenant is not willing to agree to such a variation of the terms of the tenancy as would give such access and other facilities as would permit the intended work to be carried out, or

(ii)   the nature of the intended work is such that no such variation is practicable, or

(iii)   the tenant is not willing to accept an assured tenancy of such part only of the dwelling-house (in this sub-paragraph referred to as 'the reduced part') as would leave in the possession of his landlord so much of the dwelling-house as would be reasonable to enable the intended work to be carried out and, where appropriate, as would give such access and other facilities over the reduced part as would permit the intended work to be carried out, or

(iv) the nature of the intended work is such that such a tenancy is not practicable; and

(b) either the landlord seeking possession acquired his interest in the dwelling-house before the grant of the tenancy or that interest was in existence at the time of that grant and neither that landlord (or, in the case of joint landlords, any of them) nor any other person who, alone or jointly with others, has acquired that interest since that time acquired it for money or money's worth; and

(c) the assured tenancy on which the dwelling-house is let did not come into being by virtue of any provision of Schedule 1 to the Rent Act 1977, as amended by Part I of Schedule 4 to this Act or, as the case may be, section 4 of the Rent (Agriculture) Act 1976, as amended by Part II of that Schedule.

For the purposes of this ground, if, immediately before the grant of the tenancy, the tenant to whom it was granted or, if it was granted to joint tenants, any of them was the tenant or one of the joint tenants of the dwelling-house concerned under an earlier assured tenancy . . ., any reference in paragraph (b) above to the grant of the tenancy is a reference to the grant of that earlier assured tenancy . . .

For the purposes of this ground 'registered housing association' has the same meaning as in the Housing Act 1985 . . . and 'charitable housing trust' means a housing trust, within the meaning of the Housing Association Act 1985, which is a charity, within the meaning of the Charities Act 1993.

Ground 7

The tenancy is a periodic tenancy (including a statutory periodic tenancy) which has devolved under the will or intestacy of the former tenant and the proceedings for the recovery of possession are begun not later than twelve months after the death of the former tenant or, if the court so directs, after the date on which, in the opinion of the court, the landlord or, in the case of joint landlords, any one of them became aware of the former tenant's death.

For the purposes of this ground, the acceptance by the landlord of rent from a new tenant after the death of the former tenant shall not be regarded as creating a new periodic tenancy, unless the landlord agrees in writing to a change (as compared with the tenancy before the death) in the amount of the rent, the period of the tenancy, the premises which are let or any other term of the tenancy.

Ground 8

Both at the date of the service of the notice under section 8 of this Act relating to the proceedings for possession and at the date of the hearing—

(a) if rent is payable weekly or fortnightly, at least eight weeks' rent is unpaid;

(b) if rent is payable monthly, at least two months' rent is unpaid;

(c) if rent is payable quarterly, at least one quarter's rent is more than three months in arrears; and

(d) if rent is payable yearly, at least three months' rent is more than three months in arrears;

and for the purpose of this ground 'rent' means rent lawfully due from the tenant.

Notes

1. Many of the above grounds are either self-explanatory, or duplicate those in the Rent Act discussed below. However, on a general level it is highly significant that in the 1988 Act (unlike the 1977 Act) the mandatory grounds

come first (at the very least of psychological significance!). Moreover, any legislative amendments to these grounds seem likely to tighten them up, rather than to liberalise them. (See the comments on Ground 8 below.)

2. The relationship between Grounds 1 and 2 is not unproblematic. It *appears* that the type of notice envisaged in Ground 2 is one served by a 'Ground 1' landlord, i.e. a past or future 'owner-occupier'. The idea seems to be that to facilitate repossession by a mortgagee the tenant should first have been put on guard by the landlord indicating his or her occupational interest in the property (no doubt a well-advised mortgagee would normally insist on the mortgagor creating an assured shorthold, but it has been suggested that even lets as long as six months might sometimes prove inconvenient to a mortgagor ideally wishing to sell the property and desiring to create a (very) short-term let, often to tide him or her over temporary financial difficulties. An alternative justification could be the (perceived) general social benefit in encouraging 'absentee' property owners to let empty properties until a sale is agreed. Ground 1, in itself, seems to be an amalgam of the 1977 Act cases 9, 11 and 12 (below), all adjusted to make things easier for landlords. In particular, there is no need for the landlord to demonstrate that he or she was a former owner-occupier *and* now wishes to re-occupy, merely that one *or* the other is the case (admittedly it must have been or be intended to be 'genuine' owner-occupation, i.e. as the landlord's 'only or principal home').

The court has a general discretion to 'waive' the need for the usual Ground 1 notice. In *Byle* v *Verrall* (1996) 29 HLR 436 and *Mustafa* v *Ruddock* (1997) 30 HLR 495, the Court of Appeal held that the following matters were relevant to the exercise of the discretion to dispense with the statutory notice:

(a) whether hardship would (thereby) be caused to the defendant, or not;

(b) whether hardship would (thereby) be caused to the landlord, if the notice requirement was not 'waived';

(c) whether the tenancy agreement itself indicated that security of tenure was to be limited; and

(d) whether other written (or oral) indications had been given to the tenant concerning limited security.

3. Ground 6 has no counterpart in the Rent Acts, and is both of considerable interest and some difficulty. Broadly equivalent provisions are to be found in Ground 10 of Sch. 2 of the Housing Act 1985 (concerning public sector residential tenants) and in s. 30(1)(f) of the business tenancy 'code' in the Landlord and Tenant Act 1954. There is fairly extensive case law on the 1954 Act, concerning issues such as the genuineness of the landlord's intention to demolish or reconstruct (it has been pointed out that this 'intention' need exist only up to the date possession has been obtained!).

As a curb on the pure 'speculator', it is not possible to use the ground if the landlord acquired the freehold *after* the tenancy was created. Also, if the ground is invoked the tenant is entitled to reasonable removal expenses (s. 11, 1988 Act). Overall, the objective of the ground is both clear and instructive as to the general philosophy underlying the 1988 Act; the right of a freeholder to develop and improve his property should not be curbed even if this is at the expense of removing the occupational security of the tenant. Prior to the Act, the only way that such a freeholder could secure the necessary repossession was if he or she was prepared to offer the tenant 'suitable alternative accommodation' (Rent Act 1977 s. 98(1)(a) and Sch. 15, Part IV – below).

A typical business sector case is *Fisher* v *Taylors Furnishing Stores Ltd* [1956] 2 QB 78, in which Denning LJ (as he was then) stated (at p. 84):

The court must be satisfied that the intention to reconstruct is genuine . . . that it is a firm and settled intention . . . that the reconstruction is of a substantial part of the premises, indeed so substantial that it cannot be thought a device to get possession: that the work is so extensive that it is necessary to get possession of the holding in order to do it; and that it is intended to do the work at once, and not after a time.

4.   Ground 7 is required because, whereas a statutory tenancy under the Rent Acts is personal to a tenant and *prima facie* terminates automatically on that tenant's death, an assured tenancy can, in principle, 'devolve' by will or on intestacy. More generally, in the 1988 Act rights of succession are limited to spouses or cohabitees (s. 17, below).

5.   As will be seen shortly, Grounds 10 and 11 of Sch. 2 provide for discretionary grounds of possession in rent arrears cases. Ground 8 is mandatory and must be strictly construed given the fact that there is no in-built flexibility for a court to grant suspended orders (or adjourn proceedings) conditional on an agreed arrears schedule. Above all, the arrears must still exist *both* at the date of service of the s. 8 notice *and* at the date of the hearing. The severity of Ground 8 has recently been increased by amendments contained in s. 101 of the Housing Act 1996 which reduce the period of arrears in Ground 8(a) from 13 weeks to eight weeks, and in the case of Ground 8(b) from three months to two months. Given that Ground 8 is mandatory, mitigating circumstances (for example that housing benefit is late being paid – and it has been estimated that up to one-third of all local authorities fail to pay housing benefit on time (Hansard HL Deb (1996) Vol. 572) col. 613)) appear irrelevant.

(b)   Discretionary grounds for possession

As indicated above, a prerequisite for the invocation of one of these grounds is that, in addition to a relevant ground being made out, it is seen by the court(s) as *reasonable* to grant a possession order (s. 7(4), above). Numerous judicial formulations exist concerning the approach to be adopted in adjudicating on 'reasonableness' (a concept with a long Rent Act 'pedigree'). Perhaps the most succinct is that of Lord Greene MR in *Cumming* v *Danson* [1942] 2 All ER 653, at p. 655:

the duty of the judge is to take into account all relevant circumstances as they exist at the date of the hearing. That he must do in what I venture to call a broad, common sense way as a man of the world, and come to the conclusion giving such weight as he thinks right to the various factors in the situation. Some factors may have little or no weight, others may be decisive, but it is quite wrong for him to exclude from his consideration matters which he ought to take into account.

What *is* clear is that the interests/needs/circumstances of both the landlord *and* the tenant should be considered, and that unless the first instance judge has plainly misdirected himself or herself (as was indeed the case in *Cumming v Danson*) it will be unusual for an appeal court to disturb a preliminary finding on 'reasonableness'. Equally, the court has a very wide discretion to adjourn the proceedings, or suspend any possession order actually granted. In such cases conditions as to payment of (any) rent arrears *will* normally be imposed, and other conditions *may* be imposed (generally see s. 9. above).

The grounds themselves are predominant similar to those to be found in the Rent Act 1977 and the Housing Act 1985, centering on tenant 'default', in such cases as nuisance, non-payment of rent and deterioration of the property. They have been significantly amended by the Housing Act 1996.

Housing Act 1988

SCHEDULE 2
GROUNDS FOR POSSESSION OF DWELLING-HOUSES LET ON ASSURED TENANCIES
PART II
GROUNDS ON WHICH COURT MAY ORDER POSSESSION

Ground 9

Suitable alternative accommodation is available for the tenant or will be available for him when the order for possession takes effect.

Ground 10

Some rent lawfully due from the tenant—
    (a)   is unpaid on the date on which the proceedings for possession are begun; and
    (b)   except where subsection (1)(b) of section 8 of this Act applies, was in arrears at the date of the service of the notice under that section relating to those proceedings.

Ground 11

Whether or not any rent is in arrears on the date on which proceedings for possession are begun, the tenant has persistently delayed paying rent which has become lawfully due.

Ground 12

Any obligation of the tenancy (other than one related to the payment of rent) has been broken or not performed.

Ground 13

The condition of the dwelling-house or any of the common parts has deteriorated owing to acts of waste by, or the neglect or default of, the tenant or any other person résiding in the dwelling-house and, in the case of an act of waste by, or the neglect or default of, a person lodging with the tenant or a sub-tenant of his, the tenant has not taken such steps as he ought reasonably to have taken for the removal of the lodger or sub-tenant.

For the purposes of this ground, 'common parts' means any part of a building comprising the dwelling-house and any other premises which the tenant is entitled under the terms of the tenancy to use in common with the occupiers of other dwelling-houses in which the landlord has an estate or interest.

Ground 14

The tenant or a person residing in or visiting the dwelling-house—

(a) has been guilty of conduct causing or likely to cause a nuisance or annoyance to a person residing, visiting or otherwise engaging in a lawful activity in the locality, or

(b) has been convicted of—

(i) using the dwelling-house or allowing it to be used for immoral or illegal purposes, or

(ii) an arrestable offence committed in, or in the locality of, the dwelling-house.

Ground 14A

The dwelling-house was occupied (whether alone or with others) by a married couple or a couple living together as husband and wife and—

(a) one or both of the partners is a tenant of the dwelling-house,

(b) the landlord who is seeking possession is a registered social landlord or a charitable housing trust,

(c) one partner has left the dwelling-house because of violence or threats of violence by the other towards—

(i) that partner, or

(ii) a member of the family of that partner who was residing with that partner immediately before the partner left, and

(d) the court is satisfied that the partner who has left is unlikely to return.

. . .

Ground 15

The condition of any furniture provided for use under the tenancy has, in the opinion of the court, deteriorated owing to ill-treatment by the tenant or any other person residing in the dwelling-house and, in the case of ill-treatment by a person lodging with the tenant or by a sub-tenant of his, the tenant has not taken such steps as he ought reasonably to have taken for the removal of the lodger or sub-tenant.

Ground 16

The dwelling-house was let to the tenant in consequence of his employment by the landlord seeking possession or a previous landlord under the tenancy and the tenant has ceased to be in that employment.

Ground 17

The tenant is the person, or one of the persons, to whom the tenancy was granted and the landlord was induced to grant the tenancy by a false statement made knowingly or recklessly by—

(a) the tenant, or
(b) a person acting at the tenant's instigation.

Notes

1. As under s. 98(1)(a) of the Rent Act 1977 (below), but unlike the position under the Housing Act 1985, the offering of *suitable alternative accommodation* by the landlord is an independent ground for possession (Ground 9). It remains a discretionary ground despite calls from many landlords for it to become mandatory in order to facilitate tenant transfer and enhance the scope for property redevelopment (as indeed was the case, in the Housing Bill as originally drafted). However, in the light of the mandatory Ground 6 (above), it is debatable how significant this point remains. 'Suitability' is defined by Pt III of Sch. 2 to the 1988 Act. Much of the structure and content of Pt III is similar to that in the Rent Act 1977, Sch. 15, Pt IV discussed below – the main difference lying in the (fairly obvious) substitution of 'assured tenancy' for 'protected tenancy' in relation to alternatives deemed to be suitable (assured shortholds excepted). Under s. 11(1) of the 1988 Act, a landlord must pay a tenant's reasonable removal expenses.

2. Again, in the original Housing Bill Ground 11 was to be a mandatory ground – no doubt better to deter the '11th hour' payer. As now enacted, it still provides a useful tool for landlords frustrated by a tenant who consistently heads off legal proceedings by paying off all arrears prior to the service of the possession summons. The main uncertainty is the scope of 'persistent'. It appears to encompass both the 'persistent' late payer and a particular sum 'persistently' remaining in arrears.

3. Ground 14 has been considerably widened and strengthened by the Housing Act 1996 (s. 148) in terms now identical to those in the Housing Act 1985 (Sch. 2, Ground 2 as amended). As will be discussed in relation to the 1985 Act, the aim is to arm the courts with clearer and more effective powers to deal with 'anti-social' tenants. It is likely that some of the main landlord users of this new provision will be housing associations.

4. Again, Ground 14A (inserted by s. 149 of the 1996 Act) mirrors the new public sector provision, now in Ground 2A of Sch. 2 to the 1985 Act. The definition of 'domestic' violence required to 'trigger' the new ground is somewhat narrow (significantly narrower than the new concept of 'associated person' which correspondingly triggers 'domestic violence' provisions in relation to homelessness – see the Housing Act 1996, s. 178). 'Gay' couples and others sharing a common household, but not married or cohabiting, are, in particular, not covered.

5. Ground 17 is also new, and also mirrors Housing Act 1985 provisions, although in this case Ground 5 in Sch. 2 to the Housing Act 1985 is *not* a new provision. It seems clear that the measure is designed to put housing associations and other *registered social landlords* (Pt I of the 1996 Act) in the same position as local authorities as regards those 'jumping the queue' by deceit.

Questions
1. How much effective 'security of tenure' do assured tenancies provide?
2. In relation to fixed-term assured tenancies, what type of 'provision' does s. 7(6)(b) of the Housing Act 1988 envisage being included in the tenancy agreement to facilitate termination of the original fixed term?
3. Does *Mountain* v *Hastings* require landlords to give *full* details of the basis of their possession claim in the original 's. 8' notice?
4. Is there any sanction which can be invoked against a landlord who obtains possession on the basis of Ground 6 of Sch. 2 of the Housing Act 1988 but then does *not* 'redevelop' the property?
5. Would any or all of the following potentially amount to 'common parts' in relation to Ground 13?

   (a) stairways;
   (b) corridors;
   (c) passages (in blocks of flats);
   (d) lifts;
   (e) rubbish chutes.

(ii) Assured shorthold tenancies
As discussed in chapter 2, the centrepiece of the Housing Act 1988 is the assured shorthold, a form of tenancy giving landlords maximum letting flexibility, both in terms of the rent that can be charged (subject to a few minor caveats – see below) and the ability to recover possession of the property. An assured shorthold tenant (despite a somewhat contradictory impression conveyed by the name) has no *legal* security of tenure past the first six months of the tenancy. Even during the initial six months, such a tenant is vulnerable to repossession on the same bases as any assured tenant (above). In relation to assured shortholds in fixed-term form (pre- or post-Housing Act 1996 – see chapter 2), this means Grounds 2, 8, 10–15 and 17 (1988 Act, s. 7(6)(b)). In relation to periodic (s. 19A) assured shortholds, any ground seems theoretically available.

More significantly, at the end of the original minimum six-month fixed term ('old' assured shortholds: s. 20(1) and s. 21(1), 1988 Act) or after six months have passed from the commencement of the tenancy ('new' assured shortholds: s. 21(5), 1988 Act as amended) a landlord has an absolute right to obtain possession without any ground for possession having to be shown at all. Two months' notice of the intention to repossess must be given by the landlord (s. 21(1)(b)); or in the case of continuation periodic assured shortholds, a period equal to a tenancy period if this is longer than two months (s. 21(4)(a)). However, it seems implicit that a notice can be served so as to expire on the last day of the original six months of the tenancy. No particular form is required for a s. 21 notice, although it must now be in writing (since the 1996 Act, s. 98).

Housing Act 1988

Recovery of possession on expiry or termination of assured shorthold tenancy
21.—(1) Without prejudice to any right of the landlord under an assured shorthold tenancy to recover possession of the dwelling-house let on the tenancy in accordance with Chapter I above, on or after the coming to an end of an assured shorthold tenancy which was a fixed term tenancy, a court shall make an order for possession of the dwelling-house if it is satisfied—

(a) that the assured shorthold tenancy has come to an end and no further assured tenancy (whether shorthold or not) is for the time being in existence, other than an assured shorthold periodic tenancy (whether statutory or not); and

(b) the landlord or, in the case of joint landlords, at least one of them has given to the tenant not less than two months' notice in writing stating that he requires possession of the dwelling-house.

(2) A notice under paragraph (b) of subsection (1) above may be given before or on the day on which the tenancy comes to an end; and that subsection shall have effect notwithstanding that on the coming to an end of the fixed term tenancy a statutory periodic tenancy arises.

(3) Where a court makes an order for possession of a dwelling-house by virtue of subsection (1) above, any statutory periodic tenancy which has arisen on the coming to an end of the assured shorthold tenancy shall end (without further notice and regardless of the period) on the day on which the order takes effect.

(4) Without prejudice to any such right as is referred to in subsection (1) above, a court shall make an order for possession of a dwelling-house let on an assured shorthold tenancy which is a periodic tenancy if the court is satisfied—

(a) that the landlord or, in the case of joint landlords, at least one of them has given to the tenant a notice in writing stating that, after a date specified in the notice, being the last day of a period of the tenancy and not earlier than two months after the date the notice was given, possession of the dwelling-house is required by virtue of this section; and

(b) that the date specified in the notice under paragraph (a) above is not earlier than the earliest day on which, apart from section 5(1) above, the tenancy could be brought to an end by a notice to quit given by the landlord on the same date as the notice under paragraph (a) above.

(5) Where an order for possession under subsection (1) or (4) above is made in relation to a dwelling-house let on a tenancy to which section 19A above applies, the order may not be made so as to take effect earlier than—

(a) in the case of a tenancy which is not a replacement tenancy, six months after the beginning of the tenancy, and

(b) in the case of a replacement tenancy, six months after the beginning of the original tenancy.

(6) In subsection (5)(b) above, the reference to the original tenancy is—

(a) where the replacement tenancy came into being on the coming to an end of a tenancy which was not a replacement tenancy, to the immediately preceding tenancy, and

(b) where there have been successive replacement tenancies, to the tenancy immediately preceding the first in the succession of replacement tenancies

(7) For the purposes of this section, a replacement tenancy is a tenancy—

(a) which comes into being on the coming to an end of an assured shorthold tenancy, and

(b)   under which, on its coming into being—
(i)   the landlord and tenant are the same as under the earlier tenancy as at its coming to an end, and
(ii)   the premises let are the same or substantially the same as those let under the earlier tenancy as at that time.

Notes

1. Unsurprisingly, under the shorthold 'regime', a court has no power to adjourn proceedings, suspend an order for possession, or postpone the date of possession (s. 9(6)(b)).

2. An 'accelerated' possession procedure is available to landlords seeking repossession of assured shortholds (and also assured tenancies under Grounds 1, 3, 4, and 5). In outline, no hearing is necessarily required – a district judge can make a possession order without a hearing if satisfied by the landlord's written application that the necessary legal requirements have been made out (ss. 19A and 20, plus s. 21 as appropriate). The landlord's original application (supported by affidavit) is sent to the tenant who has 14 days to reply. On receipt of the tenant's reply (or failure to reply in the time allowed) the court must decide whether to grant possession or fix a hearing date. In the former case the tenant has to vacate the dwelling-house within 14 days of the order (the courts can extend this up to six weeks if there is 'exceptional hardship'). On all this see CCR Ord. 49, r. 6A(3) and (9).

3. In serving a 's. 21' notice a landlord must, at least, make sure that he or she does not attempt to commence possession proceedings before the notice expires. In *Lower Street Properties Ltd* v *Jones* (1996) 28 HLR 877, Kennedy LJ stated (at p. 883): '. . . from the point of view of the tenant, I regard it as objectionable that having been given a period in which to leave, legal proceedings to obtain possession should be instituted . . . before that period has expired'.

4. It has been suggested (Campbell, *Roof* July/August 1997, at p. 15) that the current relationship of landlord and tenant (typically now via assured shortholds) could be made fairer via one 'simple' reform; this would be to repeal (or amend) s. 89 Housing Act 1980 which (currently) requires that a possession order must take effect within 14 days, or (if exceptional hardship is proved) within six weeks. Instead, the courts could be given the discretion to fix an appropriate date for possession, taking into account any hardship that an early possession date would cause.

(iii)   Rent Act tenancies

Rent Act tenants, a declining but still significant 'breed', continue to enjoy full security of tenure. This security is the result of substantive hurdles imposed by the Rent Act 1977 (s. 98 and Sch. 15 in particular), and procedural hurdles imposed by the Protection from Eviction Act 1977 (in particular ss. 3 and 5).

As relevant, s. 98 of the Rent Act 1977 and ss. 3 and 5 of the Protection from Eviction Act 1977 provide as follows:

Rent Act 1977

Grounds for possession of certain dwelling-houses
98.—(1)   Subject to this Part of this Act, a court shall not make an order for possession of a dwelling-house which is for the time being let on a protected tenancy or subject to a statutory tenancy unless the court considers it reasonable to make such an order and either—
(a)   the court is satisfied that suitable alternative accommodation is available for the tenant or will be available for him when the order in question takes effect, or
(b)   the circumstances are as specified in any of the Cases in Part I of Schedule 15 to this Act.
(2)   If, apart from subsection (1) above, the landlord would be entitled to recover possession of a dwelling-house which is for the time being let on or subject to a regulated tenancy, the court shall make an order for possession if the circumstances of the case are as specified in any of the Cases in Part II of Schedule 15.
(3)   Part III of Schedule 15 shall have effect in relation to Case 9 in that Schedule and for determining the relevant date for the purposes of the Cases in Part II of that Schedule.
(4)   Part IV of Schedule 15 shall have effect for determining whether, for the purposes of subsection (1)(a) above, suitable alternative accommodation is or will be available for a tenant.
(5)   . . .

Protection From Eviction Act 1977

Prohibition of eviction without due process of law
3.—(1)   Where any premises have been let as a dwelling under a tenancy which is neither a statutorily protected tenancy nor an excluded tenancy and—
(a)   the tenancy (in this section referred to as the former tenancy) has come to an end, but
(b)   the occupier continues to reside in the premises or part of them,
it shall not be lawful for the owner to enforce against the occupier, otherwise than by proceedings in the court, his right to recover possession of the premises.
(2)   In this section 'the occupier', in relation to any premises, means any person lawfully residing in the premises or part of them at the termination of the former tenancy.
(2A)   Subsections (1) and (2) above apply in relation to any restricted contract (within the meaning of the Rent Act 1977) which—
(a)   creates a licence; and
(b)   is entered into after the commencement of section 69 of the Housing Act 1980;
as they apply in relation to a restricted contract which creates a tenancy.
(2B)   Subsections (1) and (2) above apply in relation to any premises occupied as a dwelling under a licence, other than an excluded licence, as they apply in relation to premises let as a dwelling under a tenancy, and in those subsections the expressions 'let' and 'tenancy' shall be construed accordingly.
(2C)   References in the preceding provisions of this section and section 4(2A) below to an excluded tenancy do not apply to—
(a)   a tenancy entered into before the date on which the Housing Act 1988 came into force, or

(b)   a tenancy entered into on or after that date but pursuant to a contract made before that date,

but, subject to that, 'excluded tenancy' and 'excluded licence' shall be construed in accordance with section 3A below.

(3)   This section shall, with the necessary modifications, apply where the owner's right to recover possession arises on the death of the tenant under a statutory tenancy within the meaning of the Rent Act 1977 or the Rent (Agriculture) Act 1976.

Excluded tenancies and licences

3A.—(1)   Any reference in this Act to an excluded tenancy or an excluded licence is a reference to a tenancy or licence which is excluded by virtue of any of the following provisions of this section.

(2)   A tenancy or licence is excluded if—

(a)   under its terms the occupier shares any accommodation with the landlord or licensor; and

(b)   immediately before the tenancy or licence was granted and also at the time it comes to an end, the landlord or licensor occupied as his only or principal home premises of which the whole or part of the shared accommodation formed part.

(3)   A tenancy or licence is also excluded if—

(a)   under its terms the occupier shares any accommodation with a member of the family of the landlord or licensor;

(b)   immediately before the tenancy or licence was granted and also at the time it comes to an end, the member of the family of the landlord or licensor occupied as his only or principal home premises of which the whole or part of the shared accommodation formed part; and

(c)   immediately before the tenancy or licence was granted and also at the time it comes to end, the landlord or licensor occupied as his only or principal home premises in the same building as the shared accommodation and that building is not a purpose-built block of flats.

(4)   For the purposes of subsections (2) and (3) above, an occupier shares accommodation with another person if he has the use of it in common with that person (whether or not also in common with others) and any reference in those subsections to shared accommodation shall be construed accordingly, and if, in relation to any tenancy or licence, there is at any time more than one person who is the landlord or licensor, any reference in those subsections to the landlord or licensor shall be construed as a reference to any one of those persons.

(5)   In subsections (2) to (4) above—

(a)   'accommodation' includes neither an area used for storage nor a staircase, passage, corridor or other means of access;

(b)   'occupier' means, in relation to a tenancy, the tenant and, in relation to a licence, the licensee; and

(c)   'purpose-built block of flats' has the same meaning as in Part III of Schedule 1 to the Housing Act 1988;

. . .

(6)   A tenancy or licence is excluded if it was granted as a temporary expedient to a person who entered the premises in question or any other premises as a trespasser (whether or not, before the beginning of that tenancy or licence, another tenancy or licence to occupy the premises or any other premises had been granted to him).

(7)   A tenancy or licence is excluded if—

(a)   it confers on the tenant or licensee the right to occupy the premises for a holiday only, or

    (b)   it is granted otherwise than for money or money's worth.
. . .

Validity of notices to quit

5.—(1)   Subject to subsection (1B) below no notice by a landlord or a tenant to quit any premises let (whether before or after the commencement of this Act) as a dwelling shall be valid unless—

    (a)   it is in writing and contains such information as may be prescribed, and

    (b)   it is given not less than four weeks before the date on which it is to take effect.

(1A)   Subject to subsection (1B) below, no notice by a licensor or a licensee to determine a periodic licence to occupy premises as a dwelling (whether the licence was granted before or after the passing of this Act) shall be valid unless—

    (a)   it is in writing and contains such information as may be prescribed, and

    (b)   it is given not less than four weeks before the date on which it is to take effect.

(1B)   Nothing in subsection (1) or subsection (1A) above applies to—

    (a)   premises let on excluded tenancy which is entered into on or after the date on which the Housing Act 1988 came into force unless it is entered into pursuant to a contract made before that date; or

    (b)   premises occupied under an excluded licence.

The 'prescribed information' referred to in s. 5 is contained in the Notices to Quit, etc. (Prescribed Information) Regulations 1988 (SI 1988 No. 2201) which provide:

1.   If the tenant or licensee does not leave the dwelling, the landlord or licensor must get an order for possession from the court before the tenant or licensee can lawfully be evicted. The landlord or licensor cannot apply for such an order before the notice to quit or notice to determine has run out.

2.   A tenant or licensee who does not know if he has any right to remain in possession after a notice to quit or a notice to determine runs out can obtain advice from a solicitor. Help with all or part of the cost of legal advice and assistance may be available under the Legal Aid Scheme. He should also be able to obtain information from a Citizens' Advice Bureau, a Housing Aid Centre or a rent officer.

Failure to provide this information renders the notice invalid.

Notices to quit, unlike 's. 8' notices under the 1988 Act have the effect of bringing the contractual tenancy to an end, continued security being dependent on the tenant satisfying the Rent Act s. 2 conditions for a statutory tenancy (see further chapter 2). Aside from that, the Protection from Eviction Act 1977 adds to the inherent common law requirement of a notice to quit to bring a contractual tenancy to an end (below) the further requirements of a *minimum* four-week notice period, and the provision of information designed to alert tenants to their legal rights. Additionally (and of crucial importance) s. 3 requires court proceedings before *any* right to possess of a landlord can be exercised. Indeed the 'unlawfulness' of any attempt to repossess other than by court proceedings (s. 3(1)) is reinforced by s. 1(2) of the Act, which makes it a criminal offence so to do unless the person concerned proves that he believed, and had reasonable cause to believe, that the occupier had ceased to reside in the premises.

Of particular interest are the amendments introduced by the Housing Act 1988 to both ss. 3 and 5 (and so only applicable to tenancies created *on* or after 15 January 1989). In simple terms, the procedural requirements of a court order and a statutory notice to quit (although presumably not the common law requirement of a notice to quit) are inapplicable to a range of *excluded* tenancies and licences. Perhaps the most significant of these are the 'holiday lets' (s. 3A(7)) and cases where landlords share accommodation with their tenants (s. 3A(2)–(5)). In the latter case the sharing even of a toilet or bathroom with the tenant (s. 3A(5)) obviates the need for a statutory notice to quit or a court order to obtain possession.

Section 98 of the Rent Act 1977 (in conjunction with Sch. 15) introduces the substantive framework for security of tenure, in terms reasonably similar to those already discussed in relation to assured tenancies (although the emphasis in the Rent Act is considerably more towards tenant protection). Structurally the grounds for possession divide into suitable alternative accommodation, other 'discretionary' grounds and the mandatory grounds (considerably more limited than in the 1988 Act).

(a)   Suitable alternative accommodation

Rent Act 1977

SCHEDULE 15
GROUNDS FOR POSSESSION OF DWELLING-HOUSES LET ON OR
SUBJECT TO PROTECTED OR STATUTORY TENANCIES
PART IV
SUITABLE ALTERNATIVE ACCOMMODATION

3.   For the purposes of section 98(1)(a) of this Act, a certificate of the housing authority for the district in which the dwelling-house in question is situated, certifying that the authority will provide suitable alternative accommodation for the tenant by a date specified in the certificate, shall be conclusive evidence that suitable alternative accommodation will be available for him by that date.

4.   Where no such certificate as is mentioned in paragraph 3 above is produced to the court, accommodation shall be deemed to be suitable for the purposes of section 98(1)(a) of this Act if it consists of either—

(a)   premises which are to be let as a separate dwelling such that they will then be let on a protected tenancy other than one under which the landlord might recover possession of the dwelling-house under one of the cases in Part II of this Schedule, or

(b)   premises to be let as a separate dwelling on terms which will, in the opinion of the court, afford to the tenant security of tenure reasonably equivalent to the security afforded by Part VII of this Act in the case of a protected tenancy of a kind mentioned in paragraph (a) above,

and in the opinion of the court, the accommodation fulfils the relevant conditions as defined in paragraph 5 below.

5.—(1)   For the purposes of paragraph 4 above, the relevant conditions are that the accommodation is reasonably suitable to the needs of the tenant and his family as regards proximity to place of work, and either—

    (a)   similar as regards rental and extent to the accommodation afforded by dwelling-houses provided in the neighbourhood by any housing authority for persons whose needs as regards extent are, in the opinion of the court, similar to those of the tenant and of his family; or

    (b)   reasonably suitable to the means of the tenant and to the needs of the tenant and his family as regards extent and character; and

that if any furniture was provided for use under the protected or statutory tenancy in question, furniture is provided for use in the accommodation which is either similar to that so provided or is reasonably suitable to the needs of the tenant and his family.

    (2)   For the purposes of sub-paragraph (1)(a) above, a certificate of a housing authority stating—

    (a)   the extent of the accommodation afforded by dwelling-houses provided by the authority to meet the needs of tenants with families of such number as may be specified in the certificate, and

    (b)   the amount of the rent charged by the authority for dwelling-houses affording accommodation of that extent,

shall be conclusive evidence of the facts so stated.

    6.   Accommodation shall not be deemed to be suitable to the needs of the tenant and his family if the result of their occupation of the accommodation would be that it would be an overcrowded dwelling-house for the purposes of Part X of the Housing Act 1985.

    7.   Any document purporting to be a certificate of a local housing authority named therein issued for the purposes of this Schedule and to be signed by the proper officer of that authority shall be received in evidence and, unless the contrary is shown, shall be deemed to be such a certificate without further proof.

    . . .

As noted above, the Housing Act 1988 (with necessary amendments) adopts much of the structure of this in Pt III of Sch. 2, and case law under the Rent Act will remain relevant for Housing Act purposes. There is indeed a considerable body of case law on Sch. 15, Pt IV and some of the key decisions are reproduced below.

Perhaps the two most important points are, first, that the question is whether the premises offered are a *suitable alternative* not (*per se*) whether they are as good as the existing premises and, secondly, that there is considerable uncertainty about the precise meaning of the notion of 'character' (para. 5(1)(b) above).

Hill v *Rochard*
[1983] 1 WLR 478

An elderly married couple held a statutory tenancy of a period country house in which they had resided for many years. The premises contained many spacious rooms, a staff flat, outbuildings, a stable, and one and a half acres of land, including a paddock, where the tenants kept a pony. The landlords wished to obtain possession of the house and offered the tenants a modern, detached, four-bedroomed house as alternative accommodation. The house was situated in a cul-de-sac on a housing estate in a nearby country village. The garden covered one eighth of an acre and there was no stable or paddock. The tenants refused the offer and the landlords sought an order for possession in the county court on the ground that the modern house was reasonably suitable to the needs of the tenant as regards extent and character within the meaning of Sch. 15, Pt IV, para. 5(1)(b) to the Rent Act 1977 and constituted suitable alternative accommodation for the purposes of s. 98(1) of the Act. The judge found that the tenants were not ordinary tenants and for the past 15 years had not been ordinarily housed. Adopting the test whether the accommodation which was offered met the standard of the needs of an ordinary and reasonable tenant, she found that the alternative accommodation satisfied that test as regards extent and character and it would permit the tenants to live reasonably comfortably in the style of life which they liked to lead, in a reasonably similar way to that permitted by their present accommodation. She held that suitable alternative accommodation was available to the tenants, that it was reasonable to make an order for possession and, accordingly, granted the landlords an order for possession.

The tenants' appeal was dismissed by the Court of Appeal.

DUNN LJ: . . . The judge, in a careful judgment, dealt at length with these various points and made findings of fact upon them. She concluded that the tenants did not wish to move from The Grange and would use any permissible reason to prevent this coming about. These findings of fact cannot be disturbed; but complaint is made of her direction as the law. She said:

> The standard I have to adopt is that of an ordinary tenant and not one which will gratify to the full 'all the fads and fancies and preferences of the tenant'. The Rochards are not ordinary tenants and for the past 15 years they have not been ordinarily housed. They are both now in their 60s and resist a change. The accommodation offered is modern, easy to run, and by ordinary standards generous accommodation. The accommodation at Chestermaster Close does not compare exactly with that at The Grange but it does not have to. The test is does it meet the standard of the needs of an ordinary and reasonable tenant? I am satisfied that it does both as to extent and as to character.

It is said by Mr Gordon that that passage constituted a misdirection. The test, he said, is not whether the alternative accommodation offered meets the standard of needs of an ordinary and reasonable tenant: the test is whether the accommodation meets the standard of needs of these particular tenants. In considering that question regard may be had to the lifestyle of the tenants in their present accommodation, and if that lifestyle cannot be continued in the alternative accommodation offered, then that alternative accommodation is not suitable to the needs of the tenant.

In support of that submission Mr Gordon relied on two decisions of this court, the first *MacDonnell* v *Daly* [1969] 1 WLR 1482. That was a case in which the alternative accommodation offered was two of three rooms which had previously been occupied by the tenant. The judge dismissed the landlord's claim, holding that the two rooms were not suitable alternative accommodation. This court upheld the judge's finding, but Mr Gordon relies, in particular, on certain obiter dicta of Edmund Davies LJ in relation to *Briddon* v *George* [1946] 1 All ER 609, which was a case where the landlord was offering the tenant alternative accommodation which did not include a garage, whereas the premises occupied by the tenant did include a garage. Edmund Davies LJ said, at p. 1487:

> This court there held that the dwelling-house itself was the unit which fell to be considered throughout the Rent Restriction Acts, that these Acts were concerned with the provision only of a suitable habitation, and that the absence of a garage could not, therefore, be taken into consideration in deciding the suitability of the alternative accommodation offered. I venture respectfully to doubt whether the same decision would be arrived at by this court under the circumstances prevailing, not in 1946, but in 1969. One thinks of the common case of the man who went into the premises originally because they had a garage, without which they would be wholly unsuitable to him. Is it to be said in these days that to offer him premises which lack that which was an essential requirement for him when he initially went into possession and so remains, constitutes the provision of suitable alternative accommodation? Circumstances have changed so much that considerable doubts arise in my mind whether such question would be answered today as it was 23 years ago.

Mr Gordon submits that that case indicates that, in considering the suitability of needs, the court is not simply confined to the provision of suitable habitation but can also have regard to other amenities enjoyed by the tenant in his present accommodation.

He also referred us to *Redspring Ltd v Francis* [1973] 1 WLR 134, which he said established the same point. In that case the tenant, who occupied a flat in a quiet residential road, was offered alternative accommodation in a flat which, unlike the first flat, had no garden and was in a busy traffic thoroughfare with a fried fish shop next door. The county court judge made the order for possession and this court allowed the appeal, holding that what a tenant needed was somewhere where he could live in reasonably comfortable conditions suitable to the style of life which he led. Mr Gordon relied particularly on a passage in the judgment of Buckley LJ when, after referring to a concession which had been made by counsel for the landlord, he said, at p. 138:

> That concession was, in my judgment, properly made, for if a tenant who occupies accommodation in a residential area is offered other accommodation which may be physically as good as or better than the accommodation which he is required to vacate but is situated in an area which is offensive as the result of some industrial activity in the neighbourhood, which perhaps creates offensive smells or noises, or which is extremely noisy as a result of a great deal of traffic passing by, or in some other respect is clearly much less well endowed with amenities than the accommodation which the tenant is required to vacate, then it seems to me that it would be most unreal to say that the alternative accommodation is such as to satisfy the needs of the tenant with regard to its character. What he needs is somewhere where he can live in reasonably comfortable conditions suitable to the style of life which he leads, and environmental matters must inevitably affect the suitability of offered accommodation to provide him with the sort of conditions in which it is reasonable that he should live.

Sachs LJ said, at p. 140:

> In each case it is a question of fact having regard to the needs of the tenant in the circumstances as a whole. The view which I have just expressed coincides with the

tenor of those sparsely reported decisions of the court (for example, in the 'Estates Gazette') to which reference has already been made. Any other view of the meaning of the relevant words would, indeed, produce astonishing results, some of which were canvassed in the course of argument. It would result in accommodation on the third floor of premises facing on to the Edgware Road being necessarily held to be equivalent in character to a quiet third floor flat in nearby Montague Square. Another example was put in argument of a cottage in a quiet country lane which has one character and that of a cottage of identical construction which finds itself implanted in or entangled with a new motorway.

Mr Gordon submitted that those two cases supported his proposition to which I have referred, and he also drew attention to the fact that *Christie v Macfarlane*, 1930 SLT (Sh Ct) 5 had been cited in argument in *Redspring Ltd v Francis* [1973] 1 WLR 134. He pointed out that *Christie v Macfarlane* had been cited to the judge in this case and contained in it a reference to the ordinary tenant, and included the citation from *Clark v Smith* (unreported), 16 July 1920:

The alternative accommodation need not be a dwelling-house in which all the fads and fancies and preferences of the tenant shall be gratified to the full.

This citation, he said, misled the judge.

He submitted that *MacDonnell v Daly* [1969] 1 WLR 1482 and *Redspring Ltd v Francis* [1973] 1 WLR 134 show that the court is not concerned, as might appear from *Christie v Macfarlane*, 1930 SLT (Sh Ct) 5, with the needs of the ordinary tenant, but is concerned with the needs of the tenant in question, and those needs include the ability of the particular tenant, in his new accommodation, to follow the lifestyle which he had enjoyed in the old accommodation.

For myself I prefer to go first to the relevant statutory provisions before considering how they have been construed. Section 98 of the Rent Act 1977 provides:

'(1) Subject to this Part of this Act, a court shall not make an order for possession of a dwelling-house which is for the time being let on a protected tenancy or subject to a statutory tenancy unless the court considers it reasonable to make such an order and either' – and this is the material provision – '(a) the court is satisfied that suitable alternative accommodation is available for the tenant or will be available for him when the order in question takes effect . . . (4) Part IV of Schedule 15 shall have effect for determining whether, for the purposes of subsection (1)(a) above, suitable alternative accommodation is or will be available for a tenant.'

. . .

It has not been seriously suggested, in this appeal, that 2, Chestermaster Close is not suitable as regards extent. A four-bedroomed house with two living rooms is perfectly extensive enough for an elderly couple living alone, as these tenants are.

The argument in this court has revolved around the word 'character.' The sub-paragraph does not provide, and it is not necessary, that the character of the alternative accommodation should be similar to that of the existing premises. Indeed, there are, in this case, certain obvious differences between the character of The Grange and the character of 2, Chestermaster Close. 2, Chestermaster Close is a modern house and not a period house. It stands in a housing estate and does not stand alone. But the question is whether 2, Chestermaster Close is reasonably suitable to the tenants' housing needs as regards its character. In considering those needs the cases to which I have referred show that it is permissible for the court to look at the environment to which the tenants have become accustomed in their present accommodation, and to see how far the new environment differs from that. The new house is on the outskirts of a village, and the tenants will, in ordinary parlance, still be living in the country. It is not as if they have been offered accommodation on a housing estate in a town. In so far as their style of life is relevant they will still be able to enjoy the amenities of country life. Indeed, looked at from the point of view of reasonable suitability, as this court is required to do by the paragraph, many people would say that a modern house in a country village is more suitable to the needs of people of the ages of these tenants than a large isolated country house such as The Grange.

In my view the judge was right to say that these tenants were not ordinary tenants. By that I take her to mean that, accommodation aside, the present tenancy enables them to enjoy the use of certain amenities, including the paddock and outbuildings, so that they could keep their animals. Even on a liberal construction of the statutory provisions I do not think that the Rent Acts were intended to protect incidental advantages of that kind. The Rent Acts are concerned with the provision of housing and accommodation. The judge said:

> I accept Lower Almondsbury is not precisely similar to The Street, but it is a country village, many would say a pleasant country area which in my judgment will permit the Rochards to live reasonably comfortably in the lifestyle they like to lead. Not precisely in the way they can at The Grange but in a reasonably similar way. Accordingly I find the plaintiffs have satisfied me that suitable alternative accommodation is available to the Rochards.

That crucial finding followed immediately after a citation by the judge from *Redspring Ltd v Francis* [1973] 1 WLR 134 when she cited Buckley LJ's observations about the tenant needing somewhere where he can live in conditions suitable to the style of life which he leads. The judge must have had those observations of Buckley LJ in mind when she made her finding, which is directed not to the ordinary tenant but to these particular tenants. I find no fault in that finding. Nor can this court interfere with the judge's finding that it was reasonable to make an order. That was essentially a matter for the judge. She balanced the detriments, if I may so describe them, to the landlords on the one side if no order was made, against the position of the tenants if an order was made, and she came down plainly in favour of the landlords.

This court cannot interfere with a determination of that kind. I would accordingly dismiss this appeal.

A particularly controversial 'line' on the 'character' question was taken in the later case of *Siddiqui v Rashid*:

Siddiqui v Rashid
[1980] 1 WLR 1018

The tenant, a Muslim, occupied a room in a house in London under a protected tenancy and worked in Luton. The landlords of the house were the trustees of an Islamic mission. They wished to sell the house with vacant possession in order to buy a larger property for their charitable work, and accordingly offered the tenant alternative accommodation in

Luton which was reasonably suitable to the needs of the tenant as regards rental and extent and to his means and which was closer to his work. The tenant refused to move and the landlords brought proceedings in the county court for possession. The county court judge granted a possession order on the ground that the Luton premises constituted 'suitable alternative accommodation' for the purposes of s. 98(1)(a) of the Rent Act 1977 since it fulfilled the conditions as to suitability set out in para. 5 of Sch. 15 to that Act. The tenant appealed, contending that the alternative accommodation was not suitable to his needs as regards 'character' within para. 5(1)(b) because it would take him away from his friends and his local mosque and cultural centre in London.

In dismissing the tenant's appeal, the Court of Appeal held that in determining for the purposes of para. 5(1)(b) of Sch. 15 to the 1977 Act whether alternative accommodation offered to a tenant was suitable to his needs as regards 'character', environmental or peripheral matters could be taken into account only in so far as they related to the character of the property itself, since the term 'character' did not extend to such matters as the society of friends or cultural interests. On that basis, the alternative accommodation offered was suitable to the tenant's needs, and, having regard to the necessity for the landlords to sell the house for their charitable work, it satisfied the statutory requirements.

STEPHENSON LJ: . . . No question arises as to this room in Luton being reasonably suitable to the needs of the tenant as regards proximity to place of work. Equally no dispute arises as to the suitability of this room as regards rental and extent; and no question arises as to its reasonable suitability to the defendant's means. But what is in dispute is whether this room would be reasonably suitable to the needs of the defendant and his family as regards character. The judge, as I said, made an order for possession and was satisfied that it was reasonably suitable accommodation as regards character to the needs of the tenant, and he has found that it was reasonable for him to make the order.

Mr Morgan, in his interesting argument before us, has submitted that the judge was wrong on the first point, but I think he would agree that he is not able any longer to maintain that if he was right on the first point, he was wrong on the second point, or so plainly wrong, at any rate, that this court could interfere and substitute its view of what was reasonable for the judge's view.

The judge considered suitability in this way:

The [defendant] did not suggest that the alternative premises were not suitable as regards extent, but has endeavoured to persuade me that 'character' must be given a wide interpretation and that if you move a person from the place where he carries out his leisure activities and where his friends are that can be brought under the heading of character. I totally disagree. In *Redspring* v *Francis* [1973] 1 WLR 134 character was clearly defined in the headnote by reference to the premises being 'somewhere where the [tenant] could live in reasonably comfortable conditions suitable to the style of life which he led' . . . This is reflected in the judgment of Buckley LJ (at p. 138) where he went on to say that 'environmental matters must inevitably affect the suitability of offered accommodation to provide him with the sort of conditions in which it is reasonable that he should live.' . . . Having viewed

128 Oak Road, I am perfectly satisfied that the tenant could lead a perfectly good life in accordance with his present style. I am totally unable to accept the submission that the upsetting effect that the move would have and that although he would be near his work, he would be further from the mosque he so often attends and where his friends are, can be included in 'character'. I cannot be moved. I must follow the words of the statute. The character of the property refers to the property itself. I have had the advantage of seeing both properties and have made notes. (Those notes are before us) In my view, the alternative premises at Oak Road are preferable; furthermore, another room which has not been let would be available for the defendant if he wished it. Furthermore, he will have exclusive use of the kitchen, the sink and a very nice modern bathroom.' (He had had to share in the London premises.)

He then went on to consider 'reasonableness', and said:

That is more arguable, but one must consider the plaintiffs' side. They are trying to help the members of the Muslim community; they are trying to sell 148 Liverpool Road to pay back a loan to buy a larger property in the Euston area. It is obvious that they will get more for the property with vacant possession than with a tenant. I cannot accept the argument that anyone would be prepared to offer as much if the defendant were there. It is perfectly reasonable for the landlords to seek an order for possession so that they can sell the property at the best price available. The plaintiffs have amply proved their case and I make an order for possession in 28 days.

We are bound by authority not to give a very narrow construction to the word 'character' in para. 5(1)(b) of Sch. 15 to the 1977 Act. The wording of the relevant statutory provisions which this court had to consider in *Redspring* v *Francis* [1973] 1 WLR 134 was the same, and in that case this court rejected the argument that the character to which the court must have regard did not include what the county court judge in that case had called 'environmental aspects or peripheral amenities.' That was a case which in some respects resembled this. Buckley LJ, in the leading judgment, said at p. 137:

So we have to consider whether in the present case the accommodation offered at 108 Fleet Road is reasonably suitable to the needs of the tenant as regards extent and character. No point arises in this case in relation to proximity to the place of work or the means of the tenant. We are concerned only with the question whether the accommodation is reasonably suitable to her needs as regards extent and character. Extent, as I have already stated, is conceded. So the question is whether the accommodation is reasonably suited to her needs in respect of its character.

That was exactly the same position as in this case. There the judge had made an order for possession, because he took the view that equally good accommodation next to a smelly fish and chip shop and a good deal of motor traffic and noise was suitable alternative accommodation to similar premises in a quiet street not far off which Mr Francis had been occupying for 30 years. He was able to take that view because of the narrow view which he took on the meaning of the word character. In his judgment, quoted by Buckley LJ at p. 137 he had said:

The 'needs' contemplated by the paragraph 3(1)(b) of Part IV of Sch. 3 to the Rent Act 1968, cited in argument, are not the same as tastes and inclinations: they are needs of an urgent, compelling nature – space, transport, a bathroom etc. Peripheral amenities are of a different category; by this I am not saying that Mr Francis's objections are fanciful but I find that her needs are met, apart from the environmental aspect. One must look at the whole of the picture, and I have not forgotten the hospital, the fish and chip shop, the public house and the cinema.

This court held that in spite of that last sentence the judge really had forgotten, or, at any rate, put out of the picture, the hospital, the fish and chip shop, the public house and the cinema and the smells and the noises that all that the proximity of a busy road provide; and was wrong in excluding from his consideration the question whether the accommodation offered was reasonably suited to Mr Francis's needs in respect of its character. Buckley LJ lists 'environmental matters' at p. 139:

. . . environmental matters such as the smell from the fish and chip shop, the noise from the public house, noise perhaps from vehicles going to and from the hospital and matters of that kind. In so doing, with respect to the judge I think he misdirected himself. Those, I think, are all matters properly to be taken into consideration in connection with the making of such an order as was sought in this case.

Orr LJ agreed, and Sachs LJ also agreed, and added some observations to the effect that for there to be a difference in character that must of course normally relate to a difference in kind rather than a difference of lesser degree; and in that case he held that there was a difference in kind between the character of the two premises.

As was pointed out in the course of the argument, the statutory provisions say nothing of difference in character, but Mr Morgan has submitted that it was only if there could be shown to be some difference in character between the two premises that this question of unsuitability of alternative accommodation to the needs of the tenant as regards character could arise. What he submits and he did not appear in the county court, but it was submitted in the county court is that the court must look at environmental aspects, and that means the respective locations of the two premises, and see whether the tenant's needs are satisfied as regards the new location. Those needs are not merely physical needs, it was submitted, but such needs as were given in evidence here; need for a devout Muslim to keep in touch with his local mosque and cultural centre (in this case the mosque and cultural centre in Regent's Park) and need to enjoy the company of friends whom he had made in the course of his many years' residence in London. The judge was not wholly satisfied, according to a note which he made in the course of his notes of the evidence, with the defendant's evidence as to his attendances and need to attend at the Regent's Park mosque, but he ruled that the need of the defendant's to visit that mosque and the cultural centre there, and to keep in touch with his London friends, did not relate to the character of the property, as environmental aspects had to relate if they were to be a relevant consideration to the question of the suitability of the alternative accommodation.

The 1977 Act does not say that the alternative accommodation must be reasonably suitable to the needs of the tenant as regards location or, of course, as regards environment, and for my part I would regard the judge as right in this case in confining 'character' to the 'character of the property'. I find nothing in the judgment of this court in *Redspring v Francis* [1973] 1 WLR 134 to indicate that that is wrong, or to extend the meaning of 'character' beyond character of the property. The character of the property was directly affected by the environmental matters which were the subject of Mr Francis's objection to her move. I have read them from Buckley LJ's judgment; noise and smell were matters which would directly affect the tenant in the enjoyment of her property, so they could well be said to relate to the character of the property. I cannot think that Parliament intended to include such matters as the society of friends, or cultural interests, in using the language that it did in the particular word 'character'. Nor can I accept that Buckley LJ had any such considerations in mind when he referred, in the passages which he quoted from his judgment [1973] 1 WLR 134, 138, to the needs of the tenant to have 'somewhere where [the tenant] could live in reasonably comfortable conditions suitable to the style of life which he leads . . .', and referred to the accommodation providing him with the sort of conditions in which it is reasonable that he should live. To extend the character of the property to cover the two matters on which the defendant relies, namely his friends in London and his mosque and cultural centre would, in my judgment, be unwarranted. The defendant said he did not want to leave London or to live in Luton, although he worked there, but it is clear that his preference for London and objection to Luton was based on those two considerations.

In my judgment it would be impossible to say that the room in Luton was not one in which he could live in reasonably comfortable conditions suitable to the style of life which he was leading in London, or that it did not provide him with the sort of conditions in which it was reasonable that he should live.

He implied that his workmates in Luton were not as much friends of his as his friends in London, but he agreed that his workmates were friends. However that may be, I do not think that the court is required to go into such questions in considering suitability. I would therefore hold that the judge was right in the conclusion which he reached as to the reasonable suitability of the alternative accommodation in Luton which the landlords offered to the tenant.

That would not conclude the matter if Mr Morgan had felt able to challenge the judge's view of what was reasonable. The language of the judge, which I have read, when he went on to consider 'reasonableness' may not be the language in which he would have put his consideration of the matter in a reserved judgment; but I am not satisfied that he was indicating that the leisure activities and the spiritual needs of this tenant, or any tenant, would be irrelevant to the question of overall reasonableness. What he was clearly deciding was that it was perfectly reasonable for the plaintiffs to seek an order for possession and it was reasonable for him to grant it. I need not detail the evidence that was given as to the work of the mission, of the trustees who were seeking possession; but the judge was quite satisfied that they needed to sell these premises to carry on their charitable work, that they had had to borrow money to acquire the larger property which they needed to carry on that work, and that they could repay the loan if they could sell the property in which the tenant was living with vacant possession.

For these reasons, in my judgment, the judge came to the right conclusion and I would dismiss the appeal.

Notes

1. In *Macdonnell* v *Daley* [1969] 1 WLR 1482, it was held that the offer (by a landlord) of part of the tenant's existing accommodation was not *on the facts* 'suitable alternative accommodation', but that does not rule out the possibility of such an offer being 'suitable' on other facts, particularly where the extra rooms are not used or are used mostly for storage (see *Thompson* v *Rolls* [1926] 2 KB 426 and *Parmee* v *Mitchell* [1950] 2 KB 199).

2. Even if 'suitable' accommodation is offered, it must still be seen as 'reasonable' by the court to order possession (in this case – inevitably –

outright possession): s. 98(1). The general question of 'reasonableness' and discretionary grounds for possession has already been addressed in relation to *Cumming* v *Danson* and is equally applicable to the other Rent Act discretionary grounds (Rent Act 1977, Sch. 15, Pt I). However, the issue is particularly acute in 'suitable alternative accommodation' cases where no issue of tenant 'default' arises, and where the ground exists largely to cater for landlords' convenience. The issues are demonstrated well in the case of *Battlespring* v *Gates*.

Battlespring v *Gates*
(1983) 11 HLR 6

The tenant (Gates) had resided in an unmodernised maisonette for 35 years. She had brought her family up there, and lived there with her husband, who had died. There was only one other flat in the same house, which was empty. The landlords had recently purchased the property, with the intention of renovating the premises for reselling with vacant possession. They offered the tenant accommodation at a pleasanter end of the same road, in a modernised flat at a lower rent.

The tenant refused to move, and the county court declined to make an order for possession, on the grounds that it would not be reasonable to do so, taking into account both the time she had lived there and the fact that the landlords had only bought the property one year beforehand, with the intention of obtaining vacant possession and reselling. The landlords appealed, on the principal grounds that the court should not have taken their intentions, and the recent character of their purchase, into account, or placed so much weight on the tenant's objections to moving.

The Court of Appeal dismissed the appeal holding that there was no basis for saying that the lower court had erred. Both types of questions were proper to be taken into account.

WATKINS LJ: . . . The learned and experienced county court judge in the present case seems to me to have had that guidance well in mind in coming to the conclusion which he did. He expressed his reasons for arriving at his decision finally in this lucid and brief way:

> I have decided not to make the order and I base my decision on the fact that here is a tenant who has occupied the accommodation for a very long time and a landlord who has only bought the property less than one year ago, and bought it, on the evidence, with the intention of obtaining vacant possession and re-selling it. Subject to any authorities which might have been pointed out to me, I feel that that would be an unreasonable order to make.

He had earlier referred to the personal situation and feelings of the defendant, for whom he obviously felt a great deal of sympathy.

I ask myself whether it is possible to say that the judge misdirected himself in the exercise of his discretion. In reviewing the exercise of a judge's discretion in this context, it is well to bear in mind what was said by Singleton LJ in the *Cresswell* case [*Cresswell* v *Hodgson* [1951] 2 QB 92] at p. 96.

When there has been an appeal to this court on that question of reasonableness it has to be said time and time again that it is really a question of fact, and that unless the appellant can show that the judge has misdirected himself in some measure, this court cannot interfere, for the decision on that question is for the county court judge. It is for him to consider whether he thinks it reasonable to make an order.

Mr Acton-Davies submits that the judge in this case did not exercise his discretion properly; in the first place he took into account the fact that the plaintiffs were new landlords, whose only object was to make a quick profit upon the property in which the defendant now lives. That, he says, was wholly irrelevant and should not have been allowed to have influenced the judge's mind at all. If allowed to influence it, it was a factor to be used in favour of the plaintiffs, rather than against them.

Secondly, he contends that this really was a decision founded almost exclusively upon a sympathetic consideration of the defendant's objection to moving from a place which she had occupied for a very long time – the prospect of going to another and superior place notwithstanding.

Lastly he maintained that to make reference, as the judge did, to the fact that this was a recent acquisition by the plaintiffs of the relevant property, was yet another instance of his taking into account factors which should not have been allowed to influence him.

I regard the decision of the judge as the product of the exercise of a discretion which I cannot possibly fault. What in fact he did was, on the one hand, to consider the position of the plaintiffs, and properly to find that they were landlords who were simply interested in the property for the purpose of gain. There is, as he said, nothing wrong in that motive whatsoever, but that was precisely their position. It was quite unlike the situation of other landlords who seek orders for possession on the basis that they have either nowhere to live, or that the dwelling which they have at the moment is over-crowded.

Balanced against that was the personal position of this elderly defendant, which was among other things that she had occupied these premises for thirty-five years. It seems always to have been her home – all her memories are still there. I do not consider that a factor of that kind should not be allowed to influence the judge in coming to a conclusion as to whether or no it would be reasonable to turn her out – even though alternative, and suitable alternative accommodation (as he found) was available to her.

For these reasons I would dismiss this appeal.

(b)   Grounds for possession

Many of the Rent Act grounds for possession (or 'cases' as they are referred to in the legislation) mirror those in the Housing Act 1988, and they will not be reproduced in full here. Again, the grounds divide into discretionary ones and mandatory ones, with the same implications already discussed. However, the different emphasis in the Rent Act 1977 is well demonstrated by the fact that the mandatory grounds *follow* the discretionary ones and are much more limited in scope than under the Housing Act 1988. In particular, there is no equivalent to Ground 8 (two months' rent arrears) or Ground 6 (landlord redevelopment 'needs') in the Rent Act 1977. If a detailed examination of the Rent Act grounds is required, Sch. 15 to the 1977 Act should be consulted; attention is given here only to those Rent Act grounds which differ significantly from their Housing Act counterparts.

Case 2: nuisance or immoral or illegal purpose

Rent Act 1977

SCHEDULE 15
GROUNDS FOR POSSESSION OF DWELLING-HOUSES
LET ON OR SUBJECT TO PROTECTED OR STATUTORY TENANCIES
PART I
CASES IN WHICH COURT MAY ORDER POSSESSION
Case 2

Where the tenant or any person residing or lodging with him or any sub-tenant of his has been guilty of conduct which is a nuisance or annoyance to adjoining occupiers, or has been convicted of using the dwelling-house or allowing the dwelling-house to be used for immoral or illegal purposes.

This discretionary ground is considerably narrower in scope than the newly amended Ground 14 in the Housing Act 1988. The nuisance 'limb' extends only to 'adjoining occupiers' rather than to persons generally affected in the 'locality'. The illegality 'limb' does not extend to arrestable offences committed *in* the locality, nor even to arrestable offences *per se*, but only the use of the property for illegal purposes.

Indeed, the limitation of those relevantly affected by the nuisance to 'adjoining occupiers' might, on one construction, exclude even near neighbours whose property did not physically 'abut' or attach to the tenants'. Such a construction would severely limit the influence of the ground, and could lead to illogical results, such as that a person (say) 'next door but one' who was routinely 'abused' by the tenant could not in this context make his complaints felt. A wider interpretation of the phrase was, however, given in the Court of Appeal case of *Cobstone Investments Ltd v Maxim* the facts of which appear in the following extract from the judgment of Dunn LJ, at p. 607:

Cobstone Investments Ltd v Maxim
[1984] 3 WLR 606

DUNN LJ: This is an appeal from the order of Mr Seddon Cripps sitting as an assistant recorder in the West London County Court on 1 February 1984, when he ordered that the plaintiffs should recover against the defendant possession of flat 2, 12 Queen's Gate, London SW7. He postponed the operation of the order for ten weeks, which expires today.

The plaintiffs Cobstone Investments Ltd, are the owners of the whole of the premises (no. 12) and they also own the next door premises (no. 11). They bought those premises from Crofton Hotel Ltd, which occupies no. 13, in 1980. The defendant was a sitting tenant of flat 2. She had occupied that flat certainly from 1976 and before that she had occupied a flat in no. 11.

The defendant, under the terms of her lease with the Crofton Hotel, was entitled to central heating in the flat and that central heating ceased to be available at the end of 1981. The judge found that down to late 1981 when the landlords had completed the acquisition of no. 11 there was no difficulty between them and the defendant. The defendant's tenancy had been duly determined by notice to quit, so that she was holding as a statutory tenant.

The plaintiffs sought possession of the flat under Cases 1 and 2 of Sch. 15 to the Rent Act 1977. So far as Case 1 was concerned, although there had been substantial arrears of rent at the date of issue of the proceedings, the arrears had been paid off and by the end of the hearing the defendant had paid all the arrears of rent which were due. But the assistant recorder made an order under Case 2 on the ground that the defendant had been guilty of conduct which was a nuisance or annoyance to adjoining occupiers.

The allegations of annoyance extended over a period from August 1982 to May 1983. The conduct complained of was essentially verbal abuse and the use of obscene language to, effectively, the landlord (although the company, in law, owned the premises; the company was itself owned by Dr Al Shalabi) and there were also allegations of a similar nature in respect of three other tenants of no. 12, Mr Hosford, Mr Burgess and Miss Barton. The case lasted ten working days in the county court. The assistant recorder reserved his judgment. He gave a full judgment in which he reviewed the whole of the voluminous evidence which had been before him and he found eleven incidents proved, five relating to Dr Al Shalabi, four to the other tenants of no. 12, one related to a maintenance man whose name was John, and the final incident involved the attachment to the door of the defendant's flat of an abusive notice, which it was accepted had been written by the defendant but actually attached to the door by somebody else.

The occupancy of the various flats at nos 11 and 12 is of some importance. Each house consists of a basement, a ground floor and three upper storeys. In no. 11 Dr Al Shalabi uses the ground floor as an office. Although he does not live there, it was accepted that he was in occupation of that flat. He was the only person from no. 11 who made complaint. As far as no. 12 was concerned, there were no complaints from the occupier of the basement. The defendant herself occupied flat 2 on the ground floor. The first floor flat was occupied by some employees from the Iraqi Embassy. There was no complaint from them. The second floor was occupied by Mr Burgess and Miss Barton, who were complaining: and the third and top floor by Mr Hosford, who was also complaining.

Mr Pearson for the defendant, realistically made no attack on the judge's findings of fact; nor on his finding that the tenant had been guilty of conduct which constituted an annoyance. His primary ground of appeal was that the three tenants of no. 12 who did complain were not adjoining occupiers within the meaning of case 2. He submitted that the word 'adjoining' in Case 2 of Sch. 15 to the 1977 Act means that the premises must be contiguous in the sense of physically joining, or being coterminous with the defendant of whose conduct complaint is being made. Mr Pearson submitted that, in the context, the word 'adjoining' does not mean 'neighbouring'.

In support of that basic submission Mr Pearson referred us first of all to the Increase of Rent and Mortgage Interest (War Restrictions) Act 1915, which was the first of the Rent Acts and the relevant provision is in s. 1(3) where a ground for ordering possession is if the tenant has been guilty of conduct which is a nuisance or annoyance to adjoining or neighbouring occupiers. He pointed out that the word 'neighbouring' had been deleted from the relevant statutory provision and does not appear in any subsequent Act or in the Rent Act 1977, s. 5(1)(b), of the Increase of Rent and Mortgage Interest (Restrictions) Act 1920 and so, he submits, that is an indication that Parliament intended to limit the category of persons who are entitled to complain of nuisance and on whose complaints the court can order possession.

As far as the researches of counsel have been able to ascertain, there are only two decisions of the courts which are directly in point on the construction of the word 'adjoining' in the section, and they are conflicting decisions of two very experienced county court judges. The first is *Trustees of Marquess of Northampton Estate* v *Bond* [1950] EGD 122, a decision of his Honour Judge Blagden when he adopted the restrictive meaning of the word, contended for by Mr Pearson, and held that the tenants of a second-floor flat were not adjoining occupiers to the tenant of the ground-floor flat, whose conduct was relied on as constituting a nuisance, and accordingly he dismissed the claim for possession founded on complaints by the tenants.

The case the other way is *Metropolitan Railway Land Corporation* v *Burfiti* [1960] CLY 2749, a decision of his Honour Judge Harold Brown, in which the landlord claimed possession of two rooms on the ground—

> that the defendant . . . was a nuisance and annoyance to adjoining occupiers. The defendant occupied rooms on the first floor of the house. Evidence of annoyance to themselves was given by the occupiers of rooms above those of the defendant and on the second floor, and also by the occupier of rooms on the first floor, next to those of the defendant.

The report is not clear. It would appear from the short extract which I have just read that some of the premises may have been physically touching those of the defendant but I do not think that can have been the position because the judge made an order for possession. The report continues:

> *held* (1) that the meaning of 'adjoining' . . . has not been finally adjudicated and that a rather narrow construction had been placed on it; (2) that the statement in *Megarry's Rent Acts* 8th ed. (1955), p. 251 was the correct view, namely that the meaning 'contiguous' was too strict; and (3) that where there was a building in small flats where bathrooms and lavatories had to be shared it was of the utmost importance that the tenants should live in harmony and that the landlord ought to have a right to claim possession even though the persons annoyed occupied rooms not physically adjoining those of the defendant.

Mr Pearson then went on to cite a number of 19th century and early 20th century decisions based on restrictive covenants, where the covenants had sought to restrain occupiers of adjoining premises from certain activities. In those cases the word had been strictly construed as meaning absolutely contiguous, without anything in between, or in physical contact with one another, or touching one another in some part. The word had only been given a wider meaning where that could be deduced from the context of the covenant itself. However, in *Norton* v *Charles Deane Productions Ltd* (1969) 214 EG 559, Swanwick J put a wider construction on a restrictive covenant in the following terms:

> that the lessee should not do or permit to be done on the demised premises or any part thereof anything which might be, or grow to be, a source of nuisance, damage, inconvenience or annoyance to the lessors, or the owners or occupiers of any adjoining premises.

The judge held that the covenant, as he put it, 'was not really intended to have anything to do with physical contact between the houses, but was intended to protect neighbouring properties'. The complainants in that case were occupiers of premises which were opposite the premises in question and three doors away from it.

Mr Pearson submitted that, in the context of the Rent Acts, which protect the right of occupation of tenants, the word 'adjoining' should be given a narrow or restricted meaning and that, if that meaning was accepted, then none of the three tenants of no. 12 were adjoining occupiers because their premises did not physically touch flat 2. He conceded that, as there was a party wall between the tenant's flat and the flat occupied by Dr Al Shalabi at no. 11, Dr Al Shalabi was an adjoining occupier and conduct relating to him could be taken into account; but he submitted that, if the complaints of the three tenants of no. 12 were disregarded and only the complaints of Dr Al Shalabi were considered, then it was not reasonable for the judge to have made an order. It was said that the trouble started between the tenant and Dr Al Shalabi in December 1981 when the central heating was cut off, but until then there had been no difficulties between them.

I should say, in fairness to all the parties, that the absence of central heating was only one of a number of complaints which the defendant made to Dr Al Shalabi after he took over the premises, all of which the judge rejected except the complaint about central heating. It is unclear why the central heating was turned off. The fact is that the boiler from which the heating for no. 12 came was physically in no. 13, which of course remained in the ownership of the Crofton Hotel, and there is no finding in the judgment that Mr Al Shalabi deliberately cut the central heating off, although it may be that the absence of central heating was something which the tenant especially in the winter found annoying and unpleasant.

Mr West for the plaintiffs submitted that the word 'adjoining' has more than one meaning: it is not confined to physically touching but it can also include 'neighbouring'. He submitted that in this case there was a close relationship between all the tenants in no. 12. They all occupy the same building; they all share the same entrance; they all share the same common doorway; and the flat of each of them was connected by the stairs and hallway. He submitted that, in those circumstances, a wider meaning should be given to the word 'adjoining' than the narrow meaning sought to be put by Mr Pearson. He pointed out, first of all, some of the anomalies which would arise in practice if the narrow meaning was given. To take this very case, it was accepted that Dr Al Shalabi's flat at no. 11 adjoined the tenant's flat at no. 12, but it might be that conduct by the tenant in her flat would be far more annoying to other occupiers of the same building than it would be to somebody like Dr Al Shalabi who lived next door, separated by a thick and possibly soundproof party wall and with a separate entrance. He also pointed out that, if Mr Pearson's meaning was right, it would mean that you could have two tenants of flats on the same floor separated by a narrow passage or hallway and, because the flats were not touching one another the landlord could not take proceedings for possession because one of those tenants was causing annoyance to the other. He also pointed out that all the first five cases in Sch. 15 to the Rent Act 1977, which set out the grounds on which a landlord is entitled to a possession from a statutory tenant, involve cases where the landlord's interest is being adversely affected, and he submitted that the purpose of Sch. 15 was to protect the landlord's interest, and that a narrow interpretation of the word 'adjoining' would be wholly inconsistent with that. He added that, if the landlord was not able to take proceedings for possession on the ground of nuisance on the complaints of other occupiers of a building which was divided into flats, his interest might be seriously affected because he would be unable to let the other flats in the building at reasonable rents.

He drew our attention to *Lightbound v Higher Bebington Local Board* (1885) 16 QBD 577 and in particular the judgment of Bowen LJ, where the court was concerned to define the meaning of premises 'fronting, adjoining or abutting' on the street within the meaning of section 150 of the Public Health Act 1875. He referred to the passage in the judgment of Bowen LJ at p. 584 in which he indicated that it was necessary to look at the subject matter of the section and see what was its scope and object in construing the individual words which appear in the section. That approach was also adopted in *New Plymouth Borough Council v Taranaki Electric Power Board* [1933] AC 680, where the Privy Council was concerned to construe the meaning of the word 'adjoining'. Lord Macmillan, giving the judgment of the Board, said p. 682:

> Their Lordships agree with the learned judges of the Court of Appeal that the primary and exact meaning of 'adjoining' is 'conterminous.' At the same time it cannot be disputed that the word is also used in a looser sense as meaning 'near' or 'neighbouring.' But, as Lord Hewart CJ said in a recent case [*Spillers Ltd v Cardiff (Borough) Assessment Committee* [1931] 2 KB 21, 43], where the question was as to the meaning of the word 'contiguous'; 'It ought to be the rule, and we are glad to think that it is the rule, that words are used in an Act of Parliament correctly and exactly, and not loosely and inexactly. Upon those who assert that that rule has been broken the burden of establishing their proposition lies heavily. And they can discharge it only by pointing to something in the context which goes to show that the loose and inexact meaning must be preferred'.

Mr West submitted that, when one looks at the scope and purpose of the Rent Act, the broad meaning – which is admittedly a secondary meaning of that word – must strongly be preferred because of the anomalies involved in adopting the literal meaning.

This point has never previously been decided by the Court of Appeal. It is possible that that is because of a short passage in the present Vice-Chancellor's classic work, *Megarry The Rent Acts* 10th ed., (1967) p. 271, although, as we know from the judgment of Judge Harold Brown in *Metropolitan Railway Land Corporation v Burfitt* [1960] CLY 2749, it was certainly in the 8th edition which was published in 1955 and very likely earlier still. The passage states:

> The word 'adjoining' has been construed as meaning 'contiguous', so that the occupants of a second floor flat have been held not to be 'adjoining occupiers' to the ground floor flat beneath them.

Then he cites the *Trustees of Marquess of Northampton Estate v Bond* (1950) EGD 122 and continues:

> But this seems too strict a view; for one meaning of the word is 'neighbouring' and all that the context seems to require is that the premises of the adjoining occupiers should be near enough to be affected by the tenant's conduct on the demised premises.

I accept that statement as an accurate statement of the law. The premises here, which were occupied by the complainants, were in the same building as that occupied by the defendant. They were sharing the common parts, including the common entrance, with the defendant, and in my judgment they were near enough to be affected by her conduct on the premises. And that was the view that was taken by the assistant recorder, who did not have the advantage of the citations from authority which we have had, but did have various textbooks cited to him; and he expressed the view:

not only the occupiers within no. 12 upstairs, be they tenants or other persons lawfully on the premises, were adjoining within the meaning and spirit of Case 2 of Schedule 15 to the Rent Act 1977 but also the occupiers of flat 3 in no. 11 were adjoining.

I agree with the view that the assistant recorder took on that point of law, so that Mr Pearson's primary ground of appeal fails.

Abrahams v Wilson
[1971] 2 QB 88

The difficulties posed by the need (concerning the illegality 'limb') to establish that the *dwelling-house* had been *used* for an illegal purpose were dealt with in the case of *Abrahams* v *Wilson* [1971] 2 QB 88, where a tenant who had been convicted of possession of cannabis found on the premises she rented had later been sued for possession by her landlord. The county court judge refused to grant possession, and in this was supported by the Court of Appeal. In rejecting the landlord's appeal the court found that there must be a close causal relationship between the criminal conviction and a *use* of the premises involved (applying *S. Schneider Ltd* v *Abrahams* [1925] 1 KB 301). Edmund Davies LJ stated (at p. 91):

But, having said that the certificate of conviction itself makes no reference to any particular premises, it emerges from a series of cases that this fact does not prevent the circumstances which led to the conviction from being adduced in evidence. The matter was dealt with at length by this court in *S. Schneider & Sons Ltd* v *Abrahams* [1925] 1 KB 301, which was a case where a tenant had been convicted under the Larceny Act of receiving at the demised premises certain property, well knowing it to have been stolen. The place where the act of receiving occurs is in general of no materiality in law; but there it was held that the tenant, having made use of the premises in order to commit that crime, must be regarded as having been convicted of 'using' the premises for an illegal purpose within the meaning of the statutory provision then applicable, namely, section 4 of the Rent and Mortgage Interest Restrictions Act 1923. But there must be some link between the criminal conviction and the premises which are the subject-matter of the proceedings for possession, and the test applied by Bankes LJ is one which I would respectfully adopt for the purposes of the present case. Bankes LJ said at p. 306:

> I reject the argument that the section includes only offences in which use of the premises is an essential element. But I think it is necessary to show that the tenant has taken advantage of his tenancy of the premises and of the opportunity they afford for committing the offence. In this view the tenant who uses the demised premises as a coiner's den, or as a deposit for stolen goods, and is convicted of counterfeiting coin or receiving goods, would be 'convicted of using the premises for an . . . illegal purpose' within the meaning of section 4.

Scrutton LJ applied this test, at p. 309;

> Were the words meant to have their strict meaning or were they meant to cover all cases where a tenant is convicted of a crime and had used the premises to facilitate the commission of it?

He later said, at p. 310:

Giving the case the best consideration I can, I come to the conclusion that the conviction need not be for using the premises for one or another immoral or illegal purpose, and that it is enough if there is a conviction of a crime which has been committed on the premises and for the purpose of committing which the premises have been used; but that it is not enough that the tenant has been convicted of a crime with which the premises have nothing to do beyond merely being the scene of its commission.

Applying that test to the present case, I for my part would put it in this way: In proper and clear circumstances – which must be established, of course, by the landlord – a conviction of using premises for an illegal purpose, within the meaning of Case 2, can be established by proof that in the demised premises a quantity of cannabis resin was found. One must, however, look at the circumstances very carefully before an isolated finding on a single occasion is held to constitute proof of such user. The evidence produced in the civil proceedings was very unsatisfactory regarding what transpired at the criminal trial and I am not prepared to hold that user was established. But, even if it were, my conclusion in relation to Case 2 must ultimately turn upon the overriding requirement, imposed by section 10 of the Act, that no order for possession may be made by the court (even though the circumstances are such as to bring the matter clearly within any other of the Cases set out in Part I of Schedule 3) 'unless the court considers it reasonable to make the order.'

Rent Act 1977

SCHEDULE 15

PART I
CASES IN WHICH COURT MAY ORDER POSSESSION

Case 9
Landlord requires the property as a residence

Where the dwelling-house is reasonably required by the landlord for occupation as a residence for—
    (a)   himself, or
    (b)   any son or daughter of his over 18 years of age, or
    (c)   his father or mother, or
    (d)   if the dwelling-house is let on or subject to a regulated tenancy, the father or mother of his wife or husband,
and the landlord did not become landlord by purchasing the dwelling-house or any interest therein after [certain specified dates].

This needs to be seen in the light of Sch. 15, Pt III, para. 1, which states:

A court shall not make an order for possession of a dwelling-house by reason only that the circumstances of the case fall within Case 9 in Part I of this Schedule if the court is satisfied that, having regard to all the circumstances of the case, including the question whether other accommodation is available for the landlord or the tenant, greater hardship would be caused by granting the order than by refusing to grant it.

This ground (unlike Ground 1(b) of Sch. 2, the nearest Housing Act equivalent) is discretionary, but quite apart from the consequent *general* landlord need to demonstrate that is 'reasonable' to grant possession, Pt III of Sch. 15 contains a specific 'balance of inconvenience' test. This inevitably requires a court to engage in difficult (and delicate) 'balancing acts' between the claims of parties both of which may be meritorious. It seems likely that in a marginal case a court will tend to come down in a landlord's favour and the breadth of the discretion vested in a court of first instance indicates that future appeals will only rarely succeed. As Croom-Johnson LJ stated in *Manaton* v *Edwards* (1985) 18 HLR 116 (at p. 121).

When one comes to consider the issue of greater hardship, this court cannot merely upset the decision of the county court judge or recorder simply because it might have come to a different conclusion itself.

However the case is, in itself, one of those unusual instances where the first instance decision *was* overturned, primarily because the recorder had failed to recognise that there was in such cases a primary evidential burden on the tenant to establish a significant degree of hardship should possession be granted.

Rent Act 1977

SCHEDULE 15

PART II
CASES IN WHICH COURT MUST ORDER POSSESSION WHERE DWELLING-HOUSE SUBJECT TO REGULATED TENANCY

Case 11
Case 11: returning owner-occupier

Where a person (in this Case referred to as 'the owner-occupier') who let the dwelling-house on a regulated tenancy had, at any time before the letting, occupied it as his residence and—

(a) not later than the relevant date the landlord gave notice in writing to the tenant that possession might be recovered under this Case, and

(b) the dwelling-house has not [since certain specified dates] been let by the owner-occupier on a protected tenancy with respect to which the condition mentioned in paragraph (a) above was not satisfied, and

(c) the court is of the opinion that of the conditions set out in Part V of this Schedule one of those in paragraphs (a) and (c) to (f) is satisfied.

. . .

The conditions mentioned in (c) above are:

(a) that the dwelling-house is required as a residence for the owner or any member of his family who resided with him when he last occupied it as a residence; or

(b) the owner has retired from regular employment and requires the dwelling-house as a residence;

(c)   that the owner has died and the dwelling-house is required as a residence for a member of his family who was residing with him at the time of his death; or

(d)   that the owner has died and the dwelling-house is required by a successor in title as his residence or for the purpose of sale with vacant possession; or

(e)   the dwelling-house is subject to a mortgage, made by deed and granted before the tenancy, and the mortgagee:

(i)   is entitled to exercise a power of sale conferred on him by s. 101 of the Law of Property Act 1925, and

(ii)   requires the dwelling-house for the purpose of disposing of it with vacant possession in exercise of that power; and

(f)   the dwelling-house is not reasonably suitable to the needs of the owner, having regard to his place of work, and he requires it for the purpose of disposing of it with vacant possession and of using the proceeds of that disposal in acquiring, as his residence, a dwelling-house which is more suitable to those needs.

In the 1988 Act, Ground 1(a) of Sch. 2 also 'protects' the position of an owner-occupier. The crucial difference is that the landlord in such a case need give no reason(s) for seeking possession –his or her previous occupancy already limits the long-term security of the tenant. Again, the apparent requirement of prior notice for Case 11 to be effective is limited in practice by the power of the court to ignore both the relevant dates and the requirement of prior notice if it is deemed 'just and equitable' for possession to be granted. The history of Case 11 has not been free of difficulty. For example, in *Pocock* v *Steel* [1985] 1 WLR 229, the Court of Appeal ruled that the Case could not operate unless the landlord had been in occupation immediately prior to the letting in question (not easy to achieve where 'absentee' owners let through agents). This decision was swiftly reversed in the Rent (Amendment) Act 1985.

Questions
1.   Are decisions on 'suitable alternative accommodation' above all 'policy' decisions?
2.   Can you think of any reasons why the 'character' of a property extends to its immediate *physical* environment but not equally to the *community* in which it is situated, relationships, cultural associations, religious 'outlets' etc.?
3.   Could an occupier of a 'dwelling' in a different but nearby property be an 'adjoining occupier'? If not, where/how is the line to be drawn?
4.   What exactly does it mean to state (*per* Edmund Davies LJ in *Abrahams* v *Wilson* citing Banks LJ): 'I reject the argument that the section includes only offences in which use of premises is an essential element . . . but it is necessary to show that the tenant has taken advantage of the opportunity [the premises] afford for committing the offence'?

5.   Would a desire by a child of a landlord's previous marriage to occupy the premises, enable the landlord to invoke Case 9? (See *Potsos and Potsos* v *Theodotou* (1991) 23 HLR 356.)

6.   If a landlord successfully gains possession on the basis of Case 11 (condition (a)) and then almost immediately resells the property, is there anything the tenant can do?

(iv)   Common law tenancies

Tenancies falling outside the statutory schemes of the Housing Act 1988 and the Rent Act 1977 do not provide for true security of tenure. However, the Protection from Eviction Act 1977 does at least allow for a measure of procedural protection, requiring landlords seeking possession to serve notices to quit in specified forms, containing specified information and of specified duration. Moreover, court orders are generally required before repossession by a landlord can be obtained (even if no grounds for possession as such need to be shown). The relevant provisions (ss. 3 and 5) of the 1977 Act have already been cited. Tenancies coming into force on or after the commencement date of Pt I of the Housing Act 1988 (15 January 1989) are excluded from the above protection in a number of prescribed circumstances, most importantly holiday 'lets' and where the tenant shares any accommodation with the landlord (s. 3A). However, a well-advised landlord should still have in mind the inherent *common law* need to serve a notice to quit to terminate a periodic tenancy (the length of which should correspond to the 'period' of the tenancy), and that even if not legally required to go though the courts in order to recover possession it may be advisable to obtain an order given the risks attached to forcible eviction.

In *Haniff* v *Robinson* (1994) HLR 386, Woolf LJ (as he then was) stated that the object of s. 3 was to provide protection for a tenant until execution of a warrant for possession by court bailiffs. Therefore, even after a possession order has been granted a landlord had no right to resort to self-help to recover possession.

(C)   Rent control

It is here that the differences between the 1977 and the 1988 Acts are at their most stark. The guiding principle of the 1977 Rent Act is rent *control* via a system of rent officer investigation and regulation. The perception (discussed in chapter 2) that this had had the effect of 'choking off' the supply of private rented accommodation was a principal driving force behind the 1988 Act. Little direct rent control exists for assured and assured shorthold tenancies, although residual regulation by Rent Assessment Committees does survive. Common law tenancies are, of course, wholly market driven as regards rents.

(i)   Assured Tenancies

The relevant sections of the 1988 Act are ss. 13 and 14.

Housing Act 1988

Rent and other terms

Increases of rent under assured periodic tenancies

13.—(1)   This section applies to—

(a)   a statutory periodic tenancy other than one which, by virtue of paragraph 11 or paragraph 12 in Part I of Schedule 1 to this Act, cannot for the time being be an assured tenancy; and

(b)   any other periodic tenancy which is an assured tenancy, other than one in relation to which there is a provision, for the time being binding on the tenant, under which the rent for a particular period of the tenancy will or may be greater than the rent for an earlier period.

(2)   For the purpose of securing an increase in the rent under a tenancy to which this section applies, the landlord may serve on the tenant a notice in the prescribed form proposing a new rent to take effect at the beginning of a new period of the tenancy specified in the notice, being a period beginning not earlier than—

(a)   the minimum period after the date of the service of the notice; and

(b)   except in the case of a statutory periodic tenancy, the first anniversary of the date on which the first period of the tenancy began; and

(c)   if the rent under the tenancy has previously been increased by virtue of a notice under this subsection or a determination under section 14 below, the first anniversary of the date on which the increased rent took effect.

(3)   The minimum period referred to in subsection (2) above is—

(a)   in the case of a yearly tenancy, six months;

(b)   in the case of a tenancy where the period is less than a month, one month; and

(c)   in any other case, a period equal to the period of the tenancy.

(4)   Where a notice is served under subsection (2) above, a new rent specified in the notice shall take effect as mentioned in the notice unless, before the beginning of the new period specified in the notice,—

(a)   the tenant by an application in the prescribed form refers the notice to a rent assessment committee; or

(b)   the landlord and the tenant agree on a variation of the rent which is different from that proposed in the notice or agree that the rent should not be varied.

(5)   Nothing in this section (or in section 14 below) affects the right of the landlord and the tenant under an assured tenancy to vary by agreement any term of the tenancy (including a term relating to rent).

Determination of rent by rent assessment committee

14.—(1)   Where, under subsection (4)(a) of section 13 above, a tenant refers to a rent assessment committee a notice under subsection (2) of that section, the committee shall determine the rent at which, subject to subsections (2) and (4) below, the committee consider that the dwelling-house concerned might reasonably be expected to be let in the open market by a willing landlord under an assured tenancy—

(a)   which is a periodic tenancy having the same periods as those of the tenancy to which the notice relates;

(b)   which begins at the beginning of the new period specified in the notice;

(c)   the terms of which (other than relating to the amount of the rent) are the same as those of the tenancy to which the notice relates; and

(d)   in respect of which the same notices, if any, have been given under any of Grounds 1 to 5 of Schedule 2 to this Act, as have been given (or have effect as if given) in relation to the tenancy to which the notice relates.

(2)   In making a determination under this section, there shall be disregarded—

(a)   any effect on the rent attributable to the granting of a tenancy to a sitting tenant;

(b)   any increase in the value of the dwelling-house attributable to a relevant improvement carried out by a person who at the time it was carried out was the tenant, if the improvement—

(i)   was carried out otherwise than in pursuance of an obligation to his immediate landlord, or

(ii)   was carried out pursuant to an obligation to his immediate landlord being an obligation which did not relate to the specific improvement concerned but arose by reference to consent given to the carrying out of that improvement; and

(c)   any reduction in the value of the dwelling-house attributable to a failure by the tenant to comply with any terms of the tenancy.

. . .

Section 13 (broadly) governs the mechanisms underlying rent increases under assured tenancies. Section 14 (broadly) governs the degree to which rent increases can be 'pegged' and/or rents reduced. In reality, the rent assessment committee's (RAC's) powers are very limited; even if they do have power to intervene, they are confined to bringing the rent into line with the market if it is self-evidently excessive (s. 14(1)). However, it is doubtful whether most assured tenancy agreements will let the RAC 'in'. Section 13(1)(b) exempts from scrutiny any assured tenancy containing a 'rent review' clause. It can be assumed that most will contain such a clause. Further, even where no such clause exists a landlord and tenant may subsequently agree that the rent shall be increased completely outside the complex scheme of notice of rent increases and RAC scrutiny apparently provided for by s. 13. Lastly, it is clear that any powers the RAC may have apply only to proposed rent increases — the original contract rent is not open to external alteration.

(ii)   Assured shorthold tenancies

Prior to the implementation of the 1988 Act much was made of the 'choice' supposedly existing for landlords and tenants between assured tenancies (which provided for a measure of security of tenure, but at market rents) and assured shorthold tenancies (which gave no long-term security but were subject to a measure of rent control). The reality is that while assured shorthold tenancies do contain a little more in the way of real rent review than do assured tenancies, the degree of regulation falls far short of genuine rent control. Moreover, tenant insecurity means that the likelihood of most assured shorthold tenants challenging their rents is small. The relevant 1988 Act provision is s. 22.

Housing Act 1988

Reference of excessive rents to rent assessment committee

22.—(1)   Subject to section 23 and subsection (2) below, the tenant under an assured shorthold tenancy in respect of which a notice was served as mentioned in section 20(2) above may make an application in the prescribed form to a rent assessment committee for a determination of the rent which, in the committee's opinion, the landlord might reasonably be expected to obtain under the assured shorthold tenancy.

(2)   No application may be made under this section if—

(a)   the rent payable under the tenancy is a rent previously determined under this section; or

(aa)   the tenancy is one to which section 19A above applies and more than six months have elapsed since the beginning of the tenancy or, in the case of a replacement tenancy, since the beginning of the original tenancy; or

(b)   the tenancy is an assured shorthold tenancy falling within subsection (4) of section 20 above (and, accordingly, is one in respect of which notice need not have been served as mentioned in subsection (2) of that section).

(3)   Where an application is made to a rent assessment committee under subsection (1) above with respect to the rent under an assured shorthold tenancy, the committee shall not make such a determination as is referred to in that subsection unless they consider—

(a)   that there is a sufficient number of similar dwelling-houses in the locality let on assured tenancies (whether shorthold or not); and

(b)   that the rent payable under the assured shorthold tenancy in question is significantly higher than the rent which the landlord might reasonably be expected to be able to obtain under the tenancy, having regard to the level of rents payable under the tenancies referred to in paragraph (a) above.

(4)   Where, on an application under this section, a rent assessment committee make a determination of a rent for an assured shorthold tenancy—

(a)   the determination shall have effect from such date as the committee may direct, not being earlier than the date of the application;

(b)   if, at any time on or after the determination takes effect, the rent which, apart from this paragraph, would be payable under the tenancy exceeds the rent so determined, the excess shall be irrecoverable from the tenant; and

(c)   no notice may be served under section 13(2) above with respect to a tenancy of the dwelling-house in question until after the first anniversary of the date on which the determination takes effect.

(5)   Subsections (4), (5) and (8) of section 14 above apply in relation to a determination of rent under this section as they apply in relation to a determination under that section and, accordingly, where subsection (5) of that section applies, any reference in subsection (4)(b) above to rent is a reference to rent exclusive of the amount attributable to rates.

Unlike the position concerning assured tenancies, the tenant can make direct application to the RAC contending that the rent is 'excessive'. However, the RAC's powers are confined (in effect) to determining whether the rent in question significantly exceeds the local market 'norm' (s. 22(3)(b)). Issues as to whether rent levels generally in the area are 'excessive' are outside the RAC's powers. Moreover, such an application can be made only once by the tenant (s. 22(2)(a)), and can be made only during the initial fixed term of the tenancy (s. 22(2)(b)). In the (likely to be rare) instance of an RAC reducing an assured shorthold tenancy's rent they have a wide discretion to decide the date from which the new rent commences, and consequently what degree of 'overpayment' by the tenant there has been (s. 22(4)). Lastly, if the tenant leaves, the 'assured' rent ceases to bind the landlord who can agree such new rent as he chooses with the incoming tenant (unlike the position under the Rent Acts – below).

For assured shortholds coming into force after 28 February 1997, in line with the new s. 19A, s. 22 is amended by s. 100 of the Housing Act 1996 as follows:

100.—(1)   Section 22 of the Housing Act 1988 (reference of excessive rents to rent assessment committee) shall be amended as follows.
   (2)   In subsection (2) (circumstances in which no application under the section may be made) after paragraph (a) there shall be inserted—

'(aa)   the tenancy is one to which section 19A above applies and more than six months have elapsed since the beginning of the tenancy or, in the case of a replacement tenancy, since the beginning of the original tenancy; or'.

   (3)   At the end there shall be inserted—
   '(6)   In subsection (2)(aa) above, the references to the original tenancy and to a replacement tenancy shall be construed in accordance with subsections (6) and(7) respectively of section 21 above.'

In part this is a 'tidying up' provision made necessary by the fact that assured shortholds (post-28 February 1997) can be periodic as well as fixed-term. However, given that many fixed-term assured shortholds were for periods longer than the six month minimum, it further restricts tenants' rights to apply to RACs by confining such rights to six months, rather than the period of the original fixed term.

(iii)   Rent Act tenancies
As their name would suggest, here true rent control is to be found. Either party to a protected or statutory tenancy can apply to a rent officer for a fair rent to be registered on the property. The rent ultimately registered by the rent officer binds not just the parties themselves, but future tenants within the registration period (typically two years unless both parties otherwise agree or there has been a change in the condition of the premises (ss. 67(3) and (4), Rent Act 1977).

As to how a 'fair rent' is to be assessed, much discretion is left to the rent officer, under s. 70 of the Act.

Rent Act 1977

Determination of fair rent
70.—(1)   In determining, for the purposes of this Part of this Act, what rent is or would be a fair rent under a regulated tenancy of a dwelling-house, regard shall be had to all the circumstances (other than personal circumstances) and in particular to—
      (a)   the age, character, locality and state of repair of the dwelling-house, and

(b)   if any furniture is provided for use under the tenancy, the quantity, quality and condition of the furniture, and

(c)   any premium or sum in the nature of a premium which has been or may be lawfully required or received on the grant, renewal, continuance or assignment of the tenancy.

(2)   For the purposes of the determination it shall be assumed that the number of persons seeking to become tenants of similar dwelling-houses in the locality on the terms (other than those relating to rent) of the regulated tenancy is not substantially greater than the number of such dwelling-houses in the locality which are available for letting on such terms.

Some points are clear – primarily that it is the particular property, good or bad, that should be considered, even if assistance is derived from other rents in the locality (s. 70(1)). However, the 'essence' of the section is s. 70(2) which instructs the rent officer to ignore 'scarcity value'. Traditionally this had the effect of driving down fair rent determinations to significantly below typical 'market' rents in the locality. However, more recently there has been pressure from landlords to persuade rent officers to refocus their approach, based on the fact that most new rents would be market rents, and the (supposed) fact that scarcity conditions now no longer apply in most parts of the country. The issues were authoritatively considered by the Court of Appeal in the following case:

Spath Holme Ltd v Chairman of the Greater Manchester and Lancashire Rent Assessment Committee
(1996) 28 HLR 107

In December 1991, the respondent Rent Assessment Committee determined fair rents for five flats owned by the appellant. The appellant appealed to the High Court on the basis that the Committee had erred in law in failing to take account of rents agreed in respect of similar dwellings in the same block, let on assured tenancies. In November 1992, the decision was quashed by consent and remitted to the committee.

In March 1993, the matter came back before the Committee for a determination in respect of three of the original flats, and a further 13 flats which had been referred to them at various times during 1992. The fair rents requested by the appellant were £4,290 per annum for two-bedroomed flats, £3,300 per annum for one-bedroomed flats and £2,400 per annum for studios. The appellant relied on lettings on assured tenancies of one-bedroomed flats and studios within the same block as comparables. The Committee determined that the fair rents should be £2,700 per annum for the two-bedroomed flats, £2,200 per annum for the one-bedroomed flats and £1,650 per annum for the studios. In reaching their decision, the Committee refused to accept the appellant's contention that the proper basis for determining a fair rent was the market rent less scarcity, as they were not satisfied that an absence of scarcity had been made out. They also considered that assured tenants would be willing to pay a higher rent for the security of tenure afforded by their status and that the registered rent comparables had not been demonstrated to be unsound.

A further four flats were later referred to a differently constituted Committee. That Committee also refused to accept the submissions of the landlord and set the rent levels by reference to the comparables set by the earlier committee.

The appellant appealed to the High Court for an order that the decisions should be set aside and the matter remitted for redetermination. At first instance, the judge found for the appellant. The Committee appealed to the Court of Appeal.

The Court of Appeal (dismissing the appeal) held that:

(1)   In the reasons for the determination, it was evident that the committee were using the word 'fair' in relation to a fair rent in the sense of reasonable; such an approach was contrary to the judgment of Hutchinson J in *BTE Ltd* v *Merseyside and Cheshire Rent Assessment Committee* (1991) 24 HLR 514 and wrong in law;

(2)   If the method of assessment adopted is the capital value/fair yield method then the presence of a sitting tenant must be ignored as a personal circumstance for the value will depend on the tenant's personal attributes; but if the method adopted is the comparable rent payable under an assured tenancy then the security of tenure attached to a regulated tenant is not a personal attribute; there is no *a priori* reason why a circumstance which is personal in one context must be personal in all others; it seemed unlikely that Parliament could have intended that the security of tenure of such a tenancy should be disregarded, with the consequence that two tenancies having substantially the same security of tenure have to be treated as being different in that respect;

(3)   If the Committee were entitled to conclude, and was correct in its view, that tenancies enjoying security of tenure command higher rents than those which do not (as to which it was unnecessary to decide), it was wrong in law in holding that the rents for the assured tenancies would have to be discounted on that ground since like security was enjoyed by regulated tenancies and was a circumstance to be taken into account;

(4)   . . .

(5)   In this case, there was a number of flats in the same block, virtually identical to those for which a fair rent was to be determined, let on assured tenancies at, by definition, open market rents; if, in those circumstances, a Rent Assessment Committee wished to exercise its discretion to adopt some other comparable or method of assessment, they would be failing in its duty to give reasons if it did not explain why.

MORRITT LJ: . . . Before considering these submissions further there are some general points which should be noted. The first relates to the legislative background against which the authorities to which we were referred were decided. The concept of regulated tenancies and fair rents was introduced by Rent Act 1965. That Act and the

Rent Act 1968 did not apply the regime of regulated tenancies and fair rents to furnished tenancies. But the Rent Act 1974 assimilated furnished with unfurnished tenancies. From then until 1988 tenancies of residential properties at open market rents were unusual. Since January 1989 however most new tenancies have been assured tenancies which are by definition at open market rents. Thus between 1965 and 1974 most rent comparables were either open market rents for furnished tenancies or registered fair rents which were open market rents discounted for scarcity. From 1974 to 1988 the first alternative was no longer available. Since 1988 there have been old regulated tenancies and an increasing number of assured tenancies at open market rents.

Secondly there was no dispute of substance material to the facts of this case as to the accuracy of the general principles formulated by the judge at pages 27 and 28 of his judgment which I have quoted. The Chairman suggested that the fifth and sixth principles should be glossed to take account of the right of Rent Assessment Committees to use their own knowledge and experience. The landlords suggested that the expression of the second principle should recognise that in the light of the changed legislative background some preference should be accorded to the rents payable under assured tenancies.

Thirdly it was common ground and is well established that the fair rent which is to be determined is the market rent for the property in question disregarding the personal circumstances referred to in section 70(1), the specified disregards referred to in section 70(3) and discounted for any scarcity within section 70(2). The cases emphasise that the starting point is the market rent. Thus in *Mountview Court Properties* v *Devlin* (1970) 21 P & CR 689 at 691 Lord Parker LCJ referred to 'the market rent and therefore the fair rent'. In *Tormes Ltd* v *Landau* [1971] 1 QB 61 at p. 267 Lord Parker LCJ referred to 'fair rent which will be market rent less scarcity'. Similar judicial statements may be found in *Metropolitan Properties* v *Finegold* [1975] 1 WLR 349 at p. 352 and *BTE Ltd* v *Merseyside and Cheshire Rent Assessment Committee* (1991) 24 HLR 514 at 517.

In considering the arguments for the Chairman I find it necessary to put them in the context of the wider and in some respects logically prior contentions of the landlords. Thus the first question is whether the Rent Assessment Committee appreciated the nature of the fair rent they were required to determine. I have already referred to the fact that it is common ground and anyway well established that it is the market rent less the statutory disregards and discounted to remove any element of scarcity. I find it surprising that this is nowhere stated in the Reasons for the Determination paragraph 17, which I have quoted in full, is the passage in which the committee set out the principles which they consider to be applicable but make no reference to market rents.

In paragraph 21 of the Reasons, the Committee referred to the landlords' approach described as 'market rent less scarcity' requiring two important findings to be made of which the first was stated to be 'that in law section 70(2) of the Rent Act 1977 exhaustively defines the term "fair rent" for the purposes of that Act.' That is not so and even if it was intended to refer to section 70 as a whole the statement is incomplete for it ignores the important element of the market rent held to be implicit in the term fair.

I will consider later the Committee's rejection of the assured tenancy comparables on the ground that there was still an element of scarcity and security of tenure and for the moment pass over the intervening passages in the Reasons. But at paragraph 30 the committee returned to the concept of fair rents as they understood it. In the sentence 'It would be surprising therefore even if it had proved possible to accept the landlord's conclusion on the scarcity issue to find that three years or so later it would be "fair" to increase the rent by over 100 per cent as contended for by the landlord . . .' it is evident that the Committee were using the word fair in the sense of reasonable. It is common ground that such an approach is contrary to the judgment of Hutchison J in *BTE Ltd* v *Merseyside and Cheshire Rent Assessment Committee* (1991) 24 HLR 514 and wrong in law. Subject, therefore, to any different approach indicated in the passages dealing with the rejection of the assured tenancy comparables, in my view the Reasons for the Determination reveal an error of law in that the committee did not appreciate the meaning of 'fair rent' as interpreted by the courts. The possibility of this error must be borne in mind when considering the other points.

I turn then to the reasons given for rejecting the comparables on which the landlords rely. As the judge recorded here were essentially two of which the first was security of tenure. In this context the judge accepted the view of the Committee that the rents under the assured tenancies would have to be discounted. The reason was that he considered that the security of tenure enjoyed by the tenant under a regulated tenancy had to be disregarded as a personal circumstance. Thus unless the rent payable under the assured tenancy was discounted for the security of tenure the tenant enjoyed under such a tenancy the comparison of the rents would not be like for like.

The judge does not appear to have had the benefit of the argument advanced in this court by the landlords, without objection from the Chairman, to the effect that the security of tenure attaching to a regulated tenancy is substantially the same as that enjoyed by the tenant under an assured tenancy and is not a personal circumstance to be disregarded with the consequence that the rent payable under the latter does not have to be discounted on that account.

The contention that the security of tenure of a tenant under a regulated tenancy must be ignored as a personal circumstance derives from the decision of the House of Lords in *Mason* v *Skilling* [1974] 1 WLR 1437. In that case under the legislation in force in Scotland which was in all relevant respects the same as that in England the Rent Assessment Committee decided to adopt the method of assessment of a fair rent by reference to the fair yield to the landlord on the capital value of the house. The question arose, if that method were adopted, whether the house should be valued with vacant possession or with the sitting tenant. The Court of Session decided that the presence of a sitting tenant was a circumstance to be regarded so that the latter basis should be adopted. The House of Lords disagreed on the ground that though the presence of a sitting tenant was a circumstance it was a personal circumstance which was to be disregarded. At p. 1440 Lord Reid said:

It was quite true that the fact that there is a sitting tenant is a 'circumstance' but, in my opinion, it is excluded by the Act. Section 42(1) directs that regard shall be had to 'all the circumstances (other than personal circumstances)'. In my view the tenant's right to remain in possession is a personal circumstance. A right to possess a house (or anything else) appears to me to pertain to the person who has the right, whether the right is statutory or contractual. The house itself remains the same whoever is entitled to possess it. Moreover, under the Act the tenant's right to possess lasts so long, but only so long, as he complies with certain obligations. I am confirmed in this view by the fact that all the circumstances specified at the end of the subsection relate entirely to the house itself.

In *Palmer* v *Peabody Trust* [1975] 1 QB 604 the landlord was a housing trust with the consequence that the tenant did not enjoy security of tenure. The tenant claimed that the rents payable under protected tenancies were not comparable on that ground. Lord Widgery LCJ said, at p. 608.

> Furthermore I have difficulty in saying whether or not the presence of statutory security is a personal circumstance. Under the section, as I read it, personal circumstances are to be ignored. I find it difficult to say that the presence or absence of security inherent in a particular tenancy is a personal circumstance, but I do not find it necessary to decide the point finally today and it may be that we shall have to look at it on another occasion.
>
> The only authority to which we have been referred on this point is *Mason v Skilling (sub nom. Skilling v Arcari's Executrix)*, 1974 SLT 46, in the House of Lords on appeal from Scotland. The report which I have does not otherwise assist me in identifying the particular case. It was concerned with a rent assessment committee who had chosen to make their calculations of fair rent by reference to the capital value of the premises. When they came to pursue that course, the question arose: should the premises be valued as with a sitting tenant or as vacant? The House of Lords held that they were to be valued as vacant, and certainly I think that it is right that Lord Reid was positively taking the view that the presence of a sitting tenant with a right of security was a personal consideration and to be ignored on that account.
>
> However, as I have said, I do not find it necessary to decide the matter finally today. I express my doubts and difficulties on the meaning of 'personal circumstances' and it is a matter to which we may have to return.

Later at p. 609 he added

> The Act of 1968 which requires us to make this somewhat artificial assumption of no scarcity in section 46(2) does, by a side wind, in my view also require us to regard presence or absence of security as a matter which can technically be taken into account as a relevant circumstance but one which in practice can have only minimal effects, if any, on the amount of rent to be fixed.

For the landlord it is submitted that if the method of assessment adopted is the capital value/fair yield method then, as *Mason v Skilling* requires, the presence of a sitting tenant must be ignored as a personal circumstance for the value will depend on a personal attribute of the tenant namely his age. But if the method adopted is the comparable rent payable under an assured tenancy then the security of tenure attached to a regulated tenancy is not a personal attribute. For the Chairman it is submitted that such a distinction in untenable; if the circumstance is personal for one method of assessment it must be personal for the others.

I prefer the submissions for the Landlords. I see no *a priori* reason why a circumstance which is personal in one context must be personal in all others. If the method of assessment adopted is the capital value/fair yield basis, which was the case in *Mason v Skilling*, then the individual tenant and his attributes have an effect on the valuation. In the case of rent comparables the personal attributes of the individual tenant have no bearing on the assessment of the fair rent for the subject property. The relevance in this case arises from the view of the committee that tenancies to which security of tenure are attached by statute command a higher rent than those which do not. That circumstance does not appear to me to be properly described as 'personal' when the statute is requiring the determination of a fair rent 'under a regulated tenancy'. Further it seems unlikely that Parliament could have intended that the security of tenure of such a tenancy should be disregarded with the consequences that two tenancies having substantially the same security of tenure have to be treated as being different in that respect. In my view if the committee were entitled to conclude and correct in their view that tenancies enjoying security of tenure command higher rents than those which do not (as to which it is unnecessary to decide) they were wrong in law in holding that the rents for the assured tenancies would have to be discounted on that ground since the like security was enjoyed by regulated tenancies as well and was a circumstance to be taken into account.

Accordingly I pass to the second ground relied on by the committee for rejecting the rents for the assured tenancies as comparables, namely the existence of scarcity. The sentence in paragraph 26 which reads 'Furthermore if the committee were to adopt the method of "market rent less scarcity" approach contended for by the landlord it would need to be satisfied that there was virtually no scarcity in the market' if read literally is and was accepted to be wrong in law. Moreover as the judge observed the statement in paragraph 29 that the dicta in the *BTE* case 'clearly deal with the position where a decision can be made on the evidence that there is no scarcity' betrays a misunderstanding of what that case decided.

In my judgment these two passages show that the committee thought that discounted market rents could not be used to determine the fair rent. But in that they were wrong for market rent adjusted for scarcity is precisely what the fair rent is required to be. Thus in my view the second reason given for rejecting the rents payable under the assured tenancies as comparables was bad in law too.

But it goes further than that for although it is not clear what the committee thought was the use of a 'market rent less scarcity test' if it could not be used if there was scarcity it does seem to confirm the doubt I expressed earlier that the committee did not have in mind the requirement that the fair rent should be the market rent less the disregards and discounted for scarcity. If they had they must have appreciated that the existence of scarcity could not be sufficient reason to reject these comparables.

Moreover I do not accept the submission that the Rent Assessment Committee rejected the assured tenancy comparables in favour of the registered rent comparables because the former could not be applied without a discount being applied for one or both of the reasons they gave. First this is not what they said. Secondly if that was the reason then they would have needed to explain why that was a reason to reject the former when it was, as they recognised, an exercise which had to be carried out before applying the latter.

In my view all three errors of law for which the landlords contend have been made out and this appeal should be dismissed.

This conclusion does not deal with the matters of principal concern to the Chairman, namely the ability of Rent Assessment Committees to use their own knowledge and experience in deciding and applying the method they think best for the determination of the fair rent in any given case. This submission was based on the contention that the judge had misunderstood the comments of Griffiths LJ in *London Rent Assessment Committee* v *St Georges Court Ltd* (1984) 48 P & CR 230. That case concerned the rejection as comparables of the registered fair rents of other flats in the same block. It was in that context that Griffiths LJ at p. 235 stated

Of course all the circumstances would have to be taken into account when deciding on the weight to be attached to the rent of a comparable property, but, when one is dealing with a purpose-built block of flats, with flats of the same layout, one on top of another, very weighty reasons would have be to shown before it would be permissible to depart – certainly to depart substantially – from the fair rent that had very recently been assessed for one of those similar flats.

The Chairman submitted that fair rents and market rents were not the same so that there was no reason to require weighty or indeed any reasons for rejecting the latter in favour of the former.

I do not agree. First as the judge made plain in the passage in his judgment dealing with this case which I have quoted he appreciated that the dictum of Griffiths LJ related to the determination of fair rents by reference to registered fair rents. Second his comment is apt once it is realised that the fair rent to be determined is a market rent less the disregards and discounted for scarcity.

Thus, thirdly, if there is no scarcity and no disregards then the rents should be the same whether the tenancy is a regulated tenancy or an assured tenancy.

It is quite true, as the Chairman submitted, that the question of which method to adopt for ascertaining the fair rent is a matter for the Rent Assessment Committee and that in the decided cases some preference may have been shown for taking as comparables the registered fair rents of similar premises. Thus in *Mason* v *Skilling* (1974) 1 WLR 1437 at 1439 Lord Reid said:

> In my view, this section leaves it open to the rent officer or committee to adopt any method or methods of ascertaining a fair rent provided that they do not use any method which is unlawful or unreasonable. The most obvious and direct method is to have regard to registered rents of comparable houses in the area. In the initial stages this method may not be available but as the number of comparable registered rents increases the more likely it will be that it will lead to a correct result. Of course it must be open to either party to show that those comparable rents have been determined on a wrong basis but until that is shown it must be assumed that rents already determined have been rightly ascertained.

In *Western Heritable Ltd* v *Husband* [1983] AC 849 p. 859 Lord Brightman said

> There is, I think, implicit in grounds (1) and (2), the proposition that the requirement in subsection (1) of section 42 to have regard to 'all the circumstances' imposes on an assessment committee the duty to take into consideration 'a fair return on capital' as one of the 'circumstances.' I disagree. I accept that there may be the exceptional case in which a committee are justified in taking into consideration what would be a 'fair return on capital,' leaving aside the precise definition of 'capital' in this context. I do not accept that a committee's decision can be challenged as erroneous in law merely because the committee have failed to take into consideration a 'fair return on capital' but have based their decision exclusively upon comparables. The Act is concerned with the determination of a 'fair rent', that is to say, a rent which is fair to the landlord and fair to the tenant, and yield on invested capital is not an essential ingredient of that determination. If comparables are available which do not reflect or are discounted so as not to reflect, scarcity value, such comparables are the best guide to a fair rent.

But those and other similar statements were made in the legislative context to which I referred earlier. In that context the evidence of tenancies of dwelling houses at open market rents was limited.

Section 12 of the Tribunals and Inquiries Act 1971 imposes a duty on Rent Assessment Committees to give reasons for the decision. The extent to which that duty requires detailed reasons must vary with the nature of the decision and of the case generally. *cf. Metropolitan Properties Ltd* v *Lannon* [1969] 1 QB 577; *Mountview Properties Ltd* v *Devlin* (1970) 21 P & CR 689, 692; *Metropolitan Properties Ltd* v *Laufer* (1974) 29 P & CR 172; *Guppys (Bridport) Ltd* v *Sandoe* (1975) 30 P & CR 69 and *Guppys Properties Ltd* v *Knott* (1978) 30 P & CR 255.

In this case there are a number of flats in the same block on assured tenancies at, by definition, open market rents which are virtually identical to those for which a fair rent is to be determined. In my judgment if, in those circumstances, the Rent Assessment Committee wishes to exercise its discretion to adopt some other comparable or method of assessment it will be failing in its duty to give reasons if it does not explain why.

In this case the third reason given by the Rent Assessment Committee as recorded by the judge was that the registered rent comparables had not been demonstrated to be unsound. That is not, of course, a reason for rejecting the assured tenancy comparables. It is not for the court to say in advance what would be a good reason for doing so but if such a reason involves 'working through' such comparables so be it: that consequence is no ground for rejecting the validity of its cause. But it should also be noted that the registered rent comparables are not in their nature any more or less sound than the open market rent with or without discount. Any registered rent has built into it at least two variables namely the open market rent and the discount for scarcity. Each should have been considered at the time of the original determination. The assessment of the soundness of that registered rent for use as comparable would require each of those variables to be reconsidered at the time of their possible use as a comparable. In this connection it was also objected that if Rent Assessment Committees were required to give detailed reasons that might necessitate giving detailed arithmetical workings or quantifying the degree of scarcity involved contrary to statements in *Guppys Property* v *Knott (No. 1)* (1978) EGD 255 and *Metropolitan Properties Ltd* v *Laufer* (1974) 29 P & CR 172. But those statements were made in relation to the facts of those cases. It does not follow that there will not be cases in which the duty to give reasons will require such workings or quantification to be afforded.

In my judgment the Landlords have demonstrated that the Rent Assessment Committee erred in law in the three respects I have mentioned. In consequence they arrived at a decision which can properly be described as perverse. In those circumstances it is unnecessary to deal with the other matters raised by the Landlords in their Respondent Notice. For all those reasons I would dismiss both these appeals.

Notes

1.   Since *Spath Holme* the courts have returned to the practicalities of the decision for rent assessment committees on a number of occasions. The two most recent are *Curtis* v *Chairman of the London Rent Assessment Committee* [1998] 15 EG 120 and *Northumberland and Durham Property Trust Ltd* v *London Rent Assessment Committee* [1998] EGCS 56. In both cases the Court of Appeal stated, unequivocally, that a fair rent is a market rent adjusted for scarcity and disregards. Moreover, if there are market rent 'comparables' enabling the identification of a market rent as a starting point, there would normally be no need to refer to registered rent 'comparables' at all.

If a committee's assessment of a fair rent differs significantly from the market rent, the committee must provide explicit and satisfactory reasons for this disparity (including appropriate use of figures). Of course, the 'best evidence' for market rents would be the typical level of assured and assured shorthold rents in the locality, indicating that Rent Act fair rents may in practice not differ significantly from rents under Housing Act tenancies.

2. All this raises the question of whether a substantive distinction between a fair rent and a market rent is likely to disappear, or, indeed, is in the process of disappearing. The recent DETR (Department of the Environment, Transport and the Regions) Consultation Paper (May 1998) shows that between April and September 1997 increases made by rent officers were more than five percentage points higher than the increase in the retail price index (RPI) in over 86 per cent of cases. Where cases were appealed to RACs, over half of the rents were further increased, by an average of 18 per cent. It is highly significant that most of the recent landlord appeals against fair rent registrations have been in London, where (broadly) the private rented sector is thriving and scarcity levels are relatively low. The DETR in the 1998 Consultation Paper recognises that most tenants could never have anticipated increases of the magnitude currently taking place under the fair rent system. The Paper proposes using a power contained in s. 31 of the Landlord and Tenant Act 1985 to limit fair rent increases, by linking increases to the increase in the retail price index (the RPI then functioning as an index of 'affordability'). Specifically, for the first re-registration the maximum rent increase should be limited to RPI plus 10 per cent, and subsequently should be no more than RPI plus 5 per cent. (This proposal was implemented by The Rent Acts (Maximum Fair Rent) Order 1999 in force 1 February 1999.)

3. Although a detailed treatment of housing benefit is outside the scope of this book, it should be noted that the maximum rent payable (or 'eligible rent') is pegged to a rent ceiling based partly on size but also on maximum rent criteria (Housing Benefit (General) Regulations 1987 (SI 1987 No. 1971), reg. 11, as amended. In general it can be assumed that unless the size criteria are exceeded a fair rent, even a substantially increased fair rent, will be under the appropriate 'local reference rent' ceiling. Indeed, since all such rent determinations for housing benefit purposes are themselves made by rent officers, any other result would seem wholly anomalous (for rent officer powers and duties, see Housing Benefit (General) Regulations 1987, reg. 12A and the Rent Officer (Additional Functions) Order 1995). If the tenant has been claiming housing benefit since before 1 January 1996, the unamended form of reg. 11 specifically provides for registered (fair) rents being recoverable unless size criteria are exceeded. Nevertheless, a tenant who is in receipt of maximum housing benefit because he or she is unemployed may find it difficult to afford the rent (given current levels of fair rent increases) if he or she finds *some* work with consequent reduction in, or loss of, housing benefit.

Questions
1. Is there any real distinction between fair rents and market rents in the light of recent judicial decisions?
2. Given that, as its name would suggest, the Rent Act 1977 has as its principal objective rent regulation and control, are recent decisions on s. 70 of the Act substantially undermining the legislation?
3. 'Further it seems unlikely that Parliament could have intended that the security of tenure of such a tenancy should be disregarded with the

consequences that two tenancies having substantially the same security of tenure have to be treated as being different' (Morritt LJ In *Spath Holme*).
  Discuss.
4.   Currently, do you think that tenancies with greater security of tenure (i.e. assured tenancies) 'command' higher rents than those with lesser security (i.e. assured shorthold tenancies)?

(D)   Succession

In 1982, Honoré wrote (in *The Quest for Security: Employees, Tenants, Wives*, Stevens, p. 37) that protective legislation attempted to 'provide those who cannot afford to buy their own homes with a substitute for home ownership, a right to remain in occupation for at least a lifetime, and often more'. Certainly the Rent Acts, at that time, provided that statutory tenancies passed, on death, to spouses or other 'family' members and that this right to 'succeed' could apply, in many cases, even on the death of the first 'successor'. In effect this injected into the private rented sector the concept of the 'family home', providing security equivalent to the tenant's for members of the tenant's family at the time they were most vulnerable (after the tenant's death). However, even then the extent to which this wholly equated with 'home ownership' is debatable. For example, as discussed in chapter 2, a statutory tenancy is maintained only *during* the tenant's lifetime if the tenant occupies the property as his or her residence (Rent Act 1977, s. 2(1)(a)). So, however understandable the desire of a statutory tenant to assign his or her statutory tenancy to one or more of the members of his or her family during the tenant's lifetime, this was not, *per se*, allowed for in the legislation (although the 'sub-text' of a case like *Brickfield v Hughes* – see chapter 2 – is perhaps of a court's liberality in practice to such a desire). Secondly, although a statutory tenant has security of tenure *vis-à-vis* his or her landlord, this does not necessarily mean security of tenure *vis-à-vis* the particular property, since s. 98(1)(a) of the Rent Act 1977 provides that a landlord *may* be able to recover possession of property A, if willing to offer a suitable alternative property B to the tenant. Of course the longer the property had been the tenant's home the more unreasonable it *might* seem to seek eviction (see *Battlespring v Gates*, above).
  Whatever the original status of a Rent Act statutory tenancy as a true 'home' of the tenant and his or her family, the Housing Act 1988 significantly eroded it for many Rent Act tenants and substituted a much more limited right of succession in relation to statutory tenancies.

(i)   Assured tenancies
The 'core' provision is s. 17 of the Housing Act 1988:

Housing Act 1988

Succession to assured periodic tenancy by spouse
17.—(1)   In any case where—
  (a)   the sole tenant under an assured periodic tenancy dies, and

(b)   immediately before the death, the tenant's spouse was occupying the dwelling-house as his or her only or principal home, and

(c)   the tenant was not himself a successor, as defined in subsection (2) or subsection (3) below,

then, on the death, the tenancy vests by virtue of this section in the spouse (and, accordingly, does not devolve under the tenant's will or intestacy).

(2)   For the purposes of this section, a tenant is a successor in relation to a tenancy if—

(a)   the tenancy became vested in him either by virtue of this section or under the will or intestacy of a previous tenant; or

(b)   at some time before the tenant's death the tenancy was a joint tenancy held by himself and one or more other persons and, prior to his death, he became the sole tenant by survivorship; or

(c)   he became entitled to the tenancy as mentioned in section 39(5) below.

(3)   For the purposes of this section, a tenant is also a successor in relation to a tenancy (in this subsection referred to as 'the new tenancy') which was granted to him (alone or jointly with others) if—

(a)   at some time before the grant of the new tenancy, he was, by virtue of subsection (2) above, a successor in relation to an earlier tenancy of the same or substantially the same dwelling-house as is let under the new tenancy; and

(b)   at all times since he became such a successor he has been a tenant (alone or jointly with others) of the dwelling-house which is let under the new tenancy or of a dwelling-house which is substantially the same as that dwelling-house.

(4)   For the purposes of this section, a person who was living with the tenant as his or her wife or husband shall be treated as the tenant's spouse.

(5)   If, on the death of the tenant, there is, by virtue of subsection (4) above, more than one person who fulfils the condition in subsection (1)(b) above, such one of them as may be decided by agreement or, in default of agreement, by the county court shall be treated as the tenant's spouse for the purposes of this section.

Notes

1.   The s. 17 right of 'succession' applies only to periodic tenancies (not including statutory periodic tenancies), and so prior to the Housing Act 1996 could have no application to initial assured shorthold tenancies (although it could apply to 'follow on' periodic assured shortholds, see *Lower Street Properties Ltd* v *Jones* (1996) 28 HLR 877). Assured shortholds under the 1996 Act 'regime' could in principle come within s. 17 if periodic, but given the extremely limited security they provide long-term this seems a largely theoretical point.

2.   Fixed-term assured tenancies (including pre-Housing Act 1996 assured shortholds) devolve, if at all, to 'successors' only by will or via intestacy law. Interestingly, the absence of a concept equivalent to the statutory tenancy in the Housing Act 1988 (a statutory tenancy conferring only rights personal to the statutory tenant) would have meant that all assured tenancies could be 'left' in a tenant's will, in addition to any s. 17 rights that might exist. However, so long as the landlord acts relatively swiftly to seek possession, Sch. 1 Ground 7 largely blocks this particular 'loophole' (see earlier in this chapter).

3. Controversially, succession under s. 17 is limited to spouses and co-habitees and does not extend to other members of the tenant's family. This, of course, substantially undermines any concept of an assured tenancy representing a family home.

(ii)   Rent Act tenancies

Prior to the Housing Act 1988, all Rent Act tenancies were governed by the same 'regime' in s. 2(1)(b) and Sch. 1, Pt I of the 1977 Act. These provided for spouses to succeed to statutory tenancies and for other 'family' members (undefined) who had lived with the deceased tenant for six months or more also to succeed to statutory tenancies. Two 'successions' were possible. The relevant provisions were significantly amended by Sch. 4 of the Housing Act 1988 for the majority of cases still relevant today (the original rules survived where the tenant died prior to 15 January 1989).

The amended versions of s. 2(1)(b)and Sch. 1 provide as follows:

Rent Act 1977

Statutory tenants and tenancies

2.—(1)   . . .

(b)   Part I of Schedule 1 to this Act shall have effect for determining what person (if any) is the statutory tenant of a dwelling-house [or, as the case may be, is entitled to an assured tenancy of a dwelling-house by succession] at any time after the death of a person who, immediately before his death, was either a protected tenant of the dwelling-house or the statutory tenant of it by virtue of paragraph (a) above.

SCHEDULE 1
STATUTORY TENANCIES

PART I
STATUTORY TENANTS BY SUCCESSION

1.   Paragraph 2 . . . below shall have effect, subject to section 2(3) of this Act, for the purpose of determining who is the statutory tenant of a dwelling-house by succession after the death of the person (in this Part of this Schedule referred to as 'the original tenant') who, immediately before his death, was a protected tenant of the dwelling-house or the statutory tenant of it by virtue of his previous protected tenancy.

2.   If—

(1)   the survivor's spouse (if any) of the original tenant, is residing in the dwelling-house immediately before the death of the original tenant, shall, after the death, be the statutory tenant if, and so long, as he or she occupies the dwelling-house or his or her residence.

(2)   for the purpose of this paragraph a person who was living with the original tenant or his or her wife or husband shall be treated as the spouse of the original tenant.

(3)   if immediately after the death of the original tenant, there is, by virtue of sub-paragraph (2) above, more than one person who fulfills the conditions in sub-paragraph (1) above, such one of them as may be decided by agreement or, in default of agreement, by the county court, shall be treated as the surviving spouse for the purpose of this paragraph.

3.   Where paragraph 2 above does not apply, but a person who was a member of the original tenant's family was residing with him in the dwelling-house at the time of and for the period of 2 years immediately before his death then, after his death, that person or if there is more than one such person such one of them as may be decided by agreement, or in default of agreement by the county court, shall be entitled to an assured tenancy of the dwelling-house by succession. . . .

4.   A person who becomes the statutory tenant of a dwelling-house by virtue of paragraph 2 above is in this Part of this Schedule referred to as 'the first successor'.

5.   If, immediately before his death, the first successor was still a statutory tenant, paragraph 6 below shall have effect, for the purpose of determining who is the statutory tenant after the death of the first successor.

6.—(1)   Where a person who—

(a)   was a member of the original tenant's family immediately before that tenant's death, and

(b)   was a member of the first successor's family immediately before the first successor's death,

was residing in the dwelling-house with the first successor at the time of, and for the period of 2 years immediately before, the first successor's death, that person or, if there is more than one such person, such one of them as may be decided by agreement or, in default of agreement, by the county court shall be entitled to an assured tenancy of the dwelling-house by succession.

In the amended version of Sch. 1 where the original tenant dies a surviving *spouse* can succeed to a *statutory* tenancy if resident with the tenant immediately prior to the death (cohabitees are aligned with spouses for this purpose). Other 'family' members only succeed to *assured* tenancies, and then only if they have lived with the tenant for at least two years prior to the death. On the death of the first successor, very limited succession rights apply – such a successor must have been a statutory tenant, and any 'claimant' to a further succession must have been a member *both* of the original tenant's family *and* of the first successor's family, and also must have been resident in the dwelling-house for two years, up to and including the first successor's death. Even then, only succession to an assured tenancy is possible.

Notes

1.   Again the severe diminution of the rights of non-cohabitee 'family' members via the Housing Act 1988 amendments is highly controversial.

2.   In all the above there is much controversy over the width of the concept of 'member of the tenant's family'. Originally, the debate centred on the status of cohabitees. More recently it has turned on the status of 'platonic' and 'gay' relationships (see now *Fitzpatrick* v *Sterling Housing Association Ltd* [1997] 4 All ER 991). All this is discussed more fully in chapter 9.

Questions

1.   To what extent can a Rent Act tenancy be seen as representing, in legal terms, a potential family home?

2.   Can the erosion of rights of family members, other than cohabitees, under the Housing Act 1988 be justified?

4 THE ALLOCATION OF SOCIAL HOUSING

(A) Introduction

The 'social welfare' aspects of housing are seen at their clearest in the public sector. Local authorities have certain, limited duties to safeguard the interests of the homeless having local connections with their area, to provide priority access programmes to their housing stock for those with particular needs, to supervise the general housing position in their area, and to enforce housing maintenance standards in certain cases.

(B) Local authority tenants and tenancies

Paradoxically, the individual welfare of authority tenants was, until comparatively recently, safeguarded by law less than that of the private sector tenant. Perhaps it was felt that public authorities should be 'model landlords', and so until 1980 *legal* security of tenure was very limited, which was anomalous when compared to the private sector from 1919 onwards. A tenant could resist a possession order only by showing that the local authority had acted in a way in which no reasonable authority would act, and that was an effectively impossible burden of proof to discharge. Practical or '*de facto*' security was high in most local authority areas, but scope for arbitrariness and high-handedness was great. There were questionable restrictions on matters such as keeping pets, taking in lodgers and redecoration: breach of these had the ultimate sanction of eviction. However, since 1980 a package of public sector tenant's rights has been legislatively provided for, usually termed the 'tenants charter'. These rights are now contained in Pt IV of the Housing Act 1985 (ss. 79–117; and see also chapter 5).

The relationship between an authority and its tenants is more than a simple landlord/tenant one. This chapter will consider some of the facets of this issue. However, at the root of the relationship is still the existence of the tenancy with its contract and property implications, and that should be borne in mind in reading the following text and the accompanying materials which are concerned with the process leading to the creation of that relationship, i.e. the administrative process known as 'allocation'.

(C) The allocation and transfer of council tenancies

Very little new local authority housing has been built for over 20 years and so there is a limited supply available – a supply that has been greatly diminished by the sale of over one million dwellings since 1980 under the 'right to buy' policy. It has therefore become increasingly essential that authorities should have clear and fair rules for allocating this diminishing resource on the basis of need.

(i) The issue of discretion
Local authority discretion in allocation has historically been very wide. Section 21(1) of the Housing Act 1985 states that the 'general management, regulation and control of a local authority's houses is vested in and shall be exercised by the authority'. This allowed authorities to 'pick and choose their tenants at their will', see Lord Porter in *Shelley* v *LCC* [1949] AC 56. Until recently the courts allowed them considerable latitude as 'model' landlords.

Other measures did somewhat qualify the width of the discretionary power. Thus s. 22 of the 1985 Act historically stated that in selecting its tenants the authority should give a 'reasonable preference' to those living in overcrowded housing, those with large families, those in unsatisfactory conditions and the homeless. This, however, has now been repealed and replaced by the Housing Act 1996 (see further below).

Nevertheless, even under the 'old' s. 22 it was clear that authorities did not have total freedom of choice, being subject to general legal requirements imposed by the courts to observe legality, procedural propriety and rationality in the allocation of their housing.

Particular attention should be paid to the following cases:

R v *Canterbury City Council, ex parte Gillespie*
(1986) 19 HLR 7

Until 3 March 1983 the applicant and her cohabitant lived as joint secure tenants in accommodation owned by Thanet District Council. They had two children. After the breakdown of the relationship, the applicant left this accommodation and moved to her mother's home in the respondent authority's area. This accommodation was not adequate and she applied for housing from Canterbury City Council on 11 March 1983. On 25 March 1983 the applicant was awarded custody of her two children.

On 5 April 1983 the applicant was interviewed by an officer of the respondent authority and was informed that she could not be placed upon their waiting list until she relinquished the joint secure tenancy in Thanet. This position was confirmed in a letter to the applicant's solicitors on 15 July 1983 which stated 'It is the policy of my council not to accept on the housing waiting list any person who already has an interest in the title of a council dwelling elsewhere.' The applicant attempted to surrender her interest in the Thanet tenancy but this was refused because there were arrears of rent outstanding.

The applicant's solicitors wrote to the respondent authority informing them of the position. On 19 April 1984 they replied stating that 'no consideration can be given to her application until she has relinquished her interest in the tenancy.' The matter was again raised with the respondent authority in January 1985, with an explanation of why the applicant could not take legal proceedings to evict her cohabitant from the Thanet premises since, notwithstanding the custody order, he at that time had actual care of the older child.

In reply to this approach the respondent authority stated briefly that they were aware of no reason why the applicant should not return to the secure tenancy in Thanet. On 22 April 1985 leave was given to bring proceedings for judicial review. Following this the respondent authority reviewed their position and resolved to add the applicant's name to the housing waiting list upon receipt of a valid application. The application was duly sent to them and referred to their Environmental Health and Housing Policy Committee.

The committee met on 21 May 1985 and recommended as follows:

That no applicant registered on the council's housing waiting list be allocated accommodation whilst holding a joint or sole tenancy of another local authority or housing association property unless: (a) a reciprocal arrangement can be agreed with the other landlord or local authority whereby the council may nominate its own tenant or applicant for rehousing or; (b) the case may be considered as a priority within the terms of the Housing (Homeless Persons) Act 1977 or because of violence or a threat of violence the applicant is unable to return to their accommodation in another area.

On 9 July 1985 the committee met and considered the applicant's case and resolved as follows:

That because [the applicant] holds an interest in a secure tenancy with another authority, and paragraphs (a) and (b) of the policy of the council as determined do not apply, no further consideration be given to her application for rehousing for the time being.

The decision was communicated to the applicant's solicitors by a letter dated 31 July 1985 in the following terms:

... the council has now considered your client's application to be housed as opposed to being placed on the waiting list, and has decided that as she holds an interest in a secure tenancy with another local authority no further consideration be given to her application for rehousing for the time being as she contravenes the council's housing policy.

The applicant proceeded with the application for judicial review.

Held: The policy of the authority should be quashed as it constituted a rule rather than a general approach subject to exceptions which would permit each application to be individually considered; the authority had failed to apply their minds, as they should have done, to the particular problems which the applicant asserted had prevented her relinquishing her interest in her secure tenancy.

SIMON BROWN J: ... It is plain beyond argument that decisions by a local authority in the exercise of their statutory powers are reviewable by the courts on accepted principles of judicial review. If authority for that proposition were needed, then it is to be found in the Court of Appeal decision of *Bristol District Council v Clark* [1975] 1 WLR 1443. The contrary was not argued before me.

The essential basis upon which the applicant challenges the respondent's continuous stance, as manifested in their various decision letters to which I have referred throughout the long period of this dispute, is that the respondents have fettered their discretion by adopting and implementing a fixed policy which precludes their giving proper individual consideration to such cases as fall within that policy. Putting it slightly differently, the complaint is that the adoption of the policy operates as a rule and precludes the authority taking into consideration all the relevant matters upon any individual application.

. . .

The relevant law in regard to public authorities holding policies in respect of their exercise of statutory powers, is well known. Mr Watkinson, for the applicant, helpfully put before me the decisions (both at first instance and in the Court of Appeal) in the case of *Attorney General, ex rel Tilley* v *London Borough of Wandsworth* [1981] 1 All ER 1162. The essence of that dispute is to be found in the judgment of Mervyn Davies J (as he then was) as follows:

Section 1 of the 1963 Act [that being the Children and Young Persons Act] imposes a duty and confers a discretion on the local authority. The resolution in effect declares that in carrying out that duty and exercising that discretion the council will not make living accommodation available for a specified class of families. Accordingly, the council has declared a policy which it will follow in carrying out the provisions of the 1963 Act. That is to say there is a policy that whenever any case of an intentionally homeless family is before the social services committee it will not afford accommodation under the 1963 Act for that family.

That council's stance was declared by the courts to be unlawful.

. . .

There was then cited the decision of Cooke J in the case of *Stringer* v *Minister of Housing and Local Government* [1971] 1 All ER 65 as follows:

It seems to me that the general effect of the many relevant authorities is that a Minister charged with a duty of making individual administrative decision in a fair and impartial manner may nevertheless have a general policy in regard to matters which are relevant to those decisions, provided that the existence of that general policy does not preclude him from fairly judging all the issues which are relevant to each individual case as it comes up for decision.

. . .

The effect of the council's policy adopted in the instant case is, in my judgment, to exclude from consideration any applicant on the waiting list who has a secure tenancy of the kind referred to in the policy whether with another local authority or a housing association wholly irrespective of the circumstances of that tenancy and in particular of the availability of that tenancy to the applicant, save only where the express exceptions apply.

. . . [There] is nothing in the documents before me which persuades me that the council have ever applied their mind, as in my judgment they clearly should, to the particular problems which this applicant asserts have faced her in relinquishing [her] interest.

. . .

In my judgment, this challenge succeeds not essentially because the policy is intrinsically irrational, but rather because it constitutes a rule which requires to be followed slavishly rather than merely a stated general approach which is always subject to an exceptional case and which permits each application to be individually considered.

R v Port Talbot Borough Council and others, ex parte Jones
[1988] 2 All ER 208

The respondent was a borough councillor who was divorced and living outside the ward she represented. In July 1984 she applied to the council for a council house. In September the housing tenancy committee resolved that her application should be put on a priority list to be determined on its merits against the merits of others on that list. In the normal course of events the respondent, as a single person, would have been allocated a one- or two-bedroom flat and would have been likely to have had to wait about four years before being rehoused. In April 1986 however, a three-bedroom council house became available in the ward which the respondent repre- sented and under pressure from the chairman of the housing tenancy committee the borough housing officer, to whom the decision was del- egated under standing orders, offered the tenancy of the house to the respondent, who accepted it. The chairman's reasons for seeking to influence the decision were that the respondent needed the house rather than a flat because, as a councillor, she would have members of the public visiting her at home and she also needed to return to the ward she represented in time to establish her presence there before the next election. At the time the house was allocated to the respondent the waiting list for council houses was headed by a family with one child who had expressed interest in the house. The applicant, another councillor, sought judicial review of the decision to allocate the house to the respondent.

Held: The application would be granted and the decision to allocate the house to the respondent quashed, for the following reasons:

(1) Since the dominant role in reaching the decision had been taken by the chairman of the housing tenancy committee when the council's standing orders delegated the decision to the borough housing officer the decision had not been made in an authorised and lawful manner.

(2) The decision was based on irrelevant considerations, namely the chairman's wish to put the respondent in a better position to fight an election, and was an abuse of power because it was unfair to others on the housing list.

NOLAN J: . . . Whatever the true explanation or explanations may be, I can find nothing in the housing policy of the council which would justify the giving of priority to Mrs Kingdom's application on the basis of the evidence which is now before me and which was then available. It seems to me unsatisfactory, to put it no higher, that a councillor should be treated as having priority for housing without clear and specific reasons being given for that preferential treatment. . . .

There are however, in my judgment, other and broader grounds on which [the allocation] should be quashed. The most obvious is that the council's policy is to provide suitable accommodation for those on the waiting list. Mr Hale's duty under the standing orders was to act in accordance with that policy. He clearly did not do so. Counsel for [the tenant] argued that, whatever the normal policy might be, the decision to allocate the house to [the tenant] was authorised by the resolution of September 1984. But that resolution, whatever its other failings, did not authorise the allocation of a three-bedroomed house to [the tenant] in order that she should be the better able to fight an election, without regard to the needs of others who were on the list for housing and against the opinions of the council's officers. There could hardly be a clearer case of a decision which, to adopt one test propounded in *Associated Provincial Picture Houses Ltd* v *Wednesbury Corp* [1947] 2 All ER 680, [1948] 1 KB 223, was based on irrelevant considerations and ignored relevant considerations. To put it more simply, the decision was unfair to others on the housing list and was an abuse of power.

R v *London Borough of Tower Hamlets, ex parte Mohib Ali et al* (1993) 25 HLR 218

Until 1986, the respondent authority used a standard lettings criteria (SLC) for rehousing all applicants for housing, including the homeless. Amongst the criteria for letting were: that families with children under 10 years would not be housed above the fourth floor; that families would be provided with one bedroom for every two children of the same sex born within 10 years of each other; and, that the applicant's area of choice would be taken into account where possible. In June 1986, an amended lettings criteria (ALC) was adopted for homeless families, which abandoned the limitation as to floor and allowed smaller properties to be offered. The reason for the change towards homeless families was concern at the time (between two and four years) that the homeless were spending in temporary accommodation.

Concern about the policy was expressed to the respondents in 1986 by the Commission for Racial Equality, and as a result a number of safeguards were introduced. These included monitoring by a panel of members; a right of appeal against an offer; and, automatic entry onto the transfer list for those who were obliged to accept accommodation which did not conform to the SLC criteria. Subsequently, all three safeguards were abandoned, the right of appeal explicitly so in September 1991. Furthermore, the right to two offers to the homeless had been reduced to one in September 1987, despite advice to the contrary from the respondents' director of housing.

Allocation of housing was subsequently devolved to seven neighbourhoods. Within each neighbourhood, the operation of the ALC was not mandatory. Between April and September 1991, 56 per cent of lettings were made under ALC and 44 per cent under SLC. A significantly higher proportion of homeless Asian families were allocated under ALC than homeless white families who were housed. This was due in part to the fact that larger families are nearly all Bangladeshi. The majority of Bangladeshi families were not, however, homeless. Analysis of those being rehoused by the respondents indicated that between 85 and 95 per cent of Bangladeshis being housed were not homeless, while for non-Asians this figure was between 96 and 97 per cent.

The applicant Mohib Ali applied as homeless in July 1987 and a full duty towards him was accepted. He was offered a three-bedroomed maisonette on the fourth and fifth floors of a block for himself, his wife and six children aged between 1 and 18. He refused on the basis that the offer was too small, and appealed against the offer. In February 1990, his appeal was dismissed, and the respondents wrote saying that they had considered that they had discharged their duty.

Mr Ali sought judicial review.

Held:

(1)   Challenge to the policy was not out of time; it is only when a policy affects an individual that he or she can challenge it and it is only then that time starts to run;

(2)   There is nothing unlawful is seeking to reduce the use of temporary hotel accommodation for homeless persons; the degree of priority accorded to homeless persons by the respondents in their lettings policy was not unlawful, provided that their other policies in relation to the homeless were fair; the decision to adopt the amended lettings criteria was lawful;

(3)   The respondents failed to recognise the two disadvantages occurring from a move under the amended lettings criteria from bed and breakfast, namely that less suitable accommodation might be allocated and that the prospects of a family later being offered suitable permanent accommodation after having once been moved from temporary accommodation are reduced; the subsequent removal of the safeguards of monitoring, appeal and automatic entry on to the transfer list, together with the apparently arbitrary and random way in which the alternate lettings criteria operated in different neighbourhoods demonstrated unfairness and irrationality requiring intervention by the court;

(4)   There was no evidence of direct discrimination under the Race Relations Act 1976; nor did the evidence identify any improper requirement or condition within section 1(1)(b) of the 1976 Act, nor did it show considerable disproportion;

(5)   While authorities are fully entitled in exercising their statutory duties under the Race Relations Act 1976, s. 71 to pay regard to what they thought was the best interests of race relations, this did not establish any breach of s. 71 in the circumstances of this case.

ROSE LJ: . . . It is common ground that the respondents must act rationally (see per Lord Halsbury, Lord Chancellor in *Sharpe* v *Wakefield* [1891] AC 173 at 179) and must have regard to all relevant considerations, that section 71 must be broadly interpreted (see *per* Lord Roskill in *Wheeler* v *Leicester County Council* [1985] AC 1054 at 1077D–F) and that the duties under sections 21 and 22 of the Housing Act and under section 71 of the Race Relations Act cannot properly be performed without a policy subject to exceptions in relation to the housing of homeless persons (see *per* Lord Scarman with whom all other members of the House agreed in *Re Findlay* [1985] AC 318 at 335D).

. . .

The allocation of accommodation has been devolved by Tower Hamlets to its seven neighbourhoods. It is not suggested that devolution is improper. But the operation of ALC is not mandatory. It is entirely up to the neighbourhood allocation staff whether or not they apply ALC. Between April and September 1991 there was a range of variation between 49 per cent and 77 per cent in the use made of ALC by different neighbourhoods. For the same period 56 per cent of lettings were made under ALC and 44 per cent. under SLC. A significantly higher proportion of homeless Asian families than homeless white families who were housed were allocated under ALC but it is common ground, as we have said, that the larger families are nearly all Bangladeshi. The evidence from Mr Edwards of the CRE in his affidavit of September 15, 1992, paragraph 8, shows that Asian families are disproportionately likely compared with white families to receive lettings amended by area and floor level. It is correct, as Mr Pannick said, that the respondents have not chosen to reply to this on affidavit. Mr Underwood, on the other hand, was entitled, as it seems to us, to point out, as he did, that, excluding, as Mr Edwards does in his calculations, lettings amended *by* size does not accurately reflect lettings amended *because* of size, that is a suitably large property found in a different area would appear statistically as an amendment *by* area but not *because* of area; the true rationale for the amendment will, in fact, be size. Mr Edwards' reliance on figures based on amendments by reference to area and floor level is therefore, as it seems to us, flawed though we bear well in mind the comment of Browne-Wilkinson J in *Perera* v *Civil Service Commission* (1982) ICR 350 at 359 that courts do not require sophisticated statistics in this context.

It is clear that, in practice, ALC are applied in relation to Bangladeshis to a much greater extent than in relation to white homeless families. . . .

In the light of this material, Mr Pannick's first challenge, based on arbitrariness, is that the respondents have failed to adopt and apply any consistent standards or principles for the allocation of housing for the homeless. Allocation depends on the neighbourhood which makes the allocation. The safeguards which the sub committee thought necessary in 1986 have been abandoned. The respondents have abdicated their responsibility by purporting to adopt a policy which is more honoured in the breach than in the observance. The arbitrary nature of this is particularly shown in Stepney where the policy is regarded as unfair but where it is applied to 71 per cent of lettings (A302).

Mr Pannick's second submission is that the respondents have, arbitrarily, a principle which involves the less favourable treatment of the homeless compared with other persons to whom the respondents must give a reasonable preference in the allocation of accommodation . . . and also compared with persons whom the respondents have no duty to house such as those beneficially treated under the sons and daughters scheme. The only proper basis for allocation of accommodation is housing need and it is both arbitrary and irrational for the homeless uniquely not to be placed on the list for transfer to SLC accommodation.

Mr Pannick's third submission is that the treatment of Bangladeshis demonstrates a breach of section 71 of the Race Relations Act in failing to make appropriate arrangements with a view both to eliminating racial discrimination and promoting equality of opportunity and good relations between persons of different racial groups.

Fourth, Mr Pannick submits that the matters to which we have referred demonstrate both direct and indirect discrimination contrary to section 1(1) of the Race Relations Act.

As to direct discrimination, it is common ground that [this] does not depend on intention and motive but simply on whether 'but for' their race, persons would have been more favourably treated (see *R v Birmingham City Council, ex parte Equal Opportunities Commission* [1989] AC 1155 at 1194B *per* Lord Goff). Mr Pannick emphasizes the role played by the CRE in relation to the respondents and stresses that the difficulty of showing discrimination is such that the court should be ready to infer it (see *Baker v Cornwall County Council* (1990) ICR 452 at 459C). He relies on the passage in the affidavit from Mr. Edwards to which we have earlier referred.

As to indirect discrimination, he submits that there is a requirement or condition within section 1(1)(b) in that an applicant for housing who wishes to be treated under SLC must not be homeless or he must rely on the discretion of the officer and he referred us to the judgment of Browne-Wilkinson J in *Clarke v Ely* (1983) ICR 165 at 170D to 171D. He submits that a considerably lower proportion of Bangladeshi housing applicants than non-Bangladeshis can in practice comply with this requirement and that the respondents cannot justify their conduct under section 1(1)(b)(ii) in accordance with the test postulated by Balcombe LJ in *Hampson v Department of Education and Science* (1989) ICR 179 at 191F *viz*: 'An objective balance between the discriminatory effect of the condition and the reasonable needs of the party who applies the condition.' He submits that the practice has a very considerable adverse effect on Bangladeshis, particularly when applied without the safeguards thought necessary in 1986 and even though it is criticized both by the CRE and the majority of the neighbourhoods. It is not applied to applicants other than the homeless and an alternative policy would be to provide more housing stock for the homeless as the respondents' officers have suggested. The policy is to the detriment of homeless applicants who cannot comply with it because they are given accommodation less favourable than they would receive if the old lettings policy were applied.

. . . [It] is pertinent to bear in mind that, as Lord Brightman said in *R v Hillingdon Borough Council, ex parte Puhlhofer* [1986] AC 484 at 518C:

. . . . it is not . . . . appropriate that the remedy of judicial review which is a discretionary remedy, should be made use of to monitor the actions of local authorities under the Act save in the exceptional case.

A local authority's resources are limited and they use them as best they can consistent with proper performance of their statutory duties. Accordingly there is nothing unlawful in seeking to reduce the use of temporary hotel accommodation for homeless persons. And the degree of priority accorded to homeless persons by the respondents in their lettings policy was not unlawful, provided that their other policies in relation to the homeless were fair.

In our judgment the reports made to the Housing Sub Committee on June 16, 1986, and October 13, 1986, . . . were appropriate. They set out the relevant considerations, including cost, and the particular problems of larger homeless families and the high proportion of Asian families in this group. The consequent disproportionate effect of homelessness on ethnic minorities was recognised in the respondents' published policy document . . . They were entitled to take into account the fact that the majority of the Asian applicants for housing were not homeless . . . and that, as appears from paragraph 7 of [an officer's] affidavit of June 12, 1992, depending on the basis of the analysis, between 87 per cent and 95 per cent of Bangladeshis and between 96 per cent and 97 per cent of non-Asians were able to comply with the alleged requirement or condition of not being homeless relied on by the applicants as showing indirect discrimination: clearly it cannot be said that there is disproportion, still less considerable disproportion between Asians and non-Asians.

Furthermore, the shortage of units for large families available to the respondents presented a particular and serious problem.

But the need for safeguards in applying the ALC was recognized by the respondents themselves. And their analysis, as a matter of policy and in argument before this court, failed, in our judgment, to recognize the two disadvantages occurring from a move under the ALC from bed and breakfast accommodation, namely that less suitable accommodation might be allocated and that the prospects of a family being later offered suitable permanent accommodation after having once been moved from temporary accommodation are reduced. It is, no doubt, because of these disadvantages that the initial safeguards were introduced. It seems to us to follow that the removal of those safeguards, together with the apparently arbitrary and random way in which the ALC operate in different neighbourhoods, without any proffered justification, demonstrates unfairness and irrationality requiring intervention by the court.

With regard to the Race Relations Act, however, we find no evidence of direct discrimination under section 1(1)(a) or section 21: in particular there is nothing to suggest that a large Asian family is treated less favourably than a large white family. As to indirect discrimination, we have already indicated our view that the evidence before us does not identify any improper requirement or condition within section 1(1)(b) nor does it show considerable disproportion.

As to section 71 of the Act, it seems to us that the applicants' reliance on *Wheeler v Leicester City Council* [1985] AC 1054 is misconceived. The House of Lords there held that the council had been over-zealous in exercising its section 71 powers. Lord Roskill . . . said that the council were fully entitled, in exercising their statutory discretion, to pay regard to what they thought was the best interests of race relations. But this is far from establishing any breach of duty under section 71 in the circumstances with which we are concerned.

Accordingly, the ALC policy as applied to each of these applicants, that is without the safeguards originally envisaged by the respondents, must, in our judgment, be struck down on the one ground which we have indicated.

R v *Gateshead Metropolitan Borough Council, ex parte Lauder*
(1996) 29 HLR 360

In June 1995, the applicant, the mother of three children, left her home because of domestic violence. She went to live with her parents and disabled brother. Consequently, her parents' house became overcrowded within the meaning of the respondent authority's allocation policy.

On 11 September 1995 the applicant applied to the respondent authority for accommodation. The authority accepted that the applicant was unintentionally homeless. On 19 September 1995, the authority offered the applicant accommodation. The applicant refused the offer on the ground that the accommodation was not situated within one of the areas for which she had indicated a preference. On 21 September 1995, the authority decided that they had discharged their duty to the applicant under Part III of the Housing Act 1985. On 2 October 1995, the authority wrote to the applicant informing her that she had been placed on their waiting list, but that although she was entitled to points for the overcrowding in her present address, she would not be awarded those points for a period of twelve months. This decision was made under the authority's policy that:

> Where an applicant moves into a property creating either an overcrowded or medically unsuitable situation, the benefit of the overcrowded, medical and lack of amenity points will be withheld for a period of twelve months.

On 14 November 1995, the authority considered the applicant's circumstances and the possibility of awarding her the points for overcrowding before the end of the twelve-month period. They decided, however, not to depart from their earlier decision. The applicant applied for judicial review of the authority's decisions of 2 October and 14 November.
Held:

(1)   The respondent authority's policy required the authority to withhold points for a period of twelve months where an applicant moved into overcrowded property; the relevant passage in the policy unlawfully fettered the authority's discretion to consider each case on its merits;

(2)   The authority's initial decision, made on 2 October, was reached because they were satisfied that the applicant came within the terms of the relevant part of their policy; in so doing they had adopted an inflexible approach and the decision was unlawful;

(3)   The decision made on 14 November was a decision to which the authority were entitled to come in light of the information available to them and the circumstances in question; it was a decision that they could reasonably have reached.

POTTS J: . . . Reference must be made to section 22 of the Housing Act 1985 which provides, so far as material:

A local housing authority shall secure that in the selection of their tenants a reasonable preference is given to
(a)   persons occupying insanitary or overcrowded houses . . .

It is accepted that the applicant fell within category (a) as an occupant of an overcrowded house. Reference should also be made to section 106 of the Act which provides:

(1)   A landlord authority shall publish a summary of its rules—
(a)   for determining priority as between applicants in the allocation of its housing accommodation, and . . .
(2)   A landlord authority shall

(a) maintain a set of the rules referred to in subsection (1) and of the rules which it has laid down governing the procedure to be followed in allocating its housing accommodation. . .

The respondent's letting policy and points structure derives from the provisions of section 106 and is designed to effect the purpose of section 22.

Miss Markus's first point is that that part of the policy which relates to suspension of points advantage unlawfully fettered the discretion of the respondents to consider cases such as this applicant's on its merits. Miss Markus points to that passage in the policy identified above to the effect that 'the benefit of the overcrowded, medical and lack of amenity points *will be* withheld for a period of twelve months.' (my emphasis). In essence Miss Markus submits that the words 'will be' are mandatory and require the respondents to withhold overcrowding points whenever 'an applicant moves into a property creating an overcrowded situation'.

Miss Smart, on behalf of the respondents, submits that this construction cannot be justified. She argues, as I understand it, that because the passage in question requires the respondents to withhold points for a period of 12 months only, the exercise of any power under that passage imports an element of discretion.

I have been referred to a number of authorities. In the *Attorney-General ex rel Tilley* v *London Borough of Wandsworth* [1981] 1 All ER 1162 and 1169 the Court of Appeal upheld a decision of HH Judge Mervyn Davis QC, Templeman LJ saying at page 1170J:

On well-recognised principles public authorities are not entitled to fetter the exercise of a discretion or to fetter the manner in which they are empowered to discharge the many duties which are thrust on them.

. . .

That case was concerned with the Children and Young Persons Act 1963 and was remote on its facts from the present. However, Miss Markus submits that the principle is clear; the mere existence of a mandatory provision for suspension of points advantage, as in this case, raises a doubt as to whether any decision reached concerning the suspension of points could be said to be a fair decision. My attention was also drawn to *R* v *Canterbury City Council ex parte Gillespie* (1986) 19 HLR 7 in which Simon Brown J referred to the *Wandsworth* case and followed it.

I accept the applicant's submissions on this point. In my judgment that part of the lettings policy concerned with the suspension of points advantage on its face requires the respondent to withhold points for a period of 12 months where an applicant moves into overcrowded property. On its face that passage fetters the discretion of the respondent to consider each case on its merits as the Housing Act requires. As I observed during argument, and as counsel appeared to accept, the vice in the passage could easily be cured by the insertion of the word 'usually' before 'will' or by the insertion of the words 'in exceptional cases' at some appropriate point. As it is, I am satisfied that the passage in question on its face required the respondents to adopt an inflexible approach. Had I had any doubt about this the terms of the letter of October 2, would have removed it. I am satisfied the terms of that letter indicate that when the respondent initially withheld points they did so because they were satisfied without more that this applicant came within the terms of the passage complained of.

Therefore, I conclude that that part of the policy identified, that is to say that part of the policy relating to suspension of points advantage, was and is unlawful. I am further satisfied that the decision on October 2, was made in direct consequence of that policy.

[Potts J then turned to the authority's decision of 14 November when it appeared all the facts of the situation were available and were considered:]

This court does not sit as a Court of Appeal from the decision of the Chairman, Vice Chairman and Director of Housing. It is not for this court to substitute its own judgment for that of those officers of the respondents. The crucial issue for this court is whether the decision in question was one to which, on all the information identified in the passages above, the respondents were entitled to come to. In my judgment the respondents were entitled to come to this decision on the information available to them and in the circumstances in question. This was a decision taken by the Director of Housing and the Chairman and Vice Chairman of the Housing Committee, gentlemen well equipped to judge questions of housing on South Tyneside, certainly better equipped than this court. Had I been persuaded by any of the arguments advanced by Miss Markus that that decision was unlawful I would have so held. I am not so persuaded. In my judgment it was a decision that the council could reasonably have reached.

In the result the applicant succeeds in respect of the decision of October 2. She succeeds in respect of her argument concerning the respondent's letting policy and I now invite counsel to address me as to the appropriate relief.

Questions

What do these cases tell us about the attitude of the courts to housing allocation? When are the courts prepared to intervene, and on what basis? What is meant by ideas such as 'fairness', 'consistency' and 'impartiality' in this context?

Notes

1. In *R v Sutton London Borough Council, ex parte Alger* [1992] *Legal Action*, June, p. 13, a local authority's allocation rules excluded all owner-occupiers, except elderly persons in medical need, irrespective of housing need. Judicial review was sought of this, but before the case could be heard the authority abolished the restrictive rule. This was followed chronologically by *R v Islington LBC, ex parte Aldabbagh* [1994] EGCS 156. Here an authority had a policy of refusing to transfer existing tenants to new houses unless they cleared off all arrears of rent. This policy was applied irrespective of urgent medical need evidence. It was held the authority had illegally fettered its discretion.

2. A number of authorities in the late 1980s introduced revisions to allocation policies to debar those with rates or community charge debts, either by way of non-admission to the waiting list, or by a bar on actual allocation. *R v Forest Heath DC, ex parte West & Lucas* (1992) 24 HLR 85 concerned a homeless couple with a young child who were second on the waiting list for council accommodation, but who were believed by the authority to be liable for unpaid community charge (poll tax). They were informed that they would be considered for housing only once their community charge payments were brought up to date. The Court of Appeal indicated this was an abuse of power. The relevant legislation – the Local Government Act 1988 – did not entitle an authority to discriminate against

non-payers of the poll tax – in any case, other remedies for non-payment were available.

3. Students should remember that the case law is in reality an application of the general principles of administrative law – the 'Wednesbury principles' – which require authorities to stay within the limits of their powers, to behave in a procedurally correct and fair fashion, to base their decisions only on relevant considerations and, overall, to behave reasonably in the discharge of their functions.

4. Remember that the remedy by way of judicial review is (i) discretionary, (ii) theoretically serves only to quash an authority's decision and is not an allocation decision in its own right, and (iii) is available only to someone with a 'sufficient interest' in the matter in question, for example a person actually refused admission to a housing register for some irrelevant reason. Interestingly, in the *Port Talbot* case the applicant was the Leader of the Council whose special position was considered to give him a 'sufficient interest' to challenge a decision taken by his fellow council members.

Question
What is it that courts do when they strike down a housing allocation decision? Are they actually substituting their decision for that of the local authority?

(D) Anti-discrimination provisions

Under the Race Relations Act 1976 and the Sex Discrimination Act 1975, the absolute freedom of local authorities in matters of allocation is also limited, and this has not been changed by the Housing Act 1996.

Section 21 of the 1976 Act and s. 30 of the 1975 Act prohibit discrimination in relation to entry onto the housing register and allocation from that register. These rules also apply with equal force to the allocation policies of housing associations. Unlawful discrimination may be committed *directly* or *indirectly*. The former involves treating a person less favourably than others on grounds of race, sex etc., e.g., 'no black women'. However, most forms of direct discrimination are more subtle than that, e.g. allocating the least desirable properties to black people. Such policies need not be *deliberately* or *maliciously* driven – very often they result from unthinking cultural assumptions. Indirect discrimination is the act of applying a condition which, though on its face apparently neutral, has the effect that it is harder for members of minorities (or of one sex) to comply with it than members of the host population (or of the other sex). Indirectly discriminatory practices include allocating 'points' on housing waiting lists to people only according to the number of children actually living with them. This fails to consider the needs of people who have children overseas. There are few housing cases under the anti-discrimination legislation. Students should nevertheless re-read *R v London Borough of Tower Hamlets, ex parte Mohib Ali* (1993) 25 HLR 218 (above).

Question

What does this case tell us about discriminatory housing practices, and how did the Court respond?

(E)   The historic practice of local authorities in allocation

Historically allocation involved the processes of:

(a)   determining who should qualify to apply for housing;

(b)   deciding who should be allocated council housing (normally known as 'selection')

(c)   deciding which particular dwelling any such successful applicant should be offered.

It was common practice to create waiting lists (or 'housing registers') from which all general allocations of council property were made, in accordance with the particular selection scheme used. It was not uncommon for registration on/entry to a waiting list to itself be made subject to the satisfaction of conditions, typically a residential qualification.

Allocation 'off list' (normally termed 'selection') was largely done by housing officers in housing departments, but in many instances detailed policy criteria were laid down by the housing committee which consisted of elected councillors. All but the clearest cases normally entailed not only a written application for housing, but also an interview and/or home visit. Disquiet was sometimes expressed at the effect of inbuilt prejudice in some 'housing visitors', or at the use (perhaps for reason of time) of crude labelling criteria applied after such visits.

There were three broad types of selection scheme:

(a)   *'Date order' schemes*, i.e. 'First come, first served'.

(b)   *Points schemes*, i.e. homes were allocated on the basis of 'points' assessed for satisfactory certain stated criteria, e.g., so many for size of family or bedrooms needed, so many for length of time on the list, etc.

(c)   *Combined schemes*, a combination of the above.

(F)   The new law on allocation of housing accommodation

(i)   *Part VI of the Housing Act 1996*

Housing Act 1996

PART VI
ALLOCATION OF HOUSING ACCOMMODATION

Introductory

Allocation of housing accommodation

159.—(1)   A local housing authority shall comply with the provisions of this Part in allocating housing accommodation.

(2)   For the purposes of this Part a local housing authority allocate housing accommodation when they—

(a)   select a person to be a secure or introductory tenant of housing accommodation held by them,

(b)   nominate a person to be a secure or introductory tenant of housing accommodation held by another person, or

(c)   nominate a person to be an assured tenant of housing accommodation held by a registered social landlord.

(3)   The reference in subsection (2)(a) to selecting a person to be a secure tenant includes deciding to exercise any power to notify an existing tenant or licensee that his tenancy or licence is to be a secure tenancy.

(4)   The references in subsection (2)(b) and (c) to nominating a person include nominating a person in pursuance of any arrangements (whether legally enforceable or not) to require that housing accommodation, or a specified amount of housing accommodation, is made available to a person or one of a number of persons nominated by the authority.

(5)   The provisions of this Part do not apply to the allocation of housing accommodation by a local housing authority to a person who is already—

(a)   a secure or introductory tenant,

(b)   an assured tenant (otherwise than under an assured shorthold tenancy) of housing accommodation held by a registered social landlord, or

(c)   an assured tenant of housing accommodation allocated to him by a local housing authority.

(6)   The provisions of this Part do not apply to the allocation of housing accommodation by a local housing authority to two or more persons jointly if—

(a)   one or more of them is a person within subsection (5)(a), (b) or (c), and

(b)   none of the others is excluded from being a qualifying person by section 161(2) or regulations under section 161(3).

(7)   Subject to the provisions of this Part, a local housing authority may allocate housing accommodation in such manner as they consider appropriate.

The new system of housing allocation is based on four principles inherent in the legislation: consistency, fairness, transparency and challengeability. The new system of allocation is further based on four positive levels of obligation – MUST, MAY, SHOULD, COULD – and one negative level – CANNOT. Some of these exist under the statute, some under statutory instruments, some under guidance issued by the Secretary of State.

Section 22 of the Housing Act 1985 was repealed, and local housing authorities (LHAs) were placed by s. 159 of the 1996 Act under a mandatory obligation to comply with legal requirements in allocating their housing. This 'prime duty' applies:

(a)   when they *select* a person to be a secure tenant of accommodation;

(b)   when they nominate a person to be a secure tenant of accommodation held by some other body (e.g., another LHA);

(c)   when they nominate a person to be an assured tenant of accommodation held by a 'registered social landlord' (e.g., a Housing Association).

There is a single route into social housing for those entering such housing for the first time, and that route is based on *registration* followed by a *fair assessment* of need *consistently applied*.

This is the first of a number of duties, i.e. legal *requirements*. In full these are:

(a)   to comply with Pt VI of the Act – see s. 159(1);
(b)   to allocate only to qualifying persons – s. 161(1);
(c)   to establish and maintain a register – s. 162(1), (4);
(d)   to operate that register – s. 163;
(e)   to notify certain decisions and other matters, e.g., adverse decisions, rights to request reviews, times for making such requests – s. 164(5);
(f)   to notify decisions on review with, when adverse, reasons – s. 165(5);
(g)   to have a 'scheme of allocation' – s. 167(1);
(h)   to consult other 'social landlords' before making major policy changes – s. 167(7) – though what is 'major' is not defined in the legislation;
(i)   not to allocate save in accordance with the scheme – s. 167(8);
(j)   to give out information about the scheme – s. 168;
(k)   to have regard to guidance from the Secretary of State – s. 169(1). This is contained in a new Code of Guidance, that is the document which contains the 'shoulds and the coulds' – the foregoing are the 'musts'.

If legal obligations are ignored then mandamus could be obtained to compel compliance with duties, though only by a person with a 'sufficient interest' in the matter. It is arguable that any allocation of accommodation made in breach of a duty could be a nullity and would not confer any interest at all on the purported tenant.

This may appear to be a major extension of the rights of applicants for housing. However, the changes made were already the 'best practice' of the most advanced LHAs. Furthermore the 'allocations package' cannot be divorced from the changes made in relation to reducing the entitlements of otherwise homeless people (see further chapter 6).

Questions
In insisting that there should only be one route initially into permanent council accommodation were ministers pursuing a particular political agenda, and if so what? Does the elaboration of the law merely serve to disguise the fact that there is not enough good quality accommodation to go around (and why is that so?) with the consequence that it has to be rationed? In creating such a scheme, is it not the case that the end result will be that some will be excluded from being able to benefit? Remember that the new law does not ensure the building of a single new house. Is there a case for arguing that what the law should be doing is to require LHAs to assess first the unmet housing needs of their areas and then to impose on them, central government and other social landlords, such as housing associations, an obligation to meet that need? But who would pay for that new accommodation?

(ii)   Exceptions to the prime duty
Under s. 159(5) of the 1996 Act the duty will *not* apply to allocation of housing to people who are *already* secure tenants or assured tenants of housing held by a Housing Association. Likewise, there are specific exceptions in s. 160 where the mandatory obligation will not apply:

Housing Act 1996

Cases where provisions about allocation do not apply
160.—(1) The provisions of this Part about the allocation of housing accommodation do not apply in the following cases.

(2) They do not apply where a secure tenancy—

(a) vests under section 89 of the Housing Act 1985 (succession to periodic secure tenancy on death of tenant),

(b) remains a secure tenancy by virtue of section 90 of that Act (devolution of term certain of secure tenancy on death of tenant),

(c) is assigned under section 92 of that Act (assignment of secure tenancy by way of exchange),

(d) is assigned to a person who would be qualified to succeed the secure tenant if the secure tenant died immediately before the assignment, or

(e) vests or is otherwise disposed of in pursuance of an order made under—

(i) section 24 of the Matrimonial Causes Act 1973 (property adjustment orders in connection with matrimonial proceedings),

(ii) section 17(1) of the Matrimonial and Family Proceedings Act 1984 (property adjustment orders after overseas divorce, &c.), or

(iii) paragraph 1 of Schedule 1 to the Children Act 1989 (orders for financial relief against parents).

(3) They do not apply where an introductory tenancy—

(a) becomes a secure tenancy on ceasing to be an introductory tenancy,

(b) vests under section 133(2) (succession to introductory tenancy on death of tenant),

(c) is assigned to a person who would be qualified to succeed the introductory tenant if the introductory tenant died immediately before the assignment, or

(d) vests or is otherwise disposed of in pursuance of an order made under—

(i) section 24 of the Matrimonial Causes Act 1973 (property adjustment orders in connection with matrimonial proceedings),

(ii) section 17(1) of the Matrimonial and Family Proceedings Act 1984 (property adjustment orders after overseas divorce, &c.), or

(iii) paragraph 1 of Schedule 1 to the Children Act 1989 (orders for financial relief against parents).

(4) They do not apply in such other cases as the Secretary of State may prescribe by regulations.

(5) The regulations may be framed so as to make the exclusion of the provisions of this Part about the allocation of housing accommodation subject to such restrictions or conditions as may be specified.

In particular, those provisions may be excluded—

(a) in relation to specified descriptions of persons, or

(b) in relation to housing accommodation of a specified description or a specified proportion of housing accommodation of any specified description.

The Secretary of State has power to extend these exceptions by regulations which may take account of particular exceptions for particular types of accommodation (see s. 160(4) and (5)). These are the Allocation of Housing Regulations 1996 (SI 1996 No. 2753). Students should note in particular reg. 3:

Allocation of Housing Regulations 1996
SI 1996 No. 2753

Citation and commencement

1. These Regulations may be cited as the Allocation of Housing Regulations 1996 and shall come into force on [1st April] 1997 [as amended by SI 1996 No. 3122].

Interpretation

2. In these Regulations—
'the Act' means the Housing Act 1996;
'the Common Travel Area' means the United Kingdom, the Channel Islands, the Isle of Man and the Republic of Ireland collectively;
'the Convention' means the Convention relating to the Status of Refugees done at Geneva on 28th July 1951 as extended by Article 1(2) of the Protocol relating to the Status of Refugees done at New York on 31st January 1967;
'EEA national' means a national of a State which is a Contracting Party to the Agreement on the European Economic Area signed at Oporto on 2nd May 1992 as adjusted by the Protocol signed at Brussels on 17th March 1993; and
'the immigration rules' means the immigration rules within the meaning of the Immigration Act 1971.

Cases where the provisions of Part VI of the Act do not apply

3.—(1) The provisions of Part VI of the Act about the allocation of housing accommodation do not apply in the following cases.

(2) They do not apply to the allocation of housing accommodation by a local housing authority to a person who is already—

(a) a secure tenant under Part II of the Housing (Northern Ireland) Order 1983 (secure tenants) where the estate of the landlord belongs to the Northern Ireland Housing Executive,

(b) a secure tenant under Part III of the Housing (Scotland) Act 1987 (rights of public sector tenants), or

(c) an assured tenant of accommodation under Part II of the Housing (Scotland) Act 1988 (rented accommodation) (otherwise than under a short assured tenancy within the meaning given by section 32 of that Act) where the interest of the landlord belongs to—

(i) a housing association registered in the register maintained by Scottish Homes under section 3 of the Housing Associations Act 1985((the register), or

(ii) a person who acquired the accommodation (otherwise than under Part Ill of the Housing (Scotland) Act 1987) from a district council or islands council constituted under section 2 of the Local Government (Scotland) Act 1973 (constitution of councils of regions, islands areas and districts), a council constituted under section 2 of the Local Government etc. (Scotland) Act 1994 (constitution of councils), or Scottish Homes.

(3) They do not apply where a local housing authority secures the provision of suitable alternative accommodation under section 39 of the Land Compensation Act 1973 (duty to rehouse residential occupiers).

(4) They do not apply in relation to the grant of a secure tenancy under section 554 or 555 of the Housing Act 1985 (grant of tenancy to former owner-occupier or statutory tenant of defective dwelling-house).

(iii)   The obligation on LHAs

Housing Act 1996

Allocation only to qualifying persons
161.—(1)   A local housing authority shall allocate housing accommodation only to persons ('qualifying persons') who are qualified to be allocated housing accommodation by that authority.

(2)   A person subject to immigration control within the meaning of the Asylum and Immigration Act 1996 is not qualified to be allocated housing accommodation by any authority in England and Wales unless he is of a class prescribed by regulations made by the Secretary of State.

(3)   The Secretary of State may by regulations prescribe other classes of persons who are, or are not, qualifying persons in relation to local housing authorities generally or any particular local housing authority.

(4)   Subject to subsection (2) and any regulations under subsection (3) a local housing authority may decide what classes of persons are, or are not, qualifying persons.

(5)   The prohibition in subsection (1) extends to the allocation of housing accommodation to two or more persons jointly if any of them is excluded from being a qualifying person by subsection (2) or regulations under subsection (3).

(6)   The prohibition does not otherwise extend to the allocation of housing accommodation to two or more persons jointly if one or more of them are qualifying persons.

Section 161 provides that a LHA is able to allocate housing *only* to 'qualifying persons', and these are: (i) persons falling within classes to be prescribed by the Secretary of State; and (ii) subject to the foregoing, such classes as are determined to be qualifying by each LHA. The result is a general rule that before anyone can obtain a council house they have to satisfy a number of requirements:

(a)   they have to be a 'qualifying person' to be registered at all – some people will not be able to qualify;

(b)   once they have qualified and have been registered, they will have to satisfy the requirements of the particular allocation scheme in effect in the area.

There may in *most* cases be an allocation to two or more persons if only one or more of them qualifies.

(a)   Who are 'qualifying persons'?

Qualifying persons are defined under the Allocation of Housing Regulations 1996 (SI 1996 No. 2753, as amended by SI 1997 No. 631 and SI 1999 No. 2135):

Allocation of Housing Regulations 1996
SI 1996 No. 2753

Classes prescribed under section 161(2) who are qualifying persons
4. The following are the classes of persons prescribed for the purposes of section 161(2) of the Act (allocation only to qualifying persons)—

Class A—a person recorded by the Secretary of State as a refugee within the definition in Article 1 of the Convention;

Class B—a person—

(i)   who has been granted by the Secretary of State exceptional leave to enter or remain in the United Kingdom outside the provisions of the immigration rules; and

(ii)   whose leave is not subject to a condition requiring him to maintain and accommodate himself and any dependants of his without recourse to public funds;

Class C—a person who has a current leave to enter or remain in the United Kingdom which is not subject to any limitation or condition other than a person—

(i)   who has been given leave to enter or remain in the United Kingdom upon an undertaking given by another person (his 'sponsor') or persons in writing in pursuance of the immigration rules to be responsible for his maintenance and accommodation;

(ii)   who has been resident in the United Kingdom for less than five years beginning from the date of entry or the date on which the undertaking was given in respect of him, whichever date is the later; and

(iii) whose sponsor or, where there is more than one sponsor, at least one of whose sponsors, is still alive.

Class CA—a person who is—

(i)   a national of a state which is a signatory to the European Convention on Social and Medical Assistance (done in Paris on 11th December 1953) or a state which is a signatory to the Council of Europe Social Charter (signed in Turin on 18th October 1961); and

(ii)   habitually resident in the Common Travel Area.
[Inserted by SI 1997 No. 631.]

Class CB (this applies in relation to England only) — a person who left the territory of Monserrat after 1st November 1995 because of the effect on that territory of a volcanic erruption.
[Inserted by SI 1999 No. 2135.]

Classes prescribed under section 161(3) who are qualifying persons
5. The following prescribed classes of persons are qualifying persons in relation to a local housing authority for the purposes of section 161(3) of the Act (allocation only to qualifying persons)—

Class D—a person over the age of 18 years who is owed a duty by that authority under—

(i)   section 193 (duty to persons with priority need who are not homeless intentionally), or

(ii)   subsection (2) of section 195 of that Act (duties in case of threatened homelessness) where, in pursuance of the duty under that subsection, the authority secure that accommodation other than that occupied by that person when he made his application for assistance under Part VII of that Act is available for occupation by him;

Class E—a person over the age of 18 years who has within the previous two years been owed a duty by that authority under section 192(2) or 197(2) of the Act (duty to persons not in priority need who are not homeless intentionally and duty where other suitable accommodation available), except a person who has subsequently been owed a duty by that authority under section 190 of that Act (duties to persons becoming homeless intentionally).

Class EA (this applies in relation to England only) — a person who left the territory of Monserrat after 1st November 1995 because of the effect on that territory of a volcanic erruption.
[Inserted by SI 1999 No. 2135.]

Classes prescribed under section 161(3) who are not qualifying persons
6. The following prescribed classes of persons are not qualifying persons in relation to a local housing authority for the purposes of section 161(3) of the Act (allocation only to qualifying persons—

Class F—a person who is not habitually resident in the Common Travel Area other than—

(i) . . .

(ii) a worker for the purposes of Council Regulation (EEC) No. 1612/68 or (EEC) No. 1251/70;

(iii) a person with a right to reside in the United Kingdom pursuant to Council Directive No. 68/360/EEC or No. 73/148/EEC;

(iv) a person who left the territory of Monserrat after 1st November 1995 because of the effect on that territory of a volcanic eruption.

Class G—a person who is an EEA national and is required by the Secretary of State to leave the United Kingdom.
[As amended by SI 1997 No. 631 and SI 1997 No. 2046.]

Notes
The scheme is very complex. There is a group of people who are in general 'disqualified', i.e. they cannot be assisted at all. These are those persons subject to immigration control.
2. Who are 'persons subject to immigration control'? They are all those needing permission to enter this country, that is any person who, under the Immigration Act 1971, requires leave to enter or remain in the UK, whether or not such leave has been given. Such persons are defined by ss. 1 and 2 of the 1971 Act as those who do *not* have a 'right of abode' in the UK.
Persons having a right of abode in the UK are those who are UK citizens who are connected with the UK by virtue of birth, adoption, naturalisation or registration, *or* who have a parent with that connection *or* who have been (i) lawfully settled in the UK and (ii) ordinarily resident for the last five years, *or* who are Commonwealth citizens with a parent born in the UK. All those having the right of abode are 'patrials' – *it is non-patrials, i.e. in general everyone else, who are thus subject to immigration control* and who are thus excluded from housing assistance.

(b)   Ever more complexity

Some persons are *excepted* from this exclusion by being *included* in classes specified by the Secretary of State, i.e. they do qualify for assistance. Students should read regs 4 and 5 of the 1996 Regulations (above), but their outline is as follows:

There are five classes of 'excepted immigrants':

Class A – persons recorded as refugees within the meaning of the Geneva Convention on refugees;

Class B – persons granted exceptional leave to enter/remain in the UK *and* whose leave is not subject to conditions as to self maintenance and accommodation (most immigrants into this country are, however, granted exceptional leave to enter subject to conditions and so fall outside the terms of this exception);

Class C – persons whose leave to enter/remain in the UK is not subject to restriction;

Class CA – persons who are nationals of states who have signed the European Convention on Social and Medical Assistance, or the Council of Europe Social Charter, *and* who are habitually resident in the 'Common Travel Area' (see below).

Class CB – persons from Monserrat who fled from the volcanic erruption in 1995.

Secondly, there are two classes of homeless persons:

Class D – persons aged over 18 who are owed duties in respect of homelessness because they are homeless, in priority need and not intentionally homeless, or who are threatened with homelessness *and* where the LHA have discharged their duties by securing accommodation *other* than that occupied by those persons at the time they made their applications;

Class E – persons aged over 18 who in the previous 2 years have been owed a duty in respect of non-priority homelessness, except those who have subsequently become intentionally homeless.

These seven classes are all 'qualifying persons'.

However, there are then specifically created classes of 'non qualifying persons', i.e. those who cannot be 'qualifying'. The key to understanding these classes is to remember that the Government wished to exclude from 'qualifying person' status those who are subject to immigration control and, in addition, certain other people who are not subject to immigration control. However, the UK Government had to remember its obligations under the Treaty of Rome which guarantees freedom of movement for workers between EC member states, though even they can be asked to leave the UK in certain circumstances. Thus in reg. 6 Class F *excludes* all those not subject to immigration control who are also not habitually resident in the 'Common Travel Area' (the United Kingdom, the Channel Islands, the Isle of Man and the Republic of Ireland) *unless* they are workers who are moving under rules made in pursuance of the Treaty of Rome as EC regulations, or other EC residents falling within the same basic concept of freedom of movement. The consequence of this is that an 'EC worker' can qualify for housing. Class G, however, provides that an EEA national may be excluded from 'qualifying person' status if required by the Home Secretary to leave the UK. The EEA is the EC plus Iceland, Norway and Liechtenstein. Under Class F, much depends upon whether a person is or is not 'habitually resident' in the Common Travel Area.

(c) What is a habitual residence?

This concept requires factors such as the following to be taken into account in deciding a person's status:

(a) Does the person have no immediate or family ties with the UK, or has he or she spent most of his or her life outside the UK?

(b) Does the person have a permanent job in the UK?

(c) If he or she has such a job, what is its nature, is it merely seasonal (in which case it is unlikely to provide a basis for habitual residence)?

(d) Why did the person come to the UK?

(e) How long has the person been resident elsewhere and was that residence continuous?

(f) What are the person's intentions as regards staying in this country?

Figure 4.1 sets out the legislative scheme in diagrammatic form.

(d) Other qualifiers

It is for each LHA to determine who else will be allowed to qualify. Some LHAs may require those who wish to register to have been resident in their area for a prescribed period, or to have a local connection with that area (e.g., by virtue of working in it), while other authorities may exclude people from registration on the grounds of past misconduct, e.g., outstanding rent arrears or a recent record of nuisance. According to the Code of Guidance on Allocation and Homelessness, LHAs will be able to retain such restrictions on registration as they may individually wish to impose, e.g., conditions as to age, marital status, ownership of other housing/property, local connection, length of residence in an area, rent payment record, record as to the creation of nuisances. Thus authorities retain a general residuary discretion to allocate provided they otherwise comply with their duties, under s. 159(7), and there is evidence from Shelter (*Access Denied*, 1998) that 200,000 households have already been excluded from qualification by LHAs.

Question
Bearing in mind the cases already studied, how is the discretion left to authorities to be exercised; what procedural and other requirements are imposed by the courts? Is it right that anyone in need of housing should be excluded?

(iv) The housing register

Under s. 162 of the 1996 Act, each LHA is required to establish and maintain a 'housing register' of qualifying persons. That register must contain such

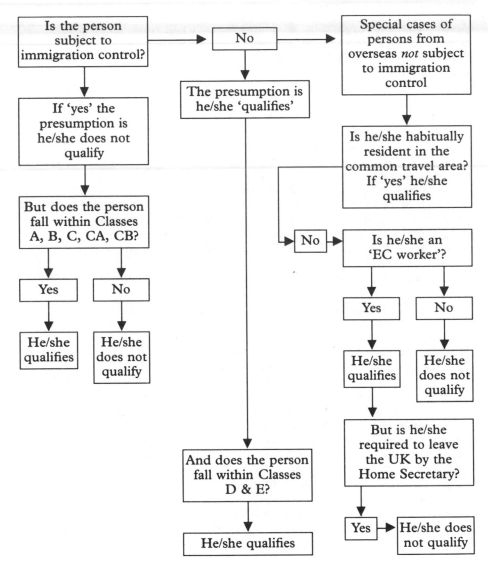

Figure 4.1   Persons qualifying for housing assistance

information about the people on it as the Secretary of State may prescribe (s. 162(4)), but otherwise the LHA is to decide what information to register and in what form the register is to be kept (s. 162(2) and (5)). It may be kept as part of a register held for other purposes or as a register maintained in common with other landlords, e.g., a common list held with housing associations of all people seeking housing in an area, *provided* it is made clear which of them is registered by the LHA – *the entries constituting the LHA's register must be distinguishable* (s. 162(3)).

The 'prescribed information' is defined by reg. 7 of the 1996 Regulations as follows:

Allocation of Housing Regulations 1996
SI 1996 No. 2753

Information in the housing register
7. A local housing authority's housing register shall contain, in relation to each qualifying person,—
    (a) the name of the qualifying person,
    (b) the number of other persons who normally reside with him as a member of his family or who might reasonably be expected to reside with him,
    (c) the number of persons falling within paragraphs (a) and (b) above who are—
        (i)   under the age of 10 years,
        (ii)   expecting a child, or
        (iii) over the age of 60 years,
    (d) the address of the qualifying person,
    (e) the date on which the qualifying person was put on the register, and
    (f) the most recent date on which an entry on the register was amended.

Question
What information has to be recorded by law, and what information could be recorded otherwise?

(G)   Registration

Housing Act 1996

Operation of housing register
163.—(1)   A person shall be put on a local housing authority's housing register if he applies to be put on and it appears to the authority that he is a qualifying person.

(2)   A local housing authority may put a person on their housing register without any application, if it appears to them that he is a qualifying person.

(3)   When a local housing authority put a person on their housing register (on his application or otherwise), they shall notify him that they have done so.

(4)   A local housing authority may amend an entry on their housing register in such circumstances as they think fit.

If they do so, they shall notify the person concerned of the amendment.

(5)   A local housing authority may remove a person from their housing register in such circumstances as they think fit.

(6)   They shall do so—
    (a) if it appears to them that he has never been a qualifying person or is no longer such a person, or
    (b) if he requests them to do so and he is not owed any duty under section 193 or 195(2) (main housing duties owed to persons who are homeless or threatened with homelessness).

(7) Before removing a person from the register, a local housing authority shall comply with such requirements, as to notification or otherwise, as the Secretary of State may prescribe by regulations.

Notification of adverse decision and right to review

164.—(1) If a local housing authority decide—

(a) not to put a person on their housing register who has applied to be put on, or

(b) to remove a person from their housing register otherwise than at his request,

they shall notify him of their decision and of the reasons for it.

(2) The notice shall also inform him of his right to request a review of the decision and of the time within which such a request must be made.

(3) A request for review must be made before the end of the period of 21 days beginning with the day on which he is notified of the authority's decision and reasons, or such longer period as the authority may in writing allow.

(4) There is no right to request a review of the decision reached on an earlier review.

(5) On a request being duly made to them, the authority shall review their decision.

(6) Notice required to be given to a person under this section shall be given in writing and, if not received by him, shall be treated as having been given if it is made available at the authority's office for a reasonable period for collection by him.

Note

Under s. 163, registrations *must* be erased in certain circumstances. However, before erasure the LHA must comply with the Secretary of State's requirements as to notification of the person and as to any other matters. The 1996 Regulations lay down the relevant requirements:

Allocation of Housing Regulations 1996
SI 1996 No. 2753

Requirements before removing a person from the housing register

8.—(1) Before removing a person from their housing register under section 163(5) of the Act (operation of housing register) a local housing authority shall give him notice in accordance with this regulation.

(2) A notice under this regulation shall—

(a) require the person to provide the authority with such information as they reasonably require to enable them to decide whether to remove him from the register,

(b) specify a period of not less than 28 days beginning with the day on which the person receives the notice within which the information must be provided, and

(c) inform the person that the authority may decide to remove him from their register if—

(i) they do not receive the information within the specified period, or

(ii) they consider that in the light of the information they receive within that period there are reasons why he should be removed.

(3) Notice required to be given to a person under this regulation shall be given in writing and, if not received by him, shall be treated as having been given if it is made available at the authority's office for a reasonable period for collection by him.

Thus where a LHA decide either *not* to register a person, or to de-register a person (other than at that person's request), they must notify the person, with reasons. The notification must inform the person of the right to seek a review of this decision and the time within which review must be sought, i.e. 21 days from notification. The right of review applies once only – there is no right to request a review of a decision reached on an earlier review (s. 164(4)). Notices are to be given in writing and may be made available via the LHA's office. The Allocation of Housing and Homelessness (Review Procedures) Regulations 1999 (SI 1999) No. 71, provide only a framework for reviews and students should read the Regulations in the light of the following paragraphs.

The Allocation of Housing and Homelessness (Review Procedures) Regulations 1999
SI 1999 No. 71

Who is to make the decision on the review?
2.—Where the decision of the authority on a review of an original decision made by an officer of the authority is also to be made by an officer, that officer shall be someone who was not involved in the original decision and who is senior to the officer who made the original decision.

PART II

The Housing Register

Notification of review procedure
3.—Following a duly made request for a review under section 164, the authority shall—

(a) notify the person concerned that he, or someone acting on his behalf, may make representations in writing to the authority in connection with the review; and

(b) if they have not already done so, notify the person concerned of the procedure to be followed in connection with the review.

Procedure on a review
4.—The authority shall, subject to compliance with the provisions of regulation 5, consider any representations made under regulation 3.

Notification of the decision on a review
5.—The period within which the authority shall notify the person concerned of the decision on a review under section 164 is eight weeks from the day on which the request for a review is made to the authority or such longer period as the authority and the person concerned may agree in writing.

(i)   Who is to take the decision on review?
The Regulations give a choice to LHAs so that:

(a)   where the review decision of the original decision is to be made by an officer of the authority, that officer must be, first, someone not involved in the original decision and, secondly, senior in rank to the officer who made the original decision; or

(b)   members of the authority may be involved.

(ii)   Review procedure

Once a 'duly made request' for a review has been received (see requirements above), LHAs must notify applicants, or their representatives, of the right to make written representations in connection with the review and (if not already done) of the procedure to be followed. LHAs must consider any representations made and must carry out the review on the basis of facts known to them *at the time of the review*. A time clearly has to be given for representations to be made, received and considered, but students should ask whether there is likely to be debate and conflict over requests for time extensions?

(iii)   Time limits

The period within which LHAs must notify applicants of decisions under s. 164 is eight weeks from the day on which a request for a review is made to the authority, *or* such longer period as LHAs and applicants may agree in writing in given cases.

The Code of Guidance indicates that LHAs should effectively invite applicants to state their grounds for requesting reviews (if not already received) and to elicit any new information applicants wish to put forward. They *may* also point out to applicants that where no representations are received in due time the LHA are entitled to decide the matter on the basis of the facts then known to them, advise applicants that representations from their representatives are acceptable and draw attention to the time period of the review. Further enquiries may have to be made during the review to elicit the most recent facts. LHAs are advised to be flexible about allowing further exchanges, and where this may lead to a delayed decision applicants may agree an extension of the time period to allow for a decision to be reached. It is important to obtain agreements for extensions of time as early as possible once significant delay is anticipated.

(iv)   How are reviews conducted?

No provision is made by the Regulations for oral hearings. The Code of Guidance indicates that they may be desirable where an applicant could be disadvantaged by being required to put everything in writing. Again there may be time implications, and hence the need for agreed extensions of time. Failure to observe good administrative practice on review may result in a maladministration investigation by the Commission for Local Administration. Failure to observe legalities may – indeed probably will – result in judicial review applications, for the only means of challenge to a review decision is by way of judicial review. There is no right of appeal to the county court.

(v)   What information is available to a registered person?

Housing Act 1996

Information about housing register

166.—(1)   A person on the housing register of a local housing authority is entitled—

(a)   to see the entry relating to himself and to receive a copy of it free of charge, and

(b)   to be given such general information as will enable him to assess how long it is likely to be before housing accommodation appropriate to his needs becomes available for allocation to him.

(2)   The fact that a person is on an authority's housing register, and the information about him included in the register, shall not be divulged to any other member of the public.

Section 166 is a 'transparency' provision. It is important where an enquiry is made that misleading information is not given, nor that any undertaking or promise appears to be given. The provision is also problematical in that enquirers are entitled only to 'general' information to enable them to assess how long they will have to wait before accommodation appropriate to their needs becomes available for allocation to them. It would not be proper for an officer to say to an enquirer: 'You are above the Smiths but below the Jones'; indeed the fact that the Smiths and Jones are on the register could not even be divulged. Furthermore the information is that which enables an assessment of the likely period of waiting to be made – but only in relation to accommodation appropriate to the given individual's needs, not in relation to council accommodation generally.

(H)   The allocation scheme

Housing Act 1996

Allocation in accordance with allocation scheme

167.—(1)   Every local housing authority shall have a scheme (their 'allocation scheme') for determining priorities, and as to the procedure to be followed, in allocating housing accommodation.

For this purpose 'procedure' includes all aspects of the allocation process, including the persons or descriptions of persons by whom decisions are to be taken.

(2)   As regards priorities, the scheme shall be framed so as to secure that reasonable preference is given to—

(a)   people occupying insanitary or overcrowded housing or otherwise living in unsatisfactory housing conditions,

(b)   people occupying housing accommodation which is temporary or occupied on insecure terms,

(c)   families with dependent children,

(d)   households consisting of or including someone who is expecting a child,

(e)   households consisting of or including someone with a particular need for settled accommodation on medical or welfare grounds, and

(f)   households whose social or economic circumstances are such that they have difficulty in securing settled accommodation.

The scheme shall also be framed so as to secure that additional preference is given to households within paragraph (e) . . . who cannot reasonably be expected to find settled accommodation for themselves in the foreseeable future.

(3)   The Secretary of State may by regulations—

(a)   specify further descriptions of people to whom preference is to be given as mentioned in subsection (2), or

(b)   amend or repeal any part of subsection (2).

(4)   The Secretary of State may by regulations specify factors which a local housing authority shall not take into account in allocating housing accommodation.

(5)   As regards the procedure to be followed, the scheme shall be framed in accordance with such principles as the Secretary of State may prescribe by regulations.

(6)   Subject to the above provisions, and to any regulations made under them, the authority may decide on what principles the scheme is to be framed.

(7)   Before adopting an allocation scheme, or making an alteration to their scheme reflecting a major change of policy, a local housing authority shall—

(a)   send a copy of the draft scheme, or proposed alteration, to every registered social landlord with which they have nomination arrangements (see section 159(4)), and

(b)   afford those persons a reasonable opportunity to comment on the proposals.

(8)   A local housing authority shall not allocate housing accommodation except in accordance with their allocation scheme.

Information about allocation scheme

168.—(1)   A local housing authority shall publish a summary of their allocation scheme and provide a copy of the summary free of charge to any member of the public who asks for one.

(2)   The authority shall make the scheme available for inspection at their principal office and shall provide a copy of the scheme, on payment of a reasonable fee, to any member of the public who asks for one.

(3)   When the authority make an alteration to their scheme reflecting a major change of policy, they shall within a reasonable period of time notify everyone on their housing register, explaining in general terms the effect of the change.

Notes

1.   Sections 167 and 168 contain the 'bare bones' of the allocation scheme. Further guidance on operating schemes is contained in the Code of Guidance issued by the Secretary of State under s. 169.

2.   The words omitted in s. 167(2) were repealed by reg. 3 of the Allocation of Housing (Reasonable and Additional Preference) Regulations 1997 (SI 1997 No. 1902) as from 1 November 1997.

(i)   How does the scheme work?

Consultation papers issued before the 1996 legislation indicated that, amongst other things:

(a)   LHAs would in general able to choose a system of allocation most appropriate to their housing situation and the supply of housing in their areas, e.g., a points scheme, or a quota based scheme;

(b)   any regulations made could in general give LHAs flexibility in determining how to make best use of local housing stock, and how to ensure a good social mix of housing occupants.

In the outcome, the legislation has not laid down too many prescriptive rules on the functioning of schemes, but note the requirement under s. 167 that allocation schemes *must be* so framed as to secure that a 'reasonable preference' is given to certain categories of people.

Questions
What are these categories? Why are they singled out for special treatment?

(ii) 'Reasonable preference' under s. 167(2)
The first category of those to be given 'reasonable preference' existed previously under s. 22 of the 1985 Act, the rest are new categories. For judicial commentary on the meaning of the expression 'reasonable preference' students should read *R v Wolverhampton MBC, ex parte Watters* (1997) 29 HLR 931 below. The meaning of the expression 'additional preference' in s. 167(2) as yet awaits judicial clarification, but it is clearly meant to ensure that those to whom it applies are to be prioritised over the other reasonable preference categories. The 'additional preference' category would certainly cover groups such as the elderly, and those with physical or learning disabilities, severe mental illness or degenerative diseases.

R v Wolverhampton MBC, ex parte Watters
(1997) 29 HLR 931

The applicant was a married woman with five children, aged between eight and 14. Until 1992, the family lived in a house let to them by the respondent authority. In September 1992, a possession order was made against them on the ground that they were in arrears of rent. At the time of the hearing of the appeal the arrears amounted to over £2,300. In 1993, after living at two other addresses, the family moved into a privately rented house. The contractual rent was £80 per week, but they were only entitled to housing benefit of £70 per week. The house was statutorily overcrowded.

In 1995, the applicant applied to the authority to be placed on their waiting list. She was informed that because there were more than two weeks' rent arrears outstanding, from her previous tenancies with the authority she would not be admitted onto the list. On 28 March 1995, the authority confirmed their decision. The applicant appealed to the authority's Housing Appeals Panel. The Panel's remit was to hear appeals where, although the applicant was in more than two weeks' arrears of rent, there was a social or medical need for which the applicant had been awarded 60 points, or the applicant had more than two weeks' worth of rent arrears but had made substantial efforts to reduce the arrears, or there was any other exceptional circumstance. On 14 March 1996, her appeal was heard. At the hearing, the authority's representative explained to the Panel that the rent arrears policy could be waived and informed them of the reasonable preference which the authority was required to accord. The appeal was dismissed. The applicant sought judicial review of the authority's decision. On 23 May 1996, the application was dismissed and the applicant appealed to the Court of Appeal.
Held:

(1) The Housing Act 1985, s. 22 required an authority to accord reasonable preference to be given to the categories of person set out in the section; the use of the word 'reasonable' envisages that other factors may diminish and even nullify the preference; this involves balancing against the statutory factors such other factors as may be relevant; an authority are entitled to take into account substantial arrears of rent due to them; in selecting tenants, when the authority consider that an applicant's rent arrears are such as to outweigh the reasonable preference which would otherwise be accorded, the applicant need not be selected;

(2) There was nothing to suggest that the respondent authority's Housing Appeals Panel regarded its power to treat the applicant's circumstances as exceptional as being so circumscribed that they could not accord to her the reasonable preference to which s. 22 of the 1985 Act entitled her; nor was there any ground for contending that the balancing exercise was not fairly conducted; the scope of the Panel's remit in considering 'exceptional circumstances' was unfettered; the authority's policy, of which the appeal process was an integral part, was sufficiently flexible to comply with s. 22.

LEGATT LJ: . . . The relevant policy of the Council is to be found in the remit of the Housing Appeals Panel, the nub of which I have recited earlier. It appears from the affidavit of Fiona Davies, the solicitor who appeared for the Council before the Panel, that she had earlier told the appellant's solicitors that there would be an Appeals Panel hearing because, independently of the result of the medical assessment for which the appellant had been referred, exceptional circumstances existed. She specifically told the appellant's representative of the wide nature of the Appeals Panel's discretion. The record of the hearing shows that Ms Davies explained that the Council's rent arrears policy could be 'waived in exceptional circumstances'. More importantly, the hearing concluded with a statement by her that 'the Housing, Act 1985 required the Local Authority to give "reasonable preference" in its housing policy to anyone who is in statutory overcrowding'. It appears likely that the emphasis was upon overcrowding because that is what the appellant's medical condition was attributed to. A subsequent letter from the appellant's solicitors to the Council continued to assert that the shortcomings in her accommodation constituted exceptional circumstances which should have resulted in her admittance to the housing waiting list.

For the appellant Mr Gallivan argued that the Council's policy is unlawful and in breach of section 22 because, although the appellant falls within three of the statutorily preferred groups, she is in fact afforded no preference whatsoever. The policy which was applied to the appellant excluded her from the waiting list because she had rent arrears of more than two weeks in respect of a former Council tenancy, unless she could establish what the Council regarded as exceptional circumstances. Since the Council selects its tenants exclusively from its housing waiting list, the appellant has no prospects of being selected as a council tenant.

Mr Gallivan submitted that because Parliament have ordained that reasonable preference is to be given, a council cannot treat it as reasonable not to grant any preference. Otherwise section 22 would be otiose. He cited several cases for incidental comments made in them. In *R v Forrest Heath DC, ex parte West and Lucas* (1991) 24 HLR 85 this Court regarded it as irrelevant to take account of non-payment of community charge, because legislation had provided other means of dealing with that indebtedness. So here the Council can distrain for rent. Mr Gallivan accepted that the existence of rent arrears is relevant, but submitted that they do not conclude the matter against the appellant, because she cannot be denied any preference whatsoever. In *R v Islington LBC, ex parte Aldebbagh* (1994) 27 HLR 1985 the Council's policy was held to be unlawful because it admitted of no exceptions and so fettered the Council's discretion. Though the policy is less rigid in the present case, Mr Gallivan submitted that there is still a danger that applicants will not have their cases considered on account of arrears of rent. In *R v Newham BC, ex parte Miah* (1995) 28 HLR 279 there was a power to choose between applicants on 'reasonable grounds'. From that Mr Gallivan argued that 'reasonable preference' must import some preference. In *R v Lambeth LBC, ex parte Njomo* (1996) 28 HLR 737 an application was allowed because of the rigidity with which the Council's policy had been applied to the applicant. Mr Gallivan relied particularly on the comment of Sedley J about the Council in that case when he said at page 742 that—

What they must not do is eclipse or distort the priority which section 22 accords.

Mr Gallivan submitted that if applicants in the first three categories of section 22 are excluded from the housing list from which a Council selects its tenants, they cannot be accorded any preference. Despite a multiplicity of examples Mr Gallivan acknowledged that on this ground of appeal his sole point was that the statutory duty to accord reasonable preference cannot be complied with if no preference is given at all.

For the Council Mr Findlay contended that, once it is conceded that a policy which takes account of rent arrears is not unlawful, a local authority is free to choose which procedure to adopt for determining preferences. Different local authorities adopt different procedures: some award points, whilst others do not allow applicants with particular shortcomings on to the waiting list. The obligation to give reasonable preference was in this case fulfilled by the consideration given to the appellant's case by the Appeals Panel. That is the means by which the Council ensured that those in any of the first three categories of section 22 were afforded reasonable preference. But reasonable preference means what it says. If two applicants are otherwise equal, but one is within one of the first three categories of section 22, that one will be preferred. It is for the Council to decide what weight to give to relevant factors. Reasonable preference is to be equated with extra weight: it cannot be determinative *per se*. Mr Findlay submitted that the Council must have power to determine whether in the circumstances an applicant's arrears outweigh the reasonable preference that has to be given; and there would be no point in taking rent arrears into account unless they could in a proper case outweigh the statutory factors.

I agree with Mr Findlay's submissions. If section 22 simply required 'preference' to be given, Mr Gallivan's argument would be correct. But it does not: it requires 'reasonable preference'. That envisages that other factors may weigh against and so diminish and even nullify the preference. In the sentence I have cited from the judgment of Sedley J in *ex parte Njomo (supra)* he asserted that the Council must not 'eclipse or distort the priority'. If he meant that the statutory preference cannot be outweighed by other relevant considerations, he was in my judgment wrong. No preference is to be given except reasonable preference. That involves balancing against the statutory factors such factors as may be relevant. So the Council is entitled to take account of substantial arrears of rent due to the Council. As the judge remarked, the Council has a duty to have regard to the financial consequences of its action and to the need to balance its housing revenue account. The answer to Mr Gallivan's sole point is that because, as is common ground, rent arrears may be taken into account in the process of selecting tenants, it follows that, when in the Council's judgment an applicant's rent arrears are such as to outweigh the reasonable preference that would otherwise avail him, that applicant will not be selected.

Mr Gallivan also attempted to show that the expression 'exceptional circumstances' was used in the Guidance Note for the Appeals Panel as though they related only to social and medical need. But the appellant's case was referred to the Appeals Panel, even though there were no sufficient grounds for an award of social points, and the doctor, to whom the appellant was referred for assessment, said that there could be no medical award of points. And the last words spoken to the Appeals Panel before the hearing ended were Ms Davis's reference to the Council's obligation under section 22.

There is nothing to suggest that the Appeals Panel regarded its power to treat the appellant's circumstances as exceptional as being so circumscribed that they could not accord her the reasonable preference to which section 22 entitled her; nor is there any ground for contending that the balancing exercise was not fairly conducted by the Appeals Panel at the hearing of the appellant's appeal. The Appeals Panel would have been entitled to pay regard to any substantial efforts to reduce arrears, even though they exceeded two weeks' arrears, and to any other exceptional circumstances, including social or medical need. The scope of 'exceptional circumstances' was unfettered. The Council's policy, of which the appeal process was an integral part, was in my judgment sufficiently flexible to comply with the Council's duty under section 22. It would be absurd if local authorities were obliged to house or rehouse tenants who, whatever their need, have persistently failed to pay their rent, and who have made no substantial efforts to reduce the arrears, and whose circumstances are not to be regarded as exceptional. For the reasons summarised by the judge [at first instance] this ground of appeal fails.

JUDGE LJ: . . . Although the effect of section 22 of the Housing Act 1985 is to produce an advantage for prospective tenants who bring themselves within the relevant criteria, they do not enjoy an automatic entitlement to be allocated local authority housing appropriate to their needs. The section is concerned with the process of 'selection' of tenants by the housing authority and there is nothing to suggest that the suitability of the prospective tenants, or indeed any other relevant considerations, are to be ignored. Even in the case of applications by those within the criteria which entitle them to preferential treatment, the express requirement that the preference should be reasonable rather than absolute entitles the housing authority, in addition, to consider any other relevant fact including the extent to and circumstances in which the applicants have failed to pay due rent or have otherwise been in breach of the obligations of their existing or earlier tenancies. Such considerations are not excluded from the selection process.

The statutory obligations imposed by section 22 therefore require that positive favour should be shown to applications which satisfy any of the relevant criteria. To use colloquial language they should be given a reasonable head start. Thereafter all the remaining factors fall to be considered in the balancing exercise inevitably required when each individual application is under consideration. If despite the head start the housing authority eventually decides on reasonable grounds that the application for a tenancy must be rejected this will not constitute a breach of the obligations imposed by section 22.

(iii)   Further reasonable preference categories
The Allocation of Housing (Reasonable and Additional Preference) Regulations 1997 SI 1997 No. 1902) made under s. 167(3) of the 1996 Act create

further classes of persons to whom a reasonable preference has to be given. Why were these additional categories added to the scheme of the statute?

Allocation of Housing
(Reasonable and Additional Preference)
Regulations 1997
SI 1997 No. 1902

Citation and commencement
1. These Regulations may be cited as the Allocation of Housing (Reasonable and Additional Preference) Regulations 1997 and shall come into force on 1st November 1997.

Further descriptions of people to whom reasonable preference is to be given
2. The following are specified as further descriptions of people to whom reasonable preference is to be given in the allocation scheme of a local housing authority—

    (a) people owed a duty by that authority under section 193 or 195(2) of the Housing Act 1996 ('the 1996 Act') or section 65(2) or 68(2) of the Housing Act 1985 (main housing duties owed to homeless persons),

    (b) people in respect of whom that authority are exercising their power under section 194 of the 1996 Act (power to secure accommodation after minimum period of duty under section 193 of that Act), and

    (c) people—

        (i) who have within the previous two years been provided with advice and assistance by that authority under section 197(2) of the 1996 Act (duty where other suitable accommodation available) or

        (ii) who are occupying accommodation secured with such advice and assistance.

(iv)   General issues relating to allocation schemes
The Secretary of State has further powers to make regulations to specify other groups of persons to whom preference is to be given, or to take away preference from any mentioned group. Regulations could in future also prevent LHAs from taking specified factors into account in the allocation of housing. Section 167(5) of the 1996 Act empowers the Secretary of State to specify procedural principles to be followed when framing an allocation scheme. See the Allocation of Housing (Procedure) Regulations 1997 (SI 1997 No. 483) below for an example of the use of this power. Students should ask why this prohibition was put in place, and should think back to *R v Port Talbot Borough Council, ex parte Jones*, above.

Allocation of Housing (Procedure) Regulations 1997
SI 1997 No. 483

Citation and commencement
1. These Regulations may be cited as the Allocation of Housing (Procedure) Regulations 1997 and shall come into force on 1st April 1997.

Interpretation
2. In these Regulations—
'allocation decision' means a decision to allocate housing accommodation;
'authority' means a local housing authority in England;
'decision-making body' means an authority or a committee or sub-committee of
an authority.

Allocation scheme procedure
3.—(1) As regards the procedure to be followed, an authority's allocation scheme
shall be framed in accordance with the principle prescribed in this regulation.

(2) A member of an authority who has been elected for the electoral division or
ward in which—

(a) the housing accommodation in relation to which an allocation decision falls
to be made is situated, or

(b) the person in relation to whom that decision falls to be made has his sole or
main residence,
shall not, at the time the allocation decision is made, be included in the persons
constituting the decision-making body.

Note
In Wales similar provision is made by SI 1997 No. 45, which, however, also
provides specifically that allocation decisions in Wales may be taken by local
authority officers except where the local housing authority determine otherwise.

As a general guiding principle LHAs are expected to give priority to those
who will need social housing over a long period: thus long-term disability,
chronic illness, etc. are more likely to attract rehousing than an acute but
temporary housing crisis.

LHAs will, however, still have to determine priority between applicants
who fall into the additional preference class and, indeed, the other reasonable
preference classes. They should act in concert with, and on the advice of,
other relevant social agencies, e.g., social services and health authorities.

In drawing up a scheme, therefore, the LHA are able to take into account a
very wide range of factors, but all the allocation criteria must be incorporated
into the scheme and made public. The characteristics of tenants may be
considered, e.g., their suitability for ensuring a good social mix on an estate, or
the length of time they have been on the register, so that where there are two
households who otherwise qualify for immediate rehousing there is some
means of determining priority between them. Most authorities now incorporate such requirements within a points scheme – date order schemes (first come,
first served) may be too rigid to enable a 'reasonable preference' to be given and
so, arguably, would not be able to meet the requirements of the legislation.

(v)   Challenges to allocation decisions
There is no section of the 1996 Act giving jurisdiction to the county court
over challenges to allocation decisions, e.g., where a LHA make an allocation
not in accordance with their scheme. In such an event it would appear that
challenge by way of judicial review would be available to someone with a

sufficient interest in the matter – perhaps a person who satisfies the scheme's requirements and who has otherwise had it indicated to him or her that the property would or could be allocated to him or her. The same would appear to be true of challenges to adverse decisions internally reviewed and confirmed. Thus the cases on s. 22 of the 1985 Act remain relevant to future practice.

(vi)   Continuing requirements for legality
There continues to be an overarching requirement to operate an allocation scheme in a lawful fashion, i.e. without illegality, procedural impropriety or irrationality. Thus there must be no absolute fetters on discretion, such as in *R v Canterbury CC, ex parte Gillespie* (1986) 19 HLR 7, or *absolutely automatic* exclusions from the register save as provided for by legislation, e.g., because an applicant has an arrears history or because of ownership of other property (see *R v Forest Heath DC, ex parte West & Lucas* (1991) 24 HLR 85 and *R v Bristol CC, ex parte Johns* (1992) 25 HLR 249). Certainly houses must not be allocated solely for party political reasons see *R v Port Talbot BC, ex parte Jones* (1987) 20 HLR 265). Apart from that, however, the breadth of the residual discretion under s. 159(7) of the 1996 Act appears to allow LHAs to consider allocating properties to those under 18, to continue the practice of making numbers of offers or one only, or to take into account historic factors affecting an applicant such as length of time spent in temporary lets. The Code of Guidance warns, nevertheless, against adopting a formulaic approach, and one way of thinking about the new system is to picture it as a three-dimensional matrix where none of the parameters is absolutely determinative. The three principal parameters or groups of parameters in any given situation will be, first, to ask what properties are available and for whom are they suitable; secondly, to determine who are the persons eligible according to scheme criteria and the general law; and then, thirdly, to determine priority as between qualifying groups *and* within groups – date order registration or points totals can be used to help in this determination but must not be used as rigid determinants.

(I)   Other allocations

LHAs allocate many of their properties to existing tenants seeking to move home for a variety of reasons – health, employment, family, etc. Such allocations (usually known as 'transfers') fall outside the terms of the 1996 Act and are in general governed by s. 106 of the Housing Act 1985, as amended by the Housing Acts 1988 and 1996 and the Local Government (Wales) Act 1994.

Housing Act 1985

Information about housing allocation
106.—(1)   A landlord authority shall publish a summary of its rules—

(a)   for determining priority as between applicants in the allocation of its housing accommodation, and

(b)   governing cases where secure tenants wish to move (whether or not by way of exchange of dwelling-houses) to other dwelling-houses let under secure tenancies by that authority or another body.

(2)   A landlord authority shall—

(a)   maintain a set of the rules referred to in subsection (1) and of the rules which it has laid down governing the procedure to be followed in allocating its housing accommodation, and

(b)   make them available at its principal office for inspection at all reasonable hours, without charge, by members of the public.

(3)   A landlord authority which is a registered housing association shall, instead of complying with paragraph (b) of subsection (2), send a set of the rules referred to in paragraph (a) of that subsection—

(a)   to the Corporation, and

(b)   to the council of any district, Welsh county or county borough or London borough in which there are dwelling-houses let or to be let by the association under secure tenancies;

and a council to whom a set of rules is sent under this subsection shall make it available at its principal office for inspection at all reasonable hours, without charge, by members of the public.

(4)   A copy of the summary published under subsection (1) shall be given without charge, and a copy of the set of rules maintained under subsection (2) shall be given on payment of a reasonable fee, to any member of the public who asks for one.

(5)   At the request of a person who has applied to it for housing accommodation, a landlord authority shall make available to him, at all reasonable times and without charge, details of the particulars which he has given to the authority about himself and his family and which the authority has recorded as being relevant to. his application for accommodation.

(6)   The provisions of this section do not apply to a landlord authority which is a local housing authority so far as they impose requirements corresponding to those to which such an authority is subject under sections 166 and 168 of the Housing Act 1996 (provision of information about housing registers and allocation schemes).

The powers of LHAs under this provision being discretionary are, of course, subject to the requirements of the general principles of administrative law which have already been considered. Particular note should be taken of the cases which follow:

R v London Borough of Tower Hamlets, ex parte Spencer
(1996) 29 HLR 64

In 1988, the applicant was granted a tenancy of a property owned by the respondent authority. In 1990, following the birth of her son, she applied for a transfer. In January 1994, she underwent an operation for a degenerative condition known as syringomelia. The condition caused her to have difficulties climbing stairs, and walking or standing for long periods of time. She suffered from headaches which could not be relieved by painkillers. At the time, the prognosis was uncertain. The applicant went to convalesce with her parents. She renewed her application for a transfer. Upon her return to the property, she discovered that she had been burgled.

The authority's medical adviser identified the applicant as being in need of a flat served by lifts. In July 1994, their Housing Management Panel placed her in a priority category for management transfer. Before an offer could be made to her, the applicant moved to live in her sister's accommodation (59 Wager Street) and applied to have the tenancy transferred to her. That application was refused.

In November 1994, an occupational therapist completed a report on the applicant which stated that her condition affected both her sensation and muscular power. The report said that although the applicant experienced pain, she had no functional problems. The therapist recommended that the applicant should not be offered a particular property (5 Verity House) which was a ground floor maisonette, which had been specially adapted for the disabled. In December 1994, despite this recommendation, the authority offered the applicant the tenancy of 5 Verity House. The applicant's solicitors wrote to the authority stating that the property was unsuitable and asking that the applicant be granted a tenancy of 59 Wager Street. On 17 January 1995, the authority replied, confirming that the applicant's medical needs would be re-assessed by the respondents' medical advisor.

On 29 March 1995, the case was considered by the Housing Management Panel. No medical re-assessment had taken place. The Panel had before them a letter from the consultant who had operated on the applicant, who was of the opinion that the applicant should be able to carry out most everyday activities, although she did experience considerable pain. The Panel also had a report from a housing officer, who explained that 5 Verity House had been offered because it was understood that the applicant's condition would deteriorate and that her longer term needs had to be taken into account. The report concluded by recommending that the applicant be offered a tenancy of her sister's flat.

On 12 April 1995, the Housing Management Panel decided that the applicant should not be offered a tenancy of her sister's property. The Panel decided that the offer would not be made because it would be contrary to the Medical Advisor's recommendation. The applicant sought judicial review of the decision.

Held:

(1) It was procedurally unfair for the Panel to rely on the original medical assessment without giving the applicant an opportunity to make representations as to the inappropriateness of doing so; it was particularly unfair, given that the respondents had represented to the applicant that an updated assessment was being obtained;

(2) In stating that an offer of 59 Wager Street would be contrary to the medical adviser's recommendation, the Panel relied on a recommendation which could not reasonably be relied on in the light of the subsequent evidence from the occupational therapist and the consultant as to the

applicant's present, improved condition; the Panel had acted irrationally in relying on these matters as grounds for rejecting the recommendation.

STEPHEN RICHARDS *(sitting as a Deputy High Court Judge)*: . . . Mr Luba, for the applicant, advances three grounds for challenging the Panel's decision of April 12: procedural unfairness, failure to give formal notification and reasons, and irrationality.

In relation to the first ground it is common ground that the council was required to observe 'basic administrative law requirements of natural justice and procedural fairness'. The case as originally formulated had been that the Panel acted unfairly in reaching its decision on the basis of a new medical assessment that had not been put to the applicant for comment. It was only after service of the council's affidavit that it emerged that there had been no new assessment. The case was then reformulated to the following effect. The applicant had been given legitimately to expect that the Panel would not reach a decision without an updated medical assessment. If the applicant had known that the Panel would proceed on the basis of the original medical assessment and without an updated assessment, she would have asked her medical advisers to comment on the original assessment (to show that it was out of date) and/or would have made representations to be put in front of the Panel as to the inappropriateness of relying on the original assessment.

There is a lot of force in that submission. The original medical assessment of May 1994, with its recommendation that the applicant be given a lifted flat served by two lifts, was based on the evidence that then existed as to the applicant's medical condition, including the evidence that she could not manage stairs and the uncertain prognosis following her operation. Happily, things had improved by the end of the year. The occupational therapist's report of November 1994 stated that the applicant at present had no functional problems. The consultant gave his opinion, in his letter of 31 January 1995, that she should be able to manage stairs and carry out most activities of daily living without significant problems other than pain. The present situation and prognosis were plainly better than they had been at the time of the original assessment.

In my judgment it was procedurally unfair in those circumstances to rely on the original medical assessment without giving the applicant an opportunity to make representations as to the inappropriateness of doing so. Unfairer still to do so after representing to the applicant in categoric terms, until the last letter before the Panel's meeting, that an updated assessment was being obtained. I would quash the Panel's resulting decision on that ground alone.

The approach adopted also goes to the substance of the Panel's decision. The first of the reasons for rejecting the Housing Officer's recommendation that the applicant be offered a tenancy of 59 Wager Street was, 'Would be contrary to Medical Adviser's recommendation', presumably on the basis that 59 Wager Street did not meet the description of property recommended in the original assessment. But that recommendation could not reasonably be relied on in the light of the recent evidence from the occupational therapist and the consultant as to the applicant's present condition. Similarly, the third of the reasons for rejecting the Housing Officer's recommendation was 'A more suitable offer [had] previously been made and refused', referring no doubt to the offer of 5 Verity House. I am prepared to accept, as Mr Crawford pressed in argument, that there was a sensible rationale behind the offer of 5 Verity House at a time when it was thought that the applicant's condition was likely to deteriorate: it was reasonable to look to the long term. The subsequent evidence about the applicant's condition and prognosis, however, undermined that rationale and flew in the face of the conclusion that premises specially adapted for a person with a much higher level of disability than the applicant were nonetheless suitable for the applicant. I do not see how a reasonable decision-making body, directing itself properly to the issues and the material before it could have relied on these matters as grounds for rejecting the recommendation. I therefore accept the thrust of Mr Luba's submissions on the third ground, irrationality, as well.

It does not follow that the applicant must now be offered 59 Wagner Street. The second reason relied on, 'Cannot condone a tenant picking properties and queue jumping', might have caused the Panel to reach the same conclusion in any event. That is not a matter for me. But the actual process of reasoning that led to the decision of 12 April was to my mind defective and fresh consideration of the case and a fresh decision are required.

Having regard to my conclusion on the first and third grounds, I do not consider it necessary to reach a conclusion on the second ground (failure to give formal notification and reasons). I doubt whether it would have got Mr Luba anywhere if he had failed on the other grounds.

In the result I shall quash the council's decision of April 12, 1995.

R v *Camden London Borough Council, ex parte Adair*
(1996) 29 HLR 236

In 1989, on the breakdown of his marriage, the respondent authority granted the applicant a secure tenancy of a three-bedroomed flat. In 1990, the applicant's girlfriend (Miss Qaddoumi) moved in with him. In February 1992, the secure tenancy was transferred into their joint names. Relations between the couple broke down. On 27 May 1994, Miss Qaddoumi obtained an interim injunction and an ouster order against the applicant requiring him to vacate the flat.

On 23 May 1994, the applicant approached the authority's District Housing Office for accommodation for himself and a new girlfriend. The applicant informed the authority that he had become involved in a dispute between two drug dealers who had made threats against him. The District Housing Office told the applicant that he would not be given temporary accommodation and advised him that he could apply to the Homeless Persons Unit. He was also given an application form for a transfer.

The applicant went to stay with friends in Scotland. Following various letters from the applicant, the authority's District Housing Office wrote to him telling him about a policy operated by the authority to assist those who were in need of re-housing as a result of breakdown in a relationship. On 17 August 1994, the applicant completed a form for consideration under the scheme. He requested a two- or three-bedroomed property for himself, his son, his current partner and her two stepdaughters. He requested housing away from the Kilburn area as he was in fear for his own safety.

On 5 January 1995, the authority wrote to the applicant to notify him of their decision not to consider him for accommodation under the scheme. The reasons given for the decision were that the applicant had applied under similar circumstances on two separate occasions and had on one occasion sublet the property offered to him and returned to live with his partner. The letter reminded the applicant that he could apply to the Homeless Persons Unit.

On 13 January 1995, the applicant was interviewed by the authority's Homeless Persons Unit. The applicant informed the authority that he suffered from anxiety and depression and was being prescribed Diazepam. An attempt was made by the assessment officer to contact the District Housing Office, but this was unsuccessful, and no further inquiries were made. On the same day, the authority decided that the applicant was homeless but was not in priority need. Their decision letter stated that they had taken into account all the evidence and set out that the applicant did not fall within the statutory categories of persons in priority need. No further reasoning or indication of the inquiries which had been made was included.

The applicant applied for judicial review of the authority's decision [amongst other things] not to grant him a transfer of his tenancy under their relationship breakdown policy.

Held:

(1)　The respondent authority had taken into account all the factors relevant to the applicant's application in refusing to offer him a transfer under their discretionary scheme for those who had suffered domestic breakdown; they were entitled to take into account the fact that the applicant had made two previous applications under the authority's discretionary policy to re-house after breakdown of relationship; the system was capable of operating unfairly to other applicants and potential applicants for housing if a person was able to use the relationship breakdown policy as a means of obtaining accommodation for a series of partners; the authority were also entitled to take into account the fact that the applicant appeared to have sublet property previously let to him by them, the weight to be given to it being a matter for the authority;

(2)　The decision letter of 5 January 1995, contained the reasons for the authority's decision; there was nothing in the circumstances of the case to justify the imposition of a legal requirement to give fuller reasoning.

STEPHEN RICHARDS (*sitting as a Deputy High Court Judge*): . . . The width of the discretion accorded to those responsible for administering . . . policy is plain and is not in dispute. The discretion must nevertheless be exercised in accordance with the normal principles of public law. Miss Shelagh MacDonald, on behalf of the applicant, challenges the council's decision on the ground that those principles were infringed in a number of respects, namely failure to take into account relevant considerations, taking into account irrelevant considerations, procedural unfairness and a failure to give reasons.

Relevant/irrelevant considerations

As regards considerations said to have been wrongly left out of account, Miss MacDonald focused in her submissions on the applicant's claim that he could not return to 182 Webheath because of threats of violence from associates of Miss

Qaddoumi, *i.e.* not just from drug dealers. The difficulty about that contention is that, although it is common ground that the applicant referred to the existence of threats against him, the council's evidence is that he did not attribute those threats to Miss Qaddoumi. As Mr McLaughlin states in his affidavit:

> It was never raised by the Applicant specifically that the threats to which he was subject came from Ms Qaddoumi, directly or indirectly. The fact that he was allegedly threatened by someone was taken into account . . .

Nor do I find any real contradiction of this in the applicant's own evidence. In his first affidavit he states:

> I told the officer that drug dealers who were acquainted with my former wife were after me because somebody I had foolishly said was trustworthy had disappeared owing them money. In addition I told her that Miss Qaddoumi knew a number of people some of whom were users and some of whom were dealers. Several of these people had made threats to the effect that if I was ever seen in Kilburn or even London 'I was dead' or 'I was history'. Subsequently I learnt that these friends of Miss Qaddoumi knew these other drug dealers.

There is nothing in that passage to suggest an allegation different in substance from the general concerns expressed by the applicant about the threat from drug-dealers. In his second affidavit, after a detailed account of the incident in which he vouched for the reliability of a cousin's boyfriend and then found himself subjected to threats of violence when the boyfriend disappeared owing money, the applicant does say: 'Threats were made about my personal safety by men who I believe were acquaintances of Ms Qaddoumi or were acting on her behalf.' This is the nearest he comes to a distinct allegation of threats of violence attributable to Miss Qaddoumi. As a distinct allegation it has little substance to it. But in any event there is nothing to show that it was made in that form to the council. I conclude that the council cannot properly be criticised for a failure to take it into consideration.

. . .

As regards the contention that the council took into account a number of considerations that it should not have taken into account, Miss MacDonald referred first to the council taking into account the fact that the applicant had made two previous applications for transfer. Specifically, as is mentioned in the council's letter of January 5, 1995 and as is explained further in the council's affidavits, account was taken of the fact that this would be the third rehousing under the relationship breakdown policy. In my judgment that is a perfectly proper consideration for the council to take into account in the exercise of a discretionary power relating to the allocation of its limited housing stock. It is plainly a housing related matter, not an extraneous consideration. It is moreover a potentially important consideration. Ms Rutherford's affidavit emphasises that the system is capable of operating unfairly to other applicants and potential applicants for housing if a person is able to use the relationship breakdown policy as a means of obtaining accommodation for a series of partners. Although no deliberate abuse of the system is alleged in the case of this applicant, it was entirely appropriate for the council to have regard to the fact that he had already benefited twice from the policy in the past.

The second allegedly irrelevant consideration was that the applicant wished to transfer because of the threats made against him by drug dealers. This is not mentioned in the decision letter and does not seem to have been given any great weight. In any event, however, I cannot accept that the reasons for wanting a transfer are irrelevant to the decision. They had been put forward by the applicant himself. In so far as it is suggested that Ms Rutherford's note of May 23, 1994 indicates that the council proceeded on the basis that the applicant was actively involved in drugs-related crime or held against him such tangential involvement as he had himself described, neither the note itself nor the affidavit evidence filed on behalf of the council supports the suggestion.

The third matter – though another matter that is not mentioned in the decision letter and does not seem to have been given great weight – was that the applicant appeared to have another family that needed rehousing. The point here was that the applicant was not simply seeking bedsit accommodation for himself as a result of his having to leave his former home following the breakdown of his relationship with Miss Qaddoumi. On his application form, as I have indicated above, he was seeking a two to three bedroom property to house his new partner and that partner's two step-daughters, as well as his own son. It is plain, in my judgment, that the council was entitled to have regard to these matters, and I do not think it necessary to say more about them.

Fourth, the council took into account the fact that the applicant seemed in the past to have sublet, in breach of his tenancy agreement, a previous property rented to him by the council. This is a matter specifically referred to in the council's letter of January 5, 1995. The applicant denies that there was any subletting, though he accepts that a friend had been allowed to stay in his property and been there by himself at weekends (when the applicant stayed with his girlfriend). Mr McLaughlin observes in his affidavit that, whilst he cannot comment on the nature of the arrangement between the applicant and his friend, the applicant had allowed the friend to stay in the premises for at least a year and the facts as they appeared to the council at the time were sufficiently conclusive for the council to serve a notice to quit on the applicant in 1986. As in the case of the first allegedly irrelevant consideration, I take the view that the council was fully entitled to take into account the previous housing history of the applicant. The weight to be given to it, as with the other factors properly taken into account, was a matter for the council.

Fifthly, the applicant complains about the council taking into account the fact that Miss Qaddoumi had obtained an injunction preventing his entering the property at 182 Webheath, and had apparently done so without his having taken any steps to defend the proceedings. But this, too, was plainly relevant to the council's decision. The applicant had himself referred to the proceedings in his letters of June 27, and July 26, 1994 . . . They were relevant to his contention that he could not return to his property at 182 Webheath, and indeed to his invocation of the relationship breakdown policy as a basis for transfer. There is no indication in the evidence that the council, in reliance on these proceedings or other matters, decided against the applicant on the basis of his conduct towards Miss Qaddoumi or more generally on the basis that he was a violent man.

That leads me to the final matter under this head, namely Ms Rutherford's observation, at the end of her note of May 23, 1994, that the applicant was 'potentially very violent'. It is obscure what prompted that observation. Perhaps one gets some hint of it in the applicant's second affidavit when, in describing the occasion, he denies using, or threatening violence but says 'I probably expressed my views fairly forcefully' and 'I certainly was very angry at the way I felt that I was being treated and I will not deny that there was an angry exchange of words . . . ' Be that as it may, Ms Rutherford's observation does not provide a basis upon which the decision can be successfully challenged, since there is no evidence that the council's decision was based on a finding as to the violence or potential violence of the applicant.

[Stephen Richards next considered the issue of alleged procedural unfairness:]

The first of the matters of which complaint is made under this head is that account was taken, without informing the applicant, of the fact that he had made two previous applications for transfer under the relationship breakdown policy. The factual accuracy of the point is not, however, disputed by the applicant; and it seems to me that the council was entitled to take the point into account in the way that it did without inviting representations on it. The position might have been different if the council had sought to draw some further inference, such as that the applicant was engaged in deliberate abuse of the system. But no such inference was drawn or relied upon.

Similar reasoning applies to other matters of which complaint is made. As to the council's reliance on the fact that the applicant had apparently sub-let his property in the past in breach of his tenancy agreement, the difference between the applicant's account and the understanding on which the council relied is not so great that anything could sensibly turn on it. As to the fact that Miss Qaddoumi had obtained an injunction against him in the Central London County Court, I have explained already that, although the proceedings were a relevant consideration, there is no indication in the evidence that the council reached its decision on the basis of the applicant's conduct towards Miss Qaddoumi or more generally on the basis that he was a violent man. I have also explained that, although account was properly taken of the threats made to the applicant by drug dealers (about which the applicant had himself informed the council), there is nothing to show that the council proceeded on the basis that the applicant had been actively involved in drug-related crime. As regards the alleged deception by which Miss Qaddoumi obtained her joint tenancy of 182 Webhouse (again a matter put forward by the applicant himself), I have found that the council dismissal of the point may have been unduly simplistic but that nothing turns on it. Accordingly, none of these matters can in my judgment provide a satisfactory foundation for a finding of procedural unfairness against the council. The situation is readily distinguishable from that in *R v London Borough of Hackney, ex parte Decordova* (1994) 27 HLR 108, to which my attention was drawn. In that case a decision was struck down for failure to put matters of concern to an applicant in circumstances where the local authority were minded to disbelieve the account given by the applicant on matters central to the decision. The present case is not one where the council disbelieved the applicant's account. Nor, as I have indicated, were the circumstances otherwise such that the council ought in fairness to have put matters to the applicant for comment before reaching its decision.

[Stephen Richards finally dealt with the issue of whether proper reasons had been given for the local authority's decision:]

Miss MacDonald's propositions of law contained a number of submissions concerning the duty to give reasons, but when it came to the facts there was little to be said under this head in relation to the first decision under challenge.

In *R v London Borough of Newham, ex parte Dawson* (1994) 26 HLR 747 it was held that the nature of the [allocation procedure] was not such as to require reasons to be given in every case, and that reasons were required only if there was something peculiar to the individual decision that called for an explanation (see also *R v Royal London Borough of Kensington & Chelsea, ex parte Grillo* (1995) 28 HLR 94). Miss Macdonald did not seek to take issue with the approach laid down in *ex parte Dawson*. She accepted that the subject-matter of [an allocation decision] was not such as to require reasons to be given as a matter of course, and that it was therefore necessary for her to point to some feature of the particular decision which called for an explanation. To my mind she was wholly unable to point to any such thing. The letter of January 5, 1995 is already a reasoned decision letter, even though it deals only with the principal aspects of the reasoning and not with the totality of the matters taken into account. I cannot find anything in the circumstances of the case that would justify the imposition of a legal requirement to give fuller reasoning.

R v Southwark London Borough Council, ex parte Melak
(1996) 29 HLR 223

In 1989, the applicant, a single mother with two children, was granted a secure tenancy by the respondent authority of a maisonette consisting of two floors. She had a back complaint which caused her difficulties in negotiating the stairs in the maisonette.

On 6 April 1992, the authority obtained a possession order against the applicant on the ground of rent arrears. The order was suspended on terms that the applicant pay the current rent and £2.15 per week off the arrears. The applicant complied with the terms of the order.

In late 1993, the applicant applied to the authority for a transfer on medical grounds. The authority carried out an assessment of the applicant's condition. The authority awarded her a number of points sufficient to qualify her for a transfer within the authority's allocations policy. On 14 September 1994, an advice centre wrote on the applicant's behalf to the authority requesting information on the progress of the application. On 4 November 1994, the authority replied stating that the application would not be actively considered because the applicant was more than four weeks in arrears of rent. The authority operated a policy under which an applicant for a transfer who owed the authority rent arrears would not be made an offer of accommodation. The policy did, however, provide that some people in a 'priority category' were exempt.

On 28 April 1995, the applicant's solicitors wrote to the authority requesting that her application be considered. The letter expressed the view that the authority's policy was too rigid and represented an unlawful fettering of their discretion. On 28 June 1995, the authority confirmed that – but for the rent arrears – the applicant would have been entitled to a transfer. The applicant applied for judicial review of the authority's refusal to process her application for a transfer.

Held: The respondent authority's policy was lawful; if properly applied to the particular features of individual applications it was entirely sound; it was not for the court to adjudicate on the soundness of the authority's housing policy; it was, however, the court's function to ensure that policy matters did not operate to exclude relevant considerations pertaining to the individual applicant; the policy had been rigidly applied by the authority as there was no indication that they had considered the applicant's individual circumstances.

SIR LOUIS BLOM-COOPER QC *(sitting as a Deputy High Court Judge)*: . . . By a letter of April 28, 1995 solicitors acting for the applicant wrote to the local authority making a further request that their client's application for a transfer to alternative accommodation should be actively considered. The solicitors referred to the letter of November 4, 1994 pointing out that its contents amounted to a 'blanket policy' which fell foul of recent judicial authority as the fettering of the discretion to treat each applicant's case for housing transfer on its merits. A reminder was sent by the solicitors on June 21, 1995, threatening judicial review proceedings. Correspondence about the applicant's medical condition took place on June 28, 1995; the applicant was awarded 20 medical points by the Medical Resources Unit, but she fell short of the 30 points needed for consideration for a Medical Needs Panel.

The impugned letter of July 25, 1995 stated:

> The Medical Resources Unit has looked at the case again and still feels that the original assessment of 20 points was correct. The Medical Resources Unit feels that she would be eligible for a move with 20 points. Unfortunately, she is suspended as a result of rent arrears. If her rent account is cleared she will be considered for a move in future.

The applicant's solicitors wrote on August 7, 1995 repeating their claim that the refusal to consider the applicant for housing transfer amounted 'to the local authority fettering its own discretion and applying a "blanket policy" to those seeking re-housing/transfers', to which the local authority replied, laconically and cryptically, on August 28, 1995:

> Unfortunately [sic], the Council do not have a blanket policy to those seeking rehousing or transfers, and do not fetter its own discretion as per your letter.

Ms Markus put her submissions concisely and cogently. She submits that the respondent's policy is clear: It will not process an application for a housing transfer, albeit the applicant is otherwise eligible, if the applicant is more than four weeks in arrears of rent in the currently-occupied property. While the respondent protested in its letter that it did not operate a 'blanket policy', the correspondence indicates the contrary. Moreover, the local authority adduces no affidavit evidence to contradict the assertion of an inflexible policy towards applicants for housing in rent arrears. Ms Markus cites authority which establishes the proposition that while a local authority may adopt a policy or rule in relation to applications for housing, it can apply such policy or rule only in the context of all the relevant factors relating to the individual applicant. The specific factors relative to this applicant would include a) the reasons for her rent arrears; b) the fact that she was paying off the arrears on a regular basis and as speedily as she reasonably could; c) the urgency of the applicant's need for more suitable accommodation, having regard to her medical condition; and d) the applicant's needs. compared with other applicants for transfers. None of these factors was ever brought into play alongside the policy rule, let alone considered on their merits.

[Having considered the relevant case law on fettering discretion, in particular *R v Canterbury City Council, ex parte Gillespie* (12986) 19 HLR 7, Sir Louis Blom-Cooper concluded: . . .]

[The local authority's policy] if properly applied to the particular features of the individual application, is entirely sound. It is not for this court to adjudicate on the soundness of a local authority's housing policy. It is this court's function, however, to ensure that policy matters do not operate in a manner that excludes relevant considerations pertaining to the individual applicant. The discretion of the local authority in determining each applicant's case must not yield to policy. Policy is an important guideline to decision-making of an applicant's own case. It must not dictate discretionary decisions.

Ms Kelly, attractively, seeks to escape the inflexible application by the respondent of its policy relating to rent arrears. First, she submits that test is here an exception to the rule – namely, 'some people in a priority category'. True that does exclude from the 'rent arrears' rule a class of applicant. But it is part of the rule and does not indicate whether those unexcluded – the non-priority category who are in rent arrears – will have their applications dealt with on their merits. The excluded class only reduces the scope of an otherwise inflexible rule. It was never suggested that this applicant was regarded as being within the 'priority category'. She fell within the 'rent arrears' category, without any special features permitting an escape from the rule.

Ms Kelly then submits that, if it be said that the local authority was applying an inflexible policy, what on earth was it doing examining the applicant's medical condition. The argument has a superficial attraction. But the answer to it is that the local authority was looking at the applicant's medical condition to gauge whether she would qualify for the Medical Needs Panel – no doubt, qualifying for the 'priority category' in the exception. Even if this indicated a degree of flexibility, it still wholly failed to take into account the applicant's rent arrears performance, to which I referred in the recital of Ms Markus' submissions.

Finally, in decorous desperation, Ms Kelly points to a letter of February 9, 1996 that states:

> The Queen v London Borough of Southwark, ex parte Mariam Melak Crown Office Ref. CO/3929/95
> Further to your letter dated 29th December 1995, I am pleased to inform you that having thoroughly considered your application for Judicial Review the Council is prepared to reconsider your client's transfer application.;

and again on February 14, 1996

> Re: ex parte Mariam Melak Crown Office Reference–3939/95
> Further to our telephone conversation yesterday. February 12, 1996, I once again reiterate that the Council having considered your application and supporting documents for judicial review, is prepared to reconsider afresh your client's application for a transfer.

This, submits Ms Kelly, demonstrates the flexible approach adopted by the local authority towards its policy. So it does, but only *ex post facto* the service of judicial review proceedings. If that approach had really been the one adopted in July and August 1995, the local authority could so easily have sworn to it on affidavit. Its response to the application for judicial review was a deafening silence. The letter of November 4, 1994, and its refusal to budge on the request to process the applicant's case for transfer-housing, leads to one conclusion only: The policy towards applicants' rent arrears was being applied rigidly.

Accordingly, this application for judicial review succeeds. Certiorari will go to quash the decision- letters of July 25, and August 28, 1995. Mandamus is unnecessary, since the local authority has expressed its willingness to reconsider the applicant's case.

R v Lambeth London Borough Council, ex parte Ashley
(1996) 29 HLR 385

The applicant was the single parent of four children (two girls and two boys) aged between seven and 14. The family lived in a two-bedroomed property owned by the respondent authority. The applicant slept in one bedroom, and the children slept in the other. The applicant applied to the authority for a transfer.

The authority operated a points system for determining priority between applicants on their waiting list. Under the terms of the authority's policy, the condition of an applicant's accommodation was only taken into account in two circumstances. First, where the authority's medical officer had assessed the applicant's circumstances and made specific recommendations, and secondly where the authority's environmental health department had deemed a room in the property to be uninhabitable.

The authority's policy also provided that where a person over three years of age had to share a bedroom with a person of the opposite sex over eight years old (the two persons not being partners), a maximum of 20 points would be awarded to the household (without consideration of the number of individuals concerned).

The applicant applied for judicial review of the authority's decisions regarding her application for a transfer on the ground that the authority's policy was unlawfully rigid.

Held:

(1) Section 22 of the Housing Act 1985 envisaged that the condition of the property in which an applicant for local authority accommodation resided should be an important factor in making a decision about the allocation of housing; the respondent authority's allocation scheme excluded consideration of the condition of the applicant's housing save in two limited circumstances; the policy unduly restricted the scope of the authority's power in a way which was inconsistent with the criteria set out in s. 22;

(2) The limitation on the number of points awarded to a household for the sharing of bedrooms between persons of the opposite sex was illogical; the scheme took no account of the number of persons affected; the scheme was rigid and inflexible and gave no consideration to individual circumstances; it was irrational in the *Wednesbury* sense.

TUCKER J: . . . Section 106 [of the 1985 Act] provides that a landlord authority shall maintain and publish rules for determining priority between applicants in the allocation of housing. In an attempt to comply with this provision, the Council, like many other local authorities, have established a points system to assist them in allocating housing accommodation between non-homeless applicants. Despite certain references in the Form 86A, the applicant's counsel, Mr Broatch, rightly concedes that the Council is entitled to take this course. But he submits that in two respects this system does not comply with the obligations under the statute.

First, paragraph 4.2.4. relates to conditions/state of property. Despite the statutory requirement to give a reasonable preference to persons occupying insanitary houses or living under unsatisfactory housing conditions, the paragraph provides that the condition of the tenant's existing property will not be taken into consideration in determining the tenant's housing need except within two sets of circumstances. The first is where the principal medical officer is assessing the tenant on medical grounds and is making specific recommendations, i.e. medical points are being given due to the current unsuitability of the existing property in terms of the floor level and availability of lifts, etc. The second is where environmental health officers have deemed that any room or rooms are currently uninhabitable and then such rooms will be disregarded for the purposes of the transfer pointing exercise.

Section 22 clearly envisages that the condition of the premises should be an important factor in making any decision about the allocation of housing. In my opinion, the Council's scheme substantially excludes such considerations being taken into account, save in the two limited situations to which the paragraph refers. In my opinion, the Council's policy, as set out in this paragraph of the scheme, unduly restricts the scope of the Council's power in a way which is inconsistent with the criteria contained in section 22. I do not regard this part of the policy as being one which contains well thought out exceptions of the kind referred to by Sedley J in other cases, notably *R* v *London Borough of Lambeth, ex parte Njomo* (1996) 28 HLR 737. I accordingly grant a declaration that this rule, in so far as it purports to limit consideration of the condition or state of the property to those two exceptions, does not represent a proper discharge by the Council of its duty under section 22(a) and (c).

The second matter complained of relates to paragraph 4.2. 10 of the scheme, described as Opposite Sex Sharing (Excluding Partners)/Children Sharing with Adults. In sub-para. (i) it is provided that where a person over three years has to share a bedroom with a person or persons of the opposite sex over eight years old, a maximum of 20 points per household will be awarded. Under this provision points are allowed, as it will be seen, not to individuals but to a household. Miss Marshall, for the respondent, submits that the entire points structure has to be applied to households, not to individuals. She says that to work, the system otherwise would be to introduce double counting which the respondents are not in a position to do, having regard to their available housing stock. I do not follow that argument. If the revision of the system results in the applicant acquiring more points, that does not necessarily entitle her to a transfer of accommodation, though it may give her priority over other applicants. In my judgment, the limitation of 20 points per household for sex separation points is plainly illogical. The scheme does not reflect what might be gross differences between different households. It takes no account, as it ought to, of the number of persons affected. The scheme is, in this regard at least, rigid and inflexible and gives no consideration to individuals.

Mr Broatch submits that the whole scheme has been treated as being absolutely determinative of the points to be awarded and the number of points being awarded as being absolutely determinative of the application for rehousing. While not being prepared to accept this criticism as applying to the whole scheme, I certainly accept it as applying to this particular paragraph relating to opposite sex sharing.

I regard this paragraph as being illogical and irrational in the *Wednesbury* sense. I accordingly declare that the paragraph is unlawful in that sense and that its application is not a proper discharge of the Council's obligations under section 22. Therefore, I quash the decisions of the Council set out in their letters of July 14, and December 19, 1995. I direct the Council to reconsider the applicant's application in accordance with the law, having regard to the condition of her present accommodation and to the allocation of points, such as will reflect the number of persons who suffer the disadvantage of opposite sex sharing of the ages set out in the rule.

R v *Wandsworth London Borough Council, ex parte Lawrie*
(1997) 30 HLR 153

Both applicants were tenants of the respondent authority. They applied separately to the authority for transfers on medical grounds. The authority's housing transfer scheme provided categories for determining priority for applications, based on a medical assessment by the authority's medical officer. The highest priority was 'Essential Medical'; the next was 'Most Advisable'. The scheme did not provide for priority to be re-assessed in the event of the applicant refusing an offer under the scheme.

In each case, the applicants, having been given Essential Medical priority, refused transfer offers and their priority was downgraded to Most Advisable. Their appeals against this were rejected by the authority.

The applicants sought judicial review of these decisions. The authority did not dispute that, since the original assessment, their housing and medical conditions had not changed but maintained that they were entitled to reconsider the priority afforded in the light of the applicants' refusals of their respective offers.

Held: The housing transfer scheme did not entitle the authority to say that if a tenant failed to accept an offer, they would no longer regard it as essential that he should be transferred.

POPPLEWELL J: . . . The London Borough of Wandsworth have a scheme called the 'Housing Transfer Scheme'. It is dated September 1990 and the purpose of it is set out in the body of the scheme in a series of answers to questions:

Why is a transfer system required?

There are a variety of reasons why tenants wish to transfer to other Council accommodation although the majority of applications are received from tenants living in dwellings which, because of changed family circumstances, are either too large or too small for their needs or which no longer suit them for medical reasons. The system of priority categories has [been] found from experience to be the best method of deciding which families have the greatest need and full details of the category system are contained elsewhere within this booklet.

The categories of priority for transfer application are these: the first category, which is called 'Residential Medical', has this definition:

Cases awarded an 'essential' medical recommendation by the Medical Officer for Environmental Health.

A category below that is: Most Advisable' medical assessment. Miss Lawrie was in December 1993 awarded the essential medical status. In the letter from the respondents to her, dated December 3, 1993, they said:

The Council's Medical Adviser has assessed the medical evidence recently submitted and I am pleased to say that she has now made an 'essential' medical recommendation. This means that we will, eventually, be able to offer you alternative accommodation.

Given the high demand for all vacancies available for re-letting it will not be possible to indicate when an offer of alternative accommodation will be made to you.

. . .

[Popplewell J then went over the facts surrounding Miss Lawrie's refusal of a house she was offered, and continued: . . .] There are two facts which are not, as I understand it, in dispute. First, that the condition of the house where she is presently residing has not altered. Secondly, that neither the medical condition of herself, nor of her children, has in any way altered. It is the respondents' contention that the

Medical Officer was entitled to take into account in reviewing the matter not merely the fact that originally she had essential medical status, nor the fact that her medical condition has not changed, but to view the original assessment in the light of the refusal to accept what the Council say is a proper alternative accommodation. It is put in this way, that by refusal she is indicating that she is happy to remain in her present accommodation and therefore it is open to the medical adviser to take the view that it is not now essential medically for her to move. It may be advisable. Her, as it were, acceptance of her present condition, implicit in her refusal to accept the alternative accommodation, indicates that she not in the essential medical category.

It is put by [counsel for the local authority] that what she says is the essential medical condition has not changed nor has the condition of her house. What has changed is the fact that she refused a suitable offer. It is a highly relevant consideration bearing directly on the urgency of a need for a transfer. Assessment of the interaction of health and housing must involve the consideration of the applicant's manifest wish either to move at all costs, or to wait in unsuitable accommodation for a property which suited her requirement.

It is submitted by [counsel for] the applicant, that having regard to the nature of the Housing Transfer Scheme what the respondents have done is contrary to the scheme. It is not suggested that it is of itself unlawful if an applicant refuses a proper alternative accommodation to downgrade that person. There has to be some form of sanction against an unreasonable refusal of alternative accommodation given the limited amount of suitable alternative accommodation. What he submits in relation to the scheme is this, that under the phrase 'How does this scheme work?' this appears:

> If your application is accepted it will be assessed and placed in one of the categories listed at the end of this booklet. If the Council's Medical Officer of Health recommends that a transfer is 'Essential' your application will be placed in the 'Essential Medical' category and will take precedence over other categories. Applications are placed in date order within each category for priority purposes. This date is the time at which your application is first placed in a specific category and not necessarily the date when you first applied for a transfer.
>
> Should I obtain a letter from my doctor if there are medical circumstances to be taken into account?
>
> No – you should complete a medical assessment form and return it to the Transfers and Applications Officer after which it will be assessed by the Medical Officer of Health.
>
> What do I do if my circumstances change?
>
> Any change in your circumstances, for example, if your family increases or decreases or your medical condition changes, should be notified immediately to the Transfers and Applications Officer since your category and transfer prospects could be affected.

The scheme is provided under the provisions of section 106 of the Housing Act 1985 and subsection (1) reads:

> A landlord authority shall publish a summary of its rules—
>   (a) for determining priority as between applicants in the allocation of its housing accommodation.

Reference was made to section 22 of the Housing Act 1985 which provides that a local housing authority may give reasonable preference to different categories of people.

Neither of those two matters seem to me to assist the Court in its determination in the instant case. . . . [There] is nothing in the scheme which indicates that if you refuse an alternative accommodation that that will give grounds for reducing, by way of penalty as it were, the top category to another category. If the borough want to operate a scheme in which they can change you from one category to another, by reason of a refusal, they must say so in their scheme and they do not. All the scheme tends to suggest is that once you have got into the essential medical category you will remain there unless there is some change in your medical condition. This is a very narrow, and I think, not very easy point.

Questions

To what extent and in what way does the case law indicate that medical and other similar evidence should be used in making determinations on requests for transfers? How may LHAs go about ensuring that they avoid rigidity in both the phrasing and the operation of their policies on transfers?

It is clear that the courts are increasingly interested in:

(a)   the way in which transfer policies are phrased and operated and, more importantly;
(b)   the *content* of those schemes. They must be flexible in themselves, i.e. flexibility must be written in and must be patent on the face of the scheme.

However, it is also clear that the courts decline to sit as appellate bodies from the decisions of LHAs. The courts will intervene only where there is clear illegality in the way the LHAs have phrased and/or are operating their policies.

(J)   Allocation policies: housing associations

Associations have to have their own selection and allocation rules, bearing in mind Housing Corporation advice on such matters and counsel from the National Federation of Housing Associations that it is important for associations to make their selection criteria clearly public as they are not democratically answerable bodies yet are in receipt of considerable public funding, *though the objects which an individual association was set up to achieve may constrain its selection and allocation policies.* (For example, an association may exist solely to house poor and elderly former Professors of Law who have fallen into reduced circumstances.) But within such constraints policies must be fairly and lawfully applied, and as a minimum there must be no racial or sexual discrimination. Note also that s. 106 of the Housing Act 1985 (above) also applies to housing associations to require them to publish their allocation rules.

Particular guidance to associations was issued by the Corporation under s. 36A of the Housing Association Act 1985 as 'The Tenants' Guarantee', which, amongst other things, stressed the need for equal opportunities policies to be pursued (see also Housing Corporation Circular HC 22/85, which further stressed that special measures may have to be taken to promote the interests of minority groups because they are often over-represented amongst those in urgent housing need). The relevant power of the Corporation to issue guidance is now found in s. 36 of the Housing Act 1996. The guiding principles upon which allocation of housing association dwellings should be based are the needs of applicants and the severity of those needs, bearing in mind specific housing difficulties affecting particular groups within society, though in general associations should try to provide open and equal access to their dwellings for all sections of the community – subject to their basic constitutions, of course. In many cases LHAs will have power to nominate tenants to housing association properties, particularly where the LHA have been instrumental in helping an association to develop housing, for example by the provision of land, or where an association has acquired its stock by voluntary transfer from the LHA. Obviously in such circumstances the nominations agreement may lay down criteria for eligibility, etc. Further guidance is found in Housing Corporation Circulars HC 36/94 and 36/96, and performance indicators issued in 1998.

5 PUBLIC SECTOR TENANTS' RIGHTS

(A) Introduction

Before the Housing Act 1980 was passed by the then newly elected Conservative Government, local authority tenants had no legal security of tenure. In practice few tenants were evicted from their homes on any grounds other than rent arrears, but even model tenants could be evicted if the local authority thought that the accommodation was underoccupied. This was only after the notice to quit requirements (which are now in s. 3 and s. 5 of the Protection from Eviction Act 1977) had been applied. (Most tenants of private sector landlords, as we saw in chapter 2, had had security since the Increase in Rent and Mortgage Interest (War Restrictions) Act 1915.) In *Shelley* v *London County Council* [1948] 2 All ER 898, the House of Lords dismissed Mrs Shelley's appeal against a possession order granted to the local authority landlords. Mrs Shelley had not broken any terms of her tenancy agreement but was served with a notice to quit her flat in Barnaby Buildings solely because the council wanted to house someone else in the property. Lord Porter stated (at p. 900): 'If, then, the general management, regulation and control of houses includes the right to oust the tenant, the local authority, in giving notice to quit, were exercising their powers under [s. 83(1), Housing Act 1936] . . . and the protection afforded to tenants of private owners does not apply . . . "management" must . . . include a right to terminate the tenancy so far as the general law allows, i.e., after due notice'. Lawton LJ followed *Shelley* in the case of *Cannock Chase DC* v *Kelly* [1978] 1 WLR 1, holding that notice to quit might be given to tenants who had paid their rent and complied with the terms of their tenancy agreements as there was a need to allocate scarce resources. The tenants in *Bristol District Council* v *Clark*

[1975] 3 All ER 976 challenged the district council, arguing that the local authority should provide evidence to the court that they required possession for the purpose of housing people under the Housing Acts. The local authority deliberately refused to provide such evidence. Lord Denning MR said (at p. 980): '. . . the corporation . . . have the general management, regulation and control of houses provided by them. This means they can pick and choose their tenants at will; they can grant tenancies and determine them by notice to quit. . . . They are not trammelled in any way by the Rent Acts.' He then went on to qualify this by saying: '. . . they must exercise [the powers] in good faith, taking into account relevant considerations. . . . It applies, I think, to a decision whether to evict a tenant or not. The local authority shall not automatically evict a man when he falls into arrear with his rent.'

It was assumed that democratically accountable public bodies would be model landlords who would treat their tenants fairly. In practice the security of council tenants may have been high, but the Report of the Committee on One Parent Families 1974, Cmnd 5629 (the Finer Report), had argued (at para. 6.90) that local authority and New Town tenants should have the basic protection of security of tenure which the Rent Acts gave to the tenants of private landlords. It wished to impose the court between the authority wanting possession and the tenant who was unwilling to go.

In addition to the lack of security, council tenants were faced with wholly one-sided tenancy agreements, or even no written agreements at all. Vast numbers of duties were often imposed on tenants – in 76 per cent of the agreements surveyed by the National Consumer Council there was no mention of *any* obligations of the council as landlord (see *Tenancy Agreements*: National Consumer Council, (1976)). Lord Wilberforce described the one-sided nature of the agreements in *Liverpool City Council* v *Irwin* [1977] AC 239 (at p. 253):

As is common with council lettings there is no formal demise or lease or tenancy agreement. There is a document headed 'Liverpool Corporation, Liverpool City Housing Dept.' and described as 'Conditions of Tenancy'. This contains a list of obligations upon the tenant – he shall do this, he shall not do that or he shall not do that without the corporation's consent. . . . At the end there is a form for signature by the tenant stating that he accepts the tenancy. On the landlord's side there is nothing, no signature, no demise, no covenant.

There were moves during the 1970s to put forward a 'Tenants' Charter' which would give statutory effect to a collection of rights for tenants including security of tenure. In June 1977 the Labour Government published *Housing Policy*, a Green Paper, Cmnd 6851, which proposed such a charter which would be 'a code of principles and practices for local authority and new town tenancies, much of which will also be relevant to housing associations' (para. 11.06). A bill was introduced the same year but failed to reach the statute book.

The question of tenants' rights was taken up by the incoming Conservative Government of 1979. It was given added impetus by the inclusion in the Conservative manifesto of the 'right to buy' commitment. It was important to define precisely who could exercise this right, so the Housing Act 1980 (now the Housing Act 1985) defined the 'secure tenant' in s. 1, and only secure tenants have the right to buy. The security of tenure provisions are now in ss. 79–81 of the Housing Act 1985.

(B)   The status of 'secure tenant'

Housing Act 1985

Secure tenancies
79.—(1)   A tenancy under which a dwelling-house is let as a separate dwelling is a secure tenancy at any time when the conditions described in sections 80 and 81 as the landlord condition and the tenant condition are satisfied.

(2)   Subsection (1) has effect subject to—

(a)   the exceptions in Schedule 1 (tenancies which are not secure tenancies),

(b)   sections 89(3) and (4) and 90(3) and (4) (tenancies ceasing to be secure after death of tenant), and

(c)   sections 91(2) and 93(2) (tenancies ceasing to be secure in consequence of assignment or subletting).

(3)   The provisions of this Part apply in relation to a licence to occupy a dwelling-house (whether or not granted for a consideration) as they apply in relation to a tenancy.

(4)   Subsection (3) does not apply to a licence granted as a temporary expedient to a person who entered the dwelling-house or any other land as a trespasser (whether or not, before the grant of that licence, another licence to occupy that or another dwelling-house had been granted to him).

The landlord condition
80.—(1)   The landlord condition is that the interest of the landlord belongs to one of the following authorities or bodies—

a local authority,

a new town corporation,

a housing action trust,

an urban development corporation, or

a housing co-operative to which this section applies.

. . .

The tenant condition
81.   The tenant condition is that the tenant is an individual and occupies the dwelling-house as his only or principal home; or, where the tenancy is a joint tenancy, that each of the joint tenants is an individual and at least one of them occupies the dwelling-house as his only or principal home.

(i)   Let as a separate dwelling
This is the key concept in the secure tenancy. Provided that the landlord and tenant conditions are fulfilled, it must be a tenancy under which a dwelling-

house is let as a separate dwelling. There are three components of this requirement: there must be 'a house', it must be a 'dwelling' and it must be 'separate'.

The term 'house' covers more than what would be called a house in everyday speech: by s. 112 of the 1985 Act, it may be part of a house, such as a flat, and may include land let together with the house although physically separated from it. The definition clearly encompasses houses, flats (whether converted from houses or in a purpose-built block), maisonettes and bungalows.

A 'dwelling' is not defined in the Act, but Rent Act decisions define it as a place where the normal functions of life such as sleeping, eating and cooking are carried out. Sharing a lavatory or a bathroom will not take the tenant outside the Act, whereas sharing a kitchen will. In *Central YMCA Housing Association* v *Goodman* (1991) 24 HLR 109, Goodman had been let a furnished room with *en suite* facilities in a hostel. He was not allowed to use any cooking apparatus in his room to which he had his own key. He was given notice to quit after living in the hostel for 14 years, as the YMCA wanted to sell the hostel to a hotel company. The Court of Appeal rejected his defence that he lived in a dwelling-house and therefore had a secure tenancy under s. 79. Dillon LJ stated that, 'this room was no more a dwelling-house than a hotel room is a dwelling-house' and rejected the notion that because the room had four walls, a ceiling and a floor and was lived in, it was a dwelling-house. Another challenge from a long-term resident to the Central YMCA Housing Association went to the Court of Appeal in the previous year. Saunders, who had been given notice to quit because of his disruptive behaviour, lived in a single bedroom and, unlike Goodman, shared the use of one of the kitchen and dining areas with 11 others. There were no cooking facilities in his room, although he did have an electric kettle in which he boiled eggs sometimes. It was held that it was not a separate dwelling as the kitchen was shared, his occupation was therefore not a secure tenancy, and possession was granted to the YMCA (*Central YMCA Housing Association Ltd* v *Saunders* (1990) 23 HLR 212).

In the private sector s. 22 of the Rent Act 1977 and s. 3 of the Housing Act 1988 specifically allow accommodation with shared facilities to be regarded as a separate dwelling. There is no equivalent section in the 1985 Act.

(ii)   The landlord condition

The landlord must be one of the public bodies listed in s. 80. The Housing Act 1988 removed the Housing Corporation, housing associations and charitable trusts from the list and in effect transferred their tenancies into the private sector; however, secure tenancies granted by such bodies before 15 January 1989 are still governed by the 1985 Act.

(iii)   The tenant condition

The tenant must be an individual. Limited companies are clearly outside the definition, and so too would be unincorporated associations such as a housing co-operative which had taken over and let out property that is soon to be demolished.

(iv)   The tenant's only or principal home
The tenant must also occupy the property as his or her 'only or principal home'. The Court of Appeal considered the ambit of this definition in the following case:

Crawley Borough Council v *Sawyer*
(1987) 20 HLR 98

Sawyer occupied a council house in Crawley from 1978 and was granted a tenancy in 1982. Early in 1985 he went to live with his girlfriend in Horsham and arranged for the electricity to be cut off in June 1985 and the gas sometime the following year. While he lived in Horsham he continued to pay the rent and the rates on the Crawley house and visited it about once a month. In May 1986 the Borough Council became aware that the house was vacant. Sawyer told the authority that he was living with his girlfriend, he was intending to buy her home jointly with her and had been contributing to the mortgage. The authority served notice to quit at the end of August 1986, which expired four weeks later. In that period Sawyer split up with his girlfriend, ceased to make mortgage payments and two weeks later moved back to Crawley. The authority sued for possession alleging that Sawyer was not occupying the dwelling-house as his only or principal home. The judge at first instance found that the premises had at all times been the defendant's principal home. The local authority appealed against that decision.

PARKER LJ: . . . The issue before the learned judge, on facts which to a very large extent were not disputed, was simply whether the tenant was or was not a secure tenant within the meaning of section 81 of the Housing Act, and I must now refer briefly to certain sections of that Act. Section 79(1) provides:

A tenancy under which a dwelling-house is let as a separate dwelling is a secure tenancy at any time when the conditions described in sections 80 and 81 as the landlord condition and the tenant condition are satisfied.

It would therefore appear that a tenancy can at one time be a secure tenancy, cease to be a secure tenancy and become a secure tenancy again if in the interim period it has not been determined. . . . Section 81 provides:

The tenant condition is that the tenant is an individual and occupies the dwelling-house as his only or principal home . . .

The judge, therefore, had to determine, and only to determine, whether the defendant satisfied the provisions of section 81. . . . It is quite plain that it is possible to occupy as a home two places at the same time, and indeed that is inherent in the wording of section 81. It is therefore plain that, if you can occupy two houses at the same time as a home, actual physical occupation cannot be necessary, because one cannot be physically in two places at the same time. . . .

Going through the whole thread of these matters is the common principle that in order to occupy premises as a home, first, there must be signs of occupation – that is to say, there must be furniture and so forth so that the house can be occupied as a home – and, secondly, there must be an intention, if not physically present, to return to it. That is the situation envisaged in the examples given by the Master of the Rolls [in *Herbert* v *Byrne* [1964] 1 All ER 882 at 886 (a Rent Act case)] of, for example, the sea captain who is away for a while. His house is left fully furnished, ready for occupation, no doubt the rent is paid in his absence, but he is not physically there and may not be for a very long period indeed.

In the present case the learned judge was, on the evidence, in my view, well entitled to hold that throughout the period the premises the subject of the action were occupied by the defendant as a home. The only question which really arose is whether it was occupied as a principal home. The learned judge considered the question. He came to the conclusion which he did on the basis that the defendant had left to live with his girlfriend but with no intention of giving up permanent residence of Cobnor Close [Crawley]. . .

. . . The position as at the time the notice to quit was served was that the girlfriend had already told him that he had to get out. He did not in fact move back into Cobnor Close until after the expiry of the notice to quit, but in my view it was well open to the learned judge to have come to the conclusion that, both when the notice to quit was served and when it expired and indeed throughout the whole period, Cobnor Close remained his principal home . . .

Accordingly I would dismiss this appeal.

Notes

1. Although Cobnor Close was regarded as Sawyer's principal home throughout the period, Parker LJ noted that the phrase 'at any time' in s. 79(1) appeared to mean that a tenancy could be a secure tenancy, cease to be a secure tenancy and then become a secure tenancy again. This was the interpretation given to the phrase in *Hussey* v *Camden LBC* (1995) 27 HLR 5, where the tenant lost security of tenure by not occupying his flat, but moved back and was living in the flat when the notice to quit expired and was able to revive the tenancy. If a tenant parts with possession or sublets the whole of the property secure status is lost and cannot be revived (s. 93(2)). In Hussey's case there was insufficient evidence that such a sub-letting had occurred as the county court judge decided that Hussey had lost security as he was not occupying the flat as his only or principal home. The Court of Appeal overturned this decision as at the date of expiry of the notice to quit Hussey was living in the property and had therefore regained security.

2. By way of contrast, the tenant in *Ujima Housing Association* v *Ansah* (1998) 30 HLR 831 said that it was his intention to return to live in the flat. He claimed he had left only because of the nuisance caused by one of his neighbours, which the housing association had ignored. He had left no clothing or personal items so the court held that objectively such an intention to return was not shown. The test of intention to return is objective rather than subjective. The Court of Appeal, no doubt, was also swayed by the amount of profit made by the tenant in letting a flat on which he paid £31.50 a week rent for the princely sum of £130 a week. The tenancy in this case

was a housing association assured tenancy, but the Housing Act 1988 lays down the same 'only or principal home' condition for assured tenancy status to be acquired (see s. 1 of the Housing Act 1988 and chapter 2).
3. It appears from s. 79(3) that licensees gain the same rights as tenants (apart from the right to buy), but the House of Lords held in *Westminster City Council* v *Clarke* [1992] 2 AC 288 that licensees must have exclusive possession to gain these rights (see chapter 1).

Questions
1. 'It is a bedroom pure and simple . . . it is not furnished for cooking and not suitable for cooking in. Mr Saunders said he sometimes boils an egg in an electric kettle, but that is far from sufficient.' (Sir Stephen Brown in *Central YMCA Housing Association* v *Saunders* (1990) 23 HLR 212)
   What would be 'sufficient' for a finding that Mr Saunders had a separate dwelling? If no regulations had existed prohibiting cooking in the room, would it have been possible for a tenant to change his or her status by installing a microwave?
2. Could a tenant sharing a bathroom have a secure tenancy under the 1985 Housing Act?
3. Section 79(3) of the Housing Act 1985 appears to allow a person with a licence to have security of tenure in the public sector. So why was Mr Clarke's notice to quit upheld? (*Westminster City Council* v *Clarke* [1992] 2 AC 288 (see chapter 1).)
4. In the light of *Hussey* v *Camden London Borough Council* (1995) 27 HLR 5, consider whether X, the tenant of a council flat, loses his secure tenant status in the following alternative situations:

   (a) X goes backpacking round the world for an indeterminate period leaving Y in possession of the flat and there is no formal agreement between X and Y.
   (b) X moves to London on a six-month employment contract which may become permanent, leaving Y in possession of the flat. Y has an agreement with X which states that Y must give up possession of the flat 'on demand' by X.
   (c) X moves in with a partner two miles away leaving Y in possession of the flat. X's parting words to Y were: 'Make yourself at home. Make sure the council get the rent on time. I doubt if I'll be back, but you never know.' No formal agreement exists between X and Y.

5. In *Crawley Borough Council* v *Sawyer* (1988) 20 HLR 98, it was decided that Sawyer never ceased to be a secure tenant of his home in Crawley. Would it have been more consistent to have decided that while Sawyer lived in Horsham with his girlfriend her house was his principal home, and that he became a secure tenant again when he returned to Crawley? Parker LJ argues that it is possible for a secure tenancy to cease to be secure for an interim period and then to become secure again as the wording of s. 79(1) states: 'A

tenancy . . . is a secure tenancy *at any time* when the . . . landlord condition and the tenant condition are satisfied' (emphasis added).

6. Do local authority social workers living in flats on the premises of a residential home for children acquire secure tenant status?

(C)   Tenancies which are not secure tenancies

Housing Act 1985

SCHEDULE 1

Long leases

1. A tenancy is not a secure tenancy if it is a long tenancy.

Introductory tenancies

1A. A tenancy is not a secure tenancy if it is an introductory tenancy or a tenancy which has ceased to be an introductory tenancy—

(a)   by virtue of section 133(3) of the Housing Act 1996 (disposal on death to non-qualifying person), or

(b)   by virtue of the tenant, or in the case of a joint tenancy every tenant, ceasing to occupy the dwelling-house as his only or principal home.

Premises occupied in connection with employment

2.—(1)   [Subject to sub-paragraph (4B)] a tenancy is not a secure tenancy if the tenant is an employee of the landlord or of—

a local authority,

a new town corporation,

[a housing action trust]

an urban development corporation, or

the governors of an aided school,

and his contract of employment requires him to occupy the dwelling-house for the better performance of his duties.

(2)   [Subject to sub-paragraph (4B)] A tenancy is not a secure tenancy if the tenant is a member of a police force and the dwelling-house is provided for him free of rent and rates in pursuance of regulations made under [section 50 of the Police Act 1996] (general regulations as to government, administration and conditions of service of police forces).

(3)   [Subject to sub-paragraph (4B)] A tenancy is not a secure tenancy if the tenant is an employee of a fire authority (within the meaning of the Fire Services Acts 1947 to 1959) and—

(a)   his contract of employment requires him to live in close proximity to a particular fire station, and

(b)   the dwelling-house was let to him by the authority in consequence of that requirement.

(4)   [Subject to sub-paragraph (4A) and (4B)] A tenancy is not a secure tenancy if—

(a)   within the period of three years immediately preceding the grant the conditions mentioned in sub-paragraph (1), (2) or (3) have been satisfied with respect to a tenancy of the dwelling-house, and

(b)   before the grant the landlord notified the tenant in writing of the circumstances in which this exception applies and that in its opinion the proposed tenancy would fall within this exception,

. . .

[(4A)   Except where the landlord is a local housing authority, a tenancy under subparagraph (4) shall become a secure tenancy when the periods during which the conditions mentioned in sub-paragraph (1), (2) or (3) are not satisfied with respect to the tenancy amount in aggregate to more than three years.

(4B)   Where the landlord is a local housing authority, a tenancy under sub-paragraph (1), (2) (3) or (4) shall become a secure tenancy if the authority notify the tenant that the tenancy is to be regarded as a secure tenancy.]

(5)   In this paragraph 'contract of employment' means a contract of service or apprenticeship, whether express or implied and (if express) whether oral or in writing.

Land acquired for development

3.—(1)   A tenancy is not a secure tenancy if the dwelling-house is on land which has been acquired for development and the dwelling-house is used by the landlord, pending development of the land, as temporary housing accommodation.

(2)   In this paragraph 'development' has the meaning given by [section 55 of the Town and Country Planning Act 1990] (general definition of development for purposes of that Act).

Accommodation for homeless persons

4.   A tenancy granted in pursuance of [any function under Part VII of the Housing Act 1996 (homelessness) is not a secure tenancy unless the local housing authority concerned have notified the tenant that the tenancy is to be regarded as a secure tenancy.]

Temporary accommodation for persons taking up employment

5.—(1)   [Subject to sub-paragraphs (1A) and (1B) a tenancy is not a secure tenancy] if—

(a)   the person to whom the tenancy was granted was not, immediately before the grant, resident in the district in which the dwelling-house is situated,

(b)   before the grant of the tenancy, he obtained employment, or an offer of employment, in the district or its surrounding area,

(c)   the tenancy was granted to him for the purpose of meeting his need for temporary accommodation in the district or its surrounding area in order to work there, and of enabling him to find permanent accommodation there, and

(d)   the landlord notified him in writing of the circumstances in which this exception applies and that in its opinion the proposed tenancy would fall within this exception;

. . .

[(1A)   Except where the landlord is a local housing authority, a tenancy under subparagraph (1) shall become a secure tenancy on the expiry of one year from the grant or on earlier notification by the landlord to the tenant that the tenancy is to be regarded as a secure tenancy.

(1B)   Where the landlord is a local housing authority, a tenancy under sub-paragraph (1) shall become a secure tenancy if at any time the authority notify the tenant that the tenancy is to be regarded as secure tenancy.]

(2)   In this paragraph—

'district' means district of a local housing authority; and

'surrounding area', in relation to a district, means the area consisting of each district that adjoins it.

Short-term arrangements

6.   A tenancy is not a secure tenancy if—

(a)   the dwelling-house has been leased to the landlord with vacant possession for use as temporary housing accommodation,

(b)   the terms on which it has been leased include provision for the lessor to obtain vacant possession from the landlord on the expiry of a specified period or when required by the lessor,

(c)   the lessor is not a body which is capable of granting secure tenancies, and

(d)   the landlord has no interest in the dwelling-house other than under the lease in question or as a mortgagee.

Temporary accommodation during works

7.   A tenancy is not a secure tenancy if—

(a)   the dwelling-house has been made available for occupation by the tenant (or a predecessor in title of his) while works are carried out on the dwelling-house which he previously occupied as his home, and

(b)   the tenant or predecessor was not a secure tenant of that other dwelling-house at the time when he ceased to occupy it as his home.

Agricultural holdings

8.—(1)   A tenancy is not a secure tenancy if—

(a)   the dwelling-house is comprised in an agricultural holding and is occupied by the person responsible for the control (whether as tenant or as servant or agent of the tenant) of the farming of the holding, or

(b)   the dwelling-house is comprised in the holding held under a farm business tenancy and is occupied by the person responsible for the control (whether as tenant or as servant or agent of the tenant) of the management of the holding.

(2)   In sub-paragraph (1) above—

(a)   'agricultural holding' means any agricultural holding within the meaning of Agricultural Holdings Act 1986 held under a tenancy in relation to which that Act applies, and

(b)   'farm business tenancy', and 'holding' in relation to such a tenancy, have the same meaning as in the Agricultural Tenancies Act 1995.

Licensed premises

9.   A tenancy is not a secure tenancy if the dwelling-house consists of or includes premises licensed for the sale of intoxicating liquor for consumption on the premises.

Student lettings

10.—(1)   [Subject to sub-paragraphs (2A) and (2B)] a tenancy of a dwelling-house is not a secure tenancy before the expiry of the period specified in sub-paragraph (3) if—

(a)   it is granted for the purpose of enabling the tenant to attend a designated course at an educational establishment, and

(b)   before the grant of the tenancy the landlord notified him in writing of the circumstances in which this exception applies and that in its opinion the proposed tenancy would fall within this exception.

. . .

(2)   A landlord's notice under sub-paragraph (1)(b) shall specify the educational establishment which the person concerned proposes to attend.

[(2A)   Except where the landlord is a local housing authority, a tenancy under sub-paragraph (1) shall become a secure tenancy on the expiry of the period specified in sub-paragraph (3) or on earlier notification by the landlord to the tenant that the tenancy is to be regarded as a secure tenancy.

(2B)   Where the landlord is a local housing authority, a tenancy under sub-paragraph (1) shall become a secure tenancy if at any time the authority notify the tenant that the tenancy is to be regarded as a secure tenancy.]

(3)   The period referred to in sub-paragraph (2A) is—

(a)   in a case where the tenant attends a designated course at the educational establishment specified in the landlord's notice, the period ending six months after the tenant ceases to attend that (or any other) designated course at that establishment;

(b)   in any other case, the period ending six months after the grant of the tenancy.

(4)   In this paragraph—

'designated course' means a course of any kind designated by regulations made by the Secretary of State for the purposes of this paragraph;

'educational establishment' means a university or [institution which provides higher education or further education (or both); and for the purposes of this definition

'higher education' and 'further education' have the same meaning as in the Education Act 1996].

(5)   Regulations under sub-paragraph (4) shall be made by statutory instrument and may make different provision with respect to different cases or descriptions of case, including different provision for different areas.

1954 Act tenancies

11.   A tenancy is not a secure tenancy if it is one to which Part II of the Landlord and Tenant Act 1954 applies (tenancies of premises occupied for business purposes).

Almshouses

12.—(1)   A licence to occupy a dwelling-house is not a secure tenancy if—

[(a)   the dwelling-house is an almshouse, and

(b)   the licence was granted by or on behalf of a charity which—

(i)   is authorised under its trusts to maintain the dwelling-house as an almshouse, and

(ii)   has no power under its trusts to grant a tenancy of the dwelling-house;

and in this paragraph 'almshouse' means any premises maintained as an almshouse, whether they are called an almshouse or not; and 'trusts', in relation to a charity, means the provisions establishing it as a charity and regulating its purposes and administration, whether those provisions take effect by way of trust or not].

Notes
1.   Paragraph 1A was inserted by Sch. 14 of the Housing Act 1996.
2.   Paragraph 12 was substituted by the Charities Act 1992.
3.   'Long leases' are defined in s. 115 of the Housing Act 1985 as tenancies for a term of over 25 years. Such leases are rare in the public sector.

(i)   Introductory tenancies

Local authorities and housing action trusts can elect to operate an introductory tenancy regime. This is a new category of tenancy brought in by the Housing Act 1996, s. 124. Where such a scheme is run, all new tenancies are for a probationary period of 12 months and other than security of tenure the tenancies have all the hallmarks of a secure tenancy, for example if the tenant dies succession by a member of the tenant's family is possible (Housing Act 1996, ss. 131–133).

The introductory tenancy regime is in Pt V of the Housing Act 1996, which is entitled 'Conduct of tenants', and has clearly been brought in as one of the measures to deal with tenants' 'anti-social behaviour'. The White Paper, *Our Future Homes*, Cm 2901, para. 3.2, put forward the purpose of this new type of tenancy: '[Introductory tenancies] would give a clear signal to new tenants that anti-social behaviour was unacceptable and that it would result in the loss of their home. It would also give reassurance to existing tenants that their authority would take prompt action to remove any new tenants acting in this way.' Although the intention may be to deal with anti-social behaviour, there appears to be nothing against a landlord giving under-occupation as the reason in the notice of proceedings.

Housing Act 1996

PART V
CONDUCT OF TENANTS
CHAPTER 1
INTRODUCTORY TENANCIES

General provisions

Introductory tenancies

124.—(1)   A local housing authority or a housing action trust may elect to operate an introductory tenancy regime.

(2)   When such an election is in force, every periodic tenancy of a dwelling-house entered into or adopted by the authority or trust shall, if it would otherwise be a secure tenancy, be an introductory tenancy, unless immediately before the tenancy was entered. into or adopted the tenant or, in the case of joint tenants, one or more of them was—

(a)   a secure tenant of the same or another dwelling-house or,

(b)   an assured tenant of a registered social landlord (otherwise than under an assured shorthold tenancy) in respect of the same or another dwelling-house.

(3)   Subsection (2) does not apply to a tenancy entered into or adopted in pursuance of a contract made before the election was made.

(4)   For the purposes of this Chapter a periodic tenancy is adopted by a person if that person becomes the landlord under the tenancy, whether on a disposal or surrender of the interest of the former landlord.

(5)   An election under this section may be revoked at any time, without prejudice to the making of a further election.

Duration of introductory tenancy

125.—(1)   A tenancy remains an introductory tenancy until the end of the trial period, unless one of the events mentioned in subsection (5) occurs before the end of that period.

(2)   The 'trial period' is the period of one year beginning with—
   (a)   in the case of a tenancy which was entered into by a local housing authority or housing action trust—
      (i)   the date on which the tenancy was entered into, or
      (ii)   if later, the date on which a tenant was first entitled to possession under the tenancy; or
   (b)   in the case of a tenancy which was adopted by a local housing authority or housing action trust, the date of adoption;
subject as follows.

(3)   Where the tenant under an introductory tenancy was formerly a tenant under another introductory tenancy, or held an assured shorthold tenancy from a registered social landlord, any period or periods during which he was such a tenant shall count towards the trial period, provided—
   (a)   if there was one such period, it ended immediately before the date specified in subsection (2), and
   (b)   if there was more than one such period, the most recent period ended immediately before that date and each period succeeded the other without interruption.

(4)   Where there are joint tenants under an introductory tenancy, the reference in subsection (3) to the tenant shall be construed as referring to the joint tenant in whose case the application of that subsection produces the earliest starting date for the trial period.

(5)   A tenancy ceases to be an introductory tenancy if, before the end of the trial period—
   (a)   the circumstances are such that the tenancy would not otherwise be a secure tenancy,
   (b)   a person or body other than a local housing authority or housing action trust becomes the landlord under the tenancy,
   (c)   the election in force when the tenancy was entered into or adopted is revoked, or
   (d)   the tenancy ceases to be an introductory tenancy by virtue of section 133(3) (succession).

(6)   A tenancy does not come to an end merely because it ceases to be an introductory tenancy, but a tenancy which has once ceased to be an introductory tenancy cannot subsequently become an introductory tenancy.

(7)   This section has effect subject to section 130 (effect of beginning proceedings for possession).

Licences
126.—(1)   The provisions of this Chapter apply in relation to a licence to occupy a dwelling-house (whether or not granted for a consideration) as they apply in relation to a tenancy.

(2)   Subsection (1) does not apply to a licence granted as a temporary expedient to a person who entered the dwelling-house or any other land as a trespasser (whether or not, before the grant of that licence, another licence to occupy that or another dwelling-house had been granted to him).

Proceedings for possession

Proceedings for possession
127.—(1)   The landlord may only bring an introductory tenancy to an end by obtaining an order of the court for the possession of the dwelling-house.

(2)   The court shall make such an order unless the provisions of section 128 apply.

(3)   Where the court makes such an order, the tenancy comes to an end on the date on which the tenant is to give up possession in pursuance of the order.

Notice of proceedings for possession

128.—(1)   The court shall not entertain proceedings for the possession of a dwelling-house let under an introductory tenancy unless the landlord has served on the tenant a notice of proceedings complying with this section.

(2)   The notice shall state that the court will be asked to make an order for the possession of the dwelling-house.

(3)   The notice shall set out the reasons for the landlord's decision to apply for such an order.

(4)   The notice shall specify a date after which proceedings for the possession of the dwelling-house may be begun.

The date so specified must not be earlier than the date on which the tenancy could, apart from this Chapter, be brought to an end by notice to quit given by the landlord on the same date as the notice of proceedings.

(5)   The court shall not entertain any proceedings for possession of the dwelling-house unless they are begun after the date specified in the notice of proceedings.

(6)   The notice shall inform the tenant of his right to request a review of the landlord's decision to seek an order for possession and of the time within which such a request must be made.

(7)   The notice shall also inform the tenant that if he needs help or advice about the notice, and what to do about it, he should take it immediately to a Citizens' Advice Bureau, a housing aid centre, a law centre or a solicitor.

Review of decision to seek possession

129.—(1)   A request for review of the landlord's decision to seek an order for possession of a dwelling-house let under an introductory tenancy must be made before the end of the period of 14 days beginning with the day on which the notice of proceedings is served.

(2)   On a request being duly made to it, the landlord shall review its decision.

(3)   The Secretary of State may make provision by regulations as to the procedure to be followed in connection with a review under this section.

Nothing in the following provisions affects the generality of this power.

(4)   Provision may be made by regulations—

(a)   requiring the decision on review to be made by a person of appropriate seniority who was not involved in the original decision, and

(b)   as to the circumstances in which the person concerned is entitled to an oral hearing, and whether and by whom he may be represented at such a hearing.

(5)   The landlord shall notify the person concerned of the decision on the review.

If the decision is to confirm the original decision, the landlord shall also notify him of the reasons for the decision.

(6)   The review shall be carried out and the tenant notified before the date specified in the notice of proceedings as the date after which proceedings for the possession of the dwelling-house may be begun.

Effect of beginning proceedings for possession

130.—(1)   This section applies where the landlord has begun proceedings for the possession of a dwelling-house let under an introductory tenancy and—

(a)   the trial period ends, or

(b)   any of the events specified in section 125(5) occurs (events on which a tenancy ceases to be an introductory tenancy).

(2)   Subject to the following provisions, the tenancy remains an introductory tenancy until—

(a)   the tenancy comes to an end in pursuance of section 127(3) (that is, on the date on which the tenant is to give up possession in pursuance of an order of the court), or

(b)   the proceedings are otherwise finally determined.

(3)   If any of the events specified in section 125(5)(b) to (d) occurs, the tenancy shall thereupon cease to be an introductory tenancy but—

(a)   the landlord (or, as the case may be, the new landlord) may continue the proceedings, and

(b)   if he does so, section 127(2) and (3) (termination by landlord) apply as if the tenancy had remained an introductory tenancy.

(4)   Where in accordance with subsection (3) a tenancy ceases to be an introductory tenancy and becomes a secure tenancy, the tenant is not entitled to exercise the right to buy under Part V of the Housing Act 1985 unless and until the proceedings are finally determined on terms such that he is not required to give up possession of the dwelling-house.

(5)   For the purposes of this section proceedings shall be treated as finally determined if they are withdrawn or any appeal is abandoned or the time for appealing expires without an appeal being brought.

Introductory Tenants (Review) Regulations 1997
SI 1997 No. 72

. . .

Right to a hearing
2.   The review under section 129 of the Housing Act 1996 of the decision to seek an order for possession of a dwelling-house let under an introductory tenancy shall not be by way of an oral hearing unless the tenant informs the landlord that he wishes to have such a hearing before the end of the time permitted under subsection (1) of that section to request a review of that decision.

Who is to carry out the review
3.—(1)   The review shall be carried out by a person who was not involved in the decision to apply for an order for possession.

(2)   Where the review of a decision made by an officer is also to be made by an officer, that officer shall be someone who is senior to the officer who made the original decision.

Review without a hearing
4.   If there is not to be a hearing the tenant may make representations in writing in connection with the review and such representations shall be considered by the landlord who shall inform the tenant of the date by which such representations must be received, which shall not be earlier than five clear days after receipt of this information by the tenant.

Review by way of a hearing
5.—(1)   Subject to the provisions of this regulation, the procedure in connection with a review by way of hearing shall be such as the person hearing the review shall determine.

(2)   A tenant who has requested a hearing has the right to—

(a)   be heard and to be accompanied and may be represented by another person whether that person is professionally qualified or not, and for the purposes of the proceedings any representative shall have the rights and powers which the tenant has under these Regulations;

(b)   call persons to give evidence;

(c)   put questions to any person who gives evidence at the hearing; and

(d)   make representations in writing.

Notice of the hearing
6.   The landlord shall give the tenant notice of the date, time and place of the hearing, which shall be not less than five days after receipt of the request for a hearing and if the tenant has not been given such notice, the hearing may only proceed with the consent of the tenant or his representative.

Absence of tenant at hearing
7.   If any person shall fail to appear at the hearing, notice having been given to him in accordance with regulation 6, the person conducting the review may, having regard to all the circumstances including any explanation offered for the absence, proceed with the hearing notwithstanding his absence, or give such directions with a view to the conduct of the further review as that person may think proper.

Postponement of hearing
8.   A tenant may apply to the landlord requesting a postponement of the hearing and the landlord may grant or refuse the application as they see fit.

Adjournment of hearing
9.   A hearing may be adjourned by the person hearing the review at any time during the hearing on the application of the tenant, his representative, or at the motion of the person hearing the review and, if a hearing is adjourned part heard and after the adjournment the person or persons hearing the review differ from those at the first hearing, otherwise than through the operation of paragraph 7, proceedings shall be by way of a complete rehearing of the case.

Absence of person hearing the review
10.   Where more than one person is conducting the review, any hearing may, with the consent of the tenant or his representative but not otherwise, be proceeded with in the absence of one of' the persons who is to determine the review.

In *Manchester City Council* v *Cochrane* [1999] *The Times,* 12 January, a local authority had granted an introductory tenancy to a couple. This was made clear in the tenancy agreement, which also clearly stated the power of the landlord to dispossess the tenant for breaches of tenancy obligations, including acts of nuisance or annoyance to other persons, or inflicting or threatening domestic violence. Using these powers the landlord served a notice in March 1998 to terminate the tenancy, and the validity of this notice was not disputed. In April 1998 the tenants requested a review of the decision to seek possession. An oral hearing was held and the tenants alleged that this was not carried out in accordance with the requirements of the Introductory Tenants (Review) Regulations 1997. After that oral hearing the landlord confirmed that they would seek possession of the dwelling-house.

The tenants sought to defend the possession action in the county court. They denied breaking their tenancy agreement and also argued that they had been denied a fair review hearing. The question for the Court of Appeal was whether as a matter of law the tenants could raise such a defence. Sir John Knox found:

(a)   The terms of the statute (the Housing Act 1996) imposed a mandatory scheme which limited the tenants' rights. Provided the council complied with the requirements of section 128 the Court was bound to make a possession order under s. 127(2).

(b)   If the tenants wished to challenge the conduct of the review they had to apply to the High Court for judicial review, and, following *Avon County Council* v *Buscott* [1988] QB 686, in such circumstances the county court could adjourn the possession proceedings if satisfied the tenants would have a real chance of being granted leave to apply for judicial review.

(c)   However, the county court could not entertain a defence to the possession proceedings based on a denial of breach of tenancy obligations, neither could it grant a stay of those proceedings based on the tenants' allegation that the landlord had failed to observe the rules of natural justice.

(d)   The county court may not review failures to exercise public duties unless Parliament has given it express authority to do so (see s. 38(3) of the County Court Act 1983); such a jurisdiction had not been granted in relation to introductory tenancies.

(e)   If the county court had jurisdiction to entertain a defence based on the invalidity of the landlord's review procedures the result could be that the tenant might achieve secure status, an undesirable result and not what was clearly intended by Parliament.

(ii)   Premises occupied in connection with employment
If the tenant is an employee and the contract of employment requires occupation of the dwelling-house 'for the better performance of his duties', the tenancy will not be secure. It would be extremely inconvenient if school caretakers living in houses on site exercised the right to buy. The next caretaker in the post would not readily be on hand to deal with emergencies.

Difficulties have arisen where the contract of employment does not expressly lay down that someone in the post *must* occupy the house, but it may be argued that such a term could be implied. In *Hughes* v *Greenwich London Borough Council* [1994] 1 AC 170, Mr Hughes was the headmaster of a boarding school for children with special educational needs. He received free board and lodging and lived in a purpose-built house in the school grounds. When the school closed and he retired he claimed to be a secure tenant, thereby having the right to buy the freehold. The borough council argued that, although it was not an express term of Mr Hughes' contract of employment that he was obliged to live in the house for the better performance of his duties, such a term could be implied. He would therefore come within the employment exceptions in Sch. 1 para. 2 of the 1985 Act and his tenancy would not be secure. Lord Lowry stated (at p. 177): 'In order that a term may be implied, there has to be a compelling reason for deeming that term to form part of the contract, and that compelling reason is missing in this case, unless it was *essential* that Mr Hughes should live in the house in order to do his job, but the facts found contradict that proposition . . . he was not required to occupy that house *for the better performance of his duties*. It is clear that the employer was providing a facility but not imposing an obligation.' Mr Hughes therefore was able to exercise the right to buy.

In contrast, in *South Glamorgan County Council* v *Griffiths* (1992) 24 HLR 334, a school caretaker lived close to the school in a house owned by the local authority. In Mr Griffiths' conditions of service a term was included: 'It shall be a condition of employment that a caretaker must reside in school accommodation where such premises are available and a tenancy agreement must be entered into.' In fact there was no formal tenancy agreement and Mr Griffiths paid only £1 a week in rent. The school closed and Mr Griffiths retired from his post as school caretaker. He was given notice to quit as the house was required for a caretaker at the community centre which had been set up in the old school. Despite the fact that there was a short period when he was occupying the house after he had retired and so was not occupying it 'for the better performance of his duties', the notice to quit was upheld by the Court of Appeal.

This exception in Sch. 1 para. 2 is not a 'once and for all' condition which must be satisfied at the start of the tenancy, or, *vice versa*, if it was satisfied earlier, circumstances can change so that it no longer applies. In *Elvidge* v *Coventry City Council* [1993] 4 All ER 903, the employee, who lived in a cottage in a country park, first worked as a water bailiff and there was no implied term that he should live in the cottage. When he was promoted to an assistant ranger post his terms of employment altered and he was required to live in the park. With his new job he came within the exclusion in Sch. 1, para. 2. The school caretaker in *Greenfield* v *Berkshire County Council* (1996) 28 HLR 691 came within the exclusion when he was employed. He was made redundant and remained in the house as the caretaker's house at his new school was still being occupied by the old caretaker. He could not cope with the travelling to his new post so he gave in his notice and therefore remained in the house for a period of months while he was not an employee of the County Council. He was given notice to quit which he resisted, as he argued that as he was no longer a caretaker he had gained security of tenure. The Court of Appeal accepted this argument and held that the tenancy did not come within the exclusion.

(iii)   Development land

Until the late 1960s certain areas of cities were declared to be clearance areas, all the properties compulsorily purchased and the owners given compensation. The housing was demolished and the local authorities then built new estates of council housing for rent. The powers were formerly contained in Housing Act 1957, Pt III, and are now in s. 289 and s. 290 of the Housing

Act 1985. This process took many months – years in some cases – with boarded-up properties lying vacant. To utilise these properties until redevelopment took place, councils licensed them to housing associations and squatters' groups. If these groups acquired secure tenancies (although possession proceedings could be brought under Ground 10, but then alternative accommodation would have to be found for the residents) the practice of using short-life housing would be put in jeopardy.

Local authority policy gradually changed after General Improvement Areas (GIAs) were introduced by the Housing Act 1969, and grants were available for private householders to improve their properties by installing modern bathrooms, internal lavatories and central heating. Although compulsory purchase is no longer used to acquire whole areas of residential properties, individual houses may still be acquired for road schemes and for community buildings such as schools. Areas of derelict industrial or former railway land are still acquired for wholesale development. In the last few years these schemes often include new housing.

Fox LJ held, in *Hyde Housing Association Ltd* v *Harrison* (1990) 23 HLR 57, at p. 58, that:

. . . paragraph 3(1) of Schedule 1, read according to its ordinary meaning in the English language, does not require that the landlord be the person who has acquired the land for development. The paragraph, it seems to me, imposes two distinct requirements. The first is that the dwelling-house must be on land which has been acquired for development. The second is that the dwelling-house is used by the landlord, pending development of the land, as temporary housing accommodation. If these two requirements are satisfied, the tenancy is not a secure tenancy.

There is, in my view, no requirement express or implied that the acquisition should have been by the landlord.

In the *Harrison* case the Department of Transport had acquired a flat as part of land required for a road development scheme. Six months later the Department licensed the land to the housing association, who in turn granted a temporary licence to Harrison. When Mr Harrison was in arrears with his rent the housing association gave him a notice to bring his licence to an end. Mr Harrison argued that he had a secure tenancy because, to come within the exception in Sch. 1, para. 3, the landlord must be the person who acquired the property for development. This was firmly rejected by the Court of Appeal.

Several other cases on this exception have reached the Court of Appeal. It was decided in *Attley* v *Cherwell District Council* (1989) 21 HLR 613 that even if the nature of the development planned altered, the exception still applied. In that case the property had been originally acquired in 1879 for a sewage works which was never built! If, however, no development at all is envisaged in the foreseeable future, the occupiers gain security (*Lillieshall Road Housing Co-operative Ltd* v *Brennan* (1991) 24 HLR 195). In the *Brennan* case the question also arose of whether the 'land' referred to in para. 3 was merely the

land on which the house stood, or whether it was all the land (in that case
29 houses) covered by the compulsory purchase order. The Court decided it
was the latter.

(iv)   Accommodation for homeless people

Paragraph 4 of Sch. 1 of the 1985 Act has been radically altered by the
Housing Act 1996, so now any tenancy granted to homeless people is
insecure. By s. 207 of the Housing Act 1996, housing can only be for a
maximum of two years unless it is in a hostel or in private sector accommodation leased by the authority. The local authority's own accommodation
cannot be allocated permanently to the homeless. The authority may, of
course, inform the tenant that the tenancy is to be regarded as a secure
tenancy.

(v)   Temporary accommodation for persons taking up employment

Many local authorities keep a small stock of property for people taking up
jobs with the authority who came from outside the area. Accommodation is
needed until they have had time to make permanent arrangements. The
amendments made by the 1996 Act differentiate between local housing
authorities and other public sector landlords. Local authority tenants remain
insecure unless the authority inform them otherwise. For all other public
sector tenants a tenancy automatically becomes secure after a year, but the
landlord can inform the tenant at any time that the tenancy has become
secure.

(vi)   Short-term arrangements

Due to the shortage of council accommodation, the practice has grown up in
some areas of local authorities leasing properties from private landlords and
then letting them in turn on a temporary basis to homeless people. This is
clearly a cheaper option than housing homeless people in bed and breakfast
accommodation in hotels. Some inner-London boroughs with large numbers
of homeless people lease properties further away from the centre in the outer
boroughs. Without such an exception private landlords would be unwilling to
lease properties to local authorities as they would not easily be able to regain
possession.

The issue addressed in *Tower Hamlets London Borough Council* v *Miah*
(1991) 24 HLR 199 was whether a licence came within Sch. 1, para. 6. The
authority owed the defendant a duty to provide permanent accommodation
with security of tenure. This duty could be fulfilled in stages – by providing
temporary accommodation to start with, giving time to find suitable permanent accommodation later. As a temporary measure the respondent was
granted a licence of a property on which Tower Hamlets had taken a licence
themselves. When served with a notice to quit Miah made two separate
arguments: first, that under s. 79(3) of the Housing Act 1985 the arrangement, despite being a licence, amounted to a secure tenancy; and, secondly,
that the exception for short-term arrangements in Sch. 1, para. 6 applied only

to leases and not to licences. The Court of Appeal held that para. 6 was intended to apply to all arrangements by which a private owner granted rights which were less than a freehold to a local authority; therefore the term 'leases' in para. 6 included licences.

(vii) Remaining exceptions in Sch. 1
The remaining exceptions include temporary accommodation during works (para. 7), agricultural holdings (para. 8), public houses (para. 9), business tenancies (para. 11), almshouses (para. 12) and lettings to students at designated courses and educational institutions (see SI 1980 No. 1407).

Questions
1.   Did it make any difference in *Hughes* v *Greenwich London Borough Council* [1994] 1 AC 170 that the school where Mr Hughes had been a headmaster had closed down?
2.   In the public sector there are six-month introductory tenants; in the private, assured shorthold tenants. Are they similar? What are the differences?
3.   The county court has a wide power to determine matters relating to homelessness decisions, including public law issues of procedural fairness. Is it logical that the jurisdiction with regard to introductory tenancies should be so limited?

(D)   Eviction procedures

Public sector tenants have security of tenure and can be evicted only if the landlord obtains a court order for possession which is served on the tenant (Housing Act 1985, s. 82). The tenancy ends on the date the court orders (s. 82(2)). The landlord has to follow the correct procedure and one of the grounds listed in Sch. 2 must exist. The procedure is in s. 83 of the Housing Act 1985, which has been completely replaced by a new s. 83, substituted by s. 147 of the Housing Act 1996. Sections 83, 83A and 84 set out below are as amended or replaced by the 1996 Act.

Housing Act 1985

Proceedings for possession or termination: notice requirements
83.—(1)   The court shall not entertain proceedings for the possession of a dwelling-house let under a secure tenancy or proceedings for the termination of a secure tenancy unless—
    (a)   the landlord has served a notice on the tenant complying with the provisions of this section, or
    (b)   the court considers it just and equitable to dispense with the requirement of such a notice.
   (2)   A notice under this section shall—
    (a)   be in a form prescribed by regulations made by the Secretary of State,
    (b)   specify the ground on which the court will be asked to make an order for the possession of the dwelling-house or for the termination of the tenancy, and

(c)   give particulars of that ground.

(3)   Where the tenancy is a periodic tenancy and the ground or one of the grounds specified in the notice is Ground 2 in Schedule 2 (nuisance or other anti-social behaviour), the notice—

(a)   shall also—

(i)   state that proceedings for the possession of the dwelling-house may be begun immediately, and

(ii)   specify the date sought by the landlord as the date on which the tenant is to give up possession of the dwelling-house, and

(b)   ceases to be in force twelve months after the date so specified.

(4)   Where the tenancy is a periodic tenancy and Ground 2 in Schedule 2 is not specified in the notice, the notice—

(a)   shall also specify the date after which proceedings for the possession of the dwelling-house may be begun, and

(b)   ceases to be in force twelve months after the date so specified.

(5)   The date specified in accordance with subsection (3) or (4) must not be earlier than the date on which the tenancy could, apart from this Part, be brought to an end by notice to quit given by the landlord on the same date as the notice under this section.

(6)   Where a notice under this section is served with respect to a secure tenancy for a term certain, it has effect also with respect to any periodic tenancy arising on the termination of that tenancy by virtue of section 86; and subsections (3) to (5) of this section do not apply to the notice.

(7)   Regulations under this section shall be made by statutory instrument and may make different provision with respect to different cases or descriptions of case, including different provision for different areas.

Additional requirements in relation to certain proceedings for possession
83A.—(1)   Where a notice under section 83 has been served on a tenant containing the information mentioned in subsection (3)(a) of that section, the court shall not entertain proceedings for the possession of the dwelling-house unless they are begun at a time when the notice is still in force.

(2)   Where—

(a)   a notice under section 83 has been served on a tenant, and

(b)   a date after which proceedings may be begun has been specified in the notice in accordance with subsection (4)(a) of that section,
the court shall not entertain proceedings for the possession of the dwelling-house unless they are begun after the date so specified and at a time when the notice is still in force.

(3)   Where—

(a)   the ground or one of the grounds specified in a notice under section 83 is Ground 2A in Schedule 2 (domestic violence), and

(b)   the partner who has left the dwelling-house as mentioned in that ground is not a tenant of the dwelling-house,
the court shall not entertain proceedings for the possession of the dwelling-house unless it is satisfied that the landlord has served a copy of the notice on the partner who has left or has taken all reasonable steps to serve a copy of the notice on that partner.

This subsection has effect subject to subsection (5).

(4)   Where—

(a)   Ground 2A in Schedule 2 is added to a notice under section 83 with the leave of the court after proceedings for possession are begun, and

(b)   the partner who has left the dwelling-house as mentioned in that ground is not a party to the proceedings,
the court shall not continue to entertain the proceedings unless it is satisfied that the landlord has served a notice under subsection (6) on the partner who has left or has taken all reasonable steps to serve such a notice on that partner.
This subsection has effect subject to subsection (5).

(5)   Where subsection (3) or (4) applies and Ground 2 in Schedule 2 (nuisance or other anti-social behaviour) is also specified in the notice under section 83, the court may dispense with the requirements as to service in relation to the partner who has left the dwelling-house if it considers it just and equitable to do so.

(6)   A notice under this subsection shall—
(a)   state that proceedings for the possession of the dwelling-house have begun,
(b)   specify the ground or grounds on which possession is being sought, and
(c)   give particulars of the ground or grounds.

Grounds and orders for possession
84. . . . (3)   Where a notice under section 83 has been served on the tenant, the court shall not make such an order on any of those grounds above unless the ground is specified in the notice; but the grounds so specified may be altered or added to with the leave of the court.

(4)   Where a date is specified in a notice under section 83 in accordance with subsection (3) of that section, the court shall not make an order which requires the tenant to give up possession of the dwelling-house in question before the date so specified.

(i)   Dispensing with the notice requirements if just and equitable
The procedure in the new s. 83 of the Housing Act 1985 is similar to the old with several important changes. First, the court can dispense with the notice requirements if it considers it just and equitable to do so (s. 83(1)(b)). The corresponding discretion for assured tenancies in s. 8 of the Housing Act 1988 was considered in *Kelsey Housing Association* v *King* (1995) 28 HLR 270, where the tenant complained about the deficiencies in the notice of possession proceedings as it did not give sufficient details of the nuisance allegations made against the tenants and their children. The court exercised its discretion and allowed dispensation of the notice, and among the factors it took into account were the events occurring after the notice had been given and the long delay (the tenant's complaint having been made six months after proceedings began). The Court of Appeal upheld the decision. Courts will probably not dispense with the need for some form of notice even in serious anti-social behaviour cases, but as *Megarry on the Rent Acts* (11th ed. Vol. 3 ('Assured Tenancies'), p. 140 (as approved by the court in *Kelsey*) said: 'This power [to dispense with the requirement of serving a possession notice] seems unlikely to be exercised unless the tenant has in some way become aware of the intended proceedings for possession, unless perhaps, his misconduct has been so grave as to invite proceedings for possession, in the sense of making such proceedings so likely that he may be taken to have expected them.'

(ii)   Notice in anti-social behaviour cases
The second change is that with cases based on Ground 2 (the anti-social behaviour ground), the possession proceedings can be started as soon as the

notice has been served and the notice must specify the date on which the tenant is to give up possession (s. 83(3)), For all the other grounds the notice must give a date after which proceedings can begin, and this date cannot be earlier than when a notice to quit would expire (see below – a minimum of four weeks).

(iii)   Notice in domestic violence cases
The third change is if the landlord is relying on Ground 2A (domestic violence). The court must be satisfied that the landlord has taken reasonable steps to serve a notice on the partner who has left (s. 83A(3)). If the partner who has departed is a tenant, a notice would have been served anyway. Lastly, a minor change in nomenclature: the old notice of intention to seek possession (NISP) has become a notice of possession proceedings (NOPP).

(iv)   Inaccurate or incomplete notices
The requirements under the old law were strictly applied; if the notice was deficient in minor particulars this could lead to the notice being held to be invalid. In *Torridge District Council* v *Jones* (1985) 18 HLR 107, the notice was in the form prescribed by the regulations that were then in force, but it stated that, 'The reasons for taking this action are non-payment of rent'. No details were given of the amount of rent owed. The Court of Appeal allowed the tenant's appeal, holding the notice was invalid as the object of the notice was to enable the tenant to put matters right before the court hearing. This notice, by not specifying the precise amount of the rent owing, did not fulfil this requirement.

In *Swansea City Council* v *Hearn* (1990) 23 HLR 284, however, the notice to quit given to the licensee, staying temporarily with her children in a hostel for the homeless, was held to be valid although it described her as a 'tenant' and the City Council as the 'landlord' (rather than the licensee and the licensor). Dillon LJ summed up by saying:

The learned assistant recorder held that certainty was necessary and that there was not sufficient certainty in this case. He considered the question whether Miss Hearn might have been confused or misled by the notice which she had received. In this court Mr Watkinson [counsel for Miss Hearn] does not put his argument in quite that way, but he says that it is important that the precise wording of the Regulations should be followed and that it has not been followed. He says also that there might perhaps be circumstances where, if the precise form were not followed, some recipient might be left in doubt. There is no suggestion that Miss Hearn herself was left in any doubt . . . I take the view that in this case the information for the tenant given in the Notice to Quit sufficiently complies with the requirements of the 1988 Regulations. In effect by virtue of the marginal notes Miss Hearn is defined as the tenant for the purposes of the notice, the Swansea City Council is defined as the landlord and the information is then complete.

Imprecise information summarising the grounds given by local housing authorities in good faith where the tenant is not misled will not invalidate the notice. In *Dudley Metropolitan Borough Council* v *Bailey* (1990) 22 HLR 424, a notice seeking possession was served with minor deviation from the wording laid down in SI 1987 No. 755; this was allowed as the notice had substantially the same effect. A figure of £145.96 for the rent arrears was given, but it was accepted that the actual rent arrears were £72.88 with the remaining sum being made up of arrears of rates and water rates. The notice was not invalidated by this honest error by the council in its description of the arrears.

(v) Notices to quit

If a landlord wishes a tenant who does not have a secure tenancy to leave, a 'notice to quit' must be served. Tenants, for their part, if they wish to leave the property, can bring any periodic tenancy, secure or insecure, to an end by serving a 'notice to quit'. A landlord's notice to a tenant must contain certain information as laid down in the Notices to Quit (Prescribed Information) Regulations 1988 (SI 1988 No. 2201). The tenant's notice to a landlord has to be in writing but does not have to be in any particular form of words. Many tenants, however, think that merely handing in the keys is sufficient. Tenants owing large sums in rent arrears sometimes abandon properties and disappear leaving no forwarding address. For all notices to quit a period of four weeks' notice must be given, which is calculated so that it includes the first day and excludes the last day. Unless there is a special term, a notice to quit should be given so that it expires at the end of any complete period of the tenancy (*Schnabel* v *Allard* [1967] 1 QB 627). Section 5 of the Protection from Eviction Act 1977 governs the validity of notices to quit.

Protection from Eviction Act 1977

Validity of notices to quit
5.—(1) Subject to subsection (1B) below no notice by a landlord or a tenant to quit any premises let (whether before or after the commencement of this Act) as a dwelling shall be valid unless—
(a) it is in writing and contains such information as may be prescribed, and
(b) it is given not less than four weeks before the date on which it is to take effect.
(1A) Subject to subsection (1B) below, no notice by a licensor or a licensee to determine a periodic licence to occupy premises as a dwelling (whether the licence was granted before or after the passing of this Act) shall be valid unless—
(a) it is in writing and contains such information as may be prescribed, and
(b) it is given not less than four weeks before the date on which it is to take effect.
(1B) Nothing in subsection (1) or subsection (1A) above applies to—
(a) premises let on an excluded tenancy which is entered into on or after the date on which the Housing Act 1988 came into force unless it is entered into pursuant to a contract made before that date, or
(b) premises occupied under an excluded licence.
(2) In this section 'prescribed' means prescribed by regulations made by the Secretary of State by statutory instrument, and a statutory instrument containing any

such regulations shall be subject to annulment in pursuance of a resolution of either House of Parliament.

(3) Regulations under this section may make different provision in relation to different descriptions of lettings and different circumstances.

Questions

1. 'Error in the particulars does not . . . invalidate the notice although it may well affect the decision of the court on its merits.' (Ralph Gibson LJ in *Dudley Metropolitan Borough Council* v *Bailey* (1990) 22 HLR 424).

Does this mean that authorities need not be wholly scrupulous about the accuracy of the particulars so long as some details are included?

2. A local authority hostel for homeless young people seeks clarification on the procedures they should legally adopt if they have a disruptive resident who they feel should be asked to leave the hostel:

(a)   Can they ask the resident to go immediately?

(b)   Do they have to serve a notice to quit under s. 5 of the Protection from Eviction Act 1977?

(c)   Do they have to obtain a court order (Housing Act 1985 Sch. 2, Ground 2)?

The young people have their own single bedrooms with wash handbasins, they share kitchens and bathrooms and have a communal lounge and garden.

The hostel has some separate 'move on' accommodation where residents have their own kitchen and bathrooms and there are no communal facilities. One resident has already stayed 12 months in this accommodation and the warden is anxious to move another resident from the main hostel on to the 'independent' living accommodation. Does the resident who has stayed 12 months have security of tenure? What procedures must be adopted if the resident refuses to go?

(E)   Grounds for possession

(i)   Introduction

To obtain a possession order the landlord must specify one of the 16 grounds in Sch. 2 to the Housing Act 1985. Some of the grounds have been amended by the Housing Act 1996. For Grounds 1 to 8 the court will make a possession order only if it would, in addition, be reasonable to make an order (s. 84(2)(a)). The Court of Appeal observed in *Manchester City Council* v *Green* [1999] January *Legal Action* 26, that in possession order cases it would be helpful if trial judges expressly referred in their judgments to reasonableness.

Housing Act 1985

SCHEDULE 2
GROUNDS FOR POSSESSION OF DWELLING-HOUSES LET UNDER SECURE TENANCIES

PART I
GROUNDS ON WHICH COURT MAY ORDER POSSESSION IF IT CONSIDERS IT REASONABLE

Ground 1

Rent lawfully due from the tenant has not been paid or an obligation of the tenancy has been broken or not performed.

Ground 2

The tenant or a person residing in or visiting the dwelling-house—
   (a)   has been guilty of conduct causing or likely to cause a nuisance or annoyance to a person residing, visiting or otherwise engaging in a lawful activity in the locality, or
   (b)   has been convicted of—
      (i)   using the dwelling-house or allowing it to be used for immoral or illegal purposes, or
      (ii)   an arrestable offence committed in, or in the locality of, the dwelling-house.

Ground 2A

The dwelling-house was occupied (whether alone or with others) by a married couple or a couple living together as husband and wife and—
   (a)   one or both of the partners is a tenant of the dwelling-house,
   (b)   one partner has left because of violence or threats of violence by the other towards—
      (i)   that partner, or
      (ii)   a member of the family of that partner who was residing with that partner immediately before the partner left, and
   (c)   the court is satisfied that the partner who has left is unlikely to return.

Ground 3

The condition of the dwelling-house or of any of the common parts has deteriorated owing to acts of waste by, or the neglect or default of, the tenant or a person residing in the dwelling-house and, in the case of an act of waste by, or the neglect or default of, a person lodging with the tenant or a sub-tenant of his, the tenant has not taken such steps as he ought reasonably to have taken for the removal of the lodger or sub-tenant.

Ground 4

The condition of furniture provided by the landlord for use under the tenancy, or in the common parts, has deteriorated owing to ill-treatment by the tenant or a person residing in the dwelling-house and, in the case of ill-treatment of a person lodging with the tenant or a sub-tenant of his, the tenant has not taken such steps as he ought reasonably to have taken for the removal of the lodger or sub-tenant.

Ground 5

The tenant is the person, or one of the persons, to whom the tenancy was granted and the landlord was induced to grant the tenancy by a false statement made knowingly or recklessly by—

(a)   the tenant, or
(b)   a person acting at the tenant's instigation.

Ground 6

The tenancy was assigned to the tenant, or to a predecessor in title of his who is a member of his family and is residing in the dwelling-house, by an assignment made by virtue of section 92 (assignments by way of exchange) and a premium was paid either in connection with that assignment or the assignment which the tenant or predecessor himself made by virtue of that section.

In this paragraph 'premium' means any fine or other like sum and any other pecuniary consideration in addition to rent.

Ground 7

The dwelling-house forms part of, or is within the curtilage of, a building which, or so much of it as is held by the landlord, is held mainly for purposes other than housing purposes and consists mainly of accommodation other than housing accommodation, and—

(a)   the dwelling-house was let to the tenant or a predecessor in title of his in consequence of the tenant or predecessor being in the employment of the landlord, or of—

a local authority
a new town corporation
[a housing action trust]
an urban development corporation, or
the governors of an aided school, and

(b)   the tenant or a person residing in the dwelling-house has been guilty of conduct such that, having regard to the purpose for which the building is used, it would not be right for him to continue in occupation of the dwelling-house.

Ground 8

The dwelling-house was made available for occupation by the tenant (or a predecessor in title of his) while works were carried out on the dwelling-house which he previously occupied as his only or principal home and—

(a)   the tenant (or predecessor) was a secure tenant of the other dwelling-house at the time when he ceased to occupy it as his home,

(b)   the tenant (or predecessor) accepted the tenancy of the dwelling-house of which possession is sought on the understanding that he would give up occupation when, on completion of the works, the other dwelling-house was again available for occupation by him under a secure tenancy, and

(c)   the works have been completed and the other dwelling-house is so available.

Notes

1.   The Housing Act 1996, s. 144 substituted a new Ground 2 (nuisance or annoyance to neighbours).

2. Section 145 of the 1996 Act inserted Ground 2A into Sch. 2 of the 1985 Act.

3. In Ground 5, s. 146 of the 1996 Act substituted the words in (a) and (b) for 'by the tenant'.

(ii) Ground 1: rent arrears or breach of a tenancy condition

(a) Rent arrears

Rent arrears is by far the most common ground for possession orders (see Gary, B., Finch, H., Prescott-Clarke, T., Cameron, S., Gilroy, R., Kirby, K., and Mountford, J., *Rent Arrears in Local Authorities and Housing Associations in England* (London: HMSO, 1994). Lord Woolf in *Access to Justice: Final Report to the Lord Chancellor on the Civil Justice System in England and Wales* (1996) has suggested that there should be a two-stage procedure in possession cases based on rent arrears. The first stage would be limited to money claims and the second would be possession proceedings where the money judgment had not been complied with. There appear to be no immediate Government plans to implement these suggestions, although further research on their practicability is being commissioned.

As the local authority's prime objective is the payment of the arrears rather than the eviction of the tenant, suspended possession orders are frequently made by the courts provided the tenant agrees to pay the current rent and the payment of the arrears by instalments. Frequently difficulties occur because of the slow processing of housing benefit claims by the same local authority as is taking the action – albeit by a separate department. The drawback to suspended possession orders is that any breach of the order, for example not paying off the arrears at the agreed rate, automatically triggers the possession order and the landlord may apply for a warrant to execute the order (*Thompson* v *Elmbridge Borough Council* (1987) 19 HLR 526).

In deciding whether the order is reasonable the court will attempt to balance the interests of the community and those of the tenant. The previous rent record of the tenant, together with reasons for non-payment such as illness or unemployment or housing benefit difficulties, will be factors to be considered. In *Woodspring* v *Taylor* (1982) 4 HLR 97, a couple in their mid-50s who had lived in their council house for over 20 years with a good payment record fell on hard times. The husband was made redundant and found it impossible to obtain employment and his wife became ill with diabetes and asthma. The rent arrears mounted when the husband received a tax bill for £500. Although the arrears were over £700 at the time of the trial and were being paid off only by a small weekly sum from the DHSS, the decision of the registrar to grant the authority a possession order was overturned on appeal.

If a possession order is granted and a warrant to execute the order is made, the tenants may become homeless if they can find nowhere else to rent. Whether they are recognised as being owed duties under the homelessness legislation will depend in part on whether they are regarded as being intentionally homeless. The crucial question will be whether the rent arrears arose through misfortune or wilful refusal to pay.

Although the factors leading to the arrears will be considered when deciding whether it is reasonable for the court to make a possession order, many tenants do not defend the proceedings and fail to appear in court. In such cases, where the arrears are a result of misfortune, the authority may owe duties under Pt VII of the Housing Act 1996. A further question is if the likelihood of homelessness is one of the factors that the court should consider when they are deciding whether to grant a possession order (see below).

If a tenant pays the full arrears before the commencement of the proceedings – in other words, between the service of the NOPP and the summons for possession – there will be no rent unpaid that is 'lawfully due' and so no possession order can be made. This point was decided under the Rent Acts, which have a similar wording to Ground 1(see chapter 3), in *Bird* v *Hildage* [1948] 1 KB 91. In another Rent Act case, *Dellenty* v *Pellow* [1951] 2 KB 858; [1951] 2 All ER 716, the position of a tenant who paid off the rent arrears after the commencement of the proceedings was considered. The court would have jurisdiction to make a possession order, but *prima facie* it would not be reasonable to make one. In that case, however, there was a long history of arrears and proceedings had been issued on a number of previous occasions so it was reasonable to make a possession order. The point was reconsidered and reconfirmed more recently in *Lee-Steere* v *Jennings* (1988) 20 HLR 1.

(b)   Breach of a tenancy condition

Tenancy agreements often contain clauses to control the activities and behaviour of the tenants in the property and the surrounding area. Clauses commonly found in local authority tenancy agreements cover matters such as the keeping of animals, the parking of trucks and caravans, the repair of cars and (in recent years) racist, sexist and homophobic harassment, as well as prohibitions on using the property for criminal activities such as drug dealing and the handling of stolen goods. Loud music played regularly into the early hours and other noisy activities may also be caught by clauses in the agreements.

When asked by a landlord to make a possession order for the breach of a tenancy condition the court must consider whether it is reasonable to make an order. It is for the landlord to prove the reasonableness of granting an order, but where there is an admitted breach of covenant and an intention to continue the breach a landlord is refused possession only in a very special case (*Green* v *Sheffield City Council* (1993) 26 HLR 349). In *Green* the court made a possession order on the ground of breach of the tenancy agreement which forbade the keeping of dogs. Mr Green had kept a dog for many years and wished to continue keeping a dog. In contrast, the tenant in *Wandsworth London Borough Council* v *Hargreaves* (1994) 27 HLR 142 had allowed petrol bombs to be made in the flat by someone who was visiting. One was thrown out of the window, and a fire causing damage costing £14,000 started from some petrol spilt in the flat. The tenant had to move out for 15 months while the flat was repaired. The Court of Appeal refused to overturn the county court judge's decision not to grant a possession order as all the circumstances had been considered. The tenant had not taken an active part in the events leading to the fire and there had been no problems since he returned to the flat so it would not be reasonable to make an order.

An alternative remedy available to landlords with tenants in breach of tenancy conditions is to apply for an injunction. In *Sutton Housing Trust* v *Lawrence* (1987) 19 HLR 520, another case concerning keeping a dog, the housing trust was granted an injunction. The court held that if the defendant could show special circumstances that the making of the order would cause him greater hardship than that caused to the landlord the injunction would be refused. Despite the tenant being a multiple sclerosis victim who argued that he needed the dog for companionship, the injunction was granted.

(iii)   Ground 2: Anti-social behaviour

For an empirical study carried out in the early 1990s before the Housing Act 1996 was even a Bill, see Hughes, D., Karn, V., and Lickess, R., 'Neighbour Disputes, Social Landlords and the Law', (1994) 16 *Journal of Social Welfare and Family Law* 201–28.

(a)   Visitors covered

Ground 2 has been amended by s. 144 of the Housing Act 1996 which broadens both the behaviour caught and the number of people affected by its provisions. Ground 2 is widened to include visitors to the dwelling-house; previously only tenants and those living with them were covered.

(b)   Professional witnesses

The words 'conduct *causing or likely to cause*' a nuisance or annoyance have been added to the description of conduct. It is no longer necessary to prove that conduct which is a nuisance or annoyance has actually occurred. It is sufficient if a third party, such as a housing official, who can act as a professional witness gives evidence that it was behaviour likely to have been a nuisance or annoyance. It had often been difficult to persuade neighbours to give evidence as they had been fearful of retaliation. For an example of intimidation, see the reaction of the defendant's husband in *Manchester City Council* v *McCann* [1998] *The Times*, 26 November. In such cases the court has the power under the County Courts Act 1984, s. 114 (which deals with 'wilful insults to a witness') to commit into custody.

(c)   People affected

Formerly action could be taken only if the nuisance or annoyance affected neighbours (as is still the case under the Rent Acts, see chapter 3), but this has been widened to include anyone visiting or otherwise engaging in a lawful activity, so racial harassment of local shopkeepers, for example, is included. A local authority are not bound to take action against tenants who misbehave. In *Hussain* v *Lancaster City Council* (1998) 31 HLR 164 a shopkeeper who was racially abused was unsuccessful when he attempted to force Lancaster City Council to take action as the court decided that the local authority were not liable in nuisance or negligence.

(d)   Geographical area

The area has also been extended. In the original Bill the description was 'in the vicinity of a dwelling-house'. This has changed to the wider 'in the locality of' the dwelling-house.

(e)   Arrestable offences included

Arrestable offences committed in, or in the locality of, the dwelling-house have been added to convictions of using the dwelling-house or allowing it to be used for immoral or illegal purposes. Arrestable offences, which are defined in s. 24 of the Police and Criminal Evidence Act 1984, include offences with fixed penalties at law and those for which adults can be imprisoned for five years or more. So offences range from taking a vehicle without the owner's consent (TWOC) to criminal damage, theft, burglary, assaults occasioning bodily harm and drug dealing. This extension enables local authorities to take action against drug dealing taking place in the common parts of an estate, whereas they had previously been limited to taking action only if dealing was taking place inside a house or flat.

(f)   Locality

The *Department of Environment, Transport and the Regions*, Circular 2/97, describes 'the locality' as the common parts of an estate. Some guidance on the ambit of 'locality' can be gathered from *Manchester City Council* v *Lawler* (1998) 31 HLR 119. In an action for possession under Grounds 1 and 2 of Sch. 2 to the Housing Act 1985, the council applied for injunctions. The tenant gave six undertakings. The undertakings were breached; one specific breach was relied on. This occurred when Lawler threatened an 11-year-old child with a knife in the local shopping centre three streets from her home. The question was whether she was in contempt of court and should therefore be committed to prison. The undertakings forbade certain activities 'in the locality of . . .'. At first instance it was held that injunctions should be worded precisely and the terms of the undertakings were unclear, and it was held that three streets from the tenant's home constituted the 'locality'. The Court of Appeal held that the extent of the locality was a matter that the court could determine as a matter of fact.

Northampton Borough Council v *Lovatt*
(1997) 30 HLR 875

The three teenage Lovatt sons admitted to a string of anti-social acts including burglary, criminal damage and racial harassment. None of these acts was committed within 100 metres of Gladstone Road where they lived with their parents. All took place on the rest of the Spencer Estate. The case was heard under the Housing Act 1985 and a possession order was granted. On appeal the main issue was the definition of 'neighbour' for the purpose of Sch. 2, Ground 2.

HENRY LJ: . . . The Housing Act, 1985 introduced the concept of 'neighbours'. On its introduction the editors of *Woodfall on Landlord and Tenant* commented:

This ground is based on Case 2, Schedule 15 to the Rent Act 1977, but 'neighbours' has been substituted for 'adjoining occupiers' to avoid arid disputes as to proximity . . .

There is, in addition, an interesting piece of legislative history. Ground 2 of Schedule 2 has been repealed and replaced by section 144 of the Housing Act, 1996. The heading to the section is 'Extension of Ground of Nuisance or Annoyance to Neighbours etc'. The new Ground reads:

Ground 2
The tenant or person residing in or visiting the dwelling-house—
    (a)   has been guilty of conduct causing or likely to cause a nuisance or annoyance to a person residing, visiting or otherwise engaging in a lawful activity in the locality, or
    (b)   has been convicted of—
        (i)   using the dwelling-house or allowing it to be used for immoral or illegal purposes, or
        (ii)   an arrestable offence committed in, or in the locality of, the dwelling-house.

It was clearly the intention of Parliament to extend the tenant's liability for nuisance. But the 1996 intention is no guide to the 1985 intention.

However, it is interesting to note that *Halsbury's Statutes'* explanatory note to the section includes the following:

The new Ground 2 substituted by this section extends the former nuisance ground in a number of ways. First, it now covers conduct, behaviour, etc., by somebody who is visiting the dwelling as well as those residing there. Secondly, it now applies to conduct which is likely to cause a nuisance or annoyance. The purpose of this is to enable third party witnesses to give evidence (for example a local authority officer) so as to overcome the problem of intimidation of potential witnesses, especially the victims of the behaviour. Thirdly, it now covers situations in which a nuisance is caused to a person visiting or otherwise engaging in a lawful activity in the locality, as well to a person residing in the locality. Fourthly, it now extends not only to cases where a tenant has been convicted of using the dwelling for immoral or illegal purposes, but also to a person convicted of an arrestable offence committing [sic] in or in the locality of the dwelling-house (HC official report SCG (Housing Bill) Columns 382–387: February 27, 1996).

And later in the same note we find:

Locality. The word 'locality' is designed to cover as wide an area as possible, while maintaining the link between the tenant's behaviour and the fact that he lives in the area. It is also designed to deal with a case where tenants do not have the same landlord: for example a tenant committing a nuisance against a neighbour could escape by virtue of the fact that he happened to be on the other side of a local authority boundary running down the middle of the road (HC official report SG (Housing Bill) Columns 384–386: February 27, 1996).

It is not contended that that Act, reflecting the concerns of Parliament in 1996, can assist us in construing the width of the protection given by Parliament in 1985. But though not relevant in this case, in any case where Parliamentary material is or may be relevant, it is convenient to have that material summarised (with references) in the notes on the section.

I turn to the construction of Ground 2. Mr Wood's [counsel for Mr and Mrs Lovatt] first submission is that Ground 2 is concerned with activities carried on by the tenant (or persons residing with him) on or at the premises which are detrimental to the peace, comfort and amenity of people living nearby.

First, he contends that the terms 'neighbours' and 'adjoining occupiers' are interchangeable. I do not agree. All adjoining occupiers are neighbours, but not all neighbours are adjoining occupiers. Neighbours is a wider word, and was intended to be – I agree with the editors of *Woodfall on Landlord and Tenant* that the intention was to avoid 'arid disputes as to proximity'. It is clearly intended to cover all persons sufficiently close to the source of the conduct complained of to be adversely affected by that conduct. In these days of amplified music, there is force in G.K Chesterton's observation:

Your next-door neighbour . . . is not a man; he is an environment.

Next, Mr Wood submits that the conduct complained of must emanate from the demised premises. He points out that most nuisances consist of unreasonable use by an occupier, and so such a limitation should be read into the Act . . . There is no warrant for reading the first part of Ground 2 as if after the word 'conduct' the qualifying words 'at the dwelling-house' were read in. There would be no sense in a law which prevented you from playing your music at maximum volume in the middle of the night from your home but permitted you to walk round your neighbourhood with your 'ghetto-blaster' at full pitch.

This example leads conveniently to the next submission. Mr Wood contends that Ground 2 is concerned with landlord and tenant 'and the use to which the tenant puts the demised premises'.

In my judgment, the restriction is not limited to his use of the premises, but his conduct in the neighbourhood, as the above example suggests . . .

The trial judge found that the purpose of the relevant legislation affecting Ground 2 was to protect the local authority's interest in the Spencer Estate, and its efficient and economic management . . .

With a public sector landlord, the case is *a fortiori*, as they are responsible for the quality of life of public sector tenants who will include many who are needy, vulnerable, isolated and probably without the ability to move from housing made a misery by the conduct of neighbours . . .

Accordingly, in my judgment the judge was right for the reasons he gave, and this appeal should be dismissed.

PILL LJ (dissenting): . . . It is common ground that the relevant provisions of the 1985 Act can apply only when the landlord is one of a number of listed public authorities or bodies (section 80). Similar grounds have however for many years appeared in statutes applying to landlords in the private sector. Case 2 in Schedule 15 Part I of the Rent Act 1977 provides:

Where the tenant or any person residing with him or any sub-tenant of his has been guilty of conduct which is a nuisance or annoyance to adjoining occupiers or has been convicted of using the dwelling-house or allowing the dwelling-house to be used for immoral or illegal purposes.

That provision is different from Ground 2 in its use of the expression 'adjoining occupiers' instead of 'neighbours'. However, I find it impossible to accept that Parliament intended a wholly different approach to Ground 2 from that in equivalent provisions in statutes covering lettings by private landlords. As enacted and before amendment, the 1985 Act applied also to some housing associations and housing cooperatives. I cannot accept that Parliament intended in the 1985 Act a broader social purpose because the landlords are public bodies.

Section 84 and Schedule 2 of the statute were intended to regulate the relationship between landlords and tenants and, in that context, to provide grounds for possession orders. It was concerned in Ground 2 to require the neighbourly use of premises and not with a sanction for general misbehaviour.

In *Cobstone Investments Ltd* v *Maxim* [1985] QB 140 this court construed the phrase 'adjoining occupiers' in the 1977 Act as referring to occupiers of premises which, while not necessarily physically touching those of the tenant complained of, were nevertheless sufficiently near to them that the occupiers were affected by the tenant's conduct on the demised premises. The point at issue was the definition of 'adjoining occupiers' but Dunn LJ expressed his conclusion by stating that they [the complainants] were 'near enough to be affected by her [the defendant's] conduct on the premises'. Dunn LJ accepted as an accurate statement of the law the passage in *Megarry, The Rent Acts* (10th ed., 1967 p. 271) that 'for one meaning of the word is "neighbouring" and all that the context seems to require is that the premises of the adjoining occupiers should be near enough to be affected by the tenant's conduct *on the demised premises*' (my emphasis). The point made was a general one and Dunn LJ and the learned author have assumed, rightly in my respectful view, that the connection between the conduct and the demised premises is necessary.

In the context of a statute dealing with the landlord and tenant relationship, the use in Ground 2 of the word 'neighbours' and in the 1977 Act 'adjoining occupiers', demonstrates a parliamentary intention to protect people living near the premises who are likely to be adversely affected by activities carried on there. I can find no broader social purpose either for the protection of other interests of the landlord or general neighbourhood protection against bad behaviour by a tenant or resident.

While I accept there may be good social reasons for granting possession orders when tenants or residents are guilty of criminal or anti-social behaviour in the general neighbourhood, I cannot accept that Ground 2 has that effect. It was not intended to deal with misconduct unconnected with the demised premises. I accept that there may be cases in which there may be conduct with a sufficient connection where the act is not committed actually on the premises. There may also be other cases covered by Ground 2, for example a conspiracy to burgle made on the premises, or the use of the premises as a headquarters for burglaries, where the anti-social behaviour is on the premises but its impact is felt elsewhere but I see a connection with the demised premises as an essential feature of Ground 2. The difficulty involved in defining what connection is required and difficulties at the borderline do not in my judgment require or permit an approach which comprehends all annoying behaviour outside or even inside the neighbourhood. The fact that a resident is guilty of anti-social behaviour in the neighbourhood, albeit criminal in character, does not of itself attract the operation of Ground 2, whether to protect the landlord's other interests or for other reasons.

(g)   Types of behaviour

Complaints of abusive and foul language were sufficient in *Woking Borough Council* v *Bystram* [1993] EGCS 208 for a suspended possession order to be granted to the local authority. The judge at first instance, however, thought that bad language was 'no doubt very much a common experience in certain areas' and refused a possession order, the decision being reversed in the Court of Appeal.

(h)   Behaviour by whom?

The single parent tenant in *Kensington & Chelsea Royal London Borough Council* v *Simmonds* (1996) 29 HLR 507 contended that she had not breached the terms of her tenancy agreement because she could not be said to have 'allowed' her 13-year-old son racially to abuse her Pakistani neighbours. Clause 22 of her tenancy agreement with the council forbade 'The tenant . . . allow[ing] members of his household to commit any act . . . cause offence to any other tenant . . . by, reason of his race, colour, ethnic origin or nationality'. Simon Brown LJ said (at p. 511):

[Clause 22] . . . No doubt the tenant here could not properly have been found to have 'allowed' Adam [her son], say, to racially abuse the Ahmeds had he merely done so once heralded, out of the blue. I am far from persuaded, however, that the judge's findings, which I have already quoted, even assuming (which I respectfully doubt) they are to be regarded as acquitting the appellant of all personal responsibility in this matter, preclude a finding that she allowed Adam to misconduct himself. The plain fact is that over a period of months she signally failed to prevent it.

It seems to me wholly inappropriate and unnecessary for the court in a case such as this to embark upon a detailed analysis of the tenant's parenting skills or a day-to-day analysis of whether she could or could not more successfully have sought to discipline and control her son. In my judgment there was ample basis here for the judge's conclusions that . . . clause 22 [was] breached. That of course founds statutory ground 1.

Statutory Ground 2
As stated, this ground was in any event satisfied. The essential submission in this regard is that, nevertheless, before any possession order could ever properly be made pursuant to this ground, the plaintiffs would have had to prove some particular degree of personal fault on the tenant's own individual part. In the case of nuisance and annoyance occasioned by an ill-disciplined and uncontrollable child in the age bracket of, say, 12 to 15 years (as in this case) namely, a case concerning a child too old to control but too young to put out of the house, that may well be impossible. The parents of such a child, submits Mr Rainey [counsel for Ms Simmonds], cannot in the result be dispossessed under this legislation.

I would firmly reject this argument. To my mind, it finds no support in the authorities or in common sense or in justice . . .

As to the justice of the position, it must be remembered that not only are the interests of the tenant and her family here at stake; so too are the interests of their neighbours. It would in my judgment be quite intolerable if they were to be held necessarily deprived of all possibility of relief in these cases, merely because some ineffectual tenant next door was incapable of controlling his or her household . . .

Of course I accept that the extent, if any, of personal blame on the tenant's part is a relevant consideration in determining whether or not a possession order should reasonably be made and the terms of any such order. To assert, however, as a proposition of law that a lack of personal blame is necessarily decisive seems to me nothing short of absurd . . .

I would unhesitatingly dismiss this appeal.

The question of potential homelessness was considered in *Bristol City Council* v *Mousah* (1997) 30 HLR 32. The local authority let a house to Mousah in November 1993. Four months later they served a notice to quit after complaints of noise and nuisance. A few days earlier the police had searched the house as it was suspected that it was being used for drug dealing, and they arrested six people using cocaine. Another police search was carried out in June 1994 and a further six people arrested for using crack cocaine. The authority served a notice of possession proceedings a few days later. Nevertheless, during a further police drugs raid in August crack cocaine was found again and two people were arrested. Mousah was not present during any of these police raids. Possession proceedings based on rent arrears and that the tenant or people living in the house had been guilty of conduct which was a nuisance to neighbours (Housing Act 1985, s. 83 and Sch. 2, Grounds 1 and 2) were started in November 1994.

By the time the case came to court in October 1995 Mousah argued that it would not be reasonable to make a possession order as he could not be held responsible for the acts of nuisance. He was not at the premises during any of the police searches as he spent time staying with his three dependent families. Also a considerable period of time had elapsed since the last incident and, lastly, he was schizophrenic and therefore vulnerable. At the trial the order was refused, on the grounds that if it was granted Mousah would become homeless, and with his medical condition might become dangerous. Mousah's psychiatrist gave evidence that eviction would have an adverse affect on his mental health.

In granting the appeal by Bristol City Council, Beldam LJ said (at p. 39):

. . . it is now well settled that this Court will only interfere with a discretionary decision on rare occasions, where, for example, a Judge has misdirected himself, where he has taken into account matters which he ought not to have taken into account, or where he has failed to take account of matters which he should have taken into account. In this case I am satisfied that the Assistant Recorder based his decision on matters which he ought not to have taken into account. It seems to me that, whilst he was perfectly entitled to consider the effect which an order for possession would have, it was wrong for him to become so involved with the possible outcome of an application by the respondent under [homelessness legislation].

Evidence has been given by the appropriate housing officer that, if the respondent applied, his application would be dealt with on its merits. That, in my view, was all that the Judge could properly take into account. Equally it seems to me the Judge paid regard to the fact that, since August 1994, the respondent had not been found to have been in breach of covenant and, in particular, Condition 24, or to have committed any offence at these premises. He regarded that as a substantial time. But the truth of the matter was that a large portion of the time was attributed to the fact that the respondent was in breach of the Court's orders for delivery of his defence, and, in any event, this was not simply an isolated occasion on which someone had been found with a small quantity of a Class B drug in the premises, as was the case in *Abrahams* v *Wilson* [1971] 2 QB 88, to which we were referred.

This was a case in which there had been a most serious offence committed over a period of three or four months at these premises, and, as I have said, the lapse of time since the last occasion was largely due to the failure of the respondent (or those who were representing him) to comply with the requirements of the Court.

For these reasons, I am satisfied that this Court is in a position to review the decision of the Assistant Recorder, to substitute its own decision and exercise its own discretion in place of the Recorder's discretion. I consider that Mr Arden's [counsel for Bristol City Council] approach to this question is correct. Where there is such a serious breach of a condition of the tenancy, it is only in exceptional cases that it could be said that it was not reasonable to make the order.

I consider that the medical report does not disclose a situation in which it is likely that the respondent will become a danger to the public. We have been referred to a passage in the evidence in which the respondent said that he desired to move to a different part of Bristol, and there would be no difficulty in his keeping in touch with the hospital authorities with whom he has now made contact.

The public interest, in my view, is best served by making it abundantly clear to those who have the advantage of public housing benefits that, if they commit serious offences at the premises in breach of condition, save in exceptional cases, an order for possession will be made. The order will assist the housing authority, who, under Section 21 of the Act, have the duty to manage the housing stock and have the obligation to manage, regulate and control allocation of their houses, for the benefit of the public. In my view the public interest would best be served by [Bristol City Council] being able in a case such as this to relet the premises to someone who will not use them for peddling crack cocaine.

For those reasons I consider that this is a case in which, taking into account the circumstances of the offence, public interest and the matters which were urged on behalf of this respondent, it is clear that the Court ought to exercise its discretion to make an order for possession. Accordingly, I would allow this appeal.

Another case where the application for a possession order was based partly on the acts of visitors to the property was *London Borough of Camden* v *Gilsenan* [1998] Housing Law Monitor, April, 6, where Camden relied on Ground 1 (rent arrears) and Ground 2 of Sch. 2 to the Housing Act 1985. The tenant allegedly had frequently caused or permitted visitors to cause severe nuisance to her neighbours because of loud music, drunkenness, rubbish throwing from balconies and even wounding in a machete attack. Camden obtained an 'unless' order: that unless Gilsenan committed no further nuisance she would be prevented from defending in the possession order proceedings. Further nuisance occurred so she was unable to defend, but at the hearing her solicitors produced a letter requesting reasonableness and stating that she undertook to refrain from further nuisance; nevertheless the possession order was granted. On appeal the possession order was upheld as there had been adequate differentiation between the acts of the tenant and those of her visitors, and the assistant recorder had been mindful of the reasonableness requirement.

(i)   Crime and Disorder Act 1998, s. 1 – anti-social behaviour orders

A local authority or the police can apply to a magistrates' court for one of these new orders under s. 1 of the Crime and Disorder Act 1998. Any person aged 10 or over who has acted in a manner that caused or was likely to cause harassment, alarm or distress to anyone who is not in the same household may be subject to an order. The orders last at least two years and cover the whole of the local government area. Orders can also cover adjoining local government areas if the areas are included in the application and consultation with the relevant local authorities and the police has taken place. Breach of an anti-social behaviour order may result in imprisonment or a fine. Whatever the definition of 'locality' in the Housing Act 1985, Sch. 2, Ground 2, it would not be as wide as the whole of a local authority area which an anti-social behaviour order would encompass.

(iv)   Ground 2A: domestic violence

This is a new ground introduced by the Housing Act 1996, s. 145. It is designed to address the problem of partners (usually women and their children) who leave accommodation because of violence or the threats of violence and where the other partner remains alone in family-sized property with a secure tenancy. The partner who has left, if homeless, would be owed duties under the homelessness legislation as she would not be intentionally homeless. If the partner leaving took children, they would be classed as being in priority need. The end result is that the local authority provide two family-sized units for one family. If the departing partner had a joint tenancy he or she can serve a notice to quit and bring the tenancy to an end (*Newlon Housing Trust* v *Alsulaimen* [1998] 3 WLR 451), but the local authority cannot force the departing partner to do this (see chapter 9). The new ground will enable local authorities to recover possession whether the tenant remaining in the property had a joint or a sole tenancy.

(v)   Ground 5: false statements to obtain a tenancy

The Court of Appeal in *Bristol City Council* v *Mousah* (above) felt that too much weight was attached to the possibility of homelessness when considering the reasonableness of making a possession order. Whether the judge had not taken enough account of the possibility of homelessness was the basis of an appeal against a possession order granted on Ground 5 (false statements made to obtain a tenancy) in *Rushcliffe Borough Council* v *Watson* (1991) 24 HLR 124. The Court of Appeal agreed with the judge's finding that if the order was granted the tenant would be in difficulties as she might be regarded as being intentionally homeless. It was felt, however, that Miss Watson, a single mother, would be able to surmount the difficulties. There was no real likelihood that she would be separated from her children and there was no other real risk to them or to her. Rushcliffe Borough Council had granted a tenancy to Miss Watson and then discovered that she had an existing housing association tenancy. On her application form she had claimed to be staying with relatives, well aware that if she was a housing association tenant she had little chance of being granted a council tenancy. The court took into account that 'reasonableness' means having regard to the interests of the parties and those of the public (*London Borough of Enfield* v *McKeon* (1986) 18 HLR 330). On the issue in *Rushcliffe* of balancing the public interest of keeping families together and the interest of local authorities allocating scarce housing resources fairly, Nourse LJ said (at p. 131):

I am quite certain that the judge recognised the public interest in keeping a family together as a unit. But since he thought that there was no real likelihood that this family would be split up, that was not something which affected his consideration of the public interest in this case. On the broader aspect of the public interest the judge was fully entitled to attach the importance which he evidently did to the policy [of discouraging deceitful applications which result in the unjust relegation on the housing list of applicants who are honest].

As His Honour Judge Brunning had said (quoted in the report at page 128) '. . . the local authority say that their's [sic] is a very difficult task in any event. There are hundreds of families at their door in inadequate accommodation who are desperate – deprived by deceptions. They say that if a deception of this kind succeeds, anyone who thinks its [sic] worth their while will try to jump the queue. The local authority cannot be expected to act as private detectives. It is essential that they should be able to rely on the accuracy of an application in such a case.

A stronger line against fraudulent applications was taken in *Shrewsbury and Atcham Borough Council* v *Evans* (1997) 30 HLR 123, where the appellant had tenancies of two local authority properties simultaneously. When Mrs Evans originally applied for a council tenancy she and her four children claimed to be living at her mother's house, which would have been grossly overcrowded with a sum total of 11 people living in the house. At the time she was in fact living with her husband and children in an expensive country farmhouse which they were buying on mortgage. After she had been granted the council tenancy her husband left her and the mortgagees threatened possession proceedings. She then applied to a different local authority on the grounds that she was being repossessed and was again granted a tenancy. At trial the judge found that it was reasonable to make a possession order. The defendant appealed on the grounds that insufficient weight had been given to the possibility of homelessness and that the family might not be able to stay together. Beldam LJ (at p. 132) said:

. . . in a case such as this, where there has been a deliberate lying to obtain public housing that only in exceptional cases would the court consider the effect of the homelessness legislation. It is not the function of the court to decide whether or not a person is intentionally homeless. That is the function of the local authority and has been entrusted to the local authority by Parliament.

Those who are on the housing list who have an equal or even greater claim to public housing would, in my view, justly be indignant to find that the court did not think it reasonable in the circumstances where someone has obtained accommodation by a deliberate and flagrant lie, to make an order for possession merely because the effect of the order would result in the occupant having to be considered by the local authority as homeless or intentionally homeless.

It seems to me, that in deciding questions of reasonableness in a case such as this, a court can, in exceptional cases take into account the nature and degree of the untrue statements which have been made and the circumstances in which they are made and whether, for example, they are deliberate or reckless. If the court had considered the matters in detail in this case it would have concluded, as the evidence showed, that this appellant had flagrantly and deliberately lied about her circumstances and had done so with the express purpose of providing herself with a higher score under to [sic] the local authority's qualifications for public housing, than she would otherwise have had, not merely a point or two more, but, according to the evidence, very substantially more.

Next, the court could reasonably, it seems to me, take into consideration the attitude of the appellant when the deception was discovered. Her attitude was to lie and lie again to deny completely that she had made the application to the District Council, suggest that this had been made by someone using her name, and when this was not wholly accepted by the officers of the respondents, to complain about the conduct of the housing officer quite unjustifiably. In my view, the court could take into account, as was said, the current position in which the appellant found herself, but at the same time it would have to have in mind, as I have previously indicated, the great importance to be attached to honesty in making application for public housing accommodation. This was the very last matter to which the judge referred and it clearly weighed with him. He said:

> It is reasonable having regard to public policy that people should not gain accommodation by making false statements.

I reach the conclusion in this appeal that apart from merely recognising that by her own conduct she had placed herself in a position in which the respondents would have to consider whether she was intentionally homeless the judge did not need to consider how she would be re-housed and, the appellant has no ground for criticising the decision of the judge. On the contrary, it seems to me, for the reasons I have given, it would have been an affront to those who put forward their claims honestly, wait patiently and rely upon the local housing authority to deal fairly with their claims, if a judge had concluded that in the circumstances of this case it was not reasonable to make an order for possession. Accordingly I would dismiss the appeal.

Questions

1. Research has shown that over half of local authority and housing association tenants owe rent (see Gary, B., Finch, H., Prescott-Clarke, T., Cameron, S., Gilroy, R., Kirby, K., and Mountford, J., *Rent Arrears in Local Authorities and Housing Associations in England*, London: HMSO, 1994). What do you think ought to be done about the problem of council tenants who are in rent arrears? The tenant could be sued for debt, but usually there are few assets to cover the arrears. There is also the remedy of 'distress for rent' which means seizing the tenant's property to pay the debt, but again tenants with high rent arrears have little property that is saleable. Is applying for a possession order the best weapon available to the local authority? Does it just result in homeless families?

2.   Are the powers in the new Ground 2 sufficiently strong that if the local authority wanted to gain possession there would be no need to use breach of the tenancy agreement? Would the following situations, where tenants have refused to remedy the matter after warnings, be covered by Ground 2:

(a)   keeping several large, barking dogs;
(b)   leaving rubbish, such as old upholstered furniture, in the back garden;
(c)   repairing cars in the forecourt of the dwelling-house?

3.   Does the interpretation of 'neighbour' in *Northampton Borough Council* v *Lovatt* (1997) 30 HLR 875 make the change of wording in Sch. 2, Ground 2 to the Housing Act 1985 – to 'persons in the locality' rather than 'neighbours' – unnecessary?
4.   Is the concept of 'locality' in the amended Sch. 2, Ground 2 a wholly subjective one? Would it be possible for appeal courts to develop some guidelines on the concept or must it simply be left to the facts of each individual case?
5.   Does the extent to which a tenant has 'allowed' another to commit acts of nuisance remain a relevant consideration under the amended form of Sch. 2, Ground 2?
6.   Local housing authority tenants face a double jeopardy if they commit criminal offences on the estate where they live: they can be evicted from their council houses as well as paying the penalty under the criminal law. Owner-occupiers do not face this double jeopardy. Is this right?

(vi)   Grounds 9–16: availability of suitable alternative accommodation
For Grounds 9–11 in Pt II of Sch. 2 to the Housing Act 1985, the court will make a possession order only if it is satisfied that there is suitable alternative accommodation available (s. 84(2)(b)). For Grounds 12–16 in Pt III of Sch. 2, the court will make an order for possession only if it considers it reasonable to do so and suitable alternative accommodation is available. Both conditions must be satisfied (s. 84(2)(c)).

Housing Act 1985

SCHEDULE 2

PART II
GROUNDS ON WHICH THE COURT MAY ORDER POSSESSION IF SUITABLE ALTERNATIVE ACCOMMODATION IS AVAILABLE

Ground 9

The dwelling-house is overcrowded, within the meaning of Part X, in such circumstances as to render the occupier guilty of an offence.

Ground 10

The landlord intends within a reasonable time of obtaining possession of the dwelling-house—

(a)   to demolish or reconstruct the building or part of the building comprising the dwelling-house, or

(b)   to carry out work on that building or on land let together with, and thus treated as part of, the dwelling-house,

and cannot reasonably do so without obtaining possession of the dwelling-house.

Ground 10A (omitted)

Ground 11

The landlord is a charity and the tenant's continued occupation of the dwelling-house could conflict with the objects of the charity.

PART III
GROUNDS ON WHICH THE COURT MAY ORDER POSSESSION IF IT
CONSIDERS IT REASONABLE AND SUITABLE ALTERNATIVE
ACCOMMODATION IS AVAILABLE

Ground 12

The dwelling-house forms part of, or is within the curtilage of, a building which, or so much of it as is held by the landlord, is held mainly for purposes other than housing purposes and consists mainly of accommodation other than housing accommodation, or is situated in a cemetery, and—

(a)   the dwelling-house was let to the tenant or a predecessor in title of his in consequence of the tenant or predecessor being in the employment of the landlord or of—

a local authority

a new town corporation

an urban development corporation, or

the governors of an aided school,

and that employment has ceased, and

(b)   the landlord reasonably requires the dwelling-house for occupation as a residence for some person either engaged in the employment of the landlord, or of such a body, or with whom a contract for such employment has been entered into conditional on housing being provided.

Ground 13

The dwelling-house has features which are substantially different from those of ordinary dwelling-houses and which are designed to make it suitable for occupation by a physically disabled person who requires accommodation of a kind provided by the dwelling-house and—

(a)   there is no longer such a person residing in the dwelling-house, and

(b)   the landlord requires it for occupation (whether alone or with members of his family) by such a person.

Ground 14

[Not applicable to local housing authority tenancies.]

Ground 15

The dwelling-house is one of a group of dwelling-houses which it is the practice of the landlord to let for occupation by persons with special needs and—

(a)   a social service or special facility is provided in close proximity to the group of dwelling-houses in order to assist persons with those special needs.

(b)   there is no longer a person with those special needs residing in the dwelling-house and—

(c)   the landlord requires the dwelling-house for occupation (whether alone or with members of his family) by a person who has those special needs.

Ground 16

The accommodation afforded by the dwelling-house is more extensive than is reasonably required by the tenant and—

(a)   the tenancy vested in the tenant by virtue of section 89 (succession to periodic tenancy), the tenant being qualified to succeed by virtue of section 87(b) (members of family other than spouse), and

(b)   notice of the proceedings for possession was served under section 83 [or where no such notice was served, the proceedings for possession were begun] more than six months but less than twelve months after the date of the previous tenant's death.

The matters to be taken into account by the court in determining whether it is reasonable to make an order on this ground include—

(a)   the age of the tenant

(b)   the period during which the tenant occupied the dwelling-house as his only or principal home, and

(c)   any financial or other support given by the tenant to the previous tenant.

(a)   Ground 9: overcrowding

Part X of the Housing Act 1985 defines overcrowding as when the number of persons sleeping in the dwelling-house is higher than 'the room standard' or 'the space standard'. The room standard is infringed when the number of living rooms and bedrooms available are insufficient for two people of opposite sexes over the age of ten not living together as husband and wife to sleep in separate rooms (s. 325, Housing Act 1985). The space standard is calculated by precise mathematical formulae based on either the number of rooms or the floor area in square feet (s. 326(3), Housing Act 1985).

The alternative accommodation offered by the landlord must be suitable for the tenant and his family; it does not have to be large enough to accommodate everyone from the overcrowded dwelling-house (Pt IV, para. 3).

(b)   Ground 10: property needed for carrying out works

Some guidance on the interpretation of Ground 10, para. (a) is provided by:

Wansbeck District Council v Marley
(1987) 20 HLR 247

The tenant's husband had been the superintendent of Humford Mill Swimming Baths and they had lived for many years in the cottage next to the pool. After the pool closed in 1974, the cottage was modernised in 1977–1978 while they were tenants. The council wished to gain possession, not to carry out any work on the cottage but because they had plans to redevelop the surrounding area, replacing the swimming pool with a paddling pool, a car park and a children's play area. The council intended that the whole area would become a country park. The cottage was needed for a warden as grants from the Countryside Commission were dependent on having a resident warden. The only construction planned was a doorway connecting the cottage to a new building which would provide facilities for visitors to the country park. There was no evidence that this work could be completed only if Mrs Marley moved out.

The first question was whether Wansbeck District Council had the requisite intention.

PURCHAS LJ: . . . [T]he intention must indeed be clearly defined and settled: see *Cunliffe* v *Goodman* [1950] 2 KB 237. Although this case was considering the meaning of the word 'intention' in the context of section 18(1) of the Landlord and Tenant Act 1927, which provided that no damage should be recovered for a breach of any covenant to repair, etc., if the tenant could show that the landlord at or shortly after the end of the tenancy intended to pull down or reconstruct the building. The section is not in terms exactly equivalent to the words of Ground 10 of the Act but, in my judgment, they provide an appropriate test in the different context. *Per* Asquith LJ at p. 254:

This leads me to the second point bearing on the existence in this case of 'intention' as opposed to mere contemplation. Not merely is the term 'intention' unsatisfied if the person professing it has too many hurdles to overcome, or too little control of events: it is equally inappropriate if at the material date that person is in effect not deciding to proceed but feeling his way and reserving his decision until he shall be in possession of financial data sufficient to enable him to determine whether the project will be commercially worthwhile.

A purpose so qualified and suspended does not in my view amount to an 'intention' or 'decision' within the principle. It is mere contemplation until the materials necessary to a decision on the commercial merits are available and have resulted in such a decision.

Asquith LJ's judgment in *Cunliffe* v *Goodman* was referred to by Viscount Simmonds in *Betty's Cafes Ltd* v *Phillips Furnishing Stores Ltd* [1959] AC 20:

In this context your Lordships have the advantage of a judgment delivered by Lord Asquith (then Asquith LJ), than whom there have been few greater masters of the English language in judicial interpretation or exposition, in *Cunliffe* v *Goodman*. I will content myself with a single short passage, though much more might be usefully cited: 'An "intention,"' said the learned Lord Justice, 'to my mind connotes a state of affairs which the party "intending" – I will call him X – does more than merely contemplate: it connotes a state of affairs which, on the contrary, he decides, so far as in him lies, to bring about, and which, in point of possibility, he has a reasonable prospect of being able to bring about, by his own act of volition.' I do not think that anything is to be gained by trying to elaborate these words, but I must fairly add that I do not at all dissent from the explanation of them which the learned Master of the Rolls has given in this case. It is a question of fact what intention a man has at a given time, difficult, it may be, to ascertain, but still a question of fact, and I think that a jury directed in such words as these could come to a fair conclusion.

. . .

Mr Richardson submitted that the whole Humford Mill Development project was a 'rolling scheme' which developed, adjusted or changed from time to time. . .

I have not been able to detect in any of the minutes [of District Council committee meetings] which have been placed before the court any reference to work required upon the cottage. The evidence of Mr Stephenson relates to a new building being erected in the garden of the cottage to which it is to be attached by a doorway. This is the only evidence of any structural impact upon the cottage . . .

For the purpose of this appeal, therefore, Ground 10 involved establishing an intention within a reasonable time of obtaining possession of the dwelling-house to carry out work on that building and that such work could not reasonably be done without obtaining possession of the dwelling-house . . .

. . . there was no evidence upon which the judge could reasonably have held that the Council had established a settled and clearly defined intention to carry out the construction adverted to . . . No doubt there had been an idea that such facilities might well be provided in due course as part of the rolling plan of development of the leisure park. However, in my judgment, this fell far short of the settled intention necessary to satisfy the test outlined by Asquith LJ and adopted in *Betty's Cafes Ltd* v *Phillips Furnishing Stores Ltd.*

However, even if the evidence before the judge was capable of supporting such an intention the Council must also establish that the work could not reasonably be done without obtaining possession of the cottage. Bearing in mind that the work is limited to the construction of a doorway connecting the existing cottage with the new facility building some specific evidence is necessary to achieve the further step of showing that the doorway involved could not be constructed without obtaining legal possession of the dwelling-house. In my judgment there was simply no evidence to support this.

Note

If a tenant is moved out under Ground 10, 'home loss payments' under the Land Compensation Act 1973, s. 29 can be claimed.

(c) Ground 11: charitable object

Ground 11 applied to pre-Housing Act 1988 tenancies granted by housing associations which are registered as charities. The charity may house people of a recognised group, e.g., mothers with dependent children or people suffering from a mental illness. If the children grow up or the residents recover from their mental problems, they will no longer fulfil the objects of the charity.

(d) Ground 13: facilities for the disabled

The court in *Freeman* v *Wansbeck District Council* [1984] 2 All ER 746 considered, albeit in the context of the right to buy, which features make the dwelling-house 'substantially different from those of ordinary dwelling-houses and which are designed to make it suitable for occupation by a physically disabled person'. Mr and Mrs Freeman's daughter suffered from spina bifida. As she had difficulty climbing stairs the council converted the larder into an inside downstairs lavatory under its powers in the Chronically Sick and Disabled Persons Act 1970. The local authority compared the house with other houses on the estate and argued that an inside lavatory downstairs was a 'special feature'.

The arguments of the local authority were rejected by Latey J sitting with Sir John Arnold P in the Court of Appeal, in the following extract (at p. 747):

The first question is whether the dwelling-house concerned has features which are substantially different from those of ordinary dwelling houses; and the second question is whether, if such features exist, they are designed to make it suitable for occupation by physically disabled persons. The local authority contended before the judge that there were features in this house which fall within the ambit of para. 3 as being substantially different from those of ordinary dwelling houses; and it says that the word 'designed' means 'intended' and that the downstairs lavatory, which it accepts is the only feature which could qualify under this paragraph, was intended to make the house suitable for occupation by physically disabled persons. . . .

I cannot find in para. 3 of Pt 1 of Sch. 1 [Housing Act 1980] anything to justify an approach of limiting the question whether or not a house has special features which are substantially different from those of ordinary dwelling houses or to entitle the authority or, for that matter, any court which has to consider it, to draw comparisons merely with other houses locally. I do not believe that that is either the natural meaning of para. 3 or was in any way intended by Parliament when one looks at the language which it has chosen.

If in fact there are no such features, as the judge rightly found in my opinion, then of course that is the end of the case. But we have been asked to consider also the second limb, and that means what is meant by the word 'designed?'

Counsel for the local authority asks us to say that that word 'designed' means intended – that and nothing more. Counsel for Mr and Mrs Freeman submits that the word 'designed' means formed in the architectural sense of the word. Of course the word 'designed' is an ambiguous word. It is possible to put either of those meanings on it, but I think that light is thrown on its real meaning in this context when one looks at para. 5(a) of Pt 1 of Sch. 1. Paragraph 5(a) reads as follows:

. . . he shall so determine if satisfied— (a) that the dwelling-house is designed or specially adapted for occupation by persons of pensionable age . . .

I find it difficult to accept the contention of counsel for the local authority that 'designed' means 'intended' there when you read it in conjunction with the following words 'or specially adapted'. It seems to me that, using one's common sense, the meaning of that phrase is that the dwelling-house was either built for occupation by persons of pensionable age or, if it was not so built for occupation by persons of pensionable age or, if it was not so built, has been specially adapted, and that surely is talking in terms of structure.

In a clear and, as I think, admirably succinct judgment the judge rejected both the contentions of the authority, and I think all becomes plain in this matter of interpretation if one exercises one's ordinary, everyday knowledge and regards the intention of the Act when it refers to features substantially different from those in ordinary dwelling houses as the sort of features we are all familiar with, such as ramps, specially widened doors, lifts, cooking surfaces at special heights for people who cannot stand up and do their cooking sitting down, and the like. At the end of it all one asks oneself this question: how (and I hope I do not put it too highly) in the name of common sense does the installation of one, small, rather cramped downstairs lavatory wholly incapable of accommodating a wheelchair fit in with what the Act envisages? The answer, in my judgment, is that it does not by any stretch of the imagination.

(vii) Suitability of the alternative accommodation

Housing Act 1985

SCHEDULE 2
GROUNDS FOR POSSESSION OF DWELLING-HOUSES LET UNDER SECURE TENANCIES

PART IV
SUITABILITY OF ACCOMMODATION

1. For the purposes of section 84(2)(b) and (c) (cases in which court is not to make an order for possession unless satisfied that suitable accommodation will be available) accommodation is suitable if it consists of premises—
   (a)   which are to be let as a separate dwelling under a secure tenancy, or
   (b)   which are to be let as a separate dwelling under a protected tenancy,
not being a tenancy under which the landlord might recover possession under one of the Cases in Part II of Schedule 15 to the Rent Act 1977 (cases where court must order possession), [or
   (c)   which are to be let as a separate dwelling under an assured tenancy which is neither an assured shorthold tenancy, within the meaning of Part I, Housing Act 1988, nor a tenancy under which the landlord might recover possession under any of the Grounds 1–5 in Schedule 2 to the 1985 Act] [added by Housing Act 1988, s. 140 and Sch. 17, para. 65]
and, in the opinion of the court, the accommodation is reasonably suitable to the needs of the tenant and his family.

2. In determining whether the accommodation is reasonably suitable for the needs of the tenant and his family, regard shall be had to—
   (a)   the nature of the accommodation which it is the practice of the landlord to allocate to persons with similar needs;
   (b)   the distance of the accommodation available from the place of work or education of the tenant and of any members of his family;
   (c)   its distance from the home of any member of the tenant's family if proximity to it is essential to that member's or the tenant's well-being;
   (d)   the needs (as regards extent of accommodation) and means of the tenant and his family;
   (e)   the terms on which the accommodation is available and the terms of the secure tenancy;
   (f)   if furniture was provided by the landlord for use under the secure tenancy, whether furniture is to be provided for use in the other accommodation, and if so the nature of the furniture to be provided.

(a) Private sector comparison

Unlike in the private sector, the availability of suitable accommodation is not *per se* a ground for possession (Rent Act 1977, s. 98(1)(a) and the Housing

Act 1988, Sch. 2 Pt II, Ground 9). Another difference between public and private housing is that the character of the proposed accommodation, i.e. the age of the property, the social standing of the area, is not one of the factors considered when deciding whether it is suitable.

(b) Suitable for the tenant and the rest of the family

The accommodation must be suitable for the tenant and the rest of the family as well. In *Wandsworth London Borough Council* v *Fadayomi* [1987] 3 All ER 474, a husband and wife who were in the throes of divorce proceedings were offered alternative accommodation. The council recognised their need for separate accommodation, but several offers of accommodation on this basis were refused. When the application for a possession order on Ground 10 came to court, as the tenancy was in Mr Fadayomi's sole name, Mrs Fadayomi's views were not sought and she was not represented. Mr Fadayomi consented for the whole family to move to alternative accommodation together. Parker LJ said (at p. 478):

It is apparent from that, in my view, that every member of the tenant's family living in the premises is a person with a potential interest in any possession proceedings. He may not in many cases desire to advance any such interest, but it is abundantly apparent, in view of the terms of this provision, that any member of the family who considers that the accommodation is unsuitable because it is too far from his place of work or too far from some other member of the family to whom it is essential he should live in close proximity may be able to advance that if he so wishes. It might well be the case that the tenant himself does not wish to raise the matter, and this section can only work in the event that the tenant does not wish to raise it if the person who has the potential right, on the wording of these provisions, himself is allowed to be joined in order to raise it.

The possession order that had been granted in the lower court was set aside as Mrs Fadayomi's interests had not been considered.

(c) Meaning of 'suitable alternative accommodation'

The following case turned on the interpretation of 'suitable alternative accommodation'.

London Borough of Enfield v French
(1984) 17 HLR 211

The tenant was under-occupying a flat that he obtained by succession from his mother. The council sought possession on Ground 16 and had to show that suitable alternative accommodation was available and that it was reasonable for the court to grant a possession order. The council offered the tenant alternative accommodation which he refused because it lacked a garden. At his present flat he had turned a wilderness into a beautiful garden with a greenhouse, a pond and an aviary. The questions posed were (i) whether the list of factors in Pt IV, para. 2 which must be taken into account when deciding whether the accommodation was suitable was an indicative or an exhaustive one, and (ii) the interpretation of the 'needs' of the tenant (para. 2(d) above).

STEPHENSON LJ: . . . The question of what is meant by 'the needs of the tenant' is not, I think, an altogether easy one to decide. Mr Stephenson, for the landlords, has put his case in two ways. I think that the judge may also have been putting it in two ways which were different and inconsistent. The first is to regard the tenant's need for a garden in which to pursue his hobbies as not the kind of need which is referred to in the statute, and when the judge said in a passage which I should have read at the end of what he said when he was dealing with alternative accommodation, namely, 'the alternative accommodation is reasonably suitable for the needs of the defendant – all his needs,' that is the view he seems to have adopted. He is satisfied that all the needs of the tenant will be met, and I think that can only mean that he was regarding the need to pursue the tenant's hobbies in the garden as a need which was so insignificant as not to be the kind of need which was contemplated by the Act.

I think it is right to consider the provisions of the Schedule as narrowing the meaning of 'needs' as it has been interpreted in superficially similar provisions of the Rent Acts. We have been referred to a number of cases on those Acts, principally to the case of *Redspring Ltd v Francis*, reported at [1973] 1 WLR 134; also to *McDonnell v Daly* [1961] 1 WLR 1483. *Warren v Austen* [1947] 2 All ER 185 and *De Markozoff v Craig* (1949) 93 SJ 693. But I think those decisions should be approached with caution, principally for two reasons; one is that the provisions of the Rent Acts required the courts to have regard to the needs of the tenant as regards extent and character of accommodation, and the words 'and character' have in my judgment been deliberately omitted from paragraph 2(d) of the Schedule; and secondly, there is in paragraph 2(a) of the Schedule a provision which finds, as far as counsel's researches go and as far as my knowledge goes, no parallel in the Rent Acts or any legislation, that in considering the needs of the tenant the court is bound to have regard to something which is no concern of the tenant at all, namely the nature of the accommodation which it is the practice of the landlord to allocate to persons with similar needs. That at once brings into consideration, as it seems to me contrary to Mr Rowlands's submission, the needs of other tenants than the tenant who is seeking to resist possession.

The other way of considering the matter is to suppose that the garden, and the tenant's use of it, are a need of the tenant. Mr Rowland derives some support for that from what is said in the judgment of Buckley LJ in the *Redspring* case about style of life. He submits that the standard and quality of a tenant's life has to be considered in the sense that the needs of the whole man have to be considered, and that it would be wrong to narrow them down simply from the considerations which I have put forward, or any other considerations, so as to exclude such a requirement, even if it is not an essential requirement, as this tenant's need to indulge his hobbies in his garden.

But, says Mr Stephenson, even if that view of the tenant's life in the garden, so to speak, is regarded as a need, what the court has to do is to consider whether the alternative accommodation – in this case, 14 Manisty Court – is reasonably suitable for his needs. and in considering that, the court is entitled to find that the alternative accommodation is reasonably suitable for those needs even if it does not meet every one of them; and the way in which Mr Stephenson asks us to uphold the judgment on this view of needs and of the evidence, is that this alternative accommodation was

reasonably suitable for the tenant's needs as a whole, even though it did not meet this particular need, and indeed deprived him of the chance of satisfying at any rate most of it.
. . .

If I had to choose between the two views, I think I would hold that it is right to regard the need for a garden and the pursuit of these hobbies in this case, as a need of the tenant; but taking that view, I am unable to say that the judge was wrong, or made any error of law or misdirected himself, in taking it into account, but in holding that it was outweighed by other considerations and by the fact, as the judge found, that all his other needs would be met by the alternative accommodation.

Questions

1. Are the listed factors as to the suitability of accommodation in Sch. 2 Pt IV a complete list of potentially relevant factors? If not, did the court in *London Borough of Enfield* v *French* (1984) 17 HLR 211 regard the garden as an irrelevant factor, or simply not a factor of sufficient importance to outweigh the other considerations?
2. If a council house had some adaptations carried out by the local authority to help an elderly person who had moved in with the family of one of her adult children, would the local authority be able to gain possession of the house under Ground 13 when the elderly person died? If it depends on the scale of the adaptations, what would the position be if (i) grab rails had been provided at strategic points in the house, (ii) a ramp had been constructed up to the front door and (iii) a special shower installed?

(F) Injunctions

Housing Act 1996

Power to grant injunctions against anti-social behaviour
152.—(1) The High Court or a county court may, on an application by a local authority, grant an injunction prohibiting a person from—
(a) engaging in or threatening to engage in conduct causing or likely to cause a nuisance or annoyance to a person residing in, visiting or otherwise engaging in a lawful activity in residential premises to which this section applies or in the locality of such premises.
(b) using or threatening to use residential premises to which this section applies for immoral or illegal purposes, or
(c) entering residential premises to which this section applies or being found in the locality of such premises.
(2) This section applies to residential premises of the following descriptions—
(a) dwelling-houses held under secure or introductory tenancies from the local authority;
(b) accommodation provided by that authority under Part VII of this Act or Part III of the Housing Act 1985 (homelessness).
(3) The court shall not grant an injunction under this section unless it is of the opinion that—
(a) the respondent has used or threatened to use violence against any person of a description mentioned in subsection (1)(a), and

(b)   there is a significant risk of harm to that person or a person of a similar description if the injunction is not granted.

(4)   An injunction under this section may—

(a)   in the case of an injunction under subsection (1)(a) or (b), relate to particular acts or to conduct, or types of conduct, in general or to both, and

(b)   in the case of an injunction under subsection (1)(c), relate to particular premises or a particular locality;

and may be made for a specified period or until varied or discharged.

(5)   An injunction under this section may be varied or discharged by the court on an application by—

(a)   the respondent, or

(b)   the local authority which made the original application.

(6)   The court may attach a power of arrest to one or more of the provisions of an injunction which it intends to grant under this section.

(7)   The court may, in any case where it considers that it is just and convenient to do so, grant an injunction under this section, or vary such an injunction, even though the respondent has not been given such notice of the proceedings as would otherwise be required by rules of court.

If the court does so, it must afford the respondent an opportunity to make representations relating to the injunction or variation as soon as just and convenient at a hearing of which notice has been given to all the parties in accordance with rules of court.

(8)   In this section 'local authority' has the same meaning as in the Housing Act 1985.

Power of arrest for breach of other injunctions against anti-social behaviour

153.—(1)   In the circumstances set out in this section, the High Court or a county court may attach a power of arrest to one or more of the provisions of an injunction which it intends to grant in relation to a breach or anticipated breach of the terms of a tenancy.

(2)   The applicant is—

(a)   a local housing authority,

(b)   a housing action trust,

(c)   a registered social landlord, or

(d)   a charitable housing trust,

acting in its capacity as landlord of the premises which are subject to the tenancy.

(3)   The respondent is the tenant or a joint tenant under the tenancy agreement.

(4)   The tenancy is one by virtue of which—

(a)   a dwelling-house is held under an introductory, secure or assured tenancy, or

(b)   accommodation is provided under Part VII of this Act or Part III of the Housing Act 1985 (homelessness).

(5)   The breach or anticipated breach of the terms of the tenancy consists of the respondent—

(a)   engaging in or threatening to engage in conduct causing or likely to cause a nuisance or annoyance to a person residing, visiting or otherwise engaging in a lawful activity in the locality,

(b)   using or threatening to use the premises for immoral or illegal purposes, or

(c)   allowing any sub-tenant or lodger of his or any other person residing (whether temporarily or otherwise) on the premises or visiting them to act as mentioned in paragraph (a) or (b).

(6)   The court is of the opinion that—

(a)   the respondent or any person mentioned in subsection (5)(c) has used or threatened violence against a person residing, visiting or otherwise engaging in a lawful activity in the locality, and

(b)   there is a significant risk of harm to that person or a person of a similar description if the power of arrest is not attached to one or more provisions of the injunction immediately.

(7)   Nothing in this section prevents the grant of an injunction relating to other matters, in addition to those mentioned above, in relation to which no power of arrest is attached.

(i)   Types of injunctions

An injunction is a court order directing someone to perform a specified act (a mandatory injunction) or to abstain from doing something (a prohibitory injunction). The Supreme Court Act 1981, s. 37 recognises the High Court's inherent power to grant injunctions, while the County Courts Act 1984, s. 38, as amended by the Courts and Legal Services Act 1990, s. 3, grants similar powers to the county court. If a local authority apply for an injunction the tenant would normally be informed, but in an emergency it is possible to obtain injunctions without notice, on affidavit evidence alone. Breach of an injunction is a contempt of court which is punishable by a fine or imprisonment. The grant of an injunction is an equitable remedy and is therefore discretionary. Injunctions can be obtained on either a permanent or an interim basis.

Lord Diplock, in the leading case *American Cyanamid Co.* v *Ethicon* [1975] AC 396, laid down the principles on which interim injunctions are granted. First, the plaintiff must satisfy the court that there is a serious question to be tried. The court should then consider the 'balance of convenience', if the plaintiff were to succeed at the trial in establishing his right to a permanent injunction, whether damages would be adequate compensation.

(ii)   Local authority use of injunctions before 1996

Before 1996, local authorities had made use of injunctions to control the behaviour of anti-social tenants. They applied to court either where there was a breach of the tenancy agreement (obtaining a contractual injunction), or under the wide-ranging powers in s. 222 of the Local Government Act 1972. There was no need for a landlord requesting an injunction for the breach of a tenancy condition to show that damage had been suffered (*Doherty* v *Allman* (1878) 3 App Cas 709). The precise wording of the terms of the tenancy agreement was strictly interpreted. In *Lewisham London Borough Council* v *Simba Tola* (1992) 24 HLR 644, the term covered nuisance committed on the housing estate. An injunction preventing harassment of council staff in the housing offices some distance from the estate was discharged on appeal. With the new express powers in the Housing Act 1996 it is likely that the powers in s. 222 of the 1972 Act will fall into abeyance.

(iii)   Changes made by the Housing Act 1996

The Housing Act 1996 has given local authorities express powers in ss. 152–155 to apply for injunctions. Section 152 gives courts powers to grant injunctions to local authorities where anyone (not solely tenants) has used, or threatened to use, violence against persons residing, visiting or engaged in lawful activity in council housing property and there is a significant risk of harm to those persons. Section 153 enables any social landlords (not just local authorities) to apply to attach a power of arrest to injunctions granted for certain breaches of tenancy agreements. These are breaches which involve violence or the threat of violence and where there is a significant risk of harm. Other breaches of tenancy agreements can still be subject to injunctions but no power of arrest can be attached. Section 155(3)–(7) are not in force yet. They will give all social landlords the power to apply for an arrest warrant at any time, provided the injunction could originally have had a power of arrest attached to it.

Sometimes councils apply for injunctions at the same time as bringing possession proceedings. This gives an opportunity to the tenants to improve their behaviour and often is enough to bring the problems to an end. Failure to respond to an injunction will make it more likely that the court will make a possession order.

(G)   Other rights of secure public sector tenants

(i)   Introduction
So far in this chapter the major right of local housing authority tenants, that of security of tenure, has been discussed. The other rights in the 'Tenants' Charter' introduced in 1980 include the rights to take lodgers, to succeed to a tenancy, to be provided with information and to be consulted. The National Consumer Council survey published in 1976, *Tenancy Agreements*, found that 93 per cent of the council tenancy agreements included in the survey prohibited lodgers and nearly all prohibited sub-letting.

(ii)   Prohibition on assignment
In general, council tenants do not have the freedom to assign (i.e. transfer) their tenancies. If they had an unfettered right, council tenancies could be assigned to those who were not in need. The right to buy has taken much former council property out of public ownership and complete freedom to assign would exacerbate the problem. Although the property would still be publicly owned, it would not be available for people on the housing register waiting to be rehoused.

The three limited exceptions to this rule against assignment are in s. 91(3) of the Housing Act 1985. The first is an exchange with another local authority or housing association tenant which accords with s. 92 of the Act. Both tenants must obtain written consent from their respective landlords and any rent arrears must be paid. Consent can be withheld only on one of the grounds listed in Sch. 3. The second exception is a transfer as a result of a property adjustment order after divorce or certain other family proceedings.

The third exception is that the tenant is allowed to assign to a person who would be qualified to succeed (see s. 87, Housing Act 1985) if the tenant died just before the assignment. To be legally binding the assignment must be by deed (s. 52, Law of Property Act 1925). In *Camden London Borough Council v Goldenberg* (1996) 28 HLR 727, Mrs Goldenberg executed a deed of assignment of the flat where she lived transferring the tenancy to her grandson. She then moved into a nursing home. The majority of the Court of Appeal thought that the grandson showed that he fulfilled the residence requirements in s. 87 of the Housing Act 1985 and so the assignment was valid. The need for a deed is shown by the salutary case of *London Borough of Croydon* v *Buston & Triance* (1991) 24 HLR 36. Mr Triance's mother had a secure tenancy of a council house for seven years. She left the property when she went to live with her new husband, leaving her son in occupation. The tenancy ceased to be a secure tenancy as the house was no longer Mrs Buston's 'only or principal home'; a contractual tenancy remained in existence. The son argued that as he had lived with his mother from time to time over the previous two years he was eligible to succeed to the tenancy under s. 87 of the Housing Act 1985. Although Mr Triance requested the council for an assignment, and his mother wanted to assign the house to him, nothing was put in writing. The council were doubtful whether the house had been Mr Triance's only or principal home for the previous 12 months. The Court of Appeal held that no assignment took place; in order to assign the property a deed must be executed and that did not happen in this case so a possession order was upheld. The Court did think, however, that if Mr Triance did show that he would have qualified this would be relevant when the council were fulfilling their duties to Mr Triance as a homeless person with a priority need.

(iii)   Succession

Housing Act 1985

Succession on death of tenant

Persons qualified to succeed tenant
87.   A person is qualified to succeed the tenant under a secure tenancy if he occupies the dwelling-house as his only or principal home at the time of the tenant's death and either—
    (a)   he is the tenant's spouse, or
    (b)   he is another member of the tenant's family and has resided with the tenant throughout the period of twelve months ending with the tenant's death;
unless, in either case. the tenant was himself a successor, as defined in section 88.

Cases where the tenant is a successor
88.—(1)   The tenant is himself a successor if—
    (a)   the tenancy vested in him by virtue of section 89 (succession to a periodic tenancy), or
    (b)   he was a joint tenant and has become the sole tenant, or
    (c)   the tenancy arose by virtue of section 86 (periodic tenancy arising on ending of term certain) and the first tenancy there mentioned was granted to another person or jointly to him and another person, or

(d)   he became the tenant on the tenancy being assigned to him (but subject to subsections (2) and (3)), or

(e)   he became the tenant on the tenancy being vested in him on the death of the previous tenant, [or

(f)   the tenancy was previously an introductory tenancy and he was a successor to the introductory tenancy.]

(2)   A tenant to whom the tenancy was assigned in pursuance of an order under section 24 of the Matrimonial Causes Act 1973 (property adjustment orders in connection with matrimonial proceedings) is a successor only if the other party to the marriage was a successor.

(3)   A tenant to whom the tenancy was assigned by virtue of section 92 (assignments by way of exchange) is a successor only if he was a successor in relation to the tenancy which he himself assigned by virtue of that section.

(4)   Where within six months of the coming to an end of a secure tenancy which is a periodic tenancy ('the former tenancy') the tenant becomes a tenant under another secure tenancy which is a periodic tenancy, and—

(a)   the tenant was a successor in relation to the former tenancy, and

(b)   under the other tenancy either the dwelling-house or the landlord, or both, are the same as under the former tenancy,

the tenant is also a successor in relation to the other tenancy unless the agreement creating that tenancy otherwise provides.

Succession to periodic tenancy

89.—(1)   This section applies where a secure tenant dies and the tenancy is a periodic tenancy.

(2)   Where there is a person qualified to succeed the tenant, the tenancy vests by virtue of this section in that person, or if there is more than one such person in the one to be preferred in accordance with the following rules—

(a)   the tenant's spouse is to be preferred to another member of the tenant's family;

(b)   of two or more other members of the tenant's family such of them is to be preferred as may be agreed between them or as may, where there is no such agreement, be selected by the landlord.

(a)   Family

Section 113 of the Housing Act 1985 defines 'family' quite widely to include a man and a woman living as husband and wife and a range of blood and steprelations. It does not extend to gay and lesbian relationships; neither are same sex couples regarded as spouses. See the discussion of family, and especially the extract from *Fitzpatrick* v *Sterling Housing Association* [1997] 4 All ER 991, in chapter 9.

The question of whether a minor can succeed to a secure tenancy was addressed in *Kingston upon Thames RLBC* v *Prince* [1998] *The Times*, 7 December. When the tenant died his daughter, Wendy Prince, had lived with him for only six months, but her daughter Marie, aged 13, had lived with her grandfather for three years. Marie, it was asserted, fulfilled the succession conditions in s. 87 of the Housing Act 1985. The local authority brought possession proceedings arguing that minors could not hold a legal estate in land and so could not succeed to a tenancy. The Court of Appeal rejected the local authority's argument and found that minors were capable of being 'persons' in housing law. Moreover, a minor could hold an equitable tenancy in any property, including a council house. Applying these principles to the case it upheld the county court judge who had decided that Wendy Prince would hold the tenancy in trust for Marie until she was 18. The tenancy would be regarded as beginning on the date of Mr Prince's death.

(b)   Residence

The residence of 12 months with the previous tenant need not be in the premises to which succession is being claimed. In *Waltham Forest London Borough Council* v *Thomas* [1992] 3 All ER 244, the defendant had lived for two and half years with his brother. First they had lived in one council house, and ten days before his brother's death they had moved to another. The brother was the sole tenant of both properties. When the council sued for possession the defendant argued that he fulfilled the residence requirements of s. 87. A unanimous House of Lords overruled *South Northamptonshire DC* v *Power* [1987] 3 All ER 831 and held that it did not require the residence to have been in the same house for the whole 12-month period. The position is different in the private sector where the successor is required to reside with the deceased tenant 'in the dwelling-house'.

Lord Templeman said (at p. 246):

My Lords, s. 87 does not stipulate that the successor must have resided at a particular house for 12 months but only that he should have resided with the deceased tenant for that period. The effect of s. 87 is to ensure that a qualified member of the tenant's family who has made his home with the tenant shall not lose his home when the tenant dies but shall succeed to that home and to the secure tenancy which protected both the tenant and the successor while the tenant was alive and which shall continue to protect the successor after the death of the tenant. In order to qualify, a successor must have resided with the tenant during the period of 12 months ending with the tenant's death. This restriction ensures that s. 87 cannot be exploited, that there will be no difficulty in identifying a genuine successor and that only bona fide claims to have been residing with the tenant shall succeed. This protection for the local authority does not require the residence to have taken place for the whole 12 months in the house to which succession is claimed. The section only requires residence with the tenant for the period of 12 months and I see no justification for implying any other requirement.

When a tenant and a potential successor move from one council house to another the tenant does not lose the protection of a secure tenancy and there is no good reason why the potential successor should lose the protection which he has obtained or is in the course of obtaining under s. 87. When a tenant who is not already a council tenant applies for a council house, the local authority, before granting a secure tenancy, finds out whether the council house will be occupied by the tenant alone or whether the council house will become the joint home of the tenant and a member of the tenant's family who has been residing with the tenant. The local authority will know whether if they let the council house to the tenant the house will also be occupied by a potential successor who has made his home with the tenant. If the tenant's death is untimely, that is to say within one year of the date of letting, there is no reason why the potential successor should lose his home if he has in fact resided with the tenant for 12 months. In the present case the respondents have been unable to suggest why the appellant should lose his home as well as his brother by reason of the death of his brother. It frequently happens that a daughter lives with a widowed parent for 20 years or more; if the parent changes council houses or moves from the private sector to a council house within one year of the death of the parent then on the death of the parent the council house will be the home which contains all the furniture and other articles which form part of the home and have been fitted into the council house by the parent and the daughter. It would be cruel if the daughter could be evicted and left to find another home for herself and for her belongings simply because of the accident of the untimely death of the parent within one year. In the absence of express language, s. 87 should not be construed in a manner which can only, as in the present case, produce unwelcome and unjustifiable distress and hardship in the event of an untimely death.

The effect of periods away interrupting the 12-month residence period was discussed in *Camden London Borough Council* v *Goldenberg* (1996) 28 HLR 727. The Court of Appeal held that when deciding whether a period of absence breaks the continuity of the 12 months residence the court must look at the nature and extent of the continuing connection with the premises and the quality of the intention to return. Mrs Goldenberg's grandson, Adam Bloom, lived with her when he arrived in Britain from Israel in 1985. He stayed four years, returning to Israel in 1989. In April 1991 he came back to London and lived with his grandmother again. He married in February 1992 but he and his wife could not afford their own accommodation in London. They 'house-sat' for a couple of months for some friends who were abroad and then lived apart as Adam moved back to his grandmother's flat. In November 1992 she executed a deed assigning the tenancy to him.

The question was whether the period of 'house-sitting' broke the 12 months residence requirement. During the 'house-sitting' episode his grandmother's flat remained his postal address and most of his possessions were kept there so he showed a continuing connection with the premises. The main difficulty was his intention after the 'house-sitting' was over to move to a flat with his wife if a suitable one could be found. As his income was low, in reality he could scarcely afford any accommodation in London so it was held that he had the intention to return to his grandmother's flat unless something unexpected turned up. Nothing did turn up so he moved back to his grandmother's flat. The Court of Appeal, by a majority, allowed the grandson's appeal and held that he could succeed to his grandmother's tenancy.

(c)   One succession only rule

Only one statutory succession is allowed, as, if the deceased was himself a successor no further succession is possible (s. 87, Housing Act 1985). 'Successor' is defined in s. 88 and includes surviving joint tenants. It does not include tenancies assigned by exchange with another council or housing association tenant, or those assigned under the provisions in the Matrimonial Causes Act 1973.

This means that, whether a tenancy begins by being a sole tenancy in the name of the husband or a joint tenancy held by husband and wife, on the husband's death it can pass to the widow. On the widow's death it cannot pass to the children even if they fulfil the residence requirements. If, on the other hand, the tenancy passed to the wife after divorce under the Matrimonial Causes Act 1973, one of the children can succeed to the tenancy on the mother's death.

On the effects of intestacy on the succession rules an instructive case is *Epping Forest District Council* v *Pomphrett* (1990) 22 HLR 475. The Pomphrett senior who lived with his family in a council house had the tenancy solely in his name. When he died intestate in 1978 no letters of administration were applied for, but his widow wrote to the council asking for the tenancy to be transferred to her name and the council agreed to 'formally transfer' the tenancy to her. On intestacy the tenancy vested in the President of the Family Division who, however, had no power to deal with it but could receive notices to quit. The family continued to live in the house until the mother's death in 1985. The two adult children who had lived there all their lives applied to succeed to the tenancy. The plaintiff council refused, arguing that this would constitute a second succession and therefore be forbidden under s. 87 of the Housing Act 1985. The council applied for a possession order but failed: when the mother became a tenant this was, in effect, a new tenancy because the father's legal estate in his periodic tenancy had vested in the President of the Family Division. As the mother had a 'new tenancy' and the children would be the first successors to this tenancy they would not be caught by the 'one succession only' rule.

(iv) Lodgers and sub-letting
Before 1980, many public sector tenancy agreements forbade taking in lodgers even with the permission of the local authority. If lodgers were allowed there was frequently an extra item added to the rent, 'a lodger charge'. Lodgers are licensees who have permission to use the property but, as they do not have exclusive possession, they are not sub-tenants.

Housing Act 1985

Lodgers and subletting
93.—(1) It is a term of every secure tenancy that the tenant—
(a) may allow any persons to reside as lodgers in the dwelling-house, but
(b) will not, without the written consent of the landlord, sublet or part with possession of part of the dwelling-house.
(2) If the tenant under a secure tenancy parts with the possession of the dwelling-house or sublets the whole of it (or sublets first part of it and then the remainder), the tenancy ceases to be a secure tenancy and cannot subsequently become a secure tenancy.

Consent to subletting
94.—(1) This section applies to the consent required by virtue of section 93(1)(b) (landlord's consent to subletting of part of dwelling-house).

(2)   Consent shall not be unreasonably withheld (and if unreasonably withheld shall be treated as given), and if a question arises whether the withholding of consent was unreasonable it is for the landlord to show that it was not.

(3)   In determining that question the following matters, if shown by the landlord, are among those to be taken into account—

(a)   that the consent would lead to overcrowding of the dwelling-house within the meaning of Part X (overcrowding);

(b)   that the landlord proposes to carry out works on the dwelling-house, or on the building of which it forms part, and that the proposed works will affect the accommodation likely to be used by the sub-tenant who would reside in the dwelling-house as a result of the consent.

(4)   Consent may be validly given notwithstanding that it follows, instead of preceding, the action requiring it.

(5)   Consent cannot be given subject to a condition (and if purporting to be given subject to a condition shall be treated as given unconditionally).

(6)   Where the tenant has applied in writing for consent, then—

(a)   if the landlord refuses to given consent, it shall give the tenant a written statement of the reasons why consent was refused, and

(b)   if the landlord neither gives nor refuses to give consent within a reasonable time, consent shall be taken to have been withheld.

(v)   Repairs and improvements

(a)   Repairs

Before 1980, many council tenancy agreements were one-sided, giving lists of the tenant's obligations but making no mention of the landlord's obligations (including those of repairing the property). *Liverpool City Council v Irwin* [1976] 2 All ER 39 is a graphic example of the former poor position of tenants – in this case the tenants of a sink estate in Liverpool where the corporation had no obligations to repair in the tenancy agreement. The House of Lords had to imply terms governing repairs.

The Housing Act 1985, s. 96 originally allowed secure tenants to recover the costs of certain repairs from the local authority after the work had been done by the tenants themselves or by building contractors that they had employed. As few tenants exercised this right the scheme was abandoned and replaced by s. 121 of the Leasehold Reform, Housing and Urban Development Act 1993 which substituted s. 96 Housing Act 1985. This enables secure tenants to apply to have 'qualifying' repairs, such as faults in the electrical, gas or water systems, carried out. 'Qualifying repairs' are listed in the Secure Tenants of Local Housing Authorities (Right to Repair) Regulations 1994 SI 1994 No. 133. The landlord must then issue a notice giving the details of the repairs, the recommended contractor and the date the work must be completed. The tenant can claim compensation if the repairs are not finished on time.

(b)   Improvements

Improvements, which are defined in s. 97(2) of the 1985 Act, require the landlord's consent (ss. 98 and 99). If the improvements have added to the value of the property or the rent the landlord could charge, the landlord may recognise this with an appropriate payment (s. 100) at the end of the tenancy. If the improvements were begun after 1 April 1994, the compensation for improvements is governed by the Leasehold Reform, Housing and Urban Development Act 1993 s. 122.

Housing Act 1985

Right to have repairs carried out

96.—(1)   The Secretary of State may make regulations for entitling secure tenants whose landlords are local housing authorities, subject to and in accordance with the regulations, to have qualifying repairs carried out, at their landlord's expense, to the dwelling-houses of which they are such tenants.

(2)   The regulations may make all or any of the following provisions, namely—

(a)   provisions that, where a secure tenant makes an application to his landlord for qualifying repair to be carried out, the landlord shall issue a repair notice—

(i)   specifying the nature of the repair, the listed contractor by whom the repair is to be carried out and the last day of any prescribed period, and

(ii)   containing such other particulars as may be prescribed;

(b)   provision that, if the contractor specified in a repair notice fails to carry out the repair within a prescribed period, the landlord shall issue a further repair notice specifying such other listed contractor as the tenant may require; and

(c)   provision that, if the contractor specified in the repair notice fails to carry out the repair within a prescribed period, the landlord shall pay the tenant such sum by way of compensation as may be determined by or under the regulations.

. . .

Tenant's improvements require consent

97.—(1)   It is a term of every secure tenancy that the tenant will not make any improvement without the written consent of the landlord.

(2)   In this Part 'improvement' means any alteration in, or addition to, a dwelling-house, and includes—

(a)   any addition to or alteration in landlord's fixtures and fittings,

(b)   any addition or alteration connected with the provision of services to the dwelling-house,

(c)   the erection of a wireless or television aerial, and

(d)   the carrying out of external decoration.

(3)   The consent required by virtue of subsection (1) shall not be unreasonably withheld, and if unreasonably withheld shall be treated as given,

(4)   The provisions of this section have effect, in relation to secure tenancies, in place of section 19(2) of the Landlord and Tenant Act 1927 (general provisions as to covenants, &c. not to make improvements without consent).

Provisions as to consents required by s. 97

98.—(1)   If a question arises whether the withholding of a consent required by virtue of section 97 (landlord's consent to improvements) was unreasonable, it is for the landlord to show that it was not.

(2)   In determining that question the court shall, in particular, have regard to the extent to which the improvement would be likely—

(a)   to make the dwelling-house, or any other premises, less safe for occupiers,

(b) to cause the landlord to incur expenditure which it would be unlikely to incur if the improvement were not made, or

(c) to reduce the price which the dwelling-house would fetch if sold on the open market or the rent which the landlord would be able to charge on letting the dwelling-house.

(3) A consent required by virtue of section 97 may be validly given notwithstanding that it follows, instead of preceding, the action requiring it.

(4) Where a tenant has applied in writing for a consent which is required by virtue of section 97—

(a) the landlord shall if it refuses consent give the tenant a written statement of the reason why consent was refused, and

(b) if the landlord neither gives nor refuses to give consent within a reasonable time, consent shall be taken to have been withheld.

Conditional consent to improvements
99.—(1) Consent required by virtue of section 97 (landlord's consent to improvements) may be given subject to conditions.

(2) If the tenant has applied in writing for consent and the landlord gives consent subject to an unreasonable condition, consent shall be taken to have been unreasonably withheld.

(3) If a question arises whether a condition was reasonable, it is for the landlord to show that it was.

(4) A failure by a secure tenant to satisfy a reasonable condition imposed by his landlord in giving consent to an improvement which the tenant proposes to make, or has made, shall be treated for the purposes of this Part as a breach by the tenant of an obligation of his tenancy.

(vi)   Right to be consulted

Housing Act 1985

Consultation on matters of housing management
105.—(1) A landlord authority shall maintain such arrangements as it considers appropriate to enable those of its secure tenants who are likely to be substantially affected by a matter of housing management to which this section applies—

(a) to be informed of the authority's proposals in respect of the matter, and

(b) to make their views known to the authority within a specified period;
and the authority shall, before making any decision on the matter, consider any representations made to it in accordance with those arrangements.

(2) For the purposes of this section, a matter is one of housing management if, in the opinion of the landlord authority, it relates to—

(a) the management, maintenance, improvement or demolition of dwelling-houses let by the authority under secure tenancies, or

(b) the provision of services or amenities in connection with such dwelling-houses;
but not so far as it relates to the rent payable under a secure tenancy or to charges for services or facilities provided by the authority.

(3) This section applies to matters of housing management which, in the opinion of the landlord represent—

(a) a new programme of maintenance, improvement or demolition, or

(b)   a change in the practice or policy of the authority,
and are likely substantially to affect either its secure tenants as a whole or a group of
them who form a distinct social group or occupy dwelling-houses which constitute a
distinct class (whether by reference to the kind of dwelling-house, or the housing
estate or other larger area in which they are situated).

(4)   In the case of a landlord authority which is a local housing authority, the
reference in subsection (2) to the provision of services or amenities is a reference only
to the provision of services or amenities by the authority acting in its capacity as
landlord of the dwelling-houses concerned.

(5)   A landlord authority shall publish details of the arrangements which it makes
under this section, and a copy of the documents published under this subsection
shall—

(a)   be made available at the authority's principal office for inspection at all
reasonable hours, without charge, by members of the public, and

(b)   be given, on payment of a reasonable fee, to any member of the public who
asks for one.

Since 1980, local authorities have been under a limited duty to consult their
secure tenants on 'housing management' matters. One of the most persistent
criticisms of public housing authorities had been their paternalism on taking
in lodgers and allowing improvements, especially in the lack of consultation
with tenants over general environmental matters and area development plans.
Section 105 gives authorities a fair amount of discretion over the matters
about which they consult their tenants and the way consultation is organised.
No detailed consultation mechanisms are laid down as s. 105(1) merely states
that the local authority 'shall maintain such arrangements as it considers
appropriate'. A case which illustrates how limited the consultation duty is in
practice is *Short* v *London Borough of Tower Hamlets* (1985) 18 HLR 171. Ms
Short, a secure tenant, was complaining about the lack of consultation with
the tenants of Waterlow Estate in Bethnal Green over the borough's plans to
sell the estate to a private developer. It was agreed by the Court of Appeal
that the tenants could have obtained an injunction if such a sale was taking
place without consulting the tenants. However, the authority had decided to
carry out a marketing exercise to find a buyer and that exercise would not
substantially affect the tenants on the estate. It does seem curious that the
decision by the council's Development Committee to carry forward the sale
of the whole estate and to abandon repair and rehabilitation of the properties
was not regarded as a matter of housing management which was covered by
s. 105.

Ralph Gibson LJ gave his reasons (at p. 184):

In explaining the reasons for that conclusion I will start with the definition of 'a matter
of housing management' in [s. 105(2)] because that is the subject of obligatory
consultation under section [105] with reference to which it is required that the
landlord authority's arrangements 'enable' secure tenants to be informed of the
authority's proposals. The duty, of which the council is said to have been in breach,
was to consider any representations made to it by secure tenants in accordance with
the consultation arrangements before making any decision on a matter of housing

management. If the impugned decision is not shown to have been made on such a matter then the council was not in breach of duty either in failing to enable the secure tenants to be informed of the council's proposals or in making a decision without first considering any representations made to it.

There are three requirements which must, in the opinion of the local authority concerned, be satisfied before any matter falls within the definition. First, the matter must relate to the management, maintenance, improvement or demolition of the dwelling-houses or to the provision of services or amenities in connection with them. The repair or redevelopment of the Waterlow Estate was clearly within that requirement. Secondly, the 'matter' must represent 'a new programme of maintenance, improvement or demolition or a *change* in the practice or policy of the authority'. On the facts of this case it was not suggested by the Council that a decision to sell the Waterlow Estate to a private developer in a package form, as proposed in principle by the Multi-Committee Report No. 54/84, did not constitute a 'new' programme of demolition, etc., or a change in the policy of the authority so as to cause the repair or redevelopment of the Waterlow Estate not to be within this requirement. It is to be noted that any change in the plans or policy of the council, made by the decision of July 27, 1983, appears to have been small so far as concerns any impact upon secure tenants as compared with the impact upon those tenants of the plans and policies of the council for the Waterlow Estate which had been established by earlier decisions of the council. Since no reliance was placed upon this aspect of the case by Mr Bowring for the council I do not examine it any further. It is noted because assessment of the extent and degree of the effect upon secure tenants of any change of policy would be relevant to the judgment which the local authority has to make upon the third requirement of the definition, namely that the matter must be, in the opinion of the local authority, 'likely substantially to affect its secure tenants as a whole or a group of them' [s. 105(3)].

The section is directed at the processes of decision of landlord authorities including local authorities. Local authorities work by committee procedures in which decisions are taken by committees to be carried out by executive actions. It seems to me that the requirement of [s. 105(3)] must be understood and applied as if such words as 'if implemented' were implied so that it reads 'is likely if implemented substantially to affect secure tenants.' The implying of such words is necessary if the purpose of the consultation provisions is to be achieved. For example, a decision by the council to sell an estate on agreed terms will not itself affect any tenant. It is the carrying out of the decision which has effect and a decision to sell may not be implemented for many different reasons. The provisions are intended to achieve consultation before decision upon matters which, if implemented, will affect tenants.

(H)   After a possession order has been granted

(i)   Court discretion

The Housing Act 1985, s. 85 gives the court a discretion to adjourn the possession proceedings; and after making an order the court can stay or suspend the execution of the order or postpone the date of possession. The court can impose conditions such as the repayment of the rent owing in cases brought on the basis of rent arrears. When the arrears have been repaid the suspended possession order becomes unenforceable. By s. 85(2) of the 1985 Act, the tenancy ends on the date given in the possession order.

If the tenant fails to leave by that date the landlord must return to court and apply for a warrant of possession. If the original possession order was suspended the tenancy does not come to an end, but if conditions were imposed and these conditions are not complied with the tenancy comes to an immediate end on the first breach of a condition without any further court order (*Thompson* v *Elmbridge Borough Council* (1987) 19 HLR 526). The landlord cannot enforce a suspended possession order without first making an application for a warrant of possession.

(ii) A new secure tenancy?

Local authority landlords often obtain a court order for possession against a secure tenant but then make an agreement with the tenant that while certain conditions are observed the order will not be executed. In *Burrows* v *Brent London Borough Council* [1996] 4 All ER 577 the House of Lords considered an appeal from Brent after the Court of Appeal had upheld the judge's at first instance declaration that Miss Burrows' agreement created a new secure tenancy. Hence the local authority would need to obtain a further possession order. As the making of an agreement after a possession order was granted was a common practice amongst local authority landlords there was an element of panic in town halls, and relief when the Court of Appeal decision was reversed.

Burrows v Brent London Borough Council
[1996] 4 All ER 577

Miss Burrows had rent arrears of £2,313, and on 29 January 1992 Brent obtained a possession order which took effect 14 days later on 12 February. A week after the possession order Miss Burrows made an agreement to pay a 'rent charge' of £2.67 a week and reduce the arrears by £3 a week. She failed to keep the agreement so Brent issued a warrant for possession for 8 June 1994 and she moved out. She commenced an action for damages for unlawful eviction, a declaration that she remained a tenant and a mandatory injunction that she be allowed back to the flat.

LORD BROWNE-WILKINSON: [After outlining the facts and establishing that Miss Burrows had a secure tenancy under ss. 79–81 Housing Act 1985, and that by s. 82 in order for a secure tenancy to be terminated by the landlord a possession order is required, Lord Browne-Wilkinson went on:]

It is important to note that the secure tenancy ends, not on the date on which possession is in fact given up, but on the date on which the order requires the defendant to give up possession.

Section 84 provides that the court shall not make an order for possession save on one of the grounds mentioned in Sch. 2 which include non-payment of rent. In addition, in the case of non-payment of rent the court must also be satisfied that it is reasonable to make the order. An order for possession cannot be made unless the ground on which an order is to be sought has been specified in a prior notice to be served on the tenant (see ss. 83 and 84(3)).

Section 85 is central to the argument in this case. It provides:

(1)   Where proceedings are brought for possession of a dwelling-house let under a secure tenancy [for the non-payment of rent] the court may adjourn the proceedings for such period or periods as it thinks fit.

(2)   On the making of an order for possession of such a dwelling-house on any of those grounds, or at any time before the execution of the order, the court may— (a) stay or suspend the execution of the order, or (b) postpone the date of possession, for such period or periods as the court thinks fit.

(3)   On such an adjournment, stay, suspension or postponement the court— (a) shall impose conditions with respect to the payment by the tenant of arrears of rent (if any) and rent or payments in respect of occupation after the termination of the tenancy (mesne profits), unless it considers that to do so would cause exceptional hardship to the tenant or would otherwise be unreasonable, and (b) may impose such other condition as it thinks fit.

(4)   If the conditions are complied with, the court may, if it thinks fit, discharge or rescind the order for possession. . . .

The argument for Miss Burrows, which the Court of Appeal accepted, is as follows. The order of 29 January 1992 directed that possessiòn should be given on 12 February 1992. Therefore, by virtue of s. 82(2), Miss Burrows' original secure tenancy terminated on that day. Yet, under the agreement of 5 February 1992 Miss Burrows remained in occupation of the house paying a 'rent charge' of £2.67 per week for such occupation. That agreement could not be effective to alter or vary the order itself, but could only take effect as an agreement to permit Miss Burrows to stay on after her existing tenancy had terminated on 12 February 1992. This right of continued occupation can only be explained on the ground that the agreement conferred on Miss Burrows a new right of occupation, either by way of a new tenancy or as a licensee, it mattered not which. If it was a new tenancy, it was a new secure tenancy; if it was only a licence, by virtue of s. 79(3) Miss Burrows enjoyed the same protection as if it were a tenancy. In either event, the new secure tenancy or a new licence could only be terminated by Brent applying to the court for a further court order terminating the new right (see s. 82(1)).

The argument for Brent before the Court of Appeal was that the agreement of 5 February was simply an agreement by Brent not to execute the possession order, provided that Miss Burrows complied with the agreed conditions. As the judge's findings demonstrated, Miss Burrows never intended that the agreement should create a tenancy and it was absurd to imagine that Brent, by granting Miss Burrows an indulgence in relation to a possession order which they had only just obtained, should have intended to create a new right of occupation necessitating a further application to the court in order to obtain possession. In the period during which Brent agreed to forbear from enforcing the order, Miss Burrows was a mere 'tolerated trespasser'.

The Court of Appeal, whilst accepting that the crucial factor in determining Miss Burrows' rights was the intention of the parties, rejected Brent's contention on the ground that it gave rise to manifest absurdities. At the rate for payment of arrears stipulated by the agreement of 5 February 1992 it would have taken Miss Burrows 14 years to pay them off during which time, if the argument of Brent was correct, she would be a mere trespasser. As a trespasser she would enjoy none of the rights of a tenant. Thus she could not require Brent to repair the house. She would have no right under the Defective Premises Act 1972. She would qualify as a homeless person under s. 58 of the 1985 Act. Brent would have no right to evict her for any breach of the covenants in her tenancy, but only for breach of the conditions contained in the agreement of 5 February 1992. On the case as presented to the Court of Appeal their conclusion was inevitable. But the significance of s. 85 was not drawn to their attention. As a result of the recent decision of the Court of Appeal in *Greenwich London BC v Regan* (1996) 28 HLR 469 Brent advanced before your lordships a far more compelling argument, viz: (1) although under s. 82(2) the original tenancy came to an end of 12 February 1992 (being the date fixed by the order for giving possession) that was not necessarily the final position; (2) under s. 85(2) the court has the power to postpone the date of possession; (3) this power to postpone the date for possession is exercisable by the court 'at any time before the execution of the order'. This shows that the power can be exercised even after the date for possession specified in the order has passed and the tenancy has thereby been terminated by virtue of s. 82(2); (4) this conclusion is re-enforced by s. 85(3)(a), which postulates that the court can make a suspended order conditional on making 'payments in respect of occupation after the termination of the tenancy (mesne profits)'. This demonstrates that there can come a time when, although the old tenancy has terminated and the former tenant has remained in possession for which he is liable to pay mesne profits as trespasser, the court can until the original order is executed make an order varying the date for giving of possession thereby reviving the previously defunct tenancy; (5) therefore, so far as the tenant is concerned, the crucial event is the execution of the order for possession. Down to that date the tenant can apply to the court for a variation of the original order substituting a new date on which possession is to be given thereby reviving the old secure tenancy. This revived tenancy will not be terminated under s. 82 until the new date for giving possession occurs; (6) that such revival of the old tenancy is possible is demonstrated by s. 85(4) which plainly assumes that on discharge or rescission of the original order for possession, the old secure tenancy will revive.

I accept this analysis of the effect of s. 85, which is largely derived from the judgment of Millett LJ in *Greenwich London BC v Regan*. In that case, an order for possession was made against a secure tenant, the order (as construed by the Court of Appeal) providing for the giving of possession to be postponed so long as arrears of rent were paid by instalments and the current rent was paid. The tenant having failed to comply with the conditions in the order, the landlord and the tenant agreed variations in the amount of the payment which were to be made. The tenant having breached the terms of the order and the agreed terms, the landlord applied for a warrant of execution. The tenant sought a stay of execution. He submitted that the old tenancy had come to an end when he failed to comply with the conditions imposed by the order (see *Thompson v Elmbridge BC* [1987] 1 WLR 1425). He then submitted, in reliance on the decision of the Court of Appeal in the instant case, that by agreeing to allow the former tenant to remain in possession the landlord had created a new tenancy or licence and therefore could not obtain possession under the old order.

The Court of Appeal in *Regan's* case, after analysing s. 85 in much the same terms as I have summarised above, posed the question whether the parties could, by agreement, revive the expired tenancy without an order of the court. The Court of Appeal held (in my view rightly) that the parties could not by agreement vary the terms of the court order. But they held that by agreeing the new conditions, the landlord waived the right to complain about failure to comply with conditions specified in the order constituted a breach of those latter conditions. Consequently, there being no breach of the conditions imposed by the order upon which the landlord could rely, the order remained in force, the date for giving possession had not passed and therefore the old tenancy had not been terminated. They distinguished the decision in the present case on the ground that they were dealing with a suspended conditional order of the court whereas in the instant case there is an immediate, unconditional order for possession.

One factor which weighed heavily with the Court of Appeal in *Regan's* case (to which I also attach importance) is the practical effect of the decision under appeal, i.e. any consensual variation of an order for possession produces a new secure tenancy or licence. Local authorities and other public housing authorities try to conduct their housing functions as humane and reasonable landlords. In so doing they frequently need to grant indulgences to their tenants to reflect changes in the tenants' circumstances. When applying for possession orders for non-payment of rent local authorities agree to the order being suspended upon the payment of arrears, the rate of payment being adjusted to meet the means of the tenant at the date of the order. If the tenant subsequently loses his job, the landlord will often be willing to reduce the rate of payment of arrears. Why should this not be done by agreement? Yet the effect of the local authority agreeing to such a reduction will be that the tenant, whilst keeping up his payments at the agreed reduced rate, will be in breach of the conditions specified by the order at the higher rate. If so his old tenancy will be terminated. On the view of the law adopted by the Court of Appeal in the present case, a new secure tenancy requiring a new order will come into existence. Similarly where, as with Miss Burrows, the court makes an immediate order for possession but the landlord grants an indulgence by agreeing not to execute the order immediately: if the Court of Appeal decision is correct, the effect of granting the indulgence is to create a new tenancy or licence and the local authority will have to obtain a new possession order. The practical result therefore will be whether that the local authority will be reluctant to make reasonable and humane concessions by agreement or in every case will have to make an application to the court to vary the existing order so as to ensure that the old tenancy is not brought to an end. I find it impossible to believe that Parliament intended to produce such an unreasonable regime, penalising sensible agreements out of court and requiring repeated applications to an already overstretched court system.
. . .

I therefore reach the conclusions that, in the absence of special circumstances, an agreement by a landlord not to enforce strictly an order for possession, whether conditional or unconditional, does not create a new secure tenancy or licence under Pt IV of the 1985 Act. Brent, by making the agreement of 5 February 1992, did not grant a new tenancy or licence to Miss Burrows as from 12 February 1992. It follows that the possession order of 29 January 1992 was properly enforced. I would therefore reverse the decisions of the Court of Appeal and the trial judge and dismiss Miss Burrows' action.

Questions

1. If council tenants are allowed to buy their houses and then sell them to whoever they wish, why should they not have a similar right to assign their tenancies?
2. Is it right that, if an elderly person who is moving into residential care agrees to assign his or her tenancy to a family member who fulfils the criteria for succession, this must be carried out by executing a deed? Does this unduly penalise people who are unaware of the legal formalities?
3. Is the concept of a 'lodger' in the Housing Act 1985, s. 93(1)(a) in effect the same as a 'licensee'? (See chapter 1.) How can one distinguish a 'partial'

sublet (requiring consent from the local authority) from a lodger arrangement (which does not)?

4.   Why do you think Ralph Gibson LJ took such a restrictive view of s. 105 of the Housing Act 1985 in *Short*? Was this a policy-led decision?

6 HOMELESSNESS

(A) The nature of the problem

Homelessness is not a new phenomenon. In the Middle Ages those lacking accommodation frequently looked to religious foundations to supply them with, albeit temporary, shelter. Following the abolition of the monasteries under Henry VIII this burden fell back on the civil authorities, though it was left to Henry's daughter Elizabeth I to pass a comprehensive 'poor law'. This made the destitute and indigent the responsibility of their home parishes, and harsh provision was made to ensure that 'sturdy beggars' could be forcibly returned to their places of origin if apprehended. Within parishes the better-off were taxed or 'rated' to pay something towards the cost of the poor, though this was an unpopular impost, and those responsible for collecting it did all they could in general to keep costs down.

It is not often appreciated that the Elizabethan Poor Law, though extensively modified, remained the essential basis of welfare provision down until the reforms of the National Assistance Act 1948. By then provision for accommodating homeless persons in workhouses owned by 'Poor Law Unions' of parishes had been made. The often harsh conditions in these establishments were graphically described by Charles Dickens in *Oliver Twist*, and by George R. Simms in his frequently parodied but nevertheless moving poem, 'It was Christmas Day in the Workhouse'.

In more recent times the problem of homelessness came to public attention in the mid 1960s with the television film 'Cathy, Come Home.' The then existing legal structure, which imposed an *obligation* on local *social service* authorities to deal with cases of emergency homelessness only – e.g. fire and flood – was unable to deal with chronic structural homelessness consequent on an increasing lack of affordable rented accommodation.

The Local Government Act 1972 gave local *housing* authorities *powers* to assist homeless persons, with a reserve power for the Secretary of State to reimpose a housing *duty* on social services authorities. The consequence was that no one was certain where the responsibility for homelessness lay and legal confusion was added to the social problem. In 1977, however, a private member's Bill, promoted by the Liberal MP Stephen Ross, drafted with the aid of Shelter and also in receipt of government assistance, was passed which imposed *duties* on local housing authorities in respect of those homeless persons who satisfied certain legal requirements. In due course this legislation (with some minor amendments) was consolidated with other housing legislation and became Pt III of the Housing Act 1985. It was under this legislation that considerable efforts were made to deal with what appeared to be an inexorably rising tide of homelessness.

Over the period 1977–87, 0.5 million people were accommodated under the law's homelessness provisions. In 1980, 8,660 persons were accepted as homeless in the first half year in London, and 7,930 in the second half year; in the rest of England the figures were 21,370 and 24,300 respectively. By 1985 the figures were 14,210 (second half – London) and 48,560 (second half) for the rest of England. These figures related to *acceptances*, not applications.

Increases in the number of acceptances of persons as 'homeless' led to a considerable expansion of the use of bed and breakfast, 'B&B', and hostel accommodation. A further consequence of the increasing incidence of homelessness was the escalating cost of dealing with the problem. The Chartered Institute of Public Finance and Accounting (CIPFA) calculated that the average cost of a case of homelessness in London dealt with by B&B accommodation was £7,670 in 1987, with hoteliers receiving a grand total of £78m.

The number of households homeless in Central London in the 1980s rose at 4 per cent pa, but in the outer boroughs the rate of increase was higher, e.g., 43 per cent in Kingston, 28 per cent in Bromley. In England in 1987, 250,000 persons were homeless according to Shelter.

Homelessness continued to rise into the 1990s apparently faster then in rural areas than in urban areas. The problem was compounded by rural poverty, inflation in rural house prices and the sale of council houses.

In 1989, the Government reviewed the law, but this was something of a legal 'damp squib'. Far from proposing any change in the law, the Government proposed to keep the existing law broadly as it was, considering, for example, the existing definitions of 'homeless' and 'priority need' to be 'adequate and appropriate'. Instead managerial change was urged to make better use of existing housing stock, closer liaison with Housing Associations, preventative advice and encouragement of those willing to provide lodgings. It was also recognised, however, that some areas needed greater assistance to provide new housing, and some mention of targeted resources was made and a newly revised Code of Guidance to ensure a greater degree of consistency between authorities' homelessness practices.

During the 1990s, according to official figures, homelessness *acceptances* declined, while the numbers of people in 'B&B' declined by two-thirds from 1991 levels. In the year ending September 1994, homelessness acceptances were down 9 per cent on the previous year, 125,640 cases in all, the peak year being 1992. The numbers in temporary accommodation were 49,330, 13 per cent down on the previous year, and the numbers in B&B were 4,740, 24 per cent down on the previous year. The more recent figures continue to show a decline in the number of households accepted as homeless. For the second quarter of 1996 the figure for England was 28,610. The figure for the second quarter of 1997 was 24,930, a decline of 11%. The final quarter figures for 1997 represent a further decline in homelessness acceptances. In England there were 24,810, a decline of 7 per cent on the previous year's figures. Even so, there were still 44,430 households in temporary accommodation – 4,240 in B&B, 9,330 in hostels and 30,860 'other' (i.e. interim housing).

The 'disincentive' effect of the changes in the law in 1996 also cannot be ignored. Prior to 1996 it was a widely held belief, amongst many housing authorities at least, that the law relating to homelessness encouraged people to present themselves as applicants because, so it was argued, that was seen as a 'fast track' route into permanent council accommodation. Certainly it was the practice of many authorities who had sufficient housing stock to utilise that to meet the needs of homeless persons. The decision of the House of Lords in *R* v *Brent LBC, ex parte Awua* [1995] 2 WLR 315 was, however, that the duty to accommodate under the pre-1996 law did not mean that authorities were under a mandatory obligation always to house homeless persons in permanent accommodation, and that was translated into a new legislative form by the 1996 Act. The *duty* now is one effectively only to accommodate temporarily, with a discretionary power to continue that accommodation once the initial two-year period of assistance is over. There is anecdotal evidence, as yet unproven by empirical research, to suggest that this change in the law has depressed the numbers of applicants to a degree.

While the decline in acceptances is to be welcomed *if* it represents a decline in real numbers of homeless people, the figures themselves are still too high and homelessness remains a major problem; furthermore, the official 'acceptance' figure may mask the situation – many people may not apply for fear of rejection.

Homelessness applications and acceptances both rose slightly in the third quarter of 1998 – 9 per cent and 7 per cent respectively – but these figures were still 26 per cent below the peak quarter for homelessness applications and acceptances in March 1992. There was also a slight (4 per cent) increase in the number of households in 'B&B' accommodation in September 1998, though that number is two-fifths of the September 1991 peak when 13,550 people were in 'B&B'.

(B)   The current law

In January 1994, 'hard-line' proposals to change the law on homelessness which had been mooted during the 1989 review were again brought forward.

The outcome was Part VII of the Housing Act 1996. Conservative Ministers accepted the local authority argument alluded to above, that the homelessness route into council accommodation had become a 'fast track' whereby the normal waiting list procedures were being evaded. The new law now provides, as already stated, a temporary entitlement only. It was, however, argued that during that temporary entitlement period otherwise homeless people, whose names would, of course, be on the housing register, would qualify for 'ordinary' allocations, but they would have to wait their turn in temporary accommodation. The Blair Government, as we shall see later, 'drew the teeth' of the 1996 Act to a degree by passing delegated legislation ensuring that homeless persons have to be given 'reasonable preference' in housing allocations. However, they have not re-introduced a primary right to accommodation and seem unlikely to do so.

Under the new law local housing authorities have both general and specific homelessness functions.

(i) General homelessness functions: advice services

Every local housing authority *must* under s. 179 ensure that advice and assistance about homelessness and its prevention are freely available to all persons in their districts; and they *may* give assistance to any person by providing advice etc., or help by way of a grant/loan, and may permit that person to use their premises, along with the provision of furniture and goods and the services of authority staff.

Section 180 further empowers the giving of financial assistance to voluntary bodies (i.e. those who seek no profit) concerned with homelessness and related matters and a local housing authority may permit such bodies to use authority premises, furniture, goods and the services of authority staff.

Under s. 181, the assistance given under ss. 179 and 180 may be subject to conditions, and undertakings *must* be given by recipients that they will use money, premises, furniture, etc. for the specified purpose for which assistance is given. In all cases there must be conditions imposed as to keeping of books and auditing of accounts, keeping records as to how money has been spent, and provision for inspection of books, etc. by the aid donor. Where assistance etc. is abused, the donor must take steps to recover from the donee an amount equal to the assistance, but must first serve notice on the donee of that amount and how it has been calculated (s. 181(5) and (6)).

(ii) Central homelessness functions

The Secretary of State may also give financial assistance under s. 180; however, his prime task is to issue guidance to authorities under s. 182, to which *they must have regard*. Although authorities are not required to adhere slavishly to the Code of Guidance, which (having initially appeared in 1977) has been revised and reissued under s. 182, they may not ignore it. It is a question of fact in each case whether or not the Code of Guidance has been considered, but where it is clear that the Code has been ignored in coming to a decision, that decision can be struck down (see *R v Newham LBC, ex parte Ojuri* [1998] *The Times*, 29th August.

(iii)   The specific homelessness function
Homeless persons can be assisted if they apply; thus there are two initial questions:

(a)   *What is 'an application'?* In *R v Chiltern DC, ex parte Roberts* (1991) 23 HLR 387, it was held that a letter from a third party may be enough provided it makes it clear what the issue is.

(b)   *Who may be an applicant?* In *Garlick v Oldham MBC* [1993] AC 509, the House of Lords laid down that a child *may* be an applicant *provided* it is (i) independent of its parents, and (ii) has the capacity to appreciate the meaning of an offer of accommodation and to make a decision on it. Thus there is no 'cut off' age such as 16. In the case of an applicant under disability, the rule is the person should either be able to make an application in person or be able to authorise another person to make it, and be able to comprehend and evaluate any offer of accommodation made.

Garlick v *Oldham MBC*
[1993] AC 509

The applicant, who was four years old, applied through his mother to the local housing authority for accommodation under Pt III of the Housing Act 1985, stating that he was in priority need under s. 59(1) of the Act. The authority refused to consider his application on the ground that it was a device to circumvent the provisions of the legislation. The High Court dismissed the applicant's request for judicial review, and the Court of Appeal dismissed his appeal. The House of Lords unanimously dismissed his further appeal, but left the doors open for more realistic 'under age' applications.

LORD GRIFFITHS: . . . Dependent children are not amongst those classified as in priority need. This is not surprising. Dependent children depend on their parents or those looking after them to decide where they are to live and the offer of accommodation can only sensibly be made to those in charge of them. There is no definition of a dependent child in the Act but the Homelessness Code of Guidance for Local Authorities, 3rd ed. (1991), to which local authorities must have regard for guidance (see section 71) suggests in paragraph 6.3 that authorities should normally include as dependent all children under 16 and all children aged 16 to 18 who are in, or about to begin, full-time education or training or who for other reasons are unable to support themselves and who live at home. This seems to me to be sensible guidance and likely to result in families being housed together until the children are reasonably mature. There will obviously be the case from time to time when a child leaves home under the age of 16 and ceases to be dependent on the parents or those with who he or she was living and such a child may be vulnerable and in priority need by virtue of section 59(1)(c): see *Kelly v Monklands District Council*, 1986 SLT 169. But however that may be, it cannot possibly be argued that a healthy four-year-old living with parents is other than a dependent child. Such a child is in my opinion owed no duty under this Act for it is the intention of the Act that the child's accommodation will be provided by the parents or those looking after him and it is to those people that the offer of accommodation must be made not to the dependent child.

I cannot accept the argument that extreme youth is a 'special reason' making the child vulnerable and thus giving it a priority need under section 59(1)(c). 'Old age' is mentioned as a cause of vulnerability but 'young age' is not. The reason of course is that already stated, Parliament has provided for dependent children by giving priority right to accommodation to their parents or those looking after them. Nor can I accept the argument that if a dependent child suffers from some disability it thereby acquires an independent priority right to accommodation. A healthy four-year-old is just as vulnerable as a disabled four-year-old from a housing point of view; neither is capable of looking after himself let alone deciding whether to accept an offer of accommodation. I am satisfied that section 59(1)(c) was not intended to confer any rights upon dependent children.

It is also to be observed that the Act imposes a duty on the authority to give written advice to the applicant and makes it a criminal offence for an applicant not to notify an authority of a change in his circumstances: see section 64 and 74. This is all part of a pattern that supports the view that the intention of this Act was to create a duty to offer accommodation to those homeless persons in priority need who can decide whether or not to accept the offer and that this does not include dependent children.

If a family has lost its right to priority treatment through intentional homelessness the parent cannot achieve the same result through the back door by an application in the name of a dependent child; if he could it would mean that the disqualification of intentional homelessness had no application to families with dependent children. If this had been the intention of Parliament it would surely have said so.

For these reasons I would dismiss the first two appeals. I wish however to point out that there are other provisions of our social welfare legislation that provide for the accommodation and care of children and of the duty of cooperation between authorities in the discharge of their duties. Section 20(1) of the Children Act 1989 provides:

> Every local authority shall provide accommodation for any child in need within their area who appears to them to require accommodation as a result of—(a) there being no person who has parental responsibility for him; (b) his being lost or having been abandoned; (c) the person who has been caring for him being prevented (whether or not permanently, and for whatever reason) from providing him with suitable accommodation or care. . . .

Once an application is made the 'legal machinery' provided under the following provisions of the 1996 Act obligates the receiving authority to make inquiries to deal with it and to decide how most appropriately to act.

Housing Act 1996

Application for assistance in case of homelessness or threatened homelessness

Application for assistance
183.—(1) The following provisions of this Part apply where a person applies to a local housing authority for accommodation, or for assistance in obtaining accommodation, and the authority have reason to believe that he is or may be homeless or threatened with homelessness.
    (2) In this Part—
      'applicant' means a person making such an application,
      'assistance under this Part' means the benefit of any function under the following
        provisions of this Part relating to accommodation or assistance in obtaining
        accommodation, and

'eligible for assistance' means not excluded from such assistance by section 185 (person from abroad not eligible for housing assistance) or section 186 (asylum seekers and their dependants).

(3)   Nothing in this section or the following provisions of this Part affects a person's entitlement to advice and information under section 179 (duty to provide advisory services).

Inquiry into cases of homelessness or threatened homelessness

184.—(1)   If the local housing authority have reason to believe that an applicant may be homeless or threatened with homelessness, they shall make such inquiries as are necessary to satisfy themselves—

(a)   whether he is eligible for assistance, and

(b)   if so, whether any duty, and if so what duty, is owed to him under the following provisions of this Part.

(2)   They may also make inquiries whether he has a local connection with the district of another local housing authority in England, Wales or Scotland.

(3)   On completing their inquiries the authority shall notify the applicant of their decision and, so far as any issue is decided against his interests, inform him of the reasons for their decision.

(4)   If the authority have notified or intend to notify another local housing authority under section 198 (referral of cases), they shall at the same time notify the applicant of that decision and inform him of the reasons for it.

(5)   A notice under subsection (3) or (4) shall also inform the applicant of his right to request a review of the decision and of the time within which such a request must be made (see section 202).

(6)   Notice required to be given to a person under this section shall be given in writing and, if not received by him, shall be treated as having been given to him if it is made available at the authority's office for a reasonable period for collection by him or on his behalf.

Notes

1.   The onus of making inquiries is on the authority not on the applicant; once told that an applicant is homeless, and having been given the source of that information, an authority cannot then refuse to make further inquiries and insist that the applicant furnish further confirmation of the facts (see *R* v *Woodspring DC, ex parte Walters* (1984) 16 HLR 73).

2.   Following *Lally* v *Kensington Royal Borough Council* [1980] *The Times*, 27 March, it is clear there is no need to make 'CID' type inquiries, but there is a need to act fairly and sympathetically, and to enable applicants to make a case out. Thus there may be a need to supply an interpreter when an applicant's first language is not English (see *R* v *Surrey Heath BC, ex parte Li* (1984) 16 HLR 79).

The authority must elicit all relevant facts, though the applicant should ensure that they know all that they might not otherwise be able to find out (see *R* v *Harrow London Borough Council, ex parte Holland* (1982) 4 HLR 108 and also *R* v *Wandsworth London Borough Council, ex parte Henderson and Hayes* (1986) 18 HLR 522).

Where an applicant's evidence is inconsistent, the inconsistency can be taken into account (*R* v *Hillingdon London Borough Council, ex parte Thomas* [1987] 19 HLR 196).

The authority are the judge of fact in inquiries and are entitled to decide which version of varying facts they wish to accept, provided it does not perversely fly in the face of all logic (*R* v *Dacorum BC, ex parte Taverner* (1988) 21 HLR 123).

A brief 10 minute interview is hardly likely to satisfy the law's requirements (see *R* v *Dacorum BC, ex parte Brown* (1989) 21 HLR 405). However, in conducting their inquiries an authority may accept hearsay advice if it is reasonable to do so, e.g., it is not obviously tittle-tattle. The authority are under no obligation to put any information received 'chapter-and-verse' to the applicant, though *they must give the applicant a fair chance to reply.* That means giving applicants the substance of allegations made against them (see *R* v *Southampton City Council, ex parte Ward* (1984) 14 HLR 89).

Matters should be put to the applicant even if received 'in confidence' (see *R* v *Poole BC, ex parte Cooper* (1995) 27 HLR 605).

Rubber stamping findings of another authority without giving an applicant a chance to explain his side is not a sufficient performance of the duty to make inquiries (see *R* v *South Herefordshire DC, ex parte Miles* (1983) 17 HLR 168).
3.   There is no clear obligation in the Act to operate a service 24 hours a day, seven days a week. However, attempts to withdraw 'out of hours' emergency cover have been blocked by court orders. In *R* v *Camden LBC, ex parte Gillan* [1988] *Independent*, 13 October, assistance from the authority's homeless persons unit was only available over a variable number of telephones, with no opportunity to meet an appropriate officer. The unit closed over weekends and was open on weekdays for half a day, so that only those who presented themselves first thing in the morning received a hearing. It was held that an authority are under a duty to take reasonable steps to hear and adjudicate upon homelessness applications. In a populous area what is 'reasonable' may amount to 24-hour cover, but each case depends on its facts. The cover provided in the present instance was clearly not reasonable.
4.   The legislation contains no timescales for decision taking, but the Code of Guidance indicates an initial assessment of the application should be made within 24 hours, and inquiries should be complete in 30 working days.

(C)   The legal concept of homelessness

Homelessness may be actual or threatened, but in both cases the core concept is that the applicant has, or will have, 'no accommodation'.

Housing Act 1996

Homelessness and threatened homelessness
175.—(1)   A person is homeless if he has no accommodation available for his occupation, in the United Kingdom or elsewhere, which he—
    (a)   is entitled to occupy by virtue of an interest in it or by virtue of an order of a court,
    (b)   has an express or implied licence to occupy, or

(c)   occupies as a residence by virtue of any enactment or rule of law giving him the right to remain in occupation or restricting the right of another person to recover possession.

(2)   A person is also homeless if he has accommodation but—

(a)   he cannot secure entry to it, or

(b)   it consists of a moveable structure, vehicle or vessel designed or adapted for human habitation and there is no place where he is entitled or permitted both to place it and to reside in it.

(3)   A person shall not be treated as having accommodation unless it is accommodation which it would be reasonable for him to continue to occupy.

(4)   A person is threatened with homelessness if it is likely that he will become homeless within 28 days.

Meaning of accommodation available for occupation

176.   Accommodation shall be regarded as available for a person's occupation only if it is available for occupation by him together with—

(a)   any other person who normally resides with him as a member of his family, or

(b)   any other person who might reasonably be expected to reside with him.

References in this Part to securing that accommodation is available for a person's occupation shall be construed accordingly.

Whether it is reasonable to continue to occupy accommodation

177.—(1)   It is not reasonable for a person to continue to occupy accommodation if it is probable that this will lead to domestic violence against him, or against—

(a)   a person who normally resides with him as a member of his family, or

(b)   any other person who might reasonably be expected to reside with him.

For this purpose 'domestic violence', in relation to a person, means violence from a person with whom he is associated, or threats of violence from such a person which are likely to be carried out.

(2)   In determining whether it would be, or would have been, reasonable for a person to continue to occupy accommodation, regard may be had to the general circumstances prevailing in relation to housing in the district of the local housing authority to whom he has applied for accommodation or for assistance in obtaining accommodation.

(3)   The Secretary of State may by order specify—

(a)   other circumstances in which it is to be regarded as reasonable or not reasonable for a person to continue to occupy accommodation, and

(b)   other matters to be taken into account or disregarded in determining whether it would be, or would have been, reasonable for a person to continue to occupy accommodation.

Meaning of associated person

178.—(1)   For the purposes of this Part, a person is associated with another person if—

(a)   they are or have been married to each other;

(b)   they are cohabitants or former cohabitants;

(c)   they live or lived in the same household;

(d)   they are relatives;

(e)   they have agreed to marry one another (whether or not that agreement has been terminated);

(f)   in relation to a child, each of them is a parent of the child or has, or has had, parental responsibility for the child.

(2)   If a child has been adopted or has been freed for adoption by virtue of any of the enactments mentioned in section 16(1) of the Adoption Act 1976, two persons are also associated with each other for the purposes of this Part if—

(a)   one is a natural parent of the child or a parent of such a natural parent, and

(b)   the other is the child or a person—

(i)   who has become a parent of the child by virtue of an adoption order or who has applied for an adoption order, or

(ii)   with whom the child has at any time been placed for adoption.

(3)   In this section—

'adoption order' has the meaning given by section 72(1) of the Adoption Act 1976;

'child' means a person under the age of 18 years;

'cohabitants' means a man and a woman who, although not married to each other, are living together as husband and wife, and 'former cohabitants' shall be construed accordingly;

'parental responsibility' has the same meaning as in the Children Act 1989; and 'relative', in relation to a person, means—

(a)   the father, mother, stepfather, stepmother, son, daughter, stepson, stepdaughter, grandmother, grandfather, grandson or granddaughter of that person or of that person's spouse or former spouse, or

(b)   the brother, sister, uncle, aunt, niece or nephew (whether of the full blood or of the half blood or by affinity) of that person or of that person's spouse or former spouse,

and includes, in relation to a person who is living or has lived with another person as husband and wife, a person who would fall within paragraph (a) or (b) if the parties were married to each other.

The issue of what it is to have 'no accommodation', while superficially straightforward, is on reflection potentially complex and has troubled the courts on many occasions since 1978. For example, although a mere licence can clearly count as 'accommodation' (see now s. 175(1)(b)), a wholly transient and insecure temporary abode may not realistically qualify. Accommodation may exist, and yet be wholly inadequate, or even a clear health risk. In the early years of the 1977 legislation, Shelter maintained a clear 'line' that the occupation of inadequate accommodation should not preclude a finding of homelessness. Given the state of much of the housing stock in the United Kingdom (discussed further in chapter 7), it is not surprising that this position was never officially adopted; but subsequent to the decision in *R v Hillingdon LBC, ex parte Puhlhofer* [1986] AC 484 (see below) there were legislative amendments providing for the requirement that to be 'accommodation' for Pt II purposes, it must be 'reasonable' for the applicant to have occupied the property in question. Of course, 'reasonableness' can entail not merely the condition of the property, but also the wide issue of whether the applicant can realistically be expected to carry on living in it. This may not be so, if he or she is under threat of violence or harassment in the area (if the applicant is under such a threat in the property itself, which can be viewed as 'domestic violence', s. 177(1) clearly indicates that it would not be reasonable to expect continued occupation).

Probably the first significant decision specifically on the 'accommodation' issue was *R* v *London Borough of Ealing, ex parte Sidhu* (although observations had been passed on the concept in earlier cases).

R v *London Borough of Ealing, ex parte Sidhu*
(1983) 2 HLR 45

HODGSON J: In this case the court is moved for judicial review in respect of the London Borough of Ealing's treatment of an application made by the applicant to the respondent local authority for accommodation under the Housing (Homeless Persons) Act 1977. The precise relief which will be granted can be decided at the end of my judgment.

The applicant is an Indian lady and she is married to Mr Sidhu. The recent history in respect of her housing problem can be stated reasonably briefly. If necessary it can be expanded from the evidence before me, and in particular from the affidavit of the applicant herself.

The applicant's marriage first ran into matrimonial difficulties as early as 1976. In 1979, because of her husband's drinking habits, the rent that they owed in respect of the Council accommodation which they occupied as tenants of the respondents ran into arrears. It was in the early part of 1980 that the applicant first learnt that her husband's arrears of rent were in the region of £240. He was the tenant, and he paid the rent, when it was paid. Because of the arrears a warning was given by the local authority. Keen to keep her home the applicant went out to work, and from then on he [sic] undertook to take over the payments of the rent, plus an amount of the arrears. She did her best but it was not good enough, and it was not good enough largely because she had perforce at times to trust her husband to make the payments, which he plainly, though unknown to her, did not do.

The matrimonial difficulties increased and violence was used by her husband to her, not only with fists but with sticks, shoes and other weapons. On 28 January, 1981 she was thrown out of the house after being assaulted by her husband. She instructed solicitors. However, shortly afterwards, though family intervention and because of promises by her husband, a reconciliation of sorts was effected.

In December 1980 the husband had been give a final warning by the local authority, and in March 1981 Mr and Mrs Sidhu, with their two young children, were evicted from their Council flat by order of the court. They both, having been evicted, applied to the local authority under the Housing (Homeless Person) Act 1977. On that application the local authority took less than 24 hours to decide that both husband and wife were intentionally homeless and to serve upon them the section 8 notice which is dated 31 March, 1981, the application having been made the previous day.

They were provided with temporary accommodation, and at the end of April 1981 they obtained accommodation in one room of a private house, for which they paid £17 per week rent. Not surprisingly, the circumstances in which they were living did not ameliorate the matrimonial difficulties. On 12 July her husband made a violent assault upon her and she had to leave the house. He came after her and persuaded her to return, but when she returned she was told that her husband had tried to get a knife, which he had been prevented from doing by the landlord's wife. The landlord's wife, not unnaturally, had already asked the family to find somewhere else to live.

On 14 July another violent assault was made upon her by her husband. As a result of that assault she left him, and she was given accommodation in which I may call colloquially a refuge for battered wives, more accurately a women's aid refuge.

That refuge is not in the London Borough of Ealing. It is, like all other refuges unhappily under extreme pressure. It is quite small, consisting of only eight bedrooms, three of which are tiny, two large and three medium size. Very frequently more than one family has to occupy the same room. The applicant was fortunate because she and her two little children were given a room of their own, and there she and her family have remained ever since.

On 21 July she returned to the room that they had previously been renting, with a police escort, to collect her belongings. When she went to collect her belongings she was told by the landlord's wife that her husband had been asked to leave, and on that occasion once again her husband was extremely abusive towards her.

On 19 August, accompanied I think I am right in saying by somebody from the refuge, she had an interview and applied for accommodation from the local authority, the respondents, under the Housing (Homeless Persons) Act 1977. She was seen by a Mrs or Miss Riding, an officer of the Homeless Families Unit of the respondent local authority. The interview was recorded thus: 'Mrs Sidhu has finally left her husband due to his violent behaviour. Now in Women's Aid. See other notes. Will help – has approached solicitor and social worker will contact us concerning this.' So it is quite clear that there was a reference then to the notes made on the previous occasion in March.

On 11 September, in the Brentford County Court, the County Court Judge made a non-molestation order and granted the applicant interim custody, care and control of the two children. A few days later the applicant heard that her husband had gone to India, and 21 September a copy of the court's order was sent to the respondent.

Mrs Sidhu had instructed solicitors, and thereafter there were some telephone conversations between her solicitors and the relevant department of the local authority. On 29 September, 1981, as a result presumably of a telephone conversation, the applicant's solicitors wrote to the local authority:

> We understand that the Authorities are not prepared to rehouse Mrs Sidhu and her two children, until a full custody order has been granted, and we would be obliged if you would kindly inform us if that is correct.

A week later the local authority replied, over the signature of Mrs Riding:

> It has been decided that Mrs Sidhu will not be considered for permanent rehousing until a full custody order has been granted. She did seek separation from her husband earlier this year but they were eventually reconciled. Mr and Mrs Sidhu were subsequently evicted from Council property for rent arrears and made intentionally homeless in March 1981. Mrs Sidhu will therefore be considered as a separate unit once legal proceedings has been completed.

From that letter it is clear that the local authority were not prepared even to contemplate doing their statutory duty under the Housing (Homeless Persons) Act 1977 until what they were pleased to call a full custody order had been granted.

In this court on behalf of the local authority some surprising, indeed in my judgment extremely bold, submissions have been made. The first is that the applicant and her two children are not homeless because they are being, as they have been for five months, accommodated by the charity of the Womens Aid organisation. It is suggested that Mrs Sidhu is not homeless because she cannot bring herself within the first sentence of Section 1(1) of the Act:

> A person is homeless for the purposes of this Act if he has no accommodation.

In my judgment that is a totally unjustified submission to make.

I am told that a County Court judge has made certain not very surprising remarks in this context. What I am told he said (and if he did not say it, it seems to me very good sense and I would be perfectly prepared to say it myself) was this.

> The Judge said it was important that refuges be seen as temporary crisis accommodation, and that women living in refuges were still homeless under the terms of the Act. If it was suggested that they were not homeless it would be necessary for voluntary organisations to issue immediate 28 days notice when women came in so that they would be under threat of homelessness. This would be totally undesirable and would simply add stress to stress. If living in crisis accommodation took women out of the 'homeless' category then the Act was being watered down and its protections would be removed from a whole class of persons that it was set up to help and for whom it was extremely important.

As I have said, I myself would be perfectly prepared to speak those words, and I adopt them without hesitation. Did I need further support for what I think is plain beyond a peradventure the correct construction of this Act, I find it in the speech of Lord Lowry in *Din* v *Wandsworth London Borough Council* (1981) 3 WLR 918. I think all I need read are two short sentences from Lord Lowry's speech at p. 933 F:

> I consider that to be homeless and to have found some temporary accommodation are not mutually inconsistent concepts. Nor does a person cease to be homeless merely by having a roof over his head or a lodging, however precarious.

. . .

Subsequently, the issue of the meaning of 'accommodation', in the context of defining homelessness, has frequently come before the courts. Perhaps the easiest way to appreciate the issue is to think of it of a 'ladder' of questions. For example:

  (a)   The first question is probably whether the premises can be seen as any kind of accommodation at all. This was, at root, the issue in *Sidhu* concerning the refuge, and this is also true in the cases of *R* v *Waveney District Council, ex parte Bowers* [1983] 1 QB 238 and *R* v *South Herefordshire DC, ex parte Miles* (1983) 17 HLR 82.

  In *Bowers*, the 'premises' consisted of a place in a Salvation Army hostel to which the applicant had to reapply each day with no guarantee of a place. The High Court (applying *Sidhu*) had no difficulty in overturning a local authority finding that he was not homeless (the authority did not appeal this point). In *Miles*, the 'premises' consisted of a hoppickers' hut, lacking all main services. At p. 92, Woolf J stated:

The accommodation in the hut in question was without any mains services and there were two rooms each measuring only 10 feet by 10 feet. According to the evidence, it was infested with rats. There was, however, a caravan nearby which did have services. The relevant committee of the respondent council were obviously concerned about the accommodation. I have little doubt that it was on the borderline of that which could be, in any circumstances, regarded as being capable of being suitable for human habitation. However, bearing in mind that that primary decision is for the Council, I have come to the conclusion that it would not be right for me to treat the accommodation as being of such a bad standard that any reasonable Council, having the information which was available to this Council, would have disregarded it for the purposes of the Act on March 10 1981. It follows, therefore, that the applicant is not entitled to have the second decision quashed. However, by April 8, 1981, the third child had been born and bearing in mind that there are now five members of the family to be housed in the hut, I have come to the conclusion, having regard to the evidence, that it was not reasonable of the Council to regard the hut as being any longer capable of being accommodation for that family now that it consisted of the mother and father, two children and the newly born baby. It was below the borderline for such a family.

(b)   Assuming that the 'premises' occupied are not so transient or lacking in basic amenities as to render any claim that they represent 'accommodation' untenable, the second question is probably the more general issue of the overall 'suitability' of the property for the applicant and (if relevant) his or her family. In *R* v *Westminster City Council, ex parte Ali* (1983) 11 HLR 83, Mr Ali had applied to Westminster for housing for himself, his wife and their five youngest children (aged one to 13). He was accepted as homeless at the time of his application, but Westminster decided that he had made himself intentionally homeless in leaving overcrowded bed-sit accommodation some months earlier. In effect they decided that it had been reasonable for Mr Ali and his family to continue living in the room, despite its overcrowding. In most respects, however, this is the same issue as whether the 'premises' had represented true 'accommodation' for Mr Ali and his family in the first place. The authority's decision was overturned in the High Court. McCullough J stated, at p. 92:

The Westminster City Council was under a statutory duty to ask itself whether it was satisfied that the accommodation at 19 Sale Place was available for Mr Ali and his family immediately before he gave it up at the end of 1981. It seems to me that either Mr Bailey never considered the question at all or he simply assumed that, because the family had been able to stay there in 1976–77 and from 1979–80, that they would be able to do so again. What Mr Ali gave up at the end of December 1981 was, on the evidence, no more than the right to share one room with another man. There was no evidence at all before the Westminster City Council that accommodation was available for him, his wife and their five children at 19 Sale Place.

I find, therefore, that no reasonable authority could, upon the material before it, have reasonably reached the conclusion that there was, as at the end of December 1981, accommodation available for this whole family at 19 Sale Place.

I think that Mr Bailey did, on the authority's behalf, consider the question of whether it would have been reasonable for the family to stay at that address, on the assumption that accommodation was there available. His thinking on the matter seems to have been as follows. 'They refused to go to the maisonette in 1977; therefore they preferred to stay in 19 Sale Place; therefore 19 Sale Place cannot have been unbearably bad to live in at that time; therefore it was reasonable for them to carry on living in 19 Sale Place in the year 1977'. So far, perhaps, so good, but then comes the error. 'Therefore it is reasonable from them to continue to live there now in 1981/82.'

That last step overlooks the increase in the number and the ages of the children. When Mr Ali refused to go and look at the maisonette he and his wife had a boy of seven, a girl of two and a four month old baby. That was the position when he decided that he would rather carry on living at 19 Sale Place until the local authority, as he hoped, offered him a house in the area in which he preferred to live.

At the end of 1981 there were children of twelve, seven, four, one and four months. By the time he applied in August 1982 they were nearly thirteen, nearly eight, five, two and one. Even if one starts from the premise that it was reasonable for husband, wife, seven year old, two year old and baby to live in one room, it does not follow that it was reasonable for husband, wife, twelve year old, seven year old, four year old, one year old and baby all to live in one room.

That anyone should regard it as reasonable that a family of that size should live in one room 10 ft x 12 ft in size, or thereabouts, is something which I find astonishing. However, the matter has to be seen in the light of s. 17(4) [of the 1977 legislation] which requires that reasonableness must take account of the general circumstances prevailing in relation to housing in the area. No evidence has been placed before me that accommodation in the area of the Westminster City Council is so desperately short that it is reasonable to accept overcrowding of this degree. In the absence of such evidence I am driven to the conclusion that this question could not properly have been determined against the applicant.

In 1983, the issue of 'accommodation' under (what was then) s. 1 of the Housing (Homeless Persons) Act 1977 was not explicitly linked to the general housing conditions of the area (unlike the equivalent issue in s. 17 concerning intentional homelessness). However, in practice the issue was always construed against the general background of area housing conditions, and the link is now explicitly made by s. 177(2) of the Housing Act 1996.

Clearly, serious overcrowding, or the 'premises' being seriously damp or otherwise 'unfit' or a health hazard, raises fundamental questions about whether the premises constitute 'accommodation' at all. Unfortunately, until 1986 (amendments introduced by s. 14(1), Housing and Planning Act 1986) there was no requirement that accommodation had to be 'reasonable'. In some cases, courts had 'fudged' the issue by stating that accommodation had (at least) to be 'appropriate' (see, for example, *R* v *Preseli DC, ex parte Fisher* (1984) 17 HLR 147, at p. 157). However, the issue was forced out into the open by the House of Lords judgment in the following case:

R v *Hillingdon LBC, ex parte Puhlhofer*
[1986] AC 484

LORD BRIGHTMAN: . . . I turn to a brief narrative of the facts. The applicants are Mr and Mrs Puhlhofer, to whom I will refer as the husband and the wife. The wife, then unmarried, applied to the London Borough of Hillingdon for assistance under the Act of 1977 in June 1983. She had a son born in April 1982 and was treated therefore as having a priority need. There was a dispute, irrelevant for present purposes, whether she was intentionally homeless. The local authority placed her in the Rosslyn Guest House, Harrow, used by the borough for homeless persons within their area. In July 1983 the husband, who was also homeless, applied to the borough for assistance. They introduced him, by way of advice and appropriate assistance, to the same guesthouse. In September 1983 the husband and the wife married. In April 1984 a child was born of the marriage. In May 1984 the husband and the wife applied jointly to the borough for assistance under the Act. At that time they and the two children were in occupation of one room at the guesthouse, on a bed-and-breakfast basis. The applicants claimed that this room was not accommodation which answered the statutory duty of the borough under the Homeless Persons Act. The housing officer disagreed. He formally notified the husband and the wife by letter dated 11 May 1984 that they were not homeless or threatened with homelessness 'because you have accommodation available for your occupation' at the guesthouse. The applicants were not satisfied with this answer and obtained leave to apply for judicial review of the local authority's decision. The relief sought by the applicants was an order of certiorari to quash the decision that they were neither homeless nor threatened with homelessness, and a declaration (so far as material) that 'the accommodation available to the applicants is such that they are homeless' within the meaning of the Homeless Persons Act.

The applicants were at the date of the application in occupation of one room at the guesthouse containing a double and a single bed, a baby's cradle, dressing table, pram and steriliser unit. There were no cooking or washing facilities in the room. There were three bathrooms in the guesthouse, the total capacity of the guest housing being 36 people or thereabouts. The applicants were in consequence compelled to eat out and to use a launderette for washing their own and the children's clothing. This expense absorbed most of their state benefit of £78 a week.

It is the submission of the applicants that a person does not have 'accommodation' within the meaning of the Act and is therefore 'homeless' if he occupies premises which either are not large enough to accommodate the family unit or lack the basic amenities of family life; such basic amenities should include not only sleeping facilities, but also cooking, washing and eating facilities. If the premises are deficient in any of these respects, they are not accommodation. The local authority have to take into account the size of the family, and whether the premises occupied are capable of being regarded as a 'home' for that family. Put shortly, 'accommodation' must provide the ordinary facilities of a residence. Therefore no local authority properly directing themselves could have formed the view that the room allotted to the applicants at the Rosslyn Guest House was 'accommodation' within the meaning of section 1, at least after the child of the marriage was born in April 1984, because it was then overcrowded in the statutory sense, and lacked both exclusive and communal facilities for cooking and clothes washing. So ran the argument for the applicants.

Before turning to the judgments of the Divisional Court and the Court of Appeal, it will be convenient to consider certain observations made in the Court of Appeal in *Parr v Wyre Borough Council* (1982) 2 HLR 71, which was decided on 3 February 1982. In that case a husband and wife, with five children, were desperate for accommodation. As a temporary expedient they acquired what was described as a motor caravanette, parked it on the promenade at Fleetwood, which was the husband's home town, and applied to the housing department for accommodation. The view taken by the housing officer was that they were not homeless because they had accommodation in keeping with their chosen mode of living. After some discussion, the housing department accepted that they were homeless and stated that they would make a suitable offer of accommodation. The offer turned out to be accommodation 200 miles away in Birmingham. It was held that the local authority could not on the facts of that case discharge their statutory duty in that manner. The importance of the case for present purposes is that observations were made in relation to the quality of the accommodation which a local authority is under a statutory duty to provide for homeless persons who qualify for accommodation, and those observations were fastened on by the trial judge in the instant case.

Lord Denning MR said, at p. 78

> It was agreed on all hands that the accommodation offered must be 'appropriate' accommodation. That means, of course, that the house – as a dwelling – must be appropriate for a family of this size. It must have enough rooms to house his wife and five children.

Eveleigh LJ spoke to the same effect, at pp. 79–80:

> I agree with my Lord that accommodation must be appropriate and whether or not it is appropriate will be a matter for the local authority to decide taking into consideration all the facts and circumstances of the case. This court may then review that decision if it comes to the conclusion that the local authority has approached the question of appropriateness upon a wrong basis.

Donaldson LJ added, at p. 82: 'both parties agreed that the word "appropriate" should be read into the Act.'

In the instant case the trial judge addressed himself first to the question whether the accommodation which the applicants were currently occupying was capable of being regarded as accommodation within section 1 of the Act. Not unnaturally, in the light of the observations of the Lords Justices in *Parr's* case, he translated this into the question 'whether – any reasonable authority could have come to the conclusion that it was appropriate.' He concluded:

> the accommodation in this case is so inappropriate . . . particularly in respect of overcrowding . . . that no reasonable local authority properly directing itself . . . could come to the conclusion that this particular accommodation was appropriate within section 1.

He accordingly quashed the decision of the local authority, and declared that the applicants were homeless persons in priority need of accommodation.

The local authority appealed, but before turning to the judgments in the Court of Appeal, I would like to put aside the Code of Guidance. I am in respectful agreement with Slade LJ (*ante*, p. 497F–G) that none of the provisions of the code give any assistance on the particular point at issue beyond that afforded by the Act itself.

Ackner LJ, who delivered the first judgment, rejected the proposition that accommodation within the meaning of section 1 of the Act must simply be 'appropriate' or 'reasonable,' *ante*, pp. 492G–493F:

> I am, however, of the opinion that to treat the word 'accommodation' as being totally unqualified does not give effect to the intention of Parliament as evinced by the statute considered as a whole . . . In my judgment the accommodation must be such that it is reasonable for the applicant and his family to continue to occupy it, having regard to the general circumstances prevailing in relation to housing in the area of the housing authority to whom he has applied. This qualification recognises:
> 1. that the standard of accommodation may be such that it is not reasonable for the

housing authority to regard it as being capable of being accommodation for the applicant and his family; and 2. that the standard cannot be lower or higher than that required by section 17 of the Act to justify an applicant being entitled to leave that accommodation without thereby becoming 'intentionally' homeless.

He concluded, *ante*, pp. 493H–494A that there was material upon which the borough were entitled to conclude, having regard to housing in their area, that it was reasonable for the Puhlhofers to continue to live in the accommodation at the guesthouse.

With great respect to Ackner LJ, I do not think that it was correct to construe 'accommodation' in section 1 by reference to section 17. The relevant subsections of section 17 read as follows:

(1) Subject to subsection (3) below, for the purposes of this Act a person becomes homeless intentionally if he deliberately does or fails to do anything in consequence of which he ceases to occupy accommodation which is available for his occupation and which it would have been reasonable for him to continue to occupy . . . (4) Regard may be had, in determining for the purposes of subsections (1) and (2) above whether it would have been reasonable for a person to continue to occupy accommodation, to the general circumstances prevailing in relation to housing in the area of the housing authority to whom he applied for accommodation or for assistance in obtaining accommodation.

The purpose of subsection (1) is simply to define the expression 'becomes homeless intentionally.' The subsection starts by making assumption that the homeless person has been in occupation of accommodation which is available for occupation both by him and (per section 16) by others reasonably expected to reside with him. It then assumes that the homeless person ceased to occupy that accommodation. Lastly, it assumes that it would have been reasonable for him to have continued to occupy that accommodation, instead of ceasing to do so. In such circumstances he 'becomes homeless intentionally.' For example, the rent of the accommodation which the homeless person has ceased to occupy may have become too great for that person to afford; in such a case the local authority may take the view that it was reasonable for him to cease to occupy it; therefore, though homeless, he is not homeless intentionally. Or the local authority may take the view that the new rent was within his means, so that by ceasing to occupy he made himself homeless intentionally. Or the accommodation which he occupied may have been up a flight of stairs, which was no longer within the physical capacity of the homeless person; so the local authority may consider that it was reasonable for him to have ceased to occupy it; he is, therefore, homeless but not intentionally. That subsection has nothing whatever to do with the inherent quality of the accommodation and does not assist to answer the question whether a person is homeless because he has no 'accommodation' properly so called. Similarly, subsection (4) has no relevance for present purposes. It simply provides a gloss on the words in subsection (1), 'which it would have been reasonable for him to continue to occupy.' In deciding whether or not it was reasonable for the homeless person to walk out of his existing accommodation, the local authority may have regard to the general circumstances prevailing in relation to housing in the locality. An example of the possible application of this subsection was given by Lord Fraser of Tullybelton in *Din (Taj)* v *Wandsworth London Borough Council* [1983] 1 AC 657, 670H–671A.

Slade LJ in his judgment also rejected the implication of 'appropriate' in section 1 of the Act. He said, *ante*, p. 495F–G:

If the legislature, in using the word 'accommodation' in that section, had intended to confine its meaning to appropriate accommodation, or to accommodation which it was reasonable for the occupant to continue to occupy, I think it would surely have said so.

Glidewell LJ added, *ante*, p. 500C–D:

If a person is occupying what would normally be regarded as accommodation (as the room occupied by [the Puhlhofers] certainly would) it is in my judgment still accommodation within section 1 however crowded or lacking in facilities it may be, and thus such a person is not 'homeless' within the Act of 1977.

He concluded, *ante*, p. 502E that there was information before the council on which they could properly reach the decision that the appellants were not homeless.

My Lords, I have summarised the judgments in the Court of Appeal with brevity but I hope without discourtesy, for the purpose of indicating the diversity of opinion expressed.

There are several features of the Act which in my respectful opinion have to be borne in mind. First, although the Act bears the word 'Housing' it its short title, it is not an Act which imposes any duty upon a local authority to house the homeless. As the long title indicates, its object is to make 'further provision as to the functions of local authorities with respect to persons who are homeless or threatened with homelessness; . . .' It is an Act to assist persons who are homeless, not an Act to provide them with homes. It is an Act which came into operation in England and Wales only four months, and in Scotland only seven months, after it was passed (section 21); not sufficient time to enable a local authority to achieve any dramatic increase in their available housing stock. It is intended to provide for the homeless a lifeline of last resort; not to enable them to make inroads into the local authority's waiting list of applicants for housing. Some inroads there probably are bound to be, but in the end the local authority will have to balance the priority needs of the homeless on the one hand, and the legitimate aspirations of those on their housing waiting list on the other hand.

In this situation, Parliament plainly, and wisely, placed no qualifying adjective before the word 'accommodation' in section 1 or section 4 of the Act, and none is to be implied. The word 'appropriate' or 'reasonable' is not to be imported. Nor is accommodation not accommodation because it might in certain circumstances be unfit for habitation for the purposes of Part II of the Housing Act 1957 or might involve overcrowding within the meaning of Part IV. Those particular statutory criteria are not to be imported into the Homeless Persons Act for any purpose. What is properly to be regarded as accommodation is a question of fact to be decided by the local authority. There are no rules. Clearly some places in which a person might choose or be constrained to live could not properly be regarded as accommodation at all; it would be a misuse of language to describe Diogenes as having occupied accommodation within the meaning of the Act. What the local authority have to consider, in reaching a decision whether a person is homeless for the purposes of the Act, is whether he has what can properly be described as accommodation within the ordinary meaning of that word in the English language.

I do not, however, accept that overcrowding is a factor to be disregarded, as Glidewell LJ (*ante* p. 500C–D) apparently thought. I agree that the statutory definition of overcrowding has no relevance. But accommodation must, by definition, be capable of accommodating. If, therefore, a place is properly capable of being regarded as accommodation from an objective standpoint, but is so small a space that it is incapable of accommodating the applicant together with other persons who normally reside with him as members of his family, then on the facts of such a case the applicant would be homeless because he would have no accommodation in any relevant sense.

In the instant case the bona fides of the borough is not in dispute. On the facts in evidence, it is in my opinion plain that the council were entitled to find that the applicants were not homeless for the purposes of the Homeless Persons Act because they had accommodation within the ordinary meaning of that expression.

. . .

The legislative amendments introduced to 'draw' some of the 'sting' of *Puhlhofer* are now to be found in s. 175(3) of the Housing Act 1996, providing that a person is only to be 'treated' as having accommodation of 'premises' which it would be 'reasonable' to expect him to continue to occupy. This reinforces the direction of cases like *Ali* (above), although, of course, it does not state, simply, that sub-standard accommodation does not count, and 'reasonableness' has to be judged in the light of all the circumstances, including family life, health issues, the ages of (any) children and local housing conditions in general (see *R v Medina BC, ex parte Dee* (1992) 24 HLR 562 and *R v Kensington and Chelsea RBC, ex parte Ben-El-Mabrouk* (1995) 27 HLR 564).

(c) A third question has come into focus since the '*Puhlhofer*' amendments: to what extent does the 'reasonableness' of continued occupation in premises depend on factors other than the physical condition and size of the premises themselves? For example, to what extent is the issue of harassment and the risk of violence from current or ex-partners relevant? The 1977 Act provided that a person was to be regarded as homeless if any attempt to occupy accommodation to which he or she had access would be likely to lead to violence or threats of violence from some other person residing in it. However, the scope of the law was widened considerably by the incorporation of a specific 'reasonableness' test, as is demonstrated clearly by the Court of Appeal decision in the next case:

R v Kensington and Chelsea RLBC, ex parte Hammell
[1989] 1 QB 518

PARKER LJ: On 12 April 1988 the appellant ('the applicant'), a divorced woman with custody of the three children of her former marriage, two boys aged 12 and 9 and a girl aged 7, applied in person to the respondent council for accommodation. She was seen by a Mr Ashton. Put it in its shortest form, the basis of her application was that, although she had a tenancy of a council house or flat in Alloa, Scotland, provided by the Clackmannan District council, she had, in January 1988, been forced to flee therefrom due to violence and harassment on the part of her ex-husband and others instigated by him. He was living with a woman who had at least one child, only a matter of some 50 yards away. Since coming to London in January, the applicant had been staying with her sister in a one-bedroomed flat in the council's area, but her sister had, not surprisingly, had enough of sharing a small flat with her and her three children and required her to leave.

Not unnaturally, the account that she gave to Mr Ashton resulted in him having reason to believe that she might (1) be homeless or threatened with homelessness and (2) have a priority need within the meaning of sections 58 (as amended by section 14 of the Housing and Planning Act 1986 and 59 of the Housing Act 1985).

The consequences of Mr Ashton forming the view that he had reason to believe as aforesaid are set out in section 62 and 63 of the Act of 1985, which provide:

62(1)   If a person (an 'applicant') applies to a local housing authority for accommodation, or for assistance in obtaining accommodation, and the authority have reason to believe that he may be homeless or threatened with homelessness, they shall make such inquiries as are necessary to satisfy themselves as to whether he is homeless or threatened with homelessness. (2) If they are so satisfied, they shall make any further inquiries necessary to satisfy themselves as to—(a) whether he has a priority need, and (b) whether he became homeless or threatened with homelessness intentionally; and if they think fit they may also make inquiries as to whether he has a local connection with the district of another local housing authority in England, Wales or Scotland.

63(1)   If the local housing authority have reason to believe that an applicant may be homeless and have a priority need, they shall secure that accommodation is made available for his occupation pending a decision as a result of their inquiries under section 62. (2) This duty arises irrespective of any local connection which the applicant may have with the district of another local housing authority.

The council had, therefore, first, a duty under section 62 to make such inquiries as were necessary to enable them to satisfy themselves as to whether the applicant was homeless or threatened with homelessness and, secondly, a duty under section 63 to secure that accommodation was made available to her and her children pending a decision as a result of the necessary inquiries under section 62.

The council did make some inquiries on the following day, 13 April, to which I shall revert hereafter, but later that day they issued a written notice under, or purporting to be under, section 64 of the Act of 1985. That section, so far as immediately material, provides:

(1)   On completing their inquiries under section 62, the local housing authority shall notify the applicant of their decision on the question whether he is homeless or threatened with homelessness. (2)   If they notify him that their decision is that he is homeless or threatened with homelessness, they shall at the same time notify him of their decision on the question whether he has a priority need . . . (4)   If the local housing authority notify the applicant— (a) that they are not satisfied that he is homeless or threatened with homelessness . . . they shall at the same time notify him of their reasons.

The notice that was given was in these terms: [His Lordship then considered the issue of the court's jurisdiction and powers. He continued:]

With those matters in mind, it is now necessary to examine in some detail the events that occurred on 12 and 13 April and the consequences of such events. First, however, I refer to section 58 of the Act of 1985. So far as relevant, section 58 reads:

(1)   A person is homeless if he has no accommodation in England, Wales or Scotland. (2)   A person shall be treated as having no accommodation if there is no accommodation which he, together with any other person who normally resides with him as a member of his family or in circumstances in which it is reasonable for

that person to reside with him—(a) is entitled to occupy by virtue of an interest in it or by virtue of an order of a court . . . (3) A person is also homeless if he has accommodation but— . . . (b) it is probable that occupation of it will lead to violence from some other person residing in it or to threats of violence from some other person residing in it and likely to carry out the threats . . .

To that section there were added in 1986, by section 14 of the Housing and Planning Act of that year, the following subsections:

(2A) A person shall not be treated as having accommodation unless it is accommodation which it would be reasonable for him to continue to occupy. (2B) Regard may be had, in determining whether it would be reasonable for a person to continue to occupy accommodation, to the general circumstances prevailing in relation to housing in the district of the local housing authority to whom he has applied for accommodation or for assistance in obtaining accommodation.

In the present instance, the duty of the council, it being plain that there was accommodation that the applicant and her children were entitled to occupy, was (1) to make inquiries necessary to satisfy themselves that 24, Menteith Court, was accommodation that it would be reasonable for the applicant to continue to occupy and (2) to house her and her children until they had completed such inquiries and so decided. It is to be noted that the section requires a positive decision to be made by the council that the accommodation is accommodation that it would be reasonable for the applicant to continue to occupy.

I go now to the council's documents to see in more detail what happened. The formal form of application signed by the applicant is followed by internal notes by the council's officers. The form reveals her present address, which is her sister's address. It reveals the names and dates of birth of her three children. It reveals the name of her tenanted property in Scotland, 24 Menteith Court, and her previous address, which had been the matrimonial home that had had to be sold during the course of the proceedings leading to the divorce as a result of which sale she had been granted a tenancy of 24, Menteith Court. There is a page that refers to medical details, but I find nothing on that of significance.

I come now to the notes of what happened when the applicant went for interview and thereafter. The notes relating to the day on which she went for interview are headed with the date, 12 April, and are in these terms:

Is at present living with sister at Adair Tower for 10 weeks – she is now asking her to leave. She has got a council tenancy in Alloa but has left there because of violence and harassment from ex-husband. [The applicant] separated from her husband and also rehoused by Alloa. Unfortunately he has now moved in with someone else opposite where [the applicant] lives. Her ex-husband not only harasses her himself [but sends] friends around to do the same. She has not got a telephone and cannot raise the alarm when he comes around. When she came to England she went to S.H.A.C. [Shelter Housing Action Centre] and they advised her to go to Hammersmith and Fulham or Royal Borough of Kensington and Chelsea and seek N.M.S. transfer.

(N.M.S. refers to a National Mobility Scheme, which is of no statutory force but which is operated by many of the councils in England, Wales and Scotland, enabling council tenants for various reasons to be transferred from one area to another.) The notes continue, setting out the name of the applicant's solicitor in Alloa and reporting the facts that she had told Mr Ashton that she had been advised by her solicitor that in order to obtain an injunction she would need a witness and that she had apparently gone to the Hammersmith and Fulham London Borough Council, who had suggested the emergency National Mobility Scheme and that she should not give up the tenancy but should go to Scotland to fill up the forms. She in fact went to Scotland for the day pursuant to that advice, filled in the forms and then returned. The note continues:

Came back and saw Hammersmith and Fulham and they said no connection (N.M.S. for them suggested Royal Borough of Kensington and Chelsea) as staying there. Case here checked. Nothing had come to us. Discovered Clackmannan District [Council] had lost papers. Served notice.

That requires a word of explanation. On her arrival in this country on 26 January, the applicant very sensibly went to the Shelter Housing Action Centre. They advised her immediately to go to Scotland and apply for a transfer under the National Mobility Scheme. She did so. Having done so, she lodged her papers with them and returned to London. That was a day trip that took place on 28 January. Thereafter, whilst waiting for a communication, nothing occurred until on 31 March she received a notice of abandonment, addressed to her sister's flat relating to the tenancy at 24, Menteith Court. That no doubt surprised her. She again sought assistance from the Housing Action Centre. They communicated with Clackmannan District Council and explained to them that they must have had the application or they would not have known that the proper place to find the applicant was at her sister's address, whereupon the council suspended the operation of the abandonment notice.

There is recorded at the bottom of the first page of these notes the following by Mr Ashton:

Spoke to Sue [Lucking] about case. She said violence was from outside the home and she considered it reasonable for her to return and seek legal assistance to protect her safety and her interests.

That concludes the notes of 12 April, and it is not surprising that, on the basis of what he there recorded, Mr Ashton concluded that there was reason to believe that the applicant might be homeless and have a priority need. Indeed, had he not so concluded, the decision would, as it seems to me, have been wholly irrational or *Wednesbury* unreasonable (*Associated Provincial Picture Houses Ltd* v *Wednesbury Corporation* [1948] 1 KB 223), but it is accepted that that conclusion was reached.

Thereupon, it became the council's duty to make the inquiries and to provide accommodation.

The position is exactly the same as was referred to by Sir David Cairns in *De Falco* v *Crawley Borough Council* [1980] QB 460, 483:

Once a housing authority have reason to believe that an applicant for housing accommodation may be homeless and may have a priority need they are obliged, if they consider that he may be intentionally homeless, to secure accommodation for him while they make inquiries about the matter: section 3(4) of the Housing (Homeless Persons) Act 1977. They must not thereafter deprive him of accommodation on the ground of intentional homelessness unless (a) they are satisfied that he is intentionally homeless (section 4(2)(b)); and (b) he has had such time as they consider will give him a reasonable opportunity of finding accommodation for himself: section 4(3)(b).

That deals with a different problem, because it was in that case intentional homelessness that arose, but the principle there stated is clearly right: once the conclusion has been reached that imposes the duty to make the inquiries and to procure accommodation, the applicant cannot be deprived of that right unless and until the inquiries have been made and the appropriate decision has been reached.

On 12 April, the notes continue as follows:

> Rang Clackmannan District Council. Spoke to Mr McAndrew, estate office. He confirmed property was still available to her. They had cancelled abandonment procedure after receiving letter from [S.]H.A.C. They were investigating problems with harassment and then they will decide to put through a N.M.S. Asked if they were aware of any damage caused by ex-husband or anyone else. He said 'no'. Rang solicitor Mr Adam of I. Allan Grant & Co. [Alloa]. He said he hadn't seen Mrs Hammell for over six months (at least). He knew she had problems in the past with her ex-husband and there was an injunction in 1986–87. He did not have to go back to courts at any time because of any breach by her ex-husband. He did confirm that injunction in Scotland did need witness before they can proceed he also added that he thought she had come down to England earlier than 10 weeks ago. When I told him that we were likely to say she was not homeless, he replied 'I am not surprised, but I cannot lie.' Spoke to Ian Mitchell – N.M.S. cannot help family units. No point in nominating . . . Section 64 prepared. Not homeless. Violence is from outside the home and it is Sue's opinion it will be reasonable.

There somewhat surprisingly, the notes end.

There is, in addition to the notes that I have already read, a note signed by the same person who signed the notice in the following terms:

> Section 64 issued. No duty – not homeless; violence occurs outside home. I appreciate the situation will be difficult for her but would suggest that she takes legal advice regarding non-molestation order if necessary with power of arrest. Also she should approach Alloa council regarding possibility of urgent management transfer. She also be offered travel warrant.

The notice itself can be attacked on a number of grounds. In the first place, the reason given was on its face bad in law. It would have been good in law until the enactment of section 58(2A) of the Act of 1985 by section 14 of the Act of 1986, but the result of that was that before the council could determine that the applicant was not homeless they had to reach a positive decision that it would be reasonable for her and her children to continue to occupy 24, Menteith Court.

Secondly, it can be attacked because there was material to show that the background reason was that the violence was outside the home and therefore did not matter. That, again, would no doubt have been a sufficient reason had it not been for the enactment of section 58(2A), because under section 58 there is provision that a person is homeless if he has accommodation but it is probable that occupation of it will lead to violence from some other person residing in it. Since, however, it is now the position that the test is reasonableness of occupation, it cannot be right in law to suggest, as the council appear to believe, that violence outside the home is not at least a very important factor going to the question of whether it is reasonable to occupy. There used to be – and, indeed, may still be – amongst the many complications of the criminal law an offence known as 'watching and besetting,' which is something quite sufficient to render life intolerable to somebody, albeit nothing takes place within the premises themselves.

Thirdly, the notice can be attacked on the ground that the real reason, albeit a bad one, was that the violence was outside the home, not the reason stated.

. . .

The Court of Appeal decided that the applicant had made out a strong *prima facie* case for judicial review of the authority's decision because the authority appeared to have come to the erroneous conclusion that violence outside the home was irrelevant. (The issues are discussed further in *R* v *Broxbourne DC, ex parte Willmoth* (1989) 22 HLR 118.)

The Housing Act 1996 further clarifies matters by providing specifically (in s. 177(1)) that it is *not* reasonable to expect continued occupation of accommodation if it is probable that this would lead to 'domestic violence'. This is further defined so as to encompass violence or threats of violence to the applicant or others residing with him or her (as members of his or her family or otherwise) by 'associated' persons. The important concept of 'associated person' (see further discussion in chapter 9) extends (via s. 178) to current or ex-partners (married or unmarried), to relatives and to anyone who lives, or has lived, with the applicant in the same household.

(d)   The final question is, probably, the most difficult. Can something be described as 'accommodation' if it is insecure, so that the applicant lives in permanent fear of being evicted from it? It *is* clear that once possession proceedings have begun (whether the applicant occupies as tenant or licensee), and it is clear that there is no defence to the claim for possession it is not reasonable to expect them to 'hang on to the bitter end' (see *R* v *Portsmouth City Council, ex parte Knight* (1984) 10 HLR 115 and *R* v *Surrey Heath DC, ex parte Li* (1984) 16 HLR 79). However, until 1996 the wider question – of whether the occupation of highly insecure, or 'unsettled', accommodation might allow the occupant to be treated as homeless – was unresolved. The issue was complicated by the fact that there was some judicial authority in support of the view that to amount to 'accommodation' breaking the chain of causation from an earlier instance of intentional homelessness, the later accommodation had to be sufficiently secure to be 'settled' (see later in this chapter and decisions such as *Lambert* v *Ealing BC* [1982] 1 WLR 550). Although this is a distinct point, it is sufficiently close to the core 'accommodation' issue to suggest that the same result could follow there also. Given that most private sector accommodation is, since the Housing Act 1988 (see chapters 2 and 3) highly insecure, guaranteeing at most short, fixed-term occupation rights (via an assured shorthold), and might therefore be seen as not representing a 'settled' home, the implication of any such result for local authorities would be serious. However, in the following House of Lords decision it was held that there was *no* absolute requirement that, to amount to 'accommodation', premises had to be occupied as a 'settled' home.

R v *Brent LBC, ex parte Awua*
[1996] 1 AC 55

LORD HOFFMANN: . . . Until certain amendments introduced by the Housing and Planning Act 1986, the Housing Act 1985 contained no definition of 'accommodation.' Its undefined meaning in the corresponding provision of the Housing (Homeless Persons) Act 1977, which was replaced by Part III of the Act of 1985, was considered by this House in *Reg.* v *Hillingdon London Borough Council, Ex parte Puhlhofer* [1986] AC 484. Lord Brightman, with whom all the rest of their Lordships agreed, said that it was impossible to imply that the accommodation should be 'appropriate or have any quality except that of being fairly described as accommodation'. As an example of shelter which would have failed this test, he instanced Diogenes' tub. The modern equivalent would be the night shelter in *Reg.* v *Waveney District Council, Ex parte Bowers* [1983] QB 238 in which the applicant could have a bed if one was available but had to walk the streets of Lowestoft by day.

Ex parte Puhlhofer was concerned with the physical quality of the accommodation rather than the period of time for which it would be available. It seems to me highly improbable, however, that, having rejected any implication as to physical suitability, your Lordships' House would have accepted the implication of a requirement that the accommodation must in some sense be settled. The Puhlhofers and their two children were living in a single small bedroom in a bed-and-breakfast guest house pending the availability of a two-bedroom flat. No one could have described their accommodation as settled. The Act deals with precariousness of tenure by the concept of being 'threatened with homelessness,' which is defined in section 58(4) as meaning that it is likely that one will become homeless within 28 days. This does not fit very easily with an implication that a person whose tenure is less precarious can be regarded as not merely threatened with homelessness but actually homeless.

The consequence of the decision in *Ex parte Puhlhofer* was that a person accommodated in conditions so intolerable that it would not be reasonable for him to continue to occupy that accommodation was not homeless although, if he actually left, he would not thereby become intentionally homeless. This produced the inconvenient result that persons living in such conditions had to put themselves on the street before they could activate the local authority's duty to provide them with accommodation. To remedy this difficulty, the 1986 amendments (by section 14(1) and (2)) introduced a definition of 'accommodation' in section 58(2A) of the Act of 1985: 'A person shall not be treated as having accommodation unless it is accommodation which it would be reasonable for him to continue to occupy.' Guidance on the quality of accommodation which a local housing authority is entitled to treat as reasonable for a person to continue to occupy is provided by section 58(2B) (as added by the Act of 1986):

> Regard may be had, in determining whether it would be reasonable for a person to continue to occupy accommodation, to the general circumstances prevailing in relation to housing in the district of the local housing authority to whom he has applied for accommodation or for assistance in obtaining accommodation.

It follows that a local authority is entitled to regard a person as having accommodation (and therefore as not being homeless) if he has accommodation which, having regard to the matters mentioned in subsection (2B), it can reasonably consider that it would be reasonable for him to continue to occupy. This produces symmetry between the key concept of homelessness in section 58(1) and intentional homelessness in section 60(1). If the accommodation is so bad that leaving for that reason would not make one intentionally homeless, then one is in law already homeless. But there is nothing in the Act to say that a local authority cannot take the view that a person can reasonably be expected to continue to occupy accommodation which is temporary. If, notwithstanding that the accommodation is physically suitable, the occupier's tenure is so precarious that he is likely to have to leave within 28 days, then he will be 'threatened with homelessness' within section 58(4). But I find it hard to imagine circumstances in which a person who is not threatened with homelessness cannot reasonably be expected to continue to occupy his accommodation simply because it is temporary.

On the other hand, the extent to which the accommodation is physically suitable, so that it would be reasonable for a person to continue to occupy it, must be related to the time for which he has been there and is expected to stay. A local housing authority could take the view that a family like the Puhlhofers, put into a single cramped and squalid bedroom, can be expected to make do for a temporary period. On the other hand, there will come a time at which it is no longer reasonable to expect them to continue to occupy such accommodation. At this point they come back within the definition of homeless in section 58(1).

I would therefore reject the submission of Mr Roger Henderson that 'accommodation' in section 58 and section 60 must be construed as 'a settled home'. There is absolutely no warrant in the language of the statute or the decision of this House in *Ex parte Puhlhofer* for implying such a concept. Yet Sir Louis Blom-Cooper and the Court of Appeal thought that the authorities required it. Where did such an idea come from?

The answer is that it comes from an altogether different context. In *Dyson v Kerrier District Council* [1980] 1 WLR 1205 Miss Fiona Dyson gave up her flat in Huntingdon and went to live in Cornwall. But the only accommodation which she had arranged for herself was a three-month winter let of a cottage in Helston. She knew that the tenancy was not protected and that she would have to leave. When she was finally evicted, she applied to the local council for accommodation on the ground that she was now homeless. The council said that she was intentionally homeless because she had given up the Huntingdon flat knowing that after the expiry of the winter let she would have nowhere to live. Miss Dyson's argument was that in applying the predecessor of section 60(1) (section 17(1) of the Act of 1977) one was concerned only with the accommodation one had been occupying at the time when one became homeless. This was the cottage in Cornwall and it was not reasonable to expect her to continue to occupy that accommodation because the court had ordered her to leave it. Brightman LJ, at p. 1214, described this as a formidable argument on the literal wording of the statute. But the Court of Appeal held that such a construction would enable people to jump the housing queues by making themselves intentionally homeless at one remove. They would only have to move into temporary accommodation and wait until evicted. The court therefore held that one was not confined to asking whether it would have been reasonable to continue to occupy the cottage in Cornwall. If it would have been reasonable to continue to occupy the flat in Huntingdon and there was a causal link between deliberately leaving that flat and her subsequent homelessness in Cornwall, then she was intentionally homeless.

What constitutes such a causal link? In *Din (Taj) v Wandsworth London Borough Council* [1983] 1 AC 657 Lord Wilberforce referred with approval to the analysis of Ackner LJ in the Court of Appeal (unreported), 23 June 1981; Court of Appeal (Civil Division) Transcript No. 372 of 1981. He summarised it, at p. 668, by saying that a disqualification on the grounds of having made oneself intentionally homeless (such as attached to Miss Dyson when she left Huntingdon) was not displaced by obtaining temporary accommodation, Ackner LJ had said (in a passage later cited by the Court of Appeal in *Lambert v Ealing Borough Council* [1982] 1 WLR 550, 557):

> To remove his self-imposed disqualification, he must therefore have achieved what can be loosely described as a 'settled residence,' as opposed to what from the outset is known (as in *Dyson's* case [1980] 1 WLR 1205) to be only temporary accommodation. What amounts to 'a settled residence' is a question of fact and degree depending upon the circumstances of each individual case.

The distinction between a settled residence and temporary accommodation is thus being used to identify what will break the causal link between departure from accommodation which it would have been reasonable to continue to occupy and homelessness separated from that departure by a period or periods of accommodation elsewhere. This jurisprudence is well-established (it was approved by this House in Din's case) and nothing I have said is intended to cast any doubt upon it, although I would wish to reserve the question of whether the occupation of a settled residence is the sole and exclusive method by which the causal link can be broken. It is the importation of the distinction between settled and temporary accommodation into other questions arising under Part III of the Act which seems to me unwarranted.

Thus there has occasionally been a tendency to treat *Dyson's* case as entailing that Miss Dyson became homeless when she left Huntingdon and remained homeless while living in her winter let in Cornwall. By this means, the notion of settled accommodation is introduced into the concept of homelessness. I cannot however accept that a lady spending Christmas in a cottage in Cornwall which she has the right to occupy for another three months (and therefore not threatened with homelessness within the meaning of section 58(4)) should somehow be deemed to be homeless. And of course *Dyson's* case implies no such thing. It decides only that her homelessness after eviction from the cottage in Cornwall is intentional because it was caused by her decision to leave the flat in Huntingdon. Some support for a contrary view can be found in the speech of Lord Lowry in *Din's* case but this opinion was not shared by the other members of the House, who analysed the case solely in terms of causation. What persists until the causal link is broken is the intentionality, not the homelessness.

I would therefore hold that 'accommodation' in section 58(1) and section 60(1) means a place which can fairly be described as accommodation (*Reg. v Hillingdon London Borough Council, Ex parte Puhlhofer* [1986] AC 484) and which it would be reasonable, having regard to the general housing conditions in the local housing authority's district, for the person in question to continue to occupy (section 58(2A) and (2B)). There is no additional requirement that it should be settled or permanent.

Notes

1. 'Accommodation' means 'a place which can fairly be described as accommodation' (see *R v Brent LBC, ex parte Awua* [1996] 1 AC 55). But to be 'available' the accommodation must be available not only to the applicant but also to all those who normally reside with him or her as a family member, or who might reasonably be expected to. It is for the authority to decide what is 'reasonable' in this context. A mere *desire* to live together may not be enough (see *R v Barking LBC, ex parte Okuneye* (1995) 28 HLR 174). Similarly, authorities must consider the risk of violence a person may run in living in a particular house: that may be sufficient to amount to a 'no accommodation' situation. Everything will, however, turn on the facts of individual cases, though authorities should investigate the issue (see *R v Broxbourne DC, ex parte Willmoth* (1989) 22 HLR 118).

2. A mere offer of a room is *not* in itself 'accommodation'. Thus in *R v Kensington & Chelsea RBC, ex parte Minton* (1988) 20 HLR 648, Mrs Minton was a live-in housekeeper who resigned and left the house. She applied as a homeless person, and the local authority contacted her former employer who indicated willingness to take her back. The authority considered that it was reasonable for her to return to the former residence and concluded that she

was not homeless. In court, however, it was held that she had *no accommodation*, as all she possessed was a mere offer of accommodation which did not amount to accommodation for the purposes of the Act.

Questions
1. What sort of issues does an authority need to address in determining whether a person has 'no accommodation'? Are they purely physical issues, or are legal issues such as the nature of occupation also relevant?
2. Consider also the following circumstances:

(a)   Does a woman living in a refuge for victims of domestic violence have 'accommodation'; and what about a person who sleeps each night in a 'night shelter'?

(b)   What is the homelessness status of a family of five living in what can only be described as a shack in the middle of a field; or of a family whose home has been completely vandalised; or of a person who is living with a friend on a 'crash pad' basis and sleeping on that friend's floor on a 'grace and favour' basis?

(D)   Eligibility for assistance

It is not enough to be 'homeless'; the applicant must also be 'eligible'. This was a qualification introduced into the law in 1996 as part of the Government's intention to exclude from housing assistance asylum seekers and certain categories of persons subject to immigration control. Similar exclusions, of course, also apply to such persons with regard to 'qualifying person' status in relation to the allocation of council housing (see chapter 4). Certain asylum seekers may still be able to obtain aid under s. 21(1)(a) of the National Assistance Act 1948 (as amended), whereunder *social services authorities* are required to provide residential accommodation for certain classes of person where this is needed by reason of age, illness, disability or other circumstances (see *R v Hammersmith & Fulham LBC, ex parte M* [1997] *The Times*, 19 February and *R v Newham LBC, ex parte Medical Foundation for the Care of Victims of Torture* [1997] *The Times*, 26 December). This obligation falls on county councils and unitary authorities where they exist (for example, Worcestershire and the City of Leicester respectively) on Metropolitan District Councils (for example, the City of Birmingham) and on London Borough Councils (for example, the City of Westminster). In effect, however, the obligation applies to persons who are effectively destitute with no means of support, and is in any case to be taken away, it seems, under the new Asylum and Immigration Bill proposed by the current Government.

Housing Act 1996

Eligibility for assistance

Persons from abroad not eligible for housing assistance
185.—(1)   A person is not eligible for assistance under this Part if he is a person from abroad who is ineligible for housing assistance.

(2)   A person who is subject to immigration control within the meaning of the Asylum and Immigration Act 1996 is not eligible for housing assistance unless he is of a class prescribed by regulations made by the Secretary of State.

(3)   The Secretary of State may make provision by regulations as to other descriptions of persons who are to be treated for the purposes of this Part as persons from abroad who are ineligible for housing assistance.

(4)   A person from abroad who is not eligible for housing assistance shall be disregarded in determining for the purposes of this Part whether another person—

(a)   is homeless or threatened with homelessness, or

(b)   has a priority need for accommodation.

Asylum-seekers and their dependants

186.—(1)   An asylum-seeker, or a dependant of an asylum-seeker who is not by virtue of section 185 a person from abroad who is ineligible for housing assistance, is not eligible for assistance under this Part if he has any accommodation in United Kingdom, however temporary, available for his occupation.

(2)   For the purposes of this section a person who makes a claim for asylum—

(a)   becomes an asylum-seeker at the time when his claim is recorded by the Secretary of State as having been made, and

(b)   ceases to be an asylum-seeker at the time when his claim is recorded by the Secretary of State as having been finally determined or abandoned.

(3)   For the purposes of this section a person—

(a)   becomes a dependant of an asylum-seeker at the time when he is recorded by the Secretary of State as being a dependant of the asylum-seeker, and

(b)   ceases to be a dependant of an asylum-seeker at the time when the person whose dependant he is ceases to be an asylum-seeker or, if it is earlier, at the time when he is recorded by the Secretary of State as ceasing to be a dependant of the asylum-seeker.

(4)   In relation to any asylum-seeker, 'dependant' means a person—

(a)   who is his spouse or a child of his under the age of eighteen, and

(b)   who has neither a right of abode in the United Kingdom nor indefinite leave under the Immigration Act 1971 to enter or remain in the United Kingdom.

(5)   In this section a 'claim for asylum' means a claim made by a person that it would be contrary to the United Kingdom's obligations under the Convention relating to the Status of Refugees done at Geneva on 28th July 1951 and the Protocol to that Convention for him to be removed from, or required to leave, the United Kingdom.

Provision of information by Secretary of State

187.—(1)   The Secretary of State shall, at the request of a local housing authority, provide the authority with such information as they may require—

(a)   as to whether a person is or has become an asylum-seeker, or a dependant of an asylum-seeker, and

(b)   to enable them to determine whether such a person is eligible for assistance under this Part under section 185 (persons from abroad not eligible for housing assistance).

(2)   Where that information is given otherwise than in writing, the Secretary of State shall confirm it in writing if a written request is made to him by the authority.

(3)   If it appears to the Secretary of State that any application, decision or other change of circumstances has affected the status of a person about whom information was previously provided by him to a local housing authority under this section, he shall inform the authority in writing of that fact, the reason for it and the date on which the previous information became inaccurate.

Homelessness Regulations 1996
SI 1996 No. 2754

The Secretary of State for the Environment, as respects England, and the Secretary of State for Wales, as respects Wales, in exercise of the powers conferred on them by sections 185(2) and (3), 194(6), and 198(4) of the Housing Act 1996 and of all other powers enabling them in that behalf, hereby make the following Regulations:

Citation and commencement
1.   These Regulations may be cited as the Homelessness Regulations 1996 and shall come into force on 20th January 1997.

Interpretation
2.   In these Regulations—
'the Act' means the Housing Act 1996;
'the 1971 Act' means the Immigration Act 1971;
'claim for asylum' means a claim made by a person that it would be contrary to the United Kingdom's obligations under the Convention for him to be removed from or required to leave the United Kingdom;
'the Common Travel Area' means the United Kingdom, the Channel Islands, the Isle of Man and the Republic of Ireland collectively;
'the Convention' means the Convention relating to the Status of Refugees done at Geneva on 28th July 1951, as extended by Article 1(2) of the Protocol relating to the Status of Refugees done at New York on 31st January 1967;
'EEA national' means a national of a State which is a Contracting Party to the Agreement on the European Economic Area signed at Oporto on 2nd May 1992 as adjusted by the Protocol signed at Brussels on 17th March 1993; and
'the immigration rules' means the immigration rules within the meaning of the 1971 Act.

Classes of persons subject to immigration control who are eligible for housing assistance
3.—(1)   The following are the classes of persons prescribed for the purposes of section 185(2) of the Act (persons subject to immigration control who are eligible for housing assistance)—
Class A—a person recorded by the Secretary of State as a refugee within the definition in Article 1 of the Convention;
Class B—a person who has made a claim for asylum which is recorded by the Secretary of State as having been made on his arrival (other than on his re-entry) in the United Kingdom from a country outside the Common Travel Area and which has not been recorded by the Secretary of State as having been determined or abandoned;
Class C—a person who becomes an asylum seeker, that is to say—
(i)   whilst that person is present in Great Britain the Secretary of State makes a declaration to the effect that the country of which that person is a national is subject to such a fundamental change in circumstances that he would not normally order the return of a person to that country; and
(ii)   that person makes a claim for asylum which is recorded by the Secretary of State as having been made within three months from the day on which that declaration was made,
provided that the claim for asylum has not been recorded by the Secretary of State as having been determined or abandoned;

Class D—a person (other than a person falling within Class B)—
    (i)   who on or before 4th February 1996 made a claim for asylum;
    (ii)   who was on that date entitled to benefit under the Housing Benefit (General) Regulations 1987; and
    (iii) either—
        (a)   whose claim has not been recorded by the Secretary of State as having been determined or abandoned; or
        (b)   whose claim has not been recorded as determined on or before 4th February 1996; and
        (aa) whose appeal in respect of that claim was pending on 5th February 1996 or was made within the time limits specified in the rules of procedure made under section 22 of the 1971 Act; and
        (bb) whose appeal in respect of that claim has not been determined or abandoned.

Class E—a person—
    (i)   who has been granted by the Secretary of State exceptional leave to enter or remain in the United Kingdom outside the provisions of the immigration rules; and
    (ii)   whose leave is not subject to a condition requiring him to maintain and accommodate himself and any dependants of his without recourse to public funds;

Class F—a person who has a current leave to enter or remain in the United Kingdom which is not subject to any limitation or condition and who is habitually resident in the Common Travel Area other than a person—
    (i)   who has been given leave to enter or remain in the United Kingdom upon an undertaking given by another person (his 'sponsor') or persons in writing in pursuance of the immigration rules to be responsible for his maintenance and accommodation;
    (ii)   who has been resident in the United Kingdom for less than five years beginning from the date of entry or the date on which the undertaking was given in respect of him, whichever date is the later; and
    (iii) whose sponsor or, where there is more than one sponsor, at least one of whose sponsors, is still alive.

Class G—a person who is—
    (i)   a national of a state which is a signatory to the European Convention on Social and Medical Assistance (done in Paris on 11th December 1953) or a state which is a signatory to the Council of Europe Social Charter (signed in Turin on 18th October 1961); and
    (ii)   habitually resident in the Common Travel Area.

Class H—a person who is on an income-based jobseeker's allowance or in receipt of income support.

  (2)   For the purposes of the description of Class H—
    (a)   'an income-based jobseeker's allowance' has the meaning given in section 1(4) of the Jobseekers Act 1995;
    (b)   'income support' has the same meaning as in the Social Security Contributions and Benefits Act 1992; and
    (c)   a person is on an income-based jobseeker's allowance—
        (i)   on any day in respect of which an income-based jobseeker's allowance is payable to him; and
        (ii)   on any day—
        (aa) in respect of which he satisfies the conditions for entitlement to an income-based jobseeker's allowance but where the allowance is not paid in accordance

with section 19 of the Jobseekers Act 1995 (circumstances in which a jobseeker's allowance is not payable); or

(bb)   which is a waiting day for the purposes of paragraph 4 of Schedule 1 to that Act and which falls immediately before a day in respect of which an income-based jobseeker's allowance is payable to him or would be payable to him but for section 19 of that Act.

Class I (this applies in relation to England only) — a person who left the territory of Monserrat after 1st November 1995 because of the effect on that territory of a volcanic erruption.

Descriptions of persons who are to be treated as persons from abroad ineligible for housing assistance
4. (1)   The following are the descriptions of persons who are to be treated for the purposes of Part VII of the Act as persons from abroad who are ineligible for housing assistance—

(a)   a person who is not habitually resident in the Common Travel Area other than—

(i)   . . .

(ii)   a worker for the purposes of Council Regulation (EEC) No. 1612/68 or (EEC) No. 1251/70;

(iii)   a person with a right to reside in the United Kingdom pursuant to Council Directive No. 68/360/EEC or No. 73/148/EEC;

(iv)   a person who has left the territory of Montserrat after 1st November 1995 because of the effect on that territory of a volcanic eruption;

(v)   a person who is on an income-based jobseeker's allowance or in receipt of income support,

(b)   a person who is an EEA national and is required by the Secretary of State to leave the United Kingdom.

(2)   Paragraph (1)(a)(v) applies to England only and the definitions in regulation 3(2)(a), (b) and (c) shall apply for the purposes of that paragraph.

Prescribed period of notice where an authority give notice that they propose to cease exercising power to secure accommodation under section 194
5.   For the purposes of section 194(6) of the Act (notice of ceasing to exercise power to secure accommodation under section 194), the prescribed period is 28 days.

Period prescribed for the purpose of conditions for referral of an application
6.   For the purposes of section 198(4)(b) of the Act (referral of case to another local housing authority), the prescribed period is the aggregate of—

(i)   five years; and

(ii)   the period between the date of the previous application and the date on which the applicant was first placed in pursuance of that application in accommodation in the district of the authority to whom the application is now made.

Notes
1.   The 1996 Regulations are set out here as amended by SI 1997 No. 631, SI 1997 No. 2046 and SI 1999 No. 2135.
2.   See also Housing Accommodation and Homelessness (Persons Subject to Immigration Control) Order 1996 SI 1996 No. 1982, as amended by SI 1997 No. 628.

3. Ineligibility is similar to lack of qualification to be allocated housing under the normal allocation principles (see chapter 4). The ineligible are basically those from abroad subject to immigration control under the Asylum and Immigration Act 1996, *unless* a member of a class of persons specified by the Secretary of State, i.e. the *exceptions* created by the Homelessness Regulations 1996, as amended by SI 1997 No. 631, SI 1997 No. 2046 and SI 1999 No. 2135. A number of people are re-qualified by the Regulations, even though initially from abroad. There then follow a number of *specifically excluded* persons. These persons are *specifically declared* to be ineligible for assistance as 'persons from abroad':

(a) Those persons not falling within classes A to I who are also not *habitually resident* in the Common Travel Area (CTA). Thus a person not habitually resident in the CTA will be ineligible. However, this exclusion does *not* apply to migrant workers from EC countries, so they *can* be assisted.

(b) Persons who are EEA nationals required by the Secretary of State to leave the UK, i.e. nationals of EC Member States plus Norway, Iceland and Liechtenstein. So even if a person is an EC migrant worker, he or she can be 'ineligible' if required to leave the UK by the Secretary of State.

4. Section 186 of the 1996 Act continues the exclusions. Asylum-seekers or their dependants not otherwise falling within s. 185, i.e. not excluded by that section from eligibility, are however, still *not eligible*, where they have *any* accommodation – *however temporary* – available for occupation in the UK. That accommodation must still, however, be 'accommodation' for the purposes of the Act.

In *Lismane* v *Hammersmith & Fulham LBC* [1998] *The Times*, 27 July, L – a Latvian – arrived in the UK in 1997 claiming to flee from persecution. She was allowed to enter and brought her son. They settled with her husband, in a single room. L was at that time pregnant. Was the room 'accommodation'? The Court of Appeal held not – the room could not count as accommodation, available for L's occupation. It was not reasonable that L should continue to occupy the accommodation, and so it was not 'accommodation' and thus L did not have any accommodation falling within s. 186 and accordingly was not excluded from eligibility by that section.

5. In *R* v *City of Westminster, ex parte Castelli* (1996) 28 HLR 616, the Court of Appeal decided that an EC national who ceases to be a qualified person in fact, but who has not been given (and overstayed) a limited leave to remain in the United Kingdom and has not been informed that the Secretary of State had decided that he should be removed, does not belong to a category of persons 'not lawfully here'; there is no obligation on such a person to apply for leave to remain, and he or she cannot properly be regarded as being in breach of the immigration laws by his or her failure to do so. (This does not, of course, prevent such a person from 'falling foul' of the requirement under s. 185(3) of the Housing Act 1996 and the Homelessness Regulations 1996 to be 'habitually resident in the Common Travel Area', effectively the United Kingdom, Eire, the Isle of Man and the Channel Islands).

Question
Consider the status for the purpose of homelessness of the following:

(a)   Ivan, who has illegally entered the UK by hiding aboard a lorry from the former Yugoslavia and evading immigration control at Dover;

(b)   Raminder, who was given only temporary permission to enter the UK from India to enable him to visit relatives, but who has now outstayed that period;

(c)   Marie, who came to the UK as a migrant worker to take up a post in a French restaurant in Leicester, but who is now required to leave the country because she has been convicted of offences connected with prostitution;

(d)   Bhaljinder, who is a relative of Raminder's, but who was born in Germany and who has German citizenship, and who has come to the UK to take up a post in marketing Asian foods in Southall in West London.

(E)   Interim duty to accommodate

Housing Act 1996

Interim duty to accommodate in case of apparent priority need
188.—(1)   If the local housing authority have reason to believe that an applicant may be homeless, eligible for assistance and have a priority need, they shall secure that accommodation is available for his occupation pending a decision as to the duty (if any) owed to him under the following provisions of this Part.

(2)   The duty under this section arises irrespective of any possibility of the referral of the applicant's case to another local housing authority (see sections 198 to 200).

(3)   The duty ceases when the authority's decision is notified to the applicant, even if the applicant requests a review of the decision (see section 202).

The authority may continue to secure that accommodation is available for the applicant's occupation pending a decision on a review.

Notes
1.   Where an authority have reason to believe that an applicant may be (i) homeless, (ii) eligible for assistance, and (iii) have a priority need they must secure accommodation for that person pending a decision as to the duty (if any) owed. This duty arises irrespective of any referral to another authority, but continues *only until* the authority's decision is notified to the applicant *even if the applicant requests a review of the decision*, though the authority *may* continue to secure accommodation pending a decision on a review.

There could be room for conflict here, i.e. the *duty* is limited in point of time and the *power* will have to be exercised according to the requirements of the *Wednesbury* principles, e.g., on the basis of relevant considerations and reasonably, etc.

2.   Note that by virtue of ss. 205 and 206 of the 1996 Act, the accommodation provided under this interim duty to accommodate must be 'suitable', i.e. there is a need to avoid unfit, overcrowded or multiply-occupied premises. Certainly the Code of Guidance argues that B&B is not suitable for families with children.

In *R v Newham LBC, ex parte Ojuri* [1998] *The Times*, 29 August, O applied as a homeless person to Newham LBC. He had a family. Pending the outcome of inquiries they were offered B&B accommodation, and Newham made it clear that they thought O was 'lucky' to be offered that – the family might have found themselves placed even further away from their original home. It was argued that Newham had failed to consider the Code of Guidance, paras 20.2, 21.15 and 21.28, which indicate that families should not be placed in B&B unless it is suitable, that the schooling of children should be considered so that they may stay in their existing school, if at all possible, and that the medical condition of the family should be considered. While the Code does not place a ban on the use of B&B if that is all that is available, authorities forced to utilise this form of accommodation should keep families so accommodated under review. Collins J found that on the facts it was clear that Newham had not taken into account the needs of the Ojuri family and had not tried to match those needs with what was available as accommodation, hence their decision had to be struck down.

(F)   Priority need for accommodation

Housing Act 1996

Priority need for accommodation
189.—(1)   The following have a priority need for accommodation—
(a)   a pregnant woman or a person with whom she resides or might reasonably be expected to reside;
(b)   a person with whom dependent children reside or might reasonably be expected to reside;
(c)   a person who is vulnerable as a result of old age, mental illness or handicap or physical disability or other special reason, or with whom such a person resides or might reasonably be expected to reside;
(d)   a person who is homeless or threatened with homelessness as a result of an emergency such as flood, fire or other disaster.
(2)   The Secretary of State may by order—
(a)   specify further descriptions of persons as having a priority need for accommodation, and
(b)   amend or repeal any part of subsection (1).
(3)   Before making such an order the Secretary of State shall consult such associations representing relevant authorities, and such other persons, as he considers appropriate.
(4)   No such order shall be made unless a draft of it has been approved by resolution of each House of Parliament.

Much of the litigation on this provision has concerned the meaning of the word 'vulnerable'. Over the years the courts have developed an understanding of the concept of vulnerability. The basic test is whether the applicant is less able to fend for himself so that he will suffer injury in circumstances where a less vulnerable person would be able to cope. This was most recently reaffirmed in *R v London Borough of Camden, ex parte Pereira* [1998] *Housing Law Monitor*, July 3. Here, however, the Court of Appeal added the 'gloss' that the test is whether the applicant is less able to fend for himself in comparison to a less vulnerable homeless person. The consequence of this gloss is that a person is not 'vulnerable' if his or her only weakness is a particular inability to find housing. What one is looking for is something that is likely to lead to physical detriment or injury.

What makes a person 'vulnerable' is thus a question of fact and degree in all cases for the local authority to decide. They should consider the frequency of affliction, however: *R v Wandsworth LBC, ex parte Banbury* (1986) 19 HLR 76.

An authority should consider all the facts of the case, and should consult relevant experts in housing and social welfare; and should not rely on the opinion of a single doctor who has neither seen nor examined the homeless person, and certainly should not 'rubber stamp' his assessment (*R v Lambeth LBC, ex parte Carroll* (1987) 20 HLR 142).

Where priority need depends on the presence of dependent children, the child(ren) in question need not live exclusively with the applicant; but much depends on the facts of each case and it is for the authority to decide with whom children 'normally reside' (*R v Lambeth LBC, ex parte Vagliviello* (1990) 22 HLR 39, and *R v Port Talbot BC, ex parte McCarthy* (1990) 23 HLR 207. There is no definition of 'dependent' in the Act. Normally a child in employment or in a YTS place is not a dependent (see *R v Kensington & Chelsea RLBC, ex parte Amarfio* (1995) 27 HLR 543).

A closer examination of two cases, *R v Lambeth LBC, ex parte Carroll* and *Ortiz v City of Westminster*, can serve to demonstrate the working out of the law and practice, in relation to the key 'vulnerability' issue.

R v Lambeth LBC, ex parte Carroll
(1987) 20 HLR 142

WEBSTER J: This is an application for judicial review by David Patrick Carroll, who seeks an order for certiorari to quash the decision of the London Borough of Lambeth, communicated by telephone by the Homeless Persons' Unit to the applicant's solicitors on June 4, 1986, that the applicant was not vulnerable and, therefore, was not in priority need within section 59 of the Housing Act 1985, so that the London Borough of Lambeth has no duty to secure the applicant accommodation pursuant to section 65 of the Housing Act 1985. He also seeks an order of mandamus that the respondent borough make appropriate inquiries into the question of whether he is vulnerable within section 59(1)(c) of the Housing Act.

It is convenient to set out the relevant statutory provisions of the Housing Act of which the first is section 59(1)(c), which is in these terms: 'The following have a priority need for accommodation (c) a person who is vulnerable as a result of old age, mental illness or handicap or physical disability or other special reason . . .' and I need not read on.

Section 62(1) provides:

If a person (an 'applicant') applies to a local housing authority for accommodation, or for assistance in obtaining accommodation, and the authority have reason to believe that he may be homeless or threatened with homelessness, they shall make such inquiries as are necessary to satisfy themselves as to whether he is homeless or threatened with homelessness.

There is no issue but that in the present case the respondents were satisfied that the applicant was homeless or threatened with homelessness.

Subsection (2) continues: 'If they are so satisfied, they shall make any further inquiries necessary to satisfy themselves as to (a) whether he has a priority need . . .' and I need not read on.

Finally, section 71(1) provides:

In relation to homeless persons and persons threatened with homelessness, a relevant authority shall have regard in the exercise of their functions to such guidance as may from time to time be given by the Secretary of State. (2) The Secretary of State may give guidance either generally or to specified descriptions of authorities.

The guidance contemplated by that section is contained in the *Housing (Homeless Persons) Act 1977 Code of Guidance* (2nd ed.) which it is common ground is to be treated as the relevant guidance given in section 71 of the 1985 Act. The only parts of the guide that I need to recite are certain passages falling under the heading 'Priority Need', which set out four categories of person for whom authorities are required to ensure that accommodation is available and, as to the third of those categories under subparagraph (c) of paragraph 2.12 at page 6 of the guide states, 'A person has priority need if he is, or his household includes one or more members who are vulnerable for one of the following reasons.' I can omit (i). Then (ii)

Mental illness or handicap of physical disability. This includes those who are blind, deaf, dumb or otherwise substantially disabled mentally or physically. Authorities are asked to take a wide and flexible view of what constitutes substantial disability, recognising that this will depend on individual circumstances. The help of the area health authority and the social service authority will be appropriate in assessing a number of these cases. (iii) Any other special reason. Authorities should have particular regard to those who are vulnerable but do not come within either of the above categories.

and then particular examples are given which are not relevant for present purposes.

The words 'substantially' and 'substantial' in that passage should probably be disregarded for the purposes, at least, of the 1985 Act, since section 59(1)(c) contains no such word and since I would not have thought it lawful for the Secretary of State by using particular words in guidance which is deemed now to be given under section 71, as I understand it, to restrict the ambit of priority need expressly defined by section 59. If the intention of the words 'substantially' and 'substantial' is simply to exclude matters de minimis, it is not open to criticism; but if as might be the case it is to be read as imposing a higher test than that expressed in section 59(1)(c), then it cannot I think lawfully do so. Although this confusion is not expressed, it is I think implicit in the judgment of Waller LJ in *R* v *Waveney District Council, ex parte Bowers* [1983] 1 QB 238 at p. 245 (which I shall cite in a moment) in which the meaning and application of the section of the Housing (Homeless Persons) Act 1977, equivalent to section 59(1)(c) of the 1985 Act, was considered. Two glosses on section 59(1)(c) itself can be gathered from that authority and another authority.

In *Bowers'* case to which I have just referred, Waller LJ giving the judgment of the Court of Appeal, says at p. 245:

It would appear from the affidavit of the local authority that particular reliance was placed on the words 'substantially disabled mentally or physically' in the Code of Guidance and that led them to the conclusion that accommodation only had to be provided for those in substantial need. It was also suggested in the course of argument that the case had to be brought within one or other of the categories mentioned in section (2)(1)(c).

I break off to say that that was the equivalent of the present section 59(1)(c). Waller LJ continued:

In our judgment this was the correct approach. The first question which has to be considered is whether or not there is vulnerability. If there is vulnerability, then does it arise from those matters which are set out within section 2(1)(c)? It may not arise from any single one but it may arise from a combination of those causes.

In an earlier passage at pp. 244–245, Waller LJ considered the meaning of vulnerable for the purpose of the section. He says:

In our opinion, however, vulnerable in the context of this legislation means less able to fend for oneself so that injury or detriment will result when a less vulnerable man will be able to cope without harmful effects.

In *R v Bath City Council, ex parte Sangermano* (1984) 17 HLR 94 at p. 97 Hodgson J said that 'the vulnerability to be considered is vulnerability loosely in housing terms or in the context of housing.' That view was adopted with approval by Russell J in *R v Wandsworth Borough Council, ex parte Banbury* (1986) 19 HLR 76 at p. 78. It is not entirely clear how in practice the view of Hodgson J, that vulnerability is to be considered loosely in housing terms or in the context of housing, is to be applied. I accept Mr Watkinson's submission that the effect of that gloss upon the section is in practice to extend the meaning given to the word 'vulnerable' by Waller LJ as if it reads 'less able to fend for oneself when homeless or in finding and keeping accommodation.'

So much for the law. The evidence before the court and (as to one part of it) before the respondents when they made their decision in June 1986 comes from three sources. As the first I take a report dated April 24, 1986 by Dr Dellaportas, which was before the respondents, or at any rate before the doctor appointed by them to consider the question of the applicant's vulnerability, in June 1986. Dr Dellaportas reported that he had seen and examined the applicant, who was 49 years old, on February 14, 1986. He reported that the applicant told him, amongst other things, that he drank six or seven pints of beer daily, but no spirits, that his past history included a fracture of the skull when he was nine years old, when he fell off a bank into a concrete yard. He told Dr Dellaportas that in 1983 he was involved in a road traffic accident, in which he sustained a fracture of his skull affecting mostly the frontal bone, which has been substantially depressed on the right.

In expressing his opinion, Dr Dellaportas wrote:

There is no doubt that as a result of the accident he sustained in 1983 he has had severe damage of the bony structures of his right orbit. This has caused him double vision which will be present indefinitely. Whether relevant orthopaedic or plastic surgery could improve his current double vision is debatable but obviously the opinion of an orthopaedic surgeon, a plastic surgeon and an ophthalmologist should be sought.

Then he ended with this paragraph:

In conclusion Mr Carroll has sustained substantial damage following the car accident he had in December 1983. This is irreversible and presents a major handicap.

The second source of information as to the applicant's condition comes from the affidavit of Deborah Cluett, a barrister employed by the North Lambeth Law Centre, and sworn in support of this application. She describes what she was told by the applicant about the car accident in 1983, which adds nothing, of course, to Dr Dellaportas' report, but she also says – and this is not contained in that report – that the applicant told her that he suffered from frequent severe headaches and that he had a drink problem which he felt aggravated his condition. That material, so far as I can tell, was never before the respondents when they made their decision in June 1986.

Finally there is a letter from Vauxhall Action for Homeless in the Community, dated February 9, 1987, which cannot therefore have been before the respondents when they made their decision. It is a social report written by a Mr D S Gibson, and includes the following information:

Mr Carroll is a friendly man inclined to play down and avoid the difficulties he faces. He would like to live in a flat of his own, but he has been unsuccessful in achieving this. He spent almost all of the last two years sleeping on a friend's floor. However, in December 1986 his friend left to return to Ireland. Since then Mr Carroll has had no fixed abode. He suffers from blurred vision and has a drink problem. It is clear that Mr Carroll's drinking exacerbates difficulties stemming from his visual disability. The following observations illustrate his ability to cope. Whilst repeatedly saying how he valued his part-time job at the day centre, Mr Carroll was unable to 'hold down' the job as a kitchen assistant. In particular any tasks requiring visual concentration, such as cooking, presented considerable difficulties and were done very slowly.

He came to the day centre with cuts and bruises on several occasions. More seriously, since losing his part-time job and his temporary accommodation he sustained a cut foot which became infected . . . it does appear that having lost his temporary home with a friend Mr Carroll has become more susceptible to injury.

These are some of the experiences that have led me to conclude that Mr Carroll's visual disability, combined with his heavy drinking makes him less able to fend for himself, to the extent that he will suffer injury in situations that a less vulnerable man would not.

[WEBSTER J then considered how the authority handled Mr Carroll's application. He continued:]

In my view, therefore, the respondent's decision of June 18, 1986 was bad in law because they failed properly to inquire into or consider the question of whether, notwithstanding the medical opinion of Dr Siva, the applicant was vulnerable for some other special reason or for a combination of one or more of the reasons set out in 59(1)(c), in that they never asked themselves the question whether in this case the obtaining of Dr Siva's opinion constituted sufficient inquiries necessary to enable them to be satisfied about the applicant's vulnerability. Moreover I think it likely, although I do not unequivocally decide, that the decision was invalid because the respondents never themselves considered the question of the applicant's priority need by or with the assistance of someone experienced in housing and social welfare matters.

Mr Watkinson's second submission is that in acting on Dr Siva's recommendation the respondents' decision was bad because that recommendation, and therefore their own decision, did not properly take into account – and the emphasis is on 'properly' – the report of Dr Dellaportas. Mr Watkinson submits that far from that report being of little value, it was the best material available because, whereas neither Dr Simon nor Dr Siva had seen the applicant and whereas the applicant's general practitioner (to whom I will assume one or both of them had spoken) had not seen the applicant since early 1985, Dr Dellaportas had seen and examined him on February 14, 1986. Although in my view this aspect of the case is most unsatisfactory, it does amount in my judgment to a contention only that the respondents and Dr Siva gave insufficient weight to Dr Dellaportas' report, and that is not a point of law. I am only just able to conclude that in this respect Dr Siva or the respondents failed to take Dr Dellaportas' report into account, although if they had failed to do so that would have been a reason for invalidating this decision. In my view, however, as I have said, the decision was invalid in any event for the reasons I have given in considering Mr Watkinson's first submission.

It is reassuring to note that the respondents have apparently, at least tentatively, themselves come to the same conclusion. In the notes before the court someone on behalf of the respondents has noted that all parties agreed that the current procedure – referral to Dr Simon – is open to question on vulnerability assessment and that the best course would be referral to the Vulnerability Panel as soon as it is convened. I am told that that Panel has not yet been convened because of the unavailability of funds, but if, as I assume, the Panel will include one or more persons experienced in housing and social welfare problems, referral to it on the question of vulnerability seems to me a most sensible course.

There remains the question of relief, which is dependent upon the exercise of my discretion. I have no doubt that the decision of June 18, 1986 must be quashed, so I make, as asked, the order of certiorari, substituting only the date of June 18, 1986 for that of June 4, 1986. I will not however in the exercise of my discretion make an order of mandamus because the respondents have made it clear in open correspondence that they are willing to assess the applicant's vulnerability again and provide interim accommodation pending the outcome of that assessment. In these circumstances it seems to me that an order of mandamus would be inappropriate.

Ortiz v *City of Westminster*
(1993) 27 HLR 364

SIMON BROWN LJ: This is an application for leave to appeal against the decision of Louis Blom-Cooper QC sitting as a deputy High Court judge on October 19, 1993, whereby he dismissed an application for judicial review of the decision of the respondent housing authority, taken in September of this year, declining to provide the applicant with secure accommodation under the homeless persons provisions of the Housing Act 1985.

For present purposes it is unnecessary to relate anything of the history of this matter beyond only this the applicant is a 24 year old woman who has had grave problems with drugs and drink; she lost her previous accommodation when she was admitted to the detoxification unit at Ealing Hospital in August; she made the application to be rehoused when she was on the point of being released from that treatment; she had two medical certificates from those concerned in her treatment, both stressing the problems that she would suffer were she not, on discharge, to acquire suitable accommodation.

The basis of her application was that she had a priority need under the provisions of section 59(1)(c) of the 1985 Act, namely as someone who is vulnerable as a result of physical disability or other special reason within the meaning of that provision.

The statutory predecessor of that provision was considered by the Court of Appeal in the case of *R* v *Waveney District Council, ex parte Bowers* [1983] 1 QB 238, in which Waller LJ in giving the judgment of the court said this:

In our opinion, however, vulnerable in the context of this legislation means less able to fend for oneself so that injury or detriment will result when a less vulnerable man will be able to cope without harmful effects.

The respondent authority, as emerged from the affidavit evidence sworn in the official review proceedings, based their decision that this applicant is not vulnerable essentially on this reason: that suitable accommodation is indeed available to her. The learned judge regarded the local authority as 'amply justified' in reaching that view, the determining passage in his judgment reading as follows:

Her undoubted troubles with drugs and alcohol no doubt make life less manageable for her, nevertheless when tested against the housing market she does not obtain the status of vulnerability. The local authority is amply justified in concluding that she is not vulnerable, not just on the basis of Dr Iwi's advice . . .

I interpose that he was the local authority's doctor whose advice was taken in the light of the two medical reports produced by the applicant.

. . . but also in the light of the evidence of the council that suitable accommodation is available to her. Any suggestion that it is not is at best speculative and contrary to the evidence.

The relevant passage of the authority's evidence as to the availability of accommodation reads thus:

Account was also taken of the accommodation which was available and it was decided that applicant was not vulnerable in the accommodation market.
The potential accommodation available consists of private lettings, bed and breakfast and hostel accommodation. Account was taken in particular in the Applicant's case of the availability of hostel accommodation. The Council had details of the accommodation, (which is supervised) which will accept and be suitable for those who have had drug addiction problems. The Council will provide details of that accommodation and will ascertain which of those hostels can offer accommodation at the requisite time.

We are told today by Mr Jones for the respondent authority that the council identified a particular hostel and indeed that arrangements were made for the applicant to attend there last Friday.
The basis upon which leave to appeal is sought in this case is that the authority, and indeed the learned deputy judge, were wrong to have regard at all to the question as to whether or not the applicant would have difficulty in securing accommodation. The essence of her case is that once she established that she had a particular need for suitable accommodation, and would suffer more than most if she failed to acquire it then that of itself was sufficient to establish that she was vulnerable within the meaning of the legislation so as to give her a priority need.
In his helpful submissions before us Mr Critchley recognises the difficulty of such an argument and very properly draws our attention to the decision of Mann J, as he then was, in *R* v *Reigate and Banstead BC, ex parte Di Dominico* (1988) 20 HLR 15 where he said this:

Vulnerable, in my judgment, means vulnerable in the housing market. There is no indication here of difficulty in finding accommodation or of maintaining the need for special accommodation. There is not one word of evidence upon those matters. There were the reports from the consultants, from the general practitioner and the observations of the medical officer. Those were before the local authority. The decision is one for them. I am quite unable to say, on the basis of the material before me, that their decision was either absurd or perverse.

He then continued by expressing the sympathy which anyone would have for such applicants, just as we have for the applicant before us.

In my judgment that approach is plainly right. In order to satisfy the test of vulnerability, as explained in the decision in *Ex parte Bowers*, an applicant must in my judgment surmount two hurdles. First, he (or she) must show that to some material extent he or she is less able to obtain suitable accommodation than the ordinary person and secondly, that if he fails to obtain it, then he will suffer more than most. It is in my judgment the first of those hurdles which the applicant so conspicuously fails to surmount in the present case. The position is strikingly different from that in *Ex parte Bowers* itself where, as the judgment recorded: 'Since the accident nobody will give him lodging . . .'

Here, for the reasons already indicated, there is no factual basis upon which the authority could conclude, let alone were bound to conclude, that this applicant would suffer peculiar difficulty in obtaining suitable accommodation. For those reasons, the learned deputy judge was undoubtedly in my judgment correct in the approach he adopted and in the conclusions he arrived at. I for my part do not think there is any worthwhile argument to pursue on appeal. I would accordingly refuse leave.

. . .

(G)   Intentional homelessness

Housing Act 1996

Duties to persons found to be homeless or threatened with homelessness

190.—(1)   This section applies where the local housing authority are satisfied that an applicant is homeless and is eligible for assistance but are also satisfied that he became homeless intentionally.

(2)   If the authority are satisfied that the applicant has a priority need, they shall—

(a)   secure that accommodation is available for his occupation for such period as they consider will give him a reasonable opportunity of securing accommodation for his occupation, and

(b)   provide him with advice and such assistance as they consider appropriate in the circumstances in any attempts he may make to secure that accommodation becomes available for his occupation.

(3)   If they are not satisfied that he has a priority need, they shall provide him with advice and such assistance as they consider appropriate in the circumstances in any attempts he may make to secure that accommodation becomes available for his occupation.

Becoming homeless intentionally
191.—(1)   A person becomes homeless intentionally if he deliberately does or fails to do anything in consequence of which he ceases to occupy accommodation which is available for his occupation and which it would have been reasonable for him to continue to occupy.

(2)   For the purposes of subsection (1) an act or omission in good faith on the part of a person who was unaware of any relevant fact shall not be treated as deliberate.

(3)   A person shall be treated as becoming homeless intentionally if—

(a)   he enters into an arrangement under which he is required to cease to occupy accommodation which it would have been reasonable for him to continue to occupy, and

(b)   the purpose of the arrangement is to enable him to become entitled to assistance under this Part,

and there is no other good reason why he is homeless.

(4)   A person who is given advice or assistance under section 197 (duty where other suitable alternative accommodation available), but fails to secure suitable accommodation in circumstances in which it was reasonably to be expected that he would do so, shall, if he makes a further application under this Part, be treated as having become homeless intentionally.

Becoming threatened with homelessness intentionally
196.—(1)   A person becomes threatened with homelessness intentionally if he deliberately does or fails to do anything the likely result of which is that he will be forced to leave accommodation which is available for his occupation and which it would have been reasonable for him to continue to occupy.

(2)   For the purposes of subsection (1) an act or omission in good faith on the part of a person who was unaware of any relevant fact shall not be treated as deliberate.

(3)   A person shall be treated as becoming threatened with homelessness intentionally if—

(a)   he enters into an arrangement under which he is required to cease to occupy accommodation which it would have been reasonable for him to continue to occupy, and

(b)   the purpose of the arrangement is to enable him to become entitled to assistance under this Part,

and there is no other good reason why he is threatened with homelessness.

(4)   A person who is given advice or assistance under section 197 (duty where other suitable alternative accommodation available), but fails to secure suitable accommodation in circumstances in which it was reasonably to be expected that he would do so, shall, if he makes a further application under this Part, be treated as having become threatened with homelessness intentionally.

(i)   The concept of intentional homelessness
The concept of intentional homelessness dates from the Housing (Homeless Persons) Act 1977, where it was inserted at a late stage in the progress of the legislation through the House of Lords. Local authorities wanted a provision to enable them to exclude obvious 'queue jumpers'. However, few pieces of legislation can have given rise to more litigation – litigation costly in terms of expense and local authority officer time.

The definition was modified in 1996 by the insertion of s. 191(3). Thus, a person *must* also be treated as becoming homeless intentionally where:

(a)   he or she enters into an arrangement under which he or she is *required* to cease to occupy accommodation which it would have been reasonable for him or her to continue to occupy; *and*

(b)   the purpose of the arrangement was to enable him or her to be entitled to assistance as homeless; *and*

(c)   there is no other 'good reason' why he or she is homeless, in other words the homelessness must arise as a result of the arrangement and for no other reason such as, say, the accommodation burning down before the arrangement 'bites'.

The object of the provision is to strike at *deliberate* 'doomed from the outset' schemes whereby an insecure short letting or licence is accepted simply to obtain the protection of the homelessness legislation.

Note also that under s. 191(4), where a person is given advice or assistance in the circumstance of suitable alternative accommodation being available (see further below), and then fails to secure suitable accommodation in circumstances in which *it was reasonably to be expected* that he or she would, that person, if he or she makes a further application, is to be treated as having become homeless intentionally. This is an instance of 'deemed' intention which will affect a subsequent application, and because of the use of the word 'reasonable' it needs to be applied carefully.

The burden clearly lies *on the authority* to 'satisfy' themselves that the homelessness was intentional: if there is any doubt, the applicant is entitled to the benefit of that doubt.

At the very heart of the concept of 'intentional homelessness' lies uncertainty. Should its application be confined to cases of *deliberate* homelessness (particularly in the light of the perceived need to ward off 'queue jumpers'), or can it be extended to any situation where the initial act or omission of the applicant is deliberate and there is an inexorable consequence of subsequent homelessness, even if that consequence was not specifically intended? An obvious example is the tenant who fails persistently to pay rent; he or she may not intend to be the subject of possession proceedings and certainly does not necessarily intend to be evicted! However, there is a 'close and intimate' relationship between the failure to pay the rent and the subsequent homelessness.

After some initial doubt, the courts soon decided that the wider view of 'deliberateness' should apply. The decisive decision was that of the Court of Appeal in the following case:

Devenport v *Salford City Council*
(1983) 8 HLR 54

FOX LJ: This is an appeal from an order of McCullough J whereby he granted certiorari to quash a resolution of the Corporation of the City of Salford ('the Corporation') that the applicants, Mr and Mrs Devenport, were intentionally homeless for the purposes of the Housing (Homeless Persons) Act 1977.

Mr and Mrs Devenport were tenants of one of the Corporation's dwellings called 77 Rowan Close. The tenancy agreement which was entered into on 22 November 1976 was, in fact, signed by Mrs Devenport only but it is common ground that they were joint tenants. The agreement was expressed to be 'on the conditions of tenancy set out overleaf'. Condition 3 provides that the tenant shall not do certain things including the following:

(P) Do or permit to be done on the premises anything which may cause annoyance or inconvenience to the (Corporation) or its tenants or the occupiers of the adjoining property.

Condition 4 provides that the tenant shall do certain things including the following:

(h) Be responsible for the orderly conduct of his family, invitees and guests on the (Corporation) estate and for any damage done by them to trees, shrubs or grassed areas or the defacement by them of any building installations or any other property belonging to the (Corporation) and pay the cost of making good such damage or defacement.

The Corporation received complaints from people living near the Devenports about the conduct of their children. As a result, on 12 September 1980 the Corporation sent the Devenports a letter. That stated:

Numerous complaints have been received about the conduct of your children thereby contravening (the Corporation's) conditions of tenancy.

I would ask your co-operation to ensure that your family maintains an accepted standard of behaviour so alleviating the necessity for me to consider any further action.

Should this appeal be ignored and no marked improvement be reported then I shall have no alternative but to recommend that legal proceedings be commenced to obtain the vacant possession of your present dwelling.

If you feel it necessary to discuss the contents of this letter then do not hesitate to telephone me . . .

The letter was signed by the Area Housing Manager. A similar letter was sent to the parents of other children of whose conduct there had been complaints.

Things did not improve. In March 1981 the Corporation received a petition signed by 237 of its tenants living at Rowan Close and elsewhere. The petition was expressed to be directed against Mr and Mrs Devenport and two of their children, Joanne and Shirley, and also against another family. The petition asked for the removal of the two families and appended a lengthy list of complaints of vandalism, assaults and violent misconduct.

On 13 April 1981 the Corporation gave to Mr and Mrs Devenport notice of intention to seek possession of 77 Rowan Close in accordance with the requirements of the Housing Act 1980. Clause 4 of that notice reads:

Possession will be sought on grounds 1 and 2 of Sched 4 to the Housing Act 1980 which reads: 'Ground 1. Obligations of the tenancy have been broken. Ground 2. The tenant or any person residing in the dwellinghouse has been guilty of conduct which is a nuisance or annoyance to neighbours'.

Section 34(1) of the Housing Act 1980 (which applied to the Devenports' tenancy) provides that:

The court shall not make an order for possession of a dwelling-house let under a secure tenancy except on one of the grounds set out in Schedule 4 to this Act . . .

The relevant part of grounds 1 and 2 in Part 1 of the 4th Schedule were sufficiently set forth in the notice.

There then followed a counter petition against the eviction of the Devenports and the other family. It was signed by about seventy people. It suggested that those who signed the previous petition were unaware that eviction was in contemplation.

Proceedings for the eviction of the Devenports and the other family were duly authorised by the Corporation on 24 April 1981 (and reaffirmed after the second petition). The proceedings were started on 9 June and claimed possession under grounds 1 and 2 of Schedule 4 to the Housing Act 1980.

Further and better particulars were delivered by the Corporation on 16 July 1981. Those particulars asserted that Mr and Mrs Devenport and certain of their children had, over a period of some years, conducted themselves in a disorderly manner on the Corporation's estate to the annoyance and inconvenience of the Corporation and their tenants. In particular the Corporation relied (inter alia) upon the following;

    (i)   Acts of vandalism by the children.

    (ii)   The threats and actual use of physical violence by Mr and Mrs Devenport against persons living in the neighbourhood.

    (iii)   Mr Devenport threatened to knife Mrs Mona James of Rowan Close and members of her family.

    (iv)   Shirley Devenport physically attacked Mrs James's son.

    (v)   Mrs Devenport and two of her children physically attacked Mrs Mona James and her daughter.

    (vi)   Mr and Mrs Devenport and their children repeatedly shouted abuse at neighbours.

    (vii)   Despite requests, Mr and Mrs Devenport had failed to control their children.

The hearing took place in the county court in August 1981. It occupied two days.

The judge found that the plaintiff's case was established and he made an order for possession in 28 days. He did not make specific findings of fact.

I come now to the immediate background to the resolution of the Corporation with which the proceedings for judicial review are concerned.

Mr and Mrs Devenport gave up possession of the premises in accordance with the judge's order and, on the same day, they made an application to the Corporation for accommodation under the Housing (Homeless Persons) Act 1977.

The Housing Manager recommended that Mr and Mrs Devenport be regarded as intentionally homeless.

The Housing Manager at the meeting of the housing committee on 25 September 1981 (a) reminded the committee that possession orders had been obtained against the Devenports and the other family and (b) reported on the position of such families for the purposes of the Housing (Homeless Persons) Act 1977 (see the minute of 25 September 1981).

On 25 September the Corporation resolved that the Devenports (and the other family) be deemed to be intentionally homeless for the purposes of the Housing (Homeless Persons) Act 1977.

Section 4 of the Act of 1977 operates if the housing authority (in this case the Corporation) 'are satisfied' that the persons became homeless intentionally. That is a matter for the Corporation. It is not a matter for the county court or for this court. If there was information before the Corporation upon which properly directed as to the requirement of the statute it could reasonably have reached the conclusion that the Devenports were intentionally homeless within the meaning of the statute then upon the principle of *Associated Provincial Picture Theatres* v *Wednesbury Corporation* [1948] 1 KB 223 the courts are not entitled to interfere.

The matter was argued before McCullough J on the basis of the misconduct of the children. And the view which the judge took of the position was this. He stated (at pp. 8 and 9 of the judgment):

It seems plain that the parents failed to control their children, but it does not necessarily follow from this that their failure was deliberate. Before one could say that such failure was deliberate one would need to be satisfied that the parents had considered the question of controlling their children, had realised they had a duty to do so and that they may have been able to achieve some control and had deliberately decided that they would not try. When one looks at the matter in this way . . . it becomes clear that there was no means by which this question could be answered in the affirmative. I do not see, in the particular circumstances here, how any corporation, any housing committee could have been satisfied that these tenants had deliberately failed to do something, or had deliberately done something themselves, as a result of which the judge made the order he did.

Counsel on behalf of Mr and Mrs Devenport support that and indeed, go further and say that there must be shown an intention on the part of the Devenports to become homeless – or, at any rate, recklessness on their part.

At this point, I turn to the language of s. 17 of the 1977 Act. Section 17(1) provides that

a person becomes homeless intentionally if he deliberately does or fails to do anything in consequence of which he ceases to occupy accommodation which is available for him.

In my opinion, the words 'homeless intentionally' are merely a formula which is given a specific meaning by the definition which follows. It is the definition which one has to construe and not the words 'homeless intentionally'. The sub-section, in my view, provides that a person becomes homeless intentionally if:

(i)   He ceases to occupy accommodation.

(ii)   That accommodation was available for his occupation.

(iii)   It would have been reasonable for him to continue to occupy it.

(iv)   The person deliberately did or failed to do something in consequence of which he ceased to occupy.

The section does not, in my opinion, require that the person should have intended to become homeless and should have done or failed to do something with the intention of becoming homeless.

We were referred to some observations of Lord Denning MR in *R v Slough BC* [1981] 1 QB 801 at p. 809 as follows:

. . . The Slough Council found that she was homeless intentionally. It was, I should have thought, a debatable point. Many people would have thought that Miss Jack's conduct however deplorable was not 'deliberate' in the sense required by s. 17(1) of the 1977 Act. She did not deliberately do anything to get herself turned out.

In my view it is not necessary to show that the tenant deliberately did something intending to get himself turned out. That seems to me to be contrary to the language of s. 17(1). The word 'deliberately' in my opinion, governs only the act or omission. There is no requirement that the person deliberately became homeless. Only that he deliberately did, or omitted to do something in consequence of which he ceased to occupy etc. That is quite a different concept. I agree with the conclusion reached on

the matter by Judge Goodall in *Robinson* v *Torbay BC* [1982] 1 All ER 726. Accordingly, in my judgment, the first question in the present case is whether the Corporation could reasonably conclude that Mr and Mrs Devenport deliberately did or failed to do something in consequence of which they became homeless. The immediate cause of Mr and Mrs Devenports' ceasing to occupy 77 Rowan Close was the order of the county court in August 1981. That order could only be made if one or both of the grounds 1 and 2 set forth in Schedule 4 to the Housing Act 1980 was established to the satisfaction of the county court. The county court judge plainly concluded that the case did come within one or both of the grounds. He specifically refers in one copy of the Note of his judgment before us to s. 34 of the 1980 Act (which directs one to Schedule 4) and in the other note to Schedule 4 itself.
. . .

But could the Corporation conclude that Mr and Mrs Devenport had deliberately done or failed to do something in consequence of which they cease to occupy?

So far as any acts of their own are concerned, I think they had. It is no doubt true that the warning letter in September 1980 related only to the conduct of the children, but it would have been obvious to Mr and Mrs Devenport that misconduct by either of them would be regarded even more seriously; many of the particularised complaints are after the warning letter.

As regards the children, Mr and Mrs Devenport were warned in the clearest terms in September 1980. So far from producing any effect it was followed by the first petition in March 1981 and, on the basis of the county court decision, continued misconduct. In my opinion there was ample evidence upon which the Corporation could conclude that Mr and Mrs Devenport deliberately failed to take any steps to control their children. In the face of the facts to which I have referred I cannot regard the bare assertion by Mrs Devenport in para 9 of her affidavit, that she and Mr Devenport have at all times used their best endeavours to control their children as sufficient evidence to the contrary. It is quite unsupported by any detailed explanation of the position at all. Whatever the position as to the acts of Mr and Mrs Devenport themselves, their omissions in relation to the children would, in my view, be quite sufficient to justify the Corporation's resolution.

I should add comments on three matters. First, I see no reason to suppose that the Corporation misdirected itself in law. The Housing Manager's analysis of the position in his report was, in my view, adequate. Secondly, Mr Hytner made a formal submission that an occupier cannot deliberately have done anything in consequence of which he ceases to occupy, if he is evicted by a court order which he opposes. But in my opinion the question is whether he deliberately did or failed to do something in consequence of which he ceases to occupy.

Thirdly, in my view the Corporation are not limited to the finding in the county court. The matter which they have to decide is not the same as that before the county court. The Corporation's task was to review all the facts as they knew them (including the decision of the county court) and reach a conclusion accordingly.

Looking at the whole matter I reach the conclusion that the facts known to the Corporation would justify it in concluding that Mr and Mrs Devenport deliberately did or failed to do acts the consequence of which was that they ceased to occupy the accommodation.
. . .

Questions
1. The intentional act must be that of the applicant, but can that arise because the applicant has acquiesced in the acts or omissions of another

family member? (Compare and contrast *R* v *Wyre Borough Council, ex parte Joyce* (1983) 11 HLR 71 and *R* v *East Northants District council, ex parte Spruce* (1988) 20 HLR 508 with *R* v *North Devon District Council, ex parte Lewis* [1981] 1 WLR 328.)

2. Intentional homelessness can arise in respect of either deliberate acts or omissions; but a failure by an evicted person to take civil action to secure reinstatement in his or her home, or a failure to pay rent or mortgage instalments, or even a court order for possession should not automatically be equated with intentional homelessness. What further question does the local authority need to ask in such circumstances? More particularly, what is meant by the word 'deliberately' in this context? Does it have the meaning it bears in criminal law, or is another meaning given by the courts?

Notes

1. Acts or omissions *in good faith* on the part of a person who is *unaware of any relevant fact* are not deliberate, but this does not cover mistakes of law, e.g., bad legal advice. It can, however, be difficult to distinguish bad advice from a genuine misapprehension of fact (see *R* v *Mole Valley DC, ex parte Burton* (1988) 20 HLR 479).

In *Burton*, a husband resigned from a job with tied accommodation. This was a deliberate act, and he was intentionally homeless. His wife then applied for rehousing. She alleged that her husband had assured her that the family would be rehoused under an agreement between his trade union and the local authorities to rehouse those employed with tied accommodation for seven years. The authority refused to consider the wife's application on this basis. It was held that they should have considered her misapprehension because it meant that she was not guilty of acquiescence.

In *Wincentzen* v *Monklands DC* [1988] SLT 259, [1988] SLT 847 Ms W was a single, homeless, epileptic teenager who until the age of 16 lived with her father but then decided to stay temporarily with her mother (who was separated from her father) while at college. Her father warned her that if she left he would not have her back. She did not believe him, but he refused to let her return. The local authority considered her intentionally homeless, but the Court found that she had acted in genuine ignorance of her father's true intention and so her acts could not be regarded as 'deliberate'. Simple lack of realisation of facts is not enough if a reasonable person would have understood them, but in this case there was a bona fide belief that the threat was not real.

2. What about criminal activities leading to a custodial sentence? In *R* v *Hounslow LBC, ex parte R* [1997] *The Times*, 25 February, R was sentenced to seven years' imprisonment for paedophile offences, and had to terminate his tenancy as he could no longer pay the rent. On his release he applied as a homeless person and was found intentionally homeless on the basis that his condition was the result of the offences which were deliberate acts in consequence of which he had ceased to occupy accommodation, etc. It was

held that, objectively, R's cessation of occupation of accommodation could have been regarded as a likely consequence of his deliberate actions.

(ii)   The chain of causation
The deliberate act or omission must be one in *consequence* of which the applicant ceased to occupy available accommodation: there must be a continuing causal connection between the deliberate act in consequence of which homelessness resulted and the homelessness existing at the date of the inquiry; but in looking at the cause of the homelessness it is necessary to have primary regard to the position *at the time when the homelessness arose*, and not to the position at the time of the application or inquiry. Sometimes it is necessary to *look beyond the most immediate cause* of the homelessness, and go back to the cessation of occupation of 'available' accommodation. The key decisions were again made relatively early in the interpretative sequence of homelessness provisions. They are, respectively, the Court of Appeal decision in *Dyson* v *Kerrier DC* and the subsequent House of Lords decision in *Din* v *Wandsworth Borough Council*.

Dyson v *Kerrier DC*
[1980] 1 WLR 1205

In September 1978 the plaintiff, who was expecting a baby, went to live with her sister in a council flat in Huntingdon where the child was born. Shortly afterwards her sister moved to Helston, but the plaintiff remained in occupation of the flat and on 2 October 1978, the council transferred the tenancy into her name. On 10 November the plaintiff signed a tenancy agreement for a 'winter let' of a flat in Helston which expired on 31 March 1979. The tenancy was not protected by the Rent Act 1977. She then surrendered the tenancy of the flat in Huntingdon. Early in 1979 she applied to the defendant council, as housing authority, for accommodation representing to them that she was homeless because her sister had left the Huntingdon flat. The council having ascertained the true position in relation to that flat, informed her through their housing officer by a letter dated 19 March, after a further application by her for accommodation, that her homelessness was going to be treated as 'self-induced'. The plaintiff failed to leave the flat at the end of the tenancy and the landlord obtained an order for possession on 18 May to take effect on 25 May. Four days before the order took effect the council informed the plaintiff that since this was a case of self-induced homelessness they would provide her with accommodation for one month from 25 May. In fact they allowed her to remain in hotel accommodation until 6 July. On 3 July they advised her formally of the decision of the housing committee on 2 July that she was homeless with a priority need but that she had become homeless intentionally.

The plaintiff brought proceedings against the council in the county court seeking declarations that she had not become homeless intentionally, that the council were in breach of their duty under s. 4(4) of the Housing (Homeless Persons) Act 1977 in failing to ensure that accommodation was available for her from 6 July 1979, an order that the council secure such accommodation was available, and damages.

BRIGHTMAN LJ (delivering the unanimous judgment of the court): . . . Two issues arise. First, did the district council correctly construe and apply section 17 in deciding that she became threatened with homelessness, and became homeless, 'intentionally'? If so, did they secure that accommodation was made available for her occupation for a period which could properly be considered as giving her a reasonable opportunity of herself securing accommodation for her occupation? The first question is the important one. If the plaintiff's homelessness could not properly be treated as 'intentional', then there is no doubt that the district council became and are liable to secure accommodation for her occupation indefinitely. The second question arises under section 4(3). It depends on whether the district council had completed their statutory inquiries under section 3 and made their decision at the time when they wrote their letter of May 21, and whether such letter was a sufficient notification to the plaintiff of their decision, or whether such decision was not made until July 2, and notified on July 3. In the latter case the period of two or three days allowed to her for making her own arrangements to secure accommodation was admittedly inadequate.

The argument on behalf of the plaintiff before the judge in the county court was that the district council were not entitled under section 17 to look at what had happened at Huntingdon. The council were only entitled to look at what the plaintiff had done or omitted to do in relation to the accommodation she was occupying immediately before she became homeless or threatened with homelessness. By taking into account what happened at Huntingdon, the district council considered matters which they were not entitled to consider on a proper interpretation of section 17. The judge came to the conclusion that section 17(1) included an act or omission deliberately contrived in respect of accommodation other than that last occupied by the applicant. Section 17(2) was to be construed in parallel manner. The district council were therefore entitled to find on March 19, 1979, that she had become threatened with homelessness intentionally; and that, when she became actually homeless, that also was 'intentional.' He also held that, as she was notified on March 19, 1979, that she was being treated as a case of intentional homelessness, she was allowed sufficient time pursuant to section 4(3) for securing her own accommodation.
. . .

As we have already indicated, counsel for the plaintiff submits that, as both subsections (1) and (2) are couched in the present tense, they relate only to the existing home, if one exists, or to the last home if none exists. That is to say, subsection (1) is directed to the case of a homeless person who loses his last home because he has done or failed to do something in consequence of which he ceases to occupy that accommodation which is available for his occupation. Subsection (2) is directed to the case of a person who is threatened with the loss of his existing home because he does or fails to do something the likely result of which is that he will be forced to leave that accommodation which is available for his occupation.

Neither subsection, it was submitted, can apply to this case. The argument is formidable. On March 19, 1979, when the district council made their decision, the plaintiff was threatened with homelessness. Therefore, the relevant subsection is subsection (2). Subsection (2) says that a person becomes threatened with homelessness 'intentionally' if he deliberately does or fails to do anything the likely result of which is that he will be forced to leave accommodation which is available for his occupation. The Huntingdon flat cannot be treated as that accommodation, because it was not accommodation which, on March 19, the plaintiff 'will be forced to leave.' She had already left it. Nor could it be said on March 19 that it was accommodation 'which is available' for the plaintiff's occupation, because it was not so available. Nor can the Helston flat be treated as accommodation within the subsection. It was not available for her after March 31, 1979. In the result, it was submitted, neither the Huntingdon flat nor the Helston flat was accommodation within subsection (2). Nor does subsection (1) apply. She did not become finally homeless until May 25, 1979. The accommodation which she then ceased to occupy was not accommodation 'which is available' for her occupation.

Although subsections (1) and (2) of section 17 are drafted in the present and future tenses, they are in fact also referring to past events. Subsection (1) reads:

> . . . a person becomes homeless intentionally if he deliberately does or fails to do anything in consequence of which he ceases to occupy accommodation which is available for his occupation and which it would have been reasonable for him to continue to occupy.

This subsection is dealing with cause and effect. The subsection states the effect first. The specified effect is the state of being homeless. The subsection specifies that effect and then describes a particular cause which, if it exists, requires the effect to be treated as intentional. The subsection therefore means

> a person becomes homeless intentionally if he deliberately has done or failed to do anything in consequence of which he has ceased to occupy accommodation which was available for his occupation and which it would have been reasonable for him to continue to occupy.

Does that formulation apply to the Huntingdon flat? In our judgment it does. The district council were entitled to reach the conclusion that the plaintiff became homeless on May 25, 1979, intentionally because she deliberately had done something (surrendered the Huntingdon tenancy) in consequence of which she ceased to occupy accommodation (the Huntingdon flat) which was available for her occupation and which it would have been reasonable for her to continue to occupy; and that, therefore, if she had not done that deliberate act she would not have become homeless on May 25.

In the result, when the plaintiff became homeless on May 25, the district council had no duty under section 4(5) to house her permanently.

We must now consider whether a similar result flows from subsection (2). By parity of reasoning this subsection means that a person becomes threatened with homelessness intentionally if he deliberately has done or failed to do anything the likely result of which is that he will be forced to leave accommodation which is available for his occupation and which it would have been reasonable for him to continue to occupy. On March 19, 1979, it could properly be said of the plaintiff that she had previously done something (surrendered the Huntingdon tenancy) the likely and indeed the inevitable result of which was that she would be forced to leave accommodation (the Huntingdon flat) which was available for her occupation and which it would have been reasonable for her to continue to occupy; as a result of which she was, on March 19, 1979, threatened with homelessness on March 31, intentionally. Therefore, the district council could properly take the view, which they did take, on March 19 that subsection (2) was satisfied.

In the result the only duty of the district council on March 19, 1979, when the plaintiff was threatened with homelessness, was to furnish advice and appropriate assistance under section 4(2), and their only duty on May 25, 1979, when she became homeless, was to secure short-term accommodation for her under section 4(3).

Din v Wandsworth Borough Council
[1983] AC 657

In 1977, Mr Din and his wife, the appellants, and their four children were occupying suitable accommodation in Wandsworth. By the middle of 1979 he was in financial difficulties and arrears of rent were mounting, but because the landlord had not begun legal proceedings against him, officials of the housing authority (at a housing aid centre) advised Mr Din to stay. Nevertheless he and his family left the premises in August 1979 when a distress warrant for non-payment of rates was served on him, moving into unsuitable accommodation in Upminster (unsuitable largely because it was overcrowded). It was accepted that by December the landlord would probably have evicted him. On 20 December the appellants applied to the housing authority for accommodation as homeless persons under the Act of 1977. That was refused on the ground that their homelessness was 'intentional' within the Act.

The appellants brought an action against the housing authority claiming damages and a mandatory injunction to house them. The judge in the county court having found in their favour, the Court of Appeal reversed his decision.

The House of Lords by a majority of 3:2 (Lords Russell and Bridge dissenting) upheld the decision of the Court of Appeal.

LORD WILBERFORCE: . . . So how does the matter stand? If one takes the words of the statute, the council has to be satisfied that the applicants became homeless intentionally (section 17). Under section 4(2)(b) their duty is limited to advice and assistance if 'they are satisfied . . . that they became homeless . . . intentionally.' The time factors here are clearly indicated: at the time of decision (the present), the local authority must look at the time (the past) when the applicants became homeless, and consider whether their action then was intentional in the statutory sense. If this was the right approach there could only be one answer: when the Dins left 56, Trinity Road their action was intentional within section 17, and the council was entitled to find that it would have been reasonable for them to continue to occupy 56, Trinity Road.

The appellants' argument against this is as follows: whatever the position may have been in July 1979 when they left 56, Trinity Road, at the time of the decision in December 1979 they would have been homeless in any event: the original cause of homelessness (even if intentional) had ceased to operate. For section 17 to apply there must be a causal nexus between the intentional action and the homelessness subsisting at the time of the decision. On the facts of the case there was not, so that the decision was wrong in law. I am unable to accept this argument.

1. It cannot be reconciled with the wording of the Act. This is completely and repeatedly clear in concentrating attention on when the appellants became homeless

and requiring the question of intention to be ascertained as at that time. To achieve the result desired by the appellants it is either necessary to distort the meaning of 'in consequence of which he ceases to occupy' (section 17(1)) or to read in a number of words. These are difficult to devise. Donaldson LJ suggests adding at the end of section 17(1) 'and still to occupy': the appellants, as an alternative 'to the date of his application.' Both are radical – and awkward – reconstructions of the section.

2.   Such an interpretation, or reconstruction, of the Act is not called for by any purposive approach. As I have pointed out, the Act reflects a complex interplay of interests. It confers great benefits upon one category of persons in need of housing, to the detriment of others. This being so, it does not seem unreasonable that, in order to benefit from the priority provisions, persons in the first category should bring themselves within the plain words. Failure to do so involves, as Mr Bruneau pointed out, greater expense for a hard pressed authority, and greater pressure on the housing stock.

3.   The appellants' interpretation adds greatly to the difficulties of the local authority's task in administering this Act. It requires the authority, as well as investigating the original and actual cause of homelessness, to inquire into hypotheses – what would have happened if the appellants had not moved, hypotheses involving uncertain attitudes of landlords, rating authorities, the applicants themselves, and even intervening physical events. The difficulty of this is well shown by the singularly imprecise and speculative evidence given as to what was likely to have happened in December 1979 – see above. This approach almost invites challenge in the courts – all the more if it is open to applicants to litigate the whole state of facts with witnesses, de novo, in the county court, but still significantly if the applicants are limited to judicial review. On the other hand the respondents' contention involves a straightforward inquiry into the circumstances in which the applicants became homeless.

4.   The appellants' argument is not assisted by the case of *Dyson* v *Kerrier District Council* [1980] 1 WLR 1205. There (as here) the applicant intentionally surrendered available accommodation in order to go to precarious accommodation (a 'winter letting') from which she was ejected and so became homeless. It was held (in my opinion, rightly) that she had become homeless in consequence of her intentional surrender. This does not in any way support an argument that a subsequent hypothetical cause should be considered to supersede an earlier actual cause. It merely decides that a disqualification for priority by reason of an intentional surrender is not displaced by obtaining temporary accommodation. As pointed out by Ackner LJ in the Court of Appeal, it can be displaced by obtaining 'settled' accommodation.

5.   It does not follow from accepting the respondents' argument that occupants who move before a notice to quit takes effect will be held to be intentionally homeless. Such cases are likely to be covered by section 1(3), referred to above.

I agree therefore with the majority of the Court of Appeal in holding that the present case falls squarely within the provisions of the Act as to intentional homelessness and that there is no justification for reading these provisions otherwise than in their natural sense.

In the result the local authority was entitled to decide, on the facts, and in law, that the appellants became intentionally homeless. I would dismiss this appeal.

Lords Fraser, and Lowry delivered concurring judgments.

Their Lordships clearly found the issue difficult, and the dissents of Lords Bridge and Russell are clear and powerful. For example, Lord Bridge stated (at p. 683):

But if a housing authority are minded to rely against an applicant on the fact that he voluntarily left accommodation on some date in the past as the cause of his present homelessness and to make that the basis of their conclusion that he became homeless intentionally, I do not see how the question how long the accommodation would otherwise have continued to be available for his occupation, hypothetical though it may be, can in all cases be avoided. In a sense perhaps it is a matter of degree. At one end of the spectrum, as already indicated, is the case (as in *Dyson*) where there was no reason to anticipate eviction from the vacated accommodation and the housing authority can properly assume that it would have remained available indefinitely. At the other end is the case where a court order for possession has already been made but the applicant, for some reason, leaves voluntarily more than 28 days before the date named in the order when, in the authority's view, it would have been reasonable for him to remain. But between these two extremes there may be an almost infinite variety of circumstances in which an occupier of residential accommodation will find himself in more or less obvious and more or less imminent danger of eviction on grounds which cannot be attributed to any earlier deliberate act or omission on his part and where he may choose to leave voluntarily rather than wait for a court order for possession to be made against him. In any such case, the housing authority, on considering a later application for accommodation under the Act, assuming they find that he left the previous accommodation prematurely, having ascertained the relevant facts, must ask themselves the question: if the applicant had not left his previous accommodation, is it likely that he would now be homeless? If they answer that question in the negative, and that conclusion is one which a reasonable authority could reasonably reach on the facts, their conclusion that the applicant became homeless intentionally will, of course, be beyond challenge in the courts. But if they simply ignore the question, they fail to take account of the relevant issue which arises as to the cause of his present homelessness, and thus proceed upon an erroneous construction of the Act.

. . .

I am not at all sorry to reach this conclusion. It would seem to me a great injustice if a homeless person in priority need having once left accommodation prematurely, no matter how short the period for which the accommodation would have remained available and in which it would have been reasonable for him to continue to occupy it, may thereafter by treated as intentionally homeless for an indefinite period and thus disqualified from claiming the major benefit which the Act confers.

Nevertheless, the majority view clearly represents the law, enabling the authority to relate back current homelessness to past intentionality unless, of course, the 'chain of causation' is too flimsy or extended, or something occurs to break it. Perhaps the most obvious way to 'break the chain' is via the acquisition of a 'settled residence' (see *Lambert* v *Ealing Borough Council* [1982] 1 WLR 550, at p. 557).

It is, however, not completely clear how secure, or prospectively longstanding, accommodation must be to count as 'settled' for this purpose, a point of some importance given that the majority of premises available in the private sector are now let on short-term assured shorthold tenancies (see chapters 2 and 3). It *is* certainly clear that the causal link can, in principle, be broken by matters other than the acquisition of a 'settled' residence. In *R* v *Brent LBC, ex parte Awua* [1996] 1 AC 55, at p. 69, Lord Hoffmann stated:

The distinction between a settled residence and temporary accommodation is thus being used to identify what will break the causal link between departure from accommodation which it would have been reasonable to continue to occupy and homelessness separated from that departure by a period or periods of accommodation elsewhere. This jurisprudence is well-established . . . and nothing I have said is intended to cast any doubt upon it, although I would wish to reserve the question of whether the occupation of a settled residence is the sole and exclusive method by which the causal link can be broken.

(For further details of this case, see p. 322.)

(iii)   Accommodation available for occupation

The vacated property must be 'accommodation' (see earlier notes) and must have been *available for occupation* by the applicant's family unit. Note that accommodation is 'available' for a person's occupation only if it is available for occupation both 'by him [*and* by] any other person who might reasonably be expected to reside with him' (Housing Act 1996, s. 176).

In *R* v *Peterborough CC, ex parte Carr* (1990) 22 HLR 207, Ms Carr, who was pregnant, left her sister's house after her sister had refused to let her boyfriend (the putative father of her child) move in. The local authority found her intentionally homeless. This was quashed. The accommodation she left was not available for her occupation because it was not also reasonably available to her boyfriend, with whom she could reasonably be expected to reside.

(iv)   Reasonableness of continued occupation

The question is whether it would have been *reasonable to stay*, not whether it was reasonable to go. It may not be reasonable to continue to occupy overcrowded or poor quality accommodation. With regard to domestic disputes, the case law seems to draw a distinction between violent and non-violent disputes: as regards the former, it may not be reasonable to continue to occupy; as regards the latter, it may nevertheless be reasonable to stay.

R v *London Borough of Wandsworth, ex parte Nimako Boateng*
(1983) 11 HLR 95

The applicant was living with her husband and child in Ghana. In March 1982, when she was pregnant with her second child, she left the matrimonial home, and went to stay with her grandparents. In June 1982, she left Ghana and came to the United Kingdom, of which she was a citizen. For a period, during which her second child was born, she was housed by relatives, and in due course applied to the local authority as homeless.

During interviews with the authority, the applicant stated that she had left her husband because he had been treating her badly, although not with violence, and that she had left him voluntarily. It appeared that her accommodation with her grandparents was not settled or secure, nor was the accommodation with relatives in this country more than of limited benefit. The applicant stated that she had wanted her second child to be born in this country, where medical facilities would be available which would have been too expensive for her in Ghana.

The authority concluded that she had become homeless intentionally in that it would have been reasonable for her to remain in occupation of the marital home, rather than to leave Ghana to come to England without settled or secure accommodation available to her here. The applicant sought judicial review of this decision.

WOOLF J: . . . The first interview that was held with the applicant on behalf of the authority was carried out by a Mrs Grzybek on 16 February 1983. The applicant explained to Mrs Grzybek why the accommodation with her sister was of limited benefit. When asked about the reasons why she left Ghana, she replied that it was because her marriage had broken down three months beforehand and she wanted to give birth to her second child in England. She was asked why this was so, and she replied that the medical facilities in Ghana would have been inadequate for her needs. On further questioning it was established that there were hospital facilities available to her, but the type of treatment that she required would have been too expensive. The applicant also dealt with the accommodation that she had shared with the grandmother.

A further interview was held with the applicant on 22 February 1983. On that occasion the accommodation which had been the matrimonial home in Ghana was discussed and she was asked to explain the circumstances leading up to her quitting that accommodation. The answer that the applicant gave was that her husband had been treating her badly. When she was asked in what form that treatment had been, she said that he had been staying away from home, sometimes several days at a time, without giving her any explanation. She was asked if her husband had ever been violent towards her. She said that she had left the accommodation voluntarily and that when she left her husband was still in occupation of it. She added that she had not been in touch with her husband since.

That account of the matter was passed to the Principal Housing Aid Officer, Mr Bruneau, who was responsible for making the decision in this case. Mr Bruneau dealt with the reasons for coming to the decision that he did in paragraph 5 of his affidavit. He said:

In reaching a decision, my decision to find the applicant intentionally homeless I considered her previous addresses both in England and Ghana. I was satisfied that there were no extraordinary reasons which had forced the applicant to flee from Ghana to England despite the obvious lack of settled, secure accommodation available on arrival in England. I did not consider her stay at her grandmother's in Ghana as settled or secure but concluded that the cause of homelessness, therefore her present state of homelessness was as a result of abandoning her marital home in Ghana. Despite incertitude towards her relationship with her husband, the applicant did not indicate any violence or fear of violence from the husband or anyone else within the marital home. That being the case, I concluded that it would have, on evidence obtained from the applicant, been reasonable for her to remain in occupation of her marital home. I therefore decided after taking account of all the facts known to the Council, that it was unreasonable for the applicant to leave Ghana to come to England.

Mr Bruneau then went on to consider the problems with regard to accommodation in the Wandsworth area, which I do not need to go into, but they were clearly relevant having regard to sub-s. (4) of s. 17 of the 1977 Act.

The first point which is taken on that reasoning of Mr Bruneau, which, if I may say so with respect, I find very comprehensive, is that he dealt with an irrelevant consideration and had clearly taken it into account, namely, the reason why the applicant left Ghana. It is submitted that what was relevant was why the applicant left the former matrimonial home.

I am afraid I do not agree with that submission. Here, one of the matters that was put to the officer who interviewed the applicant on the two occasions was that the applicant had been coming to this country apparently in order to obtain medical assistance in relation to the child which she was expecting. Of course, that could have given rise to a situation where, apart from the matrimonial difficulties, she could not reasonably have been expected to continue to occupy the matrimonial home. If there was a good reason, quite apart from the matrimonial reasons, for her leaving Ghana, that was clearly something which could cause the authority to take the view that she was not intentionally homeless. If I may take a situation where, for some political reason, perfectly satisfactory accommodation in Ghana becomes accommodation which a particular person cannot reasonably be expected to continue to occupy, that is something which, in my view, the housing authority would be entitled to take into account when considering the obligations and the duties it owes when exercising its functions under s. 17 of the Act. So it seems to me that here it was reasonable, having regard to the matters put forward by the applicant, for the local authority to look at the position in relation to why the applicant left Ghana to come to England.

Having come to the conclusion that there was nothing which justified the applicant leaving Ghana to come to England, which the authority thought would affect their position under s. 17, what they then did, if I may say so perfectly sensibly, was first of all to decide which of the accommodations in Ghana it was proper to look at: Was it the grandmother's accommodation, which was the accommodation the applicant occupied immediately before leaving Ghana, or was it the accommodation she had occupied with her husband? The authority came to a conclusion, in favour of the applicant in some ways, that it was the accommodation which was the matrimonial home because they took the view that the grandmother's accommodation was not sufficiently settled and secure to be relevant.

In considering the matrimonial accommodation, what was relevant was the marital conduct to which the applicant was subjected by her husband whilst she was living there. Of course, there could be conduct on the part of a husband, who could not be prevented from entering the home, which could make it quite impossible to say that it would reasonable for the wife to continue to occupy that accommodation. Having regard to the paragraph of the affidavit which I have read, that is quite clearly something that has been accepted by the deponent on behalf of the authority because he is assessing the quality of this particular conduct. The conclusion that he came to was that there was no fear of any violence and, on that basis, he formed the opinion that it would be reasonable for the applicant to remain in the accommodation provided by the matrimonial home, having regard to the fact that she had no secure accommodation elsewhere: the grandmother's accommodation was unsatisfactory and she had no accommodation when she came back to this country, which ultimately she decided to do.

In my opinion, that is a conclusion to which the authority were fully entitled to come. I am afraid that I fundamentally disagree with Mr Allfrey's approach to the problem because he admits as part of his third submission that here no local authority could reasonably come to the conclusion that this authority did and, what is more, as a second submission, they misdirected themselves in law in taking the view that they could come to that conclusion. As I understand Mr Allfrey's submissions – and I may be doing them an injustice (although I hope not) in dealing with them in this way – it is fundamental to his approach that you start off with the premise that it is for a wife and not a local authority to decide whether or not she can go on living with her husband. As long as she is acting in good faith when she decides to leave the matrimonial home because of her husband, that is something which the local authority must accept.

That is not the situation as I understand it. It is certainly, in my view, not the situation when it comes to somebody who is leaving a home in this country. There are all sorts of protection that a woman can get if her husband misbehaves. The local authority could perfectly properly in many cases in this country take the view that it would be reasonable for the wife to continue to occupy accommodation and to say to a wife, if she thinks it right:

> If you are having trouble with your husband, go to the appropriate authority, be it a magistrates' court or the Family Division, and get protection against your husband.

If the woman does not then take that course and chooses to leave, the authority could then take the view that it was reasonable for the lady to remain.

Section 17 of the Act could have been drawn on the basis that as long as the person was reasonable in leaving the matrimonial home, then they should not be regarded as intentionally homeless. However, that is not how s. 17 is worded. It deals with a different situation, namely, whether or not the person concerned could reasonably have continued to occupy the accommodation. That results in a different test and in a different situation. It is understandable that Parliament should have approached the matter in that restricted way because it must be borne in mind that, as in Wandsworth, there is a great scarcity of accommodation which would be appropriate for the occupation of a person who is not regarded as intentionally homeless. Housing authorities have demands made upon their accommodation not only from persons making applications under this Act, but from ordinary members of the public who are on housing lists. One result of the Act is to promote persons falling within the provisions of the Act over the heads of those who are on housing lists. Parliament clearly recognised that there were cases where that should happen. But if a person is to have the benefit of that assistance, they have got to be put before the housing authority a situation which, on investigation by the authority, indicates that the person seeking assistance is not intentionally homeless. If the housing authority, on the material they have before them, find that as a result of their investigations properly carried out, they can regard the person as intentionally homeless, then it is their duty not only to ratepayers, but to those on their housing list, to say fairly and squarely to the applicant:

> This is a case where you have rendered yourself intentionally homeless.

It follows from all that I have said in this judgment that this is an application, now that I have the evidence of the housing authority before me, which is bound to fail. Accordingly, I dismiss the application.

Further discussion of domestic violence and the reasonableness (or otherwise) of continued occupation can be found in *R* v *Kensington and Chelsea*

Royal Borough Council, ex parte Hammell [1989] 1 QB 518, and *R v Tynedale DC, ex parte McCabe* (1992) March 1992 *Legal Action* 12. In the case of violence or threats of violence outside the domestic sphere, there is some suggestion in *R v Croydon LBC, ex parte Toth* (1987) 20 HLR 576 that there will be cases where the applicant may be expected to remain and seek police protection (see O'Connor LJ, at p. 583); but this will depend entirely on the circumstances of each case (as would be expected from an issue of 'reasonableness'), as is demonstrated well by the rather extreme case of *R v Hillingdon LBC, ex parte H* (1988) 20 HLR 554, where the applicant (an ex-soldier) had been threatened and harassed by the IRA, and *R v Northampton BC, ex parte Clarkson* (1992) June 1992 *Legal Action* 16, where the authority had failed to take sufficient account of the threat posed by *sexual harassment*.

Further important issues are, first, the economic circumstances of the applicant had he or she remained in his or her previous accommodation, and (secondly) the general housing circumstances in the area to which the person has applied for accommodation (see now s. 177(2), Housing Act 1996, which links this issue both to intentional homelessness and homelessness *per se*).

As to the first issue, in *R v Royal Borough of Kensington and Chelsea, ex parte Bayani* (1990) 22 HLR 406, Nicholls LJ (concerning departure from accommodation in the Philippines) stated (at p. 417):

Mrs Bayani's contribution was one aspect of the financial picture. The other aspect was the family's financial position in the Philippines. On that the housing officer knew, from his inquiries, that Mr Bayani had employment in the Philippines, since at least 1985. The housing officer also knew that Mr Bayani's income was supplemented from Mrs Bayani's earnings. In my view, given the question to which the housing authority's inquires were directed, it was not incumbent on the housing authority to probe further in this case. The question, it will be recalled was not whether it was reasonable for Mrs Bayani to leave her home in Manilla and come to the United Kingdom temporarily for work. It may very well be that Mrs Bayani acted reasonably, and with considerable selflessness and devotion to her family, in doing so. The question facing the housing authority was a different one. The question was whether it would have been reasonable for Mrs Bayani to have remained with her family in Manilla. Only if it would have been unreasonable for her to have stayed there would she be outside the statutory definition of intentionally homeless. I suppose there might be a case in which a decision by a wife, coping with a difficult pregnancy, to remain with her husband and older child in adequate, available accommodation in her home country, where her husband was employed, rather than to leave them and travel to the United Kingdom by herself, with no secure accommodation arrangements here, in order to preserve her immigration status and her ability to supplement the family income from temporary earnings, could be castigated as unreasonable, but it would need to be an altogether remarkable and exceptional set of circumstances for that to be so. In the present case, the housing officer would know, as we all do, that comparatively modest sums of sterling sent from this country to some, less developed, countries can have a value to recipients there out of all proportion to the value such sums have here. He knew that Mrs Bayani had been coming to this country every year for some years in order to boost the family income in just that way. I consider that, given that knowledge, and given what he knew about the accommodation in Manilla, the housing officer knew enough to form a view, fairly, on the question he had to answer. He was entitled, without making further inquiries, to conclude, as he did, that the financial situation did not render it unreasonable for Mrs Bayani to live in the Philippines.

As to the second issue, in *R v Leeds City Council, ex parte Adamiec and Adamiec* (1991) 24 HLR 138, at p. 153, Webster J cited, with approval, the following affidavit from the respondent's director of housing services:

The stock of council housing within the area administered by Leeds City Council comprises approximately 83,244 properties. The Council has sold approximately 14,000 houses to tenants under the provisions of the Housing Act 1980 – about 16% of the original stock. Controls on capital financing have resulted in virtually no new council house building. The number of council houses administered by my Department are therefore steadily decreasing.

At the present time there are over 21,000 applicants on the waiting list for council accommodation. These include about 500 families who, although accorded homeless persons priority, are as yet without permanent accommodation.

The lettable voids level within this authority is no more than 0.7%

About 12,000 housing applications are received each year of which 5,000 are from applicants claiming homelessness. There are many demands for housing which the Council endeavour to satisfy. As well as discharging its duties to the homeless under the provisions of the Housing Act 1985, my Department seeks to satisfy the demands of other groups which are considered to have urgent need for housing. These include those with urgent medical need; in clearance areas; persons requiring housing under the provisions of the National Mobility Scheme; those with a confirmed social need or confirmed urgent sheltered need, and a very small number of key workers.

As well as housing unintentionally homeless persons accorded priority, the Council aims to house others with an urgent need. My Department have housed about 4,000 families since April 1990, and by March 31, 1991 it is anticipated that this figure will have risen to 5,000. Of these approximately 1,500 will be those families to whom the Council have accorded homeless persons status and have thus been housed pursuant to the provisions relating to homeless persons. The remainder are largely from those groups referred to earlier in this affidavit who also have a pressing need.

My Department works within a framework of an increasing number of applications for housing from a decreasing housing stock. It is of vital importance that only those persons or families who are genuinely unintentionally homeless are given priority for rehousing, otherwise other groups would suffer. It can be seen that for several thousand families on the waiting list there is little or no prospect of housing being offered to them for many years.

(v) Can a person found to be intentionally homeless make a subsequent application?
An applicant may not make a second application based on exactly the same facts (see *Delahaye v Oswestry BC* [1980] *The Times*, 29 July). What, however, if the facts of the applicant's circumstances change?

In *R v Harrow London Borough Council, ex parte Fahia* [1998] 3 WLR 1396, F was evicted in 1994 from her home following a possession order. She applied to Harrow who found her intentionally homeless. They accordingly owed her only a time limited duty to accommodation (see now s. 190 of the 1996 Act) and placed her in a guesthouse. That accommodation was due to end on 17 February 1994, but F did not then leave, and Harrow continued to pay her rent for a further year while she stayed there. In July 1995 Harrow decided it should no longer meet the cost of F's stay in the guesthouse, and in consequence the owner of the guesthouse told F she would have to leave. A charity asked Harrow to find F accommodation, but they argued that they were under no duty at all to assist her as there had been no change in her circumstances from the first finding of intentional homelessness. They carried out an informal investigation but concluded that the stay in the guesthouse did not break the chain of causation from her original act of intentional homelessness because she had had no settled accommodation. It was held at first instance and in the Court of Appeal that the chain of causation can be broken otherwise than by obtaining a period of settled accommodation. Harrow conceded that point in the House of Lords. Harrow, however, then argued that they were not bound to consider a second application from F unless she could show a change in circumstances which might lead to the second application being successful. The House of Lords rejected that argument. There is a *duty* to make a proper statutory inquiry once an authority have reason to believe a person may be homeless or threatened with it and may have a priority need. In the instant case F was clearly threatened with homelessness, and her application was not the same as her initial one – she had had the intervening year in the guesthouse and that changed her circumstances.

Questions
1.   The statute defines intentional homelessness in terms of 'deliberate' acts or omissions. Is there any indication anywhere else in the statutory provisions that this should not be given the meaning it bears in criminal law, namely that the person has turned his or her mind to the consequences of an activity and has desired to bring them about?
2.   Much of the definition of intentional homelessness arises from judicial interpretation of the statute. Is it acceptable that non-elected officials such as the judiciary should be responsible for such a sensitive issue of public policy?

(H)   Referral to another housing authority

Housing Act 1996

Referral of case to another local housing authority
198.—(1)   If the local housing authority would be subject to the duty under section 193 (accommodation for those with priority need who are not homeless intentionally) but consider that the conditions are met for referral of the case to another local housing authority, they may notify that other authority of their opinion.

The authority need not consider under section 197 whether other suitable accommodation is available before proceeding under this section.

(2)   The conditions for referral of the case to another authority are met if—

(a)   neither the applicant nor any person who might reasonably be expected to reside with him has a local connection with the district of the authority to whom his application was made,

(b)   the applicant or a person who might reasonably be expected to reside with him has a local connection with the district of that other authority, and

(c)   neither the applicant nor any person who might reasonably be expected to reside with him will run the risk of domestic violence in that other district.

(3)   For this purpose a person runs the risk of domestic violence—

(a)   if he runs the risk of violence from a person with whom he is associated, or

(b)   if he runs the risk of threats of violence from such a person which are likely to be carried out.

(4)   The conditions for referral of the case to another authority are also met if—

(a)   the applicant was on a previous application made to that other authority placed (in pursuance of their functions under this Part) in accommodation in the district of the authority to whom his application is now made, and

(b)   the previous application was within such period as may be prescribed of the present application.

(5)   The question whether the conditions for referral of a case are satisfied shall be decided by agreement between the notifying authority and the notified authority or, in default of agreement, in accordance with such arrangements as the Secretary of State may direct by order.

(6)   An order may direct that the arrangements shall be—

(a)   those agreed by any relevant authorities or associations of relevant authorities, or

(b)   in default of such agreement, such arrangements as appear to the Secretary of State to be suitable, after consultation with such associations representing relevant authorities, and such other persons, as he thinks appropriate.

(7)   No such order shall be made unless a draft of the order has been approved by a resolution of each House of Parliament.

Local Connection

199.—(1)   A person has a local connection with the district of a local housing authority if he has a connection with it—

(a)   because he is, or in the past was, normally resident there, and that residence is or was of his own choice,

(b)   because he is employed there,

(c)   because of family associations, or

(d)   because of special circumstances.

(2)   A person is not employed in a district if he is serving in the regular armed forces of the Crown.

(3)   Residence in a district is not of a person's own choice, if—

(a)   he becomes resident there because he, or a person who might reasonably be expected to reside with him, is serving in the regular armed forces of the Crown, or

(b)   he, or a person who might reasonably be expected to reside with him, becomes resident there because he is detained under the authority of an Act of Parliament.

(4)   In subsections (2) and (3) 'regular armed forces of the Crown' means the Royal Navy, the regular forces as defined by section 225 of the Army Act 1955, the

regular air force as defined by section 223 of the Air Force Act 1955 and Queen Alexandra's Royal Naval Nursing Service.

(5)   The Secretary of State may by order specify other circumstances in which—

(a)   a person is not to be treated as employed in a district, or

(b)   residence in a district is not to be treated as of a person's own choice.

Duties to applicant whose case is considered for referral or referred

200.—(1)   Where a local housing authority notify an applicant that they intend to notify or have notified another local housing authority of their opinion that the conditions are met for the referral of his case to that other authority—

(a)   they cease to be subject to any duty under section 188 (interim duty to accommodate in case of apparent priority need), and

(b)   they are not subject to any duty under section 193 (the main housing duty), but they shall secure that accommodation is available for occupation by the applicant until he is notified of the decision whether the conditions for referral of his case are met.

(2)   When it has been decided whether the conditions for referral are met, the notifying authority shall notify the applicant of the decision and inform him of the reasons for it.

The notice shall also inform the applicant of his right to request a review of the decision and of the time within which such a request must be made.

(3)   If it is decided that the conditions for referral are not met, the notifying authority shall secure that accommodation is available for occupation by the applicant until they have considered whether other suitable accommodation is available for his occupation in their district.

If they are satisfied that other suitable accommodation is available for his occupation in their district, section 197(2) applies; and if they are not so satisfied, they are subject to the duty under section 193 (the main housing duty).

(4)   If it is decided that the conditions for referral are met, the notified authority shall secure that accommodation is available for occupation by the applicant until they have considered whether other suitable accommodation is available for his occupation in their district.

If they are satisfied that other suitable accommodation is available for his occupation in their district, section 197(2) applies; and if they are not so satisfied, they are subject to the duty under section 193 (the main housing duty).

(5)   The duty under subsection (1), (3) or (4) ceases as provided in that subsection even if the applicant requests a review of the authority's decision (see section 202).

The authority may continue to secure that accommodation is available for the applicant's occupation pending the decision on a review.

(6)   Notice required to be given to an applicant under this section shall be given in writing and, if not received by him, shall be treated as having been given to him if it is made available at the authority's office for a reasonable period for collection by him or on his behalf.

Application of referral provisions to cases arising in Scotland

201.   Sections 198 and 200 (referral of application to another local housing authority and duties to applicant whose case is considered for referral or referred) apply—

(a)   to applications referred by a local authority in Scotland in pursuance of sections 33 and 34 of the Housing (Scotland) Act 1987, and

(b)   to persons whose applications are so transferred,

as they apply to cases arising under this Part (the reference in section 198 to this Part being construed as a reference to Part II of that Act).

Notes
1. The 'local connection' or 'referral' provisions should be only used once all the prior issues (save that under s. 197) have been determined. The basic requirements are:

(a) the applicant has no local connection with area of the authority applied to (notifying authority);
(b) there is a local connection with another local housing authority's area (notified authority) (NB: not a *greater* connection);
(c) there is no risk of domestic violence to the applicant, etc. in the area of the notified authority.

In addition, a further ground for referral is:

(d) the applicant was placed in the area of the notifying authority by the notified authority in pursuance of the notified authority's homelessness functions within the previous period of five years (see s. 198(4) and SI 1996 No. 2754, reg. 6).

Note that ground (d) is free-standing and can be relied on even if the other conditions outlined above are not met.
2. Section 199 defines basic factors for determining the existence of a 'local connection':

(a) normal residence of choice in an area;
(b) employment in an area;
(c) family associations with an area;
(d) any other special circumstances.

However, in each case whether such a connection exists is a matter of fact and (a)–(d) above must be reasonably applied to the facts in coming to a decision.
3. Section 200 lays down the duties to referred applicants. There is no interim duty to accommodate under s. 188 (see above), nor a 'main housing duty' under s. 193 (see below), but only a duty to make accommodation available for occupation by the applicant until notified of the decision whether the conditions for referral are met. If conditions are met the applicant must be informed. The applicant can request a review (see further below), but otherwise the applicant is the responsibility of the notified authority, and they must accommodate him until they decide whether or not there is other suitable accommodation for the applicant in their area; and if there is not, they come under the main housing duty. If the conditions for referral are not met *the notifying authority comes under these obligations.*

(i)   Local connection: meaning of 'normal residence'
'Normal residence' is, of course, a concept the meaning of which is open to
wide variations in interpretation. In the following case, Lord Brightman
examined the term:

R v *Eastleigh Council, ex parte Betts*
[1983] 2 AC 613

LORD BRIGHTMAN: . . . My Lords, the Housing (Homeless Persons) Act 1977
entitles a homeless person to apply to a housing authority for accommodation. If the
housing authority to whom application is made considers that the applicant has no
local connection with the area of that authority, the authority may be in a position to
transfer the statutory responsibility to another housing authority with whose area the
applicant has a local connection. The respondents to this appeal, Ronald Thomas
Betts and Vivien Anne Betts, became homeless through no fault of their own at a time
when they were living in the area of the appellants the Eastleigh Borough Council
('Eastleigh') in Hampshire. They applied to Eastleigh for accommodation. Mr and
Mrs Betts had formerly lived in the area of the Blaby District Council ('Blaby') in
Leicestershire. Both Eastleigh and Blaby are in agreement that the responsibility for
housing Mr and Mrs Betts properly belongs to Blaby. Mr and Mrs Betts, who wish
to remain in the area of Eastleigh, seek to challenge that decision by way of judicial
review. They were successful before the Court of Appeal.
   Mr Betts is 37 years of age. He was born in London, and in his early years worked
there. In 1973 he lived and worked in Dunstable. In the following year he moved to
Milton Keynes and commuted to work in London. Thereafter he lived and worked
abroad for a while. In 1978 he secured a job in Leicester and went to live in a council
house in the Blaby area. In the meantime Mr and Mrs Betts' two daughters had been
born, the elder being now aged 9 and the younger nearly 5.
   In August 1980 Mr Betts left his family temporarily in order to take up employment
with Southern Television as a film processor at their studios in Southampton. In
October he secured rented accommodation in the Eastleigh area, and Mrs Betts and
their daughters joined him there. He gave up his Blaby council house, regrettably
without giving the council any notice and with arrears of rent outstanding. Unfortunately Southern Television lost their franchise shortly afterwards and as a result Mr
Betts lost his employment. He again fell into arrears with his rent. On February 3,
1981, an order for possession was made against him, to take effect on March 3. On
February 6 he was given an interview with Mr Renouf, a senior assistant in the Estates
Management Department of Eastleigh, and he applied under the Act for accommodation.
   The immediate result of that application was that Eastleigh became under a
statutory duty to make inquiries to satisfy themselves that Mr and Mrs Betts were in
fact homeless, and to ascertain whether they had a 'priority need' for accommodation
by reason of dependent children and whether they had become homeless 'intentionally' within the meaning of the Act: section 3(1) and (2). Furthermore Eastleigh
became entitled, if they thought fit, to make inquiries as to whether the applicants had
'a local connection with the area of another housing authority': section 3(3). Eastleigh
also became under a duty to secure that temporary accommodation was made
available for occupation by Mr and Mrs Betts pending any decision which Eastleigh
might make as a result of their inquiries: section 3(4). Eastleigh has performed the

duty of securing temporary accommodation for Mr and Mrs Betts by making a dwelling-house available for them at 85 High Street, Eastleigh.

As a result of inquiries, Mr Grant, the chief housing officer of Eastleigh, had satisfied himself by February 25, 1981 (see his letter of that date), that Mr and Mrs Betts were homeless, had a priority need for accommodation, and were not homeless intentionally. Eastleigh thereby became under a duty under section 4(5) of the Act, replacing their previous duty under section 3(4), to secure that (permanent) accommodation became available for Mr and Mrs Betts subject however to section 5. Section 5 defines responsibility as between different housing authorities, and it is with this section that this appeal is concerned. In his letter of February 25, Mr Grant added

> Your application under the Act has been notified to Blaby District Council because you have lived in this borough for less than 6 months, and are not employed in this borough and do not have any relatives here. Your rehousing is therefore considered to be their responsibility.

This assessment of the situation is accepted by Blaby, but not by Mr and Mrs Betts.

. . .

The attack on Eastleigh hinges on the chief housing officer's letter of February 25, 1981, and the inference to be drawn from his statement that 'your application under the Act has been notified to Blaby District Council because you have lived in this borough for less than 6 months.' The evidence in relation to that letter is somewhat brief, but is not challenged by Mr and Mrs Betts. Mr Renouf deposed that after he had reported to Mr Grant, the chief housing officer, the result of his preliminary inquiries, Mr Grant 'confirmed that this application should be referred to the Blaby District Council under section 5 of the Act of 1977 because the applicants had no local connection with the respondents but they had a local connection with Blaby District Council.' This was elaborated by Mr Grant in his own affidavit in the following terms:

> The applicants' application for accommodation came before me on February 23, 1981, when I had to give a decision as to whether they should be offered accommodation. After considering a report from Mr Renouf, my senior assistant (estate management), I decided that the application should be referred to Blaby District Council under the section 5 of the Housing (Homeless Persons) Act 1977 as I considered that the responsibility for housing the applicants lay with that council. The decision was taken by me having regard to the wording of the Act together with the recommendations set out in the 'Agreement on Procedures for Referrals of the Homeless – Revised June 6, 1979' issued by the Association of District Councils, Association of Metropolitan Authorities and the London Borough Association . . .
>
> Upon considering the report of Mr Renouf, the crucial factor in my decision was that the applicants did not have a 'local connection' with the Borough of Eastleigh, within the meaning of section 5 of the 1977 Act. The phrase 'local connection' is defined in section 18(1) of the Act of 1977, but as section 18(1)(b) and section 18(1)(c) were not applicable, unless the applicants were 'normally resident' in the borough within the meaning of section 19(1)(a) or unless any special circumstances applied, a local connection with the respondent would not be established. In considering the question of 'normally resident' I had regard to the revised 'Agreement on Procedures for Referrals of the Homeless' which states that a 'working definition of normal resident' should be that the household has been residing 'for

at least six months in the (borough) during the previous twelve months' (clause 2.5). The applicants having only resided in the borough for some four months before the date of their application on February 6, 1981, I considered that a 'normal residence' had not been established within the meaning of the Act. The 'Revised Agreement on Procedures for Referrals of the Homeless' is in wide use by housing authorities when considering a referral under section 5 of the Act of 1977, and Blaby District Council fully accepted the working definition of normal residence.

. . .

My Lords, that is not the fundamental question. The fundamental question is the existence of a 'local connection.' In construing section 5 it is only to be expected that the emphasis falls on 'local connection,' and not on past or present residence or current employment, etc. The Act is one which enables a homeless person in certain circumstances to jump over the heads of all other persons on a housing authority's waiting list, to jump the queue. One would not expect any just legislation to permit this to be done unless the applicant has in a real sense a local connection with the area in question. I accept that 'residence' may be changed in a day, and that in appropriate circumstances a single day's residence may be enough to enable a person to say that he was normally resident in the area in which he arrived only yesterday. But 'local connection' means far more than that. It must be built up and established; by a period of residence; or by a period of employment; or by family associations which have endured in the area; or by other special circumstances which spell out a local connection in real terms.

I return to the Agreement on Procedures. Faced with section 5 of the Act, a housing authority is involved, not with the question whether the applicant is or was normally resident etc. in the area in question, but whether the applicant has a local connection with that area. Has the normal residence of the applicant in the area been of such a duration as to establish for him a local connection with the area? To answer that question speedily it is sensible for local authorities to have agreed guidelines. I see nothing in the least unreasonable with a norm of six months' residence during the previous twelve months, or three years' residence during the previous five years. Seeing that the section is concerned with a subsisting and not with a past local connection, it is also reasonable to work on the basis that, after five years have gone by, no local connection based on residence is likely to have any relevance.

So I start my conclusions on this appeal by expressing the view that paragraph 2.5 of the Agreement on Procedures is eminently sensible and proper to have been included in the agreement. Although 'an opinion' formed by a housing authority under section 5(1) must be concluded by reference to the facts of each individual case, there is no objection to the authority operating a policy or establishing guidelines, for reasons which the authority may legitimately entertain, and then applying such policy or guidelines generally to all the applications which come before them, provided that the authority do not close their mind to the particular facts of the individual case. There is ample authority that a body which is charged with exercising an administrative discretion is entitled to promulgate a policy or guidelines as an indication of a norm which is intended to be followed: see, for example, the speech of Lord Reid in *British Oxygen Co. Ltd* v *Board of Trade* [1971] AC 610.

As regards the meaning of 'normally resident' in the context of section 18(1)(a), this will take its colour from the fact that residence of any sort will be irrelevant unless and until it has been such as to establish a local connection with the area in which such residence subsists or has subsisted. I doubt whether in these circumstances any elaborate attempt at a definition of 'normally resident' will be profitable. They are ordinary English words, which in many contexts will mean what this House said 'ordinarily resident' meant in *Shah* [1983] 2 WLR 16. But they are only a subsidiary component of the formula which a housing authority will be applying under section 5 of the Act. If the residence of an applicant has been of a sufficient duration to create a local connection, no difficulty is likely to arise in deciding whether such residence was normal. But if it were necessary to decide such a point in a particular case, I do not think that the housing authority would be wrong if they applied to the words 'normally resident' the meaning which in *Shah* was attached to the words 'ordinarily resident,' remembering that the real exercise will be to decide whether the normal residence has been such as to establish a subsisting local connection.

That leaves me with a single question, which is the ultimate one in this appeal; whether Eastleigh misdirected themselves in reaching the opinion that the applicants did not have a local connection with the Eastleigh area. The onus of establishing this is upon the applicants. They rely principally on the wording of the letter of February 25, 1981, which says that Blaby have been notified 'because you have lived in this borough for less than six months.' The question before Eastleigh being whether the applicants had a local connection with the Eastleigh area as a result of residence, I see nothing whatever wrong with the decision by Eastleigh that as the applicants had lived in the area for less than six months, it was considered that they did not have a local connection with that area. It is true that the letter does not expressly refer to the absence of a local connection, only to the briefness of the residence, but it is to be observed that in his affidavit of June 21, 1982, which I have quoted, Mr Renouf attributes the decision under section 5 to lack of a local connection, which is the correct approach.

In my opinion the applicants have not made out any ground for attacking the validity of the opinion formed by Eastleigh under section 5(1). Eastleigh therefore are not under a duty under section 4(5) of the Act to house the applicants. I would allow this appeal.

(ii) 'Domestic violence': s. 198(2) and (3)
As regards the issue of potential 'domestic violence' in the area of the notified authority, a controversial conclusion was reached in *R v Bristol City Council, ex parte Browne* (the facts appear in the judgment of Lloyd J, at p. 1439):

R v Bristol City Council, ex parte Browne
[1979] 1 WLR 1437

LLOYD J: . . . I now turn to the facts of this particular case, and it is important that they should be stated in some detail. The applicant arrived in this country from Limerick in Eire on March 12, 1979. She was accompanied by her seven children. She is now 29. She was married in 1967 and lived with her husband at Tralee in County Kerry. According to her affidavits, of which we have two before us, her husband is a man given to violence. She refers to a number of incidents of violence culminating in November 1978. As a result of that incident she was advised by her doctor to leave the matrimonial home and go to the Women's Aid hostel in Limerick where she remained with her children for some four and a half months. She left that hostel in March 1979, and she says she did so because her husband had discovered her whereabouts.

At all events, the people who run the hostel in Limerick made arrangements for her to come to Bristol where they put her in touch with the Bristol Women's Aid office. She arrived by air in Bristol on March 12. They had paid her airfare of £152. She was met by a representative of the Bristol Women's Aid at the airport, and she spent her first night in England at their hostel.

The next day she visited the Bristol council's housing aid centre at 11 o'clock in the morning, accompanied by two representatives of Bristol Women's Aid. There she was presented as a homeless person. She was interviewed by two of the council's officers, Mr Jeremy Ball and Mr Rex Hodgkinson, and they started inquiries at once as provided by section 3 of the Act. They also booked accommodation for her and for her children at a local guesthouse, initially for one night, while they completed their inquiries.

There was a further discussion on the afternoon of the same day with representatives of Bristol Women's Aid when Mr Hodgkinson asked why the applicant in this case had been brought to England when they no accommodation for her. The explanation they gave was that the accommodation which they had hoped to provide for her had been taken up by three emergency admissions over the weekend.

On the next day, March 14, Mr Ball telephoned a Mr Burke, who is the community welfare officer in Tralee and is the man responsible for homeless families in that part of Ireland. Mr Burke said that if the applicant were to return to Tralee with her children he would make provision for her and her children.

The next day, March 15, Mr Hodgkinson spoke to the same Mr Burke in order to satisfy himself as to what the position was. I think it is best that I should quote from his affidavit in which he describes that conversation. He says:

> Following Mr Ball's telephone conversation with Mr Burke, the community welfare officer in Tralee on March 14, 1979, I subsequently spoke to Mr Burke on March 15, 1979, and he assured me that if the applicant returned to Tralee accommodation would be secured for her and her children upon her arrival. He indicated to me that he was fully aware of the applicant's background and volunteered information concerning her husband's illegal activities. I again asked for confirmation that should the applicant return to Tralee he would make provision for her, and he confirmed that he would. In light of this discussion, I concluded that any accommodation which Mr Burke arranged for the applicant would be arranged in the full knowledge of her husband's violent nature and that Mr Burke would have regard to the possibility of violence in arranging that accommodation.

The case was then considered by Mr Martin, the principal assistant in charge of housing aid and information services at Bristol, and the superior of Mr Ball and Mr Hodgkinson. He had in fact been in touch with the case from the start, and having discussed the matter with Mr Ball and Mr Hodgkinson, he came to the following decisions, which I quote from Mr Martin's Affidavit:

> (a) That the applicant was homeless. (b) That the applicant had a priority need. (c) That the applicant had not become homeless intentionally. (d) That the applicant did not have a local connection with the city of Bristol but that it would not be appropriate to transfer responsibility to another housing authority under section 5 of the Act as there was no relevant housing authority in England, Wales or Scotland.

He concluded on the basis of those findings that the council was under a duty to secure that accommodation became available for the applicant. Those findings and that conclusion were subsequently set out in a written notification dated March 15 which was given to the applicant in accordance with section 8 of the Act.

Mr Martin then gave consideration to the question how the council should perform its duty under the Act. Again it is best to give Mr Martin's reasons in his own words. I quote from his affidavit:

I concluded that the authorities in Tralee in Eire had with full knowledge of the facts surrounding her case indicated their willingness to accept responsibility for the applicant and that the community welfare officer charged with the responsibility of securing the health and well-being of the inhabitants of the area would not have agreed to the applicant returning if he was not able to make arrangements for the applicant to be adequately protected against any risk of violence. I therefore concluded that as the primary responsibility for the applicant rested with the Irish authorities in the country from which she had originated, and as the authorities were prepared to take responsibility for the applicant, the city council could properly carry out its duties in this way under the provisions of section 6(1)(c) of the Act, i.e. by giving such advice and assistance as would secure the applicant to obtain accommodation from some other person.

Meanwhile, while all this had been going on, the council had arranged to continue to provide accommodation for the applicant and her children at the guesthouse at a cost, we are told, of about £18 a night.

On March 16 the matter was referred to the housing committee. They had before them a report of the director of housing, and the committee determined unanimously, after what appears from the minute of the meeting to have been a full discussion of the question, that the applicant should be assisted to return to Ireland if she wished to take advantage of that assistance. The minute reads:

After further debate, it was unanimously agreed that, in view of the assurance of assistance from the community welfare officer in Tralee, Eire, Mrs Browne and her family should return to Eire and that she be assisted in an approach regarding a travel warrant.

At 5 p.m. on the same day, Mr Ball told the applicant of the committee's decision. He also told her that an appointment had been made for her to see the Department of Health and Social Security at 10 a.m. on March 19 with a view to their providing her with a travel warrant if she wished to take advantage of the assistance offered by the council to return to Eire. The applicant thereupon said that she had no wish to return to Ireland. Mr Ball also informed her that, if she did not take advantage of the council's offer of assistance, the case would be referred back to the housing committee on March 19.

The applicant failed to attend at the meeting which had been arranged with the Department of Health and Social Security at 10 a.m. on March 19. She again explained that her reason was that she had no intention of returning to Ireland.

The matter then went back to the housing committee on March 19. There was a further discussion, at the end of which it was decided to continue the provision of accommodation at the guesthouse until March 20 and not beyond. Thereafter the cost of her accommodation was defrayed jointly by Bristol Women's Aid and by Shelter for a few days until April 2, when they declined to help her further.

Just to complete the history of the matter, on April 5, there was an application to this court for leave to apply for judicial review, which was granted. On April 6 the applicant went back to the housing aid centre in Bristol and again presented herself as a homeless person. She was again interviewed, on this occasion by Mr Hodgkinson. Mr Hodgkinson again discussed the matter with Mr Martin, and it was decided to treat that application as being a fresh application notwithstanding the previous decision. Accordingly, the council prepared notification, this time dated April 6, under section 8 of the Act in identical terms to the previous notification. On the afternoon of April 6, Mr Hodgkinson informed the applicant of the council's decision. Again I think it is important to quote his precise words. He said:

I offered to provide the applicant with transport and to make funds available for her in order to purchase train and boat tickets for the return journey to Eire. The applicant told me that she would not require this assistance as she did not wish to return to Eire. I explained that bed and breakfast accommodation would be provided until the morning of Monday April 9, 1979, and that if she had any change of mind over the weekend should contact me first thing on Monday morning. I advised the applicant that if she did decide to return to Eire then she should contact the community welfare officer in Tralee.

Mr Hodgkinson also handed the applicant a letter dated April 6, 1979, from the director of housing, which read:

With reference to your visit to the housing aid centre this morning, I attach herewith the written notification as required under section 8 of the Act. This decision must be regarded by you as a final decision and is made without prejudice to this authority's view that their duty towards you has already been discharged. You have been verbally informed that I am satisfied that accommodation will be made available upon your return to the Republic of Ireland and travel and other relevant details will be provided. However, in view of the particular circumstances of your case this further assistance is being given although the city council does not consider that it is statutorily obliged to do so and no consideration will be given to any further application under the Act.

Those being the facts of the case, the sole question for our consideration is whether the council has complied with its statutory duty under the Act. That turns on the language of section 6(1) of the Act, which I have already read in full and need not read again. It provides in effect, that the council can perform its duty either by providing accommodation itself or by securing that the homeless person obtains accommodation from some other person or by giving such advice and assistance as will secure that the homeless person obtains accommodation from some other person.

In the present case, on the facts which I have recited, it is clear beyond any doubt that the council has given such advice and offered such assistance (although it has not been accepted) as would enable the applicant to obtain accommodation from Mr Burke, the community welfare officer in Tralee. It is true that there is no affidavit from Mr Burke himself, but there is no reason why we should not accept what is said by Mr Ball and Mr Hodgkinson in that respect.

Thus the question comes down to this very narrow point: is Mr Burke a 'person' within the meaning of section 6(1)(c) of the Act? In my judgment, he is. Indeed, Mr Denyer, who has appeared on behalf of the applicant, did not suggest the contrary, or at any rate did not suggest it very strenuously. Putting the question of violence on one side, Mr Denyer accepted that the council could fulfil its duty under the Act by assisting the applicant and her children to go back to Tralee, even though Tralee is outside the jurisdiction. It may well be that in most cases the person referred to in section 6(1)(c) of the Act will be a person within the area of the housing authority in question. But there is nothing in the Act which expressly so confines it; and, as I say, Mr Denyer did not strenuously argue that it should be so confined.

The real point which Mr Denyer makes is that the applicant should not, on the special facts of this case, be asked to go back to Tralee, because that is the place where she has suffered the domestic violence in the past. In that connection Mr Denyer referred us to section 5(3) and (4) of the Act, which I should now read in full:

(3) It shall be the duty of the notified authority to secure that accommodation becomes available for occupation by the person to whom the notification relates if neither he nor any person who might reasonably be expected to reside with him has a local connection with the area of the notifying authority but the conditions specified in subsection (4) below are satisfied.

(4) The conditions mentioned in subsection (3) above are (a) that the person to whom the notification relates or some person who might reasonably be expected to reside with him has a local connection with the area of the notified authority, and ' — and this is the important condition' (b) that neither he nor any such person will run the risk of domestic violence in that area.

It is not of course argued that Tralee is itself a housing authority within the meaning of the Act of 1977; nobody suggests that the conditions set out in section 5(4) apply as such. But what is suggested is that section 5(4) can and should be applied, as it were, by analogy.

There is, I think, a short answer to that submission. The fact that Tralee is the place from which the applicant has come and the place where she has suffered violence in the past does not mean that she would necessarily suffer any risk of violence if she goes back. Obviously she will not go back to the same house; but there is other accommodation in the same area. The risk involved in her going back was, in my judgment, a matter for the council to consider together with the community welfare officer in Tralee. The passages from the affidavits which I have read show that that risk was considered very carefully by the council. The view which they have formed is quite clear, namely, that accommodation can be provided in Tralee without risk to the applicant or her children. There is no material on which this court can possibly interfere with that conclusion or say that it was not justified. Mr Denyer's main point, therefore fails.

Although strictly this is not a 'local connection' case (Tralee not being a notifiable authority), the analogies are clear enough, and indeed are specifically alluded to in Lloyd J's judgment. The decision might be thought to be overly sanguine as to the lack of likelihood of violence, but the subsequent decision in *R v London Borough of Islington, ex parte Adigun* again illustrates judicial unwillingness to interfere too far with local authority judgment in this area.

R v London Borough of Islington, ex parte Adigun
(1986) 20 HLR 600

The applicant was the joint tenant with her husband of a house owned by the City of Liverpool District Council. The applicant left her husband because of his violence towards her and came to London in June 1984 to stay with a friend, who lived in the area of the respondent authority. On 18 June 1984 the applicant presented as homeless to the authority. On the interview form the authority noted that there was no local connection with their area, and that responsibility lay with Liverpool City Council.

The respondent authority contacted the Liverpool City Council and established that the applicant's husband had moved out of the property, taking his furniture with him. The property had been re-let in May 1984 and it was believed that the applicant's husband had returned to Nigeria. The respondent authority referred the application to the Liverpool City Council under the local connection provisions and so notified the applicant in August 1984. The applicant, who did not wish to return to Liverpool's area, sought judicial review of this decision.

MANN J: . . . The officer of the respondent who took the decision is Mrs Brown who has deposed as follows:

> The reasons for my decision were that Mrs Adigun had left a joint tenancy in Liverpool in April 1984 as the result of a marital dispute. I did address my mind as to whether, if Mrs Adigun returned to Liverpool, she would run the risk of domestic violence in that area. I relied on the information supplied to us by Liverpool Council that the applicant's husband had moved out of the previous matrimonial home and returned to Nigeria. Liverpool Council had also stated that they had taken possession of the previous matrimonial home and it had been re-let in May 1984. I therefore believe that I was entitled to rely on this information as being correct. Although there is no reference to violence in the form completed by Mrs E. Edwards, she told me that the marital dispute involved violence. I am fully aware of the provisions of section 5 of the 1977 Act and in considering the application and the obvious local connection with Liverpool I also considered quite specifically the allegation of domestic violence. Though there was no independent evidence of this violence I accepted for the purpose of my decision that Mrs Adigun was correct in her assertions. Had there been no other information I should not have referred the matter to Liverpool because of the requirement in section 5(1)(a). However, the inquiries made of the Liverpool District Housing Office showed that Mr Adigun had given up possession of the former home, that someone else had moved in, and that he was believed to have returned to Nigeria with his furniture. Since the authority had re-let the property on May 7, 1984 this was credible information and I believed it to be accurate; nothing that has happened since indicates it was not accurate. On that basis I concluded that there was no risk of violence if the applicant returned to Liverpool. I therefore instructed that a notice under section 8 of the Housing (Homeless Persons) Act 1977 should be served which is in the form of a letter referred to in the applicant's affidavit and is in fact dated August 2, 1984.

The applicant is and has been unwilling to return to Liverpool and is still resident in Islington. The reason for her reluctance is her fear of her husband. On her behalf three points are taken. The first is this. The decision of August 2, is flawed because the respondent did not as a matter of law have sufficient information which could have led them to be satisfied that there was no risk of domestic violence in Liverpool. The available material is that to which I have referred, that is to say the re-letting of the flat by the City of Liverpool District Council and the observation that the husband was believed to have gone to Nigeria with his furniture, and it is said that material was insufficient in point of law to negative a risk. The task of determining risk or not is the task of the local authority. (See the opening words of paragraph 5 of section 5(1).)

In considering the submission I have in mind the words of Lord Brightman in *Puhlhofer (A.P.) and Another (A.P.)* v *London Borough of Hillingdon* (February 6, 1986) where his Lordships [sic] said:

> My Lords, I am troubled at the prolific use of judicial review for the purpose of challenging the performance by local authorities of their functions under the Act.

Parliament intended the local authority to be the judge of fact. The Act abounds with the formula when, or if, the housing authority are satisfied as to this, or that, or have reason to believe this, or that. Although the action or inaction of a local authority is clearly susceptible to judicial review where they have misconstrued the Act, or abused their powers or otherwise acted perversely, I think that great restraint should be exercised in giving leave to proceed by judicial review. The plight of the homeless is a desperate one, and the plight of the applicants in the present case commands the deepest sympathy. But it is not, in my opinion, appropriate that the remedy of judicial review, which is a discretionary remedy, should be made use of to monitor the actions of local authorities under the Act save in the exceptional case. The ground upon which the courts will review the exercise of an administrative discretion is abuse of power – e.g. bad faith, a mistake in construing the limits of the power, a procedural irregularity, or unreasonableness in the *Wednesbury* sense – unreasonableness verging on an absurdity: see the speech of Lord Scarman in *R v Secretary of State for the Environment, ex parte Nottinghamshire County Council* [1986] 2 WLR 1 at p. 5. Where the existence or non-existence of a fact is left to the judgment and discretion of a public body and that fact involves a broad spectrum ranging from the obvious to the debatable to the just conceivable, it is the duty of the court to leave the decision of that fact to the public body to whom Parliament has entrusted the decision-making power save in a case where it is obvious, that the public body, consciously or unconsciously, are acting perversely.

There is material upon which the respondent could have decided as it did. No doubt criticisms could be made of the quality of that material and criticisms have been made of the quality of that material. However, in practical terms I see no other sensible course that the local authority could have adopted other than that of contacting the City of Liverpool District Council. Material was, as a result of that contact, put before Islington and I find it impossible to say that they acted perversely. The first ground, therefore, fails.

(iii) Dispute resolution procedures

Disputes over referrals between authorities are to be referred to resolution procedures. These are provided, pursuant to s. 198(5) of the 1996 Act, by a Local Authority Agreement procedure originally made in 1979. In addition there is now an Order regulating the procedure and processes for referral (for a stark illustration of the conflicts which can arise between authorities, see *R v Slough BC, ex parte Ealing LBC* [1981] QB 801).

Homelessness (Decisions on Referrals) Order 1998
SI 1998 No. 1578

Citation and commencement
1. This Order may be cited as the Homelessness (Decisions on Referrals) Order 1998 and shall come into force on the twenty eighth day after the day on which it is approved by resolution of each House of Parliament.

Arrangements for deciding whether conditions for referral are satisfied
2. The arrangements set out in the Schedule to this Order are those agreed by the Local Government Association, the Welsh Local Government Association, the Association of London Government and the Convention of Scottish Local Authorities, and

shall be the arrangements for the purposes of section 198(5) and (6)(a) of the Housing Act 1996.

Revocation of order

3.—(1)   Subject to paragraph (2), the Housing (Homeless Persons) (Appropriate Arrangements) Order 1978 ('the 1978 Order') is hereby revoked.

(2)   The 1978 Order shall remain in force for any case where a notified authority has received a notification under section 67(1) of the Housing Act 1985 or section 198(1) of the Housing Act 1996 (referral to another local housing authority) prior to the date on which this Order comes into force. [20th July 1998]

SCHEDULE

The arrangements

Appointment of person by agreement between notifying authority and notified authority

1.   Where the question whether the conditions for referral of a case are satisfied has not been decided by agreement between the notifying authority and the notified authority, the question shall be decided by a person appointed by those authorities.

Appointment of person other than by agreement between notifying authority and notified authority

2.   If within a period of 21 days commencing on the day on which the notified authority receives a notification under section 198(1) of the Housing Act 1996 a person has not been appointed in accordance with paragraph 1, the question shall be decided by a person—

   (a)   from the panel constituted in accordance with paragraph 3, and
   (b)   appointed in accordance with paragraph 4.

3.—(1)   Subject to sub-paragraph (2), the Local Government Association shall establish and maintain a panel of persons from which a person may be appointed to decide the question whether the conditions for referral of a case are satisfied.

(2)   The Local Government Association shall consult such other associations of relevant authorities as they think appropriate before—

   (a)   establishing the panel,
   (b)   inviting a person to join the panel after it has been established, and
   (c)   removing a person from the panel.

4.—(1)   The notifying authority and the notified authority shall jointly request the Chairman of the Local Government Association or his nominee ('the proper officer') to appoint a person from the panel.

(2)   If within a period of six weeks commencing on the day on which the notified authority receives a notification under section 198(1) of the Housing Act 1996 a person has not been appointed, the notifying authority shall request the proper officer to appoint a person from the panel.

Procedural requirements

5.—(1)   Subject to the following provisions of this paragraph, the procedure for deciding whether the conditions for referral of a case are satisfied shall be determined by the appointed person.

(2)   The appointed person shall invite written representations from the notifying authority and the notified authority.

(3)   The appointed person may also invite—
    (a)   further written representations from the notifying authority and the notified authority,
    (b)   written representations from any other person, and
    (c)   oral representations from any person.
(4)   If the appointed person invites representations from any person, those representations may be made by a person acting on his behalf, whether or not legally qualified.

Notification of decision

6.   The appointed person shall notify his decision, and his reasons for it, in writing to the notifying authority and the notified authority.

Costs

7.—(1)   The notifying authority and the notified authority shall pay their own costs incurred in connection with the arrangements set out in this Schedule.
(2)   Where a person has made oral representations, the appointed person may give directions as to the payment by the notifying authority or the notified authority or both authorities of any travelling expenses reasonably incurred by that person.

Meaning of 'appointed person'

8.   In this Schedule 'appointed person' means a person appointed in accordance with paragraph 1 or 4.

(I)   Duties to various classes of homeless persons

Housing Act 1996

Duty to persons not in priority need who are not homeless intentionally
192.—(1)   This section applies where the local housing authority—
    (a)   are satisfied that an applicant is homeless and eligible for assistance, and
    (b)   are not satisfied that he became homeless intentionally,
but are not satisfied that he has a priority need.
(2)   The authority shall provide the applicant with advice and such assistance as they consider appropriate in the circumstances in any attempts he may make to secure that accommodation becomes available for his occupation.

Duty to persons with priority need who are not homeless intentionally
193.—(1)   This section applies where the local housing authority are satisfied that an applicant is homeless, eligible for assistance and has a priority need, and are not satisfied that he became homeless intentionally.
This section has effect subject to section 197 (duty where other suitable accommodation available).
(2)   Unless the authority refer the application to another local housing authority (see section 198), they shall secure that accommodation is available for occupation by the applicant.
(3)   The authority are subject to the duty under this section for a period of two years ('the minimum period'), subject to the following provisions of this section.
After the end of that period the authority may continue to secure that accommodation is available for occupation by the applicant, but are not obliged to do so (see section 194).

(4)   The minimum period begins with—

(a)   if the applicant was occupying accommodation made available under section 188 (interim duty to accommodate), the day on which he was notified of the authority's decision that the duty under this section was owed to him;

(b)   if the applicant was occupying accommodation made available to him under section 200(3) (interim duty where case considered for referral but not referred), the date on which he was notified under subsection (2) of that section of the decision that the conditions for referral were not met;

(c)   in any other case, the day on which accommodation was first made available to him in pursuance of the duty under this section.

(5)   The local housing authority shall cease to be subject to the duty under this section if the applicant, having been informed by the authority of the possible consequence of refusal, refuses an offer of accommodation which the authority are satisfied is suitable for him and the authority notify him that they regard themselves as having discharged their duty under this section.

(6)   The local housing authority shall cease to be subject to the duty under this section if the applicant—

(a)   ceases to be eligible for assistance,

(b)   becomes homeless intentionally from the accommodation made available for his occupation,

(c)   accepts an offer of accommodation under Part VI (allocation of housing) or,

(d)   otherwise voluntarily ceases to occupy as his only or principal home the accommodation made available for his occupation.

(7)   The local housing authority shall cease to be subject to the duty under this section if—

(a)   the applicant, having been informed of the possible consequence of refusal, refuses an offer of accommodation under Part VI, and

(b)   the authority are satisfied that the accommodation was suitable for him and that it was reasonable for him to accept it and notify him accordingly within 21 days of the refusal.

(8)   For the purposes of subsection (7) an applicant may reasonably be expected to accept an offer of accommodation under Part VI even though he is under contractual or other obligations in respect of his existing accommodation, provided he is able to bring those obligations to an end before he is required to take up the offer.

(9)   A person who ceases to be owed the duty under this section may make a fresh application to the authority for accommodation or assistance in obtaining accommodation.

Powers exercisable after minimum period of duty under s. 193

194.—(1)   Where a local housing authority have been subject to the duty under section 193 in relation to a person until the end of the minimum period, they may continue to secure that accommodation is available for his occupation.

(2)   They shall not do so unless they are satisfied on a review under this section that—

(a)   he has a priority need,

(b)   there is no other suitable accommodation available for occupation by him in their district, and

(c)   he wishes the authority to continue securing that accommodation is available for his occupation;

and they shall not continue to do so for more than two years at a time unless they are satisfied on a further review under this section as to those matters.

The review shall be carried out towards the end of the minimum period, or subsequent two year period, with a view to enabling the authority to make an assessment of the likely situation at the end of that period.

(3) They shall cease to do so if events occur such that, by virtue of section 193(6) or (7), they would cease to be subject to any other duty under that section.

(4) Where an authority carry out a review under this section they shall make such inquiries as they consider appropriate to determine—

(a) whether they are satisfied as to the matters mentioned in subsection (2)(a) to (c), and

(b) whether any of the events referred to in subsection (3) has occurred;

and on completing the review they shall notify the applicant of their determination and of whether they propose to exercise, or continue to exercise, their power under this section.

(5) The authority may at any time, whether in consequence of a review or otherwise, give notice to the person concerned that they propose to cease exercising power under this section in his case.

(6) The notice must specify—

(a) the day on which they will cease exercising their power under this section, and

(b) any action that they intend to take as a result,

and must be given not less than the prescribed period before the day so specified.

Duties in case of threatened homelessness

195.—(1) This section applies where the local housing authority are satisfied that an applicant is threatened with homelessness and is eligible for assistance.

(2) If the authority—

(a) are satisfied that he has a priority need, and

(b) are not satisfied that he became threatened with homelessness intentionally,

they shall take reasonable steps to secure that accommodation does not cease to be available for his occupation.

This subsection has effect subject to section 197 (duty where other suitable accommodation available).

(3) Subsection (2) does not affect any right of the authority, whether by virtue of a contract, enactment or rule of law, to secure vacant possession of any accommodation.

(4) Where in pursuance of the duty under subsection (2) the authority secure that accommodation other than that occupied by the applicant when he made his application is available for occupation by him, the provisions of section 193(3) to (9) (period for which duty owed) and section 194 (power exercisable after minimum period of duty) apply, with any necessary modifications, in relation to the duty under this section as they apply in relation to the duty under section 193.

(5) If the authority—

(a) are not satisfied that the applicant has a priority need, or

(b) are satisfied that he has a priority need but are also satisfied that he became threatened with homelessness intentionally,

they shall furnish him with advice and such assistance as they consider appropriate in the circumstances in any attempts he may make to secure that accommodation does not cease to be available for his occupation.

Duty where other suitable accommodation available

197.—(1) This section applies if the local housing authority would be under a duty under this Part—

(a)   to secure that accommodation is available for occupation by an applicant, or

(b)   to secure that accommodation does not cease to be available for his occupation,

but are satisfied that other suitable accommodation is available for occupation by him in their district.

(2)   In that case, their duty is to provide the applicant with such advice and assistance as the authority consider is reasonably required to enable him to secure such accommodation.

(3)   The duty ceases if the applicant fails to take reasonable steps to secure such accommodation.

(4)   In deciding what advice and assistance to provide under this section, and whether the applicant has taken reasonable steps, the authority shall have regard to all the circumstances including—

(a)   the characteristics and personal circumstances of the applicant, and

(b)   the state of the local housing market and the type of accommodation available.

(5)   For the purposes of this section accommodation shall not be regarded as available for occupation by the applicant if it is available only with assistance beyond what the authority consider is reasonable in the circumstances.

(6)   Subsection (1) does not apply to the duty of a local housing authority under—

section 188 (interim duty to accommodate in case of apparent priority need),

section 190(2)(a) (limited duty to person becoming homeless intentionally), or

section 200(1), (3) or (4) (interim duties where case is considered for referral or referred).

(i)   The 'full' or 'main housing duty'

Under the Housing Act 1996, s. 193, where an authority are satisfied that a person is homeless, eligible, in priority need and unintentionally homeless (subject to s. 197) they *shall* secure that *accommodation* is available to the applicant unless there is a referral to another authority (see above).

This duty continues for a 'minimum period' of two years, and thereafter the authority will have a discretion to secure accommodation but are under no obligation to do so (see further below). However, the official argument is that this is a sufficient period, for the evidence is that the *average* length of time spent waiting for accommodation under ordinary allocation procedures is 1.2 years, thus, as the homeless will be able to register on ordinary housing lists, they should not be disadvantaged by the new provision.

The minimum period begins:

(a)   where an applicant is in accommodation made available under the interim duty to accommodate (i.e. s. 188), on the day the authority's decision that the duty is owed was notified to him/her;

(b)   where an applicant is in accommodation pending a referral but the referral does not proceed, on the day the applicant is notified that the conditions for referral are not met; and

(c)   in any other case, the day on which accommodation was first made available in pursuance of the authority's duty to accommodate (s. 193(4)).

Thus the duty to accommodate which existed under the previous law (Pt III of the Housing Act 1985) became in many ways a duty to accommodate temporarily with a minimum time span of two years. The authority will in any case be freed of their duty if the applicant, having been informed by the authority of the consequences of a refusal, refuses accommodation the authority are satisfied is 'suitable' for him or her *and* the authority notify the applicant that they regard themselves as having discharged their duty (s. 193(5)). (For 'suitability' see s. 210 of the 1996 Act and SI 1996 No. 3204 below.)

An authority can, however, also *cease* to be under the 'full duty' where an applicant:

(a)   ceases to be 'eligible';

(b)   becomes homeless intentionally from that accommodation made available for his or her occupation (e.g., gets thrown out of a homelessness hostel for bad behaviour);

(c)   accepts an offer of ordinary housing under the general allocation procedure;

(d)   otherwise voluntarily ceases to occupy as his or her only or principal home accommodation made available (s. 193(6)).

Furthermore, where an applicant, having been notified by the authority of the consequences of refusal as regards their homelessness duties, refuses an offer of accommodation under general allocation powers, and the authority are satisfied that the accommodation was suitable and that it was *reasonable* for him or her to accept the offer, the authority ceases to be subject to the full duty to secure accommodation. The authority must notify him or her of that within 21 days of his/her refusal (s. 193(7)). For the purposes of s. 193(7), an applicant may reasonably be expected to accept an offer of accommodation under general allocation powers even though under contractual or other obligations with regard to existing accommodation, provided that he or she is able to bring those obligations to an end before being required to take up the offer (s. 193(8)).

Where the main housing duty is terminated, or where an authority cease to be subject to it the person to whom the duty was owed may make a fresh application (s. 193(9)).

(ii)   The limited nature of the duty to accommodate
Under s. 194 of the 1996 Act, where an authority have been under the duty to accommodate *until the end of the minimum period* (not otherwise), they *may* continue to accommodate, but only where:

(a)   they have carried out a review; and

(b)   they are satisfied that the person in question has a priority need; *and*

(c)   they are satisfied that there is no other suitable accommodation available for the person's occupation in their district; *and*

(d)   the person wishes the authority to continue to secure accommodation for him or her.

That discretionary continuation of accommodation can only continue for periods of two years at a time and is subject to biennial review. The review is to be carried out towards the end of each two-year period (s. 194(2)). The authority *must*, however, cease to provide accommodation if the applicant ceases to be eligible, or becomes homeless intentionally or is allocated a home under general powers (s. 194(3)).

In carrying out the review authorities must undertake appropriate inquiries to satisfy themselves as to questions of priority need, etc., or whether any of the events which would end their obligation has happened. They must inform the person of their determination and what they propose to do in consequence.

But note that the discretionary accommodation of a person may also be ended at any time, whether in consequence of a review or not (s. 194(5)). In such a case the authority must inform the person of the day on which they will cease to exercise the power for his or her benefit and any consequential action. The person must be informed by notice which will have to be given at a prescribed time before the day on which the authority will cease to accommodate.

(iii) 'Reasonable' discharge of duties

The foregoing duties are to be *reasonably* discharged (see *R* v *Wyre BC, ex parte Parr* (1982) 2 HLR 7), i.e. there must be no oppression of, or vindictiveness towards the applicant in relation to the accommodation offered. Any property provided to be 'accommodation' must be habitable bearing in mind the applicant's health.

In *R* v *Ryedale DC, ex parte Smith* (1983) 16 HLR 66, Mr and Mrs Smith and their son lived in a caravan. They were visited by a local authority housing officer who recorded no details about Mr Smith, who was 67 and suffered from chronic fibrosis of the lungs and emphysema. The Smiths claimed that in the circumstances they were homeless, and pending determination of their case a further caravan was offered to them. This they refused. The local authority said that having refused this second caravan they were intentionally homeless. That assertion failed because the Smiths had not ceased to occupy the accommodation in question, they had never occupied it at all. However, the local authority then argued that by offering that second caravan they had discharged their duty as it was all the accommodation available at the time. It was held that offers of accommodation under the Act must be considered in the light of appropriate inquiries – inquiries the local authority had failed to make. The caravan was probably not a suitable home for an old and sick man. The Court, however, would not order the local authority to provide a council house, but ordered them to reconsider the matter in the light of proper inquiries.

Recent decisions (such as *R* v *London Borough of Enfield, ex parte Akbas* [1999] *(Housing Law Monitor,* March) indicate a continuing unwillingness to interfere too far with authorities' discharge of their duties. In the *Akbas* case an offer of 15th-floor accommodation to an apparently 'phobic' woman was still seen as 'suitable' by the High Court given the pressure on the authority's accommodation and the need to reserve flats at lower levels for those with 'serious' conditions.

Questions
The incoming Labour Government promised to address the main housing duty problem in June 1997. This they did by the Allocation of Housing (Reasonable and Additional Preference) Regulations 1997 (SI 1997 No. 1902) which came into force on 1 November 1997. Under these regulations authorities are required to modify their allocation schemes so that homeless persons are given *reasonable* preference. Thus, anyone owed the 'main housing duty' under ss. 193 or 195(2) of the 1996 Act, people being found accommodation after the 'minimum period' of the s. 193 duty *and* people who have been given advice and assistance to obtain other 'suitable accommodation' under s. 197 and who are still occupying it, *all* have to be given 'reasonable preference' in the allocation of ordinary council housing.

1.   Why is this *not* a return to the pre-1996 law?
2.   The 'official' line now is that the Housing Act 1996 did not so much change the duties to homeless persons, but rather the way in which they are to be performed. Is this so?

(J)   Right to request review of decision

Housing Act 1996

Right to request review of decision
202.—(1)   An applicant has the right to request a review of—
  (a)   any decision of a local housing authority as to his eligibility for assistance,
  (b)   any decision of a local housing authority as to what duty (if any) is owed to him under sections 190 to 193 and 195 and 197 (duties to persons found to be homeless or threatened with homelessness),
  (c)   any decision of a local housing authority to notify another authority under section 198(1) (referral of cases),
  (d)   any decision under section 198(5) whether the conditions are met for the referral of his case,
  (e)   any decision under section 200 (3) or (4) (decision as to duty owed to applicant whose case is considered for referral or referred), or
  (f)   any decision of a local housing authority as to the suitability of accommodation offered to him in discharge of their duty under any of the provisions mentioned in paragraph (b) or (e).
  (2)   There is no right to request a review of the decision reached on an earlier review.
  (3)   A request for review must be made before the end of the period of 21 days beginning with the day on which he is notified of the authority's decision or such longer period as the authority may in writing allow.
  (4)   On a request being duly made to them, the authority or authorities concerned shall review their decision.

Procedure on a review

203.—(1)   The Secretary of State may make provision by regulations as to the procedure to be followed in connection with a review under section 202.

Nothing in the following provisions affects the generality of this power.

(2)   Provision may be made by regulations—

(a)   requiring the decision on review to be made by a person of appropriate seniority who was not involved in the original decision, and

(b)   as to the circumstances in which the applicant is entitled to an oral hearing, and whether and by whom he may be represented at such a hearing.

(3)   The authority, or as the case may be either of the authorities, concerned shall notify the applicant of the decision on the review.

(4)   If the decision is—

(a)   to confirm the original decision on any issue against the interests of the applicant, or

(b)   to confirm a previous decision—

(i)   to notify another authority under section 198 (referral of cases), or

(ii)   that the conditions are met for the referral of his case,

they shall also notify him for the reasons of the decision.

(5)   In any case they shall inform the applicant of his right to appeal to a county court on a point of law, and of the period within which such an appeal must be made (see section 204).

(6)   Notice of the decision shall not be treated as given unless and until subsection (5), and where applicable subsection (4), is complied with.

(7)   Provision may be made by regulations as to the period within which the review must be carried out and notice given of the decision.

(8)   Notice required to be given to a person under this section shall be given in writing and, if not received by him, shall be treated as having been given if it is made available at the authority's office for a reasonable period for collection by him or on his behalf.

Right of appeal to county court on point of law

204.—(1)   If an applicant who has requested a review under section 202—

(a)   is dissatisfied with the decision on the review, or

(b)   is not notified of the decision on the review within the time prescribed under section 203,

he may appeal to the county court on any point of law arising from the decision or, as the case may be, the original decision.

(2)   An appeal must be brought within 21 days of his being notified of the decision or, as the case may be, of the date on which he should have been notified of a decision on review.

(3)   On appeal the court may make such order confirming, quashing or varying the decision as it thinks fit.

(4)   Where the authority were under a duty under section 188, 190 or 200 to secure that accommodation is available for the applicant's occupation, they may continue to secure that accommodation is so available—

(a)   during the period for appealing under this section against the authority's decision, and

(b)   if an appeal is brought, until the appeal (and any further appeal) is finally determined.

Allocation of Housing and Homelessness (Review Procedures) Regulations 1999
SI 1999 No. 71

PART I

General

Citation, commencement and interpretation

1.—(1) These Regulations may be cited as the Allocation of Housing and Homelessness (Review Procedures) Regulations 1999 and shall come into force on 14th February 1999.

(2) In these Regulations—

'the authority' means the local housing authority which has made the decision whose review under section 164 or 202 has been requested;

'the Decisions on Referrals Order' means the Homelessness (Decisions on Referrals) Order 1998;

'the reviewer' means—

(a) where the original decision falls within section 202(1)(a), (b), (c), (e) or (f), the authority;

(b) where the original decision falls within section 202(1)(d) (a decision under section 198(5) whether the conditions are met for referral of a case)—

(i) the notifying authority and the notified authority, where the review is carried out by those authorities;

(ii) the person appointed to carry out the review in accordance with regulation 7, where the case falls within that regulation.

(3) In these Regulations, references to sections are references to sections of the Housing Act 1996.

Who is to make the decision on the review

2. Where the decision of the authority on a review of an original decision made by an officer of the authority is also to be made by a officer, that officer shall be someone who was not involved in the original decision and who is senior to the officer who made the original decision.

PART III

Homelessness

Request for a review and notification of review procedure

6.—(1) A request for a review under section 202 shall be made—

(a) to the authority, where the original decision falls within section 202(1)(a), (b), (c), (e) or (f);

(b) to the notifying authority, where the original decision falls within section 202(1)(d) (a decision under section 198(5) whether the conditions are met for referral of a case).

(2) Except where a case falls within regulation 7, the authority to whom a request for a review under section 202 has been made shall—

(a) notify the applicant that he, or someone acting on his behalf, may make representations in writing to the authority in connection with the review; and

(b) if they have not already done so, notify the applicant of the procedure to be followed in connection with the review.

Initial procedure where the original decision was made under the Decisions on Referrals Order

7.—(1)   Where the original decision under section 198(5) (whether the conditions are met for the referral of the case) was made under the Decisions on Referrals Order, a review of that decision shall, subject to paragraph (2), be carried out by a person appointed by the notifying authority and the notified authority.

(2)   If a person is not appointed in accordance with paragraph (1) within five working days from the day on which the request for a review is made, the review shall be carried out by a person—

(a)   from the panel constituted in accordance with paragraph 3 of the Schedule to the Decisions on Referrals Order ('the panel'), and

(b)   appointed in accordance with paragraph (3) below.

(3)   The notifying authority shall within five working days from the end of the period specified in paragraph (2) request the Chairman of the Local Government Association or his nominee ('the proper officer') to appoint a person from the panel and the proper officer shall do so within seven days of the request.

(4)   The notifying authority and the notified authority shall within five working days of the appointment of the person appointed ('the appointed person') provide him with the reasons for the original decision and the information and evidence on which that decision was based.

(5)   The appointed person shall—

(a)   send to the notifying authority and the notified authority any representations made under regulation 6; and

(b)   invite those authorities to respond to those representations.

(6)   The appointed person shall not be the same person as the person who made the original decision.

(7)   For the purposes of this regulation a working day is a day other than Saturday, Sunday, Christmas Day, Good Friday or a bank holiday.

Procedure on a review

8.—(1)   The reviewer shall, subject to compliance with the provisions of regulation 9, consider—

(a)   any representations made under regulation 6 and, in a case falling within regulation 7, any responses to them; and

(b)   any representations made under paragraph (2) below.

(2)   If the reviewer considers that there is a deficiency or irregularity in the original decision, or in the manner in which it was made, but is minded nonetheless to make a decision which is against the interests of the applicant on one or more issues, the reviewer shall notify the applicant—

(a)   that the reviewer is so minded and the reasons why; and

(b)   that the applicant, or someone acting on his behalf, may make representations to the reviewer orally or in writing or both orally and in writing.

Notification of the decision on a review

9.—(1)   The period within which notice of the decision on a review under section 202 shall be given under section 203(3) to the applicant shall be—

(a)   eight weeks from the day on which the request for the review is made, where the original decision falls within section 202(1)(a), (b), (c), (e) or (f);

(b)   ten weeks from the day on which the request for the review is made, where the original decision falls within section 202(1)(d) and the review is carried out by the notifying authority and the notified authority;

(c) twelve weeks from the day on which the request for the review is made in a case falling within regulation 7.

(2) The period specified in paragraph (1) may be such longer period as the applicant and the reviewer may agree in writing.

(3) In a case falling within paragraph (1)(c), the appointed person shall notify his decision on the review, and his reasons for it, in writing to the notifying authority and the notified authority within a period of eleven weeks from the day on which the request for the review is made, or within a period commencing on that day which is one week shorter than that agreed in accordance with paragraph (2).

PART IV

Revocation

Revocation and transitional provisions

10.—(1) Subject to paragraph (2), the following provisions are hereby revoked—

(a) regulations 2 to 8 of the Allocation of Housing and Homelessness (Review Procedures and Amendment) Regulations 1996;

(b) the definition of 'the Review Regulations' in regulation 1(3) of the Allocation of Housing and Homelessness (Amendment) Regulations 1997 and regulation 6 of those Regulations.

(2) The provisions revoked by paragraph (1) shall continue in force in any case where a request for a review under section 164 or 202 is made prior to the date these Regulations come into force.

(i) *Procedure*

The right to a review is a once only matter; there is no right to request a review of an earlier review. Review requests have to be made within 21 days of the decision in question (it does not appear that they must be in writing) or such longer period as may be allowed by the authority. No doubt legal advisers usually request longer! Furthermore, there is no definition in the statute of what constitutes a request for review – is a mere expression of disappointment enough?

The legislation itself lays down no prescribed review procedures, but s. 203 empowers the Secretary of State to lay down procedures in regulations, in particular requiring reviews to be carried out by persons of appropriate seniority not involved in the original decision, and the circumstances in which an oral hearing is required and whether representation will be allowed. Where the decision is to confirm the original finding *on any issue* against the applicant's interests, or to confirm a previous decision either to refer an applicant or to inform an applicant that the conditions for referral are met, the authority must notify the applicant of the reasons for such a decision. In *all* cases the authority must inform the applicant of the right to appeal to the county court on a point of law and of the time period for making such an appeal.

(ii) *'fair and lawful' requirement*

In addition to the requirements under regulations, the procedure on review must, of course, be fair and lawful. The Code of Guidance gives supplement-

ary guidance on this issue. It points out that there is an unlimited right to ask
for a review – the applicant does not have to give grounds. Nevertheless, the
authority's notification of the review should invite the applicant to state his
or her grounds for requesting a review (if not already received) and should
elicit any new information the applicant may wish to put forward. The
authority's notification *may* also point out that if no representations are
received they will be entitled to proceed on the basis of facts known to them,
advise the applicant that representations from representatives will be accepted
and draw attention to the time period of the review. The review procedure
should also be notified to the applicant if this has not already been done. It
may be necessary for authorities to elicit further information during the
course of the review, and they are advised to be flexible in this regard, bearing
in mind, however, the need to make decisions on time, subject to obtaining
the consent of the applicant to an extension of time which may be needed if
significant delay is likely.

The Code gives advice on 'irregularity in the original decision' as meaning:

(a)   failure to take into account relevant considerations, or to ignore
irrelevant matters;
(b)   failure to base a decision on the facts;
(c)   bad faith/dishonesty;
(d)   mistake of law;
(e)   decisions contrary to the policy of the 1996 Act;
(f)   unreasonable (in the *Wednesbury* sense) decisions.

These matters may lead to an oral hearing under the regulations, of course,
but authorities *may* have oral hearings otherwise if they wish, particularly
where it is considered that the applicant would be disadvantaged by being
required to make a case in writing. But where an oral hearing is held time
limits (i.e. 56 days) must still be observed unless written agreement to an
extension is reached. Early action to obtain such agreement is counselled
wherever any significant delay is anticipated.

Good practice demands that on the review decision being made a full
statement of reasons should be given, along with notification of the right to
appeal to the county court. Failure to comply with good administrative
practice may also lay an authority open to a maladministration investigation
by the local ombudsman.

(iii)   Further challenge?

The County Court has a wide discretion under the Housing Act 1996 on the
appeal to confirm, quash or vary the decision (s. 204(3)). How will this new
provision relate to judicial review? The existence of the right of appeal on a
point of law will almost certainly preclude judicial review where all that is
alleged is misinterpretation of the statute (see *R* v *Chief Constable of Merseyside, ex parte Calveley* [1986] QB 424), because the Divisional Court will
refuse to exercise its discretion. But it is arguable that judicial review may be

available on other grounds, for example, failing to take into account relevant considerations, or coming to an utterly perverse or unreasonable decision or giving an inadequate statement of reasons where this prejudices the applicant because he cannot appreciate the case that has been made against him. In such cases there could be problems if *both* misinterpretation and, say, unreasonableness are alleged – there could be a need for both an appeal *and* a judicial review application. Furthermore, pending the outcome of an appeal the county court has no express jurisdiction to grant an interim order continuing accommodation.

In *Ali* v *Westminster City Council, Nairne* v *Camden LBC* [1998] *The Times*, 16 September, the Court of Appeal pointed out that the county court has no inherent jurisdiction to grant injunctions – unlike the High Court – and can do so only if permitted by statute. So far as homelessness is concerned the 1996 Act does not grant such a jurisdiction. Furthermore, an injunction can be granted only where there is a right to be enforced. The 'right' to accommodation comes to an end once the authority have made and notified their decision. In such circumstances the only way to challenge a decision not to continue accommodation pending an appeal is by means of an allegation of abuse of discretion via judicial review, and that means going to the High Court. Similarly judicial review may have to be sought where an authority refuses to extend the time period for a review application.

In any case where an authority is under a duty under s. 188 (interim duty in case of priority need), s. 190 (duties to the intentionally homeless) or s. 200 (cases of referral or consideration for referral), s. 204(4) gives them a *discretion* to continue the securing of accommodation during the period in which an appeal can be made and until any appeal is finally determined – including any further appeal to the Court of Appeal or House of Lords from the county court.

In *R* v *Brighton and Hove Borough Council ex parte Nacion* [1999] *The Times*, 3 February, Brighton and Hove Borough Council, acting under s. 204(4), refused to provide the applicant with accommodation pending determination of an appeal under s. 204(1). The Court of Appeal stated that it would not normally be appropriate for the Court to grant a remedy – and remember that judicial review is a discretionary remedy – in such circumstances. A remedy would, however, be appropriately granted where there was a clear abuse of power in such circumstances, for example where the authority had failed to consider whether to exercise their discretion to continue to make accommodation available.

Questions

Since the coming into force of the new internal review and appeal systems, the number of homelessness cases reaching the courts has appeared to decline quite considerably. There is anecdotal evidence – as yet unsupported by empirical research – to suggest that this may be due to the workings of the review system. When a disappointed applicant asks for a review of a decision it will usually become apparent in the course of the proceedings if the authority have made a procedural error, or misapplied the law. The review gives them the opportunity to correct their mistake – though this will not always result in the review finding in favour of the applicant. Why should this be so?

(iv)   Collateral challenge?
Is it possible to challenge a homelessness decision collaterally by means of an action for breach of statutory duty?

O'Rourke v *Camden LBC*
[1998] AC 188

Mr O'Rourke was released from prison in 1991 and applied to Camden as a homeless person, arguing that he was homeless and in priority need by virtue of vulnerability. Camden first refused to consider his application, then did so, placing him in interim accommodation. They then concluded that he was intentionally homeless and in due course evicted him. He sued for breach of statutory duty. In *Thornton* v *Kirklees MBC* [1979] QB 625, a breach of statutory duty action had been allowed in a homelessness case, and in *Cocks* v *Thanet DC* [1983] 2 AC 286 the House of Lords had stated, *obiter*, that an action might lie. However, in *O'Rourke*, when the issue rose 'head on' the House of Lords backtracked and said that there should be no recovery by way of civil action. Thus even if an authority fail to fulfil the statutory functions the matter is not actionable in tort.

LORD HOFFMANN (delivering the unanimous opinion of the House): . . . The question is whether section 63(1) [of the 1985 Act] creates a duty to Mr O'Rourke which is actionable in tort. There is no doubt that, like several other provisions in Part III, it creates a duty which is enforceable by proceedings for judicial review. But whether it gives rise to a cause of action sounding in damages depends upon whether the Act shows a legislative intention to create such a remedy. In *X (Minors)* v *Bedfordshire County Council* [1995] 2 AC 633, 731, the principles were analysed by Lord Browne-Wilkinson in a speech with which the other members of the House agreed. He said that although there was no general rule by reference to which it could be decided that a statute created a private right of action, there were a number of 'indicators.' The indicator upon which Mr Drabble, who appeared for Mr O'Rourke, placed most reliance was the common sense proposition that a statute which appears intended for the protection of a limited class of people but provides no other remedy for breach should ordinarily be construed as intended to create a private right of action. Otherwise, as Lord Simonds said in *Cutler* v *Wandsworth Stadium Ltd* [1949] AC 398, 407, 'the statute would be but a pious aspiration'.

Camden, on the other hand, says that although Part III does not expressly enact any remedy for breach, that does not mean that it would be toothless without an action for damages or an injunction in private law. It is enforceable in public law by individual homeless persons who have locus standi to bring proceedings for judicial review. Furthermore, there are certain contra-indications which make it unlikely that Parliament intended to create private law rights of action.

The first is that the Act is a scheme of social welfare, intended to confer benefits at the public expense on grounds of public policy. Public money is spent on housing the homeless not merely for the private benefit of people who find themselves homeless but on grounds of general public interest: because, for example, proper housing means that people will be less likely to suffer illness, turn to crime or require the attention of other social services. The expenditure interacts with expenditure on other public services such as education, the National Health Service and even the police. It is not simply a private matter between the claimant and the housing authority. Accordingly, the fact that Parliament has provided for the expenditure of public money on benefits in kind such as housing the homeless does not necessarily mean that it intended cash payments to be made by way of damages to persons who, in breach of the housing authority's statutory duty, have unfortunately not received the benefits which they should have done. This was the view forcibly expressed by Geoffrey Lane LJ in *Wyatt v Hillingdon London Borough Council* (1978) 76 LGR 727, 733 when the plaintiff claimed damages from his local authority for failure to provide benefits under the Chronically Sick and Disabled Persons Act 1970:

> It seems to me that a statute such as this which is dealing with the distribution of benefits – or, to put it perhaps more accurately, comforts to the sick and disabled – does not in its very nature give rise to an action by the disappointed sick person. It seems to me quite extraordinary that if the local authority, as is alleged here, provided, for example, two hours less home help than the sick person considered herself entitled to that that can amount to a breach of statutory duty which will permit the sick person to claim a sum of monetary damages by way of breach of statutory duty.

This was an unreserved judgment and I think that on reflection Geoffrey Lane LJ would have been willing to substitute 'was' for 'considered herself'. With that amendment, I would associate myself with these remarks. In *X (Minors)* v *Bedfordshire County Council* [1995] 2 AC 633, 731–732, Lord Browne-Wilkinson likewise said:

> Although regulatory or welfare legislation affecting a particular area of activity does in fact provide protection to those individuals particularly affected by that activity, the legislation is not to be treated as being passed for the benefit of those individuals but for the benefit of society in general.

A second contra-indication is that Part III of the Act of 1985 makes the existence of the duty to provide accommodation dependent upon a good deal of judgment on the part of the housing authority. The duty to inquire under section 62(1) arises if the housing authority 'have reason to believe' that the applicant may be homeless and the inquiries must be such as are 'necessary to satisfy themselves' as to whether he is homeless, whether he has a priority need and whether he became homeless intentionally. When the investigations are complete, the various duties under section 65 of the Act arise only if the authority are 'satisfied' that the applicant is homeless and the extent of those duties depends upon whether or not they are 'satisfied' as to two other matters, namely that he has a priority need and that he became homeless intentionally. If a duty does arise, the authority has a wide discretion in deciding how to provide accommodation and what kind of accommodation it will provide. The existence of all these discretions makes it unlikely that Parliament intended errors of judgment to give rise to an obligation to make financial reparation. Control by public law remedies would appear much more appropriate: see *per* Lord Browne-Wilkinson in *X (Minors)* v *Bedfordshire County Council* [1995] 2 AC 633, 747–748.

Mr Drabble said that the question of whether Parliament could have contemplated enforcement of the Part III duties by judicial review rather than private action should be considered in the light of the state of public law in 1977, when the provisions of Part II were first enacted as the Housing (Homeless Person) Act 1977. Part III is no more than a consolidation of that Act and should not be treated as either restricting or enlarging the rights which the original legislation conferred. The history of judicial review is examined in some detail by Lord Diplock in his speech in *O'Reilly* v *Mackman* [1983] 2 AC 237. After referring to some of the landmark cases on substantive administrative law such as *Ridge* v *Baldwin* [1964] AC 40, *Padfield* v *Minister of Agriculture Fisheries and Food* [1968] AC 997 and *Anisimic Ltd* v *Foreign Compensation Commission* [1969] 2 AC 147, Lord Diplock [1983] 2 AC 237, 279 said that by 1977 England had 'a developed system of administrative law'. The procedural rules had however lagged behind and an applicant for judicial review remained handicapped, in particular by the absence of discovery and cross-examination. These defects were removed by the new RSC Ord. 53, which was made by the Rules of the Supreme Court (Amendment No. 3) 1977 (SI 1977 No. 1955 (L.30)) on 21 November 1977, some four months after the Act of 1977 was passed on 20 July 1977.

There was some discussion before your Lordships as to whether the Act of 1977 should be construed against the background of public law as it stood on the date when it was passed or whether the remedies which it conferred should be regarded as ambulatory, fashioned according to the law as it stood from time to time. I would not dispute that the latter construction may in certain cases be appropriate: see *Cross, Statutory Interpretation*, 3rd ed. (1995), p. 51. The question is one of statutory construction like any other. But for the purposes of this case, I do not think that it is necessary to look further than the date on which the Act of 1977 was passed. Not only was the substantive law by that time reasonably well developed but the procedural changes which soon afterwards came into force had been recommended by the Law Commission in the Report on Remedies in Administrative Law (1976) (Law Com. No. 73) (Cmnd. 6407), published in March 1976. Even the existing procedure was in most cases adequate to provide a swift remedy for a homeless person complaining of breach of duty. Lord Diplock said in *O'Reilly* v *Mackman* [1983] 2 AC 237, 281 that:

> As [the old] Order 53 was applied in practice, as soon as the application for leave had been made it provided a very speedy means, available in urgent cases within a matter of days rather than months, for determining whether a disputed decision was valid in law or not.

Accordingly there is in my view no reason to construe the Act of 1977 on the assumption that in the absence of a remedy in damages, it would at the time it was enacted have been no more than a 'pious aspiration'. The machinery for enforcing it was in place.

The question of the appropriate remedy for breach of the duties owed under the Act of 1977 was considered by this House in *Cocks* v *Thanet District Council* [1983] 2 AC 286, which was decided on the same day as *O'Reilly* v *Mackman* [1983] 2 AC 237. Mr Cocks brought an action in the Thanet County Court, alleging that he was homeless and in priority need but that in breach of duty, the housing authority, Thanet District Council, had refused to house him. He claimed a declaration that the council was in breach of a duty, a mandatory injunction and damages. The action was transferred to the Queen's Bench Division and a preliminary issue ordered as to 'whether the proceedings were properly brought by action or could only be brought by application for judicial review.' In his judgment [1983] 2 AC 286, 292, Lord Bridge of Harwich described this as a:

procedural issue . . . which . . . will naturally fall for decision in the light of the principles expounded in the speech of my noble and learned friend, Lord Diplock, in *O'Reilly* v *Mackman* [1983] 2 AC 237.

This was, if I may say so with respect, a correct description of the way in which the issue was presented to this House. But concealed within it was a substantive question which was not present in *O'Reilly* v *Mackman*, namely whether the relief sought in the action could be claimed at all. In *O'Reilly* v *Mackman* all that was claimed was a declaration that an act, undoubtedly operating solely in public law, namely the adjudication of prison visitors, was invalid. The only question was therefore whether such relief could be claimed in an action begun by writ. In *Cocks* v *Thanet District Council*, on the other hand, the plaintiff claimed a declaration, injunction and damages on the basis that he was owed a private law duty. The first question was therefore whether such a duty existed. If it did, there could be no objection to the plaintiff pursuing a tortious cause of action by writ. On the other hand, if it did not, then the *O'Reilly* v *Mackman* question of the procedure by which he could pursue a public law remedy would arise.

Lord Bridge (with whom the other members of the House agreed) decided that no duty in private law could arise until the housing authority had made its inquiries and decided whether or not it was satisfied as to the various matters upon which the existence of the duty depended. Until the authority had declared itself so satisfied, its decision could be challenged only by judicial review. This was sufficient to dispose of the appeal. The House made a declaration that the plaintiff was not entitled to continue his proceedings 'otherwise than by application for judicial review'.

Lord Bridge went on, however, to say that a duty in private law would arise once the housing authority had made a decision in the applicant's favour. He said [1983] 2 AC 286, 292–293:

On the other hand, the housing authority are charged with executive functions. Once a decision has been reached by the housing authority which gives rise to the temporary, the limited or the full housing duty, rights and obligations are immediately created in the field of private law. Each of the duties referred to, once established, is capable of being enforced by injunction and the breach of it will give rise to a liability in damages. But it is inherent in the scheme of the Act that an appropriate public law decision of the housing authority is a condition precedent to the establishment of the private law duty.

My Lords, I must say with all respect that I cannot accept this reasoning. There is no examination of the legislative intent, the various considerations which I have discussed earlier as indicating whether or not a statute was intended to create a duty in private law sounding in damages. The fact that the housing authority is 'charged with executive functions' is treated as sufficient to establish a private law duty. No doubt because the question did not have to be decided, Lord Bridge did not undertake a careful examination of the statutory intent such as he afterwards made in *Reg.* v *Deputy Governor of Parkhurst Prison, ex parte Hague* [1992] 1 AC 58, 157–161. I feel sure that if he had, he would have expressed a different opinion.

The concept of a duty in private law which arises only when it has been acknowledged to exist is anomalous. It means that a housing authority which accepts that it has a duty to house the applicant but does so inadequately will be liable in damages but an authority which perversely refuses to accept that it has any such duty will not. This seems to me wrong. Of course a private law relationship may arise from the implementation of the housing authority's duty. The applicant may become the authority's tenant or licensee and so brought into a contractual relationship. But there seems to me no need to interpose a statutory duty actionable in tort merely to bridge the gap between the acknowledgement of the duty and its implementation.

. . .

Both in principle and on the authority of the actual decision of the House in *Cocks* v *Thanet District Council* [1983] 2 AC 286 I would therefore hold that the breach of statutory duty of which the plaintiff complains gives rise to no cause of action in private law and I would allow the appeal and restore the order of Judge Tibber striking out the action.

Note
O'Rourke seems conclusive; it is not possible 'collaterally' to challenge an adverse homelessness decision through a claim for breach of statutory duty. Moreover, although a limited right of appeal to the courts (on a point of law) is provided for by s. 204 of the Housing Act 1996, in practice successful appeals are likely to be infrequent. Moreover, the very existence of the 'review' process is, as suggested above, likely to lead to a significant decline in the number of successful applications for judicial review. Is this simply a consequence of more considered and 'objective' decision-making at authority level, or are there implications which should be of concern?

(K)   Supplementary provisions

Discharge of functions: introductory
205.—(1)   The following sections have effect in relation to the discharge by a local housing authority of their functions under this Part to secure that accommodation is available for the occupation of a person—
    section 206 (general provisions)
    section 207 (provision of accommodation by authority)
    section 208 (out-of-area placements)
    section 209 (arrangements with private landlord).

Discharge of functions by local housing authorities
206.—(1)   A local housing authority may discharge their housing functions under this Part only in the following ways—
    (a)   by securing that suitable accommodation provided by them is available,
    (b)   by securing that he obtains suitable accommodation from some other person, or
    (c)   by giving him such advice and assistance as will secure that suitable accommodation is available from some other person.
    (2)   A local housing authority may require a person in relation to whom they are discharging such functions—
    (a)   to pay such reasonable charges as they may determine in respect of accommodation which they secure for his occupation (either by making it available themselves or otherwise), or
    (b)   to pay such reasonable amount as they may determine in respect of sums payable by them for accommodation made available by another person.

Discharge of functions: provision of accommodation by the authority
207.—(1) A local housing authority shall not under section 206(1)(a) discharge their housing functions under this Part by providing accommodation other than—

(a) accommodation in a hostel within the meaning of section 622 of the Housing Act 1985, or

(b) accommodation leased to the authority as mentioned in subsection (2) below,

for more than two years (continuously or in aggregate) in any period of three years.

This applies irrespective of the number of applications for accommodation or assistance in obtaining accommodation made by the person concerned.

(2) The accommodation referred to in subsection (1)(b) is accommodation—

(a) leased to the authority with vacant possession for use as temporary housing accommodation on terms which include provision for the lessor to obtain vacant possession from the authority on the expiry of a specified period or when required by the lessor,

(b) the lessor of which is not an authority or body within section 80(1) of the Housing Act 1985 (the landlord condition for secure tenancies), and

(c) in which the authority have no interest other than under the lease in question or as a mortgagee.

(3) The authority shall not discharge such functions in relation to a person who—

(a) normally resides with another person as a member of his family, or

(b) might reasonably be expected to reside with another person,

in such a way that subsection (1) would be contravened if the functions were discharged in relation to that other person.

(4) The Secretary of State may, on the application of a local housing authority, by direction exclude or modify the operation of subsection (1) in relation to that authority if it appears to him that the authority will not otherwise be able reasonably to discharge their housing functions under this Part.

(5) Any such direction shall have effect only—

(a) with respect to applicants of a description specified in the direction, and

(b) for a period specified in the direction, which shall not exceed one year,

and may be expressed to have effect subject to any conditions specified in the direction.

(6) Where the Secretary of State gives or has given a direction under subsection (4), he may give the authority such directions as he considers appropriate as to the discharge of their housing functions under this Part in cases affected by the direction having or ceasing to have effect.

Discharge of functions: out-of-area placements
208.—(1) So far as reasonably practicable a local housing authority shall in discharging their housing functions under this Part secure that accommodation is available for the occupation of the applicant in their district.

(2) If they secure that accommodation is available for the occupation of the applicant outside their district, they shall give notice to the local housing authority in whose district the accommodation is situated.

(3) The notice shall state—

(a) the name of the applicant,

(b) the number and description of other persons who normally reside with him as a member of his family or might reasonably be expected to reside with him,

(c) the address of the accommodation,

(d) the date on which the accommodation was made available to him, and

(e)   which function under this Part the authority was discharging in securing that the accommodation is available for his occupation.

(4)   The notice must be in writing, and must be given before the end of the period of 14 days beginning with the day on which the accommodation was made available to the applicant.

Discharge of functions: arrangements with private landlord
209.—(1)   This section applies where in pursuance of any of their housing functions under this Part a local housing authority make arrangements with a private landlord to provide accommodation.

For this purpose a 'private landlord' means a landlord who is not within section 80(1) of the Housing Act 1985 (the landlord condition for secure tenancies).

(2)   If the housing function arises under section 188, 190, 200 or 204(4) (interim duties), a tenancy granted in pursuance of the arrangements to a person specified by the authority cannot be an assured tenancy before the end of the period of twelve months beginning with—

(a)   the date on which the applicant was notified of the authority's decision under section 184(3) or 198(5), or

(b)   if there is a review of that decision under section 202 or an appeal to the court under section 204, the date on which he is notified of the decision on review or the appeal is finally determined,

unless, before or during that period, the tenant is notified by the landlord (or, in the cases of joint landlords, at least one of them) that the tenancy is to be regarded as an assured shorthold tenancy or an assured tenancy other than an assured shorthold tenancy.

A registered social landlord cannot serve such a notice making such a tenancy an assured tenancy other than an assured shorthold tenancy.

(3)   Where in any other case a tenancy is granted in pursuance of the arrangements by a registered social landlord to a person specified by the authority—

(a)   the tenancy cannot be an assured tenancy unless it is an assured shorthold tenancy, and

(b)   the landlord cannot convert the tenancy to an assured tenancy unless the accommodation is allocated to the tenant under Part VI.

Suitability of accommodation
210.—(1)   In determining for the purposes of this Part whether accommodation is suitable for a person, the local housing authority shall have regard to Parts IX, X and XI of the Housing Act 1985 (slum clearance; overcrowding; houses in multiple occupation).

(2)   The Secretary of State may by order specify—

(a)   circumstances in which accommodation is or is not to be regarded as suitable for a person, and

(b)   matters to be taken into account or disregarded in determining whether accommodation is suitable for a person.

Homelessness (Suitability of Accommodation) Order 1996
SI 1996 No. 3204

Citation and commencement
1.   This Order may be cited as the Homelessness (Suitability of Accommodation) Order 1996 and shall come into force on 20th January 1997.

Matters to be taken into account

2. In determining whether it would be, or would have been, reasonable for a person to continue to occupy accommodation and in determining whether accommodation is suitable for a person there shall be taken into account whether or not the accommodation is affordable for that person and, in particular, the following matters—

(a) the financial resources available to that person, including, but not limited to—

(i) salary, fees and other remuneration;

(ii) social security benefits;

(iii) payments due under a court order for the making of periodical payments to a spouse or a former spouse, or to, or for the benefit of, a child;

(iv) payments of child support maintenance due under the Child Support Act 1991;

(v) pensions;

(vi) contributions to the costs in respect of the accommodation which are or were made or which might reasonably be expected to be, or have been, made by other members of his household;

(vii) financial assistance towards the costs in respect of the accommodation, including loans, provided by a local authority, voluntary organisation or other body;

(viii) benefits derived from a policy of insurance;

(ix) savings and other capital sums;

(b) the costs in respect of the accommodation, including, but not limited to,—

(i) payments of, or by way of, rent;

(ii) payments in respect of a licence or permission to occupy the accommodation;

(iii) mortgage costs;

(iv) payments of, or by way of, service charges;

(v) mooring charges payable for a houseboat;

(vi) where the accommodation is a caravan or a mobile home, payments in respect of the site on which it stands;

(vii) the amount of council tax payable in respect of the accommodation;

(viii) payments by way of deposit or security in respect of the accommodation;

(ix) payments required by an accommodation agency;

(c) payments which that person is required to make under a court order for the making of periodical payments to a spouse or a former spouse, or to, or for the benefit of, a child and payments of child support maintenance required to be made under the Child Support Act 1991;

(d) that person's other reasonable living expenses.

Circumstances in which accommodation is not to be regarded as suitable

3. For the purposes of section 197(1) of the Housing Act 1996 (duty where other suitable accommodation available), accommodation shall not be regarded as suitable unless the local housing authority are satisfied that it will be available for occupation by the applicant for at least two years beginning with the date on which he secures it.

Notes

1. The 1996 Order as set out here is amended by SI 1997 No. 1741.

2. Section 208 of the Housing Act 1996 provides that so far as reasonably practicable authorities are under a duty in discharging their housing functions to secure accommodation for applicants within their own districts. If, however, they secure accommodation for an applicant outside their district they must give written notice to the council of the district in question, stating the name of the applicant, the number and description of others normally residing with him as members of his family, etc., the address of the accommodation, the date on which the accommodation was made available and which function the 'finding' authority was discharging in securing the accommodation. This notice must be given within 14 days of the accommodation being made available to the applicant. What is this provision designed to achieve? Is it intended to assist authorities against applicants who move from district to district to 'escape' from findings of intentional homelessness?

7 HOUSING DISREPAIR

(A) Introduction

The state of Britain's housing leaves much room for improvement. The *English House Condition Survey 1991* (DoE, 1993) (EHCS) and the 1993 *Welsh House Condition Survey* (Welsh Office, 1994) (WHCS) indicated that a high proportion of properties in England and Wales were unfit for human habitation, according to the statutory criteria (see (C) below). For example; in England 20.5 per cent of privately rented property was unfit; 6.9 per cent of council property; 6.7 per cent of housing association property and 5.5 per cent of owner-occupied property (in Wales the respective percentages were 25.6 per cent; 15.8 per cent; 6 per cent and 11.9 per cent). Viewed in relation to the age of properties, the largest problem by far (as might be expected) related to pre-1919 properties, 16.4 per cent of all of those being unfit compared to only 5.1 per cent of post-1918 properties. Clearly, old privately rented properties represent the largest problem of all.

Of course, 'unfitness' is not the only issue in relation to disrepair (even if it is the most serious); properties may suffer from numerous minor defects which render them uncomfortable to live in, without making them unfit. Equally, properties may be 'fit' yet in some areas represent health risks for those living in them and/or potential nuisances for those living nearby. Overall, disrepair is a major social issue and the adequacy of the law to help deal with disrepair is of the utmost importance.

Unfortunately few areas of housing law are less clear and less satisfactory than the law relating to disrepair, as the recent Law Commission Report, No. 238, *Landlord and Tenant: Responsibility for State and Condition of Property*, (1996) makes very clear. The Commission lists four principal defects in the law (echoing comments in its 1992 Consultation Paper (No. 123)):

(a)   The absence of a satisfactory (legal) standard to be met by leased premises. In particular, the problem that 'repair' does not necessarily include 'improvement' (discussed further in part (B) of this chapter).

(b)   The absence of any fixed legal requirement that responsibility for the repair of the property should be specifically allocated. In some cases, neither party may be under any express or implied obligation to carry out repairs! Even in cases where responsibility for the *premises* is clear (for example, leases of dwelling-houses for terms less than seven years), there can be genuine uncertainty over the position concerning the common parts.

(c)   The remedies for the enforcement of express or implied repairing obligations were often ineffective in ensuring that needed repairs were carried out.

(d)   (Crucially) that what the Commission politely terms the 'accretion of rules, both common law and statutory' has led to law which lacks clarity, and where there is often an overlap in remedies.

This chapter, then, deals with law of great complexity and diversity, stemming from a wide variety of sources, and yet which is often ill-suited for dealing with everyday problems which tenants of older properties particularly face in relation to disrepair. Why is the law in such an ill-formed and unsatisfactory state? Above all because of the lack of any shaping or guiding principle in its development, leading to the classic scenario of piecemeal solutions, which, in the end, are often no 'solution' at all. For example, as regards unfit properties the common law developed an implied term that *furnished* premises had to be fit for habitation at the start of the tenancy (*Smith v Marrable* (1843) 11 M&W 5). Legislation took this further via s. 12 of the Housing of Working Classes Act 1885 (now s. 8, Landlord and Tenant Act 1985) so that any property within the legislation (not just furnished properties) has to be fit at the start of the tenancy, and that the landlord is under an implied obligation to *keep* the property reasonably fit during the currency of the tenancy. However, the value of this potentially very useful implied term is almost completely undermined by the fact that (despite being re-enacted in 1985) it applies only to properties where the rent does not exceed £80 per year in London and £52 per year elsewhere (ss. 8(3)(a) and 8(4), 1985 Act). As the Law Commission notes (p. 31), this makes s. 8 a 'dead letter'. The Commission cites, by way of comparison, a Rent Assessment Committee ruling whereby a fair rent had been reduced from £49 to £42 *per week* in relation to a property which was unfit for habitation and on which a repair notice was outstanding.

Meanwhile, while this provision has been allowed to 'wither on the vine' (being pegged to rent limits unchanged for over 40 years), in other areas local authority powers to deal with unfitness have been (at the very least) simplified and clarified (see part (C) of this chapter), and since 1961 all landlords of properties subject to leases of seven years or less have been subject to relatively strict implied duties to keep the properties in repair and mains installations in repair and proper working order (now s. 11, Landlord and

Tenant Act 1985) (see part (B) of this chapter). There seems very little consistency or coherence in any of this, and many other examples could be cited; for example the not infrequent lack of 'fit' between local authority powers and duties concerning housing standards and environmental health.

Even when the general tenor and purpose of the law is clear enough, its interpretation is often far from straightforward. Notable examples include the scope of s. 11 of the 1985 Act, and the meaning of 'prejudicial to health or a nuisance' in relation to housing which may amount to a statutory nuisance (see now s. 79(7), Environmental Protection Act 1990).

As if all this were not enough, many of those most affected by poor housing are (because of age, ill health, or low income) amongst those least well equipped to initiate the often complex legal steps required for dealing with the problems.

Despite its strong criticism of the current state of the law, the Law Commission does not make any sweeping reform proposals. Instead (see paras 8.35–8.39), it suggests a gradual programme of improvement by the phased introduction of a new, and relatively unrestricted, implied term of fitness for human habitation derived from s. 604 of the Housing Act 1985 (on which see part (C) of this chapter). Perhaps because of the fact of the significant burden this would place on some landlords, and the fact that this would be likely to be reflected in the rent (and consequently on housing benefit payments in many cases), there has been no government initiative to implement the proposal.

Even if the proposal were to become law, much of the ill-fitting and overlapping 'jigsaw' of private and public law measures for combating disrepair would still remain. However unsatisfactory it may be, the remainder of this chapter reflects that public/private distinction, part (B) dealing with private law and part (C) with public law.

(B)   Private law remedies for dealing with substandard housing

(i)   Introduction
Part (A) of this chapter gives an indication of the poor condition of many dwellings in this country. In addition, it can be seen from *The State of UK Housing: A fact file on dwelling conditions* (Leather and Morrison, Policy Press, 1997) that almost 20 per cent of dwellings in England faced urgent repair costs in excess of £1,000 in 1991. Poor property standards are particularly prevalent, according to the above publication, in northern English cities such as Liverpool and Manchester, rural areas and South Wales as well as some industrial parts of the English Midlands. Properties below the Wash–Bristol Channel line are, on the whole, of a higher standard, although a number of London boroughs have very high levels of unfit properties.

The purpose of this part of the chapter is to identify private law remedies available to tenants and landlords wishing to upgrade the state of repair within a given property. For the most part consideration will be given to landlord obligations, although responsibilities imposed on tenants will be explored later. A considerable part of this section concentrates on actions within the law of contract, where there is a specific agreement between the parties. It is clear that obligations may arise under this agreement, the 'contract of letting', in three main ways: through covenants expressly incorporated within the agreement itself, usually in writing; through terms implied by common law, although as will be seen these are particularly limited; or through contractual terms implied by statute, principally the Landlord and Tenant Act 1985. Also briefly considered, in this part of the chapter, are remedies which may be obtainable in the law of tort, both by tenants and others, and principally under the Occupiers' Liability Act 1957 and the Defective Premises Act 1972.

(ii)   Contractual obligations

The underlying principle at common law is 'caveat emptor' (let the buyer beware). The onus is firmly placed upon persons intending to rent a property to have inspected the premises and to have satisfied themselves of its fitness for their habitation. Thus at common law a landlord is under no general obligation to repair, unless the obligation is agreed by the parties (through an express covenant) or imposed by legislation (*Gott* v *Gandy* (1853) 1 El & Bl 845). A landlord is under no obligation to ensure unfurnished premises are fit for human habitation (*Hart* v *Windsor*) (1843) 12 M&W 68, restricting the ambit of *Smith* v *Marrable* (below)). There may indeed be situations where neither the landlord nor the tenant is liable for repairing a property (*Demetriou* v *Robert Andrews* (1990) 62 P & CR 536). In relation to furnished accommodation, however, the common law implies a contractual term that it is fit for human habitation at the date of the letting. In *Smith* v *Marrable* (1843) 11 M&W 5, the defendant rented a house for his family which was bug infested. Unsurprisingly he left the property, and upon action for the remainder of the rent Lord Abinger CB stated that 'in point of law every house must be taken to be let upon the implied condition that there was nothing about it so noxious as to render it uninhabitable'. More recently *McNerney* v *Lambeth LBC* (1988) 21 HLR 188 confirmed the limitation of *Smith* v *Marrable* to furnished lettings. The court in *McNerney* found that if fitness covenant obligations were to be extended to unfurnished flats, the initiative would have to come from the legislature not the courts.

Additionally, the courts have implied repairing obligations where it was necessary to do so to give business efficacy to the agreement.

Liverpool C.C. v *Irwin*
[1977] AC 239

A tower block contained some 70 dwellings. There was a common staircase and there were two electrically operated lifts providing access to the dwellings. The block also had an internal chute for the discharge of rubbish. The tenancy agreement between the authority and tenants imposed various obligations on the tenants but no obligations upon the authority. Problems occurred over a number of years, including defects to the common parts comprising lack of lighting on the stairs, failure of the lifts, and blockage of the rubbish chutes. The tenants protested by refusing to pay rent. The authority sought possession, with the tenants counterclaiming that the authority were under an implied repairing covenant relating to the common parts. The House of Lords decided that the authority were under an obligation to take reasonable care to maintain the common parts.

LORD WILBERFORCE: . . . My Lords, this case is of general importance, since it concerns the obligations of local authority, and indeed other, landlords as regards high-rise or multi-storey dwellings towards the tenants of these dwellings. This is a comparatively recent problem though there have been some harbingers of it in previous cases.

Haigh Heights, Liverpool, is one of several recently erected tower blocks in the district of Everton. It has some 70 dwelling units in it. It was erected ten years ago, following a slum clearance programme at considerable cost, and was then, no doubt, thought to mark an advance in housing standards. Unfortunately, it has since turned out that effective slum clearance depends on more than expenditure on steel and concrete. There are human factors involved too, and it is these which seem to have failed. The defendants moved into one of the units in this building in July 1966; this was a maisonette of two floors, corresponding to the ninth and tenth floors of the block. Access to it was provided by a staircase and by two electrically operated lifts. Another facility provided was an internal chute into which tenants in the block could discharge rubbish or garbage for collection at the ground level.

There has been a consistent history of trouble in this block, due in part to vandalism, in part to non-cooperation by tenants, in part, it is said, to neglect by the corporation. The defendants, with other tenants, stopped payment of rent so that in May 1973 the corporation had to start proceedings for possession. The defendants put in a counterclaim for damages and for an injunction, alleging that the corporation was in breach of its implied covenant for quiet enjoyment, that it was in breach of the statutory covenant implied by s. 32 of the Housing Act 1961 and that it was in breach of an obligation implied by law to keep the 'common parts' in repair. The case came for trial in the Liverpool County Court before his Honour Judge T. A. Cunliffe. A good deal of evidence was submitted, both orally and in the form of reports. The judge himself visited the block and inspected the premises; he said in his judgment that he was appalled by the general condition of the property. On 10 April 1974 he gave a detailed and careful judgment granting possession to the corporation on the claim and, on the counterclaim judgment of the appellants for £10 nominal damages. He found that the defects alleged by the defendants were established. These can be summarised as consisting of (i) a number of defects in the maisonette itself – these were significant but not perhaps of major importance; (ii) defects in the common parts, which may be summarised as continual failure of the lifts, sometimes of both at one time, lack of lighting on the stairs, dangerous conditions of the staircase with unguarded holes giving access to the rubbish chutes and frequent blockage of the chutes. He found that these had existed or been repeated with considerable frequency throughout the tenancy, had gone from bad to worse, and that while some defects in the common parts could be attributed to vandalism, not all could be so attributed. No doubt also some defects, particularly the blocking of the rubbish chutes, were due to irresponsible action by the tenants themselves. The learned judge decided that there was to be implied a covenant by the corporation to keep the common parts in repair and properly lighted, and that the corporation was in breach of this implied covenant, of the covenant for quiet enjoyment and of the repairing covenant implied by the Housing Act 1961, s. 32.

The corporation appealed to the Court of Appeal [[1975] 3 All ER 658, [1975] 3 WLR 663], which allowed the corporation's appeal against the judgment on the counterclaim. While agreeing in the result, the members of that court differed as to their grounds. Roskill and Ormrod LJJ held that no covenant to repair the common parts ought to be implied. Lord Denning MR held that there should be implied a covenant to take reasonable care, not only to keep the lifts and stairs reasonably safe, but also to keep them reasonably fit for use by the tenants and their families and visitors. He held, however, that there was no evidence of any breach of this duty. The court was agreed in holding that there was no breach of the covenant implied under s. 32 of the Housing Act 1961; the tenants did not seek to uphold the judge's decision on the covenant for quiet enjoyment, and have not done so in this House.

I consider first the tenants' claim insofar as it is based on contract. The first step must be to ascertain what the contract is. This may look elementary, even naïve, but it seems to me to be the essential step and to involve, from the start, an approach different from, if simpler than, that taken by the members of the Court of Appeal. We look first at documentary material. As is common with council lettings there is no formal demise or lease or tenancy agreement. There is a document headed 'Liverpool Corporation, Liverpool City Housing Department' and described as 'Conditions of Tenancy'. This contains a list of obligations on the tenant – he shall do this, he shall not do that, or he shall not do that without the corporation's consent. This is an amalgam of obligations added to from time to time, no doubt, to meet complaints, emerging situations, or problems as they appear to the council's officers. In particular there have been added special provisions relating to multi-storey flats which are supposed to make the conditions suitable to such dwellings. We may note under 'Further special notes' some obligations not to obstruct staircases and passages, and not to permit children under 10 to operate any lifts. I mention these as a recognition of the existence and relevance of these facilities. At the end there is a form for signature by the tenant stating that he accepts the tenancy. On the landlords' side there is nothing, no signature, no demise, no covenant: the contract takes effect as soon as the tenants sign the form and are let into possession.

We have then a contract which is partly, but not wholly, stated in writing. In order to complete it, in particular to give it a bilateral character, it is necessary to take account of the actions of the parties and the circumstances. As actions of the parties, we must note the granting of possession by the landlords and reservation by them of the 'common parts' – stairs, lifts, chutes etc. As circumstances we must include the nature of the premises, viz., a maisonette for family use on the ninth floor of a high block, one which is occupied by a large number of other tenants, all using the common parts and dependent on them, none of them having any expressed obligation to maintain or repair them.

To say that the construction of a complete contract out of these elements involves a process of 'implication' may be correct; it would be so if implication means the supplying of what is not expressed. But there are varieties of implications which the courts think fit to make and they do not necessarily involve the same process. Where there is, on the face of it, a complete, bilateral contract, the courts are sometimes willing to add terms to it, as implied terms: this is very common in mercantile contracts where there is an established usage: in that case the courts are spelling out what both parties know and would, if asked, unhesitatingly agree to be part of the bargain. In other cases, where there is an apparently complete bargain, the courts are willing to add a term on the ground that without it the contract will not work – this is the case, if not of *The Moorcock* [(1889) 14 PD 64] itself on its facts, at least of the doctrine of *The Moorcock* as usually applied. This is, as was pointed out by the majority of the Court of Appeal, a strict test – though the degree of strictness seems to vary with the current legal trend – and I think that they were right not to accept it as applicable here. There is a third variety of implication, that which I think Lord Denning MR favours, or at least did favour in this case, and that is the implication of reasonable terms. But though I agree with many of his instances, which in fact fall under one or other of the preceding heads, I cannot go so far as to endorse his principle; indeed, it seems to me, with respect, to extend a long, and undesirable, way beyond sound authority.

The present case, in my opinion, represents a fourth category or, I would rather say, a fourth shade on a continuous spectrum. The court here is simply concerned to establish what the contract is, the parties not having themselves fully stated the terms. In this sense the court is searching for what must be implied.

What then should this contract be held to be? There must first be implied a letting, that is, a grant of the right of exclusive possession to the tenants. With this there must, I would suppose, be implied a covenant for quiet enjoyment, as a necessary incident of the letting. The difficulty begins when we consider the common parts. We start with the fact that the demise is useless unless access is obtained by the staircase; we can add that, having regard to the height of the block, and the family nature of the dwellings, the demise would be useless without a lift service; we can continue that, there being rubbish chutes built in to the structures and no other means of disposing of light rubbish there must be a right to use the chutes. The question to be answered – and it is the only question in this case – is what is to be the legal relationship between landlord and tenant as regards these matters.

There can be no doubt that there must be implied (i) an easement for the tenants and their licensees to use the stairs, (ii) a right in the nature of an easement to use the lifts and (iii) an easement to use the rubbish chutes.

But are these easements to be accompanied by any obligation on the landlords, and what obligation? There seem to be two alternatives. The first, for which the council contends, is for an easement coupled with no legal obligation, except such as may arise under the Occupiers' Liability Act 1957 as regards the safety of those using the facilities, and possibly such other liability as might exist under the ordinary law of tort. The alternative is for easements coupled with some obligation on the part of the landlords as regards the maintenance of the subject of them, so that they are available for use.

My Lords, in order to be able to choose between these, it is necessary to define what test is to be applied, and I do not find this difficult. In my opinion such obligation should be read into the contract as the nature of the contract itself implicitly requires, no more, no less: a test in other words of necessity. The relationship accepted by the corporation is that of landlord and tenant: the tenant accepts obligations accordingly, in relation, inter alia, to the stairs, the lifts and the chutes. All these are not just facilities, or conveniences provided at discretion: they are essentials of the tenancy without which life in the dwellings, as a tenant, is not possible. To leave the landlord free of contractual obligation as regards these matters, and subject only to administrative or political pressure, is, in my opinion, totally inconsistent with the nature of this relationship. The subject-matter of the lease (high rise blocks) and the relationship created by the tenancy demands, of their nature, some contractual obligation on the landlord.

I do not think that this approach involves any innovation as regards the law of contract. The necessity to have regard to the inherent nature of a contract and of the relationship thereby established was stated in this House in *Lister v Romford Ice & Cold Storage Co. Ltd* [[1957] 1 All ER 125], [1957] AC 555. That was a case between master and servant and of a search for an 'implied term'. Viscount Simonds, at p. 579, made a clear distinction between a search for an implied term such as might be necessary to give 'business efficacy' to the particular contract and a search, based on wider considerations, for such a term as the nature of the contract might call for, or as a legal incident of this kind of contract. If the search were for the former, he said ([1957] 1 All ER at 133, [1957] AC at 576): 'I should lose myself in the attempt to formulate it with the necessary precision'. We see an echo of this in the present case, when the majority in the Court of Appeal, considering a 'business efficacy term', i.e. a *'Moorcock'* term, found themselves faced with five alternative terms and therefore rejected all of them. But that is not, in my opinion, the end, or indeed the object, of the search.

We have some guidance in authority for the kind of term which this typical relationship (of landlord and tenant in a multi-occupational dwelling) requires in *Miller v Hancock*. There Bowen LJ said ([1893] 2 QB 177 at 180, 181, [1891–4] All ER Rep 736 at 738, 739):

> The tenants could only use their flats by using the staircase. The defendant, therefore, when he let the flats, impliedly granted to the tenants an easement over the staircase, which he retained in his own occupation, for the purpose of the enjoyment of the flats so let. Under those circumstances, what is the law as to the repairs of the staircase? It was contended by the defendant's counsel that, according to the common law, the person in enjoyment of an easement is bound to do the necessary repairs himself. That may be true with regard to easements in general, but it is subject to the qualification that the grantor of the easement may undertake to do the repairs either in express terms or by necessary implication. This is not the mere case of a grant of an easement without special circumstances. It appears to me obvious, when one considers what a flat of this kind is, and the only way in which it can be enjoyed, that the parties to the demise of it must have intended by necessary implication, as a basis without which the whole transaction would be futile, that the landlord should maintain the staircase, which is essential to the enjoyment of the premises demised, and should keep it reasonably safe for the use of the tenants, and also of those persons who would necessarily go up and down the stairs in the ordinary course of business with the tenants; because, of course, a landlord must know when he lets a flat that tradesmen and other persons having business with the tenant must have access to it. It seems to me that it would render the whole transaction inefficacious and absurd if an implied undertaking were not assumed on the part of the landlord to maintain the staircase so far as might be necessary for the reasonable enjoyment of the demised premises.

Certainly that case, as a decision concerning a claim by a visitor, has been overruled: *Fairman v Perpetual Investment Building Society*. But I cite the passage for its common sense as between landlord and tenant, and you cannot overrule common sense.

There are other passages in which the same thought has been expressed. *De Meza v Ve-Ri-Best Manufacturing Co. Ltd* (1952) 160 EG 364 was a case of failure to maintain a lift in which Lord Evershed MR, sitting with Denning and Romer LJJ, held the landlords liable in damages for breach of an implied obligation to provide a working lift. The agreement was more explicit than the present agreement in that there was an express demise of the flat 'together with the use of the lift', but I think there is no doubt that the same demise or grant must be implied here, and if so can lead to the same result.

In *Penn* v *Gatenex Co. Ltd* ([1958] 1 All ER 712 at 720, [1958] 2 QB 210 at 227), a case about a refrigerator in a flat, Sellers LJ said, at p. 227:

> If an agreement gives a tenant the use of something wholly in the occupation and control of the landlord, for example, a lift, it would, I think, be accepted that the landlord would be required to maintain the lift, especially if it were the only means of access to the demised premises. I recognise that a lift might vary in age and efficiency, but in order to give meaning to the words 'the use of' and to fulfil them it should at least be maintained so that it would take a tenant up and down, subject to temporary breakdown and reasonable stoppages for maintenance and repairs.

That was a dissenting judgment but Lord Evershed MR ([1958] 1 All ER at 716, [1958] 2 QB at 220) made a similar observation as to lifts.

These are all reflections of what necessarily arises whenever a landlord lets portions of a building for multiple occupation, retaining essential means of access.

I accept, of course, the argument that a mere grant of an easement does not carry with it any obligation on the part of the servient owner to maintain the subject-matter. The dominant owner must spend the necessary money, for example, in repairing a drive leading to his house. And the same principle may apply when a landlord lets an upper floor with access by a staircase: responsibility for maintenance may well rest on the tenant. But there is a difference between that case and the case where there is an essential means of access, retained in the landlord's occupation, to units in a building of multi-occupation, for unless the obligation to maintain is, in a defined manner, placed on the tenants, individually or collectively, the nature of the contract, and the circumstances, require that it be placed on the landlord.

It remains to define the standard. My Lords, if, as I think, the test of the existence of the term is necessity the standard must surely not exceed what is necessary having regard to the circumstances. To imply an absolute obligation to repair would go beyond what is a necessary legal incident and would indeed be unreasonable. An obligation to take reasonable care to keep in reasonable repair and usability is what fits the requirements of the case. Such a definition involves – and I think rightly – recognition that the tenants themselves have their responsibilities. What it is reasonable to expect of a landlord has a clear relation to what a reasonable set of tenants should do for themselves.

I add one word as to lighting. In general I would accept that a grant of an easement of passage does not carry with it an obligation on the grantor to light the way. The grantee must take the way accompanied by the primeval separation of darkness from light and if he passes during the former must bring his own illumination. I think that *Huggett* v *Miers* [1908] 2 KB 278 was decided on this principle and possibly also *Devine* v *London Housing Society Ltd* [1950] WN 550. But the case may be different when the means of passage are constructed, and when natural light is either absent or insufficient. In such a case, to the extent that the easement is useless without some artificial light being provided, the grant should carry with it an obligation to take reasonable care to maintain adequate lighting – comparable to the obligation as regards the lifts. To impose an absolute obligation would be unreasonable; to impose some might be necessary. We have not sufficient material before us to see whether the present case on its facts meets these conditions.

I would hold therefore that the corporation's obligation is as I have described. And in agreement, I believe, with your Lordships, I would hold that it has not been shown in this case that there was any breach of that obligation. On the main point therefore I would hold that the appeal fails.

My Lords, it will be seen that I have reached exactly the same conclusion as that of Lord Denning MR, with most of whose thinking I respectfully agree. I must only differ from the passage in which, more adventurously, he suggests [[1975] 3 All ER at 666, [1975] 3 WLR at 672] that the courts have power to introduce into contracts any terms they thought reasonable or to anticipate legislative recommendations of the Law Commission. A just result can be reached, if I am right, by a less dangerous route.

As regards the obligation under the Housing Act 1961, s. 32, again I am in general agreement with Lord Denning MR. The only possible item which might fall within the covenant implied by this section is that of defective cisterns in the maisonette giving rise to flooding or, if this is prevented, to insufficient flushing. I do not disagree with those of your Lordships who would hold that a breach of the statutory covenant was committed in respect of the matter for which a small sum of damages may be awarded. I would allow the appeal as to this matter and dismiss it for the rest.

Note

It is important to note here that the House of Lords was not prepared to go as far as Lord Denning MR in the Court of Appeal ([1975] QB 319) in *Irwin* and imply terms it thought reasonable. The terms implied into the lease were ones of necessity, for the 'whole transaction would become futile, inefficacious and absurd' (Lord Salmon at p. 262) if no such obligations were imposed upon the authority. It is of course, equally important to note that drawing the line between necessity and mere 'reasonableness' is more art than science, and still leaves significant areas of judgment to the court of first instance.

(a)   Express covenants

The vast majority of both residential and commercial leases contain express covenants stipulating liability for repair. The crucial first question therefore is: What is meant by repair? According to Hoffmann J in *Post Office* v *Aquarius Properties Ltd* [1985] 2 EGLR 105, the word 'repair' is an ordinary word of the English language taking its meaning from the context in which it is used. Of crucial importance is to recall that a landlord, or tenant, may be placed under an obligation to repair, but not generally an obligation to improve a property. Thus, it is important to distinguish between a repair and an improvement. Denning LJ in *Morcom* v *Campbell-Johnson* [1956] 1 QB 106 portrayed the difference in the following way (at p. 115):

[I]f the work which is done is the provision of something new for the benefit of the occupier, that is, properly speaking, an improvement; but if it is only the replacement of something already there, which has become dilapidated or worn out, albeit that it is the replacement by its modern equivalent, it comes within the category of repairs and not improvements.

Brew Brothers Ltd v Snax (Ross) Ltd
[1970] 1 QB 612

The wall of a demised premises tilted towards the neighbouring garage of which the plaintiffs were occupiers. The wall was found to be in a dangerous condition and was shored up to prevent it falling down, causing an obstruction to the plaintiffs' garage forecourt. The foundations of the wall were found to have shifted because of seepage from drains below the demised premises. The plaintiffs took action against the neighbouring landlord and tenant seeking abatement of the nuisance and damages. The landlord argued that the tenants were liable for the problems caused by the wall by their failure to repair drains as required by the lease. The tenants contended that the works required were outside the ambit of a repairing covenant. The Court of Appeal found in favour of the plaintiffs, with both the landlord and tenant liable for half the costs each.

SACHS LJ: The premises with which this litigation is concerned are known as No. 396, Sutton Common Road, Sutton. They were built about 1933 as a part of some seven similar premises, which appear normally to have shops on the ground floor and living premises above. In April 1937, No. 396 was conveyed to a member of the Jackson family and thus became the property of Jackson Investments Ltd [the second defendants], to whom I will refer as 'the owners'. In the course of the Second World War a bomb dropped in the vicinity just in the rear of the neighbouring land which was then expected to become Nos. 398–408 of the above road: it produced a 15-foot crater and certain consequences relevant to this action.

After the war, for some period before 1965, the premises were occupied by tenants who, however, had got into financial difficulties by 1964 or a little earlier. By April 1964, Mr Jackson (a director of the owner company) visited the premises with a representative of Snax (Ross) Ltd [the first defendant], as a preliminary to offering that company a tenancy. Negotiations seem to have dragged on, owing to questions arising between the owners and the trustee in bankruptcy of the former tenants; but during or shortly before May 1965, came a period when the landlords were in practical although not in legal possession of the premises. Both in April 1964 and during the latter period the landlords had opportunity to inspect and to get to know the condition of the premises and indeed, to a certain degree, inspected them by their directors. Moreover, during 1965 itself they executed a considerable amount of repair work to the premises: no details are available as to what work they did but it was suggested to this court that repairs to the roof formed part of what was done.

On 30 June 1965, the owners granted to Snax (Ross) Ltd a 14 year lease, and to that company I will refer as 'tenants'. The lease contained repairing covenants to which fuller reference will have to be made: it also referred to the 32 foot flank wall on the opposite side of the premises to no. 394 as a 'party wall', although by the terms of the lease it would only become a party wall in law if premises were built next to it and abutting on to it. It is convenient simply to refer to it as 'the flank wall'.

In the summer of 1966, a large tree, probably an elm, was removed from the pavement outside the property – a removal which added to the moisture content of the clay under the foundations of no. 396. In November 1966, there was a sudden and pronounced tilting movement of the flank wall which produced a situation of imminent danger to the neighbouring area which was being used as the forecourt of a garage by the plaintiffs in this action.

Thereupon a dispute arose as between the tenants and the owners as to who was responsible to the plaintiffs for resulting damage. Shoring was immediately erected with footings in the garage premises without prejudice to who was liable for abating the nuisance. That shoring remained there for some 18 months without there being any agreement between these two parties as to who should bear the cost of the operations to which more detailed reference will be made. Hence this action.

All the above facts are common ground, as also are two further matters. First, that the movement, although precipitated by the removal of the tree, was in essence due to water having flowed from badly defective drains under one side of no. 396 so as to cause the foundations to move and the flank wall to become unstable and unsafe. Secondly, that the original cause of the fractures in the drain and its casing which resulted in the above leak stemmed from damage caused by the bomb to which reference has been made.

The main questions of fact in issue before the trial judge at the lengthy proceedings before him were: first, whether the foundations had already so shifted by June 1965, as to result in the premises being already unsafe at that time; secondly, whether the landlords ought in June 1965, to have known of that state of affairs; and thirdly, what was the extent of the work necessary to abate the nuisance and to reinstate the premises into a safe and usable condition. The trial judge found against the owners on the first two of these issues: as regards the third, he found that very extensive work was required, which included fresh foundations with underpinning or equivalent work and the rebuilding of the whole of the flank wall and part of the front and rear walls.

Mr Blundell [counsel for the landlords] pressed a careful and indeed prolonged attack on the findings of fact of the trial judge. Suffice it, at this stage, to say that this attack failed completely. To my mind not only had the trial judge ample evidence on which to base his conclusions of fact but they were, so far as one can judge from a shorthand note, correct conclusions both as to whose evidence to accept and whose evidence to reject and as to what was the appropriate set of findings in the circumstances.

On the basis of the facts as common ground and found by the trial judge, there arise for consideration points of law – which have been strenuously argued and are far from easy to resolve.

. . .

Does the taking of such a covenant of itself excuse the owners assuming it is effective in the sense that it bound the tenants to do the relevant work? Mr Blundell [counsel for the landlords] urged that it did exculpate them and relied in the main on three cases decided between 1860 and 1875 and a passage in *Clerk and Lindsell on The Law of Torts*, 12th ed. (1961), para. 1293, which contains a categorical statement in his favour – in contrast to the less dogmatic views expressed in other textbooks cited to the court. Mr Drake [counsel for the tenants], on the other hand, referred to *Mint v Good* [1951] 1 KB 517 and the cases there cited: he then submitted that even if the older authorities supported Mr Blundell's submission (which he contested) there have been such developments in the relevant law of nuisance that those authorities no longer hold good. How, then, does the law stand on this matter?

In each of the three old authorities relied on Mr Blundell, the plaintiff had brought an action against the owner of property who had let it to a tenant from whom he had taken a repairing covenant: in each case the plaintiff was *Todd v Flight* (1860) 9 CBNS 377, a case of a falling chimney. It was decided on demurrer after extensive argument. For the purposes of the demurrer the chimneys were taken to be at the date of the lease to the knowledge of the owner in a ruinous and insecure state and to have been thus kept and maintained. The court held the owner was liable. Whether the repairing covenant suffered injury from some disrepair that had existed at the date of the case. The first case at p. 383 could be or was taken into account on demurrer is not clear.

In the second case, *Gwinnell v Eamer* ((1875) LR 10 CP 658), a defective grating case, it was stated, at p. 661, that at the time of the demise the owner—

> had no knowledge of the defective state of the grating, and had no means of knowing it, and was guilty of no negligence in being ignorant of it.

The owner succeeded in his defence.

Neither of those cases decides the point in issue, That leaves for consideration *Pretty v Bickmore* (1873) LR & CP 401, a defective coal-plate case. There Brett J non-suited the plaintiff after hearing the evidence adduced on his behalf. Despite the fact that knowledge of the disrepair at the date of the lease was alleged in the statement of claim and that there was evidence led on this point, Brett J made no finding of such knowledge. As was observed in regard to this case in the considered judgment of this court in *Wringe v Cohen* [1940] 1 KB 229, 235):

> It was certainly not found that the defendant knew of the disrepair and no reference was made to his knowledge one way or the other.

. . .

Bovill CJ in *Pretty v Bickmore* did decide the point in favour of the owner the question arises as to its authority today. In *Mint v Good* [1951] 1 KB 517, Denning LJ referred at p. 527 to the remarkable development which had been taking place in this branch of the law of nuisance, and said at p. 528:

> I know that in *Pretty v Bickmore* a landlord managed to escape liability for a coal-plate which was, at the beginning of the lease, in dangerous disrepair, because he took from the tenant a covenant to repair. I doubt whether he would escape liability today.

With those doubts I respectfully agree, at any rate if it be assumed that in that case the owner had knowledge of the disrepair at the relevant date – and, perhaps, on the particular facts, even if he did not. It is indeed not the only case of that period in which views of the law were expressed which do not obtain today – compare, for instance, the judgments of the court (Denman and Lopes LJJ) in *Nelson v Liverpool Brewery Co.* (1877) 2 CPD 311, a falling chimney case, with those in *Mint v Good* [1951] 1 KB 517, on the effect of an owner customarily executing repairs for which the tenant is under no liability. (Incidentally, in the former case Lopes LJ appears to take a view of *Pretty v Bickmore* LR 8 CP 401, which does not accord with Mr Blundell's submission.)

The development of this branch of the law has since the judgment of Goddard J in *Wilchick v Marks Silverstone* [1934] 2 KB 56 proceeded on lines in some respects parallel to that of the law of negligence. Both in the judgment of Goddard J in that case and in those in subsequent cases reference is made to 'proximity' as bearing on the relevant issues. Where there is proximity and an ability to remedy the danger, is the injured person to be left only to a remedy against the tenant? This was the question posed by Goddard J in the above case and adopted by MacKinnon LJ in *Heap v Ind Coope & Allsopp Ltd* [1940] 2 KB 476, 483, 484: in each instance it was given a negative answer. Although those cases related to passers-by on the highway, I cannot see how the principle of proximity does not equally apply to neighbours – at any rate so far as known dangers are concerned: this indeed was conceded by Mr Blundell at any rate as to places where persons congregate. (It is not necessary in this case to consider unknown dangers.) A similar view of its applicability to neighbours is indicated in the judgment of Somervell LJ in *Mint v Good* [1951] 1 KB 517, 522.

Instead of the liability of an owner of premises let to a tenant depending substantially or perhaps even wholly on the terms of a tenancy agreement – a criterion rightly criticised by Megaw J in the present case – it has come to depend on more rational considerations. If the nuisance arises after the lease is granted, the test of an owner's duty to his neighbour now depends on the degree of control exercised by the owner in law or in fact for the purpose of repairs: see the judgment of Denning LJ in *Mint v Good* at p. 528, as fully agreed by Birkett LJ at p. 529. As regards nuisances of which he knew at the date of the lease, the duty similarly arises by reason of his control before that date. Once the liability attaches I can find no rational reason why it should as regards third parties be shuffled off merely by signing a document which as between owner and tenant casts on the latter the burden of executing remedial work. The duty of the owner is to ensure that the nuisance causes no injury – not merely to get somebody else's promise to take the requisite steps to abate it. (Indeed in his closing address Mr Blundell seemed to concede this point as regards certain sets of circumstances.) If the nuisance is not abated he suffers it to continue and is thus liable for its effects. He could not simply by engaging a contractor to abate a long-standing nuisance relieve himself of liability for injuries caused by that nuisance before abatement: and the same principle to my mind applies to the engagement of a tenant. It would be nothing in point if the owner chose to grant a lease on terms which excluded him from entering to abate the nuisance in accordance with his duty: whether a right of entry for that limited purpose may be necessarily implied thus need not be considered.

The owner of property in my view remains liable to third parties for the effects of a nuisance of which he has knowledge at the date of granting a lease unless excused by some further fact over and above taking a covenant to repair – although of course he may have his remedy over against the tenant when that covenant is effective. Any other view would lead to absurdities, as is indicated in *Mint v Good* at p. 528. In the instant case there is no such further fact and accordingly the owners are liable to the plaintiffs because they suffered the nuisance to continue from June 1965 to November 1966, and a fortiori they suffered it to continue during the period the shoring was erected. The owners as well as the tenants are thus liable in tort to the garage proprietors: each ought to have known of the relevant dangers: and the trial judge was right in apportioning the blame on a 50:50 basis.

Having concluded that the owners are liable in nuisance on the above basis, I prefer not to express a view whether they would in any event have been liable by virtue of their failure to abate the nuisance after making the *without prejudice* arrangements of November 1966 – a point, to my mind, of some difficulty.

The next hotly contested issue of importance was whether the extensive work executed by the owners in 1968 without prejudice to issues of liability was work of repair for which the tenant, between himself and the owners, liable to pay because of the provision of clause 2(e) of the June 1965 lease. The nature of this work was summarised in the judgment of Megaw J and is about to be referred to in the judgment of Phillimore LJ, so there is no need for me further to describe it.

This court rejected an application on behalf of the owners to adduce further evidence showing that the work in fact carried out after the trial was sufficient: but I would add that so far as my judgment is concerned the issue as to whether the tenants are liable would not be affected even if the work in fact carried out was all that was necessary for the purpose in hand. Nevertheless it is the work which the trial judge decided was necessary that has to be considered by this court.

The question whether extensive work involving the rebuilding of walls in whole or in part, of reconstructing foundations, and of underpinning, does or does not on the particular facts of an individual case fall within a repairing covenant, has provided much material for the books. In the course of argument we were appropriately and carefully referred to the plethora of authorities from *Lister v Lane* 9 Nesham [1893] 2 QB 212 with the much-cited judgment of Lord Esher MR at pp. 216–217, that:

> however large the words of the covenant, may be to repair, it is not a covenant to give a different thing from that which the tenant took when he entered into the covenant through *Lurcott v Wakely and Wheeler* [1911] 1 KB 905 to *Collins v Flynn* [1963] 2 All ER 1068, with its helpful review of many of the decisions.

In the course of their submissions counsel referred to a number of varying phrases which had been used by judges in an endeavour to express the distinction between the end-product of work which constituted repair and that of work which did not. They included 'improvement', 'important improvement', 'different in kind', 'different in character', 'different in substance', 'different in nature', 'a new and different thing', and just 'something different'. They likewise referred to another set of phrases seeking to define the distinctive quality of the fault to be rectified, such as 'inherent nature' (frequently used since *Lister v Lane and Nesham* [1893] 2 QB 212), 'radical defect in the structure', 'inherent defect' and 'inherent vice'. Each of these two sets of phrases in turn was discussed in what tended to become an exercise in semantics. Moreover, it is really not much use looking at individual phrases which necessarily deal with only one of the infinitely variable sets of circumstances that can arise.

For my part I doubt whether there is any definition – certainly not any general definition – which satisfactorily covers the above distinctions: nor will I attempt to provide one. Things which can be easily recognised are not always susceptible of simple definition. Indeed the only observation I need offer is to reject the submission that if 'inherent nature' or 'inherent defects' have to be considered, they are confined to a state of affairs due to the age of the premises or to defects that originated when the building was erected.

It seems to me that the correct approach is to look at the particular building, to look at the state which it is in *at the date of the lease*, to look at the precise terms of the lease, and then come to a conclusion as to whether, on a fair interpretation of those terms in relation to that state, the requisite work can fairly be termed repair. However large the covenant it must not be looked at in vacuo.

Quite clearly this approach involves in every instance a question of degree, as indeed Mr Blundell was constrained to agree was the correct approach, and I would in this behalf echo the words of Lord Evershed MR in *Wates v Rowland* [1952] 2 QB 12, at p. 23 when dealing with an analogous problem relating to repairs. After setting out two plain examples, he said:

> Between the two extremes, it seems to me to be largely a matter of degree, which in the ordinary case the county court judge could decide as a matter of fact, applying a common-sense man-of-the-world view.

This is the approach which seems to have been adopted by that very wise and experienced judge Lynskey J in *Sotheby v Grundy* [1947] 2 All ER 761 [at p. 762]. There in an underpinning case he found in favour of a tenant who was being called upon to turn ([1947] 2 All ER at 762):

> a building which, as originally constructed, would not last more than some 80 odd years into a building that would last for probably another 100 years

and said at p. 762 that 'in my view that does not come within the purview of the repairing covenant here'

In the upshot – 'it is 'the good sense of the agreement' that has to be ascertained' a phrase conveniently quoted from the 1842 judgment of Tindal CJ (*White* v *Nicholson* (1842) 4 Man & G 95, 98)) in *Woodfall on Law of Landlord and Tenant,* in relation to a different aspect of repairing covenants.

Having thus stated what seems to me the appropriate approach to the problem, having had the advantage of reading the judgment of Phillimore LJ on this issue, and being in agreement with what he is about to say, it suffices for me to record that to my mind the trial judge properly approached the question as being one of degree and reached the correct conclusion. I also agree with the view of Phillimore LJ that the court must look at the work required as a whole and not seek to look at component parts of that work on the doomed premises individually. Any detailed examination of the work reinforces this view.

It follows that the owners have, in my view, failed in their contentions that they are not liable to the garage proprietors in nuisance; they have also failed to show that they can recover against the tenants the damages they have claimed under the repairing covenant. Accordingly I would dismiss the appeal.

Notes

1.   In *McDougall* v *Easington DC* (1989) 21 HLR 310, the Court of Appeal had to consider whether a major works programme involving £10,000 being spent on each of a number of properties, which would ultimately increase the value of the properties from £10,000 to £18,000, amounted to repair of these properties. In order to answer this question Mustill LJ indicated three tests adopted by the courts in this area:

(a)   Do the alterations go to the whole, or substantially the whole, of the structure?

(b)   Is the effect of the work to produce a building of a wholly different character from that which was let?

(c)   What is the cost of the works in relation to the building's previous value, and what is the effect on its value and life expectancy?

These tests may be applied separately or concurrently to decide whether something was a repair.

2.   The fact that works required are costly does not automatically remove them from the ambit of repair. *Elite Investments Ltd* v *T.I. Bainbridge Silencers Ltd* (1986) 280 EG 1001 involved the repair of a roof on an industrial unit. The repair would cost in excess of £80,000. In its current state of dilapidation the unit was virtually worthless; with a repaired roof the value would be around £140,000 to £150,000. The cost of rebuilding the unit was about £1 million. Did the replacement of the roof constitute a repair? The court answered in the affirmative, as the roof was a repair under the terms of the tenant's repairing covenant. The roof would not make the unit a different entity, simply an industrial unit with a new roof. Furthermore in *Elite Investments,* Judge Baker QC found that the cost of the repair, following the decision in *Ravenseft Properties Ltd* v *Davstone (Holdings) Ltd* [1980] QB 12, should be measured against the cost of rebuilding the property, rather than the value of the repaired property.

(b) Inherent defects

The fact that a property is in a poor state of repair may be due to its original construction, a consequence, for example, of design deficiencies, or shoddy workmanship. Prior to *Ravenseft*, the predominant view had been that remedying an inherent defect could never amount to a repair.

Ravenseft Properties Ltd v Davstone (Holdings) Ltd
[1980] QB 12

A 16 storey block of maisonettes constructed from reinforced concrete with stone claddings was erected between 1958 and 1960. As was usual practice at the time the property was built, expansion joints were omitted from the structure. In 1973, part of the stone cladding became loose due to the inherent defect of not inserting expansion joints. The tenant had liability for repairs, but denied repairing obligations here for the cost of inserting the joints on the grounds that this was an inherent defect, outside the scope of the covenant to repair.

FORBES J: . . . The tenant's defence is two fold. Mr Colyer, counsel for the defendants says first, there is in that branch of landlord and tenant law concerned with repairing covenants, a doctrine of inherent defect which is applicable to such covenants to repair. This is that where wants of reparation arise which are caused by some inherent defect in the premises demised, the results of the inherent defect can never fall within the ambit of a covenant to repair. Secondly he says, that if that proposition is wrong the covenantor is still not bound to pay for any works which, in fact, remedy the inherent defect.

The landlords answer that broadly in this way. Mr Bernstein [counsel] says there is no such thing as a doctrine of inherent defect. The question is simply: 'Is what the tenant is asked to do fairly represented by the word 'repair'? and this question is to be judged as a matter of degree in each case.

The leading cases on the matter have been referred to by both counsel and I need only, I think, list them at this stage and then consider at any rate some of them in a little more detail later. They are *Proudfoot v Hart* (1890) 25 QBD 42; *Lister v Lane* [1893] 2 QB 212; *Wright v Lawson* (1903) 19 TLR 510; *Lurcott v Wakely* [1911] 1 KB 905; *Anstruther-Gough-Calthorpe v McOscar* [1924] 1 KB 716, *Pembery v Lamdin* [1940] 2 All ER 434; *Sotheby v Grundy* [1947] 2 All ER 761; *Collins v Flynn* [1963] 2 All ER 1068; and *Brew Bros Ltd v Snax (Ross) Ltd* [1970] 1 QB 612. All these cases are, I think, very well known and I do not intend to recite the facts or the judgments in detail, though there are one or two matters which will have to be considered more carefully. Of these cases it seems that it is unnecessary to consider further *Proudfoot v Hart* and *Anstruther-Gough-Calthorpe v McOscar*. They are concerned with questions of the standard of repair required under a repairing covenant rather than what is included in the term 'repair'.

One should start with *Lister v Lane* ([1893] QB 212 and the frequently quoted passage from the judgment of Lord Esher MR at pp. 216–217:

> . . . if a tenant takes a house which is of such a kind that by its own inherent nature it will in course of time fall into a particular condition, the effects of that result are not within the tenant's covenant to repair. However large the words of the covenant

may be, a covenant to repair a house is not a covenant to give a different thing from that which the tenant took when he entered into the covenant. He has to repair that thing which he took; he is not obliged to make a new and different thing, and, moreover, the result of the nature and condition of the house itself, the result of time upon that state of things, is not a breach of the covenant to repair.

From this passage and the case in general, Mr Colyer [counsel for the defendants] derives this proposition. If it can be shown that any want of reparation has been caused by an inherent defect, then that want of reparation is not within the ambit of a covenant to repair. Inherent defect he defines as an omission of something in the original design. A defect in the quality of workmanship or materials is not, he says, an inherent defect. The want of reparation Mr Colyer says, was the failure to reconstruct the wall, in that case, by providing the whole house with under-pinned foundations, and that want of reparation was directly due to the omission of proper foundations in the original construction.

I started with *Lister's* case and the well-known passage from Lord Esher MR's judgment, but Mr Colyer says that *Lister's* case itself was founded on *Soward* v *Leggatt* (1836) 7 C & P 613, and it is necessary to look briefly at that case. There the floor joists were repaired by laying them on bricks rather than on mud, as the original floor joists had been laid, and Mr Colyer seeks to found an argument from that, that any work to a building which involves a different method of construction must be regarded as giving to the landlord a different thing from that which the tenant took. But such a broad proposition cannot, I think, survive close consideration of the later case of *Lurcott* v *Wakely* [1911] 1 KB 905. It should be remembered that in that case the court was dealing with the rebuilding of the eastern external wall of a house in Hatton Garden and that what had happened was that the premises had been certified as being in a dangerous state by the district surveyor and that later in compliance with a demolition order, under the London Building Acts, the plaintiff had taken down the wall to the level of the ground floor, and then in compliance with a further notice by the district surveyor, had pulled down the remaining wall and rebuilt it with concrete foundations and damp courses in accordance with the requirements of the Act. The question was whether the tenant was liable under the repairing covenant for this work and it is clear that the wall originally lacked concrete foundations and damp courses, and that the insertion of these features in the rebuilt wall was the result of statutory notices by the local authority. Both Sir Herbert Cozens-Hardy MR and Buckley LJ regarded the matter as a question of degree rather than as one of method of construction, and clearly the method of construction was wholly different. In any event, Mr Colyer's first point depends on causation, and *Soward* v *Leggatt* (1836) 7 C & P 613 was not concerned with direct causation but turned on whether the work was an improvement or not, which is Mr Colyer's second rather than his first point.

Turning to *Wright* v *Lawson* 19 TLR 510, Mr Colyer explains that in the same way as he explained *Lister* v *Lane* [1893] 2 QB 212 case. There, he says, the want of reparation complained of by the landlord was the failure to provide a bay window supported on pillars but this failure in turn was directly due to the absence of sufficient stability in the house to support a cantilever bay window. Mr Colyer accepts that the only case in which this doctrine of inherent defect was argued was *Collins* v *Flynn* [1963] 2 All ER 1068. It is necessary therefore to look at that case, but before doing so one should, I think, look at *Sotheby* v *Grundy* [1947] 2 All ER 761 because Sir Brett Cloutman VC in *Collins* v *Flynn* deals with *Lister's* case and *Sotheby's* case in a sense together.

Now the facts in *Sotheby* case were not unimportant. The house which was the demised premises in that case was found in 1944 to have bulged and fractured walls and the house was condemned as a dangerous structure and demolished by the council. Expenses incurred by the council were recovered from the landlord who sought to recover them from the tenant as damages for breach of a repairing covenant, so the case itself was not directly concerned with work of repair but with the cost of demolition due to failure to repair. The evidence showed that in fact the house was built, in defiance of the requirements of the Metropolitan Building Act 1855, entirely without footings, or in some places, on defective footings and in consequence, and because of the defective footings, there was every likelihood that the house would, in fact, fall into the dangerous state into which it did fall.

'That very wise and experienced judge' as Sachs LJ in *Brew Bros Ltd* v *Snax (Ross) Ltd* [1970] 1 QB 612, 640 called Lynskey J, found that the wants of reparation were caused by what he called 'the inherent nature of the defect in the premises' ([1947] 2 All ER 761, 762) but nevertheless felt it incumbent upon him to consider as a matter of degree whether the finding that the tenant was liable for the works required would be asking the tenant to give the landlord something different in kind from that which had been demised. This is clearly to reject, or overlook, any argument that a want of reparation caused by inherent defect could not in any circumstances be within the ambit of the repairing covenant.

Now looking at *Collins* v *Flynn* ([1963] 2 All ER 1068), Sir Brett Cloutman deals with these points at pp. 1073, 1074:

> The last case that is really in point is *Sotheby* v *Grundy* [1947] 2 All ER 761. This was the case of a condemned house, built in or about 1861, the main walls having been built either without footings or on defective footings. The foundation had settled and this could have been avoided only by underpinning and substituting a new foundation. On the authority of Lord Esher's judgment in *Lister* v *Lane* [1893] 2 QB 212, it was held that the tenant was not liable for the cost of demolition. The expenses were incurred because of the inherent nature of the defect of the premises, and, therefore, did not come within the terms of the repairing covenant. Plainly the doctrine of liability for the defects in a subsidiary part could have nothing to do with that case. The case, as it seems to me, was on all fours with *Lister* v *Lane*. Oddly enough, Lynskey J does introduce it, in what I think is an obiter passage. He said ([1947] 2 All ER 761, 762): 'It may be that the inherent nature of the building may result in its partial collapse. One can visualise the floor of a building collapsing owning to defective joists having been put in. I do not think *Lister* v *Lane* would be applicable to such a case. In those circumstances, in my opinion, the damage would fall within the ambit of the covenant to repair, but as I say, it must be a question of degree in each particular case'.

The official referee went on to talk about what he described as 'obiter joists', referred to also in *Lister's* and *Lurcott's* cases. Then, at 1074:

> I now come to the crucial point. Do the words 'repair' and 'renew' import a liability to rebuild with newly designed foundations and footings the pier supporting the girder which in turn carries a great part of the rear wall and a part of the side wall in addition? This is manifestly a most important improvement, which, if executed by the tenant, would involve him in rendering up the premises in different condition from that in which they were demised, and on the authority of Lord Esher MR, in *Lister* v *Lane*, I do not think that the tenant is under any such obligation. Furthermore, although a suggestion of liability for removal of an inherent defect in a subsidiary part seems to have been touched on in *Sotheby* v *Grundy*, I do not think

that the obiter remarks of Lynskey J, as to defective joists have any bearing on the present case.

In these passages it seems to me that Sir Brett mis-directs himself on the ratio of *Sotheby's* case. The question of whether the inherent nature of the building might result in its partial collapse was not obiter at all. It was part of the ratio in this sense that, treating the question as a matter of degree, a partial collapse, in the view of Lynskey J, would have been of a degree which brought it within the tenant's covenant to repair, whereas a total collapse would put it outside. As, therefore, it was not a matter of part only, but of putting in new foundations in the entire building, the judge found it was not within the ambit of the covenant. Insofar as he appears to be misdirecting himself on the ratio of *Sotheby's* case, the persuasive authority of Sir Brett Cloutman's judgment in *Collins v Flynn* [1963] 2 All ER 1068 must be considerably eroded.

The remaining cases in the list are *Pembery v Lamdin* [1940] 2 All ER 434 and *Brew Bros Ltd v Snax (Ross) Ltd* [1970] 1 QB 612. Now *Pembery* was clearly a case of inherent defect but the court did not there decide that the plaintiff failed because there existed a doctrine such as that put forward by Mr Colyer. One can, I think, epitomise Slesser LJ's judgment in that case in this way. The plaintiff failed because her argument, if correct, would have involved ordering the defendant to give her a different thing from that which was demised. This is clearly, in my view a decision arrived at by considering the question as one of degree. *Brew Brothers Ltd v Snax (Ross) Ltd* [1970] 1 QB 612, though a case where the defect was not inherent (see Harman LJ, arguendo at p. 622) was nevertheless a case where at any rate a doctrine of inherent defect such as that suggested by Mr Colyer was put forward in argument by the landlord (see p. 618), and countered for the tenants ([1970] 1 QB 612 at 622). But both Sachs LJ ([1970] 1 All ER 587 at 602–603, [1970] 1 QB 612 at 640) and Phillimore LJ ([1970] 1 All ER 587 at 607, [1970] 1 QB 612 at 646) appear to indicate that, whether or not the cause of any want of reparation is an inherent defect, the question must still be regarded as one of degree in each case.

This necessarily brief review of authorities indicates quite clearly to my mind that apart from *Collins v Flynn*, which I consider of doubtful authority, the explanation of the ratio in *Lister's* case as giving the tenant a complete defence, if the cause of the want of reparation is an inherent defect, has never been adopted by any court, but on the contrary in *Pembery v Lamdin* and *Sotheby v Grundy*, the court, when dealing with wants of reparation caused by inherent defect, chose to treat the matter as one of degree, and in *Brew Brothers* the court effectively said that every case, whatever the causation, must be treated as one of degree.

I find myself, therefore, unable to accept counsel's contention for the defendants that a doctrine such as he enunciates has any place in the law of landlord and tenant. The true test is, as the cases show, that it is always a question of degree whether that which the tenant is being asked to do can properly be described as repair, or whether on the contrary it would involve giving back to the landlord a wholly different thing from that which he demised.

Thus, Forbes J identifies the true test as being one of degree, i.e. whether what is being given back is something of a wholly different character to the original letting. The fact that the need for repair was caused by an inherent defect is of little consequence. However, even if there are inherent defects in the construction of a property, there must be a 'repair' required in order for liability to arise.

Quick v Taff Ely BC
[1986] QB 809

The plaintiff was a tenant of a house let by the local authority. The house was in a very poor state with severe condensation due to the lack of insulation around the concrete window lintels, inadequate heating and problems with single-glazed metal windows. The plaintiff brought an action against the authority seeking specific performance of the authority's covenant to repair under s. 32(1) of the Housing Act 1961 (see now s. 11, Landlord and Tenant Act 1985, below).

DILLON LJ: . . . The case turns on the construction and effect of the repairing covenant in section 32 of the Act of 1961. Before I turn to that, however, I should mention one apparent oddity in the legislation. There is in section 6 of the Housing Act 1957 a provision that, in any contract for the letting of a house for human habitation at an annual rent not exceeding £80 in the case of a house in London and £52 in the case of a house elsewhere, there is to be implied a condition that the house is at the commencement of the tenancy, and an undertaking that the house will be kept by the landlord during the tenancy, fit for human habitation. That section has legislative antecedents, albeit at lower rent levels, in the Housing Act 1936, and before that in the Housing Act 1925 and before that in the Housing Town Planning etc. Act 1909. It was amended by the London Government Act 1963 as a result of the creation of the Greater London Council, but without altering the rent levels. It seems that the section as so amended has remained on the statute book ever since, but – for whatever reason – the rent levels have never been increased. Therefore, in view of inflation, the section must now have remarkably little application. It is not available to the plaintiff in the present case because his rent is too high, even though he is an unemployed tenant of a small council house.

The judge delivered a careful reserved judgment in which he reviewed many of the more recent authorities on repairing covenants, starting with *Pembery* v *Lamdin* [1940] 2 All ER 434. His ultimate reasoning seems to me to be on the following lines, viz (1) recent authorities such as *Ravenseft Properties Ltd* v *Davstone (Holdings) Ltd* [1980] QB 12 and *Elmcroft Developments Ltd* v *Tankersley-Sawyer* (1984) 270 EG 140 show that works of repair under a repairing covenant, whether by a landlord or a tenant, may require the remedying of an inherent defect in a building; (2) the authorities also show that it is a question of degree whether works which remedy an inherent defect in a building may not be so extensive as to amount to an improvement or renewal of the whole which is beyond the concept of repair; (3) in the present case the replacement of windows and the provision of insulation for the lintels does not amount to such an improvement or renewal of the whole; (4) therefore, the replacement of the windows and provision of the insulation to alleviate an inherent defect is a repair which the local authority is bound to carry out under the repairing covenant.

But, with every respect to the judge, this reasoning begs the important question. It assumes that any work to eradicate an inherent defect in a building must be a work of repair, which the relevant party is bound to carry out if, as a matter of degree, it does not amount to a renewal or improvement of the building. In effect, it assumes the broad proposition urged on us by Mr Blom-Cooper for the plaintiff that anything defective or inherently inefficient for living in or ineffective to provide the conditions of ordinary habitation is in disrepair. But that does not follow from the decisions in

Ravenseft's case [1980] QB 12 and *Elmcroft's* case 270 EG 140 that works of repair *may* require the remedying of an inherent defect.

Mr Blom-Cooper's proposition has very far-reaching implications indeed. The covenant implied under section 32 of the Act of 1961 is an ordinary repairing covenant. It does not only apply to local authorities as landlords, and this court has held in *Wainwright* v *Leeds City Council* (1984) 270 EG 1289 that the fact that a landlord is a local authority, which is discharging a social purpose in providing housing for people who cannot afford it, does not make the burden of the covenant greater on that landlord than it would be on any other landlord. The construction of the covenant must be the same whether it is implied as a local authority covenant in a tenancy of a council house or is expressly included as a tenant's or landlord's covenant in a private lease which is outside section 32. A tenant under such a lease who had entered into such a repairing covenant would, no doubt, realise, if he suffered from problems of condensation in his house, that he could not compel the landlord to do anything about those problems. But I apprehend that the tenant would be startled to be told – as must follow from Judge Francis's decision – that the landlord has the right to compel him, the tenant, to put in new windows. If the reasoning is valid, where is the process to stop? The evidence of Mr Pryce Thomas was that changing the windows and the lintels would 'alleviate' the problems, not that it would cure them. If there was evidence that double-glazing would further alleviate the problems, would a landlord, or tenant, under a repairing covenant be obliged to put in double-glazing? Mr Price Thomas said that a radiator system of heating to all rooms in the place of the warm air system was 'necessary'; if the judge's reasoning was correct, it would seem that, if the point had been properly pleaded early enough, the tenant might have compelled the local authority to put in a radiator system of heating.

In my judgment, the key factor in the present case is that disrepair is related to the physical condition of whatever has to be repaired, and not to questions of lack of amenity or inefficiency. I find helpful the observation of Atkin LJ in *Anstruther-Gough-Calthorpe* v *McOscar* [1924] 1 KB 716, 734, that repair 'connotes the idea of making good damage so as to leave the subject so far as possible as though it had not been damaged'. Where decorative repair is in question one must look for damage to the decorations but where, as here, the obligation is merely to keep the structure and exterior of the house in repair, the covenant will only come into operation where there has been damage to the structure and exterior which requires to be made good.

If there is such damage caused by an unsuspected inherent defect, then it may be necessary to cure the defect, and thus to some extent improve without wholly renewing the property as the only practicable way of making good the damage to the subject matter of the repairing covenant. That, as I read the case, was the basis of the decision in *Ravenseft* [1980] QB 12. There was an inherent defect when the building, a relatively new one, was built in that no expansion joints had been included because it had not been realised that the different coefficients of expansion of the stone of the cladding and the concrete of the structure made it necessary to include such joints. There was, however, also physical damage to the subject matter of the covenant in that, because of the differing coefficients of expansion, the stones of the cladding had become bowed, detached from the structure, loose and in danger of falling. Forbes J in a very valuable judgment rejected the argument that no liability arose under a repairing covenant if it could be shown that the disrepair was due to an inherent defect in the building. He allowed in the damages under the repairing covenant the cost of putting in expansion joints, and in that respect improving the building, because, as he put it at p. 22), on the evidence 'In no realistic sense . . . could it be said that there was any other possible way of reinstating this cladding than by providing the expansion joints which were, in fact, provided'.

The *Elmcroft* case, 270 EG 140 was very similar. There was physical damage from rising damp in the walls of a flat in a fashionable area of London. That was due to an inherent defect in that when the flat had been built in late Victorian times as a high-class residential flat, the slate damp proof course had been put in too low and was therefore ineffective. The remedial work necessary to eradicate the rising damp was, on the evidence, the installation of a horizontal damp-proof course by silicone injection and formation of vertical barriers by silicone injection. This was held to be within the landlord's repairing covenant. It was necessary in order to repair the walls and, although it involved improvement over the previous ineffective slate damp proof course, it was held that, as a matter of degree, having regard to the nature and locality of the property, this did not involve giving the tenant a different thing from that which was demised. The decision of this court in *Smedley* v *Chumley & Hawke Ltd* (1982) 44 P & CR 50 is to the same effect; the damage to a recently constructed restaurant built on a concrete raft on piles over a river could only be cured by putting in further piles so that the structure of the walls and roof of the restaurant were stable and safe on foundations made structurally stable.

The only other of the many cases cited to use which I would mention is *Pembery* v *Lamdin* [1940] 2 All ER 434. There the property demised was a ground-floor shop and basement, built 100 years or more before the demise. The landlord was liable to repair the external part of the premises and there was physical damage to the walls of the basement in that they were permeated with damp because there had never been any damp proof course. The works required by the tenant to waterproof the basement were very extensive, involving cleaning and asphalting the existing walls, building internal brick walls and laying a concrete floor. This would have involved improvement to such an extent as to give the tenant a different thing from what had been demised and it was therefore outside the repairing covenant. But Slesser LJ appears to recognise at p. 438 that repointing of the existing basement walls where the mortar had partly perished would have been within the repairing covenant.

In the present case the liability of the council was to keep the structure and exterior of the house in repair – not the decorations. Though there is ample evidence of damage to the decorations and to bedding, clothing and other fabrics, evidence of damage to the subject matter of the covenant, the structure and exterior of the house, is far to seek. Though the condensation comes about from the effect of the warm atmosphere in the rooms on the cold surfaces of the walls and windows, there is no evidence at all of physical damage to the walls – as opposed to the decorations – or the windows.

There is indeed evidence of physical damage in the way of rot in parts of the wooden surrounds of some of the windows, but (a) that can be sufficiently cured by replacing the defective lengths of wood and (b) it was palpably not the rot in the wooden surrounds which caused damage to the bedding, clothes and fabrics in the house, and the rot in the wooden surrounds cannot have contributed very much to the general inconvenience of living in the house for which the judge awarded general damages.

There was also, as I have mentioned, evidence of nails sweating in bedroom ceilings, and of some plaster perishing in a bedroom. The judge mentions the sweating nails in his judgment, but I have not found any mention of the perishing of plaster. The judge did not ask himself – since on the overall view he took of the case it was not necessary – whether these two elements of structural disrepair (since the local authority accepts for the purposes of this case in this court that the plaster was part of the structure of the house) were of themselves enough to require the replacement of the windows etc. They seem, however, to have been very minor elements indeed in the context of the case which the plaintiff was putting forward, and, in my judgment, they do not warrant an order for a new trial or a remission to the judge for further findings, save in respect of the reassessment of damages as mentioned below.

As I have already mentioned, Mr Pryce Thomas used the word 'alleviate' to describe the effect which the replacement of the windows and the facing of the lintels with insulation materials would have on the problems of condensation. At one point in his judgment the judge refers to 'the work propounded by Mr Pryce Thomas as necessary to cure the condensation problems'. This must be a slip because alleviation prima facie falls short of cure. However, as the extent of alleviation was not probed in the court below, it is inappropriate to make any further comment.

It does appear from Mr Pryce Thomas's report that the problems of condensation would have also been alleviated if the plaintiff had kept the central heating on more continuously and at higher temperatures. In that event the walls and windows would have remained warm or warmer and condensation would have been reduced. As to this, the judge appreciated that some people for financial reasons have to be sparing in their use of central heating, and he found that there was no evidence at all to suggest that the life-style of the plaintiff and his family was likely to give rise to condensation problems because it was outside the spectrum of life-styles which a local authority could reasonably expect its tenants to follow. In my judgment, that finding answers the argument that it would be anomalous or unreasonable that this house should be held to be in disrepair because the plaintiff cannot afford to keep the heating on at a high enough temperature, whereas an identical adjoining house would not be in disrepair because the tenant had a good job and so spent more on his heating. If there is disrepair which the council is by its implied covenant bound to make good, then it is no answer for the council to say that, if the tenant could have afforded to spend more on his central heating, there would have been no disrepair, or less disrepair.

But the crux of the matter is whether there has been disrepair in relation to the structure and exterior of the building and, for the reasons I have endeavoured to explain, in my judgment, there has not, quoad the case put forward by the plaintiff on condensation as opposed to the case on water penetration.

I would accordingly allow this appeal.

Despite the fact that this property was almost uninhabitable during the winter months it did not qualify as a 'repair' under the Act. The fundamental reason here is that in order for there to be a repair there had to be a disrepair. The court established that there was no evidence of damage or need for repair of the windows, or the concrete lintels or any other part of the structure or exterior of the property. Thus these parts of the house had not deteriorated and called for a repair, and, as a consequence, the tenant's action failed. Thankfully, however, the tenant and his family were rehoused by the local authority.

(iii) Statutory obligations

In addition to obligations contained within the lease and covenants imposed by the common law, Parliament has acted to impose statutory obligations on landlords. These obligations cannot be contracted out of by the parties to a lease. The major statutory provisions here are contained within the Landlord and Tenant Act 1985, specifically s. 8 and ss. 11–16. Sections 8, 11, 13 and 14 are set out below.

Landlord and Tenant Act 1985

Implied terms as to fitness for human habitation
8.—(1) In a contract to which this section applies for the letting of a house for human habitation there is implied, notwithstanding any stipulation to the contrary—

(a) a condition that the house is fit for human habitation at the commencement of the tenancy, and

(b) an undertaking that the house will be kept by the landlord fit for human habitation during the tenancy.

(2) The landlord, or a person authorised by him in writing, may at reasonable times of the day, on giving 24 hours' notice in writing to the tenant or occupier, enter premises to which this section applies for the purpose of viewing their state and condition.

. . .

Repairing obligations in short leases
11.—(1) In a lease to which this section applies (as to which, see sections 13 and 14) there is implied a covenant by the lessor—

(a) to keep in repair the structure and exterior of the dwelling-house (including drains, gutters and external pipes),

(b) to keep in repair and proper working order the installations in the dwelling-house for the supply of water, gas and electricity and for sanitation (including basins, sinks, baths and sanitary conveniences, but not other fixtures, fittings and appliances for making use of the supply of water, gas or electricity), and

(c) to keep in repair and proper working order the installations in the dwelling-house for space heating and heating water.

[(1A) If a lease to which this section applies is a lease of a dwelling-house which forms part only of a building, then, subject to subsection (1B), the covenant implied by subsection (1) shall have effect as if—

(a) the reference in paragraph (a) of that subsection to the dwelling-house included a reference to any part of the building in which the lessor has an estate or interest; and

(b) any reference in paragraph (b) and (c) of that subsection to an installation in the dwelling-house includes a reference to an installation which, directly or indirectly, serves the dwelling-house and which either—

(i) forms part of any part of a building in which the lessor has an estate or interest; or

(ii) is owned by the lessor or under his control.

(1B) Nothing in subsection (1A) shall be construed as requiring the lessor to carry out any works or repairs unless the disrepair (or failure to maintain in working order) is such as to affect the lessee's enjoyment of the dwelling-house or of any common parts, as defined in section 60(1) of the Landlord and Tenant Act 1987, which the lessee, as such, is entitled to use.]

(2) The covenant implied by subsection (1) ('the lessor's repairing covenant') shall not be construed as requiring the lessor—

(a)   to carry out works or repairs for which the lessee is liable by virtue of his duty to use the premises in a tenant-like manner, or would be so liable but for an express covenant on his part,

(b)   to rebuild or reinstate the premises in the case of destruction or damage by fire, or by tempest, flood or other inevitable accident, or

(c)   to keep in repair or maintain anything which the lessee is entitled to remove from the dwelling-house.

(3)   In determining the standard of repair required by the lessor's repairing covenant, regard shall be had to the age, character and prospective life of the dwelling-house and the locality in which it is situated.

[(3A)   In any case where—

(a)   the lessor's repairing covenant has effect as mentioned in subsection (1A), and

(b)   in order to comply with the covenant the lessor needs to carry out works or repairs otherwise than in, or to an installation in, the dwelling-house, and

(c)   the lessor does not have a sufficient right in the part of the building or the installation concerned to enable him to carry out the required works or repairs,

then, in any proceedings relating to a failure to comply with the lessor's repairing covenant, so far as it requires the lessor to carry out the works or repairs in question, it shall be a defence for the lessor to prove that he used all reasonable endeavours to obtain, but was unable to obtain, such rights as would be adequate to enable him to carry out the works or repairs.]

(4)   A covenant by the lessee for the repair of the premises is of no effect so far as it relates to the matters mentioned in subsection (1)(a) to (c), except so far as it imposes on the lessee any of the requirements mentioned in subsection (2)(a) or (c).

(5)   The reference in subsection (4) to a covenant by the lessee for the repair of the premises includes a covenant—

(a)   to put in repair or deliver up in repair,

(b)   to paint, point or render,

(c)   to pay money in lieu of repairs by the lessee, or

(d)   to pay money on account of repairs by the lessor.

(6)   In a lease in which the lessor's repairing covenant is implied there is also implied a covenant by the lessee that the lessor, or any person authorised by him in writing, may at reasonable times of the day and on giving 24 hours' notice in writing to the occupier, enter the premises comprised in the lease for the purpose of viewing their condition and state of repair.

Leases to which s. 11 applies: general rule

13.—(1)   Section 11 (repairing obligations) applies to a lease of a dwelling-house granted on or after 24th October 1961 for a term of less than seven years.

(2)   In determining whether a lease is one to which section 11 applies—

(a)   any part of the term which falls before the grant shall be left out of account and the lease shall be treated as a lease for a term commencing with the grant,

(b)   a lease which is determinable at the option of the lessor before the expiration of seven years from the commencement of the term shall be treated as a lease for a term of less than seven years, and

(c)   a lease (other than a lease to which paragraph (b) applies) shall not be treated as a lease for a term of less than seven years if it confers on the lessee an option for renewal for a term which, together with the original term, amounts to seven years or more.

(3)   This section has effect subject to—

section 14 (leases to which section 11 applies: exceptions), and section 32(2) (provisions not applying to tenancies within Part II of the Landlord and Tenant Act 1954).

Leases to which s. 11 applies: exceptions

14.—(1)   Section 11 (repairing obligations) does not apply to a new lease granted to an existing tenant, or to a former tenant still in possession, if the previous lease was not a lease to which section 11 applied (and, in the case of a lease granted before 24th October 1961, would not have been if it had been granted on or after that date).

(2)   In subsection (1)—

'existing tenant' means a person who is when, or immediately before the new lease is granted, the lessee under another lease of the dwelling-house;

'former tenant still in possession' means a person who—

(a)   was the lessee under another lease of the dwelling-house which terminated at some time before the new lease was granted, and

(b)   between the termination of that other lease and the grant of the new lease was continuously in possession of the dwelling-house or of the rents and profits of the dwelling-house; and

'the previous lease' means the other lease referred to in the above definitions.

(3)   Section 11 does not apply to a lease of a dwelling-house which is a tenancy of an agricultural holding within the meaning of the [Agricultural Holdings Act 1986] [and in relation to which that Act applies or to a farm business tenancy within the meaning of the Agricultural Tenancies Act 1995].

(4)   Section 11 does not apply to a lease granted on or after 3rd October 1980 to—

a local authority,

[a National Park authority]

a new town corporation,

an urban development corporation,

the Development Board for Rural Wales,

a [registered social landlord],

a co-operative housing association, or

an education institution or other body specified, or of a class specified, by regulations under section 8 of the Rent Act 1977 [or paragraph 8 of Schedule 1 to the Housing Act 1988] (bodies making student lettings),

[a housing action trust established under Part III of the Housing Act 1988].

(5)   Section 11 does not apply to a lease granted on or after 3rd October 1980 to—

(a)   Her Majesty in right of the Crown (unless the lease is under the management of the Crown Estate Commissioners), or

(b)   a government department or a person holding in trust for Her Majesty for the purposes of a government department.

Notes

1.   As has been alluded to in part (A) of this chapter, s. 8 is now of little practical value primarily due to Parliament's failing to increase rental limits. The Law Commission Report, No. 238, *Landlord and Tenant: Responsibility for State and Condition of Property*, at p. 36, suggests a number of reasons why rental limits have not been increased, including: extension of local authority housing; decline in private sector renting levels; and the rise in owner-occupation. In addition, at p. 37 of the Report the Commission advances other possible causes: it may be that s. 11 of the Landlord and Tenant Act 1985 is regarded as the more appropriate provision for action; and that an implied fitness term is somewhat out of date given its origins in the Housing of the Working Classes Act 1885. In any event, Parliament has not acted to raise rental levels. Thus what appears at first sight to be a particularly useful vehicle for elevating fitness and repair standards in rented properties is now of little practical assistance.

2.   Due to the severe restrictions on the ambit of s. 8, s. 11 of the 1985 Act (as amended by s. 116, Housing Act 1988) is of significantly greater importance. Section 11 applies to leases of less than seven years granted on or after 24 October 1961 (s.13(1)). Additionally of importance here is to note the need for the landlord to have notice of any defect under this implied repairing covenant before liability arises (*O'Brien* v *Robinson* [1973] AC 912).

In order to gain a fuller understanding of s. 11 of the 1985 Act, a number of key phrases are considered below.

(a)   'Keep in repair'

The requirement here upon the landlord is twofold:

(a)   to put the premises in a state of repair (if it is in disrepair) at the beginning of the tenancy;
(b)   to ensure that the dwelling-house remains in repair during the lifetime of the tenancy.

(b)   Structure and exterior

The structure of the property concerns the fabric of a building or the integrity of the dwelling-house as constructed, the essential stability and shape of the building (*Irvine* v *Moran* [1991] 1 EGLR 261). Plasterwork may be part of the structure of a property (see *Staves* v *Leeds City Council* (1992) 29 EG 119, where condensation of the plasterwork of the house led it to be in disrepair). (Contrast this case, however, with *Irvine* where the court held that internal plaster was not part of the structure of a property.)

The exterior of a house includes windows (*Quick* v *Taff Ely BC* [1986] 1 QB 809) and walls between terraced houses (*Green* v *Eales* (1841) 2 QB 225). In relation to flats, in *Campden Hill Towers* v *Gardner* [1977] QB 823 the Court of Appeal held that structure and exterior did not apply to the whole of the building containing the flat, but to the exterior of the flat itself, i.e. the outside wall of that particular flat and the outer sides of the divisions between flats. The effect of this decision was amended by s. 116 of the Housing Act 1988, inserting s. 11(1A) into the Landlord and Tenant Act (see below). Additionally, steps and a path leading to a house may be part of the house's exterior, but not slabs within a yard. Contrast *Brown* v *Liverpool Corporation* with *Hopwood* v *Cannock Chase DC*.

Brown v *Liverpool Corporation*
[1969] 3 All ER 1345

SALMON LJ: . . . I do not think that this case is by any means free from difficulty or, indeed, from doubt. I do not wish to lay down any general principle of law or any general proposition as to the construction of the Housing Act 1961, or as to the meaning of the words 'building' or 'dwelling-house'. I base my judgment on the particular facts of this case.

It is conceded that the defendant corporation let this small terraced house no. 99, Carr Lane, Liverpool, to the plaintiff, and that the letting is subject to the provisions of s. 32 of the Housing Act 1961. This house lay beneath the level of the road. The gate leading to the demised premises was on the road. There were four steps beyond that gate leading on to a concrete path 7 feet in length which led up to the front door of the house.

I look at s. 32(5) and read the material words:

Lease of a dwelling-house' means a lease whereby a building . . . is let . . . as a private dwelling, and the 'dwelling house' means that building . . .

In the particular circumstances of this case I think it proper to regard the house, with the short concrete path and steps leading to it, as being one unit. Together they formed one building and were, therefore, 'the dwelling-house'.

It is conceded by the defendant corporation that the steps and the path were demised with the house. It seems to me that the path and steps must be an integral part of the building, otherwise it would be impossible for the building to be used as a dwelling-house for it would have no access. On that narrow ground I think that the judgment of the learned county court judge can be supported.

I also think that an alternative way of putting the matter would be to say that, on the facts here, that short concrete path and those four steps were part of the exterior of the dwelling-house. Whichever way it is put – whether it is put that way or whether one says that, looking at the facts, the path, steps and house are all part of the building which was let as a private dwelling-house – it would follow that the plaintiff is entitled to succeed.

I confess that this is a conclusion at which I arrive with no reluctance. According to the learned county court judge's judgment the plaintiff, the tenant of what used to be called a small artisan dwelling, had complained again and again to the defendant corporation about the dangerous condition of one of the steps which he and his family had to use day by day, and he received continuous assurances that the defect would be remedied and the step made safe. The defendant corporation, however, did absolutely nothing to make it safe and eventually what was only to be expected happened: the plaintiff, because of the dangerous condition of the step, fell and injured himself quite severely. If the step had not been a part of the demise there would have been no answer to a claim in negligence on the facts as found by the learned judge: but as the steps were a part of the demise the defendant corporation thought it right to take the point that on the true construction of the Act they were entitled to escape liability. It is a technical point entirely devoid of merit, but which, if it were a good one, the defendant corporation would, of course, be fully entitled to take advantage of. I, however, have come to the conclusion, as did the learned county court judge, that this technical point cannot succeed, and I agree that the appeal should be dismissed.

Hopwood v Cannock Chase District Council
[1975] 1 WLR 373

CAIRNS LJ: . . . This is an appeal from a decision of Deputy Judge Lewis sitting at Stafford on 22 February 1974; he had before him an action by the plaintiff, the widow of the tenant of one of the defendants' houses, no. 57 Newman Grove, Rugeley. It was an action for damages for personal injuries which the plaintiff suffered when she fell in the back yard of the house and injured her knee.

The house is a terraced house; it is some 16 feet in width and at the back of it there is a little yard consisting first of a concrete area adjoining the house for the full width of the house and probably about five feet going out from the back of the house; then there is a row of nine paving slabs, again across the full width of the house; then next to them, on the other side, another concrete area, a rather narrower one, perhaps between two and three feet wide. Then, still further away from the house, is a garden.

At the time the plaintiff had come from the back door of the house and had walked diagonally across the first concrete area; she was intending to go and have a chat with her neighbour at the next house. But when she came to one edge of the paving slabs – it is not clear whether it was the first edge that she came to or the second edge going up on to the other piece of concrete – at one of those two places she tripped and fell; and it was common ground that there was a difference in height between the concrete and the paving slab of an inch and a half, the paving slab being lower than the concrete. The judge found that the defendants, by their servants, well knew of this condition.

The judge had however to consider whether there was any obligation on the defendants to keep this part of the premises in repair. He held that there was no such obligation, and he gave judgment for the defendants, though he assessed the damages in case there should be a successful appeal.

The plaintiff's case was founded on section 32 of the Housing Act 1961, which contains this provision:

(1) In any lease of a dwelling-house, being a lease to which this section applies, there shall be implied a covenant by the lessor—(a) to keep in repair the structure and exterior of the dwelling-house (including drains, gutters and external pipes) . . .

I need not consider (b) but it is convenient to refer to one of the definitions contained in section 32(5), reading:

'lease of a dwelling-house' which words are defined to means:

'a lease whereby a building or part of a building is let wholly or mainly as a private dwelling'; and the 'dwelling-house' means 'that building or part of a building'.

The plaintiff's case depended on whether there was an obligation on the defendants to repair this part of the premises, it being acknowledged that they were out of repair and it being found that they knew they were out of repair; it was conceded that if the obligation to repair was established, the plaintiff was entitled to succeed by reason of the provisions of section 4(1) of the Occupiers' Liability Act 1957 which provides:

Where premises are occupied by any person under a tenancy which puts on the landlord an obligation to that person for the maintenance or repair of the premises, the landlord shall owe to all persons who or whose goods may from time to time be lawfully on the premises the same duty, in respect of dangers arising from any default by him in carrying out that obligation, as if he were an occupier of the premises and those persons or their goods were there by his invitation or permission (but without any contract).

The judge said in the course of his judgment: 'It is of course plain that it is not the whole of the letting that can compose the exterior' – he used that word because, as I have already quoted, the obligation relates to the repair of the structure and the exterior of the dwelling-house. The judge went on:

One has to draw the line somewhere, it is a pretty close run thing. After considerable thought, I think that the line must fall on the other side. Steps and part of the front door are exterior – an integral part. A row of slabs not even path to the back door – they were no doubt used by the plaintiff and her husband but not sensibly in the structure or exterior. I am fortified by the thought that the Act requires a duty to repair – nothing wrong with the slabs in themselves – repair should not include raising slabs.

With regard to that last sentence it was not a point taken by counsel on behalf of the defendants, and Mr Chapman in this court has not sought to support it. Clearly, if there is an obligation to keep what I may call for convenience this back yard in repair, then the obligation would run to the length of requiring the landlords not merely to have sound slabs, but to have the slabs kept in proper position.

That, however, was not the basis of the judge's judgment; it was something which he wrongly thought fortified the view that he came to on other grounds.

In reaching his decision, he founded himself on the only reported case as far as we know that has been decided under this provision; it is the decision of the Court of Appeal in *Brown* v *Liverpool Corporation* [1969] 3 All ER 1345. That was a case in which the house had a path running to steps which went up to the road, the house being at a lower level than the road, and the plaintiff met with an accident on those steps. The question was whether the landlords had a duty under s. 32 of the Act of 1961 to keep those steps in repair, and the question that had to be considered in that case, as in this one, was: did they form part of the structure or exterior of the building?

Danckwerts LJ, giving the first judgment, first easily reached the conclusion that they did not form part of the structure and then went on in this way (at p. 1346):

On the other hand it seems to me equally clear that the seven feet of flagstones and the steps up do form part of the exterior of the dwelling-house. They are attached in that manner to the house for the purpose of access to this dwelling-house, and they are part of the dwelling-house which is necessary for the purpose of anybody who wishes to live in the dwelling-house enjoying that privilege. If they have not means of access of some sort they could not get there, and these are simply the means of access. The steps are an outside structure, and therefore, it seems to me that they are plainly part of the building, and, therefore, the covenant implied by section 32 of the Act of 1961 fits and applies to the obligations of the landlords in this case.

Salmon LJ agreed: he said (at p. 1346):

I do not think that this case is by any means free from difficulty, or, indeed, from doubt. I do not wish to lay down any general principle of law or any general proposition as to the construction of the Housing Act 1961, or as to the meaning of the words 'building' or 'dwelling-house'. I base my judgment on the particular facts of this case.

Then, after referring to the main facts and quoting section 32(5) of the Housing Act 1961 he went on:

In the particular circumstances of this case I think it proper to regard the house, with the short concrete path and steps leading to it, as being one unit. Together they formed one building and were, therefore 'the dwelling-house'. It is conceded by the defendant corporation that the steps and the path were demised with the house. It seems to me that the path and steps must be an integral part of the building, otherwise it would be impossible for the building to be used as a dwelling-house for it would have no access. On that narrow ground I think that the judgment of the learned county court judge can be supported. I also think that an alternative way of putting the matter would be to say that, on the facts here, that short concrete path and those four steps were part of the exterior of the dwelling-house. Whichever way it is put – whether it is put in that way or whether one says that, looking at the facts, the path, steps and house are all part of the building which was let as a private dwelling-house – it would follow that the plaintiff is entitled to succeed.

Sachs LJ, after quoting subsection (5), went on at p. 1347:

> For my part I have no doubt but that, as counsel for the plaintiff has correctly conceded, the definition given to 'the dwelling-house' was intended to and does exclude from the ambit of the landlord's liability those parts of the demise that are not part of the building itself. In particular, to my mind, there would normally be excluded from the ambit of those liabilities a garden or a pond, and likewise the fences round or a gate leading to such a garden or pond. Similarly, there would normally be excluded the steps leading into the garden from a road . . . The question, accordingly, is whether in this particular case, the seven feet approach with the steps at the end of it really was part of the exterior of the terrace building or whether that seven feet pathway and the steps down into it were simply part of a means of traversing a garden. That seems to me – as, indeed counsel for the plaintiff rightly contended – to be a question of degree, and a very close run thing at that.

Then, after quoting a clause of the conditions of tenancy, he said:

> In the end, however, I have come to the conclusion that the learned county court judge adopted the right approach and did treat this question as one of degree and fact. He referred specifically to the point that this concrete path was 'only seven feet long', and it seems to me that on the evidence he was entitled to come to the conclusion which he reached on this question of fact, i.e., that in all the circumstances the steps formed part of the building.

One matter on which all three members of the court founded their judgments was that in that case the path and steps formed an essential part of the means of access to the house, in that it was the only way in. In this case that certainly was not so; the ordinary means of access to the house was from the front of the house and to my mind it is very doubtful whether this yard could be regarded as a means of access to the house at all. It is true that there was a way out from one side of the yard, apparently into an alley or lane, this house being at the end of the terrace of houses; and there was also a way through from the yard into the corresponding yard of the adjoining house. But that is very far from saying, as could be said in *Brown's* case [1969] 3 All ER 1345, that it was necessary to the house as the means of access to it.

Sachs LJ in *Brown's* case went no further than to say that there were materials upon which it was open to the county court judge to reach the conclusion that he did. Here, the county court judge has reached the opposite conclusion; he did, I think, approach it as a question of degree and of fact, and it appears to me that the facts were such as entitled him to reach that conclusion. I should be prepared to go still further and say that, treating it as Danckwerts and Salmon LJJ did, as a matter of law and construction of the section, in my view the section cannot be extended beyond what was held in *Brown's* case to include a yard of this kind.

For these reasons I would dismiss this appeal.

(c)   Installations

The landlord's duty under s. 11(1)(b) and (c) is to keep the installations in proper working order. In *Wycombe Health Authority* v *Barnett* (1982) 5 HLR 84, the question arose whether a landlord was in breach of this duty by failing to lag a water pipe which burst following a cold snap. The Court of Appeal found the landlord had responsibility to ensure that the pipe was kept in reliable mechanical condition, but that this did not extend to lagging a pipe.

(d)   Amendment to s. 11: Housing Act 1988, s. 116

Section 116 of the Housing Act 1988 inserted new provisions into s. 11 of the Landlord and Tenant Act 1985, namely s. 11(1A), (1B) and (3A). The consequence of these amendments overturns the effects of the decision in *Campden Hill Towers* (see above) in respect of leases entered into after 15 January 1989. Hence the obligation to repair the structure and exterior now applies to any part of the building in which the landlord has an interest. With regard to installations to be kept in working order, this provision now encompasses any installation serving directly or indirectly the dwelling-house where it either forms part of the building, or is owned by or under the control of the landlord.

(iv)   Standards of repair

Section 11(3) of the Landlord and Tenant Act 1985 stipulates in relation to the required standard of repair that 'regard shall be had to the age, character and prospective life of the dwelling-house and the locality in which it is situated' (see *(iii)* above). Additionally, in *Proudfoot* v *Hart* (1890) 25 QBD 42, Lopes LJ stated that the standard of repair expected should be 'such repair, as having regard to the age, character and locality of the house, would make it reasonably fit for the occupation of a reasonably minded tenant of the class who would be likely to take it'.

In *Newman LBC* v *Patel* (1978) 13 HLR 77, there was agreement between the parties that the property was substandard. The authority wished to move the tenant to other accommodation. The tenant wished to remain and have the property upgraded, claiming a breach by the authority of s. 11 of the Landlord and Tenant Act 1985. The Court of Appeal found the house in very poor condition; however, as the prospective life of the house was very short they concluded that repair under s. 11 would be useless. 'Patching' repairs may at times be sufficient (*Trustees of Hungerford Charity* v *Beazeley* (1994) 26 HLR 269), although this depends on whether this mode of repair is one a sensible person would adopt. This can be seen from *Stent* v *Monmouth DC*, where repairs of this nature proved inadequate.

Stent v Monmouth DC
(1987) 19 HLR 269

Water had blown into a property through or under the front door. The authority had attempted to remedy this in a number of ways, including replacing parts of the door, followed by the provision of a new door. Ultimately, however, the problem was solved only by the installation of a purpose-built door.

STOCKER LJ: . . . This is an appeal from so much of the judgment of Mr Assistant Recorder Eifion Morgans given at Pontypool County Court on November 26 1985 as adjudged that the defendants were in breach of their duty to keep in repair the structure and exterior of a dwelling-house known as 102 Old Barn Way, Abergavenny, in the County of Gwent, by failing to prevent water penetration to the front external door of the said property. The learned judge also found that the water penetration had caused damage to the plaintiff's carpets in the sum of £250, and he awarded £100 general damages in respect of loss of amenity and £37.50 interest. Therefore, he awarded a total sum of £387.50 and interest, with costs. No issue arises on the causation or remoteness of the damage or of the amount of the damages so assessed.

The issue, which is form a simple one, but which in fact has presented numerous problems which have been skilfully argued before this court, is whether such damages admittedly caused by water penetration through or under the front door of the premises arose from the failure on the part of the appellants to carry out their obligations under the repairing covenant.

So far as the factual outline of the case is concerned, the situation is this. The premises in question, no. 102, is one of a number of similar houses in Old Barn Lane [sic] built in 1953. The respondent became a tenant in that year and was the original tenant under a weekly tenancy of those premises. He, therefore, took over the house as the first person to have that experience. The landlords at that date were the Abergavenny Council and the appellants are their successors in title. It is not entirely clear what were the precise terms of the landlords' obligations at the date of the first letting or the document in which such terms were contained, but that does not matter for the purposes of this case, since it is accepted by the appellants that they were under an obligation imposed by a covenant in the lease to keep the exterior and structure of the property in repair. There are among the documents certain printed terms of conditions of tenancy, Condition 2 of the Landlords' Obligations being:

The Landlord will repair and maintain the structure and exterior of the dwelling-house.

Mr Hague agrees that that represents the contractual obligation of the landlords in this case.

The respondent's house and the others in Old Barn Way stand on an elevated and very exposed site facing into the direction of the prevailing south-west wind. It is not disputed that the respondent's house, and for that matter others in the same row, had almost from the outset of the tenancy in 1953 suffered from the ingress of water through or under the front door. From time to time efforts were made by the appellants to rectify that situation.

The appellants rely, in support of the arguments put before this court, on the detail of the evidence given by the plaintiff, and accordingly I will now refer to that evidence.

The plaintiff having described that his front door was wet within six months after he moved in continued:

Windows, letter box and panelling in the door. I reported to the Town Hall (Rent Offices). Houses had just been built. Clerk of Works on Site – Advice was given to put a bolt on top of the door to prevent it from warping. Reported it again, time and time again, we more or less complained every time it rained. The door would become swollen, water came in via door frame. Wood of the frame and door became rotten. The workmen cut off the rotten parts and put a new one in – it happened a few times.

When the Monmouth District Council took over – Report to the Town Hall. Workmen would come and see – the problems like before. Door replaced roughly 1979. No good at all. Water still came in through the glass panel, sides and underneath. Door stuck, frame wanted doing. If you stood inside you could see outside – there was a gap rain, snow, wood lice, anything would get in.

We kept complaining, very rarely they would do anything about it. Put aluminium step below the door – no effect at all. Water stayed in the groove, rain into hall via frame and damaged the carpet. Summer 1983, new aluminium sealed door unit fitted, no problem since then. Door opens inwards, water back well beyond the first step of the staircase . . .

Then he describes the damage to his carpets, to which it is not necessary to refer. When he [was] cross-examined, he said:

For 30 years the problem remained. New house when I went there. Water started coming in through the edge of the glass and panelling. Most of the water came from under the door. There was a groove put under the door a couple of years later . . .
    Aluminium door fixed in Summer, 1983. . . .

He describes that groove in re-examination thus:

Groove a couple of inches, two inches deep. It got full up with water. No threshold or a piece of wood across the bottom of the door.

That, in outline, is the evidence that was given to the court as recorded by the learned recorder.

There was also called in support of the respondent's case a Mrs Morgan, a resident in the same street, who lived at 116 Old Barn Way. She said:

I am friendly with the plaintiff. We have had the same problem ourselves. Seen the carpet wet about two years after we moved in. Went [to the respondent's] for coffee. The problem went away when the aluminium door fitted in 1983. New door in 1979 no good. It was saturated half-way back to the hall. Bottom step of stairs began to rot . . .

So she was describing fairly succinctly a similar state of affairs as that which existed and was described by the respondent.

The appellants disclosed a certain number of their work sheets and documents which are contained in the bundle. They do not go back further than 1979. The first document records a complaint of May 11 1979 which apparently was not dealt with by work being carried out until April 13 1980. The details shown upon that job specification are:

Take off door and rehang on new frame and bed in glass door.
Fix new 6' 6" x 2' 9" door frame.
Fix 2 ADS weather strips . . . and repair doors.
Fix new mortice lock to rear door

A complaint of January 7 1980, dealt with apparently on the next day, January 8, indicates as the reported defect:

New door frame fitted recently, but wasn't completed.

Then apparently the work done was to seal around the front door-frame with Mastic. That was referring clearly to the new door fitted in 1979.

There is a further report of a complaint on June 28 1982, the defect reported being:

Front door leaking very badly, water running into hall.

The work carried out was apparently:

Remove glass in front door, re-bed four pieces of glass.
Take off defective weather board and fix new board.
Fix a storm guard threshold.

That is perhaps sufficient indication. The records from their nature are not necessarily complete or comprehensive, but it would appear, in my view, that the defects dealt with on those occasions were treated by the respondents as being repairs under the repairing covenant. Of course, that does not conclude the matter, because they may have been acting from paternalistic ideals rather than under the compulsion of legal obligation. But that does seem to be how they then dealt with it.

The plaintiff wrote a letter of complaint in 1983, and proceedings being imminent or having started, a surveyor, a Mr Frecknall, was instructed on his behalf. He gave evidence at the trial and produced his report, which included details of his inspection and his conclusion.

. . .

As has been observed, it is largely upon that report, together with the respondent's evidence, that the appellants found their case as argued in this court, and indeed before the trial judge, and it is for that reason that I have thought it proper to cite fairly extensively from those parts of the evidence.

Put very shortly at this stage, the appellants contend that the cause of the water ingress either through or under the door was not due to any defective condition of the door calling for repair under the covenant, but was due to an inherent design defect, and that accordingly the damage sustained by the respondent was due to design defects outside the ambit of the repair covenant and, therefore, cannot found a valid claim for breach of covenant in respect of the repairing obligations.

The respondent gave evidence concerning the damage and described it. It is unnecessary to relate that part of his evidence. Nor is it necessary to go in any detail into the way in which the contentions in the pleadings. It is perhaps sufficient to say that in the amended particulars of claim by para. 3 of the covenant to repair is set out, and the provisions of section 32 of the Housing Act 1961 are alleged to apply to the tenancy and the claim was founded in the alternative under the provisions of that implied term under the Housing Act. It is also contended that the provisions of section 4 of the Defective Premises Act 1972 applied and were breached. It is unnecessary to express any view on that, because neither statutory provision seems to be relevant to the real issues in this case and neither was relied upon in argument before us.

So far as the defence is concerned, the only matter of relevance seems to be that contained in subpara. (3) of para. 4 of the defence, in which it is affirmatively alleged that the defendants (that is the appellants) had responded to complaints received from the plaintiff and carried out the following repairs, being such repairs as were reasonably necessary at the time of the relevant complaint, and they are listed:

Changed the door.
Increased the width of the door stop and inserted additional capillary grooves.
Inserted normal weather stripping.

Inserted high performance weather stripping.
Inserted aluminium storm guards.

The only possible relevance of those pleadings, as it seems to me, is the point mentioned earlier, that the appellants at all times seem to have accepted that their attempts to prevent the ingress of water included those matters which might be said to involve a change in the nature of the structure itself, and accordingly attempts to deal with a latent or design defect under the provisions of the covenant.

. . .

It is again unnecessary, as it seems to me, to refer to the formal grounds of appeal, since all the relevant matters have been reflected in the cogent argument of Mr Hague before this court. Those arguments, I hope, can be summarised accurately as follows. First, and this is an important matter, that the damage did not result from disrepair, but as a result of the door not being effective in the first place. That is to say that the cause of the ingress of water was original design defect. He argued that, in such a case, a duty to repair arose only if there was an existing defect in fact which itself called for repair, and the only 'sensible' way of achieving this repair was to rectify the design defect also. (Many synonyms have, in the authorities cited, been substituted for the word 'sensible' used by counsel in his argument.) He submitted that in the instant appeal those facts did not arise, since the door could have been replaced in its original form, and the replacement of the original door would be the limit of the appellant's obligations. He agreed that those comments were subject to a general observation that it was possible that a defect calling for repairs under the covenant might be due to inherent underlying defect and was repairable as such, but that that comment was subject to the criticisms to which I have just referred. He submitted that it was not correct in law that a duty to repair applies simply because the door lets in water or is not wind and watertight. There must be some specific defect or lack of repair within the terms of the covenant that must be proved; and in this case no such specific defect or lack of repair was established. He gave as a contrasting example of that proposition that if slates of a house were loose due to defect, then there would be a liability because the house would be in disrepair in that respect, but if the slates had never been there, then, although that would give rise to the ingress of water there would be no disrepair and no liabilities. He enlarged upon those submissions in the context of various authorities to which reference has to be made. Secondly, he submitted generally that on the facts of this case such damage or lack of repair to the door as may have been proved over the years did not themselves cause the damage which was solely due to the design defect presented by the alignment of the outside step and the inside floor in conjunction with the exposed site upon which this building had been built.

Mr Gage for the respondent submitted first a general proposition that the purpose of a door is to provide access and keep out wind, water and the elements, and in the context of a private dwelling-house and of a covenant to keep in repair such a house is not in repair if the door in question does not fulfil those basic purposes. He submitted in the alternative that there was evidence of lack of repair, actual damage and actual defects in this particular door.

I therefore turn to consider the various authorities which have been cited before this court. A convenient starting point, though not chronologically the first of the cases cited, is the case of *Ravenseft Properties Ltd* v *Davstone (Holdings) Ltd* [1980] QB 12. This was a case of a building constructed of concrete with a facing of stone cladding. When constructed there were no expansion joints to deal with the differential expansion of those two materials respectively, and also the facingstones had not been properly tied in and had been erected in a way which was not a workmanlike one. The consequence of those two matters was that there was a bowing of the stone facing with a consequence of the danger of the stones falling, to the danger of persons below. The lack of the expansion joint was an inherent design factor. The failure to tie in the defective stone was a matter of defective building practice. The learned trial judge, Forbes J, held that both, in the circumstances of the case, fell within the repairing covenant.

. . .

The next case to which reference requires to be made is the case of *Quick v Taff Ely Borough Council* [1986] QB 809. This is a case upon which the appellants strongly relied. The headnote, to give the facts, reads:

The plaintiff was the tenant of a house owned by the defendant council. As a result of very severe condensation throughout the house decorations, woodwork, furnishings, bedding and clothes rotted, and living conditions were appalling. The condensation was caused by lack of insulation of window lintels, single-glazed metal-frame windows and inadequate heating. The plaintiff brought proceedings in the county court, alleging that the council was in breach of its covenant, implied in the tenancy agreement by section 32(1) of the Housing Act 1961, 'to keep in repair the structure and exterior' of the house.

I think that that is, perhaps, a sufficient résumé for present purposes.
At p. 817 between C–F, Dillon LJ, giving the first judgment of the court, said this:

The judge delivered a careful reserved judgment in which he reviewed many of the more recent authorities on repairing covenants, starting with *Pembery v Lamdin* [1940] 2 All ER 434.

Submissions had been made upon which the judge founded his judgment as follows:

(1) recent authorities such as *Ravenseft Properties Ltd v Davstone (Holdings) Ltd* [1980] QB 12 and *Elmcroft Developments Ltd v Tankersley Sawyer* (1984) 270 EG 140 show that works of repair under a repairing covenant, whether by a landlord or a tenant, may require the remedying of an inherent defect in a building; (2) the authorities also show that it is a question of degree whether works which remedy an inherent defect in a building may not be so extensive as to amount to an improvement or renewal of the whole which is beyond the [concept of repair; (3) in the present case] the replacement of windows and the provision of insulation for the lintels does not amount to such an improvement or renewal of the whole; (4) therefore, the replacement of the windows and provision of the insulation to alleviate an inherent defect is a repair which the council is bound to carry out under the repairing covenant.

He then stated, by way of comment upon those submissions:

But, with every respect to the judge, this reasoning begs the important question. It assumes that any work to eradicate an inherent defect in a building must be a work of repair, which the relevant party is bound to carry out if, as a matter of degree, it does not amount to a renewal or improvement of the building. In effect, it assumes the broad proposition urged on us by Mr Blom-Cooper for the plaintiff that anything defective or inherently inefficient for living in or ineffective to provide the conditions of ordinary habitation is in disrepair. But that does not follow from the decisions in *Ravenseft's* case [1980] QB 12 and *Elmcroft's* case, 270 EG 140 that works of repair *may* require the remedying of an inherent defect.

On p. 818 at F there appears this passage:

If there is such damage caused by an unsuspected inherent defect, then it may be necessary to cure the defect, and thus come to some extent improve without wholly renewing the property as the only practicable way of making good the damage to the subject matter of the repairing covenant. That, as I read the case, was the basis of the decision in *Ravenseft* [1980] QB 12. There there was an inherent defect when the building, a relatively new one, was built in that no expansion joints had been included because it had not been realised that the different coefficients of expansion of the stone of the cladding and the concrete of the structure made it necessary to include such joints. There was, however, also physical damage to the subject matter of the covenant in that, because of the differing coefficients of expansion, the stones of the cladding had become bowed, detached from the structure, loose and in danger of falling. Forbes J in a very valuable judgment rejected the argument that no liability arose under a repairing covenant if it could be shown that the disrepair was due to an inherent defect in the building.

That was limb 1 of the argument put before us.

He allowed in the damages under the repairing covenant the cost of putting in expansion joints, and in that respect improving the building, because, as he put it, at p. 22, on the evidence 'In no realistic sense . . . could it be said that there was any other possible way of reinstating this cladding than by providing the expansion joints which were, in fact, provided.'

That is a passage which has already been cited. Dillon LJ then goes on to consider the *Elmcroft* case, to which reference will be shortly made in this judgment; and he sets out the facts in the *Elmcroft* case.

Dillon LJ, having considered the cases of *Ravenseft* and *Elmcroft*, concluded at p. 820 at H:

But the crux of the matter is whether there has been disrepair in relation to the structure and exterior of the building and, for the reasons I have endeavoured to explain, in my judgment, there has not, quoad the case put forward by the plaintiff on condensation as opposed to the case on water penetration.

He therefore, as I understand it, rejected the submission on the basis that there was no damage which could fall within a repairing covenant other than condensation which was due to inherent causes.

. . .

It seems to me that in the *Quick* case had there been evidence that there was actual disrepair in some material respect, that is to say some respect material to the rectification, the decision might have been the other way. But, of course, I cite the case only for the dicta that it contains, and not the conclusion that might arise had the findings of fact been different from those that they were.

Neill LJ made this observation at p. 823 at E:

The authorities to which we were referred establish that, in some cases, the only realistic way of effecting the relevant repairs is to carry out some additional work which will go somewhat further than putting the property back into its former condition and will indeed result in some improvement. But this case does not fall into that category. The repair work consisting of the replacement of the defective parts of the wooden surrounds and the replacement of the areas of plaster did not

require as a realistic way of effecting those repairs the replacement of the metal
windows by wooden-framed windows or windows with PVC frames.

Mr Gage on behalf of the respondent distinguishes that case from the instant case
on the basis that the actual observable physical damage did involve or could
realistically or sensibly involve the repair also by altering the design of what has been
described as design defect.

Mr Hague relied on the case of *Foster* v *Day* (1968) 208 EG 495. For my part,
despite his argument to the contrary, I do not derive any great assistance from it, since
the judgment of Edmund Davies LJ (which is very shortly set out, in no more than
eight lines) was a matter which was clearly obiter and, in my view, begs rather than
resolves the issues before this court.

. . .

Finally, I turn to the case of *Elmcroft Developments Ltd* v *Tankersley-Sawyer* (1984)
270 EG 140. The facts were that the respondents, by their counterclaim, claimed,
inter alia, damages for breach of covenant of repair. The respondents were tenants of
flats in a block of which the appellants were the landlords. The Court of Appeal
upheld the judge's finding that the appellants were in breach of their covenants to
repair, and at p.140 there is set out the condition of the premises in question. It is said:

> He held – and this not disputed – that there was constructed into the walls what
> was intended to be a damp-proof course, consisting of slates laid horizontally. These
> existed in the external and the party walls of the flat, but, owing either to a defect
> in design or construction or bad workmanship, this layer of slates intended to be a
> damp-proof course was ineffectual because it was positioned below ground. The
> result was obvious. It allowed moisture to be drawn up from the ground by the
> capillary action, with the inevitable consequence that the flats were in a damp
> condition, rising damp resulting from what was described as the bridging of this
> damp-proof course, and parts of the interior of the main walls of the flats had been
> adversely affected up to a height of about 1 to 1½ m. The rooms in the flats were
> damp, and the plaster, decoration and woodwork needed repair or renewal.

There was then cited a graphic description of the condition of two of those flats.
The remedial work necessary was referred to on p. 141 as being:

> The remedial works necessary to eradicate rising dampness in the walls is the
> installation of a horizontal damp-proof course by silicone injection and the forma-
> tion by silicone injection of vertical barriers where the front and back external walls
> meet the dividing walls.

The court then considered and cited from the case of *Lurcott* v *Wakely* [1911] 1 KB
905, and made citations from the judgment of Fletcher Moulton LJ, first the definition
of the expression 'tenable repair', and then citing from Buckley LJ at p. 141 these
words:

> But if that which I have said is accurate, it follows that the question of repair is in
> every case one of degree, and the test is whether the act to be done is one which in
> substance is the renewal or replacement of defective parts or the renewal or
> replacement of substantially the whole.

The court then considered a passage from the judgment of Lord Evershed MR in
Wates v *Rowland* [1952] 2 QB 12, quoted by this court in *Brew Bros Ltd* v *Snax (Ross)
Ltd* [1970] 1 QB 612, as follows:

Between the two extremes, it seems to me to be largely a matter of degree, which in the ordinary case the county court judge could decide as a matter of fact, applying a common-sense man-of-the-world view; . . .

And in the *Brew Bros* case, a quotation from Sachs LJ at p. 640:

It seems to me that the correct approach is to look at the particular building, to look at the state which it is in at the date of the lease, to look at the precise terms of the lease, and then come to a conclusion as to whether, on a fair interpretation of those terms in relation to that state, the requisite work can fairly be termed repair. However large the covenant it must not be looked at *in vacuo*.

The court then cited a passage from the judgment of Forbes J in *Ravenseft Properties Ltd v Davstone (Holdings) Ltd* [1980] 1 QB 12, a passage which has already been cited in this judgment and which I, therefore, will not repeat.
. . .

One may observe there that that would appear to be an explicit approval of the judgment of Forbes J in *Ravenseft* so far as this second limb of the proposition is concerned and, accordingly, that judgment of Forbes J would, in my view, have clearly received the approbation of this court.

What are the conclusions, which should be drawn from those authorities in the light of the evidence which has been accepted by the learned judge and which has been put before us? I find from those authorities, though I must confess with some regret, since in the context of council letting of small houses it conforms in my view with common sense, that Mr Gage's first proposition is stated in terms which are indeed too wide. This is a hypothesis: if the only defect in the door was that it did not perform its primary function of keeping out the rain, and the door was otherwise undamaged and in a condition which it or its predecessors had been at the time of the letting, then it seems to me, on the authorities of *Quick* and *Aquarius*, this cannot amount to a defect for the purpose of a repairing covenant even though, as it seems to me in layman's terms, that a door which does not keep out the rain is a defective door, and one which is in need of some form of repair or modification or replacement. That seems to have been the view indeed of the appellants themselves throughout the year, since they did take steps (though, as it turned out, ineffective steps) to deal with that very problem. However, though common sense would dictate to me that a door which does not keep out the rain is not performing the primary function of a door and is, therefore, defective, and in want of repair it seems to me that insofar as the door was the original one and was wholly undamaged, if that were to be the factual position, then the first proposition of Mr Gage is expressed in terms which are too wide.

In this case, however, the factual position is that the damage undoubtedly did occur. The appellants' own documents illustrate that clearly and graphically. There was damage such as to require the replacement of the door in 1979. The same applied in 1983, and clearly this was also the position on many other occasions both prior to and between those dates. Accordingly, applying the reasoning of this court from the cases cited, and in particular *Ravenseft Properties Ltd v Davstone (Holdings) Ltd* and *Elmcroft Developments Ltd v Tankersley-Sawyer*, the former having been specifically approved by this court, in my judgment the replacement of the wooden door by a self-sealing aluminium door was a mode of repair which a sensible person would have adopted; and the same reasoning applies if for the word 'sensible' there is substituted some such word as 'practicable' or 'necessary'. The argument reflected by Ackner LJ in [the] passage recently cited from *Elmcroft* seems to me to be precisely in point here. There has been a history of nearly 30 years of difficulty with this door, the difficulty being that it did not keep the rain out, and itself became damaged; and because of the design, from time to time parts of it rotted. It became distorted. It needed accordingly replacement in order to enable it to perform its function at all, quite apart from the question of repairing obvious defects which it had exhibited.

Accordingly, in my view and upon those authorities, in this case the repair carried out in 1983 by the installation of a purpose-built, self-sealing aluminium door was one of the methods which could have been adopted much earlier, and which in my view should have been adopted. Of course, it does not follow that the self-sealing door is the only sensible way in which that object could be achieved. There may well have been others, but in my view the obligation under the covenant in this case was one which called upon the appellants to carry out repairs which not only effected the repair of the manifestly damaged parts but also achieved the object of rendering it unnecessary in the future for the continual repair of this door. Accordingly, some such steps as were in fact taken in 1983 should in my view have been carried out at any rate by 1979 and perhaps earlier, there being no suggestion either before the trial judge or before this court that the steps adopted were not ones which were known to the trade in 1979 or which were for any other reasons impracticable at that date. Accordingly, and for these reasons I agree with the conclusion of the trial judge, though perhaps the reasons that I have given are not identical with those expressed in his judgment.

I would dismiss this appeal.

Questions
1.   Given the views of Lord Denning in *Liverpool City Council* v *Irwin* [1975] 3 All ER 658, at p. 664, should the courts imply 'reasonable' terms into a contract letting, rather than merely terms of necessity?
2.   Would the installation of a new shower in a bathroom, to replace an old bath, be a repair or an improvement?
3.   One of the options for review suggested by the Law Commission in the Consultation Paper *Landlord and Tenant: Responsibility for State and Condition of Property* (No. 123, March 1992) was to link the need to maintain the demised premises directly with the purpose for which the property was let. Hence, a new duty to maintain premises imposed upon a landlord which could in whole, or part, be transferred to the tenant by agreement.

What advantages/disadvantages are there with such a proposal? (For the Commission's further views in this area, see *Landlord and Tenant: Responsibility for State and Condition of Property* (Law Com. No. 238).)
4.   Carol is a monthly tenant of Leases Ltd. The property she inhabits has for many years suffered from condensation as a result of faulty windows. The landlord, having been informed of this, has undertaken work to the windows and some of the walls suffering dampness as a result of the condensation. Leases Ltd, however, refuses to replace the windows due to the costs involved in such a venture.

Advise Carol.

(v)   Tenant obligations
The obligations of tenants in this area fall under two main heads. The tenant should act as a 'tenant-like user' and should not 'commit waste'.

(a)   Tenant-like user

A tenant is under an implied obligation to use the dwelling in a tenant-like manner. In *Warren* v *Keen*, Denning LJ shed some light on the meaning of this term:

Warren v *Keen*
[1954] 1 QB 15

DENNING LJ: . . . Apart from express contract, a tenant owes no duty to the landlord to keep the premises in repair. The only duty of the tenant is to use the premises in a husbandlike, or what is the same thing, a tenantlike manner. That is how it was put by Sir Vicary Gibb CJ in *Horsefall* v *Mather* (Holt NP 7) and by Scrutton LJ and Atkin LJ in *Marsden* v *Edward Heyes Ltd* [1927] 2 KB 7, 8. But what does it mean – 'to use the premises in a tenantlike manner'? It can, I think, best be shown by some illustrations. The tenant must take proper care of the place. He must, if he is going away for the winter, turn off the water and empty the boiler. He must clean the chimneys, when necessary, and also the windows. He must mend the electric light when it fuses. He must unstop the sink when it is blocked by his waste. In short, he must do the little jobs about the place which a reasonable tenant would do. In addition, he must of course, not, damage the house, wilfully or negligently; and he must see that his family and guests do not damage it: and if they do, he must repair it. But, apart from such things, if the house falls into disrepair through fair wear and tear or lapse of time, or for any reason not caused by him, the tenant is not liable to repair it.

The landlord sought to put upon the tenant a higher obligation. She said that the duty of the tenant was to keep the premises wind and water tight and to make fair and tenantable repairs thereto. That seems to be based on Hill and Redman *Landlord and Tenant*, 11th ed., p. 186. I do not think that is a correct statement of the obligation.

Take the first branch, 'to keep the premises wind and water tight'. Lord Tenterden in one or two cases at Nisi Prius used that expression, and it was followed by the Court of Appeal in *Wedd* v *Porter* [[1916] 2 KB 100], but it is very difficult to know what 'wind and water tight' means. I asked counsel whether there was any case to be found in the books where a tenant had been found liable for breach of that obligation . . . I wanted to see what sort of thing it had been held to cover. But there was no such case was to be found. In the absence of it, I think that the expression 'wind and water tight' is of doubtful value and should be avoided. It is better to keep to the simple obligation 'to use the premises in a tenantlike manner'.

Take the second branch, 'to make fair and tenantable repairs.' Lord Kenyon used the expression in *Ferguson* v *Anon* 1798 2 Esp 590, which is reported only by Espinasse, whose reports were notoriously defective . . . If you read the whole sentence used by Lord Kenyon, however, it is clear that he was referring only to cases where a tenant does damage himself, such as breaking the windows or the doors. Then, of course, he must repair them. The sentence used by Lord Kenyon was explained by Bankes LJ in *Marsden* v *Edward Heyes Ltd* [1927] 2 KB 1, by saying that if a tenant commits waste – that, is if he commits voluntary waste by doing damage himself – he must do such repairs to the premises as will enable them to exclude wind and water. So explained, it does not support the proposition stated in Redman.

It was suggested by Mr Willis that an action lies against a weekly tenant for permissive waste. I do not think that is so. It has been held not to lie against a tenant at will: see the *Countess of Shrewsbury's* case (1600) 5 Co Rep 13b; and, in my opinion, it does not lie against a weekly tenant. In my judgment, the only obligation on a weekly tenant is to use the premises in a tenantlike manner. That does not cover the dampness and other defects alleged in the particulars of claim. The appeal should be allowed accordingly.

(b)   Doctrine of waste

Waste is a tort falling in two types: (i) voluntary waste, and (ii) permissive waste. Voluntary waste is committed by the tenant acting in such a way as to alter the premises. In *Mancetter Developments Ltd* v *Garmeston Ltd* [1986] QB 1212, the tenant lawfully removed extractor fans and pipes. However, the tenant committed an act of waste when in removing the fans and pipes he failed to fill the holes created by their removal causing the building to cease to be weather proof, leading to damage of the property. Permissive waste incorporates an omission by the tenant leading to damage to the premises (for example, failing to clear a ditch so that foundations rot, see *Powys* v *Blagrave* (1854) 4 DeGM & G 448).

(vi)   Remedies

A tenant has a wide range of remedies available to enforce a landlord's obligations to repair, including damages, specific performance and setting off the costs of repair against rent.

(a)   Damages

Where a landlord fails to uphold a repairing covenant, express or implied, the tenant may choose to sue for damages. The principle in the award of damages is to restore the tenant, as far as money can, to the position the tenant would have been in if no breach had occurred.

Calabar Properties v *Stitcher*
[1984] 1 WLR 287

In October 1975, the tenant, Mrs Renee Stitcher, acquired a lease of a flat within a block of flats. The lease contained, amongst other things, a repairing covenant requiring the landlords to maintain the external parts of the block in good repair. From January 1976 onwards the tenant made a number of complaints, prompted by rainwater penetrating the flat causing damage and leading to the tenant's husband suffering ill health. They remained in the flat for five years until it became uninhabitable, with Mr and Mrs Stitcher having to seek accommodation elsewhere.

GRIFFITHS LJ: . . . I agree that this appeal fails for the reasons given by Stephenson LJ, but I venture to add a few words of my own because it appears to me, both from the arguments at the Bar and the way in which the judge expressed himself, that there may be a widely held belief by those practising in this field that when damages are claimed by a tenant for breach of a landlord's repairing covenant they must always be assessed by reference to the diminution in the open market value of the premises and that they can never include the cost of alternative accommodation whilst the repairs are being carried out.

The object of awarding damages against a landlord for breach of his covenant to repair is not to punish the landlord but, so far as money can, to restore the tenant to the position he would have been in had there been no breach. This object will not be achieved by applying one set of rules to all cases regardless of the particular circumstances of the case. The facts of each case must be looked at carefully to see what damage the tenant has suffered and how he may be fairly compensated by a monetary award.

In this case on the findings of the judge the plaintiff landlords, after notice of the defect neglected their obligation to repair for such a length of time that the flat eventually became uninhabitable. It was also clear that, unless ordered to do so by an order of the court, the plaintiffs had no intention of carrying out the repairs. In these circumstances the defendant had two options that were reasonably open to her: either of selling the flat and moving elsewhere or alternatively of moving into temporary accommodation and bringing an action against the plaintiffs to force them to carry out the repairs and then returning to the flat after the repairs were done. If the defendant had chosen the first option then the measure of damages would indeed have been the difference in the prices he received for the flat in its damaged condition and that which it would have fetched in the open market if the plaintiffs had observed their repairing covenant. If however, the defendant does not wish to sell the flat but to continue to live in it after the plaintiffs has carried out the necessary structural repairs it is wholly artificial to award her damages on the basis of loss in market value, because once the plaintiffs had carried out the repairs and any consequential redecoration of the interior was completed there will be no loss in market value. The defendant should be awarded the cost to which she was put in taking alternative accommodation, the cost of redecorating, and some award for all the unpleasantness of living in the flat as it deteriorated until it became uninhabitable. These three heads of damage will, so far as money can, compensate the tenant for the plaintiffs' breach.

But it was said that the court cannot award the cost of the alternative accommodation because of the decision of the Queen's Bench in *Green* v *Eales* (1841) 2 QB 225, and in particular the passage in the judgment of Lord Denman CJ in which he said at p. 238:

> We are of opinion that the defendant was not bound to find the plaintiff another residence whilst the repairs went on, any more than he would have been bound to do so if the premises had been consumed by fire.

But I take that passage to do no more than draw attention to the fact that a landlord is not in breach of his covenant to repair until he has been given notice of the want of repair and a reasonable time has elapsed in which the repair could have been carried out. If in this case the plaintiffs had sent workmen round to carry out the repairs promptly on receiving notice of the defect and the defendant for her own convenience had decided to move to a hotel whilst the repairs were carried out, she could not have claimed the cost of the hotel because the plaintiffs would not have been in breach of the repairing covenant. That Lord Denman CJ meant no more than this is I think apparent from his observation that the tenant might have had a claim on the basis that the time he had to be in alternative accommodation had been lengthened by the delay in carrying out repairs. For these reasons I do not regard *Green* v *Eales* as an authority for the proposition that there can be no claim for the costs of alternative accommodation, but if it did purport so to decide, it was in my view wrongly decided.

If the defendant in this case had claimed for the cost of alternative accommodation it would in principle have been an allowable head of damage. It would naturally have been closely investigated in the evidence: was the defendant's true reason for leaving the flat that she and her husband found the conditions intolerable, or were there other reasons for going to live in the Isle of Man; was the cost of the alternative accommodation reasonable and so forth? However, the claim was not made and I agree that it is now too late to put it forward.

The judge awarded the defendant part of the costs of the internal decorations which she had had to carry out as a result of the plaintiff's breach of covenant. In my view he should have awarded the whole of the costs of the repairs. However, he deducted one-third of the cost of repairs as a betterment element because he was attempting the unreal exercise of putting a price on the diminution in value of the flat in circumstances when there was no need to do so.

The judge was however, invited to assess damages in this way by the defendant's counsel because it was thought that the decision of the Court of Appeal in *Hewitt* v *Rowlands* 93 LJKB 1080, left no other approach to the assessment. That was a case in which a statutory tenant claimed damages against his landlord for breach of the landlord's duty to repair. The sums involved were very small and in giving directions to the registrar as to the basis on which damages should be assessed Bankes LJ said at p. 1082:

> Prima facie the measure of damage for breach of the obligation to repair *is the difference in value to the tenant* during the period between the house in the condition in which it now is and the house in the condition in which it would be if the landlord on receipt of the notice had fulfilled his obligation to repair. (My emphasis).

Whatever Bankes LJ meant by 'the difference in value to the tenant', the one thing he cannot have meant in the circumstances of that case was the diminution in the market value of the tenancy, for it was a statutory tenancy which the tenant could not sell, and thus it had no market value. In my view the difference in value to the tenant must vary according to the circumstances of the case. If the tenant is in occupation during the period of breach he is entitled to be compensated for the discomfort and inconvenience occasioned by the breach and I suspect that that is what Bankes LJ had in mind when he used the phrase 'the difference in value to the tenant' in *Hewitt* v *Rowlands* 93 LJKB 1080, 1982, for which the judge in this case awarded £3,000. If the tenant has rented the property to let it and the landlord is aware of this, then 'the difference in value to the tenant' may be measured by his loss of rent if he cannot let it because of the landlord's breach. If the tenant is driven out of occupation by the breach and forced to sell the property then 'the difference in value to the tenant' may be measured by the difference between the selling price and the price he would have obtained if the landlord had observed his repairing covenant. But each case depends on its own circumstances and *Hewitt* v *Rowlands* should not be regarded as an authority for the proposition that it is in every case necessary to obtain valuation evidence.

In my view there was no need for any valuation evidence in this case. I repeat that damages in a case such as this should include the cost of the redecoration, a sum to compensate for the discomfort, loss of enjoyment and health involved in living in the damp and deteriorating flat and any reasonable sum spent on providing alternative accommodation after the flat became uninhabitable.

The tenant has not appealed against the one-third reduction of the cost of repairs; the claim for alternative accommodation was not pleaded or argued, and for the reasons given by Stephenson LJ the heads of damage for which the tenant contended in this court are not recoverable.

Notes

1.   Thus the Court of Appeal laid down in *Calabar* a number of fundamental principles in assessing damages payable to a tenant following a landlord's breach of a repairing covenant. These were:

(a)   The object of the damages is to restore the tenant to the position the tenant would have been in if there had been no breach.

(b)   The diminution of the value of the property was not necessarily the measure of damages for a breach.

(c)   The cost of alternative accommodation may be recoverable, if the tenant is forced to leave the property by lack of repair.

(d)   The cost of repairs paid by the tenant is *prima facie* recoverable.

(e)   Compensation may be payable for discomfort, loss of enjoyment and ill-health endured following the breach.

2.   The decision in *Calabar* was subsequently applied in *McGreal v Wake* (1984) 13 HLR 107, where a tenant living in a house in disrepair successfully claimed for alternative accommodation, redecoration and the cost of storing furniture.

3.   The tenant is under a common law obligation to mitigate losses. Thus a tenant should provide prompt notice of the need for repair to the landlord. In *Minchburn v Peck* (1988) 20 HLR 392, damages were reduced where prompt notice was not given in a claim for damages for distress and discomfort.

(b)   Specific performance

In addition to the possibility of suing for damages, a tenant may decide to enforce a landlord's repairing obligation by the equitable remedy of a decree of specific performance. Action may be brought here either under the general equitable jurisdiction of the court to grant a decree, or via s. 17(1) of the Landlord and Tenant Act 1985.

In *Jeune v Queen's Cross Properties* (below), Pennycuick V-C held that although the jurisdiction of specific performance should be carefully exercised, he saw no reason why an order for specific performance should be refused where the landlord was clearly in breach of a repairing obligation and there was no question as to what needed to be done.

Jeune v Queens Cross Properties
[1974] Ch 97

PENNYCUICK V-C: In this action there are four plaintiffs, Mr Jeune, Mr Beardmore, Mrs Evans and Mrs Williams. The defendant is Queen's Cross Properties Ltd. I have before me a motion for judgment in default of the defendant's serving a defence.

The statement of claim sets out a series of underleases and assignments, the effect of which is that the leasehold reversion in the property, 117/119 Westbourne Terrace, London, W2, is vested in the defendant. The four plaintiffs are respectively tenants in possession of four flats comprised in the property. The leases contain repairing covenants binding on the landlord. The relevant covenant is set out in para. 5 of the statement of claim in the following terms:

In each of the said underleases, to which the plaintiffs will refer at the trial for their full terms and effect, the lessors covenanted, inter alia, to maintain repair and renew the structure of the aforesaid building, including the external walls thereof,

Then the statement of claim goes on:

In breach of the repairing covenants hereinbefore referred to the defendant . . . while assignee of the said reversion failed to repair, maintain and renew the structure of the aforesaid building.

These are the particulars of the breach:

Failure to reinstate the York stone balcony situate at the front of the aforesaid building at first floor level in the form in which it existed prior to its partial collapse on the 13th May 1972.

and then there is an allegation of damage and an allegation of refusal to remedy the breach.

The claim is:

1.   An order that the defendant . . . do forthwith reinstate the said balcony in the form in which it existed prior to its partial collapse on the 13th May 1972; and

2.   Damages for breach of covenant in lieu of or in addition to the aforesaid relief.

The defendant, although it entered an appearance, has not served a defence and in these circumstances the plaintiffs now move for an order in the terms of minutes annexed to the notice of motion, the first relief sought being an order:

that the defendant . . . do forthwith reinstate the York stone balcony situate at the front of the building known as No 117/119 Westbourne Terrace, London W2 in the form in which it existed prior to its partial collapse on 13th May 1972.

Now, on the face of it, common sense and justice, it seems perfectly clear that this is the appropriate relief. The defendant's repairing covenant requires it to maintain, repair and renew the structure, including the external walls. A mandatory order upon the defendant to reinstate the balcony is a much more convenient order than an award of damages leaving it to the individual plaintiffs to do the work. There is nothing burdensome or unfair in the order sought.

My only preoccupation in this matter has been in regard to a principle which I am told is stated in some textbooks to the effect that specific performance will never be ordered of repairing covenants in a lease. So far as the general law is concerned, apart from a repairing covenant in a lease, it appears perfectly clear that in an appropriate case the court will decree specific performance of an agreement to build if certain conditions are satisfied. See *Snells' Principles of Equity*, 26th edn (1966), p. 647:

The rule has now become settled that the court will order specific performance of an agreement to build if—(i) the building work is sufficiently defined by the contract, e.g. by reference to detailed plans; (ii) the plaintiff has a substantial interest in the performance of the contract of such a nature that damages would not compensate him for the defendant's failure to build; and (iii) the defendant is in possession of the land so that the plaintiff cannot employ another person to build without committing a trespass.

It is clear that all those conditions are satisfied in the present case; in particular, the balcony is not included in any of the leases.

A similar principle was enunciated in relation to tort by Lord Upjohn in *Morris* v *Redland Bricks Ltd* [1970] AC 652. In particular Lord Upjohn said AC at p. 666:

> If in the exercise of its discretion the court decides that it is a proper case to grant a mandatory injunction, then the court must be careful to see that the defendant knows exactly in fact what he has to do and this means not as a matter of law but as a matter of fact, so that in carrying out an order he can give his contractors the proper instructions.

Again in the present case there is no difficulty about that because the defendant would know what has to be done.

The difficulty arises from something which was said by Lord Eldon LC in *Hill* v *Barclay* (1810) 16 Ves Jun 402. The facts should be looked at but I will not take time reading them now. Lord Eldon LC considered whether the case was one in which forfeiture should be decreed against the plaintiff tenant and in the course of his judgment said at p. 405:

> The situation of the landlord is however very different as to rent and as to these other covenants. He may bring an ejectment upon non-payment of rent: but he may also compel the tenant to pay rent. He cannot have that specific relief with regard to repairs. He may bring an action for damages: but there is a wide distinction between damages and the actual expenditure upon repairs, specifically done. Even after damages recovered the landlord cannot compel the tenant to repair: but may bring another action. The tenant therefore, standing those actions, may keep the premises until the last year of the term; and from the reasoning of one of the cases [*Hack* v *Leonard* (1724) 9 Mod. 91] the conclusion is, that the most beneficial course for the landlord would be, that the tenant, refraining from doing the repairs until the last year of the term, should then be compelled to do them. The difficulty upon this doctrine of a court of equity is, that there is no mutuality in it. The tenant cannot be compelled to repair.

Now that decision is, I think, an authority laying down the principle that a landlord cannot obtain against his tenant an order for specific performance of a covenant to repair. It does not however apply to a landlord's covenant to repair, although it is said that there may be some other explanation for the words, 'The difficulty upon this doctrine of a court of equity is, that there is no mutuality in it.'

Counsel for the plaintiffs has looked through various textbooks on the law of landlord and tenant and assures me that, although *Hill* v *Barclay* 16 Ves Jun 402, is repeatedly cited – there is no other authority in point. It is worthwhile to refer to two passages in *Halsbury's Laws of England*, 3rd edn, vol. 23 (1958) – on landlord and tenant – it is stated, at p. 587:

> Unless the lease contains a proviso empowering the landlord to re-enter for forfeiture on breach of the covenant to repair, the landlord's remedy is an action for damages; for specific performance of such a covenant will not ordinarily be granted.

Reference is made there to *Hill* v *Barclay*. In *Halsbury*, vol. 36 (1961) the specific performance volume there is this passage, at p. 267: 'In particular, the court does not, as a rule, order the specific performance of a contract to build or repair.' It then goes on to refer to the circumstances in which specific performance of a contract to build will be granted.

There is nothing at all there inconsistent with a power in the court to make an order on a landlord to do specific work under a covenant to repair. I cannot myself see any reason in principle, why, in an appropriate case, an order should not be made against a landlord to do some specific work pursuant to his covenant to repair. Obviously, it is a jurisdiction which should be carefully exercised. But in a case such as the present where there has been a plain breach of a covenant to repair and there is no doubt at all what is required to be done to remedy the breach, I cannot see why an order for specific performance should not be made.

I propose to make an order accordingly in the terms of the minutes annexed to the notice of motion, namely:

> that the defendant company do forthwith reinstate the York stone balcony situate at the front of the building known as No 117/119 Westbourne Terrace, London W2 in the form in which it existed prior to its partial collapse on 13th May 1972.

(c)   Setting off the cost of repairs against rent

In *Lee-Parker* v *Izzet* [1971] 1 WLR 1688, it is clear that a tenant has a common law right to recoup out of future rents the cost of repairs carried out by the tenant, insofar as the repairs come within the express or implied repairing covenants of the landlord. Additionally, in *British Anzani (Felix-stowe) Ltd* v *International Marine Management (UK) Ltd* [1979] 3 WLR 451, upon being sued for unpaid rent a tenant counterclaimed for breach of a repairing covenant by the landlord. Forbes J held that the tenant here could not counterclaim at common law, as the defendant had not in fact paid out anything on repairs. However, the doctrine of equitable set-off could still be available where a tenant could demonstrate that the counterclaim was so directly or closely connected with the landlord's claim so as to go to the very foundation of that claim.

(vii)   Obligations in tort

(a)   Landlord's duty of care – common law

At common law a landlord is generally not liable to any person not party to the contract of letting for breach of a repairing covenant. Therefore members of a tenant's family who are injured as a result of a failure to repair, will not succeed in actions against the landlord (see *Cavalier* v *Pope* [1906] AC 428). An exception to this general principle, however, can be seen in *Rimmer* v *Liverpool City Council* [1985] QB 1. Here the local housing authority both designed and built a block of flats. The Court of Appeal held that the authority had, in its capacity as designer and builder, a duty of care to all persons who might reasonably be expected to be affected by the design or construction of the building. The duty imposed was to take reasonable care to see that such persons would not suffer injury as a result of defects in design or construction.

(b)   Landlord's duty of care – Occupiers' Liability Act 1957

Occupiers' Liability Act 1957

Extent of occupier's ordinary duty

2.—(1)   An occupier of premises owes the same duty, the 'common duty of care', to all his visitors, except in so far as he is free to and does extend, restrict, modify or exclude his duty to any visitor or visitors by agreement or otherwise.

(2)   The common duty of care is a duty to take such care as in all the circumstances of the case is reasonable to see that the visitor will be reasonably safe in using the premises for the purposes for which he is invited or permitted by the occupier to be there.

(3)   The circumstances relevant for the present purposes include the degree of care, and of want of care, which would ordinarily be looked for in such a visitor, so that (for example) in proper cases—

(a)   an occupier must be prepared for children to be less careful than adults; and

(b)   an occupier may expect that a person, in the exercise of his calling, will appreciate and guard against any special risks ordinarily incident to it, so far as the occupier leaves him free to do so.

(4)   In determining whether the occupier of premises has discharged the common duty of care to a visitor, regard is to be had to all the circumstances, so that (for example)—

(a)   where damage is caused to a visitor by a danger of which he had been warned by the occupier, the warning is not to be treated without more as absolving the occupier from liability, unless in all the circumstances it was enough to enable the visitor to be reasonably safe; and

(b)   where damage is caused to a visitor by a danger due to the faulty execution of any work of construction, maintenance or repair by an independent contractor employed by the occupier, the occupier is not to be treated without more as answerable for the danger if in all the circumstances he had acted reasonably in entrusting the work to an independent contractor and had taken such steps (if any) as he reasonably ought in order to satisfy himself that the contractor was competent and that the work had been properly done.

(5)   The common duty of care does not impose on an occupier any obligation to a visitor in respect of risks willingly accepted as his by the visitor (the question whether a risk was so accepted to be decided on the same principles as in other cases in which one person owes a duty of care to another).

(6)   For the purposes of this section, persons who enter premises for any purpose in the exercise of a right conferred by law are to be treated as permitted by the occupier to be there for that purpose, whether they in fact have his permission or not.

An occupier, for the purposes of the Act, is the person in control and possession of the premises. Hence a landlord retaining control over the common parts of a building, i.e. lifts, stairs, entrance hall in a block of flats, has a 'common duty of care' to ensure that a visitor to the premises is reasonably safe for the purposes he or she was invited or permitted to be on the premises. While an occupier may exclude, restrict or modify this duty of care (s. 2(1)), these exclusions are subject to the Unfair Contract Terms Act 1977. In particular, if the occupation of the premises is for the 'business purposes' of the occupier (see 1977 Act, s. 1(3)) any attempt to exclude or restrict the duty of care under the 1957 Act is subject to s. 2(1) and 2(2) of the 1977 Act. At its simplest, this means that a 'business' landlord who does (in some sense) 'occupy' the premises will not be able to disclaim liability for any death or injury caused to lawful visitors.

(c)   Landlord's duty of care – Defective Premises Act 1972

Defective Premises Act 1972

Landlord's duty of care in virtue of obligation or right to repair premises demised

4.—(1)   Where premises are let under a tenancy which puts on the landlord an obligation to the tenant for the maintenance or repair of the premises the landlord owes to all persons who might reasonably be expected to be affected by defects in the state of the premises a duty to take such care as is reasonable in all the circumstances to see that they are reasonably safe from personal injury or from damage to their property caused by a relevant defect.

(2)   The said duty is owed if the landlord knows (whether as the result of being notified by the tenant or otherwise) or if he ought in all the circumstances to have known of the relevant defect.

(3)   In this section 'relevant defect' means a defect in the state of the premises existing at or after the material time and arising from, or continuing because of, an act or omission by the landlord which constituted or would if he had had notice of the defect, have constituted a failure by him to carry out his obligation to the tenant for the maintenance or repair of the premises; and for the purposes of the foregoing provision 'the material time' means—

(a)   where the tenancy commenced before this Act, the commencement of this Act; and

(b)   in all other cases, the earliest of the following times, that is to say—

  (i)   the time when the tenancy commences;

  (ii)   the time when the tenancy agreement is entered into;

  (iii)   the time when possession is taken of the premises in contemplation of the letting.

(4)   Where premises are let under a tenancy which expressly or impliedly gives the landlord the right to enter the premises to carry out any description of maintenance or repair of the premises, then, as from the time when he first is, or by notice or otherwise can put himself, in a position to exercise the right and so long as he is or can put himself in that position, he shall be treated for the purposes of subsections (1) to (3) above (but for no other purpose) as if he were under an obligation to the tenant for that description of maintenance or repair of the premises; but the landlord shall not owe the tenant any duty by virtue of this subsection in respect of any defect in the state of the premises arising from, or continuing because of, a failure to carry out an obligation expressly imposed on the tenant by the tenancy.

(5)   For the purposes of this section obligations imposed or rights given by an enactment in virtue of a tenancy shall be treated as imposed or given by the tenancy.

(6)   This section applies to a right of occupation given by contract or any enactment and not amounting to a tenancy as if the right were a tenancy, and 'tenancy' and cognate expressions shall be construed accordingly.

Notes
1.   This provision imposes on a landlord a duty of care where under the terms of the tenancy there is an obligation towards the tenant to maintain or repair the demised premises. This obligation may be express, within the terms of the tenancy, or implied by statute. The duty is owed to everyone who may be affected by the state of the premises, thus including both the tenant and third parties. The duty is to take such care as is reasonable in the circumstances, to ensure that such persons are reasonably safe from personal injury or damage caused by a relevant defect. Under s. 4(2) the landlord must know, or ought to know, of the relevant defect. Section 4(3) defines a relevant defect which may arise as a result of, or continue because of, an act or omission on the part of the landlord constituting a breach of the repairing covenant. Additionally, where a landlord has a right to enter the premises to carry out repair he is considered by s. 4(4) to be under an obligation to the tenant for the repair.
2.   As mentioned above, under s. 4 the landlord can be liable even if he does not know of the defect, if he ought to have known of it: *Clarke v Taff Ely Borough Council* (1983) 10 HLR 44. Further, under s. 4(4), if the landlord has merely an express or implied *right* (rather than a duty) to enter and maintain or repair, failure to do the work may give rise to tortious liability: *Smith v Bradford Metropolitan Borough Council* (1982) 4 HLR 86.
3.   Note that the word 'maintenance' in s. 4 is wider in scope than the word 'repair', and could cover the curing of severe condensation even though neither the structure nor the exterior has yet been corrupted by the damp (compare the contractual position, as discussed in *Quick v Taff Ely Borough Council* [1985] 3 All ER 321).

In *McAuley v Bristol CC* (1991) 23 HLR 586, the plaintiff and her husband were joint tenants of a council house under a tenancy agreement whereby the council undertook to maintain the structure and exterior of the house in good repair. The tenants were liable for interior decoration and, by cl. 6(1a), they were to keep the premises, including the gardens, in a clean and orderly condition and to pay to the council the cost of any special cleaning rendered necessary by their failure to comply with that condition. By cl. 6(c) they were to give the council 'all reasonable facilities for entering upon the premises . . . and for any purpose which may from time to time be required by the council.' The garden at the back of the house was steep and included a flight of steps, one of which was unstable. The husband complained to the council, who took no action. The plaintiff, while standing on the step, lost her balance and fell breaking her ankle. She claimed damages from the council, and by amendment to her pleadings at the trial she claimed that the step was part of the premises within the meaning of s. 4 of the Defective Premises Act 1972 and that the council were in breach of their duty of care owed to the plaintiff under the section to ensure that the premises were reasonably safe. The assistant recorder awarded the plaintiff damages, holding that, although there was no implied obligation on the council to repair the steps under the tenancy agreement, the council had a statutory duty to do so and therefore were in breach of s. 4 of the Act of 1972.

On the council's appeal, it was held that the obligations imposed on a local authority by (as it was then) s. 32 of the Housing Act 1961 did not extend to a defect in a garden and, in the absence of a statutory duty or an express term in the tenancy agreement, the council could only be liable under s. 4(4) of the Defective Premises Act 1972 if there was an implied obligation on the council to repair a defect in the premises of a description for which the council had a right to enter the premises; that cl. 6(c) of the tenancy agreement gave the council a right of entry for any purpose the council might require and could lawfully carry out; that the basis of the agreement between the council and their tenants was that, apart from the interior decoration and keeping the house and garden clean and orderly, the council would keep the premises in a reasonable and habitable condition; that to give business efficacy to the agreement a term was to be implied that the council would carry out repair where there was a defect in the garden which exposed a tenant or visitor to a serious risk of injury; and that, accordingly, the council, having the right to enter the premises to cure the defect, were liable under s. 4 of the Act for the defective step.

The important point to note about this case is the acceptance that where there is a *general* right of entry for the landlord, *and* a general basis of agreement between the parties that the landlord will keep the premises in reasonable and habitable order, business efficacy requires an implied term that the landlord will carry out repairs where there is a defect which may expose the tenant and visitors to risk of harm. Section 4(4) of the 1972 Act can then 'seize' on this term.

(C)   Public law remedies for dealing with substandard housing

(i)   Introduction

Legislative and judicial limitations on the private contractual freedoms of landlords have never been enough by themselves to combat poor housing. In many cases tenants lack the financial resources to equip themselves for protracted litigation, and probably lack the resolve to see such litigation through. Moreover, private law solutions are piecemeal and limited, focusing on individual instances of disrepair (with the notable exception of the neglected s. 8, Landlord and Tenant Act 1985). The existence of *areas* of substandard housing also makes it unrealistic to place reliance solely on individual tenant action.

As a consequence local authorities have long possessed powers to take action to deal with unfit (and seriously defective) housing, and also with the health risks posed by poor housing. Powers to enforce unfitness notices against landlords date back to 1868 (the Artisans' and Labourers' Dwellings Act (the Torrens Act)). Powers to deal with area redevelopment notionally date back to 1875 (the Artisans' and Labourers' Dwellings Improvement Act (the Cross Act)), although true area improvement powers did not arrive until the Housing Act 1964. Powers in relation to poor health and housing derive ultimately from the Public Health Act 1936 (itself following on from the

Public Health Act 1875), although now they are to be found in the Environmental Protection Act 1990.

This section deals in detail with 'unfitness' (and the powers possessed by local authorities for dealing with it), plus the remedies available under the Environmental Protection Act 1990. Area improvement is beyond the scope of the section, although issues relating to area improvement may be mentioned in passing.

(ii)   Unfitness

The current standard of unfitness is set out in s. 604 of the Housing Act 1985, as amended by the Local Government and Housing Act 1989.

Housing Act 1985

Fitness for human habitation

604.—(1)   Subject to subsection (2) below, a dwelling-house is fit for human habitation for the purposes of this Act unless, in the opinion of the local housing authority, it fails to meet one or more of the requirements in paragraphs (a) to (i) below and, by reason of that failure, is not reasonably suitable for occupation,—

(a)   it is structurally stable;

(b)   it is free from serious disrepair;

(c)   it is free from dampness prejudicial to the health of the occupants (if any);

(d)   it has adequate provision for lighting, heating and ventilation;

(e)   it has adequate piped supply of wholesome water;

(f)   there are satisfactory facilities in the dwelling-house for the preparation and cooking of food, including a sink with a satisfactory supply of hot and cold water;

(g)   it has a suitably located water-closet for the exclusive use of the occupants (if any);

(h)   it has, for the exclusive use of the occupants (if any), a suitably located fixed bath or shower and wash-hand basin each of which is provided with a satisfactory supply of hot and cold water; and

(i)   it has an effective system for the draining of foul, waste and surface water; and any reference to a dwelling-house being unfit for human habitation shall be construed accordingly.

(2)   Whether or not a dwelling-house which is a flat satisfies the requirements in subsection (1), it is unfit for human habitation for the purposes of this Act if, in the opinion of the local housing authority, the building or a part of the building outside the flat fails to meet one or more of the requirements in paragraphs (a) to (e) below and, by reason of that failure, the flat is not reasonably suitable for occupation,—

(a)   the building or part is structurally stable;

(b)   it is free from serious disrepair;

(c)   it is free from dampness;

(d)   it has adequate provision for ventilation; and

(e)   it has an effective system for the draining of foul, waste and surface water.

(3)   Subsection (1) applies in relation to a house in multiple occupation with the substitution of a reference to the house for any reference to a dwelling-house.

(4)   Subsection (2) applies in relation to a flat in multiple occupation with the substitution for any reference to a dwelling-house which is a flat of a reference to the flat in multiple occupation.

A property is therefore 'unfit' if, in the opinion of the authority, it fails to meet one or more of the above criteria *and* by reason of that failure is not reasonably suitable for occupation. There is obviously still considerable scope for variation between authorities as to how the above criteria are evaluated and 'weighed', but the 1989 amendments do facilitate greater uniformity in practice by providing for such a 'checklist' (the 'down-side' is, of course, the possibility of an authority considering a property to be fit, despite numerous minor defects, because the listed criteria are satisfied). The difference between the old and the new fitness standards is summed up well in para. 7 of Department of the Environment Circular 6/90:

Paragraph 83 of Schedule 9 to the 1989 Act substitutes a new section 604 of the 1985 Act. The basis of the new standard remains the same in that it is a means of determining whether premises are fit for human habitation. There are however, some differences in its application. The former section 604 provided what was essentially an 'unfitness standard'. Authorities were required to look at a number of specified matters and to decide whether or not defects in respect of any one of these, or a combination of them, were sufficiently serious to make a property so defective that it was unfit for human habitation. By contrast, the new section 604 is cast more positively: it lists criteria which must be met if the premises are to be considered fit for habitation. Premises are unfit for human habitation if, in the opinion of an authority, they fail to meet one or more of these requirements and by reason of that failure are not reasonably suitable for occupation.

Annex A to the DoE circular not only reproduces the new s. 604, but also gives further guidance on the criteria:

Fitness Standard – Guidance Note
2.1   A dwelling-house is unfit for human habitation if, in the authority's view, it fails to meet any one of the requirements specified in subsection 604(1) or, where it is a flat, it so fails to meet subsection 604(1) or the building or a part of the building outside the flat fails to meet any of the requirements in subsection 604(2), and because of the failure to meet that particular requirement, it is not reasonably suitable for occupation.
2.2   In deciding whether a dwelling-house is or is not unfit, the authority should determine for each of the statutory requirements in turn, whether or not the dwelling-house is reasonably suitable for occupation because of a failure of that particular matter. In reaching this decision, the authority is asked to have regard to the general guidance note below and, specifically, the note on each particular requirement. However, in addressing each requirement, the list of items for consideration and the advice given in respect of defects mentioned under each section are not exclusive and all other relevant items will need to be considered.
2.3   The order of sections reflects the general need to maintain a conventional inspection procedure, notwithstanding the determination of each requirement individually. Defective items are frequently interrelated and the consideration of, for example, repair and the cause or reason for any disrepair may assist in identifying a failure to meet other requirements, particularly structural stability and dampness. Consequently, a thorough internal and external inspection of the whole dwelling-house and building should normally be undertaken, before determining which of the individual requirements meet or fail the standard.

2.4 In assessing fitness for human habitation, consideration should be given to the condition of all rooms and spaces in the dwelling-house and of all parts of the fabric of the building and of the fixtures which, were the accommodation rented, would normally be provided by a landlord.

. . .

2.6 For the purposes of 604(2), section 183 of the Housing Act 1985 will have effect to determine whether a dwelling-house is a flat. In determining whether a dwelling-house which is a flat is or is not unfit, the parts of the building outside the flat must satisfy subsection (2) in addition to the flat itself satisfying subsection (1). Thus, the condition of the structural elements and of the external envelope (roof, walls, etc.) of the building and of the hall, stairway, accessways and other common areas, may fall to be considered in addition to that of the particular flat, but only with regard to the matters of repair, stability, dampness, ventilation and drainage. Moreover, these matters should only be considered to the extent that they affect the particular flat in question. Consequently, the failures which fall to be addressed are generally those in the parts of the building directly affecting the flat concerned, for example, those in the particular structure or part of the building accommodating the flat and/or its primary means of access.

Further notes indicate that 'unfitness' is now primarily a health and safety issue, even though discomfort and inconvenience may be relevant factors. Emphasis is to be placed on the property itself, rather than on the situation of the current occupants, although it is emphasised that the elderly and young children are particularly vulnerable to health and safety risks.

Given how 'functional' much of the above now is, legal interest is more likely to settle on the core issue within s. 604 (s. 604(1)(b)) of 'serious disrepair', and on the various options open to local authorities for dealing with properties which are seen as unfit.

(a) Serious disrepair

The requirement that a property must be in a state of 'serious disrepair' before it can be seen as unfit (currently to be found in s. 604(1)(b)) has long been part of the law, and there have been a number of judicial observations on it. For example, in *Morgan* v *Liverpool Corporation* [1927] 2 KB 131, Atkin LJ said (at p. 145), that:

. . . if the state of repair of a house is such that by ordinary user damage may naturally be caused to the occupier, either in respect of personal injury to life or limb or injury to health then the house is not in all respects fit for human habitation.

This approach, though not commanding the assent of the remainder of the Court in *Morgan*, was expressly approved by the House of Lords in *Summers* v *Salford Corporation* [1943] AC 283. In *Summers*, a tenant sued for damages for injuries caused to her by a defective sash window. Her claim was based on the implied term of fitness for habitation (then contained in s. 2(1) of the Housing Act 1936). Despite the individual defect being relatively minor, the House of Lords found that the property was rendered statutorily 'unfit' because of it. Specifically, this was because the dangerously defective window meant that the room could not be properly ventilated, and this in itself was enough to make the property unfit. The House approved a statement by Luxmore LJ in the Court of Appeal that:

The usual method of providing ventilation for a room in a dwelling is by a window or windows, which is, or are, constructed so as to open and shut without danger to the person opening or shutting it, or them. If a room, especially a bedroom, had only one window and that window cannot be opened or shut without danger to the person seeking to perform that operation, that room may, in my opinion, be said not be fit for human habitation.

(see Lord Wright [1943] AC 283, at p. 293).

More generally, *Summers* demonstrates that 'serious disrepair' need not necessarily equate with 'falling down' or 'totally dilapidated'. As Lord Atkin states in the case (at p. 288):

The test of the obligation cannot simply be whether, with the disrepair complained of, the tenant can live in the house . . . it must not be measured by the magnitude of the repairs required. A burst or leaking pipe, a displaced slate or tile, a stopped drain, a rotten stair tread, may each of them until repair make a house unfit to live in, though each of them may be quickly and cheaply repaired . . . .

To what extent does this approach still represent the law? Nothing in the recent amendments to the 'fitness standard' invalidates it, but equally there is now much more detailed guidance given to local authorities (in DoE Circular 6/90, Annex A) which, while not inconsistent with the older case law, does appear to give greater emphasis to the overall condition of the premises:

Repair – Guidance Note
3.1   A dwelling-house is unfit for human habitation if, in the authority's view, it is in serious disrepair or, where it is a flat, it or the building or a part of the building outside the flat are in serious disrepair, and for that reason it is not reasonably suitable for occupation.
3.2   In deciding whether a dwelling-house is or is not unfit, the authority should consider whether the dwelling-house or building is currently free from items of disrepair which either individually or due to their combined effect are so severe and/or extensive that they present a risk to health and safety, or cause serious inconvenience to any occupants.
3.3   In reaching a decision, the authority should have regard, amongst other things, to the extent to which by reason of the disrepair:—
(a)   the fabric is liable to failure, dislodgement or spalling or is otherwise prejudicial to safety;
(b)   the fabric prohibits normal usage of the dwelling-house, increases the risk of falls or is otherwise prejudicial to health or safety;
(c)   the fixtures and internal surfaces are incapable of being cleansed;
(d)   the condition increases the risk of electrocution, toxic fumes, explosion or fire; and

(e) the condition increases the risk of water penetration or is otherwise prejudicial to the structural fabric.

3.4 Serious disrepair may be due to the severity of one item of disrepair, or be due to the combined effect of two or more items. A multiplicity of items, none of which, by themselves, would be sufficiently serious to provide grounds for unfitness, may well constitute serious disrepair when combined.

Once a dwelling is seen to be unfit by a local authority a duty to take action arises.

(b) Dealing with unfit properties

Under the 1989 amendments, such action as an authority decide to take should be part of an integrated area policy. Section 604A of the Housing Act 1985 now sets out the general framework for action:

Housing Act 1985

Authority to consider guidance given by Secretary of State in deciding whether to take action under sections 189, 264, 265 or 289
604A.—(1) In deciding for the purposes of section 189, 264, 265 and 289 whether the most satisfactory course of action, in respect of any dwelling-house, house in multiple occupation or building, is, if applicable,—
(a) serving notice under subsection (1) of section 189;
(b) serving notice under subsection (1A) of that section; or
(c) making a closing order under subsection (1) of section 264; or
(d) making a closing order under subsection (2) of that section with respect to the whole of a part of the building concerned; or
(e) making a demolition order under subsection (1) of section 265; or
(f) making a demolition under subsection (2) of that section; or
(g) declaring the area in which the dwelling-house, house in multiple occupation or building is situated to be a clearance area in accordance with section 289;
the local housing authority shall have regard to such guidance as may from time to time be given by the Secretary of State.

The 'guidance' referred to in s. 604A is to be found as Annex F to DoE Circular 6/90. Ostensibly, this guidance is just a factor to be taken into account, but in practice it is so detailed as to be fairly prescriptive as to the appropriate course(s) of action. The code establishes the following principles:

(a) There should be an identification of the need for action, evidenced by a survey (the *recommended* means for this is the Neighbourhood Renewal Assessment which takes into account the socio-economic characteristics of the area as well as its physical characteristics) or complaints from tenants or applications for grant aid.

(b) The authority should then consider the most satisfactory course of action, by taking into account matters such as costs, the social implications of alternative actions, area strategy factors and the views of those affected by the action.

After the above evaluation process authorities should be in a position to make a reasoned choice as to which course(s) of action to take. The most appropriate action(s) might, of course, be on an area basis, but it is the alternative actions in relation to individual unfit properties which are considered below. The alternatives under the Housing Act 1985 are (i) the serving of a repair notice (s. 189); (ii) action under s. 190 to bring properties up to reasonable standards; (iii) closing orders (s. 264) and demolition orders (s. 265).

(i)   Repair notice

Housing Act 1985

Repair notice in respect of unfit house
189.—(1)   Subject to subsection (1A) where the local housing authority are satisfied that a dwelling-house or house in multiple occupation is unfit for human habitation, they shall serve a repair notice on the person having control of the dwelling-house or house in multiple occupation if they are satisfied, in accordance with section 604A, that serving a notice under this subsection is the most satisfactory course of action.
(1A)   Where the local housing authority are satisfied that either a dwelling-house which is a flat or a flat in multiple occupation is unfit for human habitation by virtue of section 604(2) they shall serve a repair notice on the person having control of the part of the building in question if they are satisfied, in accordance with section 604A, that serving a notice under this subsection is the most satisfactory course of action.
(2)   A repair notice under this section shall—
(a)   require the person on whom it is served to execute the works specified in the notice (which may be works of repair or improvement or both) and to begin those works not later than such reasonable date, being not earlier than the twenty-eighth day after the notice is served as is specified in the notice and to complete those works within such reasonable time as is so specified, and
(b)   state that in the opinion of the authority the works specified in the notice will render the dwelling-house or, as the case may be, house in multiple occupation fit for human habitation.

A repair notice requires the execution of specified works of *repair* or *improvement* where an authority are satisfied that this is the most satisfactory course of action. Factors to 'weigh up' include: the physical condition of the property; its life expectancy as repaired; a comparison of repair costs as against other courses of action; and the condition of neighbouring properties and the overall local environment. Any person aggrieved by the service of a repair notice may appeal to the county court (s. 191). If no appeal is entered, the notice becomes final and effective 21 days after service. An appeal may be on the basis that some other person (e.g., the owner of the property) ought to execute the required works or pay for them. Alternatively, it may be on the basis that some other action (e.g., closure and demolition, below) would have been the most satisfactory course.

(ii)   Section 190 notice

Housing Act 1985

Repair notice in respect of house in state of disrepair but not unfit

190.—(1)   Subject to subsection (1B) where the local authority—
  (a)   are satisfied that a dwelling-house or house in multiple occupation is in such a state of disrepair that, although not unfit for human habitation, substantial repairs are necessary to bring it up to a reasonable standard, having regard to its age, character and locality, or
  (b)   are satisfied whether on a representation made by an occupying tenant or otherwise that a dwelling-house or house in multiple occupation is in such a state of disrepair that, although not unfit for human habitation, its condition is such as to interfere materially with the personal comfort of the occupying tenant or, in the case of a house in multiple occupation, the persons occupying it (whether as tenants or licensees),
they may serve a repair notice on the person having control of the dwelling-house or house in multiple occupation.

It might be thought inappropriate to deal with s. 190 under the general heading of 'unfitness', given that it is specifically focused on properties which are *not* unfit; but the line between 'fitness' and 'unfitness' can be a fine one and all the procedures and processes concerned with s. 190 are so closely aligned with s. 189 that it is sensible to deal with it here.

Section 190 contemplates action against two kinds of property: (i) housing which though 'fit' is in need of substantial repair; and (ii) housing which though 'fit' is in need of repair to the extent that its condition interferes with the personal comfort of occupying tenants.

Appeals procedures against the service of a s. 190 notice are, in essence, the same as regards s. 189.

Under s. 191A, authorities may execute works by agreement at the expense of the person having control of the house, or s. 193, where they may do the work and recover their costs. It should also be noted that the provisions do not apply to an authority's own houses (see *R v Cardiff City Council ex parte Cross* 1982 6 HLR 1).

(iii)   Closing and demolition orders

Housing Act 1985

Power to make closing order

264.—(1)   Where the local housing authority are satisfied that a dwelling-house or house in multiple occupation is unfit for human habitation and that, in accordance with section 604A, taking action under this subsection is the most satisfactory course of action, they shall make a closing order with respect to the dwelling-house or house in multiple occupation.

  (2)   Where the local housing authority are satisfied that, in a building containing one or more flats, some or all of the flats are unfit for human habitation and that, in accordance with section 604A, taking action under this subsection is the most

satisfactory course of action, they shall make a closing order with respect to the whole or part of the building.

(3)   In deciding for the purposes of subsection (2)—

(a)   whether to make a closing order with respect to the whole or part of the building; or

(b)   in respect of which part of the building to make a closing order;

the authority shall have regard to such guidance as may from time to time be given by the Secretary of State under section 604A.

(4)   This section has effect subject to section 300(1) (power to purchase for temporary housing use houses liable to be demolished or closed).

Power to make demolition order

265.—(1)   Where the local housing authority are satisfied that—

(a)   a dwelling-house which is not a flat, or

(b)   a house in multiple occupation which is not a flat in multiple occupation,

is unfit for human habitation and that, in accordance with section 604A, taking action under this subsection is the most satisfactory course of action, they shall make a demolition order with respect to the dwelling-house or house concerned.

(2)   Where the local housing authority are satisfied that, in a building containing one or more flats, some or all of the flats are unfit for human habitation and that, in accordance with section 604A, taking action under this subsection is the most satisfactory course of action, they shall make a demolition order with respect to the building.

(3)   This section has effect subject to sections 300(1) (power to purchase for temporary housing use houses liable to be demolished or closed) and 304(1) (listed buildings and buildings protected by notice pending listing).

Content of demolition and closing orders

267.—(1)   A demolition order is an order requiring that the premises—

(a)   be vacated within a specified period (of at least 28 days) from the date on which the order becomes operative, and

(b)   be demolished within six weeks after the end of that period or, if it is not vacated before the end of that period, after the date on which it is vacated or, in either case, within such longer period as in the circumstances the local housing authority consider it reasonable to specify.

(2)   A closing order is an order prohibiting the use of the premises to which it relates for any purpose not approved by the local housing authority.

(3)   The approval of the local housing authority shall not be unreasonably withheld, and a person aggrieved by the withholding of such approval by the authority may, within 21 days of the refusal, appeal to the county court.

Much of the above is self-explanatory – in certain cases the only 'reasonable' solution may be for the authority to issue an order for the premises to be closed, or even demolished. The Code of Guidance (paras 19–21) emphasises the physical condition of the premises; the costs of demolition/closure relative to other certain costs; local needs for buildings of the particular type; the general effect on the area and (regarding demolition) the prospective use of the cleared site. Appeals are, again, available within a 21-day period from the service of the notice (ss. 268 and 269). Once the date set by the authority for surrendering possession has passed, vacant possession can be obtained in the county court, irrespective of any security of tenure existing under the Rent Act 1977 or the Housing Act 1988 (s. 270). Sections 271 and 272 grant powers to authorities to demolish premises in default of action by their owners, and to recover their expenses.

Notes
1. Assuming that an authority strictly adhere to ministerial guidance on the issue of unfitness and the action(s) adopted for dealing with it (or at least appear to!) then much of their decision-making now appears 'judge proof'. However, judicial review remains available in principle as much to tenants as to landlords. If an authority, for example, take irrelevant factors into account their decision may be challengeable see (*R* v *Forest of Dean District Council, ex parte Trigg* (1989) 22 HLR 167). Although the case mainly turned on 'reasonable expense' issues under the 'old' s. 604 (below), there was also vulnerability because of irrelevant considerations, in this particular case the extent to which the poor drainage system in the property could affect nearby rivers (p. 173).
2. Under the 'old' law (i.e. prior to the amendments introduced by the Local Government and Housing Act 1989), once the local authority were satisfied that premises were unfit, they had then to decide whether the premises could be made fit at 'reasonable expense'. If repair at reasonable expense was possible, the process culminating in repair and rehabitation was applicable. If not, procedures leading towards closure or demolition had to be instituted. Given that the 'reasonable expense' criterion was crucial to the way unfit housing was dealt with it generated a significant amount of litigation (see, for example, *Hillbank Properties Ltd* v *Hackney LBC* [1982] 3 HLR 73). However, the provision has now been removed.
3. Procedures for dealing with statutorily unfit properties may not always operate in the best interests of tenants. The end result may be to leave a freehold owner with vacant possession or a cleared site. The tenants may qualify for rehousing by the local authority (either as homeless persons under (now) Pt VIII of the Housing Act 1996, or under the provisions of s. 39 of the Land Compensation Act 1973 – below), but they may still be compelled to spend significant periods in substandard or temporary accommodation.

Land Compensation Act 1973

Duty to rehouse residential occupiers
39.—(1) Where a person is displaced from residential accommodation on any land in consequence of—
    (a) the acquisition of the land by an authority possessing compulsory purchase powers;
    (b) the making . . . or acceptance of a housing order . . . or undertaking in respect of a house or building on the land;
    (c) where the land has been previously acquired by an authority possessing compulsory purchase powers or appropriated by a local authority and is for the time

being held by the authority for the purposes for which it was acquired or appropriated, the carrying out of any improvement to a house or building on the land or of redevelopment on the land; . . .
and suitable alternative accommodation on reasonable terms is not otherwise available to that person, then, subject to the provisions of this section, it shall be the duty of the relevant authority to secure that he will be provided with such other accommodation.

In the context of 'unfitness' this requires authorities making demolition or closing orders (plus area clearance orders) to rehouse persons displaced by them. The greatest restriction on the s. 39 obligation is that it confers no right on persons displaced to take priority over others on the housing waiting list, so that they may be condemned for a significant period to a series of short-term/temporary occupancies (see, for example, *R v Bristol Corporation, ex parte Hendy* [1974] 1 All ER 1047 and *R v East Hertfordshire DC, ex parte Smith* (1990) 23 HLR 26).
4.   In 1993, the DoE published *Monitoring the New Housing Fitness Standard*, incorporating research undertaken by the University of Warwick concerning local authority use of unfitness powers. It was found that 65 per cent of local authority inspections arose from grant enquiries, and only 19 per cent from occupiers' complaints. As regards action over 'unfit' properties, in 54 per cent of cases the initial recommendation was for a renovation grant, with repair notices being served in 23 per cent of cases and demolition or closure orders in 3 per cent. Overall, it was concluded that there was reasonable uniformity in practice between authorities, but that there was a need for further clarification in relation to structural stability, dampness, lighting, heating and ventilation.

Questions
1.   Is there any inconsistency between cases like *Summers v Salford* and the guidance in Annex A of Circular 6/90 on the issue of 'disrepair' and 'unfitness'?
2.   *Summers* and similar cases were mainly concerned with the implied term of unfitness (now s. 8, Landlord and Tenant Act 1985). The 'core' of this term is that a landlord covenants to keep premises 'reasonably fit for human habitation'. Is that exactly the same issue as in s. 604 of the Housing Act 1985?
3.   How would you advise a tenant of apparently unfit premises in relation to potential local authority involvement?

(iii)   Health and housing
Part III of the Environmental Protection Act 1990 (replacing Pt III of the Public Health Act 1936) contains a number of measures aimed at the identification and control of properties which may constitute health or other 'environmental' risks.

Environmental Protection Act 1990

PART III

STATUTORY NUISANCES AND CLEAN AIR

Statutory nuisances: England and Wales

Statutory nuisances and inspections therefor

79.—(1) [Subject to subsections (2) to (6A) below], the following matters constitute 'statutory nuisances' for the purposes of this Part, that is to say—

(a) any premises in such a state as to be prejudicial to health or a nuisance;

(b) smoke emitted from premises so as to be prejudicial to health or a nuisance;

(c) fumes or gases emitted from premises so as to be prejudicial to health or a nuisance;

(d) any dust, steam, smell or other effluvia arising on industrial, trade or business premises and being prejudicial to health or a nuisance;

(e) any accumulation or deposit which is prejudicial to health or a nuisance;

(f) any animal kept in such a place or manner as to be prejudicial to health or a nuisance;

(g) noise emitted from premises so as to be prejudicial to health or a nuisance;

[(ga) noise that is prejudicial to health or a nuisance and is emitted from or caused by a vehicle, machinery or equipment in a street;]

(h) any other matter declared by any enactment to be a statutory nuisance; and it shall be the duty of every local authority to cause its area to be inspected from time to time to detect any statutory nuisances which ought to be dealt with under section 80 below [or sections 80 and 80A below] and, where a complaint of a statutory nuisance is made to it by a person living within its area, to take such steps as are reasonably practicable to investigate the complaint.

. . .

(7) In this part—

'prejudicial to health' means injurious, or likely to cause injury, to health;

'premises' includes land and, subject to subsection (12) [and section 81A(9)] below any vessel;

. . .

Summary proceedings for statutory nuisances

80.—(1) Where a local authority is satisfied that a statutory nuisance exists, or is likely to occur or recur, in the area of the authority, the local authority shall serve a notice ('an abatement notice') imposing all or any of the following requirements—

(a) requiring the abatement of the nuisance or prohibiting or restricting its occurrence or recurrence;

(b) requiring the execution of such works, and the taking of such other steps, as may be necessary for any of those purposes, and the notice shall specify the time or times within which the requirements of the notice are to be complied with.

(2) [Subject to section 80A(1) below, the abatement notice] shall be served—

(a) except in a case falling within paragraph (b) or (c) below, on the person responsible for the nuisance;

(b) where the nuisance arises from any defect of a structural character, on the owner of the premises;

(c) where the person responsible for the nuisance cannot be found or the nuisance has not yet occurred, on the owner or occupier of the premises.

(3) [A person served with an abatement notice] may appeal against the notice to a magistrates' court within the period of twenty-one days beginning with the date on which he was served the notice.

(4) If a person on whom an abatement notice is served, without reasonable excuse, contravenes or fails to comply with any requirement or prohibition imposed by the notice, he shall be guilty of an offence.

(5) Except in a case falling within subsection (6) below, a person who commits an offence under subsection (4) above shall be liable on summary conviction to a fine not exceeding level 5 on the standard scale together with a further fine of an amount equal to one-tenth of that level for each day on which the offence continues after the conviction.

. . .

Supplementary provisions

81.—(1) [Subject to subsection (1A) below, where] more than one person is responsible for a statutory nuisance section 80 above shall apply to each of those persons whether or not what any one of them is responsible for would by itself amount to a nuisance.

[(1A) In relation to a statutory nuisance within section 79(1)(ga) above for which more than one person is responsible (whether or nor what any one of those persons is responsible for would by itself amount to such a nuisance), section 80(2)(a) above shall apply with the substitution of 'any one of the persons' for 'the person'.

. . .

(3) Where an abatement notice has not been complied with the local authority may, whether or not they take proceedings for an offence under section 80(4) above, abate the nuisance and do whatever may be necessary in execution of the notice.

(4) Any expenses reasonably incurred by a local authority in abating, or preventing the recurrence of, a statutory nuisance under subsection (3) above may be recovered by them from the person by whose act or default the nuisance was caused and, if that person is the owner of the premises, from any person who is for the time being the owner thereof; and the court may apportion the expenses between persons by whose acts or defaults the nuisance is caused in such manner as the court consider fair and reasonable.

(5) If a local authority is of opinion that proceedings for an offence under section 80(4) above would afford an inadequate remedy in the case of any statutory nuisance, they may, subject to subsection (6) below, take proceedings in the High Court for the purpose of securing the abatement, prohibition or restriction of the nuisance, and the proceedings shall be maintainable notwithstanding the local authority have suffered no damage from the nuisance.

. . .

Although 'unfitness' powers are, indirectly, to do with the health of individuals they are primarily concerned with housing standards. The Environmental Protection Act 1990, like its predecessor, is centrally concerned with the health of individuals (although of course this, in its time, may involve controls over poor housing which threatens health). Under s. 79, councils must periodically inspect their area in respect of (defined) 'statutory nuisances'. What, then, is a 'statutory nuisance'?

(a)   Statutory nuisance

The 'core' of the definition lies in s. 79(1)(a) of the 1990 Act, which states that a statutory nuisance exists when premises are 'prejudicial to health or a nuisance', 'prejudicial to health' being further defined in s. 79(7) as meaning 'injurious, or likely to cause injury, to health'. Judicial comment on these definitions, which have a long 'pedigree', is extensive. For example:

Dover District Council v Farrar
(1980) 2 HLR 32

In 1973 and 1974 the local authority constructed an estate called Friars Way Estate, consisting of 196 dwellings, of which 54 were flats. All of the houses had building regulation approval, and the standard of insulation was slightly higher than that prescribed in the regulations. Fifty-one of the houses had a gas warm air system installed, but the remaining 91 houses had an electric warm air fan-assisted heating system installed. The electric system was designed to provide adequate background heat downstairs, and to maintain the structure of the house at a satisfactory temperature. By the third winter after construction, however, the houses in which the electric system had been installed were suffering from dampness so as to be prejudicial to health. In four cases, there was some penetrating damp, but in all cases, including these four, the most serious damp was that caused by condensation. Six tenants issued proceedings against the authority under s. 99 of the Public Health Act 1936, by way of test cases. It was found that the tenants had not understood that the heating provided was intended as background heating only, and that it had been intended that supplementary systems should be used. It was further found that the electric system could not be used within their means, whether alone or when considered in conjunction with supplementary systems. If heated properly, the houses would not have suffered sufficient dampness to amount to prejudice to health. The magistrates nonetheless made a nuisance order, requiring conversion of the systems to gas, from which order the authority appealed by way of case stated.

Held by the Divisional Court (allowing the appeal): the construction of the houses and the method of heating supplied were perfectly proper and adequate and would have maintained the houses in a state which would not have been prejudicial to the health of the occupants, had the systems been used. The statutory nuisance accordingly arose because of the act or default of the tenants, even though their refusal to use the systems on account of expense was wholly understandable. The terms of the order underlined the proposition that the authority had not caused a statutory nuisance, as it could not be right to make an order which depended on the relative costs of electricity and gas at any one time.

ORMROD LJ: . . . The complainants in the Court below, the respondents here, proved, and indeed by the end of the day the appellant Council accepted, that the degree of condensation was sufficient on its own to be prejudicial to health in some of the houses. The only question therefore was the cause of the condensation and whether or not the Council as the landlord were in default in any way.

The Justices, in this admirably drafted case, set out interestingly a description of how condensation arises and what intensifies it, and they point out that it all depends on the amount of water vapour in the air. If the house is used in a certain way, the amount of water vapour in the house is likely to increase. For example using calor gas or paraffin creates substantial water vapour because the installation contains an external flue. Electrical heat does not produce any water vapour. That is a very important fact so far as this case is concerned.

Then the Justices go on to say:

During the first three years of their occupation all of the Respondents had used the electricaire system of heating less and less and had used other vapour producing methods of heating to various degrees to heat their houses.

They accepted their evidence as to that. Then they say:

We considered the Respondents to be reasonable sensible people who have taken the same course that a great many others would take if placed in the same circumstances and we find that they have not behaved unreasonably.

The Justices then found that the reason why these alternative methods of heating were adopted was because the tenants did not understand the electricaire system was for background heat only, and that they should use additional electrical heating both upstairs and downstairs. Alternatively, if they were going to use any other kind of heating, they would have to open the windows a good deal more. The tenants also found the system inadequate and that the cost was beyond their means from early in their occupation. So they preferred to heat their houses by means which they found provided the heat at the price they could afford.

One other important finding is in paragraph 21:

The electricaire system was not capable of use within their means, because they found it too costly in itself, and in addition they were expected to supply such supplementary heat as was needed, exclusively by additional electrical means.

The next finding to my mind is of great importance:

If the houses had been heated in this way regardless of cost they would not have been damp to the extent of being prejudicial to health. The construction of the houses is such that cheaper forms of heating of the tenant's choice can only be used at the cost of opening windows to such a degree as involves loss of heat and discomfort from draught.

I pause there. That finding makes it perfectly clear, and beyond any possibility of controversy, that the construction of the houses, and the method of heating supplied by the appellant Council, were perfectly proper and perfectly adequate and would have maintained these houses in a state in which there was no question of their being prejudicial to health, provided that the system supplied was used by the tenant. The only reason it was not used by the tenant, a reason one can very well understand, is that they found it too expensive. So putting it in its simplest terms, the cause of this so called statutory nuisance was the unwillingness of the tenants themselves to spend the amount of money that was required to provide themselves with adequate heating with the system provided in the first place by the appellant Council.

So we are dealing here with a case in which the cause of the condensation and hence of the dampness, hence of the mould and hence of the prejudice to health is the unwillingness, possibly inability, of the complainants themselves to afford the costs of the heating. That may be a very cogent criticism of the design adopted in these houses or of the method by which it was decided to build them. But to try to bring this under the umbrella of section 92 of the Public Health Act 1936 as 'statutory nuisance' is to extend that section, in my judgment, far too far. Obviously it was never intended to apply to a situation such as this.

On the other hand, in the next case liability for condensation under the Public Health Act 1936 was found to exist.

Greater London Council v *London Borough of Tower Hamlets* (1983) 15 HLR 54

GRIFFITHS LJ: . . . This is an appeal by way of case stated by the Greater London Council from a finding of the magistrates sitting at the Thames Magistrates' Court, on 15 September 1982, that they had been guilty of a statutory nuisance, pursuant to section 93 of the Public Health Act, 1936 and that consequently, pursuant to the provisions of that statute, they were required to abate the nuisance.

The proceedings arose out of the conditions in a flat at premises known as Withy House, in the East End of London, owned by the Greater London Council since March 1962. The findings of the magistrates were as follows. They found that the Greater London Council owned No. 1, Withy House and that an abatement notice had been served on them on 20 January 1982. They found that it had not been complied with. The nature of that abatement notice required the Greater London Council to remedy the cause of dampness in the walls of the kitchen, the floor and walls of the living room, the walls of bedroom No. 3, the walls of bedroom No. 1, the ceiling of bedroom No. 2 and the walls in the passageway.

The magistrates found, on the evidence presented before them, that there were signs of dampness on the kitchen wall adjacent to the lift shaft area and that water was running down the kitchen walls and along the lino. They also found that this was due to dampness from condensation, there being no adequate ventilation in the kitchen. There was mould growing on the walls. They found that in the living room there were signs of dampness and moisture under the carpets. In bedroom No. 1, there were traces of mould growth on the walls, and dampness. In bedroom No. 2, there was dampness and flaking paint on the ceiling. In bedroom No. 3, there was dampness and mould growth. In the passageway there were signs of dampness. Finally, they found that the dampness was caused by lack of proper ventilation and of insulation and by lack of heating, no adequate heating having been provided by the Greater London Council. They went on to say:

We found that a statutory nuisance existed in that the Greater London Council as owner of the premises, was the person by whose default the said nuisance continued.

They referred to the fact that the facts were found on the basis of the evidence that they heard in court and that the defence referred them to the unreported case of *Dover District Council* v *John Ernest Farrar and Others* which was heard in 1980. They said that they distinguished the *Dover District Council* case from the present case on the facts.

The first question on which the opinion of the High Court is sought is as follows:

(1) Whether upon the evidence before the bench of magistrates a reasonable bench could find a case proved that the premises were in such a state as to be prejudicial to health or a nuisance.

I can deal shortly with that point. The evidence of those who saw this flat late in winter revealed it to be in a shocking condition with dampness in many places, as evidenced by the magistrates' findings of fact. The Greater London Council, for reasons I find difficult to understand – although the abatement notice was served on them in January – did not have an inspection of those premises until the following June. Naturally, the conditions were very different to the conditions seen during the winter. There can be no doubt that there was ample evidence before the magistrates to entitle them to come to the conclusion that the condition of that flat was prejudicial to the health of those living within it.

It is to be observed that under section 92 of the Public Health Act, subsection (1) contains a definition of a statutory nuisance. Subsection 1(a) says:

Any premises in such a state as to be prejudicial to health.

I would answer the first question raised in this case by saying that there was evidence upon which the magistrates were entitled to find that these premises were in such a state as to be prejudicial to health and were, consequently, a statutory nuisance within the meaning of the Public Health Act.

The second question raised by the magistrates was this:

Whether upon the evidence before the Bench of Magistrates a reasonable bench could find a case proved that the Greater London Council was the person by whose default the said alleged nuisance continued.

The submission made by the Greater London Council is that the only evidence of an expert nature that was called before the magistrates, which dealt with the causes of the dampness, was the evidence of two surveyors who were called by them. The prosecutors in the case were the London Borough of Tower Hamlets. They relied upon the evidence of a Mr Seal, who is an environmental health officer and who may well be qualified to speak on the threats to health from housing conditions. However, it was submitted that he is not an expert on the causes of dampness. The other witness was the lady who had the misfortune to live in this flat.

When one looks at the evidence, there is really very little dispute between the evidence of the experts and that given by Mr Seal. It is common ground that the cause of dampness in that flat was condensation. It is not suggested that the dampness came from any other source such as, penetration, rising damp, etc. We are dealing with a condensation problem. The submission of the Greater London Council is that the sole cause of the condensation problem in the flat was due to the tenant failing to use sufficient artificial sources of heating during the winter months.

To a large extent, this submission has been founded upon the decision of this court in *Dover District Council* v *Farrar and Others* [(1980) 2 HLR 32], to which I will refer later. First, it is necessary to say a few words about the construction of the flat. We have been told that this was a building commonly described as a system-built building. It is a fairly familiar kind of construction. The ground floor of the building is at a raised level. The flat with which we are concerned is a corner flat on the ground floor. The result of the construction is that three of the sides of the flat are open to the air and the whole of the underneath of the flat is open to the air. By reason of this construction, one will see immediately that an exceptionally large part of the flat is exposed to the elements. When the flat was originally built, it was built with an open solid fuel fire in the living room. The report of one of the Greater London Council's experts attributes the extraordinary condensation problem encountered in this flat, to a large degree, to the decision to remove that open fire place, to block up the flues and to replace the fire place with an electric heater. We have been told in the course of this case that the decision to make this modification to the flat was occasioned by the discovery that the flues were defective. According to the expert, the result was that one lost the advantage of a fire being made up that would have kept heat in for most of the day. One also lost the advantage of the very considerable ventilation effect of such a fire. According to the expert, this would have assisted in combating condensation. That was a modification in design made by the landlord in a flat which, by virtue of the exposure of the whole of the bottom to the elements, was peculiarly susceptible to the cooling down of the walls, thereby creating condensation. Apparently, the Greater London Council put in one storage heater. According to the evidence of one of the experts they called, he did not think the provision of one storage heater would be sufficient to combat the condensation that might be anticipated in a flat of this construction, after such a modification had been made. However, according to the evidence of the tenant – and this was not challenged – at some time, the Greater London Council came in and removed even that one storage heater.

Of course, the experts were at this greater disadvantage. They never saw the flat in winter. They did not see how wet it was. They could see it had been wet because of all the signs – for example, the wallpaper peeling off and the existence of the mould. They did not have a chance to see the conditions in winter and they did not have a chance to appreciate the degree of heating that the tenant was using during the winter. They clearly formed the view that it must have been wholly inadequate heating. The evidence of the daughter of the tenant, who actually lived there, was quite to the contrary. Her evidence was that they used a great deal of heating in the flat. She said that they had the heating on all the time. She even described the use of three oil fires and an electric fire. During the first winter, the fires were on all the time and during the next winter, they were on all day but they were turned off at night. In cross-examination, she said that they had radiators in each bedroom. They had large oil-filled electric radiators and there were three there all the time. They also had an electric fire in addition to that. However, despite all this, in the time that they had been living there, they had had to have the kitchen and two bedrooms decorated four times and the bathroom decorated three or four times. They also had to live with soaking wet carpets.

The case of *Dover District Council* v *Farrar and Others* [(1980) 2 HLR 32], to which I now return, upon which the Greater London Council rely, was founded on very different facts. The facts in that case were that a number of houses had been built with a purpose-built electrical system installed for heating them. There was no dispute that if the system was used, the houses would not suffer condensation, and they would be habitable without any prejudice to health at all. As Ormrod LJ specifically found, the method of heating supplied by the Council was perfectly proper and perfectly adequate to maintain the houses in such a state that there would be no prejudice to health.

It is a very different state of affairs in this case. Initially, the heating system which had been installed, which, according to the Greater London Council's expert, would have been effective in combating condensation, had been removed. The flues had been blocked in. The ventilation provided had been withdrawn and in its place there

had at first been installed one night storage heater, which the expert said would have been inadequate. That was then removed. There is all the difference in the world between the *Dover* case and this case. In the *Dover* case, the court went on to hold that the cause of the condensation was a failure by the tenant to use the heating system which had been provided. They found it expensive so they chose not to use it and they used some less expensive method of heating, which did not combat the condensation which then arose. It would not have arisen had they used the heating installed for that design of house. It is understandable, in those circumstances, that the court felt that there was no evidence on which the magistrates could have found that the condensation was attributable to any fault on the part of the landlord.
. . .

To return to the case, I, for my part think that there was evidence upon which this bench of magistrates could find that it was the fault of the Greater London Council that the statutory nuisance was continuing.

(Further extensive comment can be found on the same point in *Birmingham District Council* v *Kelly* (1985) 17 HLR 572.)

So the effect on health of dampness and condensation is clearly accepted by the courts. There seems little doubt that seriously damp premises, or premises subject to intractable condensation, will normally constitute 'prejudice' to health even where the structure of the premises is unaffected. More difficult is the distribution of responsibility where the dampness/condensation results from the heating and ventilation (or lack of it) in the premises. The principle to be derived from the above cases seems to be that if the heating/ventilation system is unsuitable or inadequate and dampness and/or condensation is the consequence, the landlord *is* liable. However, if the system supplied is adequate (if used as envisaged) then even if it is very expensive to operate in this way the landlord will not be liable if the dampness or condensation results from the tenant's failure to operate the system properly.

In other cases it has been held that defective wiring in premises may be 'prejudicial to health' (*Bennett* v *Preston District Council* unreported, 1983 though see *Roof*, March/April 1984 p. 18), and that traffic noise penetrating a property made it 'prejudicial to health' (*Southwark LBC* v *Ince and Williams* (1989) 21 HLR 504). Of course, it must be borne in mind that a statutory nuisance arises only if the state of the premises as a whole is such as to be prejudicial to health or a nuisance. This may arise from a single item of serious disrepair (for example, a collapsed roof and ceiling), or from the accumulation of more minor defects. However, it is the overall effect that counts, so that even where there is disrepair the nuisance results not from the need for repair but because the defect threatens health (in the above case in allowing the 'elements' to penetrate).

The concept of 'health' obviously includes physical health, but equally obviously does *not* include (mere) interference with the tenant's comfort (*Springett* v *Harold* [1954] 1 WLR 521). Logic would indicate that mental health should be as relevant as physical health, particularly given the obvious (and medically recognised) stress associated with living in poor housing. The case law, is, however, equivocal.

Coventry City Council v Cartwright
[1975] 2 All ER 99

A local authority owned a vacant and unfenced plot of land. The authority allowed indiscriminate tipping to take place on the land. Items deposited there included large quantities of building materials, brick ends, tarmacadam, old reinforcements, earth, scrap iron, broken glass, tin cans and household refuse. The authority removed the household refuse periodically but took no action to remove the other materials dumped. A complaint was made against the authority that the accumulation of materials constituted a 'statutory nuisance' within a s. 92(1)(c) of the Public Health Act 1936 in that it was 'prejudicial to health or a nuisance'. The justices found the complaint proved, holding that the accumulation was prejudicial to health because people who went on to the land, particularly children, might hurt themselves on things which had been tipped there, such as broken glass or tin cans, and further that the pile of rubbish constituted a nuisance because of its visual impact on people living in neighbouring houses. The authority appealed.

Held by the Divisional Court (in allowing the appeal): the section was aimed at an accumulation of something which produced a threat to health in the sense of a threat of disease, vermin or the like. It followed that an accumulation could not constitute a 'nuisance' within the section merely because of its visual impact; neither could an accumulation of inert matter be 'prejudicial to public health' within the section merely because the inert matter might cause injury to persons who came on to the land.

LORD WIDGERY CJ: . . . It seems to me that the only way in which we can properly approach this case is on the basis that the justices are concerned only with the inert material and presumably that they are satisfied that the household refuse, which was dumped from time to time and then removed, plays no part in the case. I certainly approach this on the footing that it is an accumulation of inert material which is the basis of the complaint.

I have read s. 92(1)(c). It is necessary to read with it the definition of 'prejudicial to health', which is to be found in s. 343 of the same Act. The expression means 'injurious or likely to cause injury, to health'. The justices, with that law behind them and their own findings of fact, concluded that the case had been made out that there was a statutory nuisance under s. 92(1), and they put it on two clear bases.

The first was that in their opinion the tipping of materials such as are referred to in this case was dangerous to health and limb and constituted a particular hazard, especially where children were concerned who had easy access to the site. In other words, they find a threat to health from these facts on the footing that people who went to the site, and particularly if children went on to the site, might hurt themselves by reason of the physical properties present – broken glass, old tin cans and whatever it may be.

The second ground on which they found that a nuisance had been sustained was that they had regard to the visual impact of this pile of rubbish on the site, a pile of rubbish which was within view of a number of occupied houses. They found as an alternative to their first ground that the visual impact could constitute a nuisance within the meaning of s. 92(1)(c).

Counsel for the respondent, I think wisely, accepts that in this case very little turns on the reference to nuisance in this section. He says, and I agree with him, that the real question here is whether that which the justices found to exist was an accumulation prejudicial to health, and on that approach to the matter he says that the possibility of physical injury from cuts and the like is sufficient to justify the assertion that this deposit or accumulation was prejudicial to health.

For my part, I think that that is taking too wide a view of the section. The words are obviously very wide, and one should hesitate, in construing the section in proceedings such as the present, to lay down boundaries which may in another case prove to be unsuitable. But I think that the underlying conception of the section is that that which is struck at is an accumulation of something which produces a threat to health in the sense of a threat of disease, vermin or the like.

It is clear from the case that offensive 'visual impact' is not sufficient, but is the emphasis in Lord Widgery's judgment on physical injury intended to exclude arguments based on psychological injury or even distress? This seems doubtful, particularly given his comment later in the judgment (referring to *Gales* v *Morrissey* [1955] 1 WLR 110) that 'a noisy animal could be as much prejudicial to health as a smelly animal'. The better view is probably that psychological 'injury' *is* within the protection of the law.

The other 'limb' of s. 79(1)(a) is that even if not 'prejudicial to health' premises constitute a 'nuisance'. It seems that this means something more technical than mere irritation or annoyance, and that, in effect, the act(s) complained of must be either a public or a private nuisance in the technical sense. Broadly this means that either a significant and harmful interference with the rights of the public at large is being caused (public nuisance), or a substantial interference with a neighbour's use and enjoyment of his or her property is being caused (private nuisance). Older authorities had sometimes taken the view that 'nuisance' in this context could include (mere) 'interference with the personal comfort of the occupiers' (Viscount Caldecote LJ in *Betts* v *Penge UDC* [1942] 2 KB 154, at 159), but doubt was cast on this by the House of Lords in *Salford City Council* v *McNally* [1976] AC 379; and conclusively, in *National Coal Board* v *Thorne* (below) the narrower and more technical interpretation of nuisance was seen to be the correct one.

National Coal Board v *Thorne*
[1976] 1 WLR 543

WATKINS J: . . . The National Coal Board, the 'board', own premises known as 38, Roman Road, in the village of Banwen in South Wales. That village, for local government purposes, lies within the jurisdiction of the Neath Borough Council, the local authority. The local authority have the duty under section 91 of the Public Health Act 1936 to inspect from time to time property within their area for the detection of matters requiring to be dealt with under the provisions of Part III of the Act as statutory nuisances.

At some time or other an officer of the local authority inspected 38, Roman Road, Banwen, and found the place to be in a state of disrepair in that there were two defective windows, there was no stop end for a rain water gutter, and there was a defective skirting board. Those were matters reported to the local authority. They determined that a nuisance was present in the premises and, using the power which they have under section 93 of the Act, they served upon the board a notice to abate the nuisance, a notice which one supposes set out in terms the precise things which the board had to do in order to bring about an effective abatement. The board did nothing to abate the so-called nuisance so an information was laid before the local justices. A hearing followed, the result of which was that on April 4, 1975, the justices found that an abatement notice had been served on the board on January 9, 1975, by recorded delivery and the requirements of the abatement notice had not been complied with by the board. So they decided that, having regard to those findings and the state of the law as they understood it to be, they had no alternative but to issue a nuisance order. The effect of issuing a nuisance order is to compel the person upon whom it is served to comply with its terms under penalty. The penalty is laid down in the Act; it amounts to the maximum sum of £50.

Before however, the board could be expected to carry out the terms of the nuisance order, they appealed. The appeal comes to this court by way of case stated.

The justices had addressed to them argument affecting the meaning to be attached to the word 'nuisance' as it appears in section 92(1) of the Act. Nothing was said at that hearing suggestive of the fact that there had been any injury or anticipated injury to the health of persons residing either in the premises or in any premises adjoining them. The information itself was laid simply upon the basis that there was a nuisance present at the material time at the premises.

This short point, therefore, arising in this appeal is what is the meaning to be attached to the word 'nuisance'. *Betts v Penge Urban District Council* [1942] 2 KB 154 has been referred to. What happened in that case was that the landlord of a flat, of which the rent was in arrears, made no application for possession but removed the front door and some of the window sashes thereby interfering with the personal comfort of the occupier. It was held that there was a distinction between public and private nuisance which was material to the question whether a statutory nuisance under section 92(1) of the Public Health Act 1936 existed on the premises, and that it was sufficient in order to sustain a conviction of the appellant for permitting a statutory nuisance on the premises to prove that by his act or default they were in such a state as to interfere with the personal comfort of the occupiers, without necessarily being injurious to health. If the law is accurately stated in that case, then the justices in the present case, it seems to me, cannot be criticised for issuing a nuisance order, since I see no basis for assuming that they came to conclusions of fact which were not properly founded upon the evidence which came before them, and upon their findings of fact they were entitled, assuming the law is correctly stated in *Betts'* case, to proceed to make the nuisance order.

In his very able argument Mr Roch appearing for the board says that the word 'nuisance' cannot have and should not be understood to have the meaning attached to it by *Betts'* case, and that the word 'nuisance' as used in section 92(1) must be understood to equate with the same word as that is understood at common law in relation to nuisances, public or private. A public nuisance at common law has been expressed to be an act or omission which materially affects the material comfort and quality of life of a class of Her Majesty's subjects. A private nuisance has often been defined in this way: private nuisances, at least in the vast majority of cases, are interferences for a substantial length of time by owners or occupiers of property with the use or enjoyment of neighbouring property. The distinction which immediately springs to mind therefore between a private nuisance at common law and a nuisance of the kind as found by the justices in the present case is that the justices, feeling compelled to follow the decision in *Betts'* case, found that a nuisance could exist in a dwelling-house in relation to the occupier of it, whereas that notion is obviously alien to the concept of a common law private nuisance.

When the justices reached their conclusion in April 1975 *Salford City Council* v *McNally* [1975] 3 WLR 87 had not been decided. Accordingly, they had not the advantage of knowing what I now propose to quote from the speeches made in that case. Lord Wilberforce said, at p. 91:

> In dealing with each Act it is better to use its own terminology. A similar confusion occurs in some of the cases through the use of the words 'personal comfort'. These words are appropriate enough in the context of what is a 'nuisance' for the purposes of the Public Health Act (see as to this the clear judgment of Stephen J in *Bishop Auckland Local Board* v *Bishop Auckland Iron and Steel Co. Ltd* (1882) 10 QBD 138), but they are quite inappropriate in relation to the other limb 'prejudicial to health.' Health is not the same as comfort and interference with the latter does not bring a case within the 'health' limb of the Public Health Act. In my opinion *Betts* v *Penge Urban District Council* [1942] 2 KB 154 is guilty of this confusion and was wrongly decided. It was simply a case of what is now called 'harassment' and not, in my view, under the Act at all. I express no opinion upon *Coventry City Council* v *Cartwright* [1975] 1 WLR 845, which was reported after argument had been closed in the present case.

Lord Simon of Glaisdale expressly agreed with Lord Wilberforce. Lord Edmund-Davies, at p. 95 said of *Betts'* case:

> Be that as it may, no. 20 Johnson Street being at the material time undoubtedly a 'statutory nuisance', i.e. injurious to the health of the occupier, this House is not presently called upon to determine the correctness of the decision in *Betts* v *Penge Urban District Council* [1942] 2 KB 154 that, in order to sustain a conviction for permitting a statutory nuisance, it is sufficient to prove that premises were in such a state as to interfere with the *personal comfort* of the occupiers, without being injurious to their health, though for my part I think it desirable to make clear that I respectfully think it was wrongly decided.

Lord Cross of Chelsea and Lord Fraser of Tullybelton agreed with Lord Edmund-Davies.

Mr Fletcher, in common with Mr Roch, submits that the effect of these speeches is such as to cause this court to pronounce that in its opinion *Betts'* case was in fact wrongly decided and does not represent the true law upon the crucial matter of the meaning of the word 'nuisance' in section 92(1) of the Public Health Act 1936. I welcome the opportunity of saying that what Lord Wilberforce said in the *Salford* case leads me to the conclusion that *Betts* unquestionably does not express the proper law upon this question. Speaking for myself, I would adopt the words of Lord Wilberforce so as to state that a nuisance cannot arise if what has taken place affects only the person or persons occupying the premises where the nuisance is said to have taken place. A nuisance coming within the meaning of the Public Health Act 1936 must be either a private or public nuisance as understood by common law.

For that reason, it seems to me that the proper course is to direct that the order of the justices should be quashed.

This interpretation has been further supported by subsequent authority, for example *Southwark LBC* v *Ince* (1989) 21 HLR 504.

(b)   The procedure for taking action in respect of a statutory nuisance

The main emphasis of the law is 'public', typically through Environmental Health Departments. Section 80 of the 1990 Act states that where an authority are satisfied that a statutory nuisance exists, or is likely to occur or recur, they must serve an abatement notice requiring the nuisance's abatement, or prohibiting or restricting its occurrence or recurrence, and may require the execution of works or taking of steps for such purposes, specifying the time within which compliance is required. The abatement notice is to be served on the person responsible for the nuisance or on the owner, where the nuisance arises from structural defects, or the responsible person cannot be found (ss. 80(2)(b) and (c)). Failure to comply with a notice, without reasonable excuse, is an offence (s. 80(4)). An abatement notice must specify the work(s) to be done. A person served with an abatement notice has 21 days to appeal to the magistrates' court (see further the Statutory Nuisance (Appeals) Regulations 1990, SI 1990 No. 2276). An alternative to all the above is that an authority can take direct proceedings in the High Court to obtain an order against the perpetrator of the nuisance, prohibiting it or requiring its abatement or restriction (s. 81(5)).

Although the majority of statutory nuisances are dealt with by authorities, private action is possible via s. 82 of the 1990 Act.

Environmental Protection Act 1990

Summary proceedings by person aggrieved by statutory nuisances
82.—(1)   A magistrates' court may act under this section on a complaint made by any person on the ground that he is aggrieved by the existence of a statutory nuisance.

(2)   If the magistrates' court is satisfied that the alleged nuisance exists, or that although abated it is likely to recur on the same premises [or, in the case of a nuisance within section 79(1)(ga) above, in the same street], the court shall make an order for either or both of the following purposes—

(a)   requiring the defendant to abate the nuisance, within a time specified in the order, and to execute any works necessary for that purpose;

(b)   prohibiting a recurrence of the nuisance, and requiring the defendant, within a time specified in the order, to execute any works necessary to prevent the recurrence,
and may also impose on the defendant a fine not exceeding level 5 on the standard scale.

. . .

(6)   Before instituting proceedings for an order under subsection (2) above against any person, the person aggrieved by the nuisance shall give to that person such notice in writing of his intention to bring the proceedings as is applicable to proceedings in respect of a nuisance of that description and the notice shall specify the matter complained of.

(7)   The notice of the bringing of proceedings in respect of a statutory nuisance required by subsection (6) above which is applicable is—

(a)   in the case of a nuisance falling within paragraph (g) [or (ga)] of section 79(1) above, not less than three days' notice; and

(b) in the case of a nuisance of any other description, not less than twenty-one days' notice;
but the Secretary of State may, by order, provide that this subsection shall have effect as if such period as is specified in the order were the minimum period of notice applicable to any description of statutory nuisance specified in the order.

(8) A person who, without reasonable excuse, contravenes any requirement or prohibition imposed by an order under subsection (2) above shall be guilty of an offence and liable on summary conviction to a fine not exceeding level 5 on the standard scale together with a further fine of an amount equal to one-tenth of that level for each day on which the offence continues after the conviction.

Therefore any 'person aggrieved' (below) can complain to magistrates (subject to s. 82(6)), and if the latter are convinced that an alleged nuisance exists, or is likely to recur, they must make an order requiring the defendant to abate the nuisance and execute any necessary works. They may also fine the defendant. Similar provisions concerning liability attaching to 'responsible persons' or property owners apply here as with 'public' action (s. 82(4)).

A 'person aggrieved' includes anyone whose health has been injured by the nuisance, or anyone with a legal interest in the property which is permanently affected by the nuisance (although a tenant of one flat in a tower block cannot be 'aggrieved' in relation to the whole block *Birmingham City Council* v *McMahon* (1987) 19 HLR 452).

One crucial consequence of s. 82 (like its predecessor – s. 95 of the 1936 Act) is that a local authority tenant, via this route, can take 'direct action' against her/his local authority landlord (whereas, of course, the idea of a local authority taking action against themselves is implausible, even if possible(!) – see further below). This will be the case even if the authority are claiming to be using their discretion under housing legislation, for example a power to use otherwise unfit housing as temporary accommodation pending eventual demolition, and after compulsory purchase (see *Salford* v *McNally*). Once a court is satisfied (under s. 82(2)) that a statutory nuisance exists (or is likely to recur) it must make an order concerning abatement or execution of works (above), even though there must be significant discretion as to the *terms* of the order.

A good illustration of the above appears in the following case:

Coventry City Council v *Doyle*
[1981] 2 All ER 184

HODGSON J: . . . These three appeals arise out of litigation between council house tenants and their landlord, the Coventry City Council. Two of them, *Coventry City Council* v *Doyle* and *Coventry City Council* v *Quinn*, are appeals from decisions of the Coventry City magistrates who have stated cases; these are brought by the council. The third, *Clarke* v *Coventry City Council* is an appeal by case stated from the Crown Court at Coventry; this is brought by the tenant from the Crown Court decision to allow the council's appeal from the adjudication of the magistrates. We heard these cases together. They raise questions of some difficulty and importance.

The council owns a number of houses which are designated as temporary accom-modation to be used by homeless families or others who do not qualify for a regular tenancy. The houses in these cases were short life property, so that the council was naturally reluctant to spend its scarce resources on them. The tenants were members of the Coventry Temporary Tenants Association. Prior to 22nd February 1979 each had made numerous complaints to the council about the condition of their property. On that date all three preferred informations with the city magistrates against the council under s. 99 of the Public Health Act 1936, alleging that the houses they occupied constituted statutory nuisances within the meaning of s. 92(1)(a) of the Act, namely that they were in such a state as to be prejudicial to health.
. . .

The magistrates found in respect of each house that a statutory nuisance existed at the date of the preferring of the informations, i.e. 22nd February 1979. The Doyle family were moved out of their house on 9th April 1979, as the council had decided to extend and modernise their house; at the dates of the hearing work on the house had begun but was not completed. The Clarke family was still in occupation at the date of the hearing before the magistrates, but the Crown Court found that at that date the nuisance had been abated. The Quinn family were offered alternative accommodation a week or two before the date (19th November) fixed for the hearing; they moved to alternative accommodation on 2nd December, the day before the third and final hearing day.

In each case the tenants contended that, if they established that a statutory nuisance existed at the date the information was laid, then the magistrates would have to find that an offence under s. 94 had been committed, whether or not the nuisance had been abated at the date of the hearing. The council contended that the date on which the magistrates had to find that a nuisance existed was the date of the hearing and that, if no nuisance existed on that date, then the magistrates could not find that an offence had been committed, or make an order unless (and for the purpose of these appeals this is not relevant) there was a danger of recurrence. The only order the court could make, if the nuisance no longer existed at the date of hearing, was, contended the council, an order as to costs.
. . .

The submissions made on behalf of the tenants are succinctly set out in the case stated by the Crown Court. For the tenants it was contended that, following the decisions in *R v Newham Justices ex parte Hunt* [[1976] 1 WLR 420], *R v Oxted Justices, ex parte Franklin* [1976] 1 All ER 839 proceedings brought under s. 99 of the 1936 Act were criminal proceedings. Hence, in this case, proceedings were commenced by the laying of information and the issue of a summons. The matter for the court to decide was not whether the respondents had failed to comply with an abatement notice but whether 'there was a nuisance in existence in fact' (see [1976] 1 All ER 839 at 843, [1976] 1 WLR 420 at 425). It was argued by the tenants therefore that the question in this case was whether at the date of the issue of proceedings there existed in fact a statutory nuisance at the houses which they occupied.

It was further contended by the tenants that, although the law might impose a heavy burden on local authorities against whom persons issued proceedings under s. 99, such a burden was justified, given the statutory duties and responsibilities of such authorities in relation to housing. It was argued, furthermore, that to reject the tenants' submission as to the appropriate date and to accept as an alternative the date of the hearing before the magistrates would be in effect to treat the summonses as abatement notices. This would mean that local authorities could escape criminal liability by carrying out repairs or rehousing the occupier between the date proceedings were issued and the date of the hearing. This would be analogous to allowing a burglar to escape criminal liability provided he returned the goods he had stolen before the hearing of his case.

That, I think, also fairly summarises the submissions made to us by counsel for the tenants. He further pointed out that, if his argument was rejected, it would mean that a local authority would be able, by delaying the hearing as much as possible, to give itself more time to escape liability.

Counsel for the council relied on the wording of s. 94(2) and submitted that the plain meaning is that the nuisance must exist at the date of the hearing before the magistrates and that, unless it does exist or, being temporarily abated, is likely to recur, the magistrates can neither make an order nor impose a fine.

In *Northern Ireland Trailers Ltd* v *Preston Corpn* [[1972] 1 All ER 260, [1972] 1 WLR 203] the question was whether quarter sessions, when hearing an appeal from magistrates, had to have regard to the situation as it was at the date of the hearing before the magistrates or the date they heard the appeal. The court held that the relevant date was the date of the hearing before the magistrates.

In dealing with this part of the case Lord Widgery CJ said ([1972] 1 All ER 260 at 264–265, [1972] 1 WLR 203 at 208):

> The second point . . . arises in this way: there had . . . been a substantial interval of time between the date when the justices made the nuisance order . . . and the date when quarter sessions considered the appeal . . . It was not disputed below or before us that when the matter was before the magistrates' court, it was essential for the complainant to show that the alleged nuisance still existed at the time . . . and, accordingly, when the matter was before the magistrate's court, proof was directed to the existence of the nuisance at that date.

The same point arose in *London Borough of Lambeth* v *Stubbs* [1980] *The Times*, 15 May. In that case the tenant was in occupation at the date of the hearing before the magistrates but had been rehoused by the time the appeal was heard. At that date the house was no longer occupied. The court decided that the mere fact that the house was empty did not mean that the nuisance had been abated (as to this aspect of the case I shall have to return) but, in giving judgment, Stephen Brown J used these words:

> The specific ground of appeal which might have resulted, if successful, in the nuisance order being quashed related to the time at which the nuisance was alleged to have existed. I think it is clear from the decision in *Northern Ireland Trailers Ltd* v *Preston Corpn* that the relevant date is the date of the information. Accordingly the Crown Court was bound to consider the state of affairs at that date. Of course it was open to them, and indeed they acted on, the changed circumstances which had occurred since the original hearing before the justices.

The reference to the *Northern Ireland Trailers* case, the fact that it had not been contended that the relevant date was the preferring of their information and the reference at the end of the sentence to the 'original hearing before the justices' convinces me that the reference to the 'date of the information' was an understandable slip of the tongue and that what the judge meant was 'the date of the hearing of the information'.

I find it a strange argument that the words in an offence-creating statute should be construed in a way which is not their natural meaning so as to enlarge the ambit of the offence. In their plain and ordinary meaning the words of s. 94(2) say that in the relevant date for the magistrates to consider is the date of the hearing before them. In the usual case where it is the local authority which is bringing the proceedings there is not the slightest difficulty involved in giving them their natural meaning and the fact that s. 99 was badly drafted does not in my judgment warrant giving the words in s. 94 the strained meaning for which the tenants contend.

I am fortified in my view by the provisions of s. 94(3) which make an award of expenses to the local authority mandatory in cases where the nuisance has been abated at the date of hearing. If the relevant date were the date of the information, no such provision would be necessary. I think it is clear that it was just because the draftsmen realised that if the nuisance was abated at the time of the hearing the magistrates could make no order nor convict of any offence that this provision for payment of the council's costs was included.

I have no hesitation in finding that the relevant date is the date of the hearing before the magistrates. It is true that s. 99 makes no provision for the prior service of an abatement notice and that therefore its provisions do not fit neatly into the principal scheme, but this does not seem to me in any way to warrant the forced construction of the plain words of s. 93 and 94 for which counsel for the tenants contends.

. . .

As to the considerations which should influence justices in making orders under the 1936 Act, I do not think I can do better than refer to the words of Lord Widgery CJ in *Nottingham District Council* v *Newton* [1974] 2 All ER 760, [1974] 1 WLR 923. That was a case where there were difficulties as to the precise order which should be made when the final disposition of the house under a clearance order had not been decided at the time of the hearing by the court. Lord Widgery CJ after referring to the wide discretion in the court as to the order that it made, said ([1974] 2 All ER 760 at 766, [1974] 1 WLR 923 at 930):

In deciding within that wide ambit of detailed discretion just what the terms of the nuisance order should be, I have no doubt it is the duty of the justices, as common sense dictates, to look at the whole circumstances of the case and to try and make an order which is in its terms sensible and just having regard to the entire prevailing situation. They were wrong in my judgment in closing their eyes to the Housing Act proceedings and the imminence of demolition, and had they had regard to those factors as well as all the other relevant factors, it may be that they would have provided for the nuisance to be abated by perhaps March 1974 so that if the demolition proceedings had taken effect meanwhile, the danger of money being spent on the house abortively in view of the subsequent demolition would be avoided. I think the justices were very nearly right in this case, but I conclude that they were wrong in restricting the factors to which they had regard, and I think this appeal should be allowed to the extent that the case should be sent back to the justices asking them to reconsider their decision in the light of the discretion within the precise terms of s. 94(2), and in the light of all the prevailing circumstances, and endeavour to come to what seems to them to be a sensible and just conclusion.

As Waller LJ said of this passage in the *Lambeth* case:

Lord Widgery CJ was stressing at the beginning of that passage what common sense dictates. He was stressing that justices should have in mind a decision which will avoid the possibility of public money being wasted because of the subsequent demolition and saying that the conclusion should be a sensible and just one.

Notes
1.   It should always be borne in mind that statutory nuisance proceedings are criminal in nature, and that therefore the burden of proof on any 'informant' will be high (see *R* v *Newham Justices, ex parte Hunt* [1976] 1 WLR 420).
2.   In *Patel* v *Mehtab* (1980) 5 HLR 78, the court commented upon the question as to how in practice 'prejudice to health' is to be established. Above all, it was emphasised that the court should not prefer its own (lay) assessment of the facts over those of expert witnesses for the parties.
3.   As discussed above, s. 79(7) of the 1990 Act further defines 'prejudicial to health' as 'injurious, or likely to cause injury, to health'. Does this extend to aspects of a dwelling which make accidents (and therefore personal injury) more likely? In *R* v *Bristol City Council, ex parte Everett* (13 May 1998 – *Housing Law Monitor*, June 1998) Richards J thought not. The property in question had a steep internal staircase, and the tenant felt that this would cause her to fall and further aggravate an existing back injury. The court found that this did not bring the property within s. 79. This result has now been confirmed by the Court of Appeal ([1999] *The Times*, 9 March). On the facts this seems a sensible enough decision, but are all the implications equally sensible? Is it always possible to draw a clear line between a risk to health and a risk of injury? For example, a highly 'rickety' and uneven staircase could easily cause (or at least aggravate) back and pelvic injury. Is this not, in logic, equally a risk to health?
4.   As indicated above, noise can certainly amount to a statutory nuisance (as would be expected from the general law of nuisance). However, noise would have to be particularly penetrating and persistent to make the premises 'prejudicial to health' as a result (the alternative 'nuisance' limb would apply only if the noise affected neighbours). Nevertheless, in two recent cases it was, very surprisingly, held that even less serious noise penetration might constitute a breach of the covenant of 'quiet enjoyment' which is an inherent feature of a typical landlord and tenant relationship. In *Baxter* v *LB of Camden* (1998) 30 HLR 501, the Court of Appeal not only took this literal and wide view of 'quiet enjoyment', but also seemed virtually to equate it with noise nuisance. In *Southwark LBC* v *Mills* [1998] 3 WLR 9, Laddie J felt constrained by precedent to take the same approach, despite serious misgivings (with the result that Southwark Council were under an absolute duty to re-soundproof 15 flats (dating from 1919) so as to bring them fully up to modern building standards).

   Traditionally, the conventional wisdom was that 'quiet enjoyment' had nothing directly to do with the absence of noise (unless of course deliberately caused by a 'harassing' landlord!), but rather meant 'undisturbed' or 'without interference' (see, for example, Kekewich J in *Jenkins* v *Jackson* (1880) 40 Ch D 71). Typical breaches would, therefore, be the landlord who enters into tenanted property uninvited or who disturbs the tenant in possession. The Court of Appeal in *Southwark*, in overturning Laddie J has returned to the traditional view ([1998] *The Times*, 20 August). *Baxter* was seen as representing one line of authority but there was another line (see *Duke of Westminster* v *Guild* (1985) QB 688) which indicated that 'quiet enjoyment' had nothing directly to do with noise. This 'line' was to be preferred.

5.   A very recent decision on the meaning of 'statutory nuisance', which is likely to have serious financial implications for many housing authorities, is *Ockley* v *Birmingham City Council* ([1999] *The Times*, 8 January). In effect it was the potential lack of hygiene associated with the layout of the premises which constituted a nuisance and required abatement by the authority. The only lavatory in the premises was in a room too small also to accommodate a wash-hand basin, so that anyone using it either had to use the kitchen sink to wash their hands, or had to pass through the kitchen and use a bathroom on the other side. The Court of Appeal upheld a finding by Birmingham justices that the premises were 'prejudicial to health' under s. 79(1)(a) of the 1990 Act on the basis that the risk of cross-infection in the kitchen area was 'injurious, or likely to cause injury, to health' within the meaning of s. 79(7), and therefore constituted a statutory nuisance. The court noted that Birmingham City Council owned 20,000 similar properties and that many other authorities would have significant numbers of similar properties. Given that 'abatement' of the nuisance would require some structural alterations to every one of these properties to accommodate a wash-hand basin adjacent to the toilet, the financial implications are, of course, very substantial.

6.   Perhaps the most contentious issue in relation to 'public' law remedies for housing in disrepair, is the relationship between a local authority's powers under housing legislation and those under environmental protection legislation. Formally, the two codes are 'separate but equal', but as elsewhere this formula does not prevent perceptions of inequality or discrimination. Two principal issues arise:

(i)   Can local authorities be compelled to take action under one code or the other, or is their discretion as to how to proceed unconstrained?

(ii)   Can a local authority be required to take action (under either code) against themselves?

(i)   As regards the 'choice of codes' issue   Generally a discontented tenant would wish to compel a local authority to take action under housing legislation rather than under the statutory nuisance procedures. In the former case a complete eradication of the source of the problem may be required (e.g., in the case of dampness caused by lack of a damp-proof course, the insertion of such a course), whereas the nuisance procedures may result in only temporary measures to deal with the immediate problem (in the above case, perhaps using damp-proof paint or lining the walls with damp-proof paper might suffice). There are nevertheless cases where tenants might prefer a statutory nuisance approach (e.g. if unfitness procedures could result in the closure or demolition of the premises).

In *R* v *Kerrier District Council, ex parte Guppy's (Bridport) Ltd* (1975) 30 P & CR 194, the Divisional Court held that the housing legislation provisions were mandatory (then ss. 9, 16 and 69 of the Housing Act 1957). Lord Widgery CJ (at p. 198) stated:

Looking at that legislation, the applicants say that there is an obligation on the local authority to take action in respect of a house which is unfit for human habitation. If it can be made fit at reasonable expense, the action should be under section 9. If it cannot be made fit at reasonable expense, the action should be under section 16. Here, the applicants are saying: 'We do not mind which of the two, but once you accept, as you do, that the house is unfit for human habitation one or other of these is mandatory' – or so they seek to contend.

The respondent council contend that this is not a mandatory provision. They deny that they are bound to carry out either of the courses of action in respect of unfit houses which I have described as being laid down in the Act of 1957.

It is not easy for the respondents to contend that they have this discretion because the language, as I have demonstrated, is imperative in form. In each case it is said that the local authority 'shall' serve the notice in question. The fact that this is an imperative provision is somewhat reinforced, I think, by the decision in *R v Epsom and Ewell Corporation, ex parte R.B. Property Investments (Eastern) Ltd* [1964] 1 WLR 1060; [1964] 2 All ER 832. That concerned two other sections of the Housing Act 1957 [ss. 21(a) and 22(1)] which again contained a provision that the local authority should take action within a certain time. According to the headnote, the decision was that the section in question [s. 22(1)] was mandatory and that once a demolition order had become operative the local authority did not have a discretion to postpone service of the notice to quit but under sections 21 and 22 was bound to serve the notice to quit under section 22. The circumstances, of course, were quite different, but the case is illustrative of the fact that in this Act, in general, the obligations are imperative obligations, and I think that that must be much the more so where one is dealing with unfit houses which obviously ought not still to have occupiers in them and ought instead to be rendered fit as soon as possible.

Accordingly, it seems to me that the provisions are mandatory and that the respondents are not able to claim the right to take action or not as and when they think it proper. I would like to say at once that I have great sympathy with the respondents in this matter because housing authorities are notoriously in trouble at the present time due to the pressures on them. I think, however, that the Act, properly understood, means that once the condition of an unfit house is brought to their attention in the words of the section they have got to do something about it because the Act so provides.

The final contention, which I think would have been in the forefront of Mr Dinkin's argument but for a recent decision of the House of Lords, is that where local authorities have their Housing Act powers and Public Health Act powers available in relation to a given situation they have a choice as to which of those powers they will employ. If that were right, it would provide a complete answer to the applicants' case in the present application because that is the attitude which the respondents have taken. They have said: 'no, we are going to use our Public Health Act powers and not our Housing Act powers.'

This hearing was, however, adjourned for a few days so that we could have the advantage of guidance from the House of Lords which we knew was likely to come this week; it is now available in the . . . case of *Salford City Council v McNally*. In this case the problem posed by the dual systems of control of housing was extremely pertinent. Indeed, the case did raise specifically the question whether a local authority could refuse to carry out their Public Health Act powers because they had chosen to assert control under the Housing Act instead.

Lord Wilberforce, giving the leading speech, laid it down in the plainest terms that the Public Health Act code and the Housing Act code are two separate systems for securing similar objects, but that they are not in collision and that there should be no difficulty in getting them separated and distinguishing one from the other if attention is duly given to the precise language used in the two statutes.

In particular, however, it seems to me that, since this decision of the House of Lords, one cannot possible contend on behalf of the local authority that a choice has been made of the Public Health Act system over the Housing Act system or vice versa. They are separate and parallel. Each is to be enforced and carried out in its own way, and, once that is established, it seems to me to show that there is no substance in the respondents' attitude to their problems in this case.

This seems clear enough, but is it as easy to reconcile the decision with *Salford* v *McNally* [1976] AC 379 as Lord Widgery seemed to think? If two codes stand side by side, and are both mandatory, some 'reconciliation' is surely required. In *McNally* it was held that a house in a clearance area used by the authority for temporary housing was still subject to compulsory nuisance procedures as 'prejudicial to health', even though the authority were acting under Housing Act powers (then s. 48 of the Housing Act 1957). Perhaps the solution to the (apparent) dilemma can be seen through a full study of the key passage of Lord Wilberforce's judgment in *McNally* (at p. 388):

My Lords, the answer to this question, in my opinion, is manifestly in the negative. It is only necessary to perceive the respective and different purposes of the Housing Acts and of the Public Health Act 1936 to see that they are dealing with different matters and setting different standards, which may in any individual case have to be separately met. The Housing Act 1957, in that part of it which provides for clearance and redevelopment, is concerned with fitness for human habitation. This is a technical expression, to which the Act supplies its interpretation in section 4(1)(c) through a list of specific matters. The subsection states:

In determining for any of the purposes of this Act whether a house is unfit for human habitation, regard shall be had to its condition in respect of the following matters, that is to say—(a) repair; (b) stability; (c) freedom from damp; (d) natural lighting; (e) ventilation; (f) water supply; (g) drainage and sanitary conveniences; (h) facilities for storage, preparation and cooking of food and for the disposal of waste water; and the house shall be deemed to be unfit for human habitation if and only if it is so far defective in one or more of the said matters that it is not reasonably suitable for occupation in the conditions.

The Public Health Act 1936 on the other hand, is concerned with the general concepts 'prejudicial to health' and 'nuisance'; the former being defined as 'injurious, or likely to cause injury, to health.' And I do not doubt that the persons whose health is here in question may include occupiers of the house as well as members of the public. But it must be obvious that a house may well be 'unfit for human habitation' in the statutory sense without being either 'prejudicial to health' or a 'nuisance' and consequentially that the Housing Act 1957 when it authorises a house which is unfit for human habitation to be temporarily occupied as 'adequate for the time being' is not lending statutory authority to the use of a house which is prejudicial to health. In view, indeed, of the fact that houses may have to be used for accommodation, adequate for the time being, for considerable periods (in the present case seven years), it would be surprising if a local authority, in permitting such use, were held to be dispensed altogether for this period from the public health requirements.

There is therefore, in my opinion, no difficulty in reconciling the two legislative codes or in operating them side by side. Much of the apparent difficulty of so doing has been created by a confusion of terms. Thus, the judgment of the Divisional Court refers ([1975] 1 WLR 365, 369) to the purpose of the Public Health Act 1936 as being 'to prevent people from living in houses which are not fit for human habitation.' This may be confusing since, while a house which is by its condition 'prejudicial to health' is likely to be 'unfit for human habitation,' the converse is not necessarily the case. In dealing with each Act it is better to use its own terminology.

(ii)   As regards the local authority taking action against themselves   It was settled by *R* v *Cardiff City Council, ex parte Cross* (1982) 6 HLR 1 that local authorities cannot serve housing orders on themselves, principally because the legislation, with its detailed procedures for serving notice and bringing appeals, seems to presuppose at all points that more than one party will be involved. However, statutory nuisance procedures may give tenants some protection concerning seriously defective council properties. In this context magistrates may well take a more lenient view of local authority 'default', particularly if the authority can convince the court that the properties are on some planned improvement list (the court in *Birmingham District Council* v *Kelly* (1985) 17 HLR 572 encouraged magistrates to think in this way). Of course the practical difficulties of persuading the Environmental Health Department to act are considerable in such a case, but, as noted earlier, the right to direct tenant action under s. 82 of the 1990 Act may prove invaluable.

Questions
1.   On the assumption that household refuse indiscriminately dumped is highly likely to attract vermin, was the appeal in *Cartwright* successful only because the magistrates failed to focus on the correct question(s)?
2.   Is any common law nuisance inevitably a statutory nuisance under s. 79?
3.   Where an authority have a choice of remedies between the 1985 and 1990 Acts, can the courts compel them to use the latter in preference to the former? (Compare Lord Widgery CJ in *Nottingham Corporation* v *Newton* [1974] 1 WLR 923, at p. 927, with the *Encyclopaedia of Housing Law and Practice*).
4.   ' . . . it is most important that the justices should bear in mind the fact that a local authority . . . has very heavy housing responsibilities and the procedure [concerning statutory nuisance] must not be used as a method of obtaining for particular tenants benefits which they were well aware did not exist when they took the tenancies . . . and which . . . could put those tenants in a favoured position in relation to the other tenants . . . housed by the authority.' (Woolf J in *Birmingham DC* v *Kelly* (1985) 17 HLR 572)
Discuss.

8 HOUSES IN MULTIPLE OCCUPATION

(A) Introduction

The range of accommodation which may be termed a house in multiple occupation (HMO) is particularly wide. The Department of the Environment, Transport and the Regions (DETR) list six types of HMO: bedsits; shared houses; households with lodgers; purpose-built HMOs, such as halls of residence; hostels and houses used as care homes; and houses converted into self-contained flats. As will be indicated later, the range of HMO properties leads to enforcement actions in this area by a number of authorities; this chapter will, however, principally consider the role of housing authorities as enforcers of HMO standards.

A survey (Thomas, A. D., and Hedges, A., *The 1985 Physical and Social Survey of Houses in Multiple Occupation in England and Wales,* London, HMSO, 1985, p. 100) estimated that some 2.6 million people inhabit HMOs nationally, the average inhabitant being young (two-thirds are under the age of 35), single (fewer families inhabit HMOs than other types of accommodation) and generally poor (with only around 40 per cent of occupiers in full-time employment). The quality of accommodation offered is often of a most unsatisfactory nature, with (according to the aforementioned survey) 80 per cent of HMOs being unsatisfactory in terms of management, occupancy or amenity provision. Of especial concern were the four-fifths of HMOs surveyed where the means of escape from fire was either defective, inadequate or non-existent. In the five years between 1988 and 1992, 849 people died in HMO fires, with in excess of 14,000 non-fatal casualties (*Fire Statistics United Kingdom 1992,* Home Office, 1994).

Given the above, it should be of little surprise that both central and local government have been concentrating efforts, with mixed success, on the need to improve standards of accommodation generally, and fire safety standards in particular, in HMOs. This chapter will initially consider legal provisions available to raise safety and amenity standards within HMOs. The major housing legislation to facilitate this is contained within Pt XI of the Housing Act 1985, as amended by the Local Government and Housing Act 1989 and further amended by the Housing Act 1996. Before considering this, however, discussion needs to focus on establishing the meaning of 'a house in multiple occupation', in order to pinpoint the subject of legislative regulation.

(B)   Defining a house in multiple occupation

At the outset of this chapter a range of accommodation was identified as potential HMOs. It is crucial to note though that not all multiply occupied accommodation will be 'houses in multiple occupation', for the purposes of the Housing Act 1985. It is important to gain an understanding of the basic concepts in defining a HMO.

Housing Act 1985

Meaning of 'multiple occupation'
345.   In this Part 'house in multiple occupation' means a house which is occupied by persons who do not form a single household.

This definition can be most easily grasped if it is broken down into three constituent parts.

(i)   'a house'
The Housing Act 1985 does not provide a full definition of the word 'house', merely indicating, at s. 399, that a house includes a yard, garden and outhouses. However, the courts have given a wide meaning to 'house' for the purposes of s. 345.

R v *London Borough of Hackney, ex parte Evenbray*
(1987) 19 HLR 557

The applicant company owned a converted hotel and adjoining property. The hotel accommodated tourists, the next-door premises had been used since 1983 as a homeless hostel. The local authority issued a direction notice stipulating the highest permissible occupancy, which due to the condition of the property was zero. The company appealed, amongst other things that the hostel was not a house for the purposes of the Housing Act 1961. Evenbray were ultimately successful in this appeal, but of especial interest is the review of case law undertaken by Kennedy J.

KENNEDY J: . . . Mr Read, for the applicants, assisted by definitions from the *Shorter Oxford English Dictionary*, submits that whereas an hotel exists primarily for the benefit of those who are in transit, a house is a place in which people live or dwell with a degree of permanence. It is common ground that the word 'hotel' does not feature in either the 1957 Act or the 1961 Act, and such definitions of the word 'house' as can be found in those two Acts are of very little assistance. Section 189(1) of the 1957 Act I have already quoted; section 9(3) contains another inclusive definition which applies only to sections 9 to 12, and section 87, in relation to the foregoing provisions of Part IV of the Act, defines 'dwelling-house' as meaning 'any premises used as a separate dwelling.' Mr Read points out that in section 15(2) of the 1961 Act there is reference to 'individuals living on the premises,' and section 19(4)(b) refers to 'those living in the house' whereas it is normal to say that people 'stay' in an hotel.

Mr Read submits that here we have in No. 356 a building which was an integral part of an hotel, and on the facts it never ceased to be so. The respondents have, he submits, applied to it a statute which speaks only of houses, and that word is inappropriate to describe an hotel. Furthermore, Mr Read submits that it is unnecessary to give the word 'house' an unusually wide meaning in order to enable the statute to deal with the mischief it was intended to prevent. In 1957 when addressing itself to a house let in lodgings or occupied by members of more than one family Parliament concerned itself with overcrowding (see Section 90 of the 1957 Act). In 1961 it conferred further powers on local authorities in relation to such houses, which came later to be described as houses 'occupied by persons who do not form a single household,' and the part of the Act dealing with 'houses in multiple occupation' is the part which contains sections 15 and 19. In that part of the Act, submits Mr Read, the provisions are clearly aimed at problems which may arise in houses in multiple occupation. For example, inadequate facilities for the storage, preparation and cooking of food. If that problem were to arise in relation to an hotel other remedies are available without resort to housing legislation, so clearly, submits Mr. Read, Parliament did not have hotels in mind when passing sections 15 and 19 of the 1961 Act.

Section 21 of the 1961 Act is also, submits Mr. Read, of assistance. It extends the provisions of sections 12 to 15 of the Act to 'a building which is not a house but comprises separate dwellings' if two or more of the dwellings either lack sanitary conveniences or are occupied by persons who do not form a single household. That extension, submits Mr Read, could embrace an hotel, but section 21 expressly provides that 'no directions shall be given under section nineteen of this Act by virtue of this section in relation to such a building.' If, asks Mr Read, a house is any building constructed or used for human habitation, why did Parliament find it necessary to pass section 21, and when can it operate?

All of the submissions made by Mr Read to which I have referred thus far seem to me to be attractive and persuasive were it not for the history of this legislation and the wealth of authority which has grown up in relation to it, to much of which I have been helpfully referred. In *London County Council v Rowton House Company* (1898) 77 LT 693 the question was whether a hostel named Rowton House was a dwelling-house. The magistrate found as a fact that it was not, and the appeal was dismissed, but having said that the majority of public buildings such as churches, chapels and ballrooms would not be dwelling-houses Channell J continued 'but there are a few and particularly hotels, lodging houses, and so on, that would be. Those I think might be dwelling-houses notwithstanding that they are also public buildings.' In *Ross v Leicester Corporation* (1932) 30 LGR 382 it was contended in connection with a clearance scheme that the word 'dwelling-house' in section 1 of the Housing Act 1930 did not include a common lodging house. Swift J found that proposition impossible to accept and cited Channell J in the *Rowton* case.

In *Re Butler* [1939] 1 KB 570 it was held in the Court of Appeal, again in connection with a clearance scheme, that a garage or workshop with a dwelling-house above it was a 'house' within the meaning of section 25(l). of the Housing Act 1936.

[After reviewing *Okereke v Brent* LBC [1967] 1 QB 42 and *R v LB Southwark, ex parte Lewis Levy* (1983) 8 HLR 1, Kennedy J continued:]

In *R v London Borough of Camden, ex parte Rowton (Camden Town) Ltd* (1983) 10 HLR 28 McCullough J was faced with a similar problem. The local authority served notices under sections 12, 15 and 19 of the 1961 Act in relation to Arlington House, a large purpose-built hostel. The owners contended that for the purposes of those sections it was not a house. McCullough J thought that it might be possible to distinguish *Reed's* case because that case concerned a building which had obviously started life as a dwelling-house, and he found, as I do, the greatest difficulty in accepting that Parliament intended the word 'house' to bear a meaning that would bring within it every hotel and every hostel in the country, but nevertheless he felt unable to depart from the dicta in *Reed v Hastings Corporation* [(1964) 62 LGR 588] or from the decision in *Ex parte Lewis Levy Ltd.* I find myself in a similar difficulty. I accept that in one sense Mr. Reed is right when he says that there is no authority for the proposition that the word 'house' in sections 15 and 19 of the 1961 Act must be construed widely enough to embrace an hotel or a part of an hotel, but the line of reasoning which led the Court of Appeal to decide as it did in *Reed's* case compels me to accept that No. 356 Seven Sisters Road was a house for the purposes of sections 15 and 19, because it was a building constructed and used for human habitation. On the facts of the present case, it is not even possible to distinguish *Reed's* case in the way suggested by McCullough J. Therefore on the first ground on which the applicants seek relief they fail.

The consequences stemming from the analysis of the meaning of the word 'house' by Kennedy J are such that a multitude of residential property types may be HMOs, provided the property is 'fitted and used and adapted for human habitation' (see Harman LJ in *Reed v Hastings Corporation* (1964) 62 LGR 588, at p. 590). This definition incorporates self-contained flats, hotels, etc. in addition to more traditional types of houses let to a number of individuals. This diversity leads to overlapping legal provisions within the fire, (see, for example, provisions under the Fire Precautions Act 1971, as amended) housing (principally the Housing Act 1985, as amended) and health and safety sphere. Indeed it may be that a particular HMO is subject to differing regulatory regimes. Certain types of HMO accommodation require a fire certificate for the purposes of the Fire Precautions Act. However, the same HMOs may also be subject to inspection and registration by the local housing authority. Given that both these regimes allow for differing require-ments, the owner/manager of a house in multiple occupation may be required to install, for example, different fire detection systems according to the stipulations of fire precautions officers (enforcing the 1971 Act) and environ-mental health officers (enforcing the Housing Act 1985 requirements).

(ii)   'which is occupied'
This phrase has been described by Cumming-Bruce LJ in *Silbers v Southwark LBC* (1977) 122 Sol Jo 128, as simply indicating a requirement of 'living in'

a property. The words here do not require an inhabitant to have exclusive possession, thus both tenants and licensees may fall within the scope of this provision.

(iii)   *'by persons who do not form a single household'*

Simmons v *Pizzey*
[1979] AC 37

Mrs Pizzey was the owner of a refuge for battered women. The occupants of the accommodation fluctuated with people arriving at all times of the day and night. In December 1975 the local authority directed that, pursuant to s. 19(1) of the Housing Act 1961, a maximum of 36 individuals could occupy the dwelling. Counsel for Mrs Pizzey, who had breached this figure, argued that the residents constituted a single household, thus escaping the provisions of the Act.

LORD HAILSHAM OF ST. MARYLEBONE: My Lords, in this case, not without reluctance, but without doubt, I come to the conclusion that the appeal must be dismissed. The proceedings arise from a decision of the Willesden justices on an information by the respondent against the appellant alleging a breach of section 19(10) of the Housing Act 1961. The justices dismissed the information but stated a case for the opinion of the Divisional Court. The Divisional Court allowed the appeal and ordered that the case be remitted to the justices with a direction to convict, but certified that the case involved a question of law of general public importance. From the decision of the Divisional Court the appellant now appeals by leave of your Lordships' House.

The appellant is the occupier of 369, Chiswick High Road and maintains that house as a place of refuge for so-called battered wives, that is to say, to quote the judgment of Lord Widgery CJ, 'women who are ill treated by their husbands or other men with whom they are living . . . and who are in desperate straits. . . .' These come to the house, with or without their children, to find accommodation away from the home which has been rendered intolerable or dangerous to them by the violence of their partners. It is in the nature of the case that the population of number 369 is a fluctuating one, women arriving each day or each week at all hours of the day or night, and each day or each week leaving and being replaced by others.

At a meeting of Hounslow London Borough Council on or before October 21, 1975, a resolution was passed in purported exercise of the power conferred by section 19(1) of the Housing Act 1961 fixing the maximum number of persons permitted to reside in number 369 as 368, and a direction dated December 1, 1975, purporting to be made under the same section applying this maximum to the premises was afterwards made, the various formalities required by the section with regard to service of notice of intention, etc., having been duly complied with.

It was proved at the hearing that on January 14, 1976, the date of the alleged offence, the number of residents was in fact 75, and the information dated January 27 thereafter charged the appellant with a breach of section 19(10) in that she 'knowingly failed to comply with the requirements of section 19 (2)' by exceeding the maximum to this extent.

At the hearing before the justices one point and one point only was argued on behalf of the appellant. The powers, it was contended, under section 19 of the Act of 1961 could only be exercised if at the relevant times, which, the appellant contended, were the time of the direction and of the breach, it was proved that the house was in multiple occupation in the sense defined in the Act as it had been amended by the Housing Act 1969 (section 58 and Schedule 8, paragraph 2). This condition, the argument ran, was not fulfilled because, in fact, at the relevant time the residents in the house had not been proved not to 'form a single household.' which was the statutory test under the amended formula. The justices accepted this argument and found as a fact that at the relevant time the residents were in fact members of and did form a single household. The question, and the only question stated by the justices for the opinion of the Divisional Court, was whether they were entitled so to find.

The Divisional Court did not answer this question. They had before them the case of *Allen* v *Khan* [1968] 1 QB 609, decided under the Act of 1961 before the description of multiple occupation had been replaced by section 58 of the Act of 1969. This case had not been cited to the justices. On this authority and at the invitation of the present respondent (then appellant) the Divisional Court (Lord Widgery CJ and Eveleigh and Slynn JJ) held in effect that the question whether at either of the material times the house was in multiple occupation was irrelevant. Section 19 of the Act of 1961, they decided, was of general application and was not limited to houses in multiple occupation either at the time when the direction was made, or at the time when the alleged breach was committed. If this is right, of course it does not matter whether the 75 residents on January 14, 1976, did form a single household or not. It was enough that, to the knowledge of the appellant, they exceeded the permitted maximum of 36.

Accordingly, it becomes the duty of your Lordships to consider whether *Allen* v *Khan* [1968] 1 QB 609 was rightly decided, and whether it is a necessary condition of the exercise by a local authority of the powers under section 19 of the Housing Act 1961, that at one or both of the relevant times the house was in multiple occupation in the sense described in section 58 of the Housing Act 1969 and Schedule 8 to that Act. That is the first matter to be considered in this appeal.

Both at the Divisional Court and before your Lordships. the appellant also raised a new point not argued before the magistrates. This related to the form and content of the direction. It appears that, on the date of the direction, December 1, 1975, there were only 29 residents in the house. The direction however purported to be made for the purpose of 'remedying' a state of affairs calling for the service of a notice under section 15 of the Housing Act 1961 (of which more later) and not of 'preventing' such a state of affairs and, it was contended, this invalidated the proceedings since, if 36 was the correct maximum and there were only 29 residents there was nothing to 'remedy.' Admittedly, for the purposes of this point, a direction for the purpose of 'preventing' the same state of affairs would have been valid under the terms of the section, but this, it was argued, would have involved the council in different considerations. The council had elected to proceed on the basis that it was necessary to remedy a state of affairs which, ex concessis for this point, was not in existence, and therefore the whole proceeding became invalid. If in doubt whether the state of affairs existed or not, the council, it was contended, should have issued two notices, one expressed to 'prevent,' and one to 'remedy' the prescribed state of affairs. The appellant sought to strengthen this point by referring to the form prescribed in the Housing (Prescribed Forms) Regulations 1972 (SI 1972 No. 228) (Form No. 40), which appears to put the local authority to its election between 'preventing' and 'remedying.'

I now proceed to discuss the merits of the three points thus involved in the appeal. I begin by saying that I personally have no doubt that *Allen* v *Khan* [1968] 1 QB 609 was wrongly decided and the Divisional Court accordingly erred in following it. I do not think anything turns in this context on the change of phrase between 1961 and 1969 to describe multiple occupation. It took place, we were told and I accept, probably to tighten the formula as the result of *Holm v Royal Borough of Kensington and Chelsea* [1968] 1 QB 646. But whether the original or the substituted formula be used, I am satisfied that multiple occupation of the premises in question at the time of the alleged offence is an essential ingredient of an offence under section 19(10) of the Act of 1961, and with some hesitation that it is also a condition of the exercise by a local authority of its powers of issuing a direction under section 19(1).

I consider that this is apparent on a close inspection of the terms of section 19 itself which makes it a condition of the exercise of the powers that the exercise should be considered necessary 'for the purpose of preventing the occurrence of, or remedying a state of affairs calling for the service of a notice or a further notice under section 15 . . .' This clearly relates back to the provisions of section 15. and whatever else may be uncertain about the Act, the situation calling for a notice under section 15 (which permits the council to require the execution by the occupier of works in respect of specified matters) involves the condition that the house to which the notice applies must be in multiple occupation at the time of the notice. Notwithstanding that section 19 does not expressly incorporate the qualifying condition, it is my opinion that it unambiguously incorporates it by implication. It is true, as is pointed out in *Allen v Khan* [1968] 1 QB 609 and by the Divisional Court in the instant appeal, that section 19 is a 'forward looking' section envisaging the prevention of something which ex hypothesi has not yet happened. But still the situation which must be prevented is one calling for a section 15 notice, and that can only occur in respect of a house in multiple occupation.

If there were any ambiguity I think it would be resolved by the location of sections 15 and 19 in the original Act and of section 58 of the amending Act which occur in Parts II and IV respectively, each Part being headed by a description expressly referring to houses in 'multiple occupation,' and section 19 forming part of a bundle of sections (12 to 23) clearly involving multiple occupation, and, for what it is worth, clearly referring to multiple occupation in the side notes. Sections 15 and 19 are clearly companion sections. Section 15 enables the council to direct the execution of works in order to provide adequate facilities of specified kinds in houses in multiple occupation when these are thought necessary having regard to the number of persons or households involved, and section 19 enables the council to fix the maximum number of persons permitted in such houses having regard to the facilities actually provided, or (by section 67(5) of the Housing Act 1964) directed to be provided by the section 15 notice. Counsel rightly drew our attention to the fact that there are separate provisions in the principal Act (Housing Act 1957) dealing with overcrowding per se and extending to houses in single occupation.

Having thus disposed of the point decided by the Divisional Court, it becomes necessary to consider the decision of the justices having regard to the test directed to be applied in *Bracegirdle v Oxley* [1947] KB 349 and the burden of proof in criminal cases. The test of multiple occupation is whether the house was, at the material times, 'occupied by persons who do not form a single household' (see Housing Act 1969, section 58 and Schedule 8) and as I interpret *Bracegirdle v Oxley* the question which must be posed on this point is whether on the facts proved any reasonable bench of magistrates, properly directing themselves, could have come to the conclusion that the prosecution had failed to prove that the actual residents in December 1975 and January 1976 did not form a single household.

Admittedly the expression 'household' is not given a statutory definition in the Housing Acts. *The Oxford English Dictionary*, vol. 5 (1901), p. 421, gives: 'The inmates of a house collectively; an organised family, including servants or attendants dwelling in a house; a domestic establishment.' This gives some colour to the appellant's case. The trouble is that the first part of the definition would cover the inmates of any house and deprive the section of any meaning at all. The work *Words and Phrases Legally Defined*. 2nd ed. (1969), p. 379 cites the opinions of Branson J and Clauson LJ in *English* v *Western* [1940] 1 KB 145; [1940] 2 KB 156; the Australian Matrimonial Causes Act 1959, and the observations of Rand J in *Wawanesa Mutual Insurance Co.* v *Bell* [1957] SCR 581 and *Calverley* v *Gore District Fire Insurance Mutual Co.* (1959) 18 DLR (2d) 598. I do not find any of these references particularly helpful except to make clear to me what I would have supposed in any case that both the expression 'household' and membership of it is a question of fact and degree, there being no certain indicia the presence or absence of any of which is by itself conclusive.

In this case I am driven by at least three factors to place what happened in 369, Chiswick High Road outside the limits of what can be conceivably called a single household. The first is the mere size. There comes a point at which all differences of degree become differences of kind. Neither 36 nor 75 is a number which in the suburbs of London as they exist at the present time can ordinarily and reasonably be regarded as a single household. The second factor is the fluctuating character of the resident population both as regards the fact of fluctuation and the extent of it The residents were coming and going in the words of Lord Widgery CJ 'each day or each week.' The first of the Canadian cases cited above does attempt a definition which, I think rightly, implies something more durable and more intimate than the fortuitous relationship between the unhappy inmates of number 369 at the material times. The third consideration is the fact that I cannot regard a temporary place of refuge for fortuitous arrivals as ordinarily forming a household at all. These residents came from a variety of homes and may have gone to a variety of different places after leaving number 369. No doubt some would have gone back home. These would never have ceased to be members of their former household. Others will have gone to relatives. Others will have been found accommodation elsewhere. They never had the intention to use number 369 as more than a temporary harbour in a storm. Whilst they were in number 369 no doubt each looked after her own children where possible, and no doubt each conformed with the very reasonable communal organisation described in the stated case. I do not think that every community consisting of temporary migrants housed under a single roof reasonably organised constitutes or can, constitute a single household. I do not think this is necessarily true of a hostel, a monastery, or a school, but certainly not of a temporary haven in a storm.

I think the magistrates would not have come to the conclusion they did had they not, apparently, been tempted by the way in which the case was presented on behalf of the authority to treat the alternatives as being either 'separate households' or a 'single household.' They do not seem to have contemplated the possibility that this unhappy migrant and fluctuating body of residents did not form a household at all but an amorphous and fluctuating assembly of unfortunate human beings belonging to different households or to none. Had they directed their minds to this question I do not believe they could have come to the conclusion they did.

I am somewhat strengthened in this view by the history of the legislation. The original formula under the Act of 1961 expressly described multiple occupation by reference to houses let in lodgings and individuals not forming part of the same family. Clearly the tragic wives in number 369 did not form part of the same family and, on the old formula, I have no doubt that number 369 would have been held as in multiple occupation. It was changed, I believe for the reason given, to substitute the household for the family test for the unit of description. The separate reference to houses let in lodgings was, I believe, omitted not in order to make it possible that houses let in lodgings were outside the scope of the relevant sections, but because, with the tighter formula, no one supposed that the words were necessary. The reference to 'household' was substituted for 'family' not in order to widen the formula, but to tighten it so as to get rid of the decision in *Holm* v *Royal Borough of Kensington and Chelsea* [1968] 1 QB 646.

Lord Hailsham thus lays down three relevant factors for determining the meaning of a 'household': (i) the number of people living in a property; (ii) the stability of the population, whether the inhabitants fluctuated or remained relatively constant; and (iii) the nature of the accommodation (this house provided a 'temporary harbour in a storm'). Given the facts of the case, it is difficult to view the occupation by the women residing at 369 Chiswick High Road as anything other than living in more than a single household. However, the next case appears to be somewhat more arguable.

Barnes v *Sheffield CC*
(1995) 27 HLR 719

The property involved here was a turn of the century two-up two-down terrace house with two further attic rooms. At all material times the property was occupied by either four male or five female students. Sheffield issued a s. 352 notice (see (D) below) requiring the carrying out of certain works, including reasonably extensive fire precautions. Mr and Mrs Barnes successfully appealed against the service of such a notice on the grounds the house was not a HMO.

SIR THOMAS BINGHAM MR: This is an appeal against a decision of His Honour Judge Walker, sitting as a deputy judge in the Sheffield County Court on September 2, 1994. The case before the learned judge arose out of an appeal against a notice served by the Sheffield City Council on the owners of a house. No. 494 Crookesmoor Road, Sheffield. under section 352 of the Housing Act 1985. There were two issues before the judge of which the first was whether the house in question was a house in multiple occupation within the definition in section 345 of the Housing Act 1985 at the date the notice was served. The notice was served on May 22, 1992, and that was accordingly the material date for the purpose of this issue. The judge held that the house was not a house in multiple occupation and the council appeal against that decision.

The house in question is described as a small, turn of the century mid-terrace house. On the ground floor there are two rooms. One of those has at all times been used as a kitchen and dining room. The other room was between 1991 and 1992 used as a bedroom but has since then been used as a sitting room. On the first floor there is a bathroom with a lavatory and also two bedrooms. one of them small. On the second floor there are two attic bedrooms. Outside the house there is a yard with an external lavatory.

In 1990 Mr and Mrs Barnes bought this house and did it up. They then let it for the period July 1990 to July 1991 to five students. Two of those students were in their second year and three in their third year. In July 1991 the three third year students moved on and the two second year students stayed in residence. There then joined them three more students, all of them girls. One was a friend of one of the two girls: the other two were not particular friends but were students on the same course at the same university. One of the girls, who was in residence in the house for two years, was Miss Jagdeep Mann. She gave evidence at the hearing before the judge and also filled in a questionnaire describing the arrangements when she had lived in the house. As a result of a notice given to the council by the father of one of the girls, a representative of the council visited the premises and formed the view that too many people were living there, that one of the first floor bedrooms was too small to be used as a bedroom in a house without a living room, and that the shared kitchen was too small for five occupants, although big enough for four. Accordingly on May 22, 1992 the council served three notices on Mr and Mrs Barnes.

The first notice was under section 189 of the Housing Act 1985 and required larger roof lights to be installed in the two attic bedrooms. The second was under section 352 and required various works to be carried out. First, it required the fitting of a larger worktop in the kitchen; secondly, it required improvements to the outside lavatory; thirdly, it called for improvements to the fire resistance of the house, including the installation of seven half-hour fire doors, the upgrading of ceilings, the installation of a fire corridor in the ground floor front room and a system of emergency lighting for the hall and staircase; fourthly, it required additional fire precautions. including the provision of fire extinguishers and fire blankets, and a comprehensive fire alarm, heat and smoke detection system. The third notice informed the owners that the first floor rear room was below the minimum size of a bedroom in a house with a kitchen-dining room but no separate living room. At the time these notices were served Mr and Mrs Barnes had already let the house for the academic year July 1992 to July 1993 by an agreement which they had made in February. The other parties to the agreement were four young men, also students, who agreed to take the property for that year. As it happened, those four students remained in occupation after July 1993 for another year, but that is irrelevant to this narrative.

In June 1992 Mr and Mrs Barnes appealed against all three notices. I should, however, make it clear that they had done some work to comply with them. After the girls had left at the end of the summer in 1992, the Barneses had completed the work necessary to comply with the section 189 notice. They had also (in compliance with the section 352 notice) fitted the larger worktop in the kitchen: they had provided fire extinguishers and blankets; and the number of occupants had already been reduced from five to four. The appeal therefore related to the balance of the fire precaution works which were in themselves quite an expensive undertaking.

In early 1994 there was an interlocutory hearing in court at which the council agreed that the works to the outside lavatory could be omitted, that the fire corridor could be omitted on the grounds that it would make the ground floor front room too small, and that the smaller first floor room could continue to be used as a bedroom so long as the ground floor room was used as a living room. It was that issue which came before the learned judge on August 31 1994 when there was a hearing, extending into a second day, at which evidence was given.

It is common ground that. if the notice served on the owners under section 352 related to a house which was not in law a house in multiple occupation, then that was an error in the notice which provided the owners with a ground of appeal under section 353(2)(c) of the Act. The question therefore was whether on May 22, 1992 this was a house which was occupied by persons who did not form a single household.

I put it like that because the definition of 'a house in multiple occupation' is to be found in section 345(1) of the 1985 Act, which provides:

> . . . 'house in multiple occupation' means a house which is occupied by persons who do not form a single household.

The meaning of that expression has been considered by the courts on more than one occasion, in particular by the House of Lords in *Simmons v Pizzey* [1979] AC 37. The most germane passage is to be found in the speech of Lord Hailsham at p. 59Γ where, having referred to various dictionary definitions and also definitions to be found in a number of authorities, he said:

> I do not find any of these references particularly helpful except to make clear to me what I would have supposed in any case that both the expression 'household' and membership of it is a question of fact and degree. there being no certain indicia the presence or absence of any of which is by itself conclusive.

That case of course related to a refuge for battered wives, and, addressing the particular facts of that case. Lord Hailsham outlined the factors which led him to the conclusion that it could not be regarded as a single household for purposes of the relevant legislation. One of the factors was the mere size of the community which occupied the house. He pointed that the number of occupants well exceeded what could ordinarily and reasonably be regarded as a single household. The second factor to which he drew attention was the fluctuating character of the resident population both as regards the fact of fluctuation and the extent of it.

The fact that a large number of residents came and went all the time in his view indicated that this house was not occupied as a single household. He thirdly paid attention to the fact that those who did live there did so as 'a temporary harbour in a storm'. That again in his view was a relevant matter. It is, however, apparent from the passage I cited at the outset that he was setting his face against the use of any single test to answer the statutory question.

We have also been referred to the *London Borough of Hackney v Ezedinma* [1981] 3 All ER 438. That was a case which went on appeal to the Queen's Bench Divisional Court against a decision of justices, and it is apparent that both May J, who gave the main judgment. and Griffiths LJ had reservations about the factual conclusion which the justices had reached although they both thought it wrong to disturb it. So far as principle is concerned. I think the case is of very limited authority. The same is true of *Berg v Trafford Borough Council* (1987) 20 HLR 47, a decision of the Court of Appeal which is of interest but which does not throw any helpful light on the meaning of this expression. It seems, therefore, that one is essentially driven back to one's own understanding of what is meant by occupation by persons forming a single household, of course bearing in mind the legislation in which this expression appears and in particular its reference to Part XI of the 1985 Act governing houses in multiple occupation.

It is, as I think, helpful to begin by taking what is one very clear case of occupation by those forming a single household, i.e. the ordinary family consisting of parents and children with perhaps a grandmother, or a grandfather, or an aunt, or a grandchild, as the case may be. No one could doubt that in any ordinary situation such occupation would be regarded as occupation by persons forming a single household. But of course the pattern of life within that household could vary widely from family to family. In the language of monastic life, a distinction was drawn between monasteries observing a coenobitic regime as opposed to those following what was known as an idiorrhythmic regime, the distinction essentially being between those in which life was lived communally and those in which the monks essentially lived their own lives. So I think it is to some extent in families. Even if the family were one where some members went out to work before the others got up and the early-risers went to bed before the late-risers returned home so that they rarely met, one would nonetheless regard that as occupation by persons forming a single household. At the other end of the spectrum one can imagine a typical rooming house, perhaps a sizeable house with a large number of different households sharing limited facilities, such as bathrooms and lavatories, but with separate establishments as between one flat and another, with their own front doors and perhaps a high degree of anonymity as between the various occupants. Indeed, we had an appeal this morning concerning a house in an urban setting which one would have no doubt – and it was not in issue – was a house in multiple occupation with numerous households on different floors, with some communal use of facilities, but in which essentially independent lives were being led by different households within it.

Other cases, of course, will fall somewhere between the ends of that spectrum, and the question that has to be answered on the facts of any given case is whether it falls within the family kind of picture or within the typical pattern of a house in multiple occupation. There are a number of tests that can be applied, and Mr Gaunt, who represents the owners on this appeal, has suggested a number of factors. I would for my part wish to make clear that the order of these factors should not be regarded as significant and that the weight to be given to any particular factor will vary widely from case to case depending on the overall picture. It would in my judgment be wrong to do what Lord Hailsham rightly said could not be done and suggest that there was a litmus test which could be applied to determine whether a house was being occupied as a single household or not. Nonetheless, I do regard these factors, in whichever order they are taken, as being helpful.

The first factor which was suggested was the origin of the tenancy. Mr Gaunt suggested that it was relevant whether the persons living in the house came to it as a single group or whether they were independently recruited either by the landlord or by an estate agent. In each of these cases Mr Gaunt attached importance to the fact that the occupants of the house, both the girls and the boys, came as a group. In relation to the girls who lived in the house between 1991 and 1992, there were separate agreements but they all signed on the same day in the same form, and it was they who formed the group and together took on responsibility as tenants. So far as the boys are concerned it is even more clear, since they came to the property as a group and signed one agreement to which they were all party. Mr Gaunt drew attention to the evidence of the owners to the effect that they would only let to groups and not to individuals, and therefore Mr Gaunt suggested that this was a factor which pointed towards this house being occupied by persons who did form a single household.

The second matter which Mr Gaunt suggested was relevant for consideration was the question of what facilities were shared. In the case of the girl students the bathroom and WC were shared and so was the kitchen; in the case of the boys the sitting room also was shared. The suggestion that was made was that the greater the extent of the shared facilities the greater the likelihood of a single household.

That seems to me – although by no means conclusive on its own – to be a relevant consideration.

Thirdly, Mr Gaunt drew attention to the question of occupation and in particular the consideration whether the occupants were responsible for the whole house or just their particular rooms, with the responsibility for the common parts remaining with the landlord or owner. He suggested – and it seems clear – that in this case the occupants were responsible for the whole house, in particular to keep it clean and in reasonable order, and that he suggested militated in favour of a single household. So far as it goes, that also seems to me to be a correct submission.

Fourthly, he drew attention to the issue of locks, his suggestion being that the greater the extent of the tenants' ability to lock their doors and keep everybody else out the less communal the occupation looked. In this case it appears that one of the rooms had bolts on the inside but not on the outside and that another of the rooms had a lock which the tenant had put on herself, but that none of the other rooms had locks on them at all. That does. I think, point towards a degree of communality as against the more isolated and independent regime which one would expect to find in a rooming house.

Fifthly, he drew attention to the responsibility for filling vacancies, the suggestion being that when it is up to a group to do this that is more suggestive of a household, and when it is up to the landlord to fill voids that is more suggestive of independent occupiers. That does seem to me, among other tests, to be a proper one and it is plain on the facts here that the responsibility for filling vacancies rested with the groups in each case, both the girls and the boys.

Sixthly, he referred to the allocation of rooms. The submission here was that if a particular room is let by a landlord to a particular tenant, that looks more like an independent letting than a single household, whereas if a house is let and it is left to the tenants to decide who should occupy which room, then that is more suggestive of a single household. Again I agree with that suggestion so far as it goes on its own and on the facts of this case. Both during the girls' occupation and the boys' it is plain the landlord played no part in allocating rooms and left it to the students to decide who would sleep where.

Seventhly, Mr Gaunt drew attention to the size of the establishment, his suggestion being that the bigger the establishment and the more numerous the occupants the less likely it was to be a single household. This, I think, echoes the thoughts of Lord Hailsham in the case I have mentioned and it seems to me to more or less obvious. On the facts here the groups numbered five in the first instance and four in the second, and those seem to me to be very conventional sizes for a single household. That is not to say that a single household cannot be bigger, but it is to say that there was nothing about the size of these groups which suggests that they were not or could not be a single household. Mr Gaunt drew attention to the fact that when the girls were in occupation the ground floor front room was being used as a bedroom and, far from being that occupant's exclusive territory, it was the room through which everybody entering from the street had to pass. It seems to me for what it is worth that that point also is suggestive that this was a single household rather than the opposite.

Eighthly, Mr Gaunt drew attention to the stability of the group. the relevant factor here being its continuity and the extent to which it was in continuous residence without chopping and changing of personnel. Here again it seems to me that he is echoing the thinking of Lord Hailsham in *Simmons v Pizzey*, it seems to me a relevant consideration, and it seems to me on the facts here to point towards a single household, since for the period of the tenancies there was, and was intended to be, a stable group occupying the house.

Ninthly, Mr Gaunt drew attention to the mode of living, such questions as how the cooking was done. how the eating was done, who did the shopping, who was responsible for cleaning and so on. He suggested that this was a matter of relatively little importance and that the council in its approach to the matter had given this aspect a greatly' exaggerated importance. As I have indicated, I do not necessarily accept that this is by any means the least important of the factors, and I can imagine it in some cases being of considerable importance. On the facts here it is apparent that the girl students lived rather more independent existences than the boys did. They tended to shop and cook for themselves, to keep their own supplies of food in the kitchen, and to have no very clear plans for a common purse beyond sharing, at least in theory, the costs of electricity.

The boys appeared to be rather more communal and did more cooking and shopping for each other.

I appreciate the points which were made by Mr Underwood on behalf of the council and I do not, as I have indicated, accept that this is a factor of no importance, but on the facts here I cannot regard the differences in the living arrangements between the two occupancies as being in any way crucial. It is inherent in student life that different students will come and go at different times and that groups will vary in their habits so far as sharing expenses and generally mucking in are concerned, and on the facts of this particular case there is nothing in the way in which the girl students ran the house which leads me to think that they were not one household, all the other indications to my mind showing that they were. I agree with Mr Underwood that the boys were more obviously living in a communal way, but there is a little force in the criticism that the judge formed his view by paying primary attention to the period when the boys were in residence when he should have been concentrating on the occupation by the girls. His overall conclusion did not however distinguish between the two periods. He held that there had at both times been occupation by persons who did form a single household, and in that judgment he was in my view entirely correct.

I would therefore dismiss the appeal against his conclusion on that primary point and uphold his decision.

The Master of the Rolls adds a number of elements, in accretion to those in *Simmons* v *Pizzey*, to the 'factual matrix' in considering the meaning of a household for these purposes. The decision itself has caused considerable consternation to environmental health officers charged with enforcing HMO standards on behalf of housing authorities, given that a great number of student lettings are organised in a similar way to the facts in *Barnes*. Thus, at least some properties formally regarded as HMOs by environmental health departments will now fall outside the scope of legislative protection offered by Pt XI of the Housing Act 1985. In an attempt to assuage the fears of local authorities, the Court of Appeal in *Rogers* v *Islington London Borough Council* (1999) *The Times*, 30 August, reiterated that the 'label' or description placed on a house by its owner does not determine its status – in this case the 'label' was 'residential club'. Furthermore, for a group of persons to be regarded as a 'household', there must be some form of sufficient relationship recognisable between them; although that can arise where a small group of students club together to occupy a home, either for reasons of comradeship or to reduce expenses, and even though they might not all have known one another beforehand and perhaps pay their rent individually.

Questions
1.   In Scotland a HMO is defined by means of a 1991 order under s. 44 of the Civic Government (Scotland) Act 1982, as 'a house which is the only or

principal residence of more than 4 people, being persons who are not all members of the same family or of one or other of two families.'

Does this definition bring greater clarity to the HMO definition? What difficulties are envisaged by using 'family' instead of 'household'? Should there be a minimum number of inhabitants before a property could be a HMO?

2.   Are the criteria mentioned by the Master of the Rolls in *Barnes* an adequate way of establishing a single household? Are there other factors which could (should) be taken into account?

3.   Amy, Betty, Carla and Dawn are the current inhabitants of a converted office block owned by Ethel, run for young women leaving care. The population changes reasonably frequently, although some women remain in the accommodation for a number of months until they are ready to move on. All occupants have their own room, but are expected to share cleaning and cooking duties.

Is this property a HMO for the purposes of the Housing Act 1985?

(C)   Registration schemes

(i)   Introduction

Once a property has been identified as a HMO, a local authority, if they have adopted a registration scheme, will require persons specified within the scheme to register a house to which the scheme applies. A power to adopt such a scheme is provided by s. 346 of the Housing Act 1985, as amended.

Housing Act 1985

Registration schemes

346.—(1)   A local housing authority may make a registration scheme authorising the authority to compile and maintain a register for their district of houses in multiple occupation.

(2)   A registration scheme need not be for the whole of the authority's district and need not apply to every description of house in multiple occupation.

(3)   A registration scheme may vary or revoke a previous registration scheme; and the local housing authority may at any time by order revoke a registration scheme.

Contents of registration scheme

346A.—(1)   A registration scheme shall make it the duty of such person as may be specified by the scheme to register a house to which the scheme applies and to renew the registration as and when required by the scheme.

(2)   A registration scheme shall provide that registration under the scheme—

(a)   shall be for a period of five years from the date of first registration, and

(b)   may on application be renewed, subject to such conditions as are specified in the scheme, for further periods of five years at a time.

(3)   A registration scheme may—

(a)   specify the particulars to be inserted in the register.

(b)   make it the duty of such persons as may be specified by the scheme to give the authority as regards a house all or any of the particulars specified in the scheme,

(c)   make it the duty of such persons as may be specified by the scheme to notify the authority of any change which makes it necessary to alter the particulars inserted in the register as regards a house.

(4)   A registration scheme shall, subject to subsection (5)—

(a)   require the payment on first registration of a reasonable fee of an amount determined by the local housing authority, and

(b)   require the payment on any renewal of registration of half the fee which would then have been payable on a first registration of the house.

(5)   The Secretary of State may by order make provision as to the fee payable on registration—

(a)   specifying the maximum permissible fee (whether by specifying an amount or a method for calculating an amount), and

(b)   specifying cases in which no fee is payable.

(6)   An order under subsection (5)—

(a)   may make different provision with respect to different cases or descriptions of case (including different provision for different areas), and

(b)   shall be made by statutory instrument which shall be subject to annulment in pursuance of a resolution of either House of Parliament.

Note

Sections 346 and 346A were substituted by s. 65 of the Housing Act 1996.

(ii)   Model registration schemes: control and special control provisions

The Secretary of State is granted powers, under s. 346B of the Housing Act 1985, to establish model schemes of registration. This power has been exercised to devise two types of scheme: a simple notification scheme, enabling an authority to establish a list of HMOs in their area; and a scheme to which control provisions may be attached (see DoE Circular 3/97). Control provisions can either limit the number of occupants within a property (s. 347, as amended), or prevent the house from becoming a HMO (s. 348, as amended). Special control provisions are designed to prevent HMOs, by reason of their existence or the behaviour of their residents, from adversely affecting the amenity or character of the area (s. 348B). The primary purpose behind special controls has been to prevent the proliferation of so-called 'benefit hotels' in many seaside resorts.

Housing Act 1985

Control provisions

347.—(1)   A registration scheme may contain control provisions, that is to say, provisions for preventing multiple occupation of a house unless—

(a)   the house is registered, and

(b)   the number of households or persons occupying it does not exceed the number registered for it.

(2)   Control provisions may prohibit persons from permitting others to take up residence in a house or part of a house but shall not prohibit a person from taking up or remaining in residence in the house.

(3)   Control provisions shall not prevent the occupation of a house by a greater number of households or persons than the number registered for it if all of those

households or persons have been in occupation of the house without interruption since before the number was first registered.

Control provisions: decisions on applications and appeals

348.—(1) Control provisions may enable the local housing authority, on an application for first registration of a house or a renewal or variation of registration—

(a) to refuse the application on the ground that the house is unsuitable and incapable of being made suitable for such occupation as would be permitted if the application were granted;

(b) to refuse the application on the ground that the person having control of the house or the person intended to be the person managing the house is not a fit and proper person;

(c) to require as a condition of granting the application that such works as will make the house suitable for such occupation as would be permitted if the application were granted are executed within such time as the authority may determine;

(d) to impose such conditions relating to the management of the house during the period of registration as the authority may determine.

(2) Control provisions shall provide that the local housing authority shall give an applicant a written statement of their reasons where they—

(a) refuse to grant his application for first registration or for a renewal or variation of registration,

(b) require the execution of works as a condition of granting such an application, or

(c) impose conditions relating to the management of the house.

(3) Where the local housing authority—

(a) notify an applicant that they refuse to grant his application for first registration or for the renewal or variation of a registration,

(b) notify an applicant that they require the execution of works as a condition of granting such an application,

(c) notify an applicant that they intend to impose conditions relating to the management of the house, or

(d) do not within five weeks of receiving the application, or such longer period as may be agreed in writing between the authority and the applicant, register the house or vary or the registration in accordance with application,

the applicant may, within 21 days of being so notified of the end of the period mentioned in paragraph (d), or such longer period as the authority may in writing appeal to the county court.

(4) On appeal the court may confirm, reverse or vary the decision of the authority.

(5) Where the decision of the authority was a refusal—

(a) to grant an application for first registration of a house, or

(b) for the renewal or variation of the registration,

the court may direct the authority to grant the application as made or as varied in such manner as the court may direct.

(6) For the purposes of subsections (4) and (5) an appeal under subsection (3)(d) shall be treated as an appeal against a decision of the authority to refuse the application.

(7) Where the decision of the authority was to impose conditions relating to the management of the house, the court may direct the authority to grant the application without imposing the conditions or to impose the conditions as varied in such manner as the court may direct.

Control provisions: other decisions and appeals

348A.—(1) Control provisions may enable the local housing authority at any time during a period of registration (whether or not an application has been made)—

(a)   to alter the number of households or persons for which a house is registered or revoke the registration on the ground that the house is unsuitable and incapable of being made suitable for such occupation as is permitted by virtue of the registration; or

(b)   to alter the number of households or persons for which a house is registered or revoke the registration unless such works are executed within a specified time as will make the house in question suitable for such occupation as is permitted by virtue of the registration.

(2)   Control provisions which confer on a local housing authority any such power as is mentioned in subsection (1) shall provide that the authority shall, in deciding whether to exercise the power, apply the same standards in relation to the circumstances existing at the time of the decision as were applied at the beginning of the period of registration.

(3)   Control provisions may enable the local housing authority to revoke a registration if they consider that—

(a)   the person having control of the house or the person managing it is not a fit and proper person, or

(b)   there has been a breach of conditions relating to the management of the house.

(4)   Control provisions shall also provide that the local housing authority shall—

(a)   notify the person having control of a house and the person managing it of any decision by the authority to exercise a power mentioned in subsection (1) or (3) in relation to the house, and

(b)   at the same time give them a written statement of the authority's reasons.

(5)   A person who has been so notified may within 21 days of being so notified, or such longer period as the authority may in writing allow, appeal to the county court.

(6)   On appeal the court may confirm, reverse or vary the decision of the authority.

Registration schemes: special control provisions

348B.—(1) A registration scheme which contains control provisions may also contain special control provisions, that is, provisions for preventing houses in multiple occupation, by reason of their existence or the behaviour of their residents, from adversely affecting the amenity or character of the area in which they are situated.

(2)   Special control provisions may provide for the refusal or revocation of registration, for reducing the number of households or persons for which a house is registered and for imposing conditions of registration.

(3)   The conditions of registration may include conditions relating to the management of the house or the behaviour of its occupants.

(4)   Special control provisions may authorise the revocation of registration in the case of—

(a)   occupation of the house by more households or persons than the registration permits, or

(b)   a breach of any condition imposed in pursuance of the special control provisions,

which is due to a relevant management failure.

(5)   Special control provisions shall not authorise the refusal of—

(a)   an application for first registration of a house which has been in operation as a house in multiple occupation since before the introduction by the local housing authority of a registration scheme with special control provisions, or

(b)   any application for renewal of registration of a house previously registered under such a scheme,
unless there has been a relevant management failure.

(6)   Special control provisions may provide that in any other case where an application is made for first registration of a house the local housing authority may take into account the number of houses in multiple occupation in the vicinity in deciding whether to permit or refuse registration.

Notes

1.   Sections 347, 348 and 348A were substituted by s. 66 of the Housing Act 1996. Section 348B was substituted by s. 67 of the 1996 Act. Sections 348C, 348D and 348D provide the procedural and appeal mechanisms in relation to special control mechanisms. They were substituted by s. 67 of the 1996 Act, as was s. 348F which defines a 'relevant management failure' as a failure on the part of the person having control of the house, or the person managing it, to take such steps as are reasonably practicable. To prevent the existence of the house or the behaviour of its residents from adversely affecting the amenity or character of the areas where the home is situated, or a failure to reduce such an effect.

2.   Annex C1 of DoE Circular 3/97 contains a model registration scheme, as follows:

Department of the Environment Circular 3/97

ANNEX C1

The [Council Name] (Registration of Houses in Multiple Occupation) Scheme 19

The [name of Council] in exercise of their powers under sections 346 to 348A of the Housing Act 1985 and section 70(3) of the Housing Act 1996 hereby make the following scheme.

CITATION, COMMENCEMENT AND REVOCATION

1.   (1)   This scheme may be cited as the [name of Council] (Registration of Houses in Multiple Occupation) Scheme 19
     (2)   This scheme shall come into force on [date not less than 1 month from date of scheme]
     [(3)   The   Scheme 19   is hereby revoked.]

INTERPRETATION

2.   In this scheme–
     "1985 Act" means the Housing Act 1985;
     "authority" means the [name of Council];
     "house" has the same meaning as in section 399 of the 1985 Act;
     "house in multiple occupation" has the same meaning as in section 345 of the 1985 Act and "multiple occupation" shall be construed accordingly;
     "person having control" and "person managing" have the same meaning as in section 398 of the 1985 Act;
     "responsible person" means the person having control or the person managing;

"storey" excludes any storey lying wholly or mainly below the floor level of the principal entrance to the house.

AREA OF REGISTRATION

3.   This scheme shall apply to [*specify geographical area to which scheme is to apply*].

APPLICATION

4.(1)   This scheme shall not apply to–

(a)   any house in which the authority has an interest, whether freehold or leasehold;

(b)   any house subject to a control order made under section 379 of the 1985 Act;

(c)   any house used as a children's home or community home which is registered or provided under the Children Act 1989;

(d)   any house registered under the Registered Homes Act 1984;

(e)   any house which is occupied by persons who form only two households;

(f)   any house which is occupied by no more than four persons who form more than two households;

(g)   any house which is occupied by no more than three persons in addition to the responsible person and any other member of his household;

(h)   any house where the living accommodation consists entirely of self-contained flats and either–

  (i)   at least one third of the flats are either–

     (aa)   let on leases of more than 21 years and wholly occupied by the lessees and their households; or

     (bb)   wholly occupied by any freeholder of the house and his household; or

  (ii)   when the flats were created

     (aa)   the building was required to comply with the requirements relevant to fire safety contained in the Building Regulations 1985 or regulations made subsequently under section 1(1) of the Building Act 1984,

     (bb)   a building notice had been given to, or full plans deposited with, a local authority, or an initial notice or a public body's notice had been given in accordance with sections 47(1) and 54(1) respectively of the Building Act 1984, and

     (cc)   the building work in respect of the creation of the flats was carried out in accordance with any such notice or plans, whether with or without any departure from them;

(i)   any house of which the responsible person is a health service body as defined in section 519A of the Income and Corporation Taxes Act 1988;

(j)   any house of which the responsible person is a social landlord registered in accordance with Part I of the Housing Act 1996;

(k)   any house of which the responsible person is–

  (i)   a university or other institution within the higher education sector within the meaning given by section 91(5) of the Further and Higher Education Act 1992 or a college or other institution in the nature of a college in such a university or other institution;

  (ii)   an institution within the further education sector within the meaning given by section 91(3) of that Act;

  (iii)   an institution which provides a course qualifying for funding under Part I of the Education Act 1994; or

(l)   any house approved by the Secretary of State under section 27 of the Probation Services Act 1993.

(2)   For the purposes of sub-paragraph (1)(h)–

(a)   a "flat" means any part of a building which was originally constructed or subsequently adapted for occupation by a single household; and

(b)   "self-contained" means that the flat has for the exclusive use of its occupants the facilities mentioned in section 352(1A)(a) to (c) of the 1985 Act.

AUTHORITY GIVEN BY THE SCHEME

5.   Subject to paragraphs 3 and 4(1) the authority shall compile and maintain a register of all houses in multiple occupation.

PARTICULARS TO BE INSERTED IN THE REGISTER

6.   Each entry in the register in respect of a house shall contain the following particulars–

(a)   address of the house;

(b)   the number of storeys;

(c)   the number of rooms in the house;

(d)   the number of those rooms used exclusively as–

kitchens
bathrooms (with or without water closets, and with a bath or a shower);

(e)   the total number of–

fixed wash hand basins
fixed sinks
fixed baths or showers
water closets   (a) external
                (b) internal;

(f)   the name and address of the person managing the house and of any other person who is an owner, lessee or mortgagee in possession of the house or any part of it. In the case of a body corporate the address shall be the registered address and, if different, that of the secretary or other principal officer;

(g)   a description of any such person as owner, lessee, mortgagee, agent or trustee;

(h)   the number of households and persons occupying the house;

(i)   particulars of any works carried out subsequent to registration pursuant to a notice given under sections 352 or 372 or under an order made under section 377A of the 1985 Act; and

(j)   the number of households and persons for whom it is registered.

REGISTRATION

7.(1)   The responsible person of a house in multiple occupation shall apply to register the house with the authority.

(2)   On a first application for registration, the responsible person shall–

(a)   give the authority the particulars of the house specified in paragraph 6, and

(b)   pay a fee of a reasonable amount determined by the authority (not exceeding the amount specified by the Secretary of State).

(3)   Registration shall be for an initial period of five years from the date of first registration, and may be renewed for further periods of five years at a time.

(4)   On or before expiry of a period of registration, the responsible person shall apply for renewal of the registration.

(5)   On renewal of registration, the responsible person shall–

(a)   notify the authority of any changes in the particulars entered in the register in respect of the house, and

    (b)   pay a fee of one-half of the amount which would at that time have been payable for first registration of the house.

(6)   During any period of registration, the responsible person shall notify the authority of any change in the particulars entered in the register which makes it necessary to alter the particulars inserted in the register except a decrease in number registered under paragraph 6(h).

CONDITIONS FOR REGISTRATION

8.(1)   The authority may, on an application for first registration of a house or a renewal or variation of a registration–

    (a)   refuse the application on the ground that the house is unsuitable and incapable of being made suitable for such occupation as would be permitted if the application were granted;

    (b)   refuse the application on the ground that the person having control of the house or the person intended to be managing the house is not a fit and proper person;

    (c)   require as a condition of granting the application that such works as will make the house suitable for such occupation as would be permitted if the application were granted are executed within such time as the authority determine; or

    (d)   impose such conditions relating to the management of the house during the period of registration as the authority determine.

(2)   The authority shall give the applicant a written statement of their reasons where they–

    (a)   refuse to grant his application for first registration or for renewal or variation of registration;

    (b)   require the execution of works as a condition of granting such an application, or

    (c)   impose conditions relating to the management of the house.

9.(1)   The authority may, at any time during the period of registration (whether or not an application has been made)–

    (a)   alter the number of households or persons for which a house is registered on the ground that the house is unsuitable and incapable of being made suitable for such occupation as is permitted by virtue of the registration; or

    (b)   alter the number of households or persons for which a house is registered or revoke the registration unless such works are executed within a time specified by the authority as will make the house in question suitable for such occupation as is permitted by virtue of the registration.

(2)   The authority shall, in deciding whether to exercise the power under sub-paragraph (1), apply the same standards in relation to the circumstances existing at the time of the decision as were applied at the beginning of the period of registration.

(3)   The authority may revoke a registration if they consider that–

    (a)   the person having control of the house or the person managing it is not a fit or proper person, or

    (b)   there has been a breach of the conditions relating to the management of the house.

(4)   The authority shall–

    (a)   notify the responsible person of any decision by the authority to exercise a power mentioned in sub-paragraph (1) or (3) in relation to a house, and

    (b)   at the same time give them a written statement of the authority's reasons.

PROHIBITION AGAINST OVER-OCCUPATION

10.   No person shall permit another to take up residence in a house or part of a house unless

    (a)   the house is registered, and

    (b)   the number of households or persons occupying it will not as a result exceed the number registered for it.

[Date and authentication]

Notes

1.   As indicated above, the condition of many HMOs is poor, both from a fire safety and an amenity standard viewpoint. One method of locating all HMOs, and in so doing helping to enable enforcing authorities to upgrade standards in the HMO sector generally, would be to ensure that all HMOs are subject to a licensing or registration scheme. This, however, has proven to be a matter of considerable controversy. The then Department of the Environment (DoE) issued a paper on the issue of licensing (*Houses in Multiple Occupation: Consultation Paper on the Case for Licensing*, London, DoE, 1994) which highlighted arguments both for and against a national mandatory registration or licensing scheme. Ultimately, despite 76 per cent of respondents to the Consultation Paper supporting a mandatory system, the Conservative Government selected a system allowing local authorities to determine, for their area, whether registration for HMOs should take place.

2.   Upon the implementation of such a registration scheme by an authority it becomes the duty of persons specified under the scheme to register a house to which the scheme applies (s. 346A(1)). The registration scheme shall last for a period of five years and may be renewed for further five-year periods (s. 346A(2)). A fee may be charged by the authority both for the initial registration and for the renewal of registration (s. 346A(4)) (See SI 1998 No. 1812 detailing maximum permissible charges.)

3.   The current Government, following a manifesto commitment prior to the General Election 1997, have indicated a desire to move towards a national mandatory licensing scheme for all HMOs. In the interim, the DETR are encouraging all authorities to adopt registration schemes to facilitate the transition to licensing (DETR Press Notice, 22 June 1998).

(D)   Execution of general works

Section 352 of the Housing Act 1985, as amended by the Local Government and Housing Act 1989 and the Housing Act 1996, empowers a housing authority to serve a notice requiring the execution of work deemed necessary, where the premises fail to meet one of the requirements laid down in s. 352A and due to that failure the premises are considered, by the authority, not reasonably suitable for occupation by the number of persons or households within the premises. Two restrictions are placed on the issuing of notices in this area: (i) on the area of second works notices (s. 352(7)); (ii) relating to a written warning prior to the issuing of a formal notice (s. 377A).

Housing Act 1985

Power to require execution of works to render premises fit for number of occupants

352.—(1) Subject to section 365 the local housing authority may serve a notice under this section where in the opinion of the authority, a house in multiple occupation fails to meet one or more of the requirements in paragraphs (a) to (e) of subsection (1A) and, having regard to the number of individuals or households or both for the time being accommodated on the premises, by reason of that failure the premises are not reasonably suitable for occupation by those individuals or households.

(1A) The requirements in respect of a house in multiple occupation referred to in subsection (1) are the following, that is to say,—

(a) there are satisfactory facilities for the storage, preparation and cooking of food including an adequate number of sinks with a satisfactory supply of hot and cold water;

(b) it has an adequate number of suitably located water-closets for the exclusive use of the occupants;

(c) it has, for the exclusive use of the occupants, an adequate number of suitably located fixed baths or showers and wash-hand basins each of which is provided with a satisfactory supply of hot and cold water;

(d) subject to section 365, there are adequate means of escape from fire; and

(e) there are adequate other fire precautions.

(2) Subject to subsection (2A) the notice shall specify the works which in the opinion of the authority are required for rendering the house reasonably suitable—

(a) for occupation by the individuals and households for the time being accommodated there, or

(b) for a smaller number of individuals or households and the number of individuals or households, or both, which, in the opinion of the authority, the house could reasonably accommodate if the works were carried out,

but the notice shall not specify any works to any premises outside the house.

(2A) Where the authority have exercised or propose to exercise their powers under section 368 to secure that part of the house is not used for human habitation, they may specify in the notice such work only as in their opinion is required to meet such of the requirements in subsection (1A) as may be applicable if that part is not so used.

(3) The notice may be served—

(a) on the person having control of the house, or

(b) on the person managing the house;

and the authority shall inform any other person who is to their knowledge an owner, lessee, occupier or mortgagee of the house of the fact that the notice has been served.

(4) The notice shall require the person on whom it is served to execute the works specified in the notice within such period as follows, namely,—

(a) to begin those works not later than such reasonable date, being not earlier than the twenty-first day after the date of service of the notice, as is specified in the notice; and

(b) to complete those works within such reasonable period as is so specified.

(5) If the authority are satisfied that—

(a) after the service of a notice under this section the number of individuals living on the premises has been reduced to a level which will make the works specified in the notice unnecessary, and

(b) that number will be maintained at or below that level, whether in consequence of the exercise of the authority's powers under section 354 (power to limit number of occupants of house) or otherwise,
they may withdraw the notice by notifying that fact in writing to the person on whom the notice was served, but without prejudice to the issue of a further notice.

(5A) A notice served under this section is a local land charge.

(5B) Each local housing authority shall—

(a) maintain a register of notices served by the authority under subsection (1) after the coming into force of this subsection;

(b) ensure the register is open to inspection by the public free of charge at all reasonable hours; and

(c) on request, and on payment of any such reasonable fee as the authority may require, supply copies of entries in the register to any person.

(6) . . .

(7) Where a local housing authority serve a notice under this section in respect of any of the requirements specified in subsection (1A), and the works specified in the notice are carried out, whether by the person on whom the notice was served or by the local housing authority under section 375, the authority shall not, within the period of five years from the service of the notice, serve another notice under this section in respect of the same requirement unless they consider that there has been a change of circumstances in relation to the premises.

(8) Such a change may, in particular, relate to the condition of the premises or the availability or use of the facilities mentioned in subsection (1A).

Works notices: improvement of enforcement procedures
377A.—(1) The Secretary of State may by order provide that a local housing authority shall act as specified in the order before serving a works notice.

In this section a 'works notice' means a notice under section 352 or 372 (notices requiring the execution of works).

(2) An order under this section may provide that the authority—

(a) shall as soon as practicable give to the person on whom the works notice is to be served a written notice which satisfies the requirements of subsection (3); and

(b) shall not serve the works notice until after the end of such period beginning with the giving of a notice which satisfies the requirements of subsection (3) as may be determined by or under the order.

(3) A notice satisfies the requirements of this subsection if it—

(a) states the works which in the authority's opinion should be undertaken, and explains why and within what period;

(b) explains the grounds on which it appears to the authority that the works notice might be served;

(c) states the type of works notice which is to be served, the consequences of serving it and whether there is a right to make representations before, or a right of appeal against, the serving of it.

(4) An order under this section may also provide that, before the authority serves the works notice on any person, they—

(a) shall give to that person a written notice stating—

(i) that they are considering serving the works notice and the reasons why they are considering serving the notice; and

(ii) that the person may, within a period specified in the written notice, make written representations to them or, if the person so requests, make oral representations to them in the presence of a person determined by or under the order; and

(b)   shall consider any representations which are duly made and not withdrawn.

(5)   An order under this section may in particular—

(a)   make provision as to the consequences of any failure to comply with a provision made by the order;

(b)   contain such consequential, incidental, supplementary or transitional provisions and savings as the Secretary of State considers appropriate (including provisions modifying enactments relating to the periods within which proceedings must be brought).

(6)   An order under this section—

(a)   may make different provision with respect to different cases or descriptions of case (including different provision for different areas), and

(b)   shall be made by statutory instrument which shall be subject to annulment in pursuance of a resolution of either House of Parliament.

(7)   Nothing in any order under this section shall—

(a)   preclude a local housing authority from serving a works notice on any person, or from requiring any person to take immediate remedial action to avoid a works notice being served on him, in any case where it appears to them to be necessary to serve such a notice or impose such a requirement; or

(b)   require such an authority to disclose any information the disclosure of which would be contrary to the public interest.

Notes

1.   Section 352(7) and (8) were inserted by s. 71(1) of the Housing Act 1996. Section 377A was inserted by s. 76 of the 1996 Act.

2.   It is important to note here that local authorities merely have a discretion to act under s. 352, rather than a duty to do so. It may well be that the financial consequences of serving such a notice is one of the factors impacting upon an authority's decision. Before an authority serve notice upon a person having control of or managing the house (s. 353, as amended), it is incumbent upon the authority to ensure that one or more of the stipulated requirements of s. 352(1A) have been broken. The question for the housing authority therefore is: what HMO standards should be acceptable? The DoE issued Circular 12/92 giving authorities detailed guidance in this area. While the guidance is advisory, councils are aware that too great a departure from guidance may result in an appeal to the county court under s. 353 of the 1985 Act.

3.   Under s. 77 of the Housing Act 1996 the above Circular was to be replaced by a new code of practice approved by the Secretary of State. However, the DETR announced in a Press Release of 22 June 1998 that they had decided against an interim code of practice while work was ongoing with issues of licensing HMOs. Thus, it may be some time before a new code of practice is in place.

4.   An authority has the powers under s. 375 of the 1985 Act to undertake any required works themselves if a notice has not been complied with, or if, in the opinion of the authority, reasonable progress has not been made.

5.   Where an HMO is in a particularly poor state, an authority may make a control order, effectively allowing the authority to manage the property as they see fit for up to five years (s. 381(1)).

(E)   Powers to limit the number of occupants

Section 354 of the Housing Act 1985 (as amended) enables a housing authority to specify the maximum number of persons who may inhabit the house with subsisting amenities, or, if used in conjunction with the service of a notice under s. 352, to determine permissible occupation after works have been executed.

Housing Act 1985

Power to limit number of occupants of house
354.—(1)   The local housing authority may, for the purpose of preventing the occurrence of, or remedying, a state of affairs calling for the service of a notice or further notice under section 352 (notice requiring execution of works to render house fit for number of occupants)—

(a)   fix as a limit for the house what is in their opinion the highest number of individuals or households, or both, who should, having regard to the requirements set out in subsection (1A), of that section, occupy the house in its existing condition, and

(b)   give a direction applying that limit to the house.

(2)   The authority may also exercise the powers conferred by subsection (1) in relation to a part of a house; and the authority shall have regard to the desirability of applying separate limits where different parts of a house are, or are likely to be, occupied by different persons.

(3)   Not less than seven days before giving a direction under this section, the authority shall—

(a)   serve on an owner of the house, and on every person who is to their knowledge a lessee of the house, notice of their intention to give the direction, and

(b)   post such a notice in some position in the house where it is accessible to those living in the house,

and shall afford to any person on whom a notice is so served an opportunity of making representations regarding their proposal to give the direction.

(4)   The authority shall within seven days from the giving of the direction—

(a)   serve a copy of the direction on an owner of the house and on every person who is to their knowledge a lessee of the house, and

(b)   post a copy of the direction in some position in the house where it is accessible to those living in the house.

(5)   A direction may be given notwithstanding the existence of a previous direction laying down a higher maximum for the same house or part of a house.

(6)   Where the local housing authority have in pursuance of section 352 served a notice specifying the number of individuals or households, or both, which in the opinion of the authority the house could reasonably accommodate if the works specified in the notice were carried out, the authority may adopt that number in fixing a limit under subsection (1) as respects the house.

(7)   The powers conferred by this section—

(a)   are exercisable whether or not a notice has been given under section 352, and

(b)   are without prejudice to the powers conferred by section 358 (overcrowding notices).

(8)   A direction under this section is a local land charge.

Note
Section 354(8) was inserted by s. 74 of the Housing Act 1996.

(F)   Additional fire powers and duties

Part (D) above considered housing authority powers with regard to, amongst other things, the means of escape from fire and other fire precautions. Section 365 of the Housing Act 1985, as amended by the Local Government and Housing Act 1989 and the Housing Act 1996, provides additional powers for authorities where the HMO is considered a particular fire risk. Furthermore, authorities are under a *duty* to act where the property is of such a description, or is occupied in such a manner, as specified by the Secretary of State (see SI 1997 No. 230 imposing a duty relating to houses in multiple occupation comprising at least three floors. The statutory instrument lays down a number of exceptions to this duty towards three-storey HMOs, including the need for the property to be occupied by more than four persons to fall within the duty.) Before taking action under s. 365, an authority has a general discretion to consult the relevant fire authority. In addition, housing authorities are under a duty to consult a fire authority where there is a duty to take action to remedy the fire risk.

Housing Act 1985

Means of escape from fire: general provisions as to exercise of powers
365.—(1) In any case where—
    (a) the local housing authority have the power to serve a notice under subsection (1) of section 352 in respect of a house in multiple occupation, and
    (b) the reason, or one of the reasons, by virtue of which that power arises is a failure to meet the requirement in paragraph (d) or (e) of subsection (1A) of that section,
the authority shall in addition have the power for that reason to accept an undertaking or make a closing order under section 368 in respect of the house.
    (2) Where by virtue of subsection (1) the local housing authority have powers in respect of a house in multiple occupation to serve a notice under section 352(1) for the reason mentioned in subsection (1)(b) and to accept an undertaking or make a closing order under section 368, they may exercise such of those powers as appear to them appropriate; and where the house is of such description or is occupied in such manner as the Secretary of State may specify by order for the purposes of this subsection, the authority shall be under a duty to so exercise those powers.
    (2A) The local housing authority shall not serve a notice under section 352(1) for the reason mentioned in subsection (1)(b) or accept an undertaking or make a closing order under section 368 if the house is of such description or is occupied in such manner as the Secretary of State may specify by order for the purposes of this subsection.
    (3) The local housing authority shall consult with the fire authority concerned before exercising any of the powers mentioned in subsection (2)—
    (a) where they are under a duty to exercise those powers, or
    (b) where they are not under such a duty but may exercise those powers and the house is of such description or is occupied in such manner as the Secretary of State may specify by order for the purposes of this subsection.]

(4)   An order under subsection (2) (2A) or (3)—
    (a)   may make different provision with respect to different cases or descriptions of case, including different provision for different areas, and
    (b)   shall be made by statutory instrument which shall be subject to annulment in pursuance of a resolution of either House of Parliament.
    (5)   Nothing in this section affects the power of the local housing authority to serve a notice under subsection (1) of section 352 if the house also fails to meet one or more of the requirements in paragraphs (a) to (c) . . . of subsection (1A) of that section.

In addition to the powers and duties of local housing authorities, fire authorities have extensive powers under s. 10 of the Fire Precautions Act 1971, as amended by the Fire Safety and Safety of Places of Sport Act 1987. Here, where the fire authority considers premises are, or are intended to be in the future, used for sleeping accommodation (other than as a single dwelling), the authority may, if there is a serious risk to persons using the property, issue a notice prohibiting or restricting its use.

(G)   Management regulations

Section 369 of the Housing Act 1985, as amended, empowers the Secretary of State to introduce a management code to ensure the effective management of HMO properties (see SI 1990 No. 830). This code requires managers of HMOs to ensure that water supply and drainage, gas and electricity, common parts, installations in common use, living accommodation, windows and ventilation, means of escape from fire, outbuildings, refuse and litter are all managed in such a way to ensure effective provision of services for residents and the protection of public safety. A housing authority may serve a remedial works notice, if they consider that the HMO is failing to reach required standards (s. 372 of the 1985 Act).

Housing Act 1985

The Management Code
369.—(1)   The Secretary of State may, with a view to providing a code for the management of houses in multiple occupation, by regulations make provision for ensuring that the person managing a house in multiple occupation observes proper standards of management.
    (2)   Subject to subsection (2A) the regulations may, in particular, require the person managing the house to ensure the repair, maintenance, cleansing and good order of—
        all means of water supply and drainage in the house,
        all means of escape from fire and all apparatus, systems and other things provided by way of fire precautions;
        kitchens, bathrooms and water closets in common use,
        sinks and wash-basins in common use,
        common staircases, corridors and passage ways, and
        outbuildings, yards and gardens in common use,

and to make satisfactory arrangements for the disposal of refuse and litter from the house and to ensure that all means of escape from fire are kept clear of obstructions.

(2A)   The person managing the house shall only be liable by virtue of the regulations under subsection (2) to ensure the repair, maintenance, cleansing and good order of any premises outside the house if and to the extent that he has power or is otherwise liable to ensure those matters in respect of any such premises.

(3)   The regulations may—

(a)   make different provision for different types of house;

(c)   impose duties on persons who have an estate or interest in a house or part of a house to which the regulations apply as to the giving of information to the local housing authority,

(d)   impose duties on persons who live in the house for the purpose of ensuring that the person managing the house can effectively carry out the duties imposed on him by the regulations;

(e)   authorise the local housing authority to obtain information as to the number of individuals or households accommodated in the house;

(g)   contain such other incidental and supplementary provisions as may appear to the Secretary of State to be expedient.

(4)   Regulations under this section may vary or replace for the purposes of this section and of the regulations made under it the definition given in section 398 of the 'person managing' a house.

(5)   A person who knowingly contravenes or without reasonable excuse fails to comply with a regulation under this section commits a summary offence and is liable on conviction to a fine not exceeding level 5 on the standard scale.

(6)   Regulations under this section shall be made by statutory instrument which shall be subject to annulment in pursuance of a resolution of either House of Parliament.

Power to require execution of works to remedy neglect of management
372.—(1)   If in the opinion of the local housing authority the condition of a house . . . is defective in consequence of—

(a)   neglect to comply with the requirements imposed by regulations under section 369 (regulations prescribing management code)
the authority may serve on the person managing the house a notice specifying the works which, in the opinion of the authority, are required to make good the neglect.

(2)   If it is not practicable after reasonable inquiry to ascertain the name or address of the person managing the house, the notice may be served by addressing it to him by the description of 'manager of the house' (naming the house to which it relates) and delivering it to some person on the premises.

(3)   The notice shall require the person on whom it is served to execute the works specified in the notice within such period, as follows, namely,—

(a)   to begin those works not later than such reasonable date, being not earlier than the twenty-first day after the date of service of the notice, as is specified in the notice; and

(b)   to complete those works within such reasonable period as is so specified.

(4)   Where the authority serve a notice under this section on the person managing a house, they shall inform any other person who is to their knowledge an owner, lessee or mortgagee of the house of the fact that the notice has been served.

(5)   References in this section to the person managing a house have the same meaning as in section 369 (and accordingly are subject to amendment by regulations under that section).

Note
Sections 369 and 372 are set out as amended by the Local Government and Housing Act 1989. Section 369(5) was amended by s. 78(6) of the Housing Act 1996.

(H)   Overcrowding

Sections 358 to 364 of the Housing Act 1985 enable an authority to act where it appears to the authority that excessive numbers of people are being accommodated within a HMO, or in situations where excessive numbers of people are likely to be accommodated, bearing in mind the number of rooms available. An aggrieved person has 21 days to appeal to the county court which may confirm, quash or vary the notice, under s. 362.

Housing Act 1985

Service of overcrowding notice
358.—(1)   Where it appears to the local housing authority in the case of a house in multiple occupation—
    (a)   that an excessive number of persons is being accommodated on the premises, having regard to the rooms available, or
    (b)   that it is likely that an excessive number of persons will be accommodated on the premises, having regard to the rooms available.
they may serve an overcrowding notice on the occupier of the premises or on the person managing the premises, or on both.
    (2)   At least seven days before serving an overcrowding notice, the local housing authority shall—
    (a)   inform the occupier of the premises and any person appearing to them to be managing the premises, in writing, of their intention to do so, and
    (b)   ensure that, so far as is reasonably possible, every person living in the premises is informed of that intention;
and they shall afford those persons an opportunity of making representations regarding their proposal to serve the notice.
    (3)   If no appeal is brought under section 362, the overcrowding notice becomes operative at the end of the period of 21 days from the date of service, and is final and conclusive as to matters which could have been raised on such an appeal.
    (4)   A person who contravenes an overcrowding notice commits a summary offence and is liable on conviction to a fine not exceeding level 4 on the standard scale.

Appeal against overcrowding notice
362.—(1)   A person aggrieved by an overcrowding notice may, within 21 days after the date of service of the notice, appeal to the county court, which may make such order either confirming, quashing or varying the notice as it thinks fit.
    (2)   If an appeal is brought the notice does not become operative until—
    (a)   a decision on the appeal confirming the order (with or without variation) is given and the period within which an appeal to the Court of Appeal may be brought expires without any such appeal having been brought, or
    (b)   if a further appeal to the Court of Appeal is brought, a decision on that appeal is given confirming the order (with or without variation);

and for this purpose the withdrawal of an appeal has the same effect as a decision confirming the notice or decision appealed against.

(I) Duty to keep premises fit for number of occupants

Section 73 of the Housing Act 1996 inserts a new s. 353A into the 1985 Act placing a duty on the person having control of the HMO, and the persons managing it, to ensure that the issuing of a s. 352 notice (see above) is not necessary:

[Duty to keep premises fit for a number of occupants
353A.—(1) It is the duty of the person having control of a house in multiple occupation, and of the person managing it. to take such steps as are reasonably practicable to prevent the occurrence of a state of affairs calling for the service of a notice or further notice under section 352 (notice requiring execution of works to render house fit for number of occupants).

(2) A breach of that duty is actionable in damages at the suit of any tenant or other occupant of the premises, or any other person who suffers loss, damage or personal injury in consequence of the breach.

(3) A person who fails to comply with the duty imposed on him by subsection (1) commits a summary offence and is liable on conviction to a fine not exceeding level 5 on the standard scale.]

This duty was due to come into force following extensive consultation and the issuing of a new code of practice for HMOs. However, it is now understood that this section will not be commenced as it is regarded as unworkable in its present form (DETR Press Release, 22 June 1998).

Questions
1. In what way could the duty under s. 353A be considered unworkable?
2. Would it be preferable to impose mandatory requirements that no person may manage or control a HMO unless they can first show that they are a 'fit and proper' person to do so. If so, what matters should be taken into account in deciding what 'fit and proper' means?

Note
In March 1999, the DETR issued a Consultation Paper on defining and licensing HMOs in order to ensure safe and acceptable living conditions with regard to the physical state of property, the standard of management, and the fitness of the licensed landlord, e.g. whether the person is adequately trained in fire safety, or has a criminal record. Implementing change would, however, need additional legislation.

9 HOUSING AND THE FAMILY

(A) Introduction

The interface between housing law and family law, with which this chapter is concerned, is complex and uncertain. Not least amongst the uncertainties is that involved in deciding on the exact focus of coverage. The death of a partner to a relationship, or another family member, or the breakdown of a relationship have many serious consequences that are far from the sole preserve of housing law, or, indeed, of the law at all. Most of the key issues concerning (for example) property transfers between partners, or the interests of (any) children of the relationship, are clearly the concern of family law and are wholly outside the scope of this book. However, in other areas, for example the future of a tenanted family home, a housing law perspective may well be distinctive and valuable, even if there is inevitable overlap with family law issues. Moreover, there are other areas which are clearly of chief concern to housing law rather than family law, such as statutory rights of succession to tenanted property (see also chapter 3 and chapter 5) and the difficulties raised by joint tenancies.

A key issue which threads through this chapter is the shifting and relative concept of the 'family' itself. Judicial and legislative attitudes towards the scope of the idea of what can constitute a 'family' have changed enormously over the last 50 years. For example, in *Gammans* v *Ekins* [1950] 2 KB 328, a cohabiting heterosexual couple were adjudged by the Court of Appeal not to be members of the same family, for the purposes of succession to a tenancy. Asquith LJ (at p. 331) summed up the view of the court: 'To say of two people masquerading . . . as husband and wife . . . that they were members of the same family, seems to be an abuse of the English language.' By 1997, in *Fitzpatrick* v *Sterling Housing Association Ltd* [1997] 4 All ER 991, the Court of Appeal came close to deciding that a longstanding homosexual relationship could be seen as putting the 'partners' to it in a 'family' relationship for succession purposes, and the dissenting judge, Ward LJ did so decide. At p. 1023, he stated: 'In my judgment, our society has shown itself to be tolerant enough to free itself from the burdens of stereotype and prejudice . . . the common man . . . would recognise that [this] relationship was to all intents and purposes a marriage . . . They were so bound together that they constituted a family.' Judicial thinking has clearly shifted considerably from a view of the 'family' as solely a function of biology or marriage, and is certainly moving in the direction of viewing any relatively long-term and stable relationship as conferring 'family' status. Nevertheless, serious issues remain concerning the consistency of the approach of the courts and of inconsistency between differing legislative provisions.

The following material is divided into three sections: an initial section on the meaning of 'family', as seen by the courts and by legislation; a section concerned with the housing law consequences of relationship breakdown, at common law and under legislation; and, the distinct problems raised by the existence of joint tenancies between family members.

Note
Though it is confusing, in 1996, following the Family Law Act of that year, the law changed from speaking of 'cohabitees' to 'cohabitants.' This should be remembered in reading what follows.

(B) The family: a problem of definition

Most of the relevant judicial discussion of the definition of 'family' has taken place in the context of the succession provisions in the Rent Act 1977, the Housing Act 1988 and the Housing Act 1985. The detailed rules as to what types of tenancy can pass on death were considered in chapters 3 and 5, but running through all the detailed, and often highly technical, law on the subject is the general notion that succession should be available to spouses and other 'family' members and not more widely. This, in its turn, has forced the courts to return on many occasions to consider how widely 'family' should be construed for this purpose. From time to time legislative amendments have refocused the discussion, as, for example, in the Housing Act 1988 amendments to the definition of 'family' in Sch. 1 to the Rent Act 1977 (set out in chapter 3) which clarified the legal position of cohabitees. Equally, legislation is not always consistent in its approach, as a comparison of the amended Sch. 1 to the Rent Act 1977 with s. 113 of the Housing Act 1985 will demonstrate. Although the most recent case law indicates a desire in the courts to achieve a greater degree of consistency across the various statutory provisions (see *Fitzpatrick* v *Sterling Housing Association Ltd* [1997] 4 All ER 991), for ease of exposition the law is considered respectively under the Rent Act 1977, the Housing Act 1988, and the Housing Act 1985.

(i) Rent Act 1977

The relevant provisions are contained in Sch. 1 to the Rent Act 1977, as amended by Sch. 4 to the Housing Act 1988. They are set out in detail in chapter 3.

The crucial amendments introduced by the 1988 Act were that 'family' members other than spouses could succeed only to an assured tenancy, that to do so such a person must have resided with the deceased tenant for at least two years (previously six months) and that those living together 'as wife or husband' were henceforward to be treated as spouses. The last amendment is of particular importance to the question of defining 'family'. Prior to *Dyson Holdings Ltd* v *Fox* [1976] QB 503, the courts had taken a narrow approach to the definition, refusing to extend it beyond close and clearly established biological relationships. Following *Dyson*, a cohabitee of long standing qualified, provided there had been a sexual relationship, but doubts remained about the position of short-term cohabitees, even though there had been a sexual relationship (see *Helby* v *Rafferty* [1979] 1 WLR 13), and a purely platonic relationship, however longstanding, certainly did not qualify (see *Carega Properties SA* v *Sharratt* [1979] 1 WLR 928). The 1988 Act amendments remove any uncertainty concerning heterosexual couples who have been sharing a common household long enough for them to be seen to be living together 'as . . . wife or husband'. Indeed such couples now have superior status to other 'family' members, such as sons and daughters, in that, like spouses, they can succeed to a statutory tenancy and need have served no 'qualification' period prior to the death to gain such rights.

What was left uncertain by the 1988 amendments was the extent to which 'family' covered non-heterosexual relationships, in particular whether it could be extended to friends who have shared a common household for a significant period, and homosexual relationships. In the former case, *Carega Properties SA* v *Sharratt* indicated that such relationships did *not* generally convert those involved into members of a 'family'.

Carega v *Sharratt*
[1979] 1 WLR 928

In 1957, when he was aged 24, Sharratt had formed a friendship with a widow of 75. From 1958, he lived with her in a flat of which she was the contractual tenant. Initially, he paid for the use of a room in the flat, but later the widow paid the whole rent, although other expenses were shared. Neither party was dependent on the other, but a close 'platonic' relationship developed, akin to aunt and nephew. On the expiry of the contractual tenancy, in 1973, the widow became a statutory tenant. In 1976 she died, but Sharratt continued to reside in the flat.

In an action for possession by the landlords, Sharratt claimed that he had succeeded to the widow's statutory tenancy, in that he had been a member of her 'family' resident with her for the requisite six-month period (now Rent Act 1977, Sch. 3, para. 3). However, although this claim was upheld by the High Court, the Court of Appeal allowed the landlord's appeal, finding that no 'familial nexus' had come into being. The House of Lords unanimously agreed with the Court of Appeal.

LORD DIPLOCK: . . . My Lords, the only question in this appeal is one of construction of the Rent Act 1968. It is whether a person between whom and the deceased statutory tenant of a dwelling house there is no connection by way of consanguinity, of affinity, of adoption (de jure or de facto) during minority or of regular sexual intercourse (past or present) can be a member of the tenant's family within the meaning of Schedule 1, paragraph 3 to the Act, so as to entitle him to become the statutory tenant of the dwelling house by succession to the deceased.
. . .

The deceased statutory tenant of flat 48, Coleherne Court, London, SW5, of which the respondents claim possession, was Lady Salter, the widow of a High Court judge, who had died as long ago as 1929. In 1957, when she was aged 75, she first met the appellant, Mr Sharratt, who was then aged 24. They shared a mutual interest in politics and the theatre and a close friendship grew up between them. In the following year, Lady Salter suggested that Mr Sharratt should come to live in her flat at Coleherne Court. He fell in with this suggestion and for the first three years that he resided there he paid her £4 a week for bed and breakfast. After that the payments ceased. Lady Salter at all times paid the rent of the flat, but the other expenses were shared between them. This continued until her death at the age of 94 in April 1976.

The relationship between them throughout was platonic and filial. He behaved towards her as a dutiful and affectionate son and looked after her during her declining years. She would have liked to speak of him as her son, but this was not acceptable to Mr Sharratt, whose mother was still alive; so they decided that he would call her Aunt Nora and she addressed him by an affectionate nickname. There was throughout no question of his being financially dependent on her. All that he did for her over the 18 years that he resided with her in the flat had no other motive than kindness and affection.

My Lords, the bare recital of these facts makes one desirous, if one can, to gratify Mr Sharratt's wish to continue to reside in the flat where he had lived for so long before Lady Salter's death. Judge Solomon in the West London County Court, where the action by the landlords for possession of the flat was brought, felt himself able to do so.

I have come to the conclusion, he said, that Lady Salter and this defendant achieved through their relationship what must surely be regarded in a popular sense, and in common sense, as a familial nexus. That is to say, a nexus such as one would find only within a family. I am sure Shakespeare's man would say: "Yes, it is stranger than fiction, but they established a familial tie. Everyone linked to her through the blood was remote by comparison with the defendant".

The reference to Shakespeare's man is an allusion to the description 'base, common and popular' which in Langdon v Horton [1951] 1 KB 666, 669 Sir Raymond Evershed MR borrowed from Henry V, Act IV, scene 1, to describe the ordinary man mentioned by Cohen LJ in Brock v Wollams [1949] 2 KB 388, where he said, at p. 395:

The question the county court judge should have asked himself was this: Would an ordinary man, addressing his mind to the question whether Mrs Wollams was a member of the family or not, have answered 'yes' or 'no'?

This test, which does no more than say that 'family' where it is used in the Rent Acts is not a term of art but is used in its ordinary popular meaning, has been repeatedly referred to and applied in subsequent cases.

The Court of Appeal (Megaw, Lawton and Browne LJJ) unanimously reversed the judgment of Judge Solomon. Megaw LJ after quoting the 'Cohen question' went on to say, in my view quite correctly [1979] 1 WLR 3, 7:

> . . . it is for this court to decide, where such an issue arises, whether, assuming all the facts found by the judge to be correct, the question may, as a matter of law, within the permissible limits of the meaning of the phrase 'a member of the tenant's family,' be answered 'Yes'.

Megaw LJ and Lawton LJ both answered the question with a confident 'No'; and so would I. Browne LJ agreed, but rather more hesitantly. However, he also thought that the Court of Appeal was bound to allow the appeal because of two previous decisions of its own, *Gammans v Ekins* [1950] 2 KB 328 and *Ross v Collins* [1964] 1 WLR 425.

Gammans v Ekins was a case of co-habitation by an unmarried couple, a relationship which raises questions upon which I find it unnecessary and inappropriate to enter for the purpose of disposing of the instant appeal. *Ross v Collins*, on the other hand, was much like the instant case, save that the sexes of the older party, who was devotedly cared for, and the younger party who did the caring, were reversed. As my reason for dismissing the instant appeal, I would not seek to improve upon what was said there by my noble and learned friend (then Russell LJ) at p. 432:

> Granted that 'family' is not limited to cases of a strict legal familial nexus, I cannot agree that it extends to a case such as this. It still requires, it seems to me, at least a broadly recognisable de facto familial nexus. This may be capable of being found and recognised as such by the ordinary man – where the link would be strictly familial had there been a marriage, or where the link is through adoption of a minor, de jure or de facto, or where the link is 'step-', or where the link is 'in-law' or by marriage. But two strangers cannot, it seems to me, ever establish artificially for the purposes of this section a familial nexus by acting as brothers or as sisters, even if they call each other such and consider their relationship to be tantamount to that. Nor, in my view, can an adult man and woman who establish a platonic relationship establish a familial nexus by acting as a devoted brother and sister or father and daughter would act, even if they address each other as such and even if they refer to each other as such and regard their association as tantamount to such. Nor, in my view, would they indeed be recognised as familial links by the ordinary man.

I would accordingly dismiss this appeal with costs up to June 12, 1979.

The judgments in *Carega v Sharratt* are brief and narrowly focused, not attempting any extensive examination of the concept of 'family'. However, in the most recent case in this general area, *Fitzpatrick v Sterling Housing Association*, the Court of Appeal ranges very widely indeed, considering the approach of foreign jurisdictions, legislative provisions in other fields (for example, social security) and some of the academic material on the subject. The end result may not be significantly to alter the law, but, at the very least, it gives a number of indications as to how the law might develop in the future.

Fitzpatrick v Sterling Housing Association Ltd
[1997] 4 All ER 991

In 1976, Fitzpatrick moved into a flat of which Thompson was the statutory tenant. From that date onwards Fitzpatrick and Thompson maintained a close and faithful homosexual relationship together, and shared the flat on this basis. In 1986 Thompson suffered head injuries in a fall, and a subsequent stroke, which left him tetraplegic. From then on, Fitzpatrick nursed Thompson and provided him with continual care. Thompson died in 1994, and Fitzpatrick applied to take over the statutory tenancy. The landlords, who wished to re-house Fitzpatrick in smaller accommodation, refused to agree. Fitzpatrick then applied to the courts for a declaration that he was entitled to succeed to the statutory tenancy. His application was dismissed, somewhat reluctantly, by the county court. By a 2:1 majority (Ward LJ dissenting) the Court of Appeal upheld the county court judgment. However, even in the majority judgments of Waite LJ and Roch LJ there was considerable sympathy for Fitzpatrick's situation.

WAITE LJ: . . . It will be convenient at this point to pause in the narrative of statutory development and turn to the authorities embodying that interpretation. Their full significance cannot be appreciated without some reference to the social changes that were occurring during the period with which they were concerned – that is to say the mid-60s to the mid-80s – regarding the incidence of, and social attitudes towards, cohabitation outside marriage in heterosexual, and also in gay and lesbian, relationships.

Unmarried cohabitation between heterosexuals developed strikingly in scale to the point that today (according to figures helpfully supplied by the Family Policies Study Centre) 25% of all women aged between 18 and 49 are unmarried cohabitants, and in the age group most likely to cohabit (women in their late 20s and men in their late 30s) over one third of the population now cohabits. As it became more common, cohabitation lost the secretiveness with which it had sometimes been concealed by those who felt the need to give the appearances of marriage (through change of surname by deed poll for example) to their relationship. As it became more open, so attitudes toward it became less judgmental. That included the attitude of the courts, where notwithstanding that the encouragement of marriage as an institution remains a well-established head of public policy, the respect due to the sincerity of commitment involved in many such relationships is reflected in judicial terminology – terms like 'partner' now being more generally used than the once preferred references to 'common law spouse', 'mistress' or even (as will shortly be illustrated) 'living in sin'. A similar respect is reflected in The Law Commission's current consideration of steps to devise for unmarried partners procedures to ease the potential for financial dispute when such relationships break down.

In the same way, though on a lesser scale, the increasing recognition by society of the respect due to those who share orientation towards their own sex has led to a greater openness in, and the removal of public censoriousness towards, gay and lesbian cohabitation. One indicator of this has been the willingness of the court, in appropriate circumstances, to regard a partner in a gay or lesbian relationship as a suitable person to adopt a child (see (in Scotland) the opinion of the Lord President (Hope) in *T, Petitioner* 1997 SLT 724 and the judgment of Singer J in *Re W (a minor) (adoption: homosexual adopter)* [1997] 3 All ER 620). The degree of interdependence, marital in character, involved in gay or lesbian relationships has also been acknowledged in the field of equity (see *Barclays Bank plc v O'Brien* [1993] 4 All ER 417 at 431, [1994] 1 AC 180 at 198 per Lord Browne-Wilkinson).

[His Lordship then discussed *Brock v Wollams, Gammans v Ekins* and *Ross v Collins*. He continued:]

A heterosexual unmarried relationship of longstanding required consideration by this court in *Dyson Holdings Ltd v Fox* [1975] 3 All ER 1030, [1976] QB 593. A spinster lived with the statutory tenant as his wife for 21 years before his death. She took his name, and in every respect they were man and wife save that they had not gone through the marriage ceremony. The court was sympathetic to her claim to be regarded as part of the deceased tenant's family, but the decision in *Gammans v Ekins* [1950] 2 All ER 140, [1950] 2 KB 328 stood in the way. Lord Denning MR was in favour of dealing with it head-on and holding that it could not – or in the light of later authority could no longer – be supported. The preference of the majority of the court was to distinguish it by treating it as correct according to the social conditions of its time, but holding that in current social conditions 'family' had acquired a wider connotation. James LJ said ([1975] 3 All ER 1030 at 1035, [1976] QB 503 at 511):

> Between 1950 and 1975 there have been many changes in the law effected by statute and decisions of the courts. Many changes have their foundation in the changed needs and views of society. Such changes have occurred in the field of family law and equitable interests in property. The popular meaning given to the word 'family' is not fixed once and for all time. I have no doubt that with the passage of years it has changed.

There are observations to like effect in the judgment of Bridge LJ. It is important, however, to note of that case that on the actual ratio of the decision upon its facts (as opposed to the grounds for distinguishing earlier authority) there was unanimity between the judges. That ratio was expressed by Lord Denning MR in this sentence ([1975] 3 All ER 1030 at 1035, [1976] QB 503 at 509):

> . . . we should hold that a couple who live together as man and wife for 20 years are members of the same family, whether they have children or not.

Although the rationale of the *Dyson* case was doubted by another division of this court in *Helby v Rafferty* [1978] 3 All ER 1016, [1979] 1 WLR 13, it was held to be binding. On the particular facts of that case (an unmarried couple who made no attempt at pretence of marriage, because the woman wanted to retain her independence, and who even attempted at times to conceal the depth of their attachment) it was held that the trial judge had been justified in declining to regard the couple as a 'family'.

When the unusual case of a widow of 75 sharing her protected flat with a young man of 25 with whom she maintained a close but platonic friendship came before the House of Lords in *Carega Properties SA (formerly Joram Developments Ltd) v Sharratt* [1979] 2 All ER 1084, [1979] 1 WLR 928, the facts were regarded as too exceptional to justify treating the case as an opportunity for a consideration by the House of the rightness of the decision in *Dyson Holdings Ltd v Fox* [1975] 3 All ER 1030, [1976] QB 503. The judge had answered 'the Cohen question' (as it had by then come to be called) with a Yes, but the Court of Appeal answered it with a No, and the House of Lords agreed. The points of principle that emerge from the case are Viscount Dilhorne's statement ([1979] 2 All ER 1084 at 1087, [1979] 1 WLR 928 at 932) that the meaning to be given to the phrase 'a member of the original tenant's family' is a question of law, that 'family' is a word whose content so varies with its context that it is for the judge to construe the statute and for him to state his conclusion as to the meaning (in its ordinary natural sense) and of the word in the particular context, and that 'family' must be read as meaning something more than 'household'.

In *Watson* v *Lucas* [1980] 3 All ER 647, [1980] 1 WLR 1493 this court was concerned with a heterosexual relationship between the tenant and a married man who never divorced his wife, both parties continuing to use their true names and making no attempt to pretend married status. The *Dyson* case, though once more criticised, was again held to be binding, and the majority (Oliver LJ dissenting) held that the trial judge had been wrong to regard the man's continuing married status and the use by both parties of their original surnames as negativing the 'family' status of their relationship. Stephenson LJ described the ratio of *Dyson* in these terms ([1980] 3 All ER 647 at 652, [1980] 1 WLR 1493 at 1499–1450):

> . . . I understand the ratio of the majority decision as holding that a union between a man and a woman, which in all the circumstances, known and unknown to the ordinary man, looks permanent and stable to him, creates a family unit and both parties are members of it, whether or not it consists of more than those two.
> . . .

Sefton Holdings Ltd v *Cairns* (1987) 20 HLR 124 concerned a woman statutory tenant whose parents had taken in a 23 year old orphan girl (the claimant) during the last war and ever thereafter treated her as a daughter. When the parents died, the tenant and the claimant remained in the house, where they regarded each other as sisters. After the death of the tenant many years later, the claimant obtained a holding from the judge that she was a member of the tenant's family. That was reversed on appeal. The case was held to be analogous to *Ross* v *Collins* [1964] 1 All ER 861, [1964] 1 WLR 425 from which the passage already quoted in the judgment of Russell LJ was cited with approval by Lloyd LJ, who said that it covered the facts of that case. He later added ((1987) 20 HLR 124 at 127–128):

> . . . there is a distinction between *being* a member of the family and living *as* a member of the family. There is no doubt that the defendant lived as a member of the family, and that may be why the judge decided this case in her favour. But the question we have to ask ourselves is not whether she lived as a member of the family, but whether she was a member of the family. I am clear that she was not, and that the man in the street would take the same view. (Lloyd LJ's emphasis).

That completes the authorities decided down to 1987 in the Rent Act jurisdiction. It will have been noted that they all concern claims to familial status for relationships that were either platonic or heterosexual. There is no decision in that area of the law, as to the right of a partner in a gay or lesbian relationship to be accorded the status of member of the other partner's 'family' for succession purposes under the Rent Acts.

Such a question did, however, arise during that period in regard to the right of such a partner to succeed to a secure tenancy of a local authority letting. The case was *Harrogate BC* v *Simpson* (1984) 17 HLR 205. The claimant (defending proceedings for possession by the local authority) had lived with the deceased secure tenant in a lesbian relationship for some years and was so living at the date of her death. It will be remembered that in the secure tenancy regime membership of the 'family' is specifically defined. It was accepted that the claimant could not bring herself within any other head of that definition and that she could succeed (if at all) only under the head, which reads (s. 50(3) of the 1980 Act): 'A person is a member of another's family . . . if they live together as husband and wife'. Watkins LJ (at 209) recited the argument of the claimant's counsel as follows:

> Mr Allan suggests that the manifestations of the living together of husband and wife following a marriage ceremony are easily recognisable and are for the most part similar to a state where two women live together in a lesbian relationship. He says that in both there may be mutual love, monogamy, some degree of public acknowledgement of their condition of living, faithfulness by one to the other, a permanence of relationship, sexual relations of some kind, a shared surname, a joint household and, in the case of man and woman, of course, children. Save for the bearing of children, he maintains that all or nearly all of those manifestations can appear from the living together of two women. So, if the appearance of things is the test, there is no earthly reason why the Act is not complied with when two women live together in the state in which the late Mrs Rodrigo and the defendant were living. They should be held to be living as husband and wife. We are told that, not only did they so regard and describe themselves, but they behaved in some ways (outwardly at any rate) as though one was the husband and the other was the wife. Mrs Rodrigo was the masculine partner apparently and wore men's clothing, and the defendant was the female counterpart. Mr Allan places reliance upon the word 'as' which is contained in the final words of section 50(3). By the appearance of that word in its context it is to be understood that Parliament was indicating, not only that the provisions were intended to apply to persons who were married in the formal sense, but also to unions which gave the appearance of two people living together in a kind of matrimonial state. Much has happened, he further maintains, over the last decade or more to change people's opinions about what before that time were considered to be repugnant sexual relationships. Nowadays nobody blanches at the fact that two women who are lesbians live together, or two men who are homosexuals. It is not a crime for men in most circumstances to behave in that way, and, so far as lesbians are concerned, a crime in no circumstance.

He then referred to the *Dyson* case, from which he quoted, and stated his conclusion in these terms (at 210):

> Mrs Davies, who appears for the plaintiffs, contends that, if Parliament had wished homosexual relationships to be brought into the realm of the lawfully recognised state of a living together of man and wife for the purpose of the relevant legislation, it would plainly have so stated in that legislation, and it has not done so. I am bound to say that I entirely agree with that. I am also firmly of the view that it would be surprising in the extreme to learn that public opinion is such today that it would recognise a homosexual union as being akin to a state of living as husband and wife. The ordinary man and woman, neither in 1975 [a reference to the date of *Dyson*] nor in 1984, would in my opinion not think even remotely of there being a true resemblance between those two very different states of affairs.

Ewbank J (the other member of the court) said (at 210):

> I agree that the expression 'living together as husband and wife' . . . is not apt to include a homosexual relationship. The essential characteristic of living together as husband and wife, in my judgment, is that there should be a man and a woman . . .

. . .

Overseas authority
The New York City Rent and Eviction Regulations contain a provision that upon the death of a rent-control tenant the landlord may not dispossess: 'either the surviving spouse of the deceased or some other member of the deceased tenant's family who has been living with the tenant'.

In *Braschi* v *Stahl Associates Co.* (1989) 544 NYS 2d 784 the New York Supreme Court held that a surviving male partner in a gay relationship with the deceased tenant was eligible to claim protection under the regulations. The Appellate Division reversed the decision, holding that protection applied only to 'family members within traditional, legally recognised familial relationships'. The Court of Appeals of New York allowed an appeal from that holding, declaring, by a majority of four to two, that 'the Legislature intended to extend protection to those who reside in households having all the normal familial characteristics. The [appellant] should therefore be allowed the opportunity to prove that he and [the deceased tenant] had such a household'. In remitting the case for a determination on that issue, the court (at 790, per Justice Titone) said:

> . . . it is the totality of the relationship as evidenced by the dedication, caring and self-sacrifice of the parties which should, in the final analysis control. Appellant's situation provides an example of how the rule should be applied.

The approach of the judge in this case
It was common ground that the judge was required, when construing the phrase 'a member of the original tenant's family', to apply the general interpretive principle of *Dyson* – i.e. to construe the term 'family' in its popular modern meaning, taking into account changed social attitudes and the changed needs and views of society. He held that in adopting that approach he was bound to look for a familial link, following the approach of Russell LJ in *Ross* v *Collins* [1964] 1 All ER 861, [1964] 1 WLR 425 which he held to be of general application and not limited to the context of a non-sexual relationship. Applying the actual ratio of *Dyson* (as confirmed in *Watson* v *Lucas* [1980] 3 All ER 647, [1980] 1 WLR 1493), he held that the relevant familial link for this purpose was that between husband and wife – which means (when applied to the context of an unmarried relationship) that the relationship must give to the ordinary man the appearance of a couple living as man and wife. After saying that in this respect the *Braschi* decision appeared to show a difference of approach between the law of New York and that of England he stated his conclusion in these terms:

> I fully accept that a cohabiting relationship between members of the same sex of a permanent and stable kind would properly be regarded nowadays, whether in 1996 or 1994, by the man in the street as just as lasting and socially valuable a relationship as that between husband and wife. But, in my judgment, for the reasons I have attempted to give, this does not entitle me, even in construing the word 'family' in a popular sense as required by *Dyson*, to find that such a relationship falls within such definition. In my judgment, such a decision falls to be made by Parliament and not by the courts. It will be for others to decide whether Parliament should look at this question, but perhaps, in the light of the Court of Appeal's observations in [*R* v *Ministry of Defence, ex parte Smith* [1996] 1 All ER 257, [1996] QB 517], it might be appropriate for it to do so.

. . .

'Members of the original tenant's family'
The applicability of this phrase has provided the central issue in the appeal. Can a sexual partner of the same sex be described as a member of his or her family?

Mr Chapman for the landlord charity accepts, as he did before the judge, the interpretative principle of *Dyson,* namely that the court is bound to give to the term 'member of the family' whatever connotation it demands in current popular thought and speech. He submits, however, that the judge was right to regard himself as constrained by authority to hold that when a sexual relationship between strangers in blood is relied on as constituting a family relationship, the attachment must bear the hallmark of the familial nexus represented either by marriage or by unmarried cohabitation of the kind that occurs between husband and wife. For that he relies on the ratio of the decisions in *Dyson* and *Watson* v *Lucas* [1980] 3 All ER 647, [1980] 1 WLR 1493 and the attributes of a familial relationship approved in *Ross* v *Collins* [1964] 1 All ER 861, [1964] 1 WLR 425. The requirement that the partners should be living as husband and wife necessarily imports a male and female relationship and precludes its application to relationships between persons of the same sex. Mr Chapman also submitted that the judge's decision has the advantage of harmonising the two regimes of statutory and secure tenancies. He reminded us, finally, that Rent Act legislation, though it fulfils a public interest in the social control of land for the benefit of those least able to afford accommodation, is nevertheless by its nature expropriatary in its interference with rights of ownership of land, and should therefore, he submitted, be construed restrictively by adopting an interpretation of 'family membership' which limits, rather than enlarges, the range of potential successors to a statutory tenant.

Mr Luba urges that, on the contrary, Parliament must be deemed to have known what it was about when the decision was taken, at the time of the 1988 amendments to Sch. 1, to leave the expression 'member of . . . the family' to be interpreted broadly, in the sense approved in *Dyson* – a decision which formed an important part of the case law in operation when those changes were made. Such an interpretation, in the light of modern social attitudes and conditions, can lead, he submits, to only one result. If unmarried heterosexual partners in a permanent relationship are capable of being held (as they were in *Dyson* and *Watson* v *Lucas*) to be members of the former tenant's family, what reason can there be in logic or humanity for declining to accord the same status to a partner in a lesbian or gay relationship?

Conclusion
If endurance, stability, interdependence and devotion were the sole hallmarks of family membership, there could be no doubt about this case at all. Mr Fitzpatrick and Mr Thompson lived together for a longer period than many marriages endure these days. They were devoted and faithful, giving each other mutual help and support in a life which shared many of the highest qualities to be found in heterosexual attachments, married or unmarried. To adopt an interpretation of the statute that allowed all sexual partners, whether of the same or opposite sex, to enjoy the privilege of succession to tenancies protected by the Rent Acts would, moreover, be consistent not only with social justice but also with the respect accorded by modern society to those of the same sex who undertake a permanent commitment to a shared life.

The survey which I have undertaken in this judgment shows, however, that the law in England regarding succession to statutory tenancies is firmly rooted in the concept of the family as an entity bound together by ties of kinship (including adoptive status) or marriage. The only relaxation, first by court decision and then by statute, has been a willingness to treat heterosexual cohabitants as if they were husband and wife. That was a restrictive extension, offensive to social justice and tolerance because it excludes lesbians and gays. It is out of tune with modern acceptance of the need to avoid any discrimination on the ground of sexual orientation. In that respect I wholly agree with the comments of Ward LJ. The question is: how is it to be put right?

Discrimination is not, unfortunately, the only arbitrary feature in this area of the law. Endemic within its system is a high risk of harsh or anomalous results – excluding from rights of succession many deserving instances of common households in which the survivor would have a strong moral case to succeed to the tenancy. Friends of longstanding (widowers or spinsters for example) who share accommodation in old age without any sexual element in their relationship, but who often give and receive much the same kind of devoted care as we have admired in this case, are (and always have been) excluded. If succession rights are to be extended to couples of the same sex in a sexually based relationship, would it be right to continue to exclude friends? If friends are to be included, how is the stability and permanence of their household to be defined?

These questions have to be judged in the light of a further policy consideration – fairness to home-owners. Every enlargement of the class of potential successors to rent controlled tenancies involves a deeper invasion of rights of house-owners to possession of their own property. That there is a need to reconcile these competing social priorities is something on which it would be easy to find a broad consensus. The difficulty arises when it comes to finding ways and means. At that point opinions are bound to vary, and a political judgment may in the end become necessary. That is what makes the process of reconciliation a task better suited to the legislative function of Parliament than to the interpretative role of the courts.

The law of succession to Rent Act protected tenancies is, in short, arbitrary and discriminatory. No one today would attempt to defend the favour it accords, outside the marriage tie, to heterosexual relationships over same-sex households. Few would support the potential for unfairness involved in a law which gives automatic succession rights to wives (however faithless) and children (however feckless) and at the same time denies any hope of succession to friends, however devoted their loyalty to the joint household. The judge was nevertheless right, in my view, to resist the temptation to change a bad law by giving it a new linguistic twist. He correctly acknowledged that such changes could only be made by Parliament.

They are changes which will certainly need to be made, if Parliament is to fulfil its function of reflecting the spirit of our times – in particular the spirit which recognises the value of all abiding relationships, the heterosexual, the lesbian, the gay – or even those which are not sexually based at all. As the law now stands, however, I feel bound, notwithstanding the respect and sympathy to which Mr Fitzpatrick is entitled, to dismiss the appeal.

WARD LJ (dissenting):

My approach to the question of construction

(1) I begin with the purpose of the 1977 Act, which is essentially to give tenants fair rents and a status of irremovability. In *Curl* v *Angelo* [1948] 2 All ER 189 at 192 Lord Greene MR described 'the real fundamental object of the Act' to be 'protecting a tenant from being turned out of his home'. In *Lloyd* v *Sadler* [1978] 2 All ER 529 at 537–538, [1978] QB 774 at 790 Lawton LJ said:

The object of the Rent Act 1968 was to give security of tenure to persons . . . The 1968 Act took away many of the landlord's rights at common law and was intended to do so for the benefit of tenants.

As Lord Greene MR had said earlier in *Cumming* v *Danson* [1942] 2 All ER 653 at 654, the Acts were 'for the protection of tenants and not Acts for the penalising of landlords'. The teleological interpretation supports the conclusion that there is no justification for limiting the class of persons entitled to the benefit of the 1977 Act on the basis that the interference with the landlord's right to possession should be curtailed because the Act has a penal effect: on the contrary, the broad purpose of the Act is to preserve the family home for tenants and their successors. Consequently, those who occupy the property as their home should wherever it is possible – but of course not beyond that – be given protection against eviction.

(2) As I have already explained, the words of this Act must be given their contemporary meaning. Professor Ronald Dworkin expressed the point well in *Law's Empire* (1986) p. 348, when he said:

> [The judge] interprets not just the statute's text but its life, the process that begins before it becomes law and extends far beyond that moment . . . [the judge's] interpretation changes as the story develops.

Since families are dynamic, the statutory interpretation must equally reflect the motive forces, physical or moral, affecting behaviour and change in domestic organisation. On reading Professor Zimmermann's article, 'Statutes and the Common Law: A Continental Perspective' [1997] CLJ 315 at 323, I realise, with some apprehension (but with some pleasure at the recollection of it), how close I am to a return to Celsus *The Digest of Justinian* D 1, 3, 17, whose rule of interpretation was 'Scire leges non hoc est verba earum tenere, sed vim ac potestatem': to know the laws is not a matter of sticking to their words, but of grasping their force and tendency.

(3) Since the inception of the Rent Acts in or before 1920, the home of members of the tenant's family has been preserved for them. As the decided cases show, the meaning of family has been progressively extended. The movement has been away from the confines of relationships by blood and by marriage to the reality of family life, and from de jure to de facto relationships. We need to analyse how that has come to pass. In 1950 Mr Ekins was not a member of Mrs Smith's family because, per Asquith LJ, the decisions which bound them limited membership of the same 'family' to three relationships: first that of a child; secondly those constituted by way of legitimate marriage like that between a husband and wife; and thirdly relationships whereby one person becomes in loco parentis to another. In that case the masquerade as husband and wife was not enough. The form of their relationship – an unmarried couple – overcame the substance of the way they functioned akin to a married couple. By 1976 Mrs Fox had become a member of the family because the ordinary man recognised that this was not a relationship, per James LJ, 'of a casual or intermittent character . . . bearing indications of impermanence (as) would not come within the popular concept of a family unit'. The trend in the cases, as I see them, is to shift the focus, or the emphasis, from structure and components to function and appearance – what a family does rather than what it is, or putting it another way, a family is what a family does. I see this as a functionalist approach to construction as opposed to a formalist approach. Thus, whether the *Carega Properties* test is satisfied, i.e. whether there is 'at least a broadly recognisable de facto familial nexus', or a conjugal nexus, depends on how closely the alternative family or couple resemble the traditional family or husband and wife in function if not in precise form.

(4) We do not have (or should I say we do not *yet* have?) the equivalent of the Canadian Charter of Rights and Freedoms which enables the judges to strike down offensive discriminatory legislation. I must, therefore, be faithful to Parliament's sovereign will. Nevertheless, I am entitled to presume that Parliament always intends to conform to the rule of law as a constitutional principle and accordingly to respect the constitutional rights of the individual to enjoy equality under the law. I agree with

the majority of the Canadian Supreme Court in *Egan* v *Canada* (1995) 124 DLR (4th) 609 at 631, where L'Heureux-Dubé J said:

> Equality, as that concept is enshrined as a fundamental human right within s. 15 of the Charter, means nothing if does not represent a commitment to recognising each person's equal worth as a human being, regardless of individual differences. Equality means that our society cannot tolerate legislative distinctions that treat certain people as second-class citizens, that demean them, that treat them as less capable for no good reason, or that otherwise offend fundamental human dignity.

If, therefore, there is doubt about the ordinary meaning of the words of the statute, I would strain to place upon them that construction which produces a dignified result consistent with the purpose of the Act.

(5)   To exclude same-sex couples from the protection the 1977 Act proclaims the inevitable message that society judges their relationship to be less worthy of respect, concern and consideration than the relationship between members of the opposite sex. The fundamental human dignity of the homosexual couple is severely and palpably affected by the impugned distinction. The distinction is drawn on grounds relating to their personal characteristics, their sexual orientation. If the law is as my Lords state it to be, then it discriminates against a not insignificant proportion of the population who will justly complain that they have been denied their constitutional right to equal treatment under the law.

(6)   There being no remedy to cure such injustice, my approach will, therefore, be to say that if I find the statute ambiguous, or even if I left in doubt as to its meaning, then I should err on the side of preventing that discrimination.

Was the appellant living with the original tenant as his wife or husband?

(1)   'As' means 'in the manner of' and suggests how the couple functioned, not what they were. I agree with the test of Woolf J in *Crake* v *Supplementary Benefits Commission, Butterworth* v *Supplementary Benefits Commission* [1982] 1 All ER 498 at 502 which, so far as I can tell, was not referred to this court in *Harrogate BC* v *Simpson* (1984) 17 HLR 205. There being no dispute but that the appellant and the deceased were living together, it is 'necessary to go on and ascertain in so far as this is possible, the manner in which and why they (were) living together in the same household'. If asked, 'Why?', would not both they and also the heterosexual couple equally well reply, 'Because we love each other and are committed to devote comfort and support to each other'. I can readily envisage that the immediate response to the question, 'How do you two live together?'' may well be, 'As a gay couple'. But when the next question is asked, 'In what manner do you, a gay couple, live together?' would their answer be any different from that given by the heterosexual couple save only in the one respect that in their case their sexual relations are homosexual, not heterosexual? No distinction can sensibly be drawn between the two couples in terms of love, nurturing, fidelity, durability, emotional and economic interdependence – to name but some and no means all of the hallmarks of a relationship between a husband and his wife.

(2)   With regard to the only distinguishing feature, sexual activity, that is a function of the relationship of a husband and his wife, a man and his mistress and it is a function of homosexual lovers. That the activity takes place between members of different sexes or of the same sex is a matter of form not function. Since the test I would apply is functionalistic, the formalistic difference can be ignored.

. . .

Was the appellant a member of the original tenant's family?
. . .

(2) Hoggett (Hale J), Pearl (Judge Pearl), Cooke and Bates state in their work *The Family, Law and Society* (4th edn, 1996) p. 1:

In the England of the 1990s, we must not assume that the answer to the question 'What is a family?' is necessarily going to produce a simple and straightforward response . . . The following extract comes from the Judicial Studies Board's *Handbook on Ethnic Minority Issues* (1994) . . . 'Despite the fact that these images may have some basis in reality, as rigid stereotypes they can be misleading and dangerous. They over-generalise certain tendencies, and conceal the existence of considerable diversity in family composition among Britain's minority ethnic communities. They also do nothing to help with understanding why there may be differences in family patterns between ethnic groups'.

Should one not, therefore, also question the validity of a heterosexual stereotype for the family?

(3) The test has to be whether the relationship of the appellant to the deceased was one where there is at least a broadly recognisable de facto familial nexus. I would not define that familial nexus in terms of its structures or components: I would rather focus on familial functions. The question is more what a family does rather than what a family is. A family unit is a social organisation which functions through its linking its members closely together. The functions may be procreative, sexual, sociable, economic, emotional. The list is not exhaustive. Not all families function in the same way. Save for the ability to procreate, these functions were present in the relationship between the deceased and the appellant.

(4) Whilst there clearly is no right of self-determination it cannot be immaterial to have regard to the view the parties have of their own relationship. If the officious commuter on the Clapham omnibus had paid a visit to the deceased's household, asked all the relevant questions about their relationship and asked the deceased finally, 'What is Mr Fitzpatrick to you? Is he one of the family?', it seems to me to be inconceivable that the deceased would not have testily suppressed him by replying, 'Of course he is'. I doubt whether the ordinary man would be surprised by the answer as he apparently would have been hearing Ms Simpson. I am quite certain that he would not treat the answer as an abuse of the English language. Indeed, I am satisfied that the ordinary man is liberated enough to accept in 1997, or even in 1994, looking broadly at the appellant's life and comparing it with the other rich patterns of family life he knows, that the bond between the appellant and the deceased was de facto familial.

(5) I would therefore conclude that if, which is my preferred view, they were not living as a husband and his wife would live, then at least they were living as members of a family.

Conclusions
Writing on 'Financial Rights in Relationships outside Marriage: a Decade of Reforms in Australia' [1995] IJLF 233 Professor Bailey-Harris says:

A pluralist society requires the law not merely to tolerate but rather to recognise and support diversity in family formation – in other words to authenticate a range of family forms.

In my judgment, our society has shown itself to be tolerant enough to free itself from the burdens of stereotype and prejudice in all their subtle and ugly manifestations.

The common man may be vaguely disapproving of the homosexual relationship which
is not for him but, having shrugged his shoulders, he would recognise that the
relationship was to all intents and purposes a marriage between those partners. They
lived a life akin to that of any husband and wife. They were so bound together that
they constituted a family.

. . .

Notes

In *Fitzpatrick v Sterling Housing Association Ltd* [1999] *The Times*, 2 November the House of Lords, three to two, supported Ward LJ's dissenting
judgment in the Court of Appeal and held that within the context of the Rent
Act 1977 Mr Fitzgerald could succeed as a member of Mr Thompson's
family. Giving his verdict Lord Slynn was at pains to point out that Mr
Fitzgerald succeeded only on the basis of being a family member, there was
no question of him succeeding as a spouse, for that word refers only to
heterosexual partners who are legally married or whose relationship is the
effective equivalent of marriage. However, so far as the word 'family' within
the context of the Rent Acts was concerned the Courts had over the years
adopted a flexible approach to extend its meaning beyond legally binding
relationships. What the courts have looked for as the hallmarks of a sufficient
relationship are a degree of mutual interdependence, of the sharing of lives,
of caring, love, commitment and support. These are *presumed* to exist within
legal relationships. In the case of de facto relationships they have to be *proved*
to exist. However, the extent of the word 'family' has to be determined by
present day conditions and attitudes, not by those prevalent in 1920 when
the word was first introduced into the Rent Acts. Relying on decisions in
other contexts such as *R v Ministry of Defence, ex parte Smith* [1996] QB 517
and *Barclays Bank plc v O'Brien* [1994] 1 AC 180, Lord Slynn continued that
attitudes towards same sex relationships have changed, and as a matter of law
a same sex partner may now be able to establish a familial link for the
purposes of the Rent Act 1977. Even though references to family and family
life under the European Convention for the Protection of Human Rights and
Fundamental Freedoms have not yet led the European Court of Human
Rights to accept claims by same sex partners to family rights, Lord Slynn
considered that Convention case law was still at an early stage of development, and that in any case it could not impinge on the power of the House
of Lords to decide the meaning of a UK statutory provision.

Lord Slynn then went on to argue that for a familial relationship to be
established a same sex partner must be able to establish the indicia of a
relationship as outlined above. Something transient and superficial is not
enough, even if it is intimate, furthermore neither will mere cohabitation by
friends as a matter of convenience. So far as the 1977 Act and its purposes
is concerned, Lord Slynn argued that two people of the same sex may be
regarded as having established membership of a family, and that was certainly
so on the facts of the present case. Lords Clyde and Nicholls came to similar
conclusions.

Lord Hutton, dissenting, argued that as it was clear as recently as 1988, when the Housing Act of that year clarified the meaning of 'spouse' for the purposes of the Rent Act 1977, that Parliament did not intend to confer succession rights on homosexual partners by that route, that it was somewhat artificial to conclude that such a partner could gain protection under the alternative 'family' route. Furthermore, if the purpose of the legislation is to provide security for those who live together in relationships of mutual affection, love and support, why should it not extend to those whose relationships have no sexual element? Lord Hutton therefore concluded that the question of whether for the purposes of the Rent Act 1977 a homosexual should be regarded as a member of his partner's family, or indeed whether the law should be more generally changed to protect homosexual partners, should be a matter for Parliament to decide. Lord Hobhouse similarly dissented.

(ii)   Housing Act 1988

The relevant provisions are contained in s. 17 of the Housing Act 1988, which is set out in detail in chapter 3. As noted there, rights of succession under the 1988 Act are far more limited than under the Rent Act 1977. Only 'spouses' (inclusive of heterosexual relationships under s. 17(4)) can succeed to the tenancy and not any other 'family' member. The definition of putative spouse in s. 17(4) clearly excludes homosexual relationships, so that any parliamentary reconsideration of 'family' under the Rent Act should presumably include an equivalent reconsideration of s. 17.

(iii)   Housing Act 1985

Secure tenancies (as discussed in chapter 5) devolve by law to spouses and family members (see s. 87 and s. 89, Housing Act 1985). Further, there is an absolute right to assign the tenancy to anyone who would have been qualified to succeed to the secure tenancy on death (s. 91(3)(c), Housing Act 1985). This is in clear contrast with the private sector position (for example, under s. 15 of the Housing Act 1988 it is an implied term of every assured tenancy that no assignment of the tenancy is permissible without the landlord's consent). In addition, s. 113 of the Housing Act 1985 appears to adopt a helpfully wide definition of 'family'.

Housing Act 1985

Member of a person's family

113.—(1)   A person is a member of another's family within the meaning of this Part if—

(a)   he is the spouse of that person, or he and that person live together as husband and wife, or

(b)   he is that person's parent, grandparent, child, grandchild, brother, sister, uncle, aunt, nephew or niece.

(2)   For the purpose of subsection (1)(b)—

(a)   a relationship by marriage shall be treated as a relationship by blood,
(b)   a relationship of the half-blood shall be treated as a relationship of the whole blood,
(c)   the stepchild of a person shall be treated as his child, and
(d)   an illegitimate child shall be treated as the legitimate child of his mother and reputed father.

There is little doubt that this explicitness is, in general, helpful in removing much of the uncertainty encountered in the private sector. Moreover, the definition, in general, adopts a wide ('extended'?) view of the 'family' encompassing both blood and marriage relationships and clearly including heterosexual cohabitees. However, there is a clear anomaly in that such cohabitees do not acquire the same status as married couples, but rather are treated in the same way as all other 'family' members in that 12 months' residence with the deceased tenant prior to the death is required before succession rights arise.

More generally, could it be that the very explicitness of s. 113 is a barrier to any judicial desire to reflect changing views as to the meaning of 'family'? The *Dyson* v *Fox* approach, applied in the private sector (with varying degrees of enthusiasm) since 1975, allows the courts to reflect changing 'popular' attitudes as to the meaning of 'family', the concept being statutorily undefined. Section 113, on the other hand, appears to provide a definitive and all-inclusive list of those relationships which can be treated as 'family' ones for Housing Act 1985 purposes. Specifically, since homosexual relationships are not mentioned, *must* they be seen as implicitly *excluded*, particularly since heterosexual cohabitation is specifically *included*? This was certainly the view of the Court of Appeal in *Harrogate BC* v *Simpson* (1984) 17 HLR 205. In particular, at p. 210, Watkins LJ stated: 'Mrs Davies who appears for the plaintiffs, contends that, if Parliament had wished homosexual relationships to be brought into the realm of the lawfully recognised state of a living together of man and wife for the purpose of the relevant legislation, it would plainly have so stated in that legislation, and it had not done so. I am bound to say that I entirely agree with that'.

When the Housing Act 1996 was before Parliament, Glenda Jackson MP proposed amendments to both s. 113 of the Housing Act 1985 and s. 17(4) of the Housing Act 1988 expressly to include homosexual relationships. Initially these were accepted by the Standing Committee considering the Bill, but they were later withdrawn after the Minister (David Curry) agreed to issue guidance to local authorities that they should normally grant a tenancy to the surviving partner of a relationship (whether homosexual or heterosexual) either in the same home, or in suitable alternative accommodation. The Minister further took the view that a preferable solution would be for a joint tenancy to have been granted in the first place (see later in this chapter), but that he understood that this would not always have occurred (276 HC Official Report coll. 985–986). The guidance referred to by the Minister was subsequently issued as Annex C to the Code of Guidance on Parts VI and VII of the Housing Act 1996 (for the remainder of the Code, see chapter 4):

The decision in *Fitzpatrick* specifically only referred to the position under the Rent Act 1977, and was facilitated by the lack of a definition of 'family' under that Act. It is extremely hard to see how, even adopting the most purposive of interpretations, the Courts could get round the highly preclusive wording of section 113 of the 1985 Act. On the traditional construction basis of 'expressio unius est exclusius alterius' only persons falling within the literal wording of section 113 can be regarded as 'family'. This is most unfortunate because a yawning void, in legal terms at least, now opens up between those parts of the private rented sector still enjoying Rent Act protection and the public sector, and the rights of same sex couples will thus vary according to the nature of their landlord and the date of commencement of the tenancy. This can hardly be logically defended, and it is of little comfort to anyone that administrative practice *may* supply the law's omissions. Urgent attention should now be given to ensuring that the rights of same sex partners are brought into line with those who are legally married or whose cohabitation is recognised as the de facto equivalent of marriage. Indeed the time may be not too far distant when the United Kingdom could follow the example of the Netherlands and give recognition to all 'registered unions' irrespective of the sex of the partners.

Annex C
Local Authority Joint Tenancies

1.   This guidance is about the allocation of joint tenancies by local housing authorities.

2.   The Secretary of State for the Environment considers that joint tenancies can play an important role in ensuring the effective use and equitable allocation of housing.

3.   In situations where the members of a household have a long-term commitment to the home, for example a married couple or when adults share accommodation as friends or unpaid live-in carers, local authorities should normally grant a joint tenancy. In this way the ability of other adult members of the household to remain in the accommodation on the death of the tenant would not be prejudiced.

4.   Local authorities will wish to be assured:
— of the likely continuance of such arrangements; and
— that there are no adverse implications from the joint tenancy for good use of authorities' housing stock, for authorities' ability to continue to provide for housing need and in particular for their being able to discharge the priority of housing families and vulnerable people.

5.   It is good practice for local authorities to ensure that applicants for housing (whether new applicants or existing sole tenants) are made aware that they can be granted joint tenancies. If an authority declines to grant a joint tenancy, it should inform the applicants in writing of its reasons for refusal.

6.   Where a member of a household dies and there is another member of that household who does not have the right to succeed to the tenancy, who either:
— had been living with the tenant for the year before the tenant's death, or
— had been looking after the tenant, or
— had accepted responsibility for the tenant's dependants
the local authority should grant a tenancy to the remaining person or persons, either in the same home or in suitable alternative accommodation, where the local authority

is satisfied that this is a priority when viewed in the context of the other demands on their housing stock and the housing need in their area.
7. This guidance replaces that in Department of the Environment Circular 7/96 'Local Authority Joint Tenancies', which is hereby withdrawn.

Empirical evidence is awaited as to how far local authority practice is now in line with this guidance. Prior to the guidance there was an admitted 'lack of uniformity . . . in how they respond to such situations' (see David Curry in the HC Official Report, above). It is particularly worrying that the guidance applies only where the authority consider it a priority to offer accommodation. There is also inevitable doubt over the exact interpretation to be given to 'member of a household' in para. 6.

Questions
1. 'The concept of the family is an entity bound together by ties of kinship . . .' (Waite LJ in *Fitzpatrick* v *Sterling HA*). Does this mean that Waite LJ (and Roch LJ who adopted this definition) felt that a homosexual relationship was *not* one involving 'kinship'?
2. If a judge interprets legislation passed in 'Year X', from a position of perceived public attitudes in 'Year Z' (as did Ward LJ in *Fitzpatrick*), is he in danger of 'second-guessing' what view Parliament itself might take of the issue in 'Year Z'?
3. In the light of Annex C (above) and the absence of legislative amendments to the Housing Act 1988 or the Rent Act 1977, the position of the homosexual partner of a deceased tenant may well differ depending on the type of tenancy held by the deceased. Can this be justified?
4. On the assumption that amending legislation (as above) *is* eventually introduced, do you think that it should extend to:

(a) partners in homosexual relationships;
(b) carers;
(c) friends who have lived together for at least one year?

(C)   Housing and relationship breakdown

The sharing of accommodation by couples, married or unmarried, homosexual or heterosexual, raises important questions as to the housing rights thereby acquired by the partners to the relationship. During the subsistence of the relationship such questions remain largely academic, but once the relationship comes under strain, or finally breaks down, the distribution and allocation of housing rights between the (ex) partners is a matter of crucial importance. Family law has tended to concentrate on owner-occupied property, whereas the focus here (as elsewhere in this book) is on the rented sector. As will be seen, however, many 'domestic' provisions are, in this area, much the same whether the 'home' involved is rented or owner-occupied. A factor of key significance is the existence (or otherwise) of a joint tenancy between the partners. This is discussed separately in part (D) of this chapter, and it should be assumed, in general, in this part that no joint tenancy exists.

For clarity of exposition the following discussion is divided between 'short-term' remedies, where the partners may still be living together despite their difficulties, and 'long-term' remedies, where the partners appear to have finally separated. In practice significant overlaps exist between the two areas.

(i) Short-term remedies

At common law the sole responsibilities and rights concerning the tenancy reside in the tenant. There appears to be no legal way that the non-tenant partner can protect his or her interests by (say) forcing the tenant spouse to pay the rent or take remedial action concerning repairs. Of course, in practice, in the still all too common situation of the non-tenant partner being a woman with children, it is highly likely that a local authority or registered social landlord would in practice accept rent from her, while seeking to deal with the male tenant's recalcitrance themselves. The Housing Benefit (General) Regulations 1987 (SI 1987 No. 1971 as amended), reg. 6, deems as 'liable' to pay rent a partner of tenant who is not paying, so that the partner can personally make a housing benefit claim.

A non-tenant spouse does at least have the common law right to occupy and use the matrimonial home during the subsistence of the marriage. This right is significantly reinforced by legislation (previously s. 1 of the Matrimonial Homes Act 1983, now (with minor modification) s. 30 of the Family Law Act 1996).

Family Law Act 1996

Rights concerning matrimonial home where one spouse has no estate, etc.
30.—(1) This section applies if—
    (a)   one spouse is entitled to occupy a dwelling-house by virtue of—
        (i)   a beneficial estate or interest or contract; or
        (ii)   any enactment giving that spouse the right to remain in occupation; and
    (b)   the other spouse is not so entitled.
    (2)   Subject to the provisions of this Part, the spouse not so entitled has the following rights ('matrimonial home rights')—
    (a)   if in occupation, a right not to be evicted or excluded from the dwelling-house or any part of it by the other spouse except with the leave of the court given by an order under section 33;
    (b)   if not in occupation, a right with the leave of the court so given to enter into and occupy the dwelling-house.
    (3)   If a spouse is entitled under this section to occupy a dwelling-house or any part of a dwelling-house, any payment or tender made or other thing done by that spouse in or towards satisfaction of any liability of the other spouse in respect of rent, mortgage payments or other outgoings affecting the dwelling-house is, whether or not it is made or done in pursuance of an order under section 40, as good as if made or done by the other spouse.
    (4)   A spouse's occupation by virtue of this section—
    (a)   is to be treated, for the purposes of the Rent (Agriculture) Act 1976 and the Rent Act 1977 (other than Part V and sections 103 to 106 of that Act), as occupation by the other spouse as the other spouse's residence, and

(b)   if the spouse occupies the dwelling-house as that spouse's only or principal home, is to be treated, for the purposes of the Housing Act 1985 and Part I of the Housing Act 1988, as occupation by the other spouse as the other spouse's only or principal home.

(5)   If a spouse ('the first spouse')—

(a)   is entitled under this section to occupy a dwelling-house or any part of a dwelling-house, and

(b)   makes any payment in or towards satisfaction of any liability of the other spouse ('the second spouse') in respect of mortgage payments affecting the dwelling-house, the person to whom the payment is made may treat it as having been made by the second spouse, but the fact that that person has treated any such payment as having been so made does not affect any claim of the first spouse against the second spouse to an interest in the dwelling-house by virtue of the payment.

(6)   If a spouse is entitled under this section to occupy a dwelling-house or part of a dwelling-house by reason of an interest of the other spouse under a trust, all the provisions of subsections (3) to (5) apply in relation to the trustees as they apply in relation to the other spouse.

(7)   This section does not apply to a dwelling-house which has at no time been, and which was at no time intended by the spouses to be, a matrimonial home of theirs.
. . .

The rights conferred by s. 30 on a non-tenant spouse ('matrimonial home rights' – formerly known as 'statutory rights of occupation') are considerable. They include:

(a)   a right not to be evicted or excluded from the dwelling (owner-occupied or tenanted) by the other spouse except with leave of the court;

(b)   a right to tender rent or other payment for occupation of the dwelling;

(c)   a right, with leave of the court, to re-enter the dwelling, if not in occupation.

Occupation by the non-tenant spouse is sufficient to satisfy the 'residence' test for a Rent Act statutory tenancy and the 'only or principal home' test for a Housing Act 1985 secure tenancy and a Housing Act 1988 assured tenancy (see s. 30(4)).

Section 30, like its predecessors, significantly strengthens the position of a non-tenant spouse. In itself, it does nothing to assist the position of co-habitees, heterosexual or homosexual. Further reinforcement of the rights of non-tenant spouses is provided for by s. 33 of the Family Law Act 1996.

Family Law Act 1996

Occupation orders where applicant has estate or interest etc. or has matrimonial home rights

33.—(1)   If—

(a)   a person ('the person entitled')—

(i)   is entitled to occupy a dwelling-house by virtue of a beneficial estate or interest or contract or by virtue of any enactment giving him the right to remain in occupation, or

(ii)   has matrimonial home rights in relation to a dwelling-house, and

(b)   the dwelling-house—

(i)   is or at any time has been the home of the person entitled and of another person with whom he is associated, or

(ii)   was at any time intended by the person entitled and any such other person to be their home,

the person entitled may apply to the court for an order containing any of the provisions specified in subsections (3), (4) and (5).

(2)   If an agreement to marry is terminated, no application under this section may be made by virtue of section 62(3)(e) by reference to that agreement after the end of the period of three years beginning with the day on which it is terminated.

(3)   An order under this section may—

(a)   enforce the applicant's entitlement to remain in occupation as against the other person ('the respondent');

(b)   require the respondent to permit the applicant to enter and remain in the dwelling-house or part of the dwelling-house;

(c)   regulate the occupation of the dwelling-house by either or both parties;

(d)   if the respondent is entitled as mentioned in subsection (1)(a)(i), prohibit, suspend or restrict the exercise by him of his right to occupy the dwelling-house;

(e)   if the respondent has matrimonial home rights in relation to the dwelling-house and the applicant is the other spouse, restrict or terminate those rights;

(f)   require the respondent to leave the dwelling-house or part of the dwelling-house; or

(g)   exclude the respondent from a defined area in which the dwelling-house is included.

(4)   An order under this section may declare that the applicant is entitled as mentioned in subsection (1)(a)(i) or has matrimonial home rights.

(5)   If the applicant has matrimonial home rights and the respondent is the other spouse, an order under this section made during the marriage may provide that those rights are not brought to an end by—

(a)   the death of the other spouse; or

(b)   the termination (otherwise than by death) of the marriage.

(6)   In deciding whether to exercise its powers under subsection (3) and (if so) in what manner, the court shall have regard to all the circumstances including—

(a)   the housing needs and housing resources of each of the parties and of any relevant child;

(b)   the financial resources of each of the parties;

(c)   the likely effect of any order, or of any decision by the court not to exercise its powers under subsection (3), on the health, safety or well-being of the parties and of any relevant child; and

(d)   the conduct of the parties in relation to each other and otherwise.

(7)   If it appears to the court that the applicant or any relevant child is likely to suffer significant harm attributable to conduct of the respondent if an order under this section containing one or more of the provisions mentioned in subsection (3) is not made, the court shall make the order unless it appears to it that—

(a)   the respondent or any relevant child is likely to suffer significant harm if the order is made; and

(b)   the harm likely to be suffered by the respondent or child in that event is as great as, or greater than, the harm attributable to conduct of the respondent which is likely to be suffered by the applicant or child if the order is not made.

(8)   The court may exercise its powers under subsection (5) in any case where it considers that in all the circumstances it is just and reasonable to do so.

. . .

Unlike s. 30, s. 33 significantly expands the scope of its predecessor, s. 1(2) and (3) of the Matrimonial Homes Act 1983, above all by having at its foundation not only 'matrimonial homes rights', arising under s. 30 and applicable only to spouses, but also rights arising by virtue of 'a beneficial estate or interest or contract' (s. 33(1)(a)(i)). The most obvious way for such rights to arise in relation to a non-spouse partner is via a joint tenancy.

The orders which a court can make under s. 33 are diverse, and its discretion is wide (s. 33(6)), although specific attention is directed to the needs of (any) children of the relationship and the conduct of the parties, and an order *shall* be made if 'significant harm' would otherwise be likely to result to the applicant or any 'relevant child' (s. 33(7)). The main orders (under s. 33(3)) are to:

(a)   enforce the applicant's right to remain in occupation;
(b)   suspend or restrict the other partner's right to occupy the dwelling;
(c)   require the other partner to leave the dwelling.

As applied to tenanted property, this means that a non-tenant spouse with 'matrimonial homes rights', or (for example) a joint tenant cohabitant can apply for an order excluding the tenant from the dwelling (s. 33(3)) or some part of it.

Although such 'occupation' orders do not settle the long-term disposition of the tenancy (or other matrimonial home) they remain highly controversial, both in their existence (overturning, even if only temporarily, entrenched property rights) and in their application. A detailed discussion of the relevant case law is outside the scope of this book, being properly the preserve of family law, but it is now clear that, although a major factor, the welfare of children is not of overriding significance (see s. 33(6)). The Law Commission in its report *Domestic Violence and the Occupation of the Family Home* (1992) (No. 207) rejected suggestions that regulatory orders should be governed by a 'welfare paramountcy' test, and this is reflected in s. 33. What *is* clear is that the 'balance of harm' test in s. 33(7) will often be decisive. Of particular interest from a housing law perspective is s. 33(6)(a), referring to the 'housing needs and housing resources . . . of the parties'. Under the previous law it had been held (*Wooton* v *Wooton* [1984] FLR 871) that the prospect of the parties being re-housed by a local authority was a relevant factor, so that an application by a wife might be refused if the local authority had a statutory obligation to re-house (see now Chapter VII of the Housing Act 1996 in chapter 6). This of course increases the risk that the courts are being used as levers to 'prise open' the doors of public housing. Correspondingly, a court will not make an order merely to aid an authority in obtaining possession of a dwelling where it is clear that the applicant partner will not return if the tenant is excluded (*Warwick* v *Warwick* (1982) 1 HLR 139). For the most authoritative discussion of the predecessor provisions to s. 33, see *Richards* v *Richards* [1984] AC 174.

All the above presupposes that the applicant partner has 'matrimonial home' or other 'occupational' rights, which will not be the case for all spouses and will only be the case for those partners in non-marital relationships who do have joint tenancies. Prior to the Family Law Act 1996, the main legislative protection for non-marital partners lay in the well-known Domestic Violence and Matrimonial Proceedings Act 1976, which applied (s. 1(2)) equally to marriages and heterosexual cohabitation. The law is now contained in s. 36 of the Family Law Act 1996.

Family Law Act 1996

One cohabitant or former cohabitant with no existing right to occupy

36.—(1)   This section applies if—

(a)   one cohabitant or former cohabitant is entitled to occupy a dwelling-house by virtue of a beneficial estate or interest or contract or by virtue of any enactment giving him the right to remain in occupation;

(b)   the other cohabitant or former cohabitant is not so entitled; and

(c)   that dwelling-house is the home in which they live together as husband and wife or a home in which they at any time so lived together or intended so to live together.

(2)   The cohabitant or former cohabitant not so entitled may apply to the court for an order under this section against the other cohabitant or former cohabitant ('the respondent').

(3)   If the applicant is in occupation, an order under this section must contain provision—

(a)   giving the applicant the right not to be evicted or excluded from the dwelling-house or any part of it by the respondent for the period specified in the order; and

(b)   prohibiting the respondent from evicting or excluding the applicant during that period.

(4)   If the applicant is not in occupation, an order under this section must contain provision—

(a)   giving the applicant the right to enter into and occupy the dwelling-house for the period specified in the order; and

(b)   requiring the respondent to permit the exercise of that right.

(5)   An order under this section may also—

(a)   regulate the occupation of the dwelling-house by either or both of the parties;

(b)   prohibit, suspend or restrict the exercise by the respondent of his right to occupy the dwelling-house;

(c)   require the respondent to leave the dwelling-house or part of the dwelling-house; or

(d)   exclude the respondent from a defined area in which the dwelling-house is included.

(6)   In deciding whether to make an order under this section containing provision of the kind mentioned in subsection (3) or (4) and (if so) in what manner, the court shall have regard to all the circumstances including—

(a)   the housing needs and housing resources of each of the parties and of any relevant child;

(b)   the financial resources of each of the parties;

(c)   the likely effect of any order, or of any decision by the court not to exercise its powers under subsection (3) or (4), on the health, safety or well-being of the parties and of any relevant child;

(d)   the conduct of the parties in relation to each other and otherwise;

(e)   the nature of the parties' relationship;

(f)   the length of time during which they have lived together as husband and wife;

(g)   whether there are or have been any children who are children of both parties or for whom both parties have or have had parental responsibility;

(h)   the length of time that has elapsed since the parties ceased to live together; and

(i)   the existence of any pending proceedings between the parties—

(i)   for an order under paragraph 1(2)(d) or (e) of Schedule 1 to the Children Act 1989 (orders for financial relief against parents);

(ii)   relating to the legal or beneficial ownership of the dwelling-house.

(7)   In deciding whether to exercise its powers to include one or more of the provisions referred to in subsection (5) ('a subsection (5) provision') and (if so) in what manner, the court shall have regard to all the circumstances including—

(a)   the matters mentioned in subsection (6)(a) to (d); and

(b)   the questions mentioned in subsection (8).

(8)   The questions are—

(a)   whether the applicant or any relevant child is likely to suffer significant harm attributable to conduct of the respondent if the subsection (5) provision is not included in the order; and

(b)   whether the harm likely to be suffered by the respondent or child if the provision is included is as great as or greater than the harm attributable to conduct of the respondent which is likely to be suffered by the applicant or child if the provision is not included.

(9)   An order under this section—

(a)   may not be made after the death of either of the parties; and

(b)   ceases to have effect on the death of either of them.

(10)   an order under this section must be limited so as to have effect for a specified period not exceeding six months, but may be extended on one occasion for a further specified period not exceeding six months.

. . .

In part, s. 36, like the remainder of Pt IV of the Family Law Act 1996, can be seen as a further legislative response to the problem of 'domestic violence', and as a successor to the abortive Family Homes and Domestic Violence Bill 1995. It is largely based on the Law Commission recommendations in its 1992 Report *Domestic Violence and the Occupation of the Family Home* (Law Com. No. 207). The *overall* aim of Pt IV is to replace the former 'hotchpotch' of provisions with a more coherent and structured code, and this is demonstrated very well by s. 36. Under the previous law cohabitees lacking joint tenant status had to rely on the 'domestic violence' provisions of the Domestic Violence and Matrimonial Proceedings Act 1976 to obtain 'non-molestation' orders and 'ouster' orders and had no access to the more clear-cut orders generally available to spouses. Now the provisions in s. 36 for occupation orders are, at least, comparable with those available under s. 30 and s. 33 to those with 'matrimonial home' rights. However, complete consistency has not been achieved, in that in deciding whether to make an order courts should consider (amongst other things):

(a)   the nature of the parties' relationship (s. 36(6)(e)), limited (via s. 41(2)) by the fact that they 'have not given each other the commitment involved in marriage';

(b)   the length of time they have lived together (s. 36)(6)(f)); and

(c)   whether there are any children of the relationship (s. 36(6)(g)).

Moreover, whereas under s. 33(10) orders can be for any period, under s. 36(10) they are limited to a maximum of six months (although they can be extended, once, for a further six months).

Although s. 36 provides for a much clearer and less 'stop gap' approach than the previous law (on which see *Wooton* v *Wooton* [1984] FLR 871 and *Thurley* v *Smith* [1984] FLR 875), there is still obvious reluctance wholly to equate the position of cohabitants and spouses, and non-heterosexual relationships are still not encompassed. However, the provisions in Pt IV of the 1996 Act dealing specifically with domestic violence, for example s. 42 (non-molestation orders), do extend more widely to cover anyone 'associated' with the respondent. 'Associated person' is defined by s. 62 of the Act in terms identical to those in s. 178 of the Housing Act 1996 (see chapter 6) and includes (s. 62(3)) anyone who 'live[s] or [has] lived in the same household', as the respondent 'otherwise than merely by reason of one of them being the other's employee, tenant, lodger or boarder'. This appears to cover homosexual relationships, and also friends sharing a dwelling as joint tenants.

Notes

1.   Section 30 of the Family Law Act 1996 protects the 'matrimonial home' rights of spouses and joint tenant partners. Section 30(4) buttresses these rights by providing that, if the tenant spouse leaves, continued occupation by the non-tenant spouse satisfies the 'residence' and 'only or principal home' conditions under the Rent Act 1977 and the Housing Acts 1985 and 1988. The position of a non-tenant cohabitant remains considerably weaker. In the typical case, such a person probably possesses only a licence, lacking the necessary 'exclusive possession' to claim even sub-tenant status (see chapter 1 and *Monmouth BC* v *Marlog* (1995) 27 HLR 30). Moreover, even in the unlikely event of a sub-tenancy existing it would seem to lack protected tenant status (s. 12, Rent Act 1977) or assured tenant status (Sch. 1, para. 10, Housing Act 1988) because the tenant partner would be a 'resident landlord' (see generally on this chapter 2). It is even doubtful whether the Protection from Eviction Act 1977 applies in the majority of cases since there will be a sharing of 'accommodation' with the landlord/licensor (s. 3A of the Protection from Eviction Act 1977). Therefore, if no protection can be found under the Family Law Act 1996, the non-tenant partner can be removed from the property simply by being served with 'reasonable' notice, and without even the protection of a court order being required.

If the tenant partner departs leaving the other in occupation, although in practice the position of the non-tenant partner may be treated sympathetically, in theory his or her position is weak. It is even doubtful whether any new tenancy will arise, where the landlord accepts 'rent' from the 'deserted' partner, unless a clear new agreement can be inferred. This might depend on the terms on which the 'rent' is accepted (purely 'concessionary' or otherwise) and over how long a period it is accepted. The issues are discussed in *Marcroft Wagons v Smith* [1951] 2 KB 496, where a landlord accepted rent from a daughter on the death of her mother, the statutory tenant of the dwelling, for a period of approximately five months. The Court of Appeal upheld a county court ruling that she remained a mere licensee and that no new tenancy had come into being. Evershed MR stated (at p. 501): '. . . I should be extremely sorry . . . [if] . . . A landlord could never grant to a person in the position of the defendant any kind of indulgence, particularly in circumstances such as existed in March 1950, when the defendant lost her mother'. Subsequently, in *Westminster City Council v Basson* (1991) 23 HLR 225, a similar approach was adopted specifically in relation to a 'deserted' cohabitee. Westminster had granted a joint secure tenancy to a Mr and Mrs Simpson in 1977. In 1984, Mrs Simpson moved out, and (subsequently) Basson moved in living with Mr Simpson as 'husband and wife'. The relationship broke down and Mr Simpson moved out in February 1985. The authority continued to accept money from Basson for her occupation and use of the property, but as early as September 1985 had stated that they regarded her occupation 'as 'unlawful' and that they did not intend to create 'a tenancy or a licence akin to a tenancy'. Possession proceedings were commenced only in November 1986, but despite the long delay the Court of Appeal upheld a county court ruling that no tenancy had come into being.

2.   Spouses *with* 'matrimonial home' rights also have rights in possession proceedings, so long as they remain in occupation, to apply for adjournments, stays, suspensions or postponements of the proceedings even if the tenancy would otherwise be terminated as a result of the proceedings (see s. 85(5), Housing Act 1985 and s. 9(5), Housing Act 1988).

3.   Section 35 of the Family Law Act 1996 gives the court powers to make occupation orders where the applicant is divorced from the respondent, and the latter is the one who retains a right to occupy the dwelling-house. The structure of s. 35 is very similar to ss. 30 and 33 concerning current spouses, but further factors are introduced (for example, the length of time that has elapsed since the parties last lived together and since the divorce) and (as with s. 36) orders are limited to a maximum of six months.

(ii) Long-term rights and remedies

Here, the concern of the law is less intervention to deal with the immediate crises inherent in the breakdown of a relationship, and more to settle the long-term consequences of the final breakdown of the relationship. The resolution of the property interests of the parties is, then, one aspect of the overall financial position which they are to be left in. Unsurprisingly the law has always been much clearer concerning spouses than other relationships. The key legislative provision has for many years been s. 24 of the Matrimonial Causes Act 1973, which grants the court extensive jurisdiction to adjust the property rights of parties on the breakdown of a marriage, and to order one party to transfer property to the other. Since amendments introduced by Sch. 2 to the Family Law Act 1996, s. 24 of the 1973 Act contains the basic powers to adjust property rights, and the orders themselves are contained in s. 21(2) of the 1973 Act. For this purpose a secure tenancy is as much 'property' as an owner-occupied dwelling, since s. 91(3)(b) of the Housing Act 1985 specifically allows assignments of secure tenancies by courts using their s. 24 powers. In the case of private sector tenancies it is much more doubtful whether the courts have 'property transfer' powers since, generally, assignments are permissible only with the consent of the landlord (see, for example, s. 15 of the Housing Act 1988). However, the courts have wider and more 'tailored' powers to transfer tenancies under s. 53 of and Sch. 7 to the Family Law Act 1996.

Family Law Act 1996

Transfer of certain tenancies
53.   Schedule 7 makes provision in relation to the transfer of certain tenancies on divorce etc. or on separation of cohabitants.

SCHEDULE 7
TRANSFER OF CERTAIN TENANCIES ON DIVORCE ETC. OR
ON SEPARATION OF COHABITANTS

PART I
GENERAL

Interpretation

1.   In this Schedule—
'cohabitant', except in paragraph 3, includes (where the context requires) former cohabitant;
'the court' does not include a magistrates' court,
'landlord' includes—
(a)   any person from time to time deriving title under the original landlord; and
(b)   in relation to any dwelling-house any person other than the tenant who is, or (but for Part VII of the Rent Act 1977 or Part II of the Rent (Agriculture) Act 1976) would be, entitled to possession of the dwelling-house;
'Part II order' means an order under Part II of this Schedule;
'a relevant tenancy' means—
(a)   a protected tenancy or statutory tenancy within the meaning of the Rent Act 1977;
(b)   a statutory tenancy within the meaning of the Rent (Agriculture) Act 1976;

(c) a secure tenancy within the meaning of section 79 of the Housing Act 1985; or

(d) an assured tenancy or assured agricultural occupancy within the meaning of Part I of the Housing Act 1988;

'spouse', except in paragraph 2, includes (where the context requires) former spouse; and

'tenancy' includes sub-tenancy.

Cases in which the court may make an order

2.—(1) This paragraph applies if one spouse is entitled, either in his own right or jointly with the other spouse, to occupy a dwelling-house by virtue of a relevant tenancy.

(2) At any time when it has power to make a property adjustment order under section 23A (divorce or separation) or 24 (nullity) of the Matrimonial Causes Act 1973 with respect to the marriage, the court may make a Part II order.

3.—(1) This paragraph applies if one cohabitant is entitled, either in his own right or jointly with the other cohabitant, to occupy a dwelling-house by virtue of a relevant tenancy.

(2) If the cohabitants cease to live together as husband and wife, the court may make a Part II order.

4. The court shall not make a Part II order unless the dwelling-house is or was—

(a) in the case of spouses, a matrimonial home; or

(b) in the case of cohabitants, a home in which they lived together as husband and wife.

Matters to which the court must have regard

5. In determining whether to exercise its powers under Part II of this Schedule and, if so, in what manner, the court shall have regard to all the circumstances of the case including—

(a) the circumstances in which the tenancy was granted to either or both of the spouses or cohabitants or, as the case requires, the circumstances in which either or both of them became tenant under the tenancy;

(b) the matters mentioned in section 33(6)(a), (b) and (c) and, where the parties are cohabitants and only one of them is entitled to occupy the dwelling-house by virtue of the relevant tenancy, the further matters mentioned in section 36(6)(e), (f), (g) and (h); and

(c) the suitability of the parties as tenants.

PART II
ORDERS THAT MAY BE MADE

References to entitlement to occupy

6. References in this Part of this Schedule to a spouse or a cohabitant being entitled to occupy a dwelling-house by virtue of a relevant tenancy apply whether that entitlement is in his own right or jointly with the other spouse or cohabitant.

Protected, secure or assured tenancy or assured agricultural occupancy

7.—(1) If a spouse or cohabitant is entitled to occupy the dwelling-house by virtue of a protected tenancy within the meaning of the Rent Act 1977, a secure tenancy within the meaning of the Housing Act 1985 or an assured tenancy or assured agricultural occupancy within the meaning of Part I of the Housing Act 1988, the court may by order direct that, as from such date as may be specified in the order, there shall, by virtue of the order and without further assurance, be transferred to, and vested in, the other spouse or cohabitant—

(a)   the estate or interest which the spouse or cohabitant so entitled had in the dwelling-house immediately before that date by virtue of the lease or agreement creating the tenancy and any assignment of that lease or agreement, with all rights, privileges and appurtenances attaching to that estate or interest but subject to all covenants, obligations, liabilities and encumbrances to which it is subject; and

(b)   where the spouse or cohabitant so entitled is an assignee of such lease or agreement, the liability of that spouse or cohabitant under any covenant of indemnity by the assignee express or implied in the assignment of the lease or agreement to that spouse or cohabitant.

(2)   If an order is made under this paragraph, any liability or obligation to which the spouse or cohabitant so entitled is subject under any covenant having reference to the dwelling-house in the lease or agreement, being a liability or obligation falling due to be discharged or performed on or after the date so specified, shall not be enforceable against that spouse or cohabitant.

(3)   If the spouse so entitled is a successor within the meaning of Part IV of the Housing Act 1985, his former spouse or former cohabitant (or, if a separation order is in force, his spouse) shall be deemed also to be a successor within the meaning of that Part.

(4)   If the spouse or cohabitant so entitled is for the purpose of section 17 of the Housing Act 1988 a successor in relation to the tenancy or occupancy, his former spouse or former cohabitant (or, if a separation order is in force, his spouse) is to be deemed to be a successor in relation to the tenancy or occupancy for the purposes of that section.

(5)   . . .

(6)   In this paragraph, references to a separation order being in force include references to there being a judicial separation in force.

Statutory tenancy within the meaning of the Rent Act 1977

8.—(1)   This paragraph applies if the spouse or cohabitant is entitled to occupy the dwelling-house by virtue of a statutory tenancy within the meaning of the Rent Act 1977.

(2)   The court may by order direct that, as from the date specified in the order—

(a)   that spouse or cohabitant is to cease to be entitled to occupy the dwelling-house; and

(b)   the other spouse or cohabitant is to be deemed to be the tenant or, as the case may be, the sole tenant under that statutory tenancy.

(3)   The question whether the provisions of paragraphs 1 to 3, or (as the case may be) paragraphs 5 to 7 of Schedule 1 to the Rent Act 1977, as to the succession by the surviving spouse of a deceased tenant, or by a member of the deceased tenant's family, to the right to retain possession are capable of having effect in the event of the death of the person deemed by an order under this paragraph to be the tenant or sole tenant under the statutory tenancy is to be determined according as those provisions have or have not already had effect in relation to the statutory tenancy.

. . .

Section 53 and Sch. 7 repeal and replace s. 7 and Sch. 1 to the Matrimonial Homes Act 1983. The crucial difference between the old and the new law is that the new law extends to cohabitants, indeed (except in para. 3) to former cohabitants, as the context requires. It expressly applies to Rent Act tenancies, secure tenancies and assured tenancies. In all such cases, the court may (as regards the matrimonial home, or dwelling in which the cohabitants lived together as husband and wife) order a transfer of the appropriate tenancy held by the respondent partner to the applicant partner. The court may also direct that some compensation be paid by the transferee partner to the transferor partner (taking account of the overall financial position of the parties): Sch. 7, para. 10). In deciding whether to make an order, the court is specifically directed to consider s. 33(6)(a) to (c) and s. 36(6)(e), (f) and (g). These have already been discussed. In addition (Sch. 7, para. 5(c)) the court is directed to have regard to the suitability of the parties as tenants.

Where the court makes a transfer under Sch. 7, there is no assignment and therefore the consent of the landlord is not required. Paragraph 14, however, provides that rules of court shall be made requiring the court, before it makes an order, to give the landlord an opportunity of being heard. A particular issue on which the landlord may well wish to be 'heard' is that of rent arrears. Where a joint tenancy becomes a sole tenancy, after a relationship breakdown, most landlords will look to the 'survivor' for the arrears (in the survey by Kay, A., Legg, C., and Foot, J., *The 1980 Tenants Rights in Practice*, 83 per cent of local authorities did so) and all have the power to do so. However, in the case of a sole tenant the tenant alone is responsible for rent arrears (like any other debt), and a 'successor' tenant, whether a 'successor' because of death, assignment, or under Sch. 7, has no responsibility for arrears. It is not uncommon for local authority landlords, in particular, still to look to the incoming tenant to discharge arrears (22 per cent of local authorities surveyed by Key, Legg and Foot), but it is very doubtful whether such a 'requirement' is legally enforceable. Moreover, Sch. 7, para. 7(2) clearly states that any 'obligation' of the former tenant is not enforceable against the transferee (implicitly precluding any arrears liability in the transferee) and specific powers are given to *the court* under Sch. 7, para. 11, to direct that the transferor and transferee are to be jointly and severally liable for obligations concerning the dwelling. Arguably, in the light of all this, a local authority pressing a transferee tenant to discharge arrears is guilty of maladministration.

The extension of these 'tailored' tenancy transfer powers to cohabitants applies irrespective of whether there are children of the relationship or not. In addition, the Children Act 1989, s. 15 and Sch. 1 give the courts powers to order the transfer of property between partners (married or unmarried) for the benefit of children of the relationship. In *K* v *K* [1992] 1 WLR 530 this was held to include tenanted or owner-occupied property.

Questions
1. Prior to Pt IV of the Family Law Act 1996, the Law Commission stated that the existing civil remedies were 'complex, confusing and lack integration' (Law Comm 207 (1992)). To what extent do the provisions in Pt IV provide for a clearer and more coherent structure?

2. Many of the provisions in Pt IV and Sch. 7 extend legal protection to heterosexual cohabitants. However, only the specific 'domestic violence' provisions extend to other relationships. Should the provisions have been extended further to encompass homosexual relationships generally?

3. Even as regards heterosexual relationships, complete consistency has not been provided for in Pt IV. What justification(s) can be given, for example, for limiting orders under s. 36 to six months, in the typical case?

4. Section 41(2) of the Family Law Act 1996 states that, 'where the court is required to consider the nature of the parties' relationship, it is to have regard to the fact that they have not given each other the commitment involved in marriage'. Do you think that this provision is either 'useless . . . or pernicious' (Earl Russell *Hansard*, HL Vol. 570, col. 115)?

(D) Joint tenancies

As has been noted at several points already in this chapter, joint tenant status confers significant advantages on non-spouse partners in particular. A joint tenancy occurs wherever more than one person in a dwelling *shares a tenancy*. Joint tenants do not possess separate parts of the property, they are all equally entitled to joint exclusive possession of the whole of it. Joint tenants, collectively, possess one tenancy. Of course, not all those living under one roof class as joint tenants; they may hold separate tenancies from the same landlord; they may hold separate non-exclusive licences (see generally chapter 1), one may be the tenant and the other(s) joint tenant(s) of that person (or perhaps joint licensees of that person). Perhaps the clearest recent discussion of these issues is to be found in *A. G. Securities* v *Vaughan* [1990] 1 AC 417 which was discussed extensively in chapter 1. The House of Lords unanimously ruled that the separate occupiers of the flat lacked all the ingredients necessary for the creation of a joint tenancy; their interests started on different days, on different documents and for different periods. In the words of Lord Bridge (at p. 453): 'The four respondents acquired their contractual rights to occupy the flat in question, and undertook their relevant obligations by separate agreements . . . made at different times and on different terms. These rights and obligations having initially been several, I do not understand by what legal alchemy they could ever become joint.'

Assuming joint tenancy status is acquired or expressly conferred, none of the difficulties already discussed for one partner on the death of the other, or on the breakdown of the relationship, arises. No question of 'succession' or 'assignment' needs to be discussed. Instead, the surviving tenant simply holds in his or her own name the tenancy formerly held by all the tenants jointly. On the other hand, the 'joint and several' nature of a joint tenancy means that each joint tenant is liable for the actions of the others and, in particular, each is liable for the whole rent of the premises. Therefore a 'surviving' joint tenant can be held accountable for all the arrears which have accrued in relation to the tenancy.

All landlords, public or private, have the power to grant joint tenancies, whether the tenancies in question are protected, assured or secure. Private sector landlords seem increasingly to favour joint tenancies, not least because of the control it gives them over rent in particular. In the public sector, as noted earlier in this chapter, Annex C to the Code of Guidance on Parts VI and VII, Housing Act 1996 advises local authorities 'normally' to grant a joint tenancy where the members of a household have a long-term commitment to the home, whether as married couples, as friends, in other relationships or even as live-in carers. Moreover, the authority should inform applicants in writing of their reasons if they refuse to grant a joint tenancy.

Generally joint tenants have collective responsibilities, and normally they must act together. Therefore, if joint tenants wish to surrender a fixed-term lease they must all act together to do so. As Somervell LJ stated in *Leek and Moorlands Building Society* v *Clark* [1952] 2 QB 788, at p. 794: 'They all have the right to the full term, and all must concur if this right is to be abandoned'. However, it now seems that is *not* the case concerning the service of notices to quit, and in the context of local authority tenancies in particular, this has proved to be a point of considerable importance in recent years.

(i)   Joint tenants and notices to quit: the issues
Prior to the Housing Act 1980, it was common for local authority landlords to issue a notice to quit against a deserted joint tenant before granting a new sole tenancy. Since the 1980 Act, however, the authority must show grounds for possession before the joint secure tenancy can be brought to an end, and possession can be obtained by the landlord only via a court order (s. 82, Housing Act 1985 and generally chapter 5). What if the authority try a different approach and come to an understanding with the deserted joint tenant that *he or she* will serve a notice to quit on the authority, following the expiry of which the authority will re-grant a sole tenancy to the tenant? The issues came to a head in the following case:

Greenwich LBC v McGrady
[1983] 46 P & CR 223

SIR JOHN DONALDSON MR: This is an appeal from the decision of His Honour Judge James at the Woolwich County Court granting the plaintiffs, the Greenwich London Borough Council, possession of 170, Nightingale Vale, SE18, against the defendant. The point is a very short one indeed, but is not without interest. It is whether, where there is a letting to joint tenants, the act of one of the joint tenants in giving notice to quit both brings the tenancy to an end and deprives the other joint tenant of the protection of the Housing Act 1980.

The facts were these. On October 25, 1976, the local authority let these premises to Mr and Mrs McGrady on a joint weekly tenancy. In 1980, there were divorce proceedings, and the parties separated. On May 11, 1981, Mrs McGrady gave the authority a notice to quit taking effect on June 15, that being one of the periodic tenancy days. Mr McGrady refused to leave, and proceedings were brought in the county court. The registrar found in favour of the defendant, but on appeal the judge found for the local authority.

The law can for practical purposes be taken from the decision of this court in *Leek and Moorlands Building Society* v *Clark* [[1952] 2 QB 788; [1952] 2 All ER 492, CA].

In that case, the husband had bought a long leasehold interest jointly held by himself and his wife. He then purported to sell with vacant possession, and the court was concerned with whether the sale constituted an effective surrender of that long leasehold interest. It was held that it did not. Somervell LJ, however, in a reserved judgment delivered as the judgment of the court, reviewed the general position of joint tenants, relying in particular on *Doe d. Aslin* v *Summersett* [(1830) 1 B & Ad 135, 109 ER 738], in which Lord Tenterden CJ had adverted to the position of joint tenants on a periodic tenancy. It is quite clear that this court was approving the earlier case. Somervell LJ quoted the *ratio* of the earlier decision in the following passage:

'Upon a joint demise by joint tenants' that is, the lessors in that case 'upon a tenancy from year to year, the true character of the tenancy is this, not that the tenant holds of each the share of each so long as he and each shall please, but that he holds the whole of all so long as he and all shall please, and as soon as any one of the joint tenants . . . gives a notice to quit, he effectively puts an end to that tenancy.'

Later, he adverted again to *Doe d. Aslin* v *Summersett* and said:

That case, for reasons which we have given, is not in our view an exception to the rule we have just stated. It is an illustration, in a highly technical field, of the general principle that if a joint enterprise is due to terminate on a particular day, all concerned must agree if it is to be renewed or continued beyond that day. To use Lord Tenterden's phrase, it will only be continued if 'all shall please.'

In my judgment, it is clear law that, if there is to be a surrender of a joint tenancy – that is, a surrender before its natural termination – then all must agree to the surrender. If there is to be a renewal, which is the position at the end of each period of a periodic tenancy, then again all must concur. In this case, Mrs McGrady made it quite clear by her notice to quit that she was not content to renew the joint tenancy on and after June 15, 1981. That left Mr McGrady without any tenancy at all, although it was faintly argued by Mr Osman that on, as he put it, the severance of a joint tenancy the joint tenant who did not concur was left with a sole tenancy. That cannot be the law, and no authority has been cited in support of it.

The only point that remains is whether Mr McGrady is entitled to the protection of the Act of 1980 on the ground that what was a secure contractual tenancy has been brought to an end. The short answer to that is that the Act of 1980 operates to give security where landlords give notice to quit; it does not give security where tenants give notice to quit. The relevant sections are sections 32 and 28; I do not think that I need quote them.

For those reasons, in my judgment, the judge was entirely correct in his decision and I would dismiss the appeal.

The reasoning in *McGrady* (that a periodic joint tenancy requires the continued desire of all the joint tenants that it should continue, so that a notice to quit by one of them effectively brings the joint tenancy to an end) was approved by the House of Lords in the next case:

Hammersmith and Fulham LBC v *Monk*
[1992] 1 All ER 1

LORD BRIDGE: My Lords, the issue in this appeal is whether a periodic tenancy held by two or more tenants jointly can be brought to an end by a notice to quit by one of the joint tenants without the consent of the others. It arises for determination in the following circumstances. The appellant, Mr Monk, and Mrs Powell were granted by the respondent council a weekly tenancy of a flat at 35 Niton Street, London SW6, where they cohabited. The tenancy was terminable by four weeks' notice to expire on a Monday. In 1988 Mr Monk and Mrs Powell fell out and Mrs Powell left the flat. She consulted the respondent, who agreed to rehouse her if she would terminate the tenancy of the flat by giving an appropriate notice, which she did. The notice was given without Mr Monk's knowledge or consent but the council immediately notified him that the tenancy had been determined and in due course brought proceedings in the West London County Court to recover possession. Judge Roger Cooke held that Mrs Powell's notice to quit was ineffective to determine the tenancy and dismissed the claim. The Court of Appeal (Slade, Nicholls and Bingham LJJ) ((1990) 61 P & CR 414) allowed the respondent's appeal and made an order for possession. Mr Monk now appeals by leave of your Lordships' House.

In a previous decision of the Court of Appeal, *Greenwich London BC* v *McGrady* (1982) 81 LGR 288 it was held that a notice to quit given by one of two joint tenants without the consent of the other was effective to determine the periodic tenancy to which it related. Much of the argument before the Court of Appeal in the present case was directed to the question whether the court was free to reach a conclusion at variance with *McGrady* on the grounds: (1) that an earlier decision of the Court of Appeal, *Howson* v *Buxton* (1928) 97 LJKB 749, was, as the judge had held, binding authority to the opposite effect; or (2) that, in any event the decision in *McGrady's* case was given per incuriam. The judgment of Slade LJ, with which Bingham LJ agreed, examined these issues very thoroughly and reached the conclusion that *Howson* v *Buxton* was not authority for the proposition sought to be derived from it and that *McGrady* was binding on the court. Nicholls LJ approached the issue more radically and held, both on principle and in reliance on a long line of authority prior to the decision in *McGrady*, that a joint periodic tenancy could be determined by a notice to quit given by one joint tenant.

Your Lordships are not technically bound by any previous decision and before examining the relevant authorities I think it helpful to consider whether the application of first principles suggests the answer to the question at issue. For a large part of this century there have been many categories of tenancy of property occupied for agricultural, residential and commercial purposes where the legislature has intervened to confer upon tenants extra-contractual rights entitling them to continue in occupation without the consent of the landlord, either after the expiry of a contractual lease for a fixed term or after notice to quit given by the landlord to determine a contractual periodic tenancy. It is primarily in relation to joint tenancies in these categories that the question whether or not notice to quit given by one of the joint tenants can determine the tenancy is of practical importance, particularly where, as in the instant case, the effect of the determination will be to deprive the other joint tenant of statutory protection. This may appear an untoward result and may consequently provoke a certain reluctance to hold that the law can permit one of two joint tenants unilaterally to deprive his co-tenant of 'rights' which both are equally entitled to enjoy. But the statutory consequences are in truth of no relevance to the question which your Lordships have to decide. That question is whether, at common law, a contractual periodic tenancy granted to two or more joint tenants is incapable of termination by a tenant's notice to quit unless it is served with the concurrence of all the joint tenants. That is the proposition which the appellant must establish in order to succeed.

As a matter of principle I see no reason why this question should receive any different answer in the context of the contractual relationship of landlord and tenant than that which it would receive in any other contractual context. If A and B contract with C on terms which are to continue in operation for one year in the first place and thereafter from year to year unless determined by notice at the end of the first or any subsequent year, neither A nor B has bound himself contractually for longer than one year. To hold that A could not determine the contract at the end of any year without the concurrence of B and vice versa would presuppose that each had assumed a potentially irrevocable contractual obligation for the duration of their joint lives, which, whatever the nature of the contractual obligations undertaken, would be such an improbable intention to impute to the parties that nothing less than the clearest express contractual language would suffice to manifest it. Hence, in any ordinary agreement for an initial term which is to continue for successive terms unless determined by notice, the obvious inference is that the agreement is intended to continue beyond the initial term only if and so long as all parties to the agreement are willing that it should do so. In a common law situation, where parties are free to contract as they wish and are bound only so far as they have agreed to be bound, this leads to the only sensible result.

Thus the application of ordinary contractual principles leads me to expect that a periodic tenancy granted to two or more joint tenants must be terminable at common law by an appropriate notice to quit given by any one of them whether or not the others are prepared to concur. But I turn now to the authorities to see whether there is any principle of the English law of real property and peculiar to the contractual relationship of landlord and tenant which refutes that expectation or whether the authorities confirm it.

. . .

In *Doe d. Aslin* v *Summersett* (1830) 1 B & AD 135, the freehold interest in land let on a yearly tenancy was vested jointly in four executors of a will to whom the land had been jointly devised. Three only of the executors gave notice to the tenant to quit. It was held by the Court of King's Bench that the notice was effective to determine the tenancy. Delivering the judgment, Lord Tenterden CJ said (1 B & AD 135 at 140–141:

> Upon a joint demise by joint-tenants upon a tenancy from year to year, the true character of the tenancy is this, not that the tenant holds of each the share of each so long as he and each shall please, but that he holds the *whole* of *all* so long as he *and all* shall please; and as soon as any one of the joint-tenants gives a notice to quit, he effectually puts an end to *that* tenancy; the tenant has a right upon such a notice to give up *the whole*, and unless he comes to a new arrangement with the other joint-tenants as to their shares, he is compellable so to do. The hardship upon the tenant, if he were not entitled to treat a notice from one as putting an end to the tenancy as to the whole, is obvious; for however willing a man might be to be sole tenant of an estate, it is not very likely he should be willing to hold undivided shares of it; and if upon such a notice the tenant is entitled to treat it as putting an end to the tenancy as to the whole, the other joint-tenants must have the same right. It cannot be optional on one side, and on one side only.

Now it was rightly pointed out in argument that part of the reasoning in this passage was dictated by considerations derived from the incidents of joint land tenure at law which were swept away by the reforming legislation of 1925. But this can in no way detract from the validity of the proposition emphasised in the judgment that the yearly tenant of a property let to him by joint freeholders 'holds the *whole* of *all* so long as he *and all* shall please.' This by itself is a sufficient and independent ground for the conclusion of the court that notice to quit by any one joint freeholder was effective to determine the tenancy. Precisely the same reasoning would apply to the operation of a notice to quit by one of two or more joint yearly tenants.

Summersett's case was followed in *Doe d. Kindersely* v *Hughes* (1840) 7 M & W 139 and *Alford* v *Vickery* (1842) Car & M 280, both cases in which the validity of a notice to determine a yearly tenancy given to the tenant without the concurrence of one or more of the joint landlords was affirmed. It is interesting that throughout the 19th century there is no reported case in the books where the effect of notice to quit given by one of two or more joint holders of the tenant's interest under a yearly or other periodic tenancy was ever called in question. I do not however find this surprising. The law was probably regarded as settled after *Summersett's* case, but, in any event, before the advent of statutory protection of tenants' rights of occupation, in the case of a notice to quit given by one of two or more joint periodic tenants the parties would in most cases have had little incentive to litigate. If the landlord was content that the other tenants should remain, there would have been nothing to litigate about. If the landlord wished to recover possession, he could do so by giving his own notice to quit.

In this century the English cases directly in point are *Howson* v *Buxton* (1928) 97 LJKB 749, *Leek and Moorlands Building Society* v *Clark* [1952] 2 QB 788 and *Greenwich London BC* v *McGrady* (1982) 81 IGR 288.

. . .

These then are the principles and the authorities which the appellant seeks to controvert. In the light of the careful analysis in the judgment of Slade LJ, 89 LGR 357, 366–369 of *Howson* v *Buxton* 97 LJ KB 749, which I gratefully adopt and need not repeat, it is now rightly accepted that the case affords no greater support for the appellant than can be derived from the obiter dictum of Scrutton LJ, who said with reference to a notice to determine a yearly tenancy at p. 752:

> I personally take the view that one joint tenant cannot give a notice to terminate the tenancy unless he does so with the authority of the other joint tenant . . .

Despite the eminence of the author of this observation, I do not feel able to give any weight to it in the absence of any indication of the reasoning on which it is based.

There are three principal strands in the argument advanced for the appellant. First, reliance is placed on the judgment in *Gandy* v *Jubber* (1865) 9 B & S 15, for the proposition that a tenancy from year to year, however long it continues, is a single term, not a series of separate lettings. The case arose out of an action for damages by a plaintiff who had been injured by a defective iron grating which was out of repair so as to amount to a nuisance. The property was occupied by a yearly tenant but the claim was brought against the reversioner, who was held liable by the Court of Queen's Bench. The defendant appealed to the Court of Exchequer Chamber on the ground that it was not alleged that the defendant knew of the nuisance, nor that it had existed prior to the commencement of the yearly tenancy. The argument is reported, see 5 B & S 485. Judgment was reserved, but before it was delivered the case was settled and Erle CJ announced at p. 494: '. . . it will not be necessary to deliver the judgment we have prepared.' The undelivered judgment in the defendant's favour is nevertheless reported and has always been regarded as authoritative. The passage relied on reads at p. 18:

> There frequently is an actual demise from year to year so long as both parties please. The nature of this tenancy is discussed in 4 Bac. Abr tit. *Leases and Terms for Years*, pp. 838, 839, 7th edn, and this article has always been deemed to be the highest authority being said to be the work of CB Gilbert. It seems clear that the learned

author considered that the true nature of such a tenancy is that it is a lease for two years certain, and that every year after it is a springing interest arising upon the first contract and parcel of it, so that if the lessee occupies for a number of years, these years, by computation from time past, make an entire lease for so many years, and that after the commencement of each new year it becomes an entire lease certain for the years past and also for the years so entered on, and that it is not a reletting at the commencement of the third and subsequent years. We think this is the true nature of a tenancy from year to year created by express words, and that there is not in contemplation of law a recommencing or reletting at the beginning of each year.

It must follow from this principle, Mr Reid submits, that the determination of a periodic tenancy by notice is in all respects analogous to the determination of a lease for a fixed term in the exercise of a break clause, which in the case of joint lessees clearly requires the concurrence of all. But reference to the passage from Bacon's *Abridgement* 7th edn, vol. IV, p. 839, on which the reasoning is founded shows that his analogy is not valid. The relevant passage reads:

A parol lease was made *de anno in annum, quamdiu ambabus partibus placuerit*; it was adjudged that this was but a lease for a year certain, and that every year after it was a springing interest, arising upon the first contract and parcel of it; so that if the lessee had occupied eight or ten years, or more, these years, by computation from the time past, made an entire lease for so many years; and if rent was in arrear for part of one of those years, and part of another, the lessor might distrain and avow as for so much rent arrear upon one entire lease, and need not avow as for several rents due upon several leases, accounting each year a new lease. It was also adjudged, that after the commencement of each new year, this was become an entire lease certain for the years past, and also for the year so entered upon; so that neither party could determine their wills till that year was run out, according to the opinion of the two judges in the last case. And this seems no way impeached by the statute of frauds and perjuries, which enacts, that no parol lease for above three years shall be accounted to have any other force or effect than of a lease only at will: for at first, this being a lease certain only for one year, and each accruing year after being a springing interest for that year, it is not a lease for any three years to come, though by a computation backwards, when five or six or more years are past, this may be said a parol lease for so many years; but with this the statute has nothing to do, but only looks forward to parol leases for above three years to come.

Thus the fact that the law regards a tenancy from year to year which has continued for a number of years, considered retrospectively, as a single term in no way affects the principle that continuation beyond the end of each year depends on the will of the parties that it should continue or that, considered prospectively, the tenancy continues no further than the parties have already impliedly agreed upon by their omission to serve notice to quit.

The second submission for the appellant is that, whatever the law may have been before the enactment of the Law of Property Act 1925, the effect of that statute, whereby a legal estate in land vested in joint tenants is held on trust for sale for the parties beneficially entitled, coupled with the principle that trustees must act unanimously in dealing with trust property is to reverse the decision in *Summerset's* case, 1 B & Ad 135 and to prevent one of two joint tenants determining a periodic tenancy without the concurrence of the other. It is unnecessary to consider the position where the parties beneficially entitled are different from those who hold the legal interest.

But where, as here, two joint tenants of a periodic tenancy hold both the legal and the beneficial interest, the existence of a trust for sale can make no difference to the principles applicable to the termination of the tenancy. At any given moment the extent of the interest to which the trust relates extends no further than the end of the period of the tenancy which will next expire on a date for which it is still possible to give notice to quit. If before 1925 the implied consent of both joint tenants, signified by the omission to give notice to quit, was necessary to extend the tenancy from one period to the next, precisely the same applies since 1925 to the extension by the joint trustee beneficiaries of the periodic tenancy which is the subject of the trust.

Finally, it is said that all positive dealings with a joint tenancy require the concurrence of all joint tenants if they are to be effective. Thus, a single joint tenant cannot exercise a break clause in a lease, surrender the term, make a disclaimer, exercise an option to renew the term or apply for relief from forfeiture. All these positive acts which joint tenants must concur in performing are said to afford analogies with the service of notice to determine a periodic tenancy which is likewise a positive act. But this is to confuse the form with the substance. The action of giving notice to determine a periodic tenancy is in form positive; but both on authority and on the principle so aptly summed up in the pithy Scottish phrase 'tacit relocation' the substance of the matter is that it is by his omission to give notice of termination that each party signifies the necessary positive assent to the extension of the term for a further period.

For all these reasons I agree with the Court of Appeal that, unless the terms of the tenancy agreement otherwise provide, notice to quit given by one joint tenant without the concurrence of any other joint tenant is effective to determine a periodic tenancy.

From this it is clear, that a secure tenancy can be effectively terminated by the service of a notice to quit by one of the former joint tenants. However, other decisions of the courts have emphasised difficulties hidden within the apparent simplicity of this, and, in particular, the formalities which need to be satisfied before the procedure can operate effectively.

(ii)   Joint tenants and notices to quit: the difficulties
As soon as *Greenwich* v *McGrady* was reported, the general academic view was that extreme care needed to be taken both by local authorities and by the deserted (partner) joint tenant, most typically a woman. The first issue to arise judicially came in *Parsons* v *Parsons* [1983] 1 WLR 1390, in which Donald Rattee QC, then sitting as a deputy High Court judge, stated (at p. 1400) that while the general *McGrady* principle seemed to be a sound one:

. . . it may be that if in a particular case the service of notice to quit by one joint tenant of the reversion to a periodic tenancy involved the joint tenants or some of them in a liability greater than the resultant increase in value of the reversion, those injured would have a claim in breach of trust against the joint tenant serving the notice: compare *Megarry and Wade, the Law of Real Property*, 4th ed. (1975), pp. 394–5, though I do not understand why the authors say in that passage that service of a notice to quit by one joint tenant will *usually* be a breach of trust.

This difficulty stems from the fact that all jointly held land (including assured and secure tenancies) is subject to an implied trust, and the joint tenants are trustees for themselves. If one of the joint tenants, therefore, acts detrimentally to the interests of the other(s) under the trust, it can be argued that he or she can be liable for any financial loss thereby incurred. Moreover, under s. 26(3) of the Law of Property Act 1925, one trustee was obliged to consult with and, as consistent with the general interests of the trust, give effect to the wishes of the other(s). It could obviously be argued that a failure by one joint tenant to consult with the other joint tenant(s) before serving a notice to quit could amount to a breach of s. 26(3). The issues came to a head in *Crawley BC v Ure*:

Crawley BC v Ure
[1996] QB 13

GLIDEWELL LJ: This is an appeal by the defendant, Mr Ure, against a decision of Judge Hammerton given in Horsham County Court on 8 February 1993 when he gave judgment for the plaintiffs, the Crawley Borough Council, and ordered Mr Ure to give possession of a flat, 156B, Three Bridges Road, Three Bridges, Crawley, West Sussex.

The material facts can be stated quite shortly. Mr and Mrs Ure were married on 12 October 1983 in the Philippines, both having previously been married and having children by their previous marriages. On 19 June 1986 Mr and Mrs Ure were granted a joint tenancy by the borough council of the flat to commence on 20 June 1986 on a weekly tenancy, the rent being due on each Monday, but subject to the statutory requirement that the tenancy could only be terminated on not less than four weeks' notice. In April 1990 Mr Ure started to work for Iraqi Airways and not long afterwards he had the grave misfortune to be taken a hostage at the start of the Gulf War. In October 1990 he was released, and presumably returned to the United Kingdom at that stage. On 16 August 1991 Mrs Ure and her daughter left the matrimonial home and have not since lived there. At some time after that, Mrs Ure started divorce proceedings. She and her daughter moved into accommodation which is variously described in the papers as a 'refuge' or 'emergency accommodation.' The judge specifically made no finding about the events which led to her leaving or the reasons why she left, though he did find that Mr Ure did not wish her to leave. On 15 September 1991 Mr Ure's son moved into the flat to live with him. In response to a letter dated 13 September which dealt with an application made by Mr Ure for housing benefit, Mr Ure informed the borough council that Mrs Ure had left on 16 August. As joint tenant Mrs Ure was entitled to continue to occupy the property; obviously she had a legal right to do so. She did not apply for an order to oust her husband from the matrimonial home. At some stage she applied to the council for assistance or accommodation as a homeless person under Part III of the Housing Act 1985. Presumably she was advised that, while she remained the joint tenant of the flat, she was not homeless, since she had an interest in the property, and thus she was not within the definition of a homeless person in section 58(2) of the Act. She would only come within the provisions if she satisfied one of the requirements in section 58(3). As far as the matters there set out are concerned, they are matters about which the judge specifically made no finding in this case, that is to say as to whether there had been any violence by the husband. However, it was suggested to Mrs Ure by the council, or by an officer of the council, that she could give a notice which would have the effect of terminating her tenancy of the flat. She therefore did so. On 6 April 1992 she gave a notice to the council in a form provided to her by them and which thus, in form, reads as though it was drafted as a notice given by the council rather than by a tenant; it starts:

> I, Irene Ure, hereby give you, Crawley Borough Council, four weeks' notice of my intention to quit and deliver up on Monday, 4 May 1992, or on the day on which a completed period of my tenancy next expires after the end of four weeks from the date of the service of this notice possession of the premises known as 156B, Three Bridges Road, Three Bridges, Crawley, West Sussex.

She did not inform her husband either beforehand that she intended to give such a notice or immediately afterwards that she had given it, and it follows that she did not have his consent to her seeking to terminate the tenancy in that way.

At one stage in these proceedings a point was taken about the form of the notice, but that is not pursued in this appeal.

The council submit that the wife's notice had the effect of terminating the tenancy. Mr Ure refused to leave the property. The council therefore brought proceedings against him in the county court. Originally they proceeded by way of an originating application for summary judgment under Order 24 of the County Court Rules 1981 (SI 1981 No. 1687 (L.20)). That failed, but as a result of that application, on 12 October 1992, Judge Kennedy QC sitting in Horsham County Court, ordered that the council should file amended particulars of claim. He then made other orders requiring there to be pleadings in the action, and that it should proceed as an action on pleadings, and gave other directions. The action thereafter proceeded in the ordinary way. Various defences were raised by Mr Ure, but in the event the judge decided against Mr Ure on all of them and gave judgment for the council as I have already indicated.

Only one of the arguments raised in the defence is repeated in this appeal.

. . .

Mr Berry, for Mr Ure, accepts of course that [*Hammersmith and Fulham LBC* v *Monk*] [1992] 1 AC 478 is binding authority for the proposition that in principle a notice to quit given by one of two joint tenants without the consent of the other is nevertheless effective to terminate the tenancy. He takes up, however, the suggestion made by Lord Browne-Wilkinson and, earlier, by Slade LJ that in some circumstances the joint tenant who serves the notice may be doing so in breach of trust. Mr Berry's argument can be summarised as follows. (1) By section 36 of the Law of Property Act 1925 a joint tenancy is held on trust for sale. The joint tenants in the present circumstances are both trustees and beneficiaries. (2) Although he now accepts (or at least does not argue to the contrary) that the service of the notice to quit itself was not a breach of trust, section 26(3) of the Law of Property Act 1925 required a joint tenant who wished to terminate the joint tenancy first to consult the other joint tenant, that is to say consult Mr Ure. (3) Mrs Ure did not consult her husband and thus acted in breach of trust. (4) If she had consulted, Mr Ure could have (a) objected to her terminating the tenancy and (b) sought a property adjustment order under section 24 of the Matrimonial Causes Act 1973 which, if it were granted, would have had the effect of vesting the joint tenancy in him alone. (5) The council, who advised and indeed encouraged Mrs Ure to serve the notice to quit, were thus parties to her breach of trust. It follows, submits Mr Berry, that the council, despite what was said by Slade LJ in *Metall and Rohstoff AG* v *Donaldson Lufkin & Jenrette Inc* [1990] 1 QB 391 in this court, were guilty of the tort of procuring a breach of trust, and, since it is a basic principle that equity will not allow a wrongdoer to take advantage of his own wrong, that is precisely what the council, in suing Mr Ure for possession and indeed in accepting the notice to quit served by Mrs Ure, were doing. Thus they should not have been allowed to succeed in their action for possession.

The passage in the judgment of Slade LJ in the *Metall and Rohstoff* case to which I have just referred is at p. 481, where, delivering the judgment of the court, he said in relation to an argument that there was a tort of procuring a breach of trust:

The principles of the law of trusts, in particular those expounded by Lord Selbourne LC in *Barnes* v *Addy* (1874) LR 9 Ch App 244, are quite sufficient to deal with those persons who incite a breach of trust or wrongfully meddle with trust assets or interfere with the relationship of trustee and beneficiary. We know of no authority supporting the existence of the alleged tort and can see no sufficient justification for the introduction of a new tort of this nature.

In reply to Mr Berry's submissions Mr Arden, for the council, submits, firstly, that the joint tenancy in this case was not held on trust for sale. The parties' interest in the property had no capital value. Therefore in practice it was not capable of being sold. Therefore there could not be a trust for sale. The last stage of this attractively simple argument is, in my view, wrong. It disregards the clear words of section 36(1) of the Law or Property Act 1925, and I do not find it necessary to say any more about it, with all due respect to Mr Arden.

However, his second argument demands more detailed consideration. This relates to the effect of section 26(3) of the Law of Property Act 1925. Section 26(1) of that Act provides:

If the consent of more than two persons is by the disposition made requisite to the execution of a trust for sale of land, then, in favour of a purchaser, the consent of any two of such persons to the execution of the trust or to the exercise of any statutory or other powers vested in the trustees for sale shall be deemed sufficient.

I need not refer to subsection (2).

Subsection (3) (as substituted by section 7 of, and the Schedule to, the Law of Property (Amendment) Act 1926), which is the critical subsection, provides:

Trustees for sale shall so far as practicable consult the persons of full age for the time being beneficially interested in possession in the rents and profits of the land until sale, and shall, so far as consistent with the general interest of the trust, give effect to the wishes of such persons . . .

If that subsection applied to the circumstances of this case Mrs Ure, in her capacity as a trustee for sale, was required to consult Mr Ure as a person beneficially interested in possession and, so far as consistent with the general interests of the trust, to give effect to his wishes; that did not require necessarily that she should follow his wishes, but at least she was required to consider them.

To whom and to what types of transaction, therefore, does section 26(3) apply? Mr Arden submits that what it requires is consultation by the trustees, or a trustee, with the beneficiaries or another beneficiary before either the execution of the trust for sale or 'the exercise of any statutory or other powers vested in the trustees for sale' – that last phrase coming from subsection (1). In this respect Mr Arden accepts, as I do, the correctness of the decision of Bennett J in *In re Jones; Jones* v *Cusack-Smith* [1931] 1 Ch 375. Bennett J summed up his judgment (which was a commendably short judgment in total) firstly by posing at the beginning the question he was seeking to answer, which was, at p. 377:

Must trustees for sale consult the persons of full age for the time being entitled in possession to the rents and profits of the land on the occasion of the exercise of any of their statutory trusts and powers, or is their duty limited to consulting the beneficiaries when they propose to exercise the trust for sale?

He answered that question, at p. 378:

> It seems that, there being nothing expressed to limit subsection (3) or to indicate that subsection (3) is to have a different meaning from subsections (1) and (2), I ought to adopt an interpretation which would make the whole section hang together, and the result is that the answer to the question is that the trustees must consult the beneficiaries, not only in the exercise of the trust for sale, but also in the exercise of all other trusts and powers arising under the Settled Land Act 1925 and the Law of Property Acts, and the additional or larger powers conferred by the settlement upon the trustees or otherwise.

However, Mr Arden submits that what that subsection requires is consultation before a trustee does what Lord Bridge in the passage I have already read from *Monk's* case [1992] 1 AC 478, 490–491 described as a 'positive act'. It is clear, says Mr Arden, from the decision in *Monk's* case that a notice by a joint tenant that she was not willing for the tenancy to continue beyond the end of the current four-week period was not, in substance, a 'positive act.' Thus, section 26(3) did not apply so as to require prior consultation to the giving of such a notice. Mr Berry, in reply, said that, though Lord Bridge said that in substance it was not a 'positive act', he accepted that in form the giving of a notice was such an act, and that that was sufficient to bring it within the ambit of section 26(3).

In my judgment Mr Arden's argument is correct. I can see that a regime which required that, where a council dwelling is occupied on a joint tenancy either joint tenant must consult with the other before taking any action which would have the effect of terminating the tenancy, might well be thought to have merit. But as Nicholls LJ said in the passage I quoted from his judgment in *Monk's* case, 89 LGR 357, 382–383, the point here at issue applies to all periodic tenancies. We cannot carve out an exception from the general law which is to apply only to tenants of residential property let by local authorities or similar authorities. In my judgment, therefore, Mr Berry's argument fails at this critical point. We need not therefore express any opinion about his further detailed argument, that in the short passage from the judgment of the court in the *Metall and Rohstoff AG* case [1990] 1 QB 391, 481, where Slade LJ said he knew of no authority supporting the existence of the alleged tort, he was speaking per incuriam. I specifically make no comment about Mr Berry's submissions to that effect.

Despite Mr Berry's persuasive argument, I would therefore dismiss this appeal.

Hobhouse and Aldous LJJ concurred with this approach, which seems to be decisive. In effect, the obligation to consult only arises where one trustee wishes to do something positive about the property; a desire to not proceed with a tenancy is negative and so is not subject to consultation. The 'breach of trust' argument seemed generally to founder on the same point. The only continuing doubt on the matter is provided by the fact that, on 1 January 1997, s. 26(3) was replaced by s. 11 of the Trusts of Land and Appointment of Trustees Act 1996. However, it seems doubtful whether there is sufficient difference in the content of s. 11 compared with s. 26(3) to lead to a different result.

Even if the interests of the other joint tenant(s) do not appear to be protected by the 'breach of trust' argument, the courts have proved sensitive, in general, to the injustices which an inflexible application of the *McGrady* principle can cause. In particular, the House of Lords' acceptance of the *McGrady* principle in *Monk* leaves a cohabiting joint tenant highly vulnerable to vindictive action by a disaffected partner (acting either wholly independently, or in collusion with the landlord authority). The origins of *McGrady* lie, as indicated above, in the understandable desire of many local authorities to rationalise housing tenure and the realities of how a property may be currently occupied. The inability of an authority simply to 'switch' the tenancy from the absentee tenant partner to the partner in occupation must be highly frustrating. However, the principle applies in non-meritorious cases, as much as in meritorious ones. It does not even preclude the partner in *desertion* attempting to remove the tenancy rights of the other, by the service of a notice to quit. The issues came to a head in the following case:

Hounslow LBC v *Pilling*
(1993) 25 HLR 305

In 1991, the plaintiffs granted the defendant and a Miss Doubtfire a secure joint tenancy of a flat. The recitals to the agreement stated that: 'If the tenancy granted is a joint tenancy the rights and liabilities of the tenant apply both jointly and individually.' By clause 14 of the agreement the tenant was obliged: 'to give the Council four weeks' written notice or such lesser period as the Council may accept when the tenant wishes to end the tenancy and give possession of the premises.'

In September 1991, following incidents of domestic violence, Miss Doubtfire left the premises permanently. The plaintiffs had a domestic violence policy whereby they undertook to rehouse any tenant who was proved to have been a victim of violence, provided that the victim surrendered his or her tenancy. On December 6, 1991, Miss Doubtfire wrote to the plaintiffs with respect to the flat stating 'I wish to terminate my tenancy . . . with immediate effect.'

On December 11, 1991, the plaintiffs wrote to the defendant stating:

The Council has received a letter ending the tenancy of 107 Highfield. It is now accepted, and from December 9, 1991, you are no longer a council tenant and should find somewhere else to live. You have no right to remain at 107 Highfield and have become an illegal occupier.

The defendant refused to give up possession and possession proceedings were taken against him. In March 1992 , the district judge made an order for possession which was affirmed on appeal by the judge. The defendant appealed to the Court of Appeal which allowed the appeal.

NOURSE LJ: . . . In this case Mr Luba, for the defendant, has raised several points on the notice by which he seeks to show that it was not an appropriate notice for the purposes of the decision in *Monk*. He has argued, for example, that it is ambiguous in its terms; that it is not clear that it was intended to take effect immediately; and that, if it was, it was not a valid notice within clause 14, because there was no 'period' between the giving of the notice and the date or time when it was expressed to take effect. So far as those and other arguments in the same vein are concerned, I would reject them. I think that the terms of Miss Doubtfire's letter of December 6, 1991 were such that it was capable of taking effect as an immediate notice to quit.

Whether it did take effect as a notice to quit is quite a different matter. It was expressed to take effect immediately and it was accepted as taking effect on Monday, December 9; that is to say, on a day on which the tenancy could not have been determined by a notice to quit given on Friday, December 6. Accordingly, argues Mr Luba, it was not a notice to quit properly so called. It was a notice purporting to be given in exercise of a break clause contained in the lease, namely that contained in clause 14.

In my judgment that argument is correct and the decision of the House of Lords in *Monk* is distinguishable on that ground. All that that case decided was that the continuation of a periodic joint tenancy beyond the end of each period of it depends on the joint will of the tenants, so that if one of them gives notice determining it at the end of a period it does not continue. Here the notice purported to determine the tenancy not at the end of a period but in the middle of one. On the assumption, which I certainly make, that clause 14 permitted notice to be given for an immediate determination, the effect of Miss Doubtfire's letter of December 6, and the council's acceptance of it was to determine the tenancy on December 9, and not on December 16. I therefore agree with Mr Luba that the notice was not a notice to quit, but one operating a break clause in the tenancy agreement. Such a notice could not be given by one only of the joint tenants, see *Re Viola's Indenture of Lease* (1909) 1 Ch 244.

That is indeed the case and that *Monk* should be distinguished on that ground appears clearly from the speech of Lord Bridge. At p. 490G, he said:

Finally, it is said that all positive dealings with a joint tenancy require the concurrence of all joint tenants if they are to be effective. Thus, a single joint tenant cannot exercise a break clause in a lease, surrender the term, make a disclaimer, exercise an option to renew the term or apply for relief from forfeiture. All these positive acts which joint tenants must concur in performing are said to afford analogies with the service of notice to determine a periodic tenancy which is likewise a positive act. But this is to confuse the form with the substance. The action of giving notice to determine a periodic tenancy is in form positive; but both on authority and on the principle so aptly summed up in the pithy Scottish phrase 'tacit relocation' the substance of the matter is that it is by his omission to give notice of termination that each party signifies the necessary positive assent to the extension of the term for a further period.

The invalidity of the notice is in itself a sufficient basis for deciding this case in favour of the defendant. However, Mr Luba submits that, even if it had been valid at common law, it would have been rendered invalid by section 5(1) of the Protection from Eviction Act 1977, which, as amended by section 32 of the Housing Act 1988, is in these terms:

5(1). Subject to subsection (1B) below, no notice by a landlord or a tenant to quit any premises let (whether before or after the commencement of this Act) as a dwelling shall be valid unless—

    (a) it is in writing and contains such information as may be prescribed, and

(b)   it is given not less than 4 weeks before the date on which it is to take effect.

No other part of the section is material. It is to be observed that section 5(1) applies as much to a notice to quit given by a tenant as to one given by a landlord. Accordingly, on the assumption that Miss Doubtfire's notice to quit was otherwise valid, it would nevertheless appear to have been invalidated by this provision. However, that was not the view taken by Judge Marder. He thought that the case was concluded against the defendant by the decision of this court in *Elsden* v *Pick* [1980] 1 WLR 898.

That was a case under section 23(1) of the Agricultural Holdings Act 1948, now section 25(1) of the Agricultural Holdings Act 1986, which provides:

A notice to quit an agricultural holding or part of an agricultural holding shall (notwithstanding any provision to the contrary in the contract of tenancy of the holding) be invalid if it purports to terminate the tenancy before the expiry of twelve months from the end of the then current year of tenancy.

It will be seen that that wording is much the same as that of section 5(1). Mr Luba did not seek to draw a distinction grounded on any material difference in wording.

In *Elsden* v *Pick* the tenant held under an agricultural tenancy determinable on one year's notice in writing expiring on April 6, in any year. On April 7, 1977, he gave notice determining the tenancy on a date which was treated as being 6 April 1978. The date on which the tenancy was determined was not crucial because on any footing the notice had been given one day late and was accordingly invalid. However, at the request of the tenant the landlords' agent agreed to treat it as valid, notwithstanding that it was short. Later the tenant, having regretted his previous action, contended that the notice was ineffective to determine the tenancy. The landlords brought proceedings for a declaration that they were entitled to possession of the holding in April 1978. Their claim failed at first instance, but succeeded in this court.

Elsden v *Pick* is authority for two propositions: first, that a provision in a tenancy agreement which enables either party to determine the tenancy on notice shorter than that required by section 23(1) of the 1948 Act is an unlawful attempt to contract out of the provisions of the Act and on that ground invalid; secondly, and on the other hand, that in relation to the operation of a given notice to quit its invalidity can be cured by the agreement of both parties to treat it as valid. Both these points are clearly dealt with in the judgment of Brightman LJ, at p. 907G, where he said:

What section 23 means is that a short notice to quit is invalid as against the recipient. A tenant is not bound to accept less than the statutory 12 months' notice to quit served by his landlord (nor vice versa) even if the tenancy agreement so provides. If the tenant chooses to do so, he can simply ignore a short notice served on him and resist any attempt by the landlord to recover possession on the strength of it. But if the tenant wishes to do so, he can bind himself to accept it. The parties are entitled to agree that the notice shall be treated in all respects as if it were a notice of the statutory length. If the parties so agree, the tenancy will come to an end on the agreed date by virtue of the defective notice to quit which it is agreed shall be treated as valid. Such an agreement could not effectively be made before a notice to quit is served, because the parties cannot agree that the tenancy shall be capable of being terminated by a short notice. Neither the landlord nor the tenant can bind himself in advance to accept a short notice from the other of them. That would be a 'provision to the contrary' in, or supplemental to, the contract of tenancy and would not be effective. But once an invalid notice has been served, which the recipient is entitled to ignore, I see nothing in section 23 to prohibit an agreement between landlord and tenant that the notice shall be followed by the same consequences as if it were valid.

The judgments of Shaw and Buckley LJJ were to the same effect. In my view the second part of Brightman LJ's observations precisely cover this case.

Here clause 14 contains an agreement that the tenancy may be determined by notice to quit given by the tenant if the period of notice is (a) four weeks or (b) such lesser period as the council may accept. The parties therefore agreed under (b) that the tenancy should in certain circumstances be determined by less than the four weeks' notice required by section 5(1). Notwithstanding Mr Cottle's arguments to the contrary, that is clearly an agreement to contract out of the provisions of section 5(1).

The case is therefore comparable with *Elsden* v *Pick*, but with one crucial difference. In *Elsden* v *Pick* the agreement to treat the invalid notice to quit as being valid was made between the landlords and the sole tenant. That agreement was held to be sufficient to take the case outside the statutory protection. Here the council are asking us to hold that the protection afforded by section 5(1) can be brought to an end by an agreement made between them and only one of two joint tenants. It is obvious that such an agreement cannot deprive the other joint tenant of the protection to which he is entitled under the Act. That is not a point which can be elaborated.

For these reasons I would also decide the second point in favour of the defendant. I would allow the appeal and discharge the district judge's order for possession.

Stuart-Smith and Waite LJJ concurred.

Superficially this decision is a technical one, on the question as to whether a clause in a tenancy agreement can override the provisions of the Protection from Eviction Act 1977, and whether the notice given in the instant case was a notice to quit, or one operating a 'break' clause in the tenancy agreement (in which case *McGrady/Monk* had no application). However, the reasoning of Nourse LJ is 'result orientated' and he is clearly influenced by the perceived injustice of a unilateral destruction of the 'domestic' rights of the remaining joint tenant (there are echoes here of Lord Browne-Wilkinson's view in *Monk* that a 'property based' perspective of the landlord and tenant relationship in this sort of case led to a 'revulsion against [one joint tenant] being able unilaterally to terminate [the other joint tenant's] rights in his home': [1992] 1 AC 491). Following *Pilling*, parties intending to use the *McGrady / Monk* approach must be very wary of the difference between a 'break' clause and a notice to quit. To be 'on the safe side', the notice should clearly be of a minimum four weeks' duration, be not shorter than the periodic length of the tenancy, and should be given so as to expire on the anniversary date of the tenancy. Indeed, a local authority who, under the mistaken belief that a joint tenancy had been validly terminated by one joint tenant, refuse the other joint tenant admission to the premises will be liable in damages under s. 27 of the Housing Act 1988 for unlawful eviction and cannot rely on the 'reasonable cause' defence under s. 27(8). This is demonstrated by *Wandsworth LBC* v *Osei-Bonsu*, (1998) *The Times*, 4 November. A joint secure tenancy had been granted by Wandsworth to the plaintiff and his wife in March 1989. The parties separated in January 1990, the wife and five children moving into bed and breakfast accommodation, following complaints of domestic violence against her husband. The wife subsequently obtained a non-molestation order and an 'ouster' injunction, and in February the plaintiff vacated the property. On 30 April, as part of an arrangement with the authority to transfer her to alternative accommodation, the wife served a notice to quit on the council. However, this notice was set to expire on 14 May, less than the 28 days required under s. 5 of the Protection from Eviction Act 1977. At the time (this being before the decision in *Pilling*) the authority took the view that the notice had been valid and had effectively terminated the joint tenancy. The plaintiff was refused readmission to the property, which was subsequently re-let, and the wife was rehoused elsewhere. Following *Pilling* the notice was seen to be invalid and the eviction unlawful. The Court of Appeal confirmed an award of substantial damages to the plaintiff (whilst reducing the amount from £30,000 to £10,000). It appears that the only sensible course for an authority unsure of their legal ground, is not to attempt eviction without being completely sure that the Protection from Eviction Act 1977 has been complied with.

The final difficulty in applying *McGrady/Monk* is the uneasy relationship between the (apparently) conclusive effect of a valid notice to quit served by one joint tenant, and any injunction which might already exist under 'domestic' legislation guaranteeing (at least in the short term) the rights of the *other* joint tenant in the property. Given that it is most often a woman (with children) who serves the notice to quit as part of a rehousing agreement with the authority landlord, and that it is most often that (any) injunctions would also favour such a female partner, the point may not arise frequently, but it did 'surface' in the next case:

Harrow LBC v Johnstone
[1997] 1 WLR 459

The defendant and his wife were joint tenants of a house owned by the plaintiff council. The wife commenced divorce proceedings in 1992. They both continued to live in the house. In February 1994 the wife left, taking the children of the marriage with her. On an *ex parte* application by the defendant pursuant to the Domestic Violence and Matrimonial Proceedings Act 1976 the judge made an order restraining the wife from using or threatening violence against the defendant or harassing or interfering with him, and from excluding or attempting to exclude him from the house. The wife applied to the council for rehousing. The council, pursuant to their policy of not providing accommodation to someone who already had a council tenancy, suggested that she should serve notice to quit on them. They were then unaware of the injunction granted to the defendant. The wife gave notice to quit, and the defendant, having received a copy, told the council about the injunction. He remained in occupation of the house, and the council brought proceedings against him for possession.

The judge dismissed the claim, holding that by giving the notice to quit the wife had acted in breach of the injunction and was in contempt of court; and that by bringing the proceedings for possession when they were aware of the injunction the council had aided and abetted the wife in that breach and were also in contempt of court, and that the proceedings were an abuse of the process of the court. The Court of Appeal by a majority dismissed the council's appeal. However, the House of Lords unanimously allowed the council's further appeal holding that the injunction had been directed at preventing the wife from molesting the defendant and at excluding him from the exercise of occupation rights under the joint tenancy *while it existed*. It had not been intended to prohibit the wife from serving a notice to quit. Therefore, the wife and the council had not acted in breach of the injunction and so had not been in contempt of court. As a consequence, the wife's notice to quit had been effective to terminate the joint tenancy, and the defendant had no defence to the claim for possession.

LORD MUSTILL: . . . My Lords it seems to me quite beyond doubt that, absent the special procedural background, the wife's notice to the council of 22 March 1994 was effective to allow the joint tenancy to terminate on the expiry of the notice. I am unable to see how clause 19 of the tenancy agreement could lead to any other result, nor has anything in the Act of 1985 been identified which could alter the position. The husband's right to remain in occupation, and the security of tenure which he had hitherto enjoyed, came to an end on the due date for renewal. Other things being equal, the husband remained in the house without legal warrant, and the council was entitled to take steps to remove him.

The question is whether, in the particular circumstances, other things were indeed equal. The husband maintains that they were not, for two quite distinct reasons. The first depends on the injunction of 3 February 1994. It is said that, by giving the notice of 22 March 1994, the wife was in breach of the injunction and that all the subsequent acts of the wife and council are either inherently flawed or were abusive and hence unenforceable.

An examination of this argument must begin with the terms of the injunction. Did the requirement that the wife should not 'exclude or attempt to exclude' the husband from the house prohibit her from notifying the council that the tenancy would not be renewed?

. . .

The husband's application was led by an affidavit alleging that the wife had assaulted him and locked him out of the house. The application was typed on a printed form reciting the Act of 1976. It invited the court to make orders:

That [the wife] be forbidden . . . from: (1) To use or threaten to use violence upon the applicant. (2) To harass threaten pester or otherwise interfere with the applicant. (3) To leave and not return to the former matrimonial home situated and known as 5 Waghorn Road, Kenton, Harrow, Middlesex. (4) To remove or attempt to remove the children of the family from the day to day care of the applicant or attempt to remove from the jurisdiction.

and concluded with the words: 'and that the respondent not prevent the applicant from returning to 5, Waghorn Road . . .'

Regrettably, even on this second appeal neither side is able to provide any information about what happened when this application came before the judge. It is not even known whether the ex parte application was followed, as it should have been, by inter partes proceedings; and if so, with what result. What we do know, however, is that an injunction was made in the terms already recited: an injunction which so far as is known the wife has never sought to discharge or vary.

My Lords, reading this application together with the statute which it invoked and with the terms of the order as made it is in my view absolutely plain that the prohibition against excluding the husband was not intended to be a mandatory order requiring the wife to co-operate in maintaining in force the rights created by the joint tenancy pending the adjustment of those rights on a future date in proceedings not yet started. The application was made at a time of crisis when the husband had been locked out of the house and wanted to get back in. His concern was that his wife had excluded him from the exercise of the rights of occupation which he undoubtedly possessed under the joint tenancy. There is no sign in the documents of an apprehension on his part that the rights themselves were under threat and would require protection by an order requiring the wife to keep the tenancy in being. If the court was to grant something on the lines of a mandatory *Mareva*-like injunction the first step was to ask for one. This the husband did not do. Instead he invited the court to make an order designed to ensure that the molestation of which she was accused did not happen again. The Act of 1976 was the right vehicle for such an order, and although the injunction actually issued did not follow precisely the wording of the Act I have no doubt that this was the foundation of the order which Judge Krikler intended to make and did make. As such it was concerned with the exercise of rights under the tenancy and not with the continued existence of the rights themselves.

On this view the husband's first line of argument fails at the outset.

. . .

Counsel for the husband [then argued] to this effect. Faced with a spouse who showed real signs of desiring a permanent end to the marriage the council should have foreseen that there already were, or in the future might be, proceedings in which the court would be called on to address the proprietary rights of the spouses, including the valuable (if vulnerable) security of tenure of the house; it should also have foreseen that that destruction of the tenure would cause irreparable damage to the husband, since the loss of his tenancy coupled with the rehousing of the wife might critically determine the question of where the young children lived; even if it was not at first in possession of enough information to form a judgment the council should have informed itself by making inquiries; and having done so should have abstained from joining with the wife in any course of action which might put out of the husband's reach the possibility of obtaining some kind of relief in any proceedings which he or the wife might, in the parlous state of the marriage, ultimately come to begin.

My Lords, I acknowledge the appeal of this argument in human terms. We know insufficient of the marital discord to say that the wife was in the wrong, but at least there was sufficient merit on the husband's side for him (rather unusually, given the reversal of gender) to obtain an anti-molestation order which the wife has never tried to displace. Nevertheless, I see no ground to treat the notice by the wife as ineffectual, and still less to convict the council of a wrongful intention to frustrate the ends of justice. Exactly what passed between the council and the wife has never been investigated, as it should have been if they were to be held in contempt. One may, however, test the matter by envisaging a situation where the wife came to the council and simply asked to be rehoused; where the official explained that this could not be done because she was already a tenant; where she told the official that she no longer wanted to keep the joint tenancy in being and asked what to do; where the official recommended that she should take legal advice; and where her lawyer, familiar with the principle of *Hammersmith and Fulham London Borough Council* v *Monk* [1992] 1 AC 478, prepared the notice which was in fact served. Would it be possible to say that anyone involved had acted in contempt of court? Surely not. All one needs, then, to reach the present case is to telescope the course of events. The contrast between this case and *Attorney-General* v *Times Newspapers Ltd* [1992] 1 AC 191 is obvious. There the newspaper defiantly acted in detriment to the obvious interests of justice. Here, the council simply carried through the logic of its housing policy, that one person could not have two council tenancies at the same time. I find it impossible to hold that by putting its statutory duty as housing authority before the interests of a matrimonial relationship of which it was not the guardian the council contemptuously subverted the authority of the court or intentionally nullified the aims of any legal proceedings. This being so I can see no ground upon which it could be held that the dealings of the council with the wife and the husband were completely ineffectual, leaving the parties in the same position as if the notice had never been given. The conclusion is to my mind inescapable that by the time the matter reached Judge Hunter the interest of the husband under the tenancy had come to an end by effluxion of time, so that there was no longer any ground on which he could deny the council the right to resume possession of the house.

These conclusions are sufficient to dispose of the appeal.

Johnstone was specifically concerned with an injunction under s. 1 of the Domestic Violence and Matrimonial Proceedings Act 1976, focusing on the immediate difficulties produced by violence or potential violence in a 'domestic' context (see now s. 33(3), s. 35(5), s. 36(5) and s. 42, Family Law Act 1996). Nothing in the injunction purported to resolve the longer-term 'disposition' of the tenancy, a fact which 'opened the door' for the service of the notice to quit by the wife. Equally, once a court order is made providing for such 'disposition' the resultant transfer of the tenancy rules out any scope for the (ex) joint tenant subsequently to serve a notice to quit (see s. 24, Matrimonial Causes Act 1973 (as amended) and Sch. 7, Family Law Act 1996).

What of a tenant spouse who intends to apply for an 'occupation' order transferring the tenancy into his or her sole name? Is it a defence to a landlord's claim for possession, subsequent to the service of a notice to quit by the other joint tenant, for a joint tenant to argue that he or she intended to apply for an order transferring the tenancy? The most recent authority indicates that the answer is 'no'.

Newlon Housing Trust v *Alsulaimen*
[1999] 1 AC 313

Husband and wife held a joint assured weekly tenancy of a property where they lived until the wife left and commenced divorce proceedings. On 1 November 1995 the wife served on the landlords a notice to quit the premises. The notice expired on 4 December 1995 but the husband continued to live there. In March 1996 the landlords commenced proceedings for possession of the premises. At the hearing the husband sought an adjournment on the ground that he proposed to make an application under (what was then) s. 24 of the Matrimonial Causes Act 1973 for a property adjustment order transferring the joint tenancy into his sole name. The judge refused the adjournment on the ground that the application was too late. The Court of Appeal reversed the judge's decision and ruled that the husband had a good prospect of obtaining a transfer of the tenancy and that justice required that he be given an opportunity to pursue his application. However, the House of Lords unanimously allowed the land-lord's appeal, holding that a notice to quit simply caused the tenancy to terminate 'by effluxion of time' and did not involve any 'disposition' of property. Therefore, the courts had no power to set aside the notice to quit for the purpose of making a property adjustment order.

LORD HOFFMANN: . . . The concession before the Court of Appeal was that the court could make an order setting aside the termination of the tenancy on the ground that it was a 'disposition' of property by the wife made with the intention of defeating the husband's claim for a property adjustment order. Your Lordships gave Mr Andrew Arden, who appeared for the trust, leave to withdraw this concession and he submitted that the termination of a tenancy by the effluxion of a notice to quit was not a disposition of property at all. It followed that the court had no power to resurrect the joint tenancy and accordingly there was no property in respect of which an adjustment order could be made. In those circumstances, there could be no defence to the claim for possession.

The question is therefore whether the termination of a tenancy can be a disposition of property. 'Disposition' is a familiar enough word in the law of property and ordinarily means an act by which someone ceases to be the owner of that property in law or in equity: see the formulation of Mr R. O. Wilberforce QC in *Grey v Inland Revenue Commissioners* [1960] AC 1, 18. In some contexts it may include the case in which the property ceases to exist. It is unnecessary to decide whether it has such an extended meaning in this case. There are contrary indications, namely that section 37 contemplates, first, that the disposition will be capable of being set aside and secondly, that the beneficiary of the disposition may be able to show that he took in good faith and without notice. On the other hand, I feel sure that 'disposition' was intended to include the surrender of a subsisting proprietary interest, such as a tenancy for years or for life, so as to merge in the reversion or remainder: see *Inland Revenue Commissioners v Buchanan* [1958] Ch 289, 296, per Lord Goddard CJ. But, be that all as it may, I think it is essential to the notion of a disposition of property in this context that there is property of which the disponor disposes, whether to someone else or not. It is this property which the court can restore to his estate by setting aside the disposition.

One asks, then, whether the effect of the termination of the tenancy by notice was to dispose of any property belonging to the wife. What property did she hold at the time she gave the notice? The answer is: a joint interest in a weekly tenancy of the flat. In considering the nature of that interest, it is important to bear in mind that, in English law, rights of property in land are four-dimensional. They are defined not only by reference to the physical boundaries of the property but also by reference to the time for which the interest will endure. Thus a life interest in a property is an item of property with a temporal dimension, ceasing to exist on the death of the tenant for life. When that event happens, no property passes from the tenant for life to the remainderman. The latter's interest falls into possession but he becomes entitled to possession by virtue of his own interest and not by having acquired that of the tenant for life. The same is true when a lease for a term of years terminates by effluxion of time. The tenant does not dispose of his interest. At the moment when it expires, he has no property of which he can dispose. It ceases to exist and the landlord's reversion falls into possession.

The analysis of a periodic tenancy by Lord Bridge of Harwich in *Hammersmith and Fulham London Borough Council* v *Monk* [1992] 1 AC 478 demonstrates that what I have said of a tenancy for a term of years is equally true of a periodic tenancy. It also comes to an end by effluxion of time, namely the expiry of the last period for which the tenant or tenants have been willing for it to continue. The respondents invite your Lordships to treat the notice to quit as an act which is dispositive, or at any rate destructive, of the tenancy. But this, as Lord Bridge said, at p. 490, is to 'confuse the form with the substance.' The notice merely signifies that the tenant is not willing to consent to the continuation of the tenancy beyond the date at which it could otherwise expire. In the absence of such consent, it terminates by effluxion of time in the same way as a tenancy for a term of years.

Mr Buckhaven, who appeared for the respondents, invited your Lordships to give a purposive construction to section 37. It was, he said, intended to give the court power to undo any dissipation of assets by one of the parties to the marriage. In many cases, a periodic tenancy would be one of the most important assets. Although in legal theory the tenancy might be said to have ceased to exist, the flat was still there. There was no physical problem about ordering a reinstatement of the tenancy and the courts should not let mere conceptual difficulties stand in their way.

I would certainly not wish to give section 37(2) a construction which defeats its evident purpose, but I am far from confident that the legislation was meant to have the broad effect for which Mr Buckhaven contends. The difference in section 37(2) between the language of paragraph (a), which confers the power to grant restraining orders in advance, and paragraph (b), which deals with past transactions, is very striking. The restraining power applies not only when a party is about to make 'any disposition' but also to transfer out of the jurisdiction or 'otherwise deal with' any property. Paragraph (b), on the other hand, deals only with dispositions.

. . . if the periodic tenancy had still been in existence, the court would have had power to order its transfer to the husband . . . But since it has duly expired, I do not think that it can be revived and the husband therefore has no answer to the claim for possession.

In part, Lord Hoffmann's reasoning is of general application, focusing as it does on the consequences for property rights of the valid service of a notice to quit. It also turns on his analysis of the precise wording of s. 37 of the Matrimonial Causes Act 1973, in particular the meaning of 'reviewable disposition' in s. 37(2)(b). The Matrimonial Causes Act provisions survive (with some amendments) the implementation of the Family Law Act 1996. Moreover, the point seems to be even clearer under the 'tailored' tenancy transfer provisions, now contained in Sch. 7 of the Family Law Act 1996, which apply only if 'one spouse [or cohabitant] is entitled, either in his own right or jointly with the other spouse, to occupy a dwelling-house by virtue of a relevant tenancy' (Sch. 7, para. 2). Once the notice to quit has expired, it seems that no 'relevant tenancy' continues to exist (see the analogy with *Thompson* v *Elmbridge BC* (1987) 19 HLR 526).

Notes

1. The *McGrady/Monk* principle applies as much to assured tenancies under the Housing Act 1988, as it does to secure tenancies under the Housing Act 1985. In both cases the statutory forms of tenancy subsist until (amongst other things) the notice to quit served by one of the joint tenants expires. However, the principle does not apply to Rent Act tenancies. A notice to quit will have the effect of bringing the contractual protected joint tenancy to an end, but this, in its turn, gives rise to a statutory joint tenancy under s. 2 of the Rent Act 1977. Statutory tenancies, having no contractual basis, cannot be brought to an end by notices to quit, but only by a court possession order pursuant to s. 98 of and Sch. 15 to the Rent Act 1977. Indeed notices to quit are wholly inapplicable to statutory tenancies (s. 3(4), Rent Act 1977). Even if only one of the (former) joint tenants remains in the property, his or her rights as a statutory tenant continue (*Lloyd* v *Sadler* [1978] 1 QB 774).

2. In *Hammersmith LBC* v *Monk*, although Lord Browne-Wilkinson concurred in the decision of the House of Lords, he did so with some misgivings. As he puts it (at p. 491): '. . . there are two instinctive reactions to this case which lead to diametrically opposite conclusions. The first is that the flat in question was the joint home of the appellant and Mrs Powell: it therefore cannot be right that one them unilaterally can join with the landlords to put an end to the other's rights in the home. The second is that the appellant and Mrs Powell undertook joint liabilities on tenants for the purpose of providing themselves with a joint home and that once the desire to live together has ended, it is impossible to require that the one who quits the home should continue indefinitely to be liable for the discharge of the obligations to the landlord under the tenancy agreement'. Putting the 'instinctive reaction' in a theoretical context, he later states that 'the revulsion against Mrs Powell being able unilaterally to terminate the appellant's rights in his home is property based . . . the other reaction is contract based: Mrs Powell cannot be held to a tenancy contract which is dependent for its continuance on the will of the tenant'. In the end, he was sufficiently satisfied that the 'contract' approach was the correct one.

3. One uncertainty left by *Newlon Housing Trust* v *Alsulaimen* is the legal position in the (far from unlikely) scenario of one of the joint tenants becoming aware that the other was *about* to serve a notice to quit, thereby ending their property rights. Clearly if the application for a tenancy transfer is heard by the courts before (any) notice to quit expires there is no difficulty, since there is still a tenancy in existence to be transferred. However, is the giving of a notice to quit a 'dealing' with the property which, in any event, can be 'restrained' by the courts (under s. 37(2)(a), Matrimonial Causes Act 1973) so as to 'protect' the right to apply for a judicial tenancy transfer? Unfortunately, Lord Hoffmann expressly states no view on this point ([1999] 1 AC at p. 319), so leaving the matter to be resolved in the future by the courts. Very recently in *Bater* v *Greenwich London Borough Council and Another* [1999] *The Times*, 28th September, the Court of Appeal followed the *Alsulaimen* decision and held the Court has no jurisdiction under s. 37(2)(b) of the Matrimonial Causes Act 1973 to set aside a unilateral notice to terminate a joint tenancy by one of two joint tenants in a matrimonial dispute. This is because such a notice is not a disposition of property within the terms of the subsection. However, Thorp LJ went on, though alone on the point, to argue that under s. 37(2)(a) there is jurisdiction to intervene where a unilateral notice is about to be served as that is a situation where the server of the notice is attempting 'otherwise [to] deal with any property'. He also argues that the court has an inherent jurisdiction to deal with acts or omissions by either side in a divorce either before or after the issue of divorce proceedings if such acts or omissions are able to harass or molest the other side or could affect adversely the welfare of any child. Equally such a power exists to prevent acts whose consequence would be to diminish the power of the court to distribute or redistribute assets in order to promote the welfare of any child or to secure the financial future of any financially dependent applicant. He then went on to argue that a similar jurisdiction exists in relation to unmarried joint tenants provided they have children under the wordships powers of the court and the powers of the Children Act 1989. The powers of the court could be activated by practitioners in family proceedings seeking undertakings from the other side where a joint tenancy is involved not to deal with it in any way detrimental to the interest of their client until the future of the property is decided by the court. Such an undertaking could then be brought to the notice of the landlord, and, if necessary, could be reinforced or superseded by an injunction from the court which could be served on the landlord preventing service of a unilateral notice.

If Thorpe LJ's arguments are correct, and Roch and Lloyd LJJ expressed no opinion on the point, then a 'race' could begin in disputes between joint tenants as to who can get which procedure under way first; either that of a unilateral notice to quit, or that under s. 37(2)(a) restraining, or seeking an undertaking not to serve, such a notice.

4.   Although the tenant's unlawful eviction claim succeeded in *Wandsworth LBC* v *Osei-Bonsu*, the Court of Appeal also held that, in such a case, a 'wronged' tenant had to choose between statutory damages and a continuing right to possession of the property. If, at the trial, a tenant elected for statutory damages, the tenancy would properly be deemed to have ended, albeit unlawfully, at the time of the eviction.

5.   Since *McGrady* the law on joint tenancies and notices to quit has become increasingly complex. Since 1992 the area has been considered three times by the House of Lords and on numerous occasions by the Court of Appeal, and yet uncertainties still remain. In many ways the current law is something of a 'blunt instrument', facilitating a sensible 'regularising' of housing arrangements where spouses with children have been deserted, or have fled the home because of domestic violence, yet also providing an opportunity for vindictive action by disaffected partners. Moreover, the *McGrady/Monk* principle operates only when there is a joint tenancy and does nothing to assist a non-tenant partner. It is likely that most local authority and social landlords *do* grant joint tenancies to partners of all descriptions today

(particularly in the light of Annex C, Code of Guidance to Parts VI and VII, Housing Act 1996), but the practice is still not universal. Another approach has often been thought to be the creation of a new ground for possession against a secure tenant who is guilty of violence; and to some extent this is now provided for by the Housing Act 1996 which, via s. 145 and s. 149 (in force 12 February 1997), creates a new Ground 2A in Sch. 2 to the Housing Act 1985 and a new Ground 14A in Sch. 2 to the Housing Act 1988. Both new grounds apply to married couples and heterosexual cohabitants, but not to homosexual relationships. They apply equally to sole and joint tenancies. It must be demonstrated that one partner has left the property in question because of violence (or threats of violence) to themselves or a member of their family in residence at the relevant time, *and* that the partner who has left is unlikely to return. The grounds are discretionary, thus requiring the landlord to demonstrate that it is reasonable to grant possession. No doubt the existence of appropriate arrangements for rehousing the partner who has left because of violence will often be a relevant factor. In the case of the Housing Act 1988, the new Ground 14A applies only to social landlords (for example, housing associations).

Questions
1. Could it be argued that where a local authority landlord accepts a unilateral notice to quit without giving warning to the other tenant, it amounts to maladministration?
2. If Lord Browne-Wilkinson in *Monk* is correct in believing that a 'contract' analysis and a 'property' analysis lead to different results, is there any conclusive reason why the 'contract' analysis should be preferred?
3. In so far as the decisions in *Johnstone* and *Alsulaimen* allow 'ouster' orders to be overridden and 'property transfer' rights to be abrogated, is the law in need of statutory reform? If so, what reform(s) do you think would be most desirable?
4. Would it be improper for a local authority or registered social landlord to refuse to *consider* (as appropriate) Ground 2A or Ground 14A as an alternative to *McGrady/Monk*?

Index